1 Reading and Writing in College
1. Reading to learn *3*
2. Writing to learn *12*
3. Joining the academic conversation *21*
4. Reading arguments *32*
5. Planning a research project *50*
6. Finding sources *59*
7. Evaluating sources *78*
8. Synthesizing and summarizing sources *90*

2 Writing with Sources
9. Planning and drafting *99*
10. Organizing and developing arguments *114*
11. Paragraphs *131*
12. Integrating and using sources ethically *146*
13. Revising and editing *158*
14. Designing documents *171*
15. Oral presentations *186*

3 Clarity and Style
16. Emphasis *193*
17. Parallelism *200*
18. Variety and details *202*
19. Appropriate and exact language *206*
20. Completeness *220*
21. Conciseness *221*

4 Sentence Parts and Patterns
22. Parts of speech *229*
23. The sentence *235*
24. Phrases and subordinate clauses *240*
25. Sentence types *244*
26. Verb forms *246*
27. Verb tenses *257*
28. Verb mood *262*
29. Verb voice *264*
30. Agreement of subject and verb *266*
31. Pronoun case *272*
32. Agreement of pronoun and antecedent *277*
33. Reference of pronoun to antecedent *281*
34. Adjectives and adverbs *284*
35. Misplaced and dangling modifiers *292*
36. Sentence fragments *297*
37. Comma splices and fused sentences *301*
38. Mixed sentences *305*

5 Punctuation
39. End punctuation *311*
40. Comma *313*
41. Semicolon *324*
42. Colon *326*
43. Apostrophe *328*
44. Quotation marks *332*
45. Other marks *336*

6 Spelling and Mechanics
46. Spelling and the hyphen *343*
47. Capital letters *348*
48. Italics or underlining *352*
49. Abbreviations *354*
50. Numbers *357*

7 Writing in the Disciplines
51. MLA documentation and format *365*
52. APA documentation and format *422*
53. Chicago documentation *456*
54. CSE documentation *470*

Glossary of Usage *477*
Glossary of Terms *491*
Index *502*
Culture and Language Guide *544*

Inside the back cover:
Detailed C
Editing Sy

The Little, Brown
Handbook, Brief Version

Seventh Edition

Jane E. Aaron

Michael Greer
University of Arkansas at Little Rock

Executive Producer and Publisher: Aron Keesbury
Content Producer: Barbara Cappuccio
Content Developer: David Kear
Portfolio Manager Assistant: Christa Cottone
Senior Product Marketing Manager: Michael Coons
Product Marketing Manager: Nicholas Bolt
Content Producer Manager: Ken Volcjak
Content Development Manager: Joanne Dauksewicz
Art/Designer: Cenveo® Publisher Services
Digital Studio Course Producer: Elizabeth Bravo
Full-Service Project Management: Cenveo® Publisher Services
Compositor: Cenveo® Publisher Services
Printer/Binder: LSC Communications, Inc.
Cover Printer: Phoenix Color
Cover Designer: Preston Thomas, Cadence Design Studio

Copyright © 2020, 2017, 2014 by Pearson Education, Inc., 221 River Street, Hoboken, NJ 07030. All Rights Reserved. Printed in the United States of America. This publication is protected by copyright, and permission should be obtained from the publisher prior to any prohibited reproduction, storage in a retrieval system, or transmission in any form or by any means, electronic, mechanical, photocopying, recording, or otherwise. For information regarding permissions, request forms, and the appropriate contacts within the Pearson Education Global Rights & Permissions Department, please visit www.pearsoned.com/permissions/.

PEARSON, ALWAYS LEARNING, and Revel are exclusive trademarks owned by Pearson Education, Inc., or its affiliates in the United States and/or other countries.

Unless otherwise indicated herein, any third-party trademarks that may appear in this work are the property of their respective owners and any references to third-party trademarks, logos, or other trade dress are for demonstrative or descriptive purposes only. Such references are not intended to imply any sponsorship, endorsement, authorization, or promotion of Pearson's products by the owners of such marks, or any relationship between the owner and Pearson Education, Inc., or its affiliates, authors, licensees, or distributors.

Library of Congress Cataloging-in-Publication Data

Names: Aaron, Jane E., author. | Greer, Michael, 1961- author.
Title: The Little, Brown compact handbook / Jane E. Aaron, Michael Greer.
Description: Tenth edition. | [New York, New York] : [Pearson], [2019] |
   Includes index.
Identifiers: LCCN 2018045791| ISBN 0135298237 (Student Edition : Tabbed) |
   ISBN 9780135298237 (Student Edition : Tabbed)
Subjects: LCSH: English language—Grammar—Handbooks, manuals, etc. | English
   language—Rhetoric—Handbooks, manuals, etc.
Classification: LCC PE1112 .A23 2019b | DDC 808/.042--dc23 LC record
available at https://lccn.loc.gov/2018045791

Access Code Card
ISBN 10:   0-13-518072-4
ISBN 13: 978-0-13-518072-3

Revel Combo Card
ISBN 10:   0-13-547356-X
ISBN 13: 978-0-13-547356-6

Rental Edition
ISBN 10:   0-13-529823-7
ISBN 13: 978-0-13-529823-7

Loose-Leaf Edition
ISBN 10:   0-13-529821-0
ISBN 13: 978-0-13-529821-3

Instructor's Resource Copy
ISBN 10:   0-13-529812-1
ISBN 13: 978-0-13-529812-1

Preface

LB Brief combines reliable, authoritative coverage of grammar, style, and mechanics with a new focus on critical reading and writing with sources.

Many student writers today enter college unprepared for the rigors of reading longer academic texts. They struggle to read textbooks, scholarly journals, and formal arguments. As they move into research and source-based writing assignments, this lack of skill and practice in critical reading translates into real difficulty with writing—teachers see papers that do not integrate and synthesize sources well, lack focus, and are poorly organized.

LB Brief is designed around the assumption that reading and writing are deeply intertwined, and that addressing student challenges with reading can directly improve their writing. Whether they are writing short response papers, discussing a reading in an online forum, or writing a formal research paper, students need strategies and skills for reading to learn, writing to learn, and connecting their reading to their writing.

What's new in the 7th edition

For this edition, Parts 1 and 2 have been completely re-organized to begin with critical reading and a focus on academic, source-based writing.

Part 1, *Reading and Writing in College*, provides instruction in core skills in critical reading, grounded in important recent research by scholars including Beth L. Hewett and Ellen C. Carillo. Chapters in Part 1 assume that most college writing involves reading and responding to sources in some way, and provides practical strategies that students can apply to any college writing assignment.

Chapter 1, Reading to Learn, is entirely new to this edition. The chapter demonstrates reading strategies students can use when reading to learn, with an emphasis on how to work with and respond to difficult texts. Chapter 1 encourages and demonstrates an active, reflective reading process.

Chapter 2, Writing to Learn, also entirely new to this edition, demonstrates processes for using annotation, taking notes, summarizing, analyzing, and collaborating to respond to readings. The chapter shows how a student uses these strategies in detail as she works through her initial responses and later analysis of a reading.

Part 2, *Writing with Sources*, combines a focus on critical reading with an overview of the writing process. While it includes many of the familiar steps in the composing process, it does so with an attention to the way in which college writers engage and negotiate texts as part of their own writing process.

Parts 3 through 7 provide the time-tested clarity and usability of the *Little, Brown* trademark coverage of clarity, style, grammar, mechanics, and documentation.

Chicago Manual of Style documentation (Chapter 53) and CSE documentation (Chapter 54) have been added to broaden the coverage of research writing to include disciplines in the humanities and natural sciences.

New sample student papers: All of the student samples in the book, from short works in progress to complete papers, are new to this edition. More than 60 student samples are included. The topics and sources used in these new sample papers are timely and attuned to student interests, including:

- Sample critical analysis of a text (analyzing an essay on selfies from *Psychology Today*) (Chapter 4)
- Sample critical analysis of a visual (a Web advertisement for *Savethefood.com*) (Chapter 4)
- Sample proposal argument on online courses (Chapter 10)
- Sample research paper in MLA style on sustainable agriculture (Chapter 51)
- Sample research paper in APA style on perceptions of mental illness on college campuses (Chapter 52)

New digital interactive applications and exercises pay particular attention to the following aspects: 1. awareness of and understanding of the elements of the rhetorical situation, helping students see these elements in sample texts and as part of their own writing assignments and practices; 2. transferability of skills and concepts outside of this course into other subject areas and contexts (in a WRAC sense and for public and professional writing); 3. exploratory writing activities to build and practice writing skills, using scaffolded writing activities ("draft a sample argument paragraph"; "draft an introduction based on your thesis" for example), and 4. multimodal literacy and writing.

A handbook for many purposes

The handbook gives students a solid foundation in the goals and requirements of college writing.

- The chapter on academic writing includes a greatly expanded overview of common academic genres, such as responses, critical analyses, arguments, informative and personal writing, and research papers and reports. The discussion highlights key features of each genre and points students to examples in the handbook.
- Eleven examples of academic writing in varied genres appear throughout the handbook, among them a new informative essay

and a new social-science research report documented in APA style.
- Emphasizing critical analysis and writing, the expanded chapter on critical reading and writing includes a student's analysis of a Web advertisement and a revised discussion of writing critically about texts and visuals.
- Pulling together key material on academic integrity, Chapter 3 on academic writing and Chapter 12 on plagiarism discuss developing one's own perspective on a topic, using and managing sources, and avoiding plagiarism. Other chapters throughout the handbook reinforce these important topics.
- Synthesis receives special emphasis wherever students might need help balancing their own and others' views, such as in responding to texts.
- Parts 2 and 7 give students a solid foundation in research writing and writing in the disciplines (literature, other humanities, social sciences, natural and applied sciences), along with extensive coverage of documentation in MLA, Chicago, APA, and CSE styles.

A reference for research writing and documentation

With detailed advice, the handbook always attends closely to research writing and source citation. The discussion stresses using the library Web site as the gateway to finding sources, managing information, evaluating and synthesizing sources, integrating source material, and avoiding plagiarism.

- Coverage of developing a working bibliography groups sources by type, reflecting a streamlined approach to source material throughout the handbook.
- The discussion of libraries' Web sites covers various ways that students may search for sources—catalog, databases, and research guides.
- A discussion of keywords and subject headings helps students develop and refine their search terms.
- A discussion of gathering information from sources stresses keeping accurate records of source material, marking borrowed words and ideas clearly, and using synthesis.
- A chapter on documenting sources explains key features of source documentation, defines the relationship between in-text citations and a bibliography, and presents the pros and cons of bibliography software.
- The discussion of evaluating sources—library, Web, and social media—helps students discern purposes and distinguish between reliable and unreliable sources. Case studies show

the application of critical criteria to sample articles and Web documents.
- The extensive chapter on avoiding plagiarism discusses deliberate and careless plagiarism, shows examples of plagiarized and revised sentences, and gives updated advice about avoiding plagiarism with online sources.
- A research paper-in-progress on sustainable agriculture follows a student through the research process and culminates in an annotated paper documented in MLA style.

An updated guide to documentation

The extensive coverage of four common documentation styles—MLA, Chicago, APA, and CSE—reflects each style's most recent version.

- Updated, annotated samples of key source types illustrate MLA and APA documentation, showing students how to find the bibliographical information needed to cite each type and highlighting the similarities and differences between print and database sources.
- The chapter on MLA documentation reflects the new 8th edition of the *MLA Handbook*. In addition, the sample paper and other examples that show MLA style have been updated to reflect the latest MLA guidelines.
- A complete social-science research report shows APA style in the context of student writing.
- The discussion of CSE documentation reflects the new 8th edition of *Scientific Style and Format: The CSE Manual for Authors, Editors, and Publishers*.
- For all styles, color highlighting makes authors, titles, dates, and other citation elements easy to grasp.

A reference for writing as a process

The handbook takes a practical approach to assessing the writing situation, generating ideas, developing the thesis statement, revising, and other elements of the writing process.

- An expanded discussion of thesis covers using the thesis statement to preview organization.
- A reorganized presentation of revising and editing distinguishes revising clearly as a step separate from editing.
- A revised discussion of preparing a writing portfolio gives an overview of common formats and requirements.
- Chapter 11 on paragraphs offers new, relevant examples illustrating paragraph development.
- A revised and streamlined chapter on presenting writing focuses on essential information related to document design, visuals and other media, and writing for online environments.

A reference on usage, grammar, and punctuation

The handbook's core reference material reliably and concisely explains basic concepts and common errors and provides hundreds of annotated examples from across the curriculum.

- Dozens of new and revised examples clarify and test important concepts.
- Two common trouble spots—sentence fragments and passive voice—are discussed in great detail and illustrated with examples.
- Examples in Chapter 19 on appropriate language show common shortcuts of texting and other electronic communication and how to revise them for academic writing.
- Summary and checklist boxes provide quick-reference help with color highlighting to distinguish sentence elements.

A guide to visual and media literacy

The handbook helps students process nonverbal information and use it effectively in their writing.

- A student's analysis of a Web advertisement illustrates critical thinking about a visual.
- Updated and detailed help with preparing or finding illustrations appears in Chapter 14 on document design and Chapter 6 on finding sources.
- Thorough discussions of critically reading advertisements, graphs, and other visuals appear in Chapter 4 on critical reading, Chapter 10 on argument, and Chapter 12 on working with sources.

A guide for culturally and linguistically diverse writers

At sections labeled Culture and Language, the handbook provides extensive rhetorical and grammatical help, illustrated with examples, for writers whose first language or dialect is not Standard American English.

- Fully integrated coverage, instead of a separate section, means that students can find what they need without having to know which problems they do and don't share with native SAE speakers.

An accessible reference guide

The handbook is an open book for students, with a convenient lay-flat binding, tabbed dividers, and many internal features that help students navigate and use the content.

- A clean, uncluttered page design uses color and type to clearly distinguish parts of the book and elements of the pages.

- A brief table of contents on the first page of the book provides an at-a-glance overview of the book, while a detailed table of contents appears inside the back cover.
- Color highlighting in boxes and on documentation models distinguishes important elements.
- A very accessible organization groups related problems so that students can easily find what they need.
- Annotations on both visual and verbal examples connect principles and illustrations.
- Dictionary-style headers in the index make it easy to find entries.

Revel

Revel is an interactive learning environment that deeply engages students and prepares them for class. Media and assessment integrated directly within the authors' narrative lets students read, explore interactive content, and practice in one continuous learning path. Thanks to the dynamic reading experience in Revel, students come to class prepared to discuss, apply, and learn from instructors and from each other.

Learn more about Revel

www.pearson.com/revel

Pearson English Assignments Library

Available with your adoption of any © 2019 or © 2020 Pearson English course in Revel is the English Assignments Library comprising 500 essay and Shared Media prompts:

- A series of 300 fully editable essay assignments invites students to write on compelling, wide-ranging writing topics. You can choose from an array of writing prompts in the following genres or methods of development: Argument/Persuasion; Comparison/Contrast; Critique/Review; Definition; Description; Exposition; Illustration; Narration; Process Analysis; Proposal; and Research Project. Assignments can be graded using a rubric based on the WPA Outcomes for First-Year Composition. You can also upload essay prompts and/or rubrics of your own.
- Two hundred Shared Media assignments ask students to interpret and/or produce various multimedia texts to foster multimodal literacy. Shared Media activities include analyzing or critiquing short professional videos on topics of contemporary interest; posting brief original videos or presentation slides; and sharing original images—such as posters, storyboards, concept maps, or graphs.

Revel Combo Card

The Revel Combo Card provides an all-in-one access code and loose-leaf print reference (delivered by mail).

Supplements

Make more time for your students with instructor resources that offer effective learning assessments and classroom engagement. Pearson's partnership with educators does not end with the delivery of course materials; Pearson is there with you on the first day of class and beyond. A dedicated team of local Pearson representatives will work with you not only to choose course materials but also to integrate them into your class and assess their effectiveness. Our goal is your goal—to improve instruction with each semester.

Pearson is pleased to offer the following resource to qualified adopters of *LB Brief*. This supplement is available to instantly download from Revel or on the Instructor Resource Center (IRC). Please visit the IRC at www.pearson.com/us to register for access.

- POWERPOINT PRESENTATION Make lectures more enriching for students. The accessible PowerPoint Presentation includes a full lecture outline and photos and figures from the textbook and Revel edition. Available on the IRC.

Acknowledgments

Instructors around the country have provided valuable feedback and suggestions. For the 7th edition, many thanks to the following for their time and insight: Michael Blaine, Delaware Technical Community College; John Jarvis, Bay Path College; Genesis Downey, Owens Community College; Anthony Edgington, University of Toledo; and Joshua Austin, Cumberland County College.

My first and most important debt of gratitude is to Jane E. Aaron, whose work through many editions of this handbook leaves me with some very large shoes to fill. I can only hope to carry on her legacy of quality, accuracy, and usefulness. Having pored over every page of this handbook many times now, I continue to be awed by its gentle, guiding awareness of the needs of student writers.

Karon Bowers at Pearson and Carolyn Merrill and Aron Keesbury at Ohlinger Publishing Services have guided the project throughout this revision cycle. Cynthia Cox and Joanne Dauksewicz at Ohlinger have been there every step and every page of the way through the editorial and production processes. David Kear has been a wonderful contributor of ideas, energy, clarity, and creativity as development editor, keeping both sanity and humor intact through a long and challenging publishing journey.

The Little, Brown Handbook, Brief Version

Part 1

Reading and Writing in College

1 Reading to Learn *3*
2 Writing to Learn *12*
3 Joining the Academic Conversation *21*
4 Reading Arguments *32*
5 Planning a Research Project *50*
6 Finding Sources *59*
7 Evaluating Sources *78*
8 Synthesizing and Summarizing Sources *90*

Part 1
Reading and Writing in College

1 Reading to Learn 3
   1.1 The reading-writing connection 3
   1.2 Processes for reading 5
   1.3 Rhetorical reading 7
   1.4 Reading journals and reading reflections 11
   1.5 Discussing readings 11

2 Writing to Learn 12
   2.1 Reading into writing 13
   2.2 Writing to respond 16
   2.3 Discovering and exploring ideas 18
   2.4 Writing to share and collaborate 19

3 Joining the Academic Conversation 21
   3.1 Purpose and audience 22
   3.2 Genre 23
   3.3 Writing with sources 26
   3.4 Academic language 28
   3.5 Communication in academic settings 30

4 Reading Arguments 32
   4.1 Techniques of critical reading 32
   4.2 Summarizing 36
   4.3 Critical response 38
   4.4 Visual analysis 40
   4.5 Writing a critical analysis 46
   4.6 Sample critical analysis 48

5 Planning a Research Project 50
   5.1 The process of research writing 51
   5.2 Research questions 52
   5.3 Search strategies 53
   5.4 Working bibliographies 56

6 Finding Sources 59
   6.1 Search strategies 60
   6.2 Reference works 63
   6.3 Books and periodicals 64
   6.4 Web search strategies 69
   6.5 Social media 72
   6.6 Government publications 73
   6.7 Visuals and media 73
   6.8 Primary research 75

7 Evaluating Sources 78
   7.1 Relevance and reliability 78
   7.2 Library sources 79
   7.3 Web sites 82
   7.4 Other online sources 88

8 Synthesizing and Summarizing Sources 90
   8.1 Interacting with sources 91
   8.2 Synthesizing sources 92
   8.3 Summary, paraphrase, and quotation 93

Chapter 1
Reading to Learn

	Learning Objectives
1.1	Explain how reading and writing are interrelated.
1.2	Describe how to vary reading processes for different kinds of texts.
1.3	Apply concepts of audience, purpose, and situation to reading texts.
1.4	Use reading journals and reflections to develop awareness of your reading processes.
1.5	Use class discussions and online forums to share responses to what you read.

1.1 The Reading-Writing Connection

1.1   Explain how reading and writing are interrelated.

True or false: the best way to read a textbook chapter is to start at the beginning and closely read through the chapter, line by line, all the way to the end? False—especially if you are reading the chapter for the first time. Try this instead: page, scroll, or swipe through this chapter quickly, reading only the main headings at the beginning of each section. Take a moment to do that, then come back here.

What do you notice? By reading the titles of each section of the chapter, you were able to discover what the chapter covers. You now have in mind a picture of what the chapter as a whole is about. Pre-reading or previewing a text, as you just did, is an effective reading strategy for many types of long-form texts.

Take a moment to think about all of the different kinds of texts you have read today. If you are like most college students, you have probably read a number of different kinds of texts, from text messages and social-media posts to longer articles or chapters in your textbooks. Maybe an instructor sent an e-mail about a class assignment, or you read through a thread of your classmates' work on an online discussion forum. Did you read all of these different texts in the same way?

You might not be in the habit of thinking much about how you read, because your focus is on getting the information—you are thinking about *what* you are reading rather than *how*. You may think of learning *how* to read as something we do as children. Many people associate learning to read with learning to ride a bicycle: once you learn how to do it, you will always be able to pick up a bicycle

read 1.1

or a text and go. This perception can limit your ability to grow as a reader, particularly when it comes to reading difficult academic texts, as college courses ask you to do. It turns out that reading is a complex skill, much like writing, and readers benefit from repeated practice, investigation, and self-reflection.

Most of the writing you will do in college involves writing about and with other texts. You may be asked to summarize texts, compare and contrast different viewpoints on a topic, and build arguments based on research. You will be expected to consider diverse points of view, find points of similarity and difference among multiple sources, and present your own interpretations in the context of those sources.

Writing from sources, or research-based writing, is a core skill in many fields. Successfully transitioning from high school to college-level research writing requires a higher level of critical reading skills. You may be a proficient writer, but if you are asked to compose a research essay based on scholarly sources in your discipline, you'll need to be confident about where to start and how to proceed.

Teachers and scholars in the fields of rhetoric and composition have recognized for some time that reading and writing are interrelated. Most formal college writing tasks depend on reading and responding to texts—and the best way to become a better reader is to write about what you read, because reading and writing are deeply connected.

What are some of the different ways that you might use reading and writing together in the process of composing an assignment for a college course?

- **Read texts from different points of view.** For example, read as a sympathetic reader, looking for points of agreement; then, read as a resistant reader, looking for points of disagreement.
- **Write about texts in different ways.** For example, write a summary, analysis, response, or synthesis of one or more readings.
- **Respond to readings.** Consider how your own ideas or experiences compare and contrast with those of the author.
- **Evaluate sources.** Evaluating sources for credibility, relevance, and quality is a key form of critical reading and writing.
- **Generate questions about a topic.** Asking questions is an important part of reading well and leads directly into research and writing.
- **Conduct research.** College research often requires you to read difficult sources written by scholars of a particular discipline, identify key ideas from those sources, and draw conclusions about them.

Because reading and writing are deeply connected, practicing these skills and reflecting on your thought process will help you improve as both a reader and a writer.

1.2 Processes for Reading

1.2 Describe how to vary reading processes for different kinds of texts.

Think about the processes you use to read different kinds of texts. Do you read a novel the same way you read an assigned chapter in a course textbook? When reading something assigned for a course, you may be hunched over a desk, highlighter in hand, searching for key concepts and ideas that you might be tested on. Reading a novel for pleasure, you may sit back or even recline in bed or on a couch. You are probably not highlighting or taking notes when you are reading for fun. While many readers are not consciously aware of these differences, the processes and strategies readers use vary from one kind of text to another.

Take a moment to reflect on your own reading processes. Imagine, first, that you have been assigned to read a chapter from a textbook in a course like chemistry or economics or some other subject that you find especially challenging.

- How do you prepare to do that reading?
- How do you feel about it?
- Where are you as you do the reading?
- What do you visualize when you think of yourself doing this reading?

Now think about reading something that you chose to read for yourself and ask yourself the same questions. (It can be a useful exercise to write down your answers to these questions, too, especially if your instructor has assigned a reading journal or blog.) Reflecting on your own reading processes may feel odd or uncomfortable at first, because you may have taken reading for granted in the past. Researchers who study reading, however, point to the value of this kind of self-reflection, which is called *metacognition*—thinking about thinking. Good readers, just like good writers, are aware of their thought processes as they read and write.

You have probably had the experience of trying to power through a long, difficult assigned reading when you are tired or distracted. Your eyes move over the words on the page (or screen), but by the time you get to the end, you have little memory of what you read. This kind of disengaged or "fake reading" might allow you to check the box and tell yourself you have completed the assignment, but it will be of little value to you later. Paying attention to your own thought process as you read can help you shift from disengaged to engaged reading, which in turn will increase your comprehension and memory of what you have read. Use some of the idea starters here to prompt your thinking. Write down your responses and use them to suggest things to note or annotate in the reading as well.

> **read 1.2**
>
> ## Reflecting on your reading
>
> As you read, use these idea starters to become aware of your thought processes:
>
> I'm thinking _____.
> I'm noticing _____.
> I'm feeling _____.
> I'm wondering _____.

Different kinds of texts require different reading processes. Reading processes can be divided into three main types:

- **Functional reading:** Reading to complete a task or perform a function. Examples include instructions for a class assignment, an e-mail with procedures for registering for classes, or a quick-start guide for setting up a new laptop.
- **Reading to learn:** Reading to learn new things, both formally (for school and work, for example) and informally (to develop skills in sports or cooking, for example). Examples include course textbooks, professional books, academic articles, self-help books, and tutorials or how-to guides.
- **Reading for entertainment:** Reading to relax, escape, unwind, and enjoy. Examples include fiction, graphic novels, blogs, or magazines.

In college writing courses, your primary focus is usually on reading to learn. Becoming aware of when you are shifting between types of reading is important. Using functional reading processes may not work well when you are reading to learn. When you conduct functional reading, your goal is to complete a task and find information quickly. If you apply the same process to reading a textbook in a new discipline, you will probably discover that the reading is harder and you are only capturing a few fragmentary ideas or concepts. When you are confronted with new and difficult readings in a field that is new to you, you need to apply conscious strategies for reading to learn.

> ## Strategies for getting started when reading difficult texts
>
> - **Reflect on your challenges.** Becoming aware of your thought processes when reading is important to making progress. Remember that reading, like writing, is a skill that requires effort and practice.

> What kind of reading is hard for you? Why? Have you ever tried different ways of reading?
> - **Suspend judgment.** Do not expect to understand or "get it" the first time. Keep moving forward through the text and enjoy the process of discovery. You can always come back to the text later to read it more closely.
> - **Look for patterns.** Some texts may confound you with technical jargon and references to ideas and concepts that you are not familiar with. Watch for patterns like repeated words and phrases, ideas that come up again and again, or examples that are used repeatedly. These patterns offer important evidence of what is important in the text, even if you are not comprehending every detail.
> - **Identify parts and relationships.** Headings, subheadings, paragraph breaks, and other visual cues in a text can help. In some fields, every article follows a similar structure, with an abstract, introduction, methods, results, and conclusion. These parts can help you begin to understand how the text is organized and what the relationships among the parts may be.

1.3 Rhetorical Reading

1.3 Apply concepts of audience, purpose, and situation to reading texts.

Reading and writing do not take place in a vacuum. People create texts to serve different purposes in different situations. The field of *rhetoric* studies the ways in which texts are used in various cultural and social settings to create meaning. Rhetoric first began as scholars started to think about why some texts (or speeches) are more persuasive than others. Rhetoricians like Aristotle investigated how and why some arguments worked more effectively than others, and their thinking was one of many different foundations upon which the discipline of rhetoric was built over centuries. Today, we have a rich body of scholarship and learning that can help identify the elements of effective persuasion and that offers strategies for rhetorical reading.

1.3.1 Elements of rhetoric

Every text has a specific *purpose*. In academic settings, many texts are composed for the purpose of reporting on new knowledge and research. A sociologist, for example, might report on a new study about teens' use of social media. A scholarly text may also have a persuasive purpose: that sociologist, for example, may want to argue that previous studies were flawed or based on faulty assumptions.

Every text also has a specific *audience*. A textbook, for example, is written for an audience of students in a particular course. In many cases, you are the intended audience for such texts. Sometimes the audience for a text is obvious. An article published in a journal of electrical engineering is probably written for an audience of electrical engineers. In that case, as a student, you are only beginning to enter into the field or profession, and you may not yet be as comfortable with the language and ideas as an electrical engineer with 25 years of experience in the field.

A third primary element of rhetoric is *context* or *situation*. Every text is written in a particular time and place, often in response to other texts and events happening in the world. The sociologist writing about teen use of social media, for example, may be writing in the context of a growing awareness or alarm about connections between excessive social media use and depression or suicide. The text may be shaped by other research, as well as by debates and conversations happening outside of the academy, and by social and political trends.

Purpose, *audience*, and *context* are three primary elements of any rhetorical situation. The *genre* or type of text (proposal or blog post, for example) and the *medium* (written report or slide presentation, for example) are also elements of the writing situation that shape the ways you read and respond to a text. Whenever you begin a composing project, you need to analyze the situation in which you are working. Using the rhetorical situation as part of the composing process for a writing project is discussed in 8.1 and 8.2. As a reader, you also need to develop an awareness of the rhetorical situation for the texts you read.

To read a text rhetorically, begin by asking questions about the text:

- **Who is the author?** What do I know about this author?
- **Who is the audience for this text?** What level of expertise and knowledge about the subject is assumed of the audience? How can I tell?
- **What is the purpose of this text?** Look for key words like *propose*, *argue*, *analyze*, or *assert*, which indicate an explicit purpose.
- **What do I know about the context?** When was the text published? Where was it published? Does the text refer to other articles? to world events?

1.3.2 Rhetorical reading strategies

To answer questions like these, you may need to apply some additional reading strategies. You may not be able to immediately identify all of these elements of a rhetorical situation, especially if you are reading an advanced scholarly text. These strategies include using *prior knowledge*, *inference*, and *questioning*.

Consider the following example, a paragraph from a business book called *Theory Z*, by William Ouchi.

> The *shinkansen* or "bullet train" speeds across the rural areas of Japan giving a quick view of cluster after cluster of farmhouses surrounded by rice paddies. This particular pattern did not develop purely by chance, but as a consequence of the technology peculiar to the growing of rice, the staple of the Japanese diet. The growing of rice requires the construction and maintenance of an irrigation system, something that takes many hands to build. More importantly, the planting and the harvesting of rice can only be done efficiently with the cooperation of twenty or more people. The "bottom line" is that a single family working alone cannot produce enough rice to survive, but a dozen families working together can produce a surplus. Thus the Japanese have had to develop the capacity to work together in harmony, no matter what the forces of disagreement or social disintegration, in order to survive.
> —William Ouchi, *Theory Z*

Prior knowledge refers to the knowledge and experience you bring to a text as a reader. Your own background knowledge contributes to what you read and the meaning you discover through your reading. The first sentence of the sample paragraph makes references to a bullet train speeding across rural Japan. If you have been to Japan, have ridden on a bullet train, or are Japanese yourself, you will have background knowledge that allows you to quickly fill in details to complete the picture. You bring meaning to the text that another reader may not. Similarly, if you have a background in economics or business, when you read the sentences about the "bottom line" and the development of communal farming, you bring to the text knowledge of group dynamics and business practices that help you understand the idea that Ouchi is presenting in this paragraph.

Reading rhetorically, and applying the strategy of prior knowledge, you make conscious connections to your own prior knowledge about a topic. You may also revise your thinking about a topic as a result of what you read. "*I used to think* _____, *but now I've learned that* _____." Reflecting on what you know about a topic and what you bring to a text is a useful strategy to apply when confronting a particularly difficult reading.

Sometimes you may be confronted with a text on a topic you know little about. If your prior knowledge about a topic is limited, you may face special challenges when reading a text on that topic. For example, consider a reader who encounters the Ouchi reading about Japan with no knowledge of Japanese culture and geography and no background in business or management theory. To that reader, the reading would be almost impenetrable at first. Most college writers face this challenge from time to time, especially when they need to read and consult scholarly sources written for specialists in a field. When this happens, the first step is simply to recognize that you are working with a subject about which you have limited background knowledge. You can't expect to immediately grasp all the meaning and subtleties that an experienced specialist would. That does not mean you should give up and abandon the reading. By using the strategies of *inference* and *questioning*, you can begin to build your knowledge about the reading and make progress toward understanding its main ideas.

Inferences are educated guesses or predictions. As you read, you are constantly making inferences. You make predictions about where the text is going, what examples may be coming next, and how the author's ideas are going to unfold. It's impossible to read without making inferences. From the moment you read the title of an article, you begin to make inferences about the article. As you read through the text, you revise and adjust your expectations, making new inferences along the way. *Reading inferentially* makes this process conscious. Start by looking for textual cues like the title, abstract, key words, headings, and visual elements that call special attention to themselves. Then move on to consider details and elements of the text that you can use to infer larger ideas about the meaning of the text.

For example, the sample paragraph above comes from the book *Theory Z*, which has a subtitle: *How American Businesses Can Meet the Japanese Challenge*. What can you infer from this subtitle? You might predict that the author is going to explain what "the Japanese challenge" is and that he is going to make an argument that is intended for an audience of American business readers. That inference helps you when you get to the sentence describing how "the Japanese have had to develop the capacity to work together in harmony." You infer that this idea of "working together in harmony" is part of the author's argument about Japanese business. You can infer that perhaps Ouchi is making the case that American businesses need to adopt similar ideas about harmony and communal work. Reading inferentially is a key part of interpretation and comprehension.

Asking questions as you read is one of the most effective strategies for engaging and staying attuned to a reading. Questions based on the rhetorical elements can inform your process of understanding a text. These questions are especially important when conducting research; they help you assess and evaluate a source.

- When was this written? By whom? For what purpose?
- How is this text useful or relevant to my own purposes?

Asking questions about context and prior knowledge is another way to connect what you are reading to what you already know.

- How does this compare to other things I have read on this topic?
- How does this change my thinking about the topic?
- What other questions does this reading motivate me to ask?

1.4 Reading Journals and Reading Reflections

1.4 Use reading journals and reflections to develop awareness of your reading processes.

Some college writing instructors will ask you to keep a reading journal. The practice of sustained, informal writing about what you read is a powerful tool for improving your skills as a reader—and as a writer. Because reading is a complex, learned skill, it pays to work consciously to develop an awareness of your own habits and thought processes as a reader. A reading journal is about you as a reader more than it is about the subjects you read about. When keeping a reading journal, avoid the temptation to simply repeat what the reading says, or to share your opinion on the topic of the reading. Instead, use the informal journal entries to identify, track, and reflect on the reading practices you use. Use these questions as starting points.

Reflecting on your reading practices

- What parts of this reading are clear to me, and what parts are challenging?
- What background knowledge do I bring to this text?
- What reading approach will I employ first and why?
- How far does this approach take me?
- What does this reading approach allow me to notice in the text?
- What other approaches do I need to use in order to construct meaning that achieves the goal of my task or assignment?
- How might this reading experience be useful as I read texts in my other courses?

1.5 Discussing Readings

1.5 Use class discussions and online forums to share responses to what you read.

Experienced readers know that discussion with other readers is one of the most valuable ways to develop insight about a text. Even a brief, informal discussion about a reading can help you see new things, clarify your own perspective, and see a reading through other readers' views. Each reader brings a different set of prior knowledge and experience to a text, each reader will connect with different details in a text and draw distinctively different inferences from them, and each reader will formulate different questions about a text. A college course provides a unique opportunity to share your responses to what you read.

In live class discussions, resist the temptation to draw conclusions or state opinions too hastily. You may have a strong reaction to a reading and want to share your interpretations. Instead, try to frame your comments around specific details in the text. Describe what you noticed in the reading and explain how specific details and language in the reading led you to make inferences or connected to other things you have read. You will learn more from a discussion if you remain open-minded and listen carefully to what others describe about their experiences and inferences during the reading.

In an online forum, your instructor will often pose a specific question about a reading and ask you to compose a thread that responds to that question. For example, an online discussion forum about the William Ouchi paragraph (1.3) might ask:

> According to Ouchi, how does the history and practice of rice farming in Japan lead to a particular model of business practices? How has the agricultural history of Japan shaped the social and economic ideas practiced in Japanese business today? What does Ouchi want to emphasize about the Japanese model?

To respond to this discussion prompt, apply the strategies presented in this chapter. You might consider how your own prior knowledge helps you to amplify words or images used in the reading. You might focus on specific keywords in the reading and in the instructor's questions to draw inferences about the concepts you are expected to learn in the class. As in a live classroom discussion, remember to focus on specific details in the reading and avoid the temptation to offer the "correct" interpretation or opinion about a text. Reading to learn is a practice that depends on your willingness to suspend judgment and become aware of yourself as a reader.

Chapter 2
Writing to Learn

Learning Objectives

2.1 Use annotation and note-taking strategies to move from reading to writing.
2.2 Write summaries to clarify and organize responses to readings.
2.3 Analyze readings to discover and explore ideas.
2.4 Use collaboration and discussion to develop ideas around readings.

2.1 Reading into Writing

2.1 Use annotation and note-taking strategies to move from reading to writing.

Writing to learn is a way to explore, discover, and connect ideas *before* you commit to sharing them with other readers. Writing to learn is different from writing to communicate. When you write to learn, your only audience is yourself; when writing to communicate, you develop and shape your ideas for wider audiences.

Writing to learn is related to *prewriting*. Prewriting is part of the planning stage of many writers' processes, and includes brainstorming, outlining, mind-mapping, and other invention strategies (see Chapter 9). Writing to learn can be a bridge from reading into writing. Taking notes, writing comments in the margins of a text, and using visual thinking are all forms of writing to learn. Summarizing and paraphrasing are also useful techniques for writing to learn.

Adopting and applying strategies for writing to learn will prepare you to compose more formal research projects. It can be tempting to read sources quickly in a form of "idea mining" in order to identify a few sentences to use as quotations in a paper. In contrast, writing-to-learn strategies help writers take a step back to consider and respond to sources *before* selecting quotations and integrating them into an informative or persuasive composition. Like some of the reading techniques presented in Chapter 1, strategies for writing to learn are valuable because they help you to develop a deeper, more complete understanding of what you have read. Most writers find that drafting and revising move more smoothly as a result of writing-to-learn strategies.

Writing-to-learn techniques can be used to prepare for more formal *critical reading* and analysis projects. Sometimes writing to learn precedes critical reading; sometimes writing to learn and critical reading overlap, as a writer moves back and forth between grappling with a text and analyzing its argument. Writing to learn and critical reading can be seen as a set of critical thinking tools that can be used together by writers who are responding to arguments and developing research-based compositions. Critical reading is presented in Chapter 4, which includes a sample rhetorical analysis essay based on the reading presented in this chapter.

Student Carmen Samsara was assigned to write a research-based essay on a topic related to media and culture for her interpersonal communication course. Samsara decided to focus on the topic of selfies and the popularity of taking self-portraits on smartphones and sharing them on social media. She found an essay called "What Your Selfies Say about You," written by Peggy Drexler, PhD, and published in *Psychology Today* magazine. Drexler's essay follows. Read through the essay carefully and consider your initial reactions and questions.

What Your Selfies Say About You

Earlier this week, a Texas mother of four, Kimberly Hall, made national headlines with her online manifesto to teenage girls prone to taking and posting self-portraits on social media. "Who are you trying to reach?" the mom asked. "What are you trying to say?" Girls who keep this sort of thing up, the mom went on to write, will be blocked in her household, because "Did you know that once a male sees you in a state of undress, he can't ever un-see it? You don't want the Hall boys to only think of you in this sexual way, do you? Neither do we."

Though her post is rife with sexism—the post runs beneath a photograph of her own three boys shirtless on the beach and includes no mention of the responsibility of the viewer, or her sons, in how he/they respond to such images—Hall makes a valid point. Ever since smartphones came equipped with cameras that face not just outward but also backward at the user, the self-portrait—dubbed the "selfie"—has taken over social media, particularly Instagram. (It's popular on dating sites, as well.) Because of the selfie's close-up nature, it's far more intimate than, say, the portrait your sister took of you standing in front of the Grand Canyon. Many selfies carry sexual undertones, especially since the majority of selfies are, obviously, user-approved, and designed to leave a positive impression or elicit a positive response. But it's not just technology that has driven the selfie—and it's not only teenage girls and singles using it to take control of how they present themselves to the world.

Sarabeth, a 40-year-old, married chief operating officer of a digital media company, routinely wove magazine-worthy photographs of herself lounging seductively on the beach, laughing by candlelight, and snuggling with her kids into her Instagram feed. They weren't all posed, though all were flawless, and served to project a certain image, that of money, power, and love of what, by all visual accounts, was her amazingly fun-filled life. "I don't put much thought into what I post other than if it's a nice photograph of a meaningful moment, I like to share it," she told me. "But no, if I look god-awful, that's not a photo that will see the light of day."

On the surface, the trend is sort of affirming, if undeniably self-absorbed: Women, whether rich and powerful like Sarabeth or otherwise, increasingly have a healthy image of themselves. That's a good thing. *Girls* creator Lena Dunham is a big fan of the selfie, both on social media and through her show—which shares with selfies a confessional quality. On TV, Dunham's character often appears naked or in various states of undress; in real life, her Instagram selfies aren't necessarily flattering by typical standards. They challenge the "Hollywood ideal" and that, too, is a good thing, especially when size 0 celebrities dominate so much of the modern day visual barrage. The more we see a range of body types, the better.

And yet selfies are also a manifestation of society's obsession with looks and its ever-narcissistic embrace. There's a sense that selfie subjects feel as though they're starring in their own reality shows, with an inflated sense of self that allows them to believe their friends or followers are interested in seeing them lying in bed, lips pursed, in a real-world headshot. It's like looking in the mirror all day long, and letting others see you do it. And that can have real and serious implications. Excessive narcissism, studies have found, can have adverse effects on marriage and relationships, parenting, and the workplace. One study found a link between excessive narcissism and violence.

What's more, a recent study out of the U.K. found that the selfie phenomenon may be damaging to real-world relationships, concluding that both excessive photo sharing and sharing photos of a certain type—including self-portraits—makes people less likeable. The same study found that increased frequency of sharing self-portraits is related to a decrease in intimacy with others. For one thing, putting so much emphasis on your own looks can make others feel self-conscious about theirs in your presence. The pressure to be "camera-ready" can also heighten self-esteem issues and increase feelings of competition among friends.

The trick with selfies may be to look at why you're taking them—and what they do for you. Posting affirming selfies can be empowering. They can help readjust the industry standard of the beauty ideal. But they can also help reinforce the idea that what matters most in this world is how things, and people, look. For Sarabeth, the problem she noticed first, before she even noticed her increasing fixation with her own appearance and that of her family, was the fact that she was so busy controlling her image that she'd often miss the moment in real life. Capturing something on camera took priority over reacting to something in person. "Documenting the experience took precedence over living it," she said. "And finally I realized, well, how can I expect others to pay attention to what's happening in my life when I can't even say the same for myself?"

—Peggy Drexler PhD

Samsara had a strong reaction to Drexler's essay. For her, the opening paragraph touched on a number of themes that she had been talking about with her friends and in some of her classes. Her first step was to write informally about the essay to identify why she was having such a strong reaction. She knew that she was expected to deliver a scholarly paper, not an opinionated rant, so she wanted to sort out what she was feeling about the topic and Drexler's approach to it. Writing to learn helped her to discover and identify these reactions.

To record her initial response to Drexler's essay, Samsara reread and annotated the text, noting in the margins specific words and sentences in the opening paragraph that were important to her understanding of Drexler's perspective on selfies.

Earlier this week, a Texas mother of four, Kimberly Hall, made national headlines with her online manifesto to teenage girls prone to taking and posting self-portraits on social media. "Who are you trying to reach?" the mom asked. "What are you trying to say?" Girls who keep this sort of thing up, the mom went on to write, will be blocked in her household, because "Did you know that once a male sees you in

Why start with a mother? Why not interview the girls posting selfies?

National? I guess this topic touches a nerve.

Why not ask them? Drexler seems to agree with the mom here.

Hall is very protective of her sons!

a state of undress, he can't ever un-see it? You don't want the Hall boys to only think of you in **this sexual way**, do you? Neither do we."

Why assume that are always sexua that what this is

Carmen Samsara decided to write about her responses to the Drexler essay in her reading journal. She knew that writing informally about what she was reading would help her to sort out her reactions as well as to identify some issues and questions to explore further in her research. Samsara used writing to learn to move from an initial response to a more focused series of questions about the topic in the reading. Notice that by the end of this journal entry, Samsara has begun to formulate a question that will guide her ongoing research for the interpersonal communication assignment.

> Peggy Drexler seems to take the viewpoint that selfies are bad and self-indulgent. She starts by talking about this mother who wrote a "manifesto" for young women who were posting selfies that her sons might see. Why does she assume that selfies are always posted by girls? Don't the sons post them too? Are selfies always about looking good and seduction? Drexler uses the term narcissism and talks about how selfies are related to self-esteem. Do women with low self-esteem post more selfies? Are they more risky and risque? I know there is a connection there. Is there any research on how selfies can be positive or self-affirming?

2.2 Writing to Respond

2.2 **Write summaries to clarify and organize responses to readings.**

Writing a summary of a reading can help you move from an initial response to a deeper understanding of a text. Summarizing leads to a broader engagement with the ideas in a reading, and helps you move beyond the "idea-mining" stage. Summaries are brief restatements, in your own words, of the ideas in a reading. A summary captures the essence of a reading. Summaries differ from informal journal responses, because instead of writing about your reactions to the text, your goal is to objectively state, in brief, what the reading says.

Sometimes you may need to summarize an entire essay in one sentence. A one-sentence summary can be used later to develop a point about a reading, or to introduce a quotation.

A process for summarizing readings

1. Write one sentence to summarize each paragraph in the reading.
2. Combine those sentences into a short paragraph.
3. Condense that paragraph into a single sentence.

Carmen Samsara applied a three-step process to develop a one-sentence summary of Peggy Drexler's essay about selfies. First, she wrote one sentence to summarize each paragraph in the essay.

1. A Texas mother wrote a manifesto and threatened to block girls who posted sexualized selfies that her sons might see on social media.
2. The manifesto is sexist but makes a valid argument about how teenage girls are using selfies to present themselves to boys and each other.
3. A 40-year-old professional woman also posts selfies that present a glamorized image of herself to others.
4. Selfies can be affirming even if they are self-absorbed, and some women are using them to challenge body stereotypes.
5. Selfies can be linked to social problems like narcissism and might also be responsible for relationship problems in families and at work.
6. A recent study concluded that excessive selfie-sharing can harm intimacy and make people feel self-conscious and competitive with each other.
7. Selfies can be empowering, but only if they are shared consciously and thoughtfully.

Carmen Samsara then took the sentences she had written, pasted them into a single paragraph, and then revised that paragraph to improve its coherence and flow (see 11.2 and 11.3 on paragraph unity and coherence).

> Young girls and older women alike use selfies, sometimes sexualized, to present an idealized image of themselves for others to view. These selfies can be affirming even if they are self-absorbed; some women are using them to challenge body stereotypes. Selfies do have a dark side and can be linked to social problems like narcissism and low self-esteem. Selfies might also be responsible for relationship problems in families and at work. A recent study concluded that excessive selfie-sharing can harm intimacy and make people feel self-conscious and competitive with each other. Selfies can be empowering, but only if they are shared consciously and thoughtfully.

Using this process, Samsara developed a one-paragraph summary that she could include in her paper later, if she decided to focus on the Drexler reading as one of her key sources. (Note that she would need to include a complete citation for the Drexler essay. Summaries of other writers' ideas need to be documented so readers know the source of the ideas.)

In a final step, Samsara condensed her summary paragraph into a single sentence that she might use later to introduce a quotation or briefly note Drexler's source in her paper.

> The popular trend of selfie-sharing by women is concerning because it is tied to sexualized body stereotypes and narcissistic behavior, but selfies can be used in affirming ways if shared intentionally and consciously.

2.3 Discovering and Exploring Ideas

2.3 Analyze readings to discover and explore ideas.

Analyzing means taking something apart in order to discover how its parts work. Analysis is a necessary part of almost any formal college writing assignment because it helps you move from simply reporting on what a text says to making your own argument about what it means and why it's important. Analysis is the basis of **critical reading** (covered in detail in Chapter 4). When writing a summary, your goal is to objectively restate the author's ideas; when writing an analysis, you seek to present your own opinion or thesis about the author's ideas.

Critical analysis essays (sometimes called **rhetorical analysis** papers) are common assignments in college writing courses. A complete sample student critical analysis paper appears in section 4.6. Analysis can also be used as a writing-to-learn strategy, as Carmen Samsara did in her work on selfies for her interpersonal communication course.

Samsara moved from summary to analysis in several steps. Once she developed a one-paragraph summary of the essay by Drexler, she chose a single short passage from the essay to focus on. In her analysis, notice how she pays close attention to the language of the passage, attending to its tone and construction. Selecting a few specific details, she uses analysis to connect the passage to the essay as a whole. Moving through this process helped her become aware of the relationship between language, style, and meaning in the essay. Writing this kind of informal analysis for herself also made her more aware of her own reading strategies.

1. Write a one-paragraph summary of the text.

   Young girls and older women alike use selfies, sometimes sexualized, to present idealized images of themselves for others to view. These selfies can be affirming even if they are self-absorbed; some women are using them to challenge body stereotypes. Selfies do have a dark side and can be linked to social problems like narcissism and low self-esteem. Selfies might also be responsible for relationship problems in families and at work. A recent study concluded that excessive selfie-sharing can harm intimacy and make people feel self-conscious and competitive with each other. Selfies can be empowering, but only if they are shared consciously and thoughtfully.

2. Select a single short passage from the text (three to five sentences) to analyze in detail.

   And yet selfies are also a manifestation of society's obsession with looks and its ever-narcissistic embrace. There's a sense that selfie subjects feel as though they're starring in their own reality shows, with an inflated sense of self that allows them to believe their friends or followers are interested in seeing them lying in bed, lips pursed, in a real-world headshot. It's like looking in the mirror all day long, and letting others see you do it. And that can have real and serious implications. Excessive narcissism, studies have found, can have adverse effects on marriage and relationships, parenting, and the workplace. One study found a link between excessive narcissism and violence.

> The key word in Peggy Drexler's essay on selfies is *narcissism*. Defined by psychologists as excessive self-interest or self-regard, narcissism is at the root of everything wrong with the popularity of selfies, especially among women, according to Drexler. Her descriptions are heavily loaded with negative value judgments. She describes women who post selfies as if they are "starring in their own reality shows" and argues that they have "an inflated sense of self." Her portrayal of the typical selfie describes women "lying in bed, lips pursed." From this characterization, she draws the conclusion that selfies, because they are essentially narcissistic, have negative effects on marriages, families, and workplace relationships. She even goes so far as to suggest a link to violent behavior.

3. Interpret the passage to connect it to the essay as a whole.

Interpretation implies an evaluation or assessment of the meaning of a text. Samsara followed a process to move from *description* (summary) to *analysis*, and then to *interpretation*. In the final paragraph of her informal analysis, she reflects on the significance of Drexler's argument.

In the last paragraph of her essay, Drexler suggests that selfies can sometimes be shared in a more empowering or affirming way. Her conclusion seems to me to swerve away from most of what she says in the body of her essay, and it leaves me with a lot of unanswered questions. What does Drexler mean when she says that selfies are empowering if women "look at why you're taking them—and what they do for you"? She does not explain how to do that. My initial reaction to her essay was to want to disagree with everything she said, because her view seemed condescending and dismissive to young women who like to share selfies. While I still disagree with her, I see now that she has helped me to identify an idea I want to research further in my paper. How can young women take ownership of their selfies and share them in empowering and affirming ways?

2.4 Writing to Share and Collaborate

2.4 Use collaboration and discussion to develop ideas around readings.

Class discussions, whether in-person or online, provide important opportunities for writing to learn. The process of developing and clarifying your responses to a reading often happens through dialogue.

For example, you might write a post for an online discussion in which you take on the voice and style of the author of one of the texts you have read. Writing in the voice of Peggy Drexler, for example, Carmen Samsara posted the following on her class discussion forum where students were sharing their work in progress on their research papers.

> Most young women and girls post selfies because they are obsessed with their own appearance and how they are seen by others. Our culture's obsession with body image and sex draws women into a narcissistic cycle where they post and share more revealing and erotic images of themselves. Selfie sharing is about looking good for men and competing with other women. Selfies are a major concern in interpersonal communication because they focus on image and appearance over substance, and the dishonesty inherent in glamorizing yourself for the camera can do real harm to women's relationships at home and in the workplace.

Carmen Samsara's instructor suggested another creative way to use a discussion forum to help her use writing to discover and clarify her thinking about interpersonal communication and social media. During one week of the research project, students were assigned to write a dialogue of sources, in which they wrote an imaginary dialogue between two authors of sources they had read. Samsara's interest in the topic of identity and technology in selfie-sharing led her to the work of Sherry Turkle, whose book *Alone Together: Why We Expect More from Technology and Less from Each Other* became an important source for her research project. She decided to write a dialogue between Turkle and Drexler. Using writing to learn in this way helped her to identify points of agreement and commonality among her sources.

Drexler: I spoke with one woman who said that she became so obsessed with controlling her image and presenting her experiences for the camera, she forgot to actually have the experience in the first place. She was like an actor in the play of her own life.

Turkle: My research has shown some of the same things. I like to call it simulation. Technology, especially social media, has made us so aware of how we look through the lens that we lose track of ourselves in real life. As I argue in my book, technology promises to connect us and provide intimacy and closeness. But it often does the opposite. We are more connected with simulations of life and less connected with each other.

Drexler: Do you think there is a way to break out of the obsessive cycle? Can people, especially women, take back control and use technologies like selfies and smartphones to form more affirming and healthy connections?

Turkle: I would like to think so, Peggy, but I am not optimistic. I've been studying how humans use technology for more than 20 years. Most of what I have seen is that technology draws us apart and presents us with images instead of intimacy.

Reflections are another way to use writing-to-learn strategies in online or live discussions. Reflections require you to step back and to observe and share your own thought processes as you read, write, and develop ideas. Carmen Samsara recognized that she had moved some distance from her original angry response to the Drexler essay.

> Reflection: describe how you met the requirements of the reading analysis assignment by listing the observations about the passage and the implications drawn from them; comment on the difficulties and what you are proud of.
>
> My reading analysis focused on the word "narcissism" because I discovered that was the key idea behind Drexler's overall argument. I connected some specific terms and showed how a lot of the language in the reading used negative connotations about women's use of selfies. She wrote about women as if every selfie had to be a bedroom shot. The biggest challenge for me was in seeing that there might be another angle to what Drexler was saying. My initial reaction was really negative and I thought the entire point of the reading was to criticize women for posting selfies. By looking closely at how Drexler was open to the idea that selfies could sometimes be empowering, I was able to find some ideas and questions to explore further in my research project.

Chapter 3
Joining the Academic Conversation

Learning Objectives

- **3.1** Determine your purpose and audience.
- **3.2** Use common academic genres in college writing.
- **3.3** Use sources ethically.
- **3.4** Use academic language.
- **3.5** Communicate with instructors and classmates.

3.1 Purpose and Audience

3.1 Determine your purpose and audience.

Like any writing, academic writing occurs in a particular situation created by your assignment and by your subject, purpose, audience, and genre. The assignment and subject will be different for each project, but some generalizations can be made about the other elements.

3.1.1 Purpose

For most academic writing, your general purpose will be to explain something or to make an argument. If your purpose is explanatory, you aim to explain your subject by analyzing, describing, or reporting on it so that readers understand it as you do. If your purpose is argumentative, you aim to gain readers' agreement with a debatable idea about the subject.

Your specific purpose—including your subject and how you hope readers will respond—depends on the genre, the kind of writing that you're doing. For instance, in a literature review for a biology class, you want readers to understand the research area you're covering, the recent contributions made by researchers, the issues needing further research, and the sources you consulted. Not coincidentally, these topics correspond to the major sections of a literature review. In following the standard format, you both help to define your purpose and begin to meet the discipline's (and thus your instructor's) expectations.

Your specific purpose will be more complex as well. You take a course to learn about a subject and the ways experts think about it. Your writing, in turn, contributes to the discipline through the knowledge you uncover and the lens of your perspective. At the same time, as a student you want to demonstrate your competence with research, evidence, format, and other requirements of the discipline.

3.1.2 Audience

Many academic writing assignments will specify or assume an educated audience or an academic audience. Such readers look for writing that is clear, balanced, well organized, and well reasoned. Other assignments will specify or assume an audience of experts on your subject, readers who look in addition for writing that meets the subject's requirements for claims and evidence, organization, language, format, and other qualities.

Much of your academic writing will have only one reader besides you: the instructor of the course for which you are writing. Instructors fill two main roles as readers:

- **They represent the audience you are addressing.** They may actually be members of the audience, as when you address academic

readers or subject matter experts. Or they may imagine themselves as members of your audience—reading, for instance, as if they sat on the city council. In either case, they're interested in how effectively you write for the audience.
- **They serve as coaches,** guiding you toward achieving the goals of the course and, more broadly, toward the academic aims of building and communicating knowledge.

Like everyone else, instructors have preferences and peeves, but you'll waste time and energy trying to anticipate them. Do attend to written and spoken directions for assignments, of course. But otherwise view your instructors as representatives of the community you are writing for. Their responses will be guided by the community's aims and expectations and by a desire to teach you about them.

3.2 Genre

3.2 Use common academic genres in college writing.

A *genre* is a type of writing. Genres take certain forms and follow certain conventions in order to meet readers' expectations. As a reader, you expect different things from a research report than you would from an editorial, for example. Research reports are one example of a genre that is common in academic settings.

Sometimes the genre is prescribed, such as the literature review mentioned earlier, with its standard content and format. Other assignments imply the genre, such as those that ask you to analyze, explain, compare, and argue. In these cases your responses would most likely be conventional academic essays—introduction, thesis statement, supporting paragraphs, conclusion—that analyze and compare in order to explain or argue.

Whether genre is specified or implied in your assignment, you are being asked to demonstrate your ability to write competently in that genre. The following sections describe genres commonly assigned in college courses and point out examples of each genre. You can get a good sense of how other writers work with genre conventions by studying the descriptions here and the samples with their surrounding explanations and annotations.

3.2.1 Reading responses

A reading response assignment may ask you to write about a written text or a visual image. Reading responses require close reading, summary, and analysis. (For more on analyzing and responding to texts and visuals, see Chapter 4.)

- **Personal response to a reading:** Use your own experiences, observations, and opinions to explain how and why you agree or disagree (or both) with the author's argument. A personal-response essay usually includes a thesis statement that conveys the essence of your response, a brief summary of the author's main points, and your own main points of agreement or disagreement.

- **Critical analysis of a text or a visual:** Closely examine a text or visual, identifying and describing important elements of the work and analyzing how the elements contribute to the whole. Often a critical analysis also includes evaluation of the quality and significance of the work. The genre gives an arguable thesis stating your interpretation, a brief summary or description of the work, and examples from the text or visual as support for your thesis and main points.

3.2.2 Arguments

Proposal arguments, position arguments, and evaluation arguments are common genres of argument assigned in college courses. Written arguments contain an arguable thesis statement—a claim reasonable people can disagree over—usually with support for its main points and acknowledgment of opposing views. Arguments often, but not always, involve research.

- **Proposal argument:** Define a problem, give a solution, explain how the solution can be implemented, and respond to possible objections to the solution.
- **Position argument:** Seek to convince readers to agree with your position on a debatable issue such as lowering the drinking age or requiring community service. A position argument introduces the issue, conveys your position in a thesis statement, makes claims and gives evidence to support your position, and responds to views different from your own. Depending on the assignment, your evidence may be personal or gathered from research or both.
- **Evaluation argument:** Judge whether something is good or effective and provide an evaluation based on criteria you define. Reviews of books, films, video games, and other cultural experiences are examples of evaluation arguments you might be asked to write in a college course.

3.2.3 Informative essays

In college courses, informative essays seek to teach readers about a subject. In the social, natural, and applied sciences, informative genres include summaries and case studies in addition to research-based writing. Informative essays require you to explore a subject in depth and provide information readers may not know. Informative essays often involve research.

- **Informative essay:** Explain a subject such as a situation or a process. Typically, an informative essay begins with an introduction and a thesis statement that previews your major points and then supports the thesis in the body paragraphs with evidence to clarify the subject.
- **Informative research paper or report:** Draw on research to explain a subject, answer a question, or describe the results of a survey or an experiment. This genre includes research papers, research reports, and laboratory reports.

3.2.4 Personal essays

A personal essay often narrates the writer's experience or describes a person or place, usually in vivid detail. What makes a personal essay interesting is the insight the writer provides, showing why the subject is significant to the writer and to readers. Personal essays can take the form of a profile of a person, a description of a place, or a narrative of an event.

A **literacy narrative** is a particular kind of personal essay, focused on narrating the writer's experience with learning to read and write.

3.2.5 Research papers and reports

Most research projects involve reporting information or results, interpreting a range of views on a topic, or analyzing a problem and arguing for a solution.

- **Research paper:** Develop an informative or argumentative thesis statement, draw on and cite multiple sources to support the thesis, and emphasize synthesis of your sources' views and data from your own perspective.
- **Research report:** Explain your own original research or your attempt to replicate someone else's research. A research report generally includes an abstract (or summary), an introduction describing your research and reviewing prior research on the subject, a description of methods, the results, discussion of the results, and a list of any sources you have cited.

Strategies for writing in academic genres

- **Develop a main point for your writing.** Most academic papers center on a main point, or thesis, and support that thesis with evidence. Depending on the genre you are writing in, the main point may be an opinion, a summary of findings, or a conclusion based on primary research you have conducted, such as an experiment or a survey.

(continued)

Strategies for writing in academic genres

(continued)

- **Support the main point with evidence, drawn usually from your reading, personal experience, or primary research.** The kinds of evidence will depend on the discipline and type of paper.
- **Synthesize your own and others' ideas.** College writing often involves researching and interacting with the works of other writers—being open to their ideas, responding to them, questioning them, comparing them, and using them to answer questions. Such interaction requires you to read critically and to synthesize, or integrate, others' ideas with your own.
- **Use academic language.** Unless your instructor specifies otherwise, choose formal, standard English. (For more on academic language, see 3.4.)
- **Document sources fully, including online sources.** Academic writers build on the work of others by citing borrowed ideas and information. Always record the publication information for your sources, put other writers' words in quotation marks, and cite the source of every quotation, paraphrase, and summary. *Not* acknowledging sources is plagiarism. (See 3.3 for more on using and acknowledging sources.)
- **Organize clearly within the framework of the type of writing you are using.** Develop your ideas as simply and directly as your purpose and content allow. Relate sentences, paragraphs, and sections clearly so that readers always know where they are in the paper's development.

3.3 Writing with Sources

3.3 Use sources ethically.

You can build your credibility as a writer by using sources ethically. Academic integrity is the foundation of academic knowledge building. Trusting in one another's honesty allows students and scholars to examine and extend the work of other scholars, and it allows teachers to guide and assess the progress of their students.

3.3.1 Avoiding plagiarism

Many writing assignments will require you to consult sources such as journal articles, Web sites, and books. These works belong to their creators; you are free to borrow from them *if* you do so with integrity. That means representing the sources accurately—not misinterpreting or distorting what they say. It also means crediting the sources—not plagiarizing, or presenting the sources' ideas and information as if they were your own. On most campuses, plagiarism is a punishable offense.

Plagiarism can be deliberate or careless:

- **Deliberate plagiarism** is outright cheating: copying another writer's sentence or idea and passing it off as your own, buying a

paper from an online store, or getting someone else to write a paper for you.
- **Careless plagiarism** is more common among students, often arising from inattentive or inexperienced handling of sources. For instance, you might cut and paste source information into your own ideas without clarifying who said what, or you might present a summary of a source without recognizing that parts of it are actually quoted. In these cases the plagiarism is unintentional, but it is still plagiarism.

3.3.2 Developing perspective on a subject

Consider your own knowledge and perspective on a subject before you start to research. This forethought will make it easier for you to recognize other authors' perspectives and to treat them fairly in your writing—whether or not you agree with them.

- **Before you consult sources, gauge what you already know and think about your subject.** Give yourself time to know your own mind before looking to others for information. Then you'll be able to reflect on how the sources reinforce, contradict, or expand what you already know.
- **Evaluate sources carefully.** Authors generally write from particular perspectives, and some are more overt about their biases than others. You needn't reject a source because it is biased; indeed, often you'll want to consider multiple perspectives. But you do need to recognize and weigh the writer's position.
- **Treat sources fairly.** Represent an author's ideas and perspectives as they were originally presented, without misunderstanding or distortion. Be careful in paraphrasing and summarizing not to misrepresent the author's meaning. Be careful in editing quotations not to omit essential words.

3.3.3 Managing sources

You can avoid plagiarism by keeping close track of the sources you consult, the ideas that influence your thinking, and the words and sentences you borrow—and by carefully citing the sources in your writing. If these habits are unfamiliar to you, keep the following list handy:

- **Keep track of source information as you read.** Get in the habit of always recording publication information (author, title, date, and so on) of any source you read as well as any ideas you glean from it.
- **Be careful with quotations.** If you cut and paste a portion of an article, Web site, or other source into your document, put quotation marks around it so that you don't mix your words and the source's words accidentally. Check any quotation that you use in your own writing against the original source.

- **Use your own words in paraphrases and summaries.** A paraphrase or summary presents the ideas of a source but not in the exact words of the original and not in quotation marks. You will be less likely to use the source author's words (and thus plagiarize) if you look away from the source while you write down what you remember from it. Note, though, that you must still cite the source of a summary or paraphrase, just as you do with a quotation.
- **Cite your sources.** As you draft, be conscious of when you're using source information and be conscientious about clearly marking where the borrowed material came from. In your final draft you'll use a particular style of citation within your text to refer to a detailed list of sources at the end. This book presents four documentation styles: MLA style for English and some other humanities (Chapter 51); APA style for the social sciences (Chapter 52); Chicago style for history, philosophy, and some other humanities (Chapter 53); and CSE style for the natural and applied sciences (Chapter 54).

3.4 Academic Language

3.4 Use academic language.

American academic writing relies on a dialect called standard American English. The dialect is also used in business, government, the media, and other sites of social and economic power where people of diverse backgrounds must communicate with one another. It is "standard" not because it is better than other forms of English, but because it is accepted as the common language, much as the dollar bill is accepted as the common currency.

In writing, standard English varies a great deal, from the formality of an academic research report to the more relaxed language of this handbook to informal e-mails between coworkers. Even in academic writing, standard English allows much room for the writer's own tone and voice, as these passages on the same topic show:

More formal

Drawn-out phrasing, such as *widespread problem of obesity among Americans.*

More complicated sentence structures, such as *take strong issue with the food industry, citing food manufacturers and fast-food chains that create and advertise. . . .*

More formal vocabulary: *responsibility, children, television.*

Responsibility for the widespread problem of obesity among Americans depends on the person or group describing the problem and proposing a solution. Some people believe the cause lies with individuals who make poor eating choices for themselves and parents who feed unhealthy foods to their children. Others take strong issue with the food industry, citing food manufacturers and fast-food chains that create and advertise food that is high in sugar, fat, and sodium. Still others place responsibility on American society as a whole for preferring a sedentary lifestyle centered on screen-based activities such as watching television and using computers for video games and social interaction.

Less formal

Who or what is to blame for the obesity epidemic depends on who is talking and what they want to do about the problem. Some people blame consumers for making bad choices and parents for feeding their kids unhealthy foods. Others demonize food manufacturers and fast-food chains for creating and advertising sugary, fatty, and sodium-loaded food. Still others point to Americans generally for spending too much time in front of screens watching TV, playing video games, or going on *Facebook*.

More informal phrasing, such as *obesity epidemic*.

Less complicated sentence structures, such as *demonize food manufacturers and fast-food chains for creating and advertising*. . . .

More informal vocabulary: *blame, kids, TV*.

Academic language, as these examples illustrate, has several common features:

- **Its formality varies depending on the writer's voice and audience.** For instance, the first passage might reflect the writer's preference for more formal language and also an audience of experts in the field who expect a serious, measured approach. Addressing peers instead of experts, the same writer might still sound more formal than the second writer does—perhaps retaining the formal vocabulary—but might also shorten sentences and tighten phrasing.
- **It follows the conventions of standard English for grammar and usage.** These conventions are detailed in guides to the dialect, such as this handbook.
- **It uses a standard vocabulary,** not one that only some groups understand, such as slang, an ethnic or regional dialect, or another language.
- **It *does not use* the informalities of everyday speech, texting, and instant messaging.** These informalities include incomplete sentences, slang, no capital letters, and shortened spellings (*u* for *you*, *b4* for *before*, *thru* for *through*, and so on).
- **It generally uses the third person (*he, she, it, they*).** The first-person *I* is sometimes appropriate to express personal opinions, but academic writers tend to avoid it and allow conclusions to speak for themselves. The first-person *we* can connect with readers and invite them to think along, but, again, many academic writers avoid it. The second-person *you* is appropriate only in addressing readers directly (as in this handbook), and even then it may seem condescending or too chummy. Definitely avoid using or implying *you* in conversational expressions such as *You know what I mean* and *Don't take this the wrong way*.
- **It is authoritative and neutral.** In the examples about obesity, the writers express themselves confidently, not timidly, as in *Explaining the causes of obesity requires the reader's patience because*. . . . The writers also refrain from hostility (*The food industry's callous attitude toward health* . . .) and enthusiasm (*The food industry's clever and appealing advertisements* . . .).

At first, the diverse demands of academic writing may leave you groping for an appropriate voice. In an effort to sound fresh and confident, you may write too casually, as if speaking to friends or family:

> **Too casual**
> Getting to the truth about the obesity epidemic in the US requires some heavy lifting. It turns out that everyone else is to blame for the problem—big eaters, reckless corporations, and all those Americans who think it's OK to be a couch potato.

In an effort to sound "academic," you may produce wordy and awkward sentences:

> **Wordy and awkward**
> The responsibility for the problem of widespread obesity among Americans depends on the manner of defining the problem and the proposals for its solution. In some discussions, the cause of obesity is thought to be individuals who are unable or unwilling to make healthy choices in their own diets and parents who similarly make unhealthy choices for their children.

The cure for writing too informally or too stiffly is to read academic writing so that the language and style become familiar, and to edit your own writing so that it sounds similar. With experience and practice, you will develop a voice that is sufficiently formal but still authentic and natural, as in the obesity examples.

Culture and language

If your first language or dialect is not standard American English, you know well the power of communicating with others who share your language. Learning to write standard English in no way requires you to abandon your first language. Like most multilingual people, you are probably already adept at switching between languages as the situation demands—speaking one way with your relatives, say, and another way with an employer. As you practice academic writing, you'll develop the same flexibility with it.

3.5 Communication in Academic Settings

3.5   Communicate with instructors and classmates.

As a member of an academic community, you will not only write papers and projects, but also write directly to instructors, classmates, and other people at your school via e-mail, course-management systems such as *Blackboard* and *Canvas*, and other electronic media. Your written communication with instructors and classmates will rarely be as formal as assigned writing, but it will also rarely be as informal as a text to a friend, a tweet, or a comment on *Facebook*.

Even in a short e-mail, your message will receive a better hearing if you present yourself well and show respect for your reader(s). Figure 3.1 illustrates an appropriate mix of formality and informality when addressing an instructor:

Figure 3.1 E-mail message

To: cmwhite@cms.edu

Subject: Research paper planning conference — *Uses subject line to describe the content of the message.*

Dear Professor White: — *Addresses instructor formally with title and last name.*

I am in your 8:10 English 111 class, and I'm writing to schedule a planning conference — *Provides context for request.* to discuss possible subjects for my research paper. I recently read an article about smoking in movies, and I'm interested in pursuing the topic for my research paper. — *Uses complete sentences and words.* However, I know I'll have to narrow the topic, and I'm not sure how to do that. Would you be available to meet sometime between 11:00 and 1:00 next Tuesday or Thursday?

Sincerely,

Rachel Rogers — *Signs with full name and phone number.*
292-8954

Here are guidelines for such communication:

- **Use the medium your instructor prefers.** Don't text, tweet, or use a social-networking site unless you're invited to do so. Federal law requires instructors to use campus e-mail (not personal e-mail or social media) to discuss grades with students.
- **Use names.** In the body of your message, address your reader(s) by name if possible. Unless your teachers instruct otherwise, always address them formally, using *Professor, Dr., Ms.,* or *Mr.,* as appropriate, followed by the last name. Sign off with your own name and contact information.
- **Pay attention to tone.** Don't use all capital letters, which SHOUT. And use irony or sarcasm only cautiously: in the absence of facial expressions, either one can lead to misunderstanding.
- **Pay attention to correctness.** Especially when you write to instructors, avoid the shortcuts of texting and tweeting, such as incomplete sentences and abbreviations (*u* for *you, r* for *are,* and so on). Proofread for errors in grammar, punctuation, and spelling.
- **Send messages only to the people who need them.** As a general rule, avoid sending messages to many recipients at once—all the students in a course, say—unless what you are writing applies to all of them. Before you hit *Reply All* in response to a message, ensure that "all" want to see the response.

- **Guard your own and others' privacy.** Online tools allow us to broadcast hurtful information about others—and allow others to do the same to us. Before you post a message about yourself or someone else, consider whether it's worthwhile and who will see it, not only now but in the future. When forwarding messages, make sure not to pass on previous private messages by mistake.
- **Don't write anything that you would not say face to face or would not write in a printed letter.** Electronic messages can be saved and forwarded and can be retrieved in disputes over grades and other matters.

Chapter 4
Reading Arguments

Learning Objectives

4.1 Use techniques of critical reading.
4.2 Summarize texts.
4.3 Develop a critical response.
4.4 View visuals critically.
4.5 Write a critical analysis.
4.6 Examine a sample critical analysis.

4.1 Techniques of Critical Reading

4.1   Use techniques of critical reading.

In college, much of your critical thinking will focus on written texts (a short story, a journal article, a blog) or on visual or multimedia texts (a photograph, an advertisement, a film). Like all subjects worthy of critical consideration, such works operate on at least three levels:

1. What the creator actually says or shows.
2. What the creator does not say or show but builds into the work, intentionally or not.
3. What you think in response.

Discovering each level of the work involves a number of reading techniques that are discussed in this chapter. Writing-to-learn techniques can be used to prepare for more formal critical reading. Writing-to-learn strategies use informal writing to explore and discover ideas presented in readings. Applying writing-to-learn techniques will help you clarify your initial responses, develop research questions, and build an understanding of how a text works as a whole. Sometimes writing to learn precedes critical reading; sometimes writing to learn and critical reading overlap as a writer moves back and forth between grappling with a text and analyzing its argument. Chapter 2 demonstrates a series of writing-to-learn strategies and follows a student through an initial encounter with a text. Writing to learn and critical reading can be seen as a set of critical thinking tools that can be used together by writers who are responding to arguments and developing research-based compositions.

Culture and language

The idea of reading critically may require you to make some adjustments if readers in your native culture tend to seek understanding or agreement more than engagement from what they read. Readers of English use texts for all kinds of reasons, including pleasure, reinforcement, and information. But they also read questioningly, to uncover the author's motives (*What are this author's biases?*), test their own ideas (*Can I support my point of view as well as this author supports hers?*), and arrive at new knowledge (*Why is the author's evidence so persuasive?*).

4.1.1 Previewing the material

When reading texts, it is worthwhile to **skim** before reading word for word, forming expectations and preliminary questions. Previewing will make your close reading more informed and fruitful.

- **Gauge length and level.** Is the material brief and straightforward so that you can read it in one sitting, or will it require more time?
- **Check the facts of publication.** Does the date of publication suggest currency or datedness? Does the publisher or publication specialize in scholarly articles, popular books, or something else? For a Web publication, who or what sponsors the site—an individual? a nonprofit organization? a government body? a college or university?
- **Look for content cues.** What do the title, introduction, headings, illustrations, conclusion, and other features tell you about the topic, the author's approach, and the main ideas?

- **Learn about the author.** Does a biography tell you about the author's publications, interests, biases, and reputation in the field? If there is no biography, what can you gather about the author from his or her words? Use a Web search to trace unfamiliar authors.
- **Consider your preliminary response.** What do you already know about the topic? What questions do you have about either the topic or the author's approach to it? What biases of your own—for instance, curiosity, boredom, or an outlook similar or opposed to the author's—might influence your reading of the work?

4.1.2 Reading

Reading is itself more than a one-step process. You want to understand the first level on which the text operates—what the author actually says—and begin to form your impressions.

First reading

The first time through new material, read as steadily and smoothly as possible, trying to get the gist of what the author is saying.

- **Read in a place where you can concentrate.** Choose a quiet environment away from distractions such as music or talking.
- **Give yourself time.** Rushing yourself or worrying about something else you have to do will prevent you from grasping what you read.
- **Try to enjoy the work.** Seek connections between it and what you already know. Appreciate new information, interesting relationships, forceful writing, humor, and good examples.
- **Make notes sparingly during this first reading.** Mark major stumbling blocks—such as a paragraph you don't understand—so that you can try to resolve them before rereading.

Culture and language

If English is not your first language and you come across unfamiliar words, don't stop and look up every one. You will be distracted from an overall understanding of the text. Instead, try to guess the meanings of the unfamiliar words by using context clues, such as examples and synonyms of the words. Be sure to circle the words and look them up later. You may want to keep a vocabulary log of the words, their definitions, and the sentences in which they appeared.

Rereading and annotating

After a first reading, plan on at least one other. This time read *slowly*. Your main concern should be to grasp the content and how it is constructed. That means rereading a paragraph if you didn't get the point, or using a dictionary to look up words you don't know.

Use the tips below to highlight and annotate a text:

- **Distinguish main ideas from supporting ideas.** Mark the central idea (the thesis), the main idea of each paragraph or section, and the evidence supporting ideas.
- **Note key terms.** Understand both their meanings and their applications.
- **Identify the connections among ideas.** Be sure you see why the author moves from point A to point B to point C and how those points work together to support the central idea. It often helps to outline the text or summarize it.
- **Distinguish between facts and opinions.** Especially when reading an argument, mark the author's opinions as well as the facts on which the opinions are based.
- **Add your own comments.** In the margins or separately, note links to other readings or to class discussions, questions to explore further, possible topics for your writing, and points you find especially strong or weak.

An example of critical reading

The following samples show how a student, Carmen Samsara, approached Peggy Drexler's essay on selfies. (You can read Drexler's essay in 2.1.) After her first reading, Samsara went through Drexler's text more slowly, adding comments and questions in the margin and writing about the essay in her journal. Following are samples of her annotations and her journal entries.

Student's annotations

Earlier this week, a Texas mother of four, Kimberly Hall, made national headlines with her online manifesto to teenage girls prone to taking and posting self-portraits on social media. "Who are you trying to reach?" the mom asked. "What are you trying to say?" Girls who keep this sort of thing up, the mom went on to write, will be blocked in her household, because "Did you know that once a male sees you in a state of undress, he can't ever un-see it? You don't want the Hall boys to only think of you in this sexual way, do you? Neither do we."

Fact-Hall's post made national news
Strong word!

The woman in Texas seems to think all selfies are sexual? Charged language

Though her post is rife with sexism—the post runs beneath a photograph of her own three boys shirtless on the beach and includes no mention of the responsibility of the viewer, or her sons, in how he/they respond to such images— Hall makes a valid point. Ever since smartphones came equipped with cameras that face not just outward but also

Author's opinion, critical of Hall

Drexler also seems to agree with Hall on this opinion

crit 4.2

backward at the user, the self-portrait-dubbed the "selfie"—has taken over social media, particularly Instagram. (It's popular on dating sites, as well.) Because of the selfie's close-up nature, it's far more intimate than, say, the portrait your sister took of you standing in front of the Grand Canyon. Many selfies carry sexual undertones, especially since the majority of selfies are, obviously, user-approved, and designed to leave a positive impression or elicit a positive response. But it's not just technology that has driven the selfie—and it's not only teenage girls and singles using it to take control of how they present themselves to the world.

Developing her m idea here: definir selfies

Shifting to a nev idea

For her journal entries, Samsara created a two-column table on her computer. She used the left column to record ideas in Drexler's essay that she found thought provoking; then in the right column she responded to some of those ideas with her own comments and questions.

Student's journal entries

Text	Responses
Selfies are taking over social media and becoming popular with many groups (2)	It's easy to see this. Maybe there are some statistics about number of selfies posted?
Selfies are more intimate than other photos and often sexual in nature (2)	Selfies can be sexual, but can't they also be friends just sharing funny photos, too?
The selfie trend can be affirming, but it is often self-absorbed as well (4)	Key question: How can you tell when a selfie is affirming vs. when it is narcissistic?
Selfies may be damaging to real-world relationships (6)	I want to hear more about this; not sure I am convinced. Can't selfies also build relationships?

4.2 Summarizing

4.2 Summarize texts.

A good way to master the content of a text and to see its strengths and weaknesses is to **summarize** it—that is, to distill it to its main points, in your own words.

Writing a summary

- **Understand the meaning.** Look up words or concepts you don't know so that you understand the author's sentences and how they relate to one another.
- **Understand the organization.** Work through the text to identify its sections—single paragraphs or groups of paragraphs focused

on a single topic. To understand how parts of a work relate to one another, try drawing a tree diagram or creating an outline.
- **Distill each section.** Write a one- or two-sentence summary of each section you identify. Focus on the main point of the section, omitting examples, facts, and other supporting evidence.
- **State the main idea.** Write a sentence or two capturing the author's central idea.
- **Support the main idea.** Write a full paragraph (or more, if needed) that begins with the central idea and supports it with the sentences that summarize sections of the work. The paragraph should concisely and accurately state the thrust of the entire work.
- *Use your own words.* By writing, you re-create the meaning of the work in a way that makes sense for you. You also avoid plagiarism.
- *Cite the source.* When summarizing a text in writing for others, always acknowledge the source.

crit
4.2

Summarizing even a passage of text can be tricky. Here we'll look at attempts to summarize the following material from an introductory biology textbook.

Original text

As astronomers study newly discovered planets orbiting distant stars, they hope to find evidence of water on these far-off celestial bodies, for water is the substance that makes possible life as we know it here on Earth. All organisms familiar to us are made mostly of water and live in an environment dominated by water. They require water more than any other substance. Human beings, for example, can survive for quite a few weeks without food, but only a week or so without water. Molecules of water participate in many chemical reactions necessary to sustain life. Most cells are surrounded by water, and cells themselves are about 70–95% water. Three-quarters of Earth's surface is submerged in water. Although most of this water is in liquid form, water is also present on Earth as ice and vapor. Water is the only common substance to exist in the natural environment in all three physical states of matter: solid, liquid, and gas. —Neil A. Campbell and Jane B. Reece, *Biology*

The first attempt to summarize the passage accurately restates ideas in the original, but it does not pare the passage to its essence:

Draft summary

Astronomers look for water in outer space because life depends on it. It is the most common substance on Earth and in living cells, and it can be a liquid, a solid (ice), or a gas (vapor).

The work of astronomers and the three physical states of water add color and texture to the original, but they are asides to the key concept that water sustains life because of its role in life. The following revision narrows the summary to this concept:

> **Revised summary**
> Water is the most essential support for life, the dominant substance on Earth and in living cells, and a component of life-sustaining chemical processes.

When Carmen Samsara summarized Peggy Drexler's essay on selfies she first drafted the following sentence:

> **Draft summary**
> Selfies can have both detrimental and beneficial effects on your personal life, your reputation, and your relationships.

Rereading the sentence and Drexler's paragraphs, Samsara saw that this draft was overly general and missed some of the main ideas in Drexler's essay. She realized that Drexler's point is more complicated than that, and rewrote her summary:

> **Revised summary**
> As the phenomenon continues to grow, selfie subjects should consider how and why they are using their images on social media to determine if the overall effects are detrimental or beneficial to their personal life, reputation, or relationships.

Using your own words when writing a summary not only helps you understand the meaning but also constitutes the first step in avoiding plagiarism. The second step is to cite the source when you use the summary in something written for others.

4.3 Critical Response

4.3 Develop a critical response.

Once you've grasped the content of what you're reading—what the author says—then you can turn to understanding what the author does not say outright but suggests or implies, or even lets slip. At this stage you are concerned with the purpose or intention of the author and with how he or she carries it out.

Critical thinking and reading consist of four overlapping operations: analyzing, interpreting, synthesizing, and (often) evaluating.

4.3.1 Analyzing

Analysis is the separation of something into its parts or elements, the better to understand it. To see these elements in what you are reading, begin with a question that reflects your purpose in analyzing the text: why you're curious about it or what you're trying to make out of it. This question will serve as a kind of lens that highlights some features and not others.

Analyzing Peggy Drexler's essay on selfies you might ask these questions:

Questions for analysis	Elements
What is Drexler's position on selfies?	References to selfies: content, words, tone
How does Drexler support her assertions about selfies?	Support: evidence, such as anecdotes, research, and examples

4.3.2 Interpreting

Identifying the elements of something is only a start: you also need to interpret the meaning or significance of the elements and of the whole. Interpretation usually requires you to infer the author's **assumptions**—opinions or beliefs about what is or what could or should be. (*Infer* means to draw a conclusion based on evidence.)

Assumptions are pervasive: we all adhere to certain values, beliefs, and opinions. But assumptions are not always stated outright. Speakers and writers may judge that their audience already understands and accepts their assumptions; they may not even be aware of their assumptions; or they may deliberately refrain from stating their assumptions for fear that the audience will disagree. That is why your job as a critical thinker is to interpret what the assumptions are.

Peggy Drexler's essay on selfies is based on certain assumptions, some obvious, some not so obvious. She assumes, for example, that most selfie-takers are women, specifically young women. While commenting on the possibly self-affirming value of selfies, Drexler seems to assume that the practice is "a manifestation of society's obsession with looks and its ever-narcissistic embrace." From these statements and others, you can infer the following:

> Drexler assumes that the majority of selfie-takers are young women, posting and sharing selfies to make themselves look good to other women and attractive to men.

4.3.3 Synthesizing

If you stopped at analysis and interpretation, critical thinking and reading might leave you with a pile of elements and possible meanings but no vision of the whole. With **synthesis** you make connections among the parts of the text *or* between the text and other texts. You consider the text through the lens of your knowledge and beliefs, drawing conclusions about how the text works as a whole.

Sometimes you'll respond directly to a text. The statement below, about Peggy Drexler's essay "What Your Selfies Say About

> Drexler states that the selfie trend is "sort of affirming, if undeniably self-absorbed," allowing women to build a healthy self-image and challenging the notion that women must be a size 0 to be beautiful.

Often synthesis will take you outside the text to its surroundings. The following questions can help you investigate the context of a work:

- **How does the work compare with similar works?** How have other writers responded to Drexler's views on selfies?
- **How does the work fit into the context of other works by the same author or group?** How do Drexler's views on selfies typify, or not, the author's other writings on psychology and popular culture?
- **What cultural, economic, or political forces influence the work?** What other examples might Drexler have given to illustrate her views about selfies and relationships?
- **What historical forces influence the work?** How have selfies become more popular in recent years?

4.3.4 Evaluating

Critical reading and writing often end at synthesis: you form and explain your understanding of what the work says and doesn't say. If you are also expected to **evaluate** the work, however, you will go further to judge its quality and significance:

- **Collect and test your judgments.** Determine that they are significant and that they apply to the whole work.
- **Turn the judgments into assertions**—for instance, *The poet creates fresh, intensely vivid images* or *The author does not summon the evidence to support his case*.
- **Support these statements with evidence from the text**—mainly quotations and paraphrases.

Evaluation takes a certain amount of confidence. You may think that you lack the expertise to cast judgment on another's work, especially if the work is difficult or the author well known. True, the more informed you are, the better a critical reader you are. But conscientious reading and analysis will give you the internal authority to judge a work *as it stands* and *as it seems to you,* against your own unique bundle of experiences, observations, and attitudes.

4.4 Visual Analysis

4.4 View visuals critically.

Every day we are surrounded by visuals—pictures on billboards, advertisements on social media, graphs in textbooks, and charts on Web sites, to name just a few examples. Most visuals slide by without our noticing them, or so we think. But visuals, sometimes even more than text, can influence us covertly. Their creators have purposes, some worthy, some not, and understanding those purposes requires critical reading. The method parallels that in the previous sections for reading text critically: write while reading, preview, read for comprehension, analyze, interpret, synthesize, and (often) evaluate.

4.4.1 Previewing a visual

Your first step in exploring a visual is to form initial impressions of its origin and purpose and to note its distinctive features. This previewing process is like the one for previewing a text:

- **What do you see?** What is most striking about the visual? What is its subject? What is the gist of any text or symbols? What is the overall effect of the visual?
- **What are the facts of publication?** Where did you first see the visual? Was it created especially for that location or for others as well? What can you tell about when the visual was created?
- **What do you know about the person or group that created the visual?** For instance, was the creator an artist, scholar, news organization, or corporation? What seems to have been the creator's purpose?
- **What is your preliminary response?** What about the visual interests, confuses, pleases, or disturbs you? Are the form, style, and subject familiar or unfamiliar? How might your knowledge, experiences, and values influence your reception of the visual?

If possible, print a copy of the visual or copy it into your reading journal file, and write comments in the visual's margins or separately.

4.4.2 Reading a visual

Reading a visual requires the same level of concentration as reading a text. Try to answer the following questions about the visual. If some answers aren't clear at this point, skip the question until later.

- **What is the purpose?** Is the visual mainly explanatory, conveying information, or is it argumentative, trying to convince readers of something or to persuade them to act? What information or point of view does it seem intended to get across?
- **Who is the intended audience?** What does the source of the visual, including its publication facts, tell about the creator's expectations for readers' knowledge, interests, and attitudes? What do the features of the visual itself add to your impression?
- **What do any words or symbols add?** Whether located on the visual or outside it (such as in a caption), do words or symbols add information, focus your attention, or alter your impression?

42 Reading arguments

crit
4.4

- **What action, change, people, places, or things are shown?** Does the visual tell a story? Do its characters or other features tap into your knowledge, or are they unfamiliar?
- **What is the form of the visual?** Is it a photograph, advertisement, painting, graph, diagram, cartoon, or something else? How do its content and apparent purpose and audience relate to its form?

Figure 4.1 shows how Randall Dempsey annotated an advertisement he saw on the Web. (He copied the ad into a document and added a text box for his annotations.)

Figure 4.1 Annotation of an advertisement

Egg carton on the left, one egg missing, placed to the right of the container.

Egg is stamped like a food carton with a sell-by date.

Black type in all caps to the right presents information about food waste and water use.

What is *Savethefood.com*? What is NRDC and what is their role in sponsoring this ad?

4.4.3 Analyzing a visual

Elements for analysis

As when analyzing a written work, you analyze a visual by identifying its elements. The visual elements you might consider appear in the following box. Few visuals include all the elements, and you can narrow the list further by posing a question about the visual you are reading, as discussed after the box.

Elements of visuals

- **Emphasis:** Most visuals pull your eyes to certain features: a graph line moving sharply upward, a provocative figure, bright color, thick lines, and so on.
- **Narration:** Most visuals tell stories, whether in a sequence (a TV commercial or a graph showing changes over time) or at a single moment (a photograph, a painting, or a pie chart). Sometimes dialog or a title or caption contributes to the story.

- **Point of view:** The creator of the visual influences responses by taking into account both the viewer's physical relation to the subject—for instance, whether it is seen head-on or from above—and the viewer's assumed attitude toward the subject.
- **Arrangement:** Pattern, foreground versus background, and separation can contribute to the visual's meaning and effect.
- **Color:** Color can direct the viewer's attention, convey the creator's attitude, and suggest a mood.
- **Characterization:** The qualities of figures and objects—sympathetic or not, desirable or not—reflect their roles in the visual's story.
- **Context:** The source of a visual affects its meaning, whether it is a graph from a scholarly journal or a car ad on the Web.
- **Tension:** Visuals often communicate a problem or seize attention with features that seem wrong, such as misspelled or misaligned words, distorted figures, or controversial relations between characters.
- **Allusions:** An **allusion** is a reference to something the audience is likely to recognize and respond to. Examples include a cultural symbol such as a dollar sign, a mythological figure such as a unicorn, or a familiar movie character such as Darth Vader from *Star Wars*.

Question for analysis

You can focus your analysis of elements by framing your main interest in the visual as a question. Randall Dempsey concentrated his analysis of the *Savethefood.com* ad by asking the question *Does the ad move viewers to reduce food waste?* The question led Dempsey to focus on some elements of the ad and ignore others:

Elements of the ad	Responses
Emphasis	The red font on the egg grabs the viewer, placing emphasis on the message: best if used.
Narration	In just a few words, the ad sends a message. Trashing food costs more than just the wasted food. It appeals to the viewer's desire to protect our natural resources.
Point of view	The viewer is looking down on the egg and the egg carton, giving the viewer a sense of power over the situation.
Color	The red font directs the viewer's attention to the message. It also gives the message a sense of urgency. The black font suggests the seriousness of the message.
Characterization	The use of all capital letters throughout the ad reflects the seriousness of the message. The viewer must pay attention to the message and act accordingly.
Allusion	The font used on the egg and the black box alludes to the best-if-used-by dates that would be familiar to anyone who has shopped in a grocery store.

crit 4.4

Sample Web pages for analysis

The screen shots in Figure 4.2 are from *AIDS Clock*, an interactive Web site sponsored by the United Nations Population Fund (*www.unfpa.org/aids_clock*). The top image is the home page, displaying a traditional world map. The bottom image appears when viewers click on "Resize the map": now each country's size reflects the number of its people who live with HIV, the virus that causes AIDS. (For example, South Africa grows while the United States shrinks.) The large blue number at the top changes every 12 seconds to give the total number of people living with HIV in the world at that moment. Try to answer the questions in the annotations above the screen shots.

4.4.4   Interpreting a visual

The strategies for interpreting a visual parallel those for interpreting a written text. In this process, you look more deeply at the elements, considering them in relation to the likely assumptions and intentions of the visual's creator. You aim to draw reasonable inferences about *why* the visual looks as it does. Here's a reasonable inference about the *Savethefood.com* advertisement:

> The *Savethefood.com* ad is designed to prevent food waste by persuading people to act.

This inference is supported by the text in the ad: "Just don't waste it."

4.4.5   Synthesizing ideas about a visual

With synthesis you take analysis and interpretation a step further to consider how a work's elements and underlying assumptions relate and what the overall message is. You may also want to view the visual in the larger context of similar images, advertisements, or art works on related topics.

Placing a visual in its context often requires research. For instance, to learn more about the assumptions underlying the *Savethefood.com* advertisement and the goals of the larger ad campaign, Randall Dempsey visited the *Savethefood.com* Web site. The following entry from his reading journal synthesizes this research and his own ideas about the ad:

> The *Savethefood.com* ad is part of a larger campaign designed to prevent food waste by persuading people to act. Viewers who go to the *Savethefood.com* Web site can find additional statistics related to food waste as well as suggestions on reducing individual food waste. Viewers can find recipes made with commonly wasted food and guidelines for short-term and long-term food storage. Viewers also have an option to join the National Resources Defense Council, the ad's sponsor. The ad with the egg and carton is designed to attract viewers by making the issue appear important and urgent.

Figure 4.2 Elements of Web pages

Emphasis and color: What elements on these pages draw your attention? How does color distinguish and emphasize elements?

Narration: What story do the two Web pages tell? What does each map contribute to the story? What does the blue number contribute? (Notice that the number changes from the first screen to the second.)

Arrangement: What does the arrangement of elements on the pages contribute to the story being told?

Tension: How do you respond to the distorted map in the second image? What does the distortion contribute to your view of the Web site's effectiveness?

Context: How does knowing the Web site's sponsoring organization, the United Nations Population Fund, affect your response to these images?

AIDS Clock Web pages, 2014

4.4.6 Evaluating a visual

If your critical reading moves on to evaluation, you'll form judgments about the quality and significance of the visual: Is the message of the visual accurate and fair, or is it distorted and biased? Can you support, refute, or extend the message? Does the visual achieve its apparent purpose, and is the purpose worthwhile? How does the visual affect you?

4.5 Writing a Critical Analysis

4.5   Write a critical analysis.

Many academic writing assignments ask for **critical analysis**, or a **critique**, in which you write critically about texts or visuals. As you form a response to a work, you integrate its ideas and information with yours to come to your own conclusions. As you write your response, you support your ideas about the work by citing evidence from it.

Critical writing is *not* summarizing. You might summarize to clarify a text or a visual for yourself, and you might briefly summarize a work in your larger piece of writing. But in critical writing you go further to bring your own perspective to the work.

4.5.1 Deciding how to respond

When an assignment asks you to respond directly to a text or a visual, you might take one of the following approaches to decide on your position:

- **Agree with and extend the ideas expressed in the work,** exploring related ideas and providing additional examples.
- **Agree with some of the ideas but disagree with others.**
- **Disagree with one or more ideas.**
- **Explain how the work achieves a particular effect,** such as balancing opposing views or conveying a mood.
- **Analyze the overall effectiveness of the work**—for example, how well a writer supports a thesis with convincing evidence or whether an advertisement succeeds in its unstated purpose.

4.5.2 Shaping a critical analysis

You will likely have an immediate response to at least some of the texts and visuals you analyze: you may agree or disagree strongly with what the author says or shows. But for some other responses, you may need to use the process of critical reading described in 4.1 to take notes on the text, summarize it, and develop a view of it. Then, as you write, you can use the tips in the following box to convey your response to readers.

Responding to a text

- **Make sure your writing has a point**—a central idea, or thesis, that focuses your response.
- **Include a very brief summary if readers may be unfamiliar with your subject.** But remember that your job is not just to report what the text says or what a visual shows; it is to *respond* to the work from your own critical perspective.
- **Center each paragraph on an idea of your own that supports your thesis.** Generally, state the idea outright, in your own voice.
- **Support the paragraph idea with evidence from the text**—quotations, paraphrases, details, and examples.
- **Conclude each paragraph with your interpretation of the evidence.** As a general rule, avoid ending paragraphs with source evidence; instead, end with at least a sentence that explains what the evidence shows.

4.5.3 Emphasizing synthesis in your response

Following the suggestions in the preceding box will lead you to show readers the synthesis you achieved as you developed a critical response to the text or visual. That is, you integrate your perspective on the work with that of the author or creator in order to support a conclusion of your own.

A key to synthesis is deciding how to present evidence from your critical reading or viewing. Especially when you are writing about a relatively unfamiliar subject, you may be tempted to let a text or other source do the talking for you through extensive summary or quotations. However, readers of your academic writing will expect to see you managing ideas and information to make your points.

A typical paragraph of text-based writing follows the pattern outlined in the preceding box: the writer's own idea, evidence from the text, and the writer's interpretation of the evidence. You can see this pattern in the following paragraph:

> The most fundamental and debatable assumption underlying Drexler's essay is that selfies can be equally good and bad for the subject's personal life and relationships, depending on the intent of the selfie-taker. Well, Drexler suggests this assumption, but she really doesn't support it. ⎯ Writer's idea
>
> She provides only anecdotal evidence that suggests a positive overall benefit to selfies while providing multiple links to peer-reviewed research on the detrimental impact of selfies on marriage and relationships, parenting, and the workplace. Moreover, her argument appears to

48 Reading arguments

focus solely on the effect of selfies on women. In her introduction, she discusses selfie use among teenage girls before discussing the selfies of a 40-year-old woman in a later paragraph. Then, she states that selfies "challenge the 'Hollywood ideal'"—a good thing in her opinion since "size 0 celebrities dominate so much of the modern day visual barrage." — **Evidence**

Obviously, Drexler is primarily concerned with the use of selfies among women despite numerous studies that suggest a link between selfie-taking men and narcissism, violence, and psychopathy. Overall, Drexler is only touching the surface of the selfie phenomenon. — **Interpretation**

By failing to include a discussion of men in the article, she persists in the stereotype that she claims to be fighting—the idea that "only teenage girls and singles [are] using it to take control of how they present themselves to the world." — **Interpretation**

By relying on anecdotal evidence and failing to include men in her essay, Drexler undermines her argument. — **Writer's conclusion**

4.6 Sample Critical Analysis

4.6 Examine a sample critical analysis.

The following essay by student Carmen Samsara responds to Peggy Drexler's "What Your Selfies Say About You" (2.1). Samsara arrived at her response through the process of critical reading outlined in this chapter and then by gathering and organizing her ideas, developing a thesis about Drexler's text that synthesized Drexler's ideas and her own, and supporting her thesis with evidence from her own experience and from Drexler's text.

Touching the Surface

Introduction

In the essay "What Your Selfies Say About You" author and psychology professor Peggy Drexler suggests that selfies can be either good or bad for the selfie-taker's personal life, relationships, and reputation, depending on the intent of the selfie-taker. Drexler wants her readers to believe that "the trick with selfies may be to look at why you're taking them—and what they do for you" (par. 7). Does Drexler provide evidence of her assertion to lead the reader to agree with her argument? The answer is no. She uses limited empirical evidence because hard evidence on the effect of selfies is less common than anecdotal experiences, leading to conclusions filled with gender bias and sexism. Moreover, she does not include the response of the viewer in her conclusions despite the inherently social aspect of the selfie.

Summary of Drexler's essay

Samsara's critical question

Thesis statement

Drexler's portrait of taking selfies as a female-dominated act is questionable and problematic. Her initial anecdote is rife with sexism. A Texas mother demands that girls stop posting images of themselves because boys (namely her sons) might see them and think sexual thoughts. Drexler suggests that the woman has a valid point about selfies, stating that "many selfies carry sexual undertones, especially since the majority of selfies are . . . designed to leave a positive impression or elicit a positive response" (par. 2). What empirical evidence does Drexler use to support this assertion? None.

> First main point
>
> Evidence for first point: paraphrases and quotations from Drexler's text

In another anecdote, Drexler discusses the selfies of a 40-year-old woman who takes "magazine-worthy photographs of herself lounging seductively on the beach, laughing by candlelight, and snuggling with her kids into her Instagram feed" (par. 3). The woman states that she posts selfies without much thought but admits that she wouldn't post an image that showed her in a poor light. She later admits that "her increasing fixation with her own appearance and that of her family" (par. 7) was ultimately preventing her from experiencing the important moments in her life.

> Evidence for first point: additional example and quotation from Drexler's text

Drexler draws a conclusion based on these two anecdotes: the selfie trend is "sort of affirming, if undeniably self-absorbed," allowing women to build a healthy self-image and challenging the notion that women must be a size 0 to be beautiful (par. 4). While these are noble causes, Drexler doesn't really support this conclusion with strong evidence. It appeals to the readers' common sense, drawing to mind all the sexualized selfie images that they've seen on their social media. Yet it is just as likely that the readers only remember the sexualized images while the nonsexualized images are quickly forgotten.

> Transition to second main point
>
> Second main point

Drexler admits that selfies "are also a manifestation of society's obsession with looks and its ever-narcissistic embrace" (par. 5). She suggests that selfie-taking can not only make the selfie-taker less likable but also "have adverse effects on marriage and relationships, parenting, and the workplace" as well as a possible link between excessive narcissism and violence. She provides numerous links to peer-reviewed studies to support these assertions. Yet she fails to mention that many of these studies suggest a strong link between selfie-taking men and narcissism, violence, and psychopathy. By failing to include men in her discussion of the issue, she persists in the stereotype that she claims to be fighting—the idea that "only teenage girls and singles [are] using it to take control of how they present themselves to the world" (par. 2).

> Third main point
>
> Evidence for third point

Yet throughout the discussion of the anecdotal and empirical evidence, Drexler fails to address how the viewers' response to the images affects the overall impact of the act. She mentions briefly that the Texas mother

> Conclusion of third point: Drexler's omissions

included no mention of any responsibility that her sons have regarding how they respond to the "sexualized" images. Despite this obvious (and likely, more manageable) solution to the Texas mother's concerns, Drexler suggests that the woman's point is still valid; women (teenage girls, in this case) must be hyperaware of the image that they portray so that they do not inadvertently arouse the attention of men in their communities. It's akin to suggesting that a woman causes her own rape by how she dresses. It's sexist and offensive, further undermining Drexler's argument that the selfie-taker controls the message.

Acknowledgment of Drexler's concerns

Summary of three main points and return to the overall theme in the introduction

Drexler writes with conviction, and her concerns are valid: selfie-takers should examine why they post self-images and what they want to receive from the act. However, the essay's flaws make it unlikely that Drexler could convince her audience that selfie-takers can truly control the message, especially when so much of the message depends on who is viewing it. Moreover, by focusing on women and anecdotal evidence, she only touches the surface of the selfie phenomenon, ultimately undermining her argument.

Work Cited

Drexler, Peggy. "What Your Selfies Say About You." *Psychology Today*, 16 Sept. 2013, www.psychologytoday.com/blog/our-gender-ourselves/201309/what-your-selfies-say-about-you.

—Carmen Samsara (student)

Chapter 5
Planning a Research Project

Learning Objectives

- **5.1** Create a plan for your research project.
- **5.2** Find a researchable subject and question.
- **5.3** Set goals for finding sources.
- **5.4** Prepare a working bibliography.

5.1 The Process of Research Writing

5.1 Create a plan for your research project.

Research writing gives you a chance to work like a detective solving a case. The mystery is the answer to a question you care about. The search for the answer leads you to consider what others think about your subject, but you do more than simply report their views. You build on them to develop and support your own opinion, and ultimately you become an expert in your own right. Your investigation will be more productive and enjoyable if you take the steps described in this chapter.

Research writing is a *writing* process:

- You work within a particular situation of subject, purpose, audience, genre, and other factors.
- You gather ideas and information about your subject.
- You focus and arrange your ideas.
- You draft to explore your meaning.
- You revise to develop and shape your writing.
- You edit to refine and polish your writing.

Although the process seems neatly sequential in this list, you know from experience that the stages overlap—that, for instance, you may begin drafting before you've gathered all the information you expect to find, and then while drafting you may discover a source that causes you to rethink your approach. Anticipating the process of research writing can free you to be flexible in your search and open to discoveries.

A thoughtful plan and systematic procedures can help you follow through on the diverse activities of research writing. One step is to make a schedule like the one below that apportions the available time to the necessary work. You can estimate that each segment marked off by a horizontal line will occupy *roughly* one-quarter of the total time—for example, a week in a four-week assignment or two weeks in an eight-week assignment. The most unpredictable segments are the first two, so get started early enough to accommodate the unexpected.

Scheduling steps in research writing

Complete by:

_____ 1. Setting a schedule and beginning a research journal
_____ 2. Finding a researchable subject and question
_____ 3. Setting goals for sources
_____ 4. Finding print and electronic sources, and making a working, annotated bibliography

(continued)

Scheduling steps in research writing

(continued)

___	5. Evaluating and synthesizing sources
___	6. Gathering information from sources, often using summary, paraphrase, and direct quotation
___	7. Taking steps to avoid plagiarism
___	8. Developing a thesis statement and creating a structure
___	9. Drafting the paper, integrating summaries, paraphrases, and direct quotations into your ideas
___	10. Citing sources in your text
___	11. Revising and editing the paper
___	12. Finalizing text citations and preparing the list of works cited or references
___	13. Preparing the final manuscript
___	Final paper due

Keeping a research journal

While working on a research project, carry a notebook or a computer with you at all times to use as a **research journal,** a place to record your activities and ideas. In the journal's dated entries, you can write about the sources you consult, the leads you want to pursue, and any difficulties you encounter. Most important, you can record your thoughts about sources, leads, dead ends, new directions, relationships, and anything else that strikes you. The act of writing in the journal can expand and clarify your thinking. To avoid mixing up your thoughts and those of others, keep separate notes on what your sources actually say.

5.2 Research Questions

5.2   Find a researchable subject and question.

Begin with an assigned subject or one that you want to explore and learn more about (perhaps one you've already written about without benefit of research); then narrow the subject to a manageable size by asking questions about it. Selecting and limiting a subject for a research paper can present special opportunities and problems.

5.2.1   Appropriate subject

When you settle on a subject, ask the following questions about it. For each requirement, there are corresponding pitfalls.

- **Are ample sources of information available on the subject?**

  Avoid a very recent subject, such as a newly announced medical discovery or a breaking story in today's news, unless you are placing it in a larger context.

- **Does the subject encourage research in the kinds and number of sources required by the assignment?**

  Avoid (*a*) a subject that depends entirely on personal opinion and experience, such as the virtues of your hobby, and (*b*) a subject that requires research in only one source, such as a straight factual biography.

- **Will the subject lead you to an objective assessment of sources and to defensible conclusions?**

  Avoid a subject that rests entirely on belief or prejudice, such as when human life begins or why women (or men) are superior. Your readers are unlikely to be swayed from their own beliefs.

- **Does the subject suit the length of the paper assigned and the time given for research and writing?**

  Avoid a broad subject that has too many sources to survey adequately, such as a major event in history.

5.2.2 Research question

Asking a question or questions about your subject opens avenues of inquiry. In asking questions, you can consider what you already know about the subject, explore what you don't know, and begin to develop your own perspective.

Try to narrow your research question so that you can answer it in the time and space you have available. The question *How does human activity affect the environment?* is very broad, encompassing issues as diverse as pollution, distribution of resources, climate change, population growth, land use, biodiversity, and the ozone layer. In contrast, the question *How can sustainable agriculture help the environment?* or *How, if at all, should carbon emissions be taxed?* is much narrower. Each question also requires more than a simple *yes* or *no* answer, so that answering, even tentatively, demands thought about pros and cons, causes and effects.

As you read and write, your question will probably evolve to reflect your increasing knowledge of the subject, and eventually its answer will become your main idea, or thesis statement.

5.3 Search Strategies

5.3 Set goals for finding sources.

Before you start looking for sources, consider what you already know about your subject and where you are likely to find information on it.

5.3.1 Your own knowledge

Discovering what you already know about your topic will guide you in discovering what you don't know. Take some time at the start to write down everything you know about the subject: facts you have learned; opinions you have heard or read elsewhere; and, of course, your own opinions. Use one of these discovery techniques discussed to explore and develop your ideas: keeping a journal, observing your surroundings, freewriting, brainstorming, mind mapping, or asking questions.

When you've explored your thoughts, make a list of questions for which you don't have answers, whether factual (*How many farms in the United States practice sustainable agriculture?*) or more open-ended (*Are sustainable farming practices better for the environment?*). These questions will give you clues about the sources you need to look for first.

5.3.2 Kinds of sources

For many research projects, you'll want to consult a mix of sources. You may start by seeking the outlines of your topic—the range and depth of opinions about it—in reference works and articles in popular periodicals or through a Web search. Then, as you refine your views and your research question, you'll move on to more specialized sources, such as scholarly books and periodicals and your own interviews or surveys.

The mix of sources you choose depends heavily on your subject. For example, Brandon Sele, a student researching the environmental effects of sustainable farming practices, required the use of recent sources because environmentally friendly practices are relatively new to the industry. Your mix of sources may also be specified by your instructor or limited by the requirements of your assignment.

Sources through the library or the open Web

The print and electronic sources available at your library or through its Web site—mainly reference works, books, and articles in periodicals—have two big advantages over most of what you'll find on the open Web: library sources are cataloged and indexed for easy retrieval; and they are generally reliable, having been screened first by their publishers and then by the library's staff. In contrast, the retrieval systems of the open Web are more difficult to use effectively, and the sources themselves tend to be less reliable because most do not pass through any screening before being posted. (There are many exceptions, such as online scholarly journals and reference works. But these sources are generally available through your library's Web site as well.)

Most instructors expect research writers to consult library sources. But they'll accept sources from the open Web, too, if you have used them judiciously. Even with its disadvantages, the Internet can be a valuable resource for primary sources, current information, and a diversity of views.

Primary and secondary sources

Use **primary sources** when they are required by the assignment or are appropriate for your subject. Primary sources are documents and objects that were created during the period you are studying. They consist of firsthand or original accounts, such as works of literature, historical documents (letters, speeches, and so on), eyewitness reports (including articles by journalists who are on location), reports on experiments or surveys conducted by the writer, and sources you originate (interviews, experiments, observations, or correspondence).

Many assignments will allow you to use **secondary sources,** which report and analyze information drawn from other sources, often primary ones. Examples include a reporter's summary of a controversial issue, a historian's account of a battle, a critic's reading of a poem, and a psychologist's evaluation of several studies. (Sometimes a secondary source may actually be your primary source, as when you analyze a historian's account or respond to a critic's interpretation.) In themselves, secondary sources may contain helpful summaries and interpretations that direct, support, and extend your own thinking. However, most research-writing assignments expect your own ideas to go beyond those in such sources.

Scholarly and popular sources

The scholarship of acknowledged experts is essential for depth, authority, and specificity. Most instructors expect students to emphasize scholarly sources in their research. But the general-interest views and information of popular sources can provide everyday examples, anecdotes, and stories that can help you apply scholarly approaches to your subject, and they can provide context for very recent topics.

Use the following guidelines to determine whether a source is scholarly or popular:

- **Check the title.** Is it technical, or does it use a general vocabulary?
- **Check the publisher.** Is it a scholarly journal (such as *Cultural Geographies*) or a publisher of scholarly books (such as Oxford University Press), or is it a popular magazine (such as *Consumer Reports* or *Time*) or a publisher of popular books (such as Vintage)?
- **Check the length of periodical articles.** Scholarly articles are generally much longer than magazine and newspaper articles.
- **Check the author.** Search the Web for the author. Is he or she an expert on the topic?

- **Check the URL.** A Web site's URL, or electronic address, includes an abbreviation that can tell you something about the origin of the source: scholarly sources usually end in *edu*, *org*, or *gov*, while popular sources usually end in *com*. (See 6.4 for more on types of online sources.)
- **Check for sources.** Scholarly authors cite their sources formally in notes or a bibliography.

Older and newer sources

For most subjects, a combination of older, established sources (such as books) and current sources (such as newspaper articles, interviews, or Web sites) will provide both background and up-to-date information.

- **Check the publication date.** Only historical subjects or very current subjects require an emphasis on one extreme or another.

Impartial and biased sources

Seek a range of viewpoints. Sources that attempt to be impartial can offer an overview of your subject and trustworthy facts. Sources with clear biases can give you a range of views about a subject and enrich your understanding of it. Of course, to discover bias, you may have to read the source carefully, but you can infer quite a bit just from a bibliographical listing.

- **Check the author.** Do a Web search to find out more about the author. Is he or she a respected researcher (thus more likely to be objective) or a leading proponent of a certain view (less likely to be objective)?
- **Check the title.** It may reveal something about point of view. (Consider these contrasting titles: "The Myth of Sustainable Meat" versus "Green Agriculture: Features and Agricultural Policy Measures for the Transition to a Sustainable Agriculture.")

Sources with helpful features

Depending on your topic and how far along your research is, you may want to look for sources with features such as illustrations (which can clarify important concepts), bibliographies (which can direct you to other sources), and indexes (which can help you develop keywords for electronic searches).

5.4 Working Bibliographies

5.4 Prepare a working bibliography.

To track where sources are, compile a **working bibliography** as you uncover possibilities. When you have a substantial file—say,

10–30 sources—you can decide which ones seem most promising and look them up first.

5.4.1 Source information

When you turn in your paper, you will be expected to attach a list of the sources you have used. Your list must include all the information needed to find the sources, in a format that readers can understand. The box below shows the information you should record for each type of source so that you will not have to retrace your steps later.

Recording source information meticulously will help you avoid careless plagiarism because you will be less likely to omit the information in your paper. Careful records will also help you avoid omitting or mixing up numbers, dates, and other data when it's time to write your citations.

5.4.2 Annotations

Your instructor may ask you to prepare an **annotated bibliography** as part of the research process or as a separate assignment. Creating annotations converts your bibliography into a tool for assessing sources, helping you discover gaps that may remain in your sources and helping you decide which sources to pursue in depth.

As you find and evaluate each source, record not only its publication information but also the following:

- **What you know about the content of the source.** Periodical databases and book catalogs generally include abstracts, or summaries, of sources that can help with this part of the annotation.
- **How you think the source may be helpful in your research.** Does it offer expert opinion, statistics, an important example, or a range of views? Does it place your subject in a historical, social, or economic context?
- **Your assessment of the source.** Consider how reliable the source is and how it might fit into your research.

Taking the time with your annotations can help you discover gaps that may remain in your sources and will help you decide which sources to pursue in depth. The following entry from an annotated bibliography (Figure 5.1) shows one student's annotation of a source, including a summary, a note on the source features the student thought would be helpful, and an assessment of the source's strength and weakness for his purposes.

Figure 5.1 Annotated bibliography entry with assessment

McWilliams, James E. "The Myth of Sustainable Meat." *The New York Times,* 13 Apr. 2012, p. A31.

Counters the push for sustainable meat sources like free-range chickens and grass-fed beef. Argues that universal acceptance of sustainable meat practices would cause additional environmental damage (deforestation, methane production in grass-fed cows) as more resources (land) would be required for the practice. Also suggests that economic incentives would push meat and dairy producers back to current practices as overhead costs rise. Provides a possible counterargument for sustainable agricultural practices.

Compelling argument but lacks sufficient citations for the claims in the op-ed. Additional research revealed that the author promotes a vegan lifestyle. Appropriate for broad concepts, but more data needed to support the claims.

— Publication info for source
— Summary of source working bibliog
— Idea on possible source
— Assessment of s

Information for a working bibliography

For a print or electronic book
Library call number
Name(s) of author(s), editor(s), translator(s), and other contributors
Title and subtitle
Publication data: (1) place of publication; (2) publisher's name; (3) date of publication; (4) title of any database or Web site used to reach the book; (5) publisher and date of any Web site used to find the book
Other important data, such as edition or volume number
Format (print, Web, Kindle file, etc.)
DOI or complete URL (see the note below)

For periodical articles in print, in online databases, or in Web journals
Name(s) of author(s)
Title and subtitle of article
Title of periodical
Publication data: (1) volume number and issue number (if any) in which the article appears; (2) date of issue; (3) page numbers on which article appears
Title of any database used to reach the source
DOI or complete URL (see the note below)

For Web material and other electronic sources

Name(s) of author(s) and other contributors
Title and subtitle of source
Title of Web site
Publication data: publisher and date of publication
Any publication data for the source in another medium (print, film, etc.)
Format of online source (Web site or page, podcast, e-mail, etc.)
Date you consulted the source
Title of any database used to reach the source
Complete URL or DOI (see the note below)

For other sources

Name(s) of author(s) or creator(s) and other contributors
Title of the source
Title of any larger work of which the source is a part (TV series, album, etc.)
Publication or production data: (1) publisher's or producer's name; (2) date of publication, release, or production; (3) identifying numbers (if any)
Format or medium (live performance, lecture, DVD, map, TV episode, etc.)

DOIs and URLs: Documentation styles generally require DOIs (Digital Object Identifiers) or URLs for citations of electronic sources. Always record the DOI (if one is available) and the complete URL so that you'll have whatever is needed for your final citation of a source.

Chapter 6
Finding Sources

Learning Objectives

6.1 Develop a strategy for finding sources.
6.2 Find reference works.
6.3 Find books and periodicals.
6.4 Find sources on the Web.
6.5 Find sources using social media.
6.6 Find government publications.
6.7 Find visuals, audio, and video.
6.8 Conduct primary research.

6.1 Search Strategies

6.1   Develop a strategy for finding sources.

6.1.1   Start with your library's Web site

As you conduct academic research, your library's Web site will be your gateway to ideas and information. Always start with your library's Web site, not with a public search engine such as *Google*.

As you look for sources, avoid the temptation to seek a "silver bullet"—that is, to locate two or three perfect sources that already say everything you want to say about your subject. Instead of merely repeating others' ideas, read and synthesize many sources so that you enter into a dialog with them and develop your own ideas.

Advantages of a library search

The library site will lead you to vast resources, including books, periodical articles, and reference works that aren't available on the open Web. More important, every source you find on the library site will have passed through filters to ensure its value. A scholarly journal article, for instance, undergoes at least three successive reviews: subject-matter experts first deem it worth publishing in the journal; then a database vendor deems the journal worth including in the database; and, finally, your school's librarians deem the database worth subscribing to.

Start with the library's Web site, but don't stop there. Many books, periodicals, and other excellent sources are available only on library shelves, not online, and most instructors expect research papers to be built to some extent on these resources. When you spot promising print sources while browsing the library's online databases, make records of them and then look them up at the library.

6.1.2   Finding print and electronic resources through your library

Your library's Web site will lead you to many kinds of print and electronic resources suitable for academic research.

- **The library catalog.** Searchable from the library's Web site, the catalog is a database that lists all the resources the library owns or subscribes to. At many libraries, the catalog finds books, e-books, and the titles of periodicals but not individual articles within online databases. At other libraries, the catalog functions as a centralized search engine that covers all the library's holdings and subscriptions and locates articles within online databases. Either type of catalog may also include the holdings at other libraries in your college's system or in your state.
- **Online databases.** Also searchable from the library's Web site are online databases which include a wide range of source types,

from journal collections and full-text resources, to reference works and primary sources. Your library's Web site will likely list databases alphabetically and by discipline. (You may discover some of the same databases on the open Web, but unless you retrieve articles through your library's Web site, you will probably have to pay for what you find.) As you use a database, be aware of what it does and does not offer, and keep track of whether you are looking at an article, a book, an archival document, or something else. Ask a librarian if you're not sure.
- **Research guides.** Some libraries provide guides that direct users to resources on particular subjects, such as twentieth-century English literature or social psychology.
- *Google Scholar.* Available on the open Web, *Google Scholar* is a search engine that seeks out scholarly books and articles. It is particularly useful for subjects that range across disciplines, for which discipline-specific databases can be too limited. *Google Scholar* can connect to your library's holdings if you set it to do so under Scholar Preferences. Keep in mind, however, that *Google Scholar*'s searches may list books that are unavailable to you and articles that you cannot obtain in full text. Your library is still the best resource for material that is easily available to you, so begin there.

A tip for researchers

Take advantage of two valuable resources offered by your library:

- **An orientation,** which will introduce you to the resources available through your library and help you navigate the library's Web site.
- **Reference librarians,** whose job it is to help you and others navigate the library's resources. All libraries offer face-to-face consultations, and many offer e-mail and chat services. Even very experienced researchers often consult reference librarians.

6.1.3   Developing search terms

Take time early in your research to develop search terms that describe your subject effectively. For this step, it helps to understand the difference between keywords and subject headings:

- **Keywords** are the terms you type when you begin a search. In a library catalog or an online database, a keyword search looks for that word (or words) in titles, authors, and subject headings and sometimes within lists of keywords supplied by the author or in user tags added by readers. On the open Web, a keyword search looks for your terms anywhere in the record. In either case, the process is entirely automatic, so as a researcher your

challenge is to find keywords that others have used to describe the same subject.
- **Subject headings** (also called *subject terms*) tell you what a source is about. They are assigned to books and articles by people who have read the sources and categorized them, so they can be more efficient than keywords at finding relevant sources. To find subject headings, use and refine your keywords until you find a promising source. On the source's full record, check the list of subject headings to see how the source is categorized. Building the subject headings that most closely match your subject into your search terms can improve your searches.

6.1.4 Refining search terms

Databases, catalogs, and search engines provide systems that you can use to refine your search terms for your purposes. The basic operations appear in the following box, but resources do differ. For instance, some assume that *AND* should link keywords, while others provide options specifying "Must contain all the words" and other equivalents for the operations in the box. You can learn a search engine's system by consulting its Advanced Search page.

You will probably have to use trial and error in developing your terms because library catalogs, databases, and search engines may all use slightly different words to describe your subject. If you are having trouble finding appropriate sources, try using subject headings, and be flexible in your search terms. The process is not busywork—far from it. Besides leading you eventually to worthwhile sources, it can also teach you a great deal about your subject: how you can or should narrow it; how it is and is not described by others; what others consider interesting or debatable about it; and what the major arguments are.

Ways to refine keywords

Most databases and many search engines work with **Boolean operators,** terms or symbols that allow you to expand or limit your keywords and thus your search.

- Use *AND* or + to narrow the search by including only sources that use all the given words. The keywords *sustainable AND agriculture* request only the sources in the shaded area:

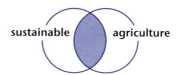

- Use *NOT* or – ("minus") to narrow the search by excluding irrelevant words. *Sustainable AND agriculture NOT industrial* excludes sources that use the word *industrial*:

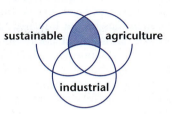

- Use *OR* to broaden the search by giving alternative keywords. *Sustainable AND agriculture OR farming* allows for sources that use a synonym for *agriculture*:

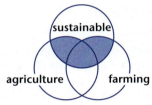

- **Use quotation marks or parentheses to form search phrases.** For instance, *"urban agriculture"* requests the exact phrase, not the separate words. Only sources using the phrase *urban agriculture* would turn up in a search.
- **Use wild cards to permit different versions of the same word.** In *consum**, for instance, the wild card * indicates that sources may include *consume, consumer, consumerism,* and *consumption* as well as *consumptive, consumedly,* and *consummate*. The example suggests that you have to consider all the variations allowed by a wild card and whether it opens up your search too much. If you seek only two or three from many variations, you may be better off using *OR: consumption OR consumerism*. (Note that some systems use ?, :, or + for a wild card instead of *.)
- **Be sure to spell your keywords correctly.** Some search tools will look for close matches or approximations, but correct spelling gives you the best chance of finding relevant sources.

6.2 Reference Works

6.2   Find reference works.

Reference works, available through your library and on the open Web, include encyclopedias, dictionaries, digests, bibliographies, indexes, atlases, almanacs, and handbooks. Your research *must* go beyond these sources, but they can help you decide whether your topic really interests you and whether it meets the requirements for a research paper. Preliminary research in reference works can also help you develop keywords for electronic searches and can direct you to more detailed sources on your topic.

The Web-based encyclopedia *Wikipedia* (at *wikipedia.org*) is one of the largest reference sites on the Internet. Like any encyclopedia, *Wikipedia* can provide background information for research on a topic. But unlike other encyclopedias, *Wikipedia* is a **wiki,** a kind of Web site that can be contributed to or edited by anyone. Ask your instructor whether *Wikipedia* is an acceptable source before you use it. If you do use it, you must carefully evaluate any information you find.

6.3 Books and Periodicals

6.3 Find books and periodicals.

6.3.1 Finding books

Your library's catalog is searchable via the library's Web site. Unless you seek a specific author or title, you'll want to search for books by using keywords or subject headings. In a keyword search, you start with your own search terms. In a subject-heading search, you use the headings on the records of promising sources to locate similar sources. Figure 6.1 shows the complete record for a book, including the subject headings and the call number for finding the book on the library's shelves.

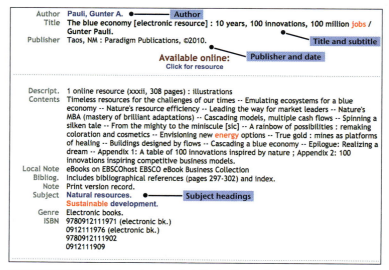

Figure 6.1 Full catalog record

Source: © Innovative Interfaces Incorporated. Used with permission.

6.3.2 Finding periodicals

Periodicals include newspapers, academic journals, and magazines, either print or online. Newspapers are useful for detailed accounts of past and current events. Journals and magazines can be harder to distinguish, but their differences are important. Most college instructors expect students' research to rely more on journals than on magazines.

Journals	Magazines
Examples	
American Anthropologist, Journal of Black Studies, Journal of Chemical Education	*National Geographic, Time, Rolling Stone, Sports Illustrated*
Availability	
Mainly college and university libraries, either on library shelves or in online databases	Public libraries, newsstands, bookstores, the open Web, and online databases
Purpose	
Advance knowledge in a particular field	Express opinion, inform, or entertain
Authors	
Specialists in the field	May or may not be specialists in their subjects
Readers	
Often specialists in the field	Members of the general public or a subgroup with a particular interest
Source citations	
Source citations always included	Source citations rarely included
Length of articles	
Usually long, 10 pages or more	Usually short, fewer than 10 pages
Frequency of publication	
Quarterly or less often	Weekly, biweekly, or monthly
Pagination of issues	
May be paged separately (like a magazine) or may be paged sequentially throughout an annual volume so that issue Number 3 (the third issue of the year) could open on page 373 (for example)	Paged separately, each issue beginning on page 1

Periodical databases

Periodical databases index articles in journals, magazines, and newspapers. Often these databases include abstracts, or summaries, of the articles, and they may offer the full text of the articles as well. Your library subscribes to many periodical databases and to services that

Selection of databases

To decide which databases to consult, you'll need to consider what you're looking for:

- **Does your research subject span more than one discipline?** Then start with a broad database such as *Academic Search Complete*, *ProQuest Research Library*, or *JSTOR*. A broad database covers many subjects and disciplines but does not index the full range of periodicals in each subject. If your library offers a centralized search engine that searches across multiple databases, you can start there.
- **Does your research subject focus on a single discipline?** Then start with a discipline-specific database such as *Historical Abstracts*, *MLA International Bibliography*, *Biological Abstracts*, or *Education Search Complete*. A specific database covers few subjects but includes most of the available periodicals in each subject. If you don't know the name of an appropriate database, the library's Web site probably lists possibilities by discipline.
- **Do you need primary sources?** Some specialized databases collect primary sources—for instance, historical newspapers, literary works not available in print, diaries, letters, music recordings, album liner notes. To determine whether you have access to such materials through your library, consult the list of databases on your library's Web site and read the descriptions to find out what each offers.
- **Which databases most likely include the kinds of resources you need?** The Web sites of most libraries provide lists of databases organized alphabetically and by discipline. Some libraries also provide research guides, which list potentially helpful databases for your search terms. To determine each database's focus, check the description of the database or the list of indexed resources. The description will also tell you the time period the database covers, so you'll know whether you also need to consult older print indexes at the library.

Database searches

When you first search a database, use your own keywords to locate sources. The procedure is illustrated in Figures 6.2, 6.3, and 6.4. Your goal is to find at least one source that seems just right for your subject so that you can see what subject headings the database itself uses for such sources. Picking up one or more of those headings for your search terms will focus and speed your search.

Many databases allow you to limit your search to so-called peer-reviewed or refereed journals—that is, scholarly journals

Figure 6.2 Initial keyword search of a periodical database

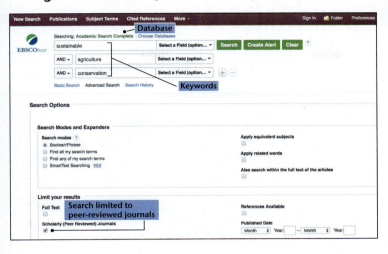

Figure 6.3 Partial keyword search results

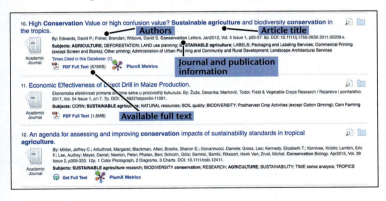

whose articles have been reviewed before publication by experts in the field and then revised by the author. Limiting your search to peer-reviewed journals can help you navigate huge databases that might otherwise return scores of unusable articles.

The use of abstracts

In Figure 6.4, the full article record shows a key feature of many databases' periodical listings: an **abstract** that summarizes the article. By describing research methods, conclusions, and other information, an abstract can tell you whether you want to pursue

68 Finding sources

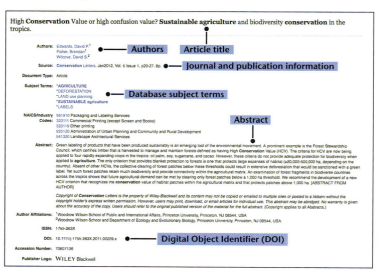

Figure 6.4 Full article record with abstract

an article and thus save you time. However, the abstract cannot replace the actual article. If you want to use the work as a source, you must consult the full text.

Helpful databases

The following list includes databases to which academic libraries commonly subscribe. Some of these databases cover much the same material, so your library may not subscribe to all of them.

EBSCOhost Academic Search. A periodical index covering magazines and journals in the social sciences, sciences, arts, and humanities. Many articles are available full-text.

InfoTrac Expanded Academic. The Gale Group's general periodical index covering the social sciences, sciences, arts, and humanities as well as national news periodicals. It includes full-text articles.

LexisNexis Academic. An index of news and business, legal, and reference information, with full-text articles. *LexisNexis* includes international, national, and regional newspapers, news magazines, legal and business publications, and court cases.

ProQuest Research Library. A periodical index covering the sciences, social sciences, arts, and humanities, including many full-text articles.

Locations of periodicals

Many article listings you find will include or link directly to the full text of the article, which you'll be able to read online and print or e-mail to yourself. If the full text is not available online, usually you can click on a link within the article record to see whether your library has the article in print or another format. Recent issues of periodicals are probably held in the library's periodical room. Back issues are usually stored elsewhere, either in bound volumes or on film that requires a special machine to read. A librarian will show you how to operate the machine.

6.4 Web Search Strategies

6.4 **Find sources on the Web.**

As an academic researcher, you enter the Web in two ways: through your library's Web site and through public search engines such as *Google* and *Bing*. The library entrance, covered in the preceding sections, is your main path to the books and periodicals that, for most subjects, should make up most of your sources. The open Web, discussed here, can lead to a wealth of information and ideas, but it also has disadvantages that limit its usefulness for academic research:

- **The Web is a wide-open network.** Anyone with the right tools can place information on the Internet, and even a carefully conceived search can turn up sources with widely varying reliability: journal articles, government documents, scholarly data, term papers written by high school students, sales pitches masked as objective reports, wild theories. You must be especially diligent about evaluating open-Web sources.
- **The Web changes constantly.** No search engine can keep up with the Web's daily additions and deletions, and a source you find today may be updated or gone tomorrow. You should not put off consulting an online source that you think you may want to use.
- **The Web is not all-inclusive.** Most books and many periodicals are available only via the library, not directly via the Web.

Disadvantages of an open-Web search

Google and other public search engines do have benefits: they may seem more user-friendly than the library's Web site; they can help you get a quick sense of how your subject is talked about; and they may locate some reliable and relevant sources for your research.

However, for academic research these search engines have more drawbacks than benefits. They are not geared toward academic research, so most of the sources they find will be unusable for your project. And the sources will not be filtered as library materials are: no one ensures their basic reliability. In the end, a library Web search will be more efficient and more effective than an open-Web search.

6.4.1 Public search engines

To find sources on the Web, you use a **search engine** that catalogs Web sites in a series of directories and conducts keyword searches. For a good range of sources, try out more than a single search engine, perhaps as many as four or five, because no search engine can catalog the entire Web. In addition, most search engines accept paid placements, giving higher billing to sites that pay a fee. These so-called sponsored links are usually marked as such, but they can compromise a search engine's method for arranging sites in response to your keywords.

Customized searches

The home page of a search engine includes a field for you to type your keywords into. Generally, it will also include an *Advanced Search* link that you can use to customize your search. For instance, you may be able to select a range of dates, a language, or a number of results to see. *Advanced Search* will also explain how to use operators such as *AND*, *OR*, and *NOT* to limit or expand your search.

Search records

No matter which search engine you use, your Web browser includes functions that allow you to keep track of Web sources and your search:

- **Use *Favorites* or *Bookmarks* to save site addresses as links.** Click one of these terms near the top of the browser screen to add a site you want to return to. A favorite or bookmark remains on file until you delete it.
- **Use *History* to locate sites you have visited before.** The browser records visited sites for a certain period, such as a single online session or a week's sessions. (After that period, the history is deleted.) If you forgot to bookmark a site, you can click History or Go to locate your search history and recover the site.

6.4.2 A sample search

Figures 6.5 and 6.6 illustrate how the refinement of keywords can narrow a search to maximize the relevant hits and minimize the irrelevant ones. Brandon Sele, a student researching the environmental effects of sustainable farming practices, started on *Google* with the keywords *sustainable agriculture*. But the search returned more than *6.5 million* items, with the first page including sponsored sites and other advertisers (see Figure 6.5). Sele realized he had to alter his strategy to get more useful results. He experimented with combinations of synonyms and narrower terms. The keywords *"sustainable agriculture" environmental impact* did refine the search but still produced 130,000 results.

Figure 6.5 First *Google* search results

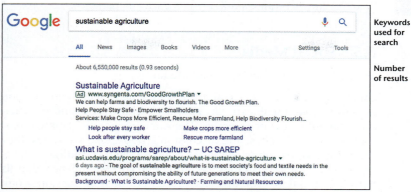

Source: © 2016 Google Inc, used with permission. Google and the Google logo are registered trademarks of Google Inc.

From *Google*'s *Advanced Search* help, Sele learned that he could specify what he wanted to see in the URLs of sources. Adding *site:.gov* limited the results to government sites, whose URLs end in *.gov*. With *"sustainable agriculture" environmental impacts site:.gov*, Sele received 25,600 results (see Figure 6.6). Although the number was still large, the government origin combined with *Google*'s criteria for ranking sources gave Sele confidence that he would easily find sources to serve his needs. He continued to limit the search by replacing *site:.gov* with *site:.org* (nonprofit organizations), *site:.edu* (educational institutions), and *site:.com* (commercial organizations).

Figure 6.6 *Google* results with refined keywords

Source: © 2016 Google Inc, used with permission. Google and the Google logo are registered trademarks of Google Inc.

Sele's Web search illustrates the trial-and-error approach required to refine keywords so that they locate worthwhile sources. Almost any Web search will require similar persistence and patience.

6.5 Social Media

6.5 Find sources using social media.

Online sources that you reach through social media can put you directly in touch with experts and others whose ideas and information may inform your research. These media include e-mail, blogs, social-networking sites, and discussion groups. Like Web sites, they are unfiltered, so you must always evaluate them carefully.

If your paper includes social-media correspondence that is not already public—for instance, an e-mail or a discussion-group posting—ask the author for permission to use it. Doing so advises the author that his or her ideas are about to be distributed more widely and lets the author verify that you have not misrepresented the ideas.

6.5.1 E-mail

As a research tool, e-mail allows you to communicate with others who are interested in your topic. You might, for instance, carry on an e-mail conversation with a teacher at your school or interview an expert in another state to follow up on a scholarly article he or she published.

6.5.2 Blogs and social-networking sites

Blogs are Web sites on which an author or authors post time-stamped comments, generally centering on a common theme, in a format that allows readers to respond to the writer or to one another. You can find directories of blogs at *blogcatalog.com*.

Somewhat similar to blogs, microblogging sites such as *Twitter* and *Tumblr* are increasingly being used by organizations, businesses, individuals, and even scholars to communicate with others.

Like all other social media discussed in this section, blogs and pages on social-networking sites must be evaluated carefully as potential sources. Some are reliable sources of opinion and evolving scholarship, and many refer to worthy books, articles, Web sites, and other resources. But just as many are little more than outlets for their authors' gripes or self-marketing.

6.5.3 Discussion lists

A **discussion list** (sometimes called a **listserv** or just a **list**) uses e-mail to connect individuals who are interested in a common subject, often with a scholarly or technical focus. By sending a question to an appropriate list, you may be able to reach scores of people who know something about your topic. For an index of discussion lists, see *tile.net/lists*.

Begin research on a discussion list by consulting the list's archive to ensure that the discussion is relevant to your topic and to see whether your question has already been answered. Always evaluate messages you receive. Although many contributors are reliable experts, almost anyone with an Internet connection can post a message.

6.5.4 Web forums and newsgroups

Web forums and newsgroups are more open and less scholarly than discussion lists, so their messages require even more diligent evaluation. **Web forums** allow participants to join a conversation simply by selecting a link on a Web page. For a directory of forums, see *delphiforums.com*. **Newsgroups** are organized under subject headings such as *soc* for social issues and *biz* for business. For a directory of newsgroups, see *giganews.com*.

6.6 Government Publications

6.6 Find government publications.

Government publications provide a vast array of data, reports, policy statements, public records, and other historical and contemporary information. For US government publications, consult the Government Printing Office's *GPO Access* at *www.gpoaccess.gov*. Also helpful is *www.usa.gov*, a portal to a range of documents and information.

Many federal, state, and local government agencies post important publications—legislation, reports, press releases—on their own Web sites. You can find lists of sites for various federal agencies by using the keywords *United States federal government* with a search engine. Use the name of a state, city, or town with *government* for state and local information.

6.7 Visuals and Media

6.7 Find visuals, audio, and video.

Visuals, audio, and video can be used as both primary and secondary sources in a research project. A painting, an advertisement, or a video of a speech might be the subject of your writing and thus a primary source. A podcast of a radio interview with an expert on your subject or a college lecture might serve as a secondary source. Because many of these sources are unfiltered—they can be posted by anyone—you must always evaluate them as carefully as you would any source you find on the open Web.

You must also cite every visual, audio, and video source fully in your paper, just as you cite text sources, with author, title, and publication information. In addition, some sources will require that you seek permission from the copyright holder, such as a publisher or a photographer. To avoid having to seek permission, you can search Web sites such as *Google*, *Flickr Creative Commons*, and *Wikimedia Commons* for media that are not protected by copyright. On *Google*, for instance, go to "Search tools" and select "Labeled for reuse." Consult a librarian at your school if you have questions.

6.7.1 Visuals

To find visuals, you have a number of options:

- **Scout for visuals while reading print or online sources.** While you are examining your sources, you may see charts, graphs, photographs, and other visuals that can support your ideas. When you find a visual you may want to use, photocopy or download it so you'll have it available later.
- **Create your own visuals,** such as photographs or charts.
- **Use an image search engine.** Web search engines can be set to find visuals, and they allow you to restrict your search to visuals that don't require reuse permission. Although search engines can find scores of visuals, the results may be inaccurate or incomplete because the sources surveyed often do not include descriptions of the visuals. (The engines search file names and any text accompanying the visuals.)
- **Use a public image database.** The following sites generally conduct accurate searches because their images are filed with information such as a description of the visual, the artist's name, and the visual's date:

    Digital Public Library of America. Maps, documents, photographs, advertisements, and more from libraries throughout the United States.
    Duke University, *Ad*Access*. Print advertisements spanning 1911–55.
    Library of Congress, *American Memory*. Maps, photographs, prints, cartoons, and advertisements documenting the American experience.
    Library of Congress, *Prints and Photographs Online Catalog.* Visuals from the library's collection, including those available through *American Memory*.
    New York Public Library Digital Gallery. Maps, drawings, photographs, and paintings from the library's collection.

- **Use a public image directory.** The following sites collect links to image sources:

    Art Project—Google Cultural Institute. Selections of fine art from major museums in the United States and Europe.

Cultural Politics: Resources for Critical Analysis. Sources on advertising, fashion, magazines, toys, and other artifacts of popular culture.
MuseumLink's Museum of Museums. Links to museums all over the world.
Yale University Robert B. Haas Family Arts Library, *Image Resources.* Sources on the visual and performing arts.

- **Use a library database.** Your library may subscribe to the following resources:

  ARTstor. Museum collections and a database of images typically used in art history courses.
  Associated Press, *AccuNet/AP Multimedia Archives.* Historical and contemporary news images.
  Grove Art Online. Art images and links to museum sites.

Many visuals you find will be available at no charge for copying or downloading, but some sources do charge a fee for use. Before paying for a visual, check with a librarian to see if it is available elsewhere for free.

6.7.2 Audio and video

Audio and video, widely available on the Web and on disc, can provide your readers with the experience of "being there." For example, if you write about the media response to the *I Have a Dream* speech of Martin Luther King, Jr., and you will submit your paper electronically, you might insert links to the speech and to TV and radio coverage of it.

- **Audio files** such as podcasts, Webcasts, and CDs offer radio programs, interviews, speeches, lectures, and music. They are available on the Web and through your library. Online sources of audio include the Library of Congress's *American Memory*, the *Internet Archive*, and *Podcastdirectory.com*.
- **Video files** capture performances, speeches and public presentations, news events, and other activities. They are available on the Web and on DVD or Blu-ray disc from your library. Online sources of video include the Library of Congress's *American Memory*, *YouTube*, and the *Internet Archive*, which include commercials, historical footage, current events, and much more. Search engines such as *Google* are also good sources of video.

6.8 Primary Research

6.8   Conduct primary research.

For some papers, you will need to conduct primary research to support, extend, or refute the ideas of others. For example, if you were writing about cyberbullying among college students, you might want to survey students on your campus as well as consult published research on the subject. Three common forms of primary research are personal interviews, surveys, and observations.

6.8.1 Personal interviews

An interview can be especially helpful for a research project because it allows you to ask questions precisely geared to your topic. You can conduct an interview in person, over the telephone, or online. An in-person interview is preferable if you can arrange it because you can see the person's expressions and gestures as well as hear his or her tone.

Here are a few guidelines for interviews:

- **Call or write for an appointment.** Tell the person exactly why you are calling, what you want to discuss, and how long you expect the interview to take. Be true to your word on all points.
- **Prepare a list of open-ended questions to ask**—perhaps ten or twelve for a one-hour interview. Do some research on these questions before the interview to discover background on the issues and your subject's published views on the issues.
- **Pay attention to your subject's answers** so that you can ask appropriate follow-up questions. Take care in interpreting answers, especially if you are online and thus can't depend on facial expressions, gestures, and tone of voice to convey the subject's attitudes.
- **Keep thorough notes.** Take notes during an in-person or telephone interview, or record the interview if you have the equipment and your subject agrees. For online interviews, save the discussion in a file of its own.
- **Verify quotations.** Before you quote your subject in your paper, check with him or her to ensure that the quotations are accurate.
- **Send a thank-you note immediately after the interview.** Promise your subject a copy of your finished paper, and send the paper promptly.

6.8.2 Surveys

Asking questions of a defined group of people can provide information about respondents' attitudes, behaviors, backgrounds, and expectations. Use the following tips to plan and conduct a survey:

- **Decide what you want to find out.** The questions you ask should be dictated by your purpose. Formulating a **hypothesis** about your subject—a generalization that can be tested—will help you refine your purpose.

- **Define your population.** Think about the kinds of people your hypothesis is about—for instance, college men or preschool children. Plan to sample this population so that your findings will be representative.
- **Write your questions.** Surveys may contain closed questions that direct the respondent's answers (checklists and multiple-choice, true/false, or yes/no questions) or open-ended questions that allow brief, descriptive answers. Avoid loaded questions that reveal your own biases or make assumptions about subjects' answers.
- **Test your questions.** Use a few respondents with whom you can discuss the answers. Eliminate or recast questions that respondents find unclear, discomforting, or unanswerable.
- **Tally the results.** Count the actual numbers of answers, including any nonanswers.
- **Seek patterns in the raw data.** Such patterns may confirm or contradict your hypothesis. Revise the hypothesis or conduct additional research if necessary.

6.8.3 Observation

Observation can be an effective way to gather fresh information on your subject. You may observe in a controlled setting—for instance, watching children at play in a child-development lab. Or you may observe in a more open setting—for instance, watching the interactions among students in a cafeteria on your campus. Use these guidelines for planning and gathering information through observation:

- **Be sure that what you want to learn *can* be observed.** You can observe people's choices and interactions, but you would need an interview or a survey to discover people's attitudes or opinions.
- **Allow ample time.** Observation requires several sessions of several hours in order to be reliable.
- **Record your impressions.** Throughout the observation sessions, take careful notes on paper, a computer, or a mobile device. Always record the date, time, and location for each session.
- **Be aware of your own bias.** Such awareness will help you avoid the common pitfall of seeing only what you expect or want to see.

Chapter 7
Evaluating Sources

Learning Objectives

7.1 Evaluate sources for relevance and reliability.
7.2 Evaluate library sources.
7.3 Evaluate Web sites.
7.4 Evaluate other online sources.

7.1 Relevance and Reliability

7.1 Evaluate sources for relevance and reliability.

Before you gather information and ideas from sources, scan them to evaluate what they have to offer, how reliable they are, and how you might use them. As you evaluate each source, add an assessment of it to your annotated bibliography.

In evaluating sources, you need to consider how they come to you. The sources you find through the library, both in print and on the Web, have been previewed for you by their publishers and by the library's staff. They still require your critical reading, but you can have some confidence in the information they contain. With online sources you reach directly, however, you can't assume similar previewing, so your critical reading must be especially rigorous.

Not all the sources you find will prove worthwhile: some may be irrelevant to your project, and others may be unreliable. Gauging the relevance and reliability of sources is the essential task of evaluating them.

Questions for evaluating sources

Relevance
- **Does the source devote some attention to your subject?** Does it focus on your subject or cover it marginally? How does it compare to other sources you've found?
- **Is the source appropriately specialized for your needs?** Check the source's treatment of a topic you know something about to ensure that it is neither too superficial nor too technical.
- **Is the source up to date enough for your subject?** When was the source published? If your subject is current, your sources should be, too.

Reliability

- **Where does the source come from?** Did you find it through your library or directly through the Internet? Is the source popular or scholarly?
- **Is the author an expert in the field?** Check the author's credentials in a biography (if the source includes one), in a biographical reference, or by a keyword search of the Web.
- **What is the bias of the source?** How do the author's ideas relate to those in other sources? What areas does the author emphasize, ignore, or dismiss?
- **Is the source fair, reasonable, and well written?** Does it provide sound reasoning and a fair picture of opposing views? Is the tone calm and objective? Is the source logically organized and error-free?
- **Are the claims well supported, even if you don't agree with the author?** Does the author provide accurate, relevant, representative, and adequate evidence to back up his or her claims? Does the author cite sources, and, if so, are they reliable?

7.2 Library Sources

7.2 Evaluate library sources.

To evaluate sources you find through your library—either in print or on the library's Web site—look at dates, titles, summaries, introductions, headings, author biographies, and any source citations. The criteria that follow expand on the most important tips in the "Questions for evaluating sources" box. In the "Evaluating library sources" box, you can see how student Brandon Sele applied these criteria to two print sources, a magazine article and a journal article, that he consulted while researching sustainable agriculture.

Identify the origin of the source.

Check whether a library source is popular or scholarly. Scholarly sources, such as refereed journals and university press books, are generally deeper and more reliable. But some popular sources, such as firsthand newspaper accounts and books for a general audience, are often appropriate for research projects.

Check the author's expertise.

The authors of scholarly publications tend to be experts whose authority can be verified. Check the source to see whether it contains a biographical note about the author; check a biographical reference, or check the author's name in a keyword search of the Web. Look for other publications by the author and for his or her job and/or any affiliations, such as teacher at a university, researcher with a nonprofit organization, or writer for popular magazines.

Evaluating library sources

Consider the sample pages from two library sources that Brandon Sele considered for his paper on sustainable agriculture.

Macdonald, "Blueprint for the Bio-Economy," *Pulp and Paper Canada*

Origin
Article by Cindy Macdonald published in *Pulp and Paper Canada*, a trade magazine published by a company called Annex Business Media.

Author
Macdonald is listed on the first page of the article as the chief editor of *Pulp and Paper Canada*. No other information about her is provided in the article.

Bias
The publication is a trade magazine, intended to promote innovations in technology, management, and financing in the paper industry.

Reasonableness and writing
Presents a summary of a report on options for renewal of the forest products industry. The information is reasonable but does not appear to have been peer reviewed.

Source citations
Includes quotations and summaries of information from the Forest Products Association of Canada, but does not include a list of works cited.

Assessment
Unreliable for academic research: The article is informative but not scholarly. No evidence of formal peer review. The magazine is explicitly written to support and promote commercial products and companies.

Curreli et al., "Solar Energy as a Form Giver for Future Cities," *Energies*

Article by Alessandra Curreli and others, published in *Energies*, an open-access journal published by MDPI, a scholarly journal publisher located in Switzerland.

The authors are based in the department of Architecture and Energy at the School of Architecture in Barcelona, Spain. E-mail addresses are provided for the authors.

Presents a balanced view of the topic based in scientific research. The research reported in the article was supported by the Spanish Ministry of Economy. A formal statement declares that the authors have no conflicts of interest and can report objectively.

The article is written as an objective report in social-science format, exploring multiple perspectives with extensive scholarly research.

Includes 35 cited sources, most from scholarly journals published in Europe and the United Kingdom, dating from 1984 to 2016.

Reliable for academic research: The article comes from a scholarly journal, the authors are experts in the field, they discuss many views and concede some, and source citations confirm evidence from reliable sources.

Library sources **81**

Unreliable source for academic research: An article by Cindy Macdonald, published in *Pulp and Paper Canada*.

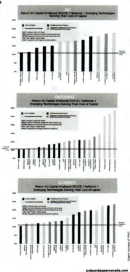

src 7.2

Reliable source for academic research: An article by Alessandra Curreli et al., published in the journal *Energies*.

Source: Page shot of last page of article: Solar Energy as a Form Giver for Future Cities; Energies 2016, 9, 544; doi:10.3390/en9070544 www.mdpi.com/journal/energies

Identify the author's bias.

Every author has a point of view that influences the selection and interpretation of evidence. You may be able to learn about an author's bias from biographies, citation indexes, and review indexes. But also look at the source itself. How do the author's ideas relate to those in other sources? What areas does the author emphasize, ignore, or dismiss? When you're aware of sources' biases, you can acknowledge them in your writing and try to balance them.

Determine whether the source is fair, reasonable, and well written.

Even a strongly biased work should present solid reasoning and give balanced coverage to opposing views—all in an objective tone. Any source should be organized logically and should be written in clear, error-free sentences. The absence of any of these qualities should raise a warning flag.

Analyze support for the author's claims.

Whether or not you agree with the author, his or her evidence should be accurate, relevant to the argument, representative of its context, and adequate for the point being made. The author's sources should themselves be reliable.

7.3 Web Sites

7.3 Evaluate Web sites.

The same critical reading that helps you evaluate library sources will help you evaluate Web sites that you reach directly. You would not use a popular magazine such as *People* in academic research—unless, say, you were considering it as a primary source in a paper analyzing popular culture. Similarly, you would not use a celebrity's Web site, a fan site, or a gossip site as a source unless you were placing it in a larger academic context.

   Even Web sites that seem worthy pose challenges for evaluation because they have not undergone prior screening by editors and librarians. On your own, you must distinguish scholarship from corporate promotion, valid data from invented statistics, well-founded opinion from clever propaganda.

   To evaluate a Web document, you'll often need to travel to the site's home page to discover the author or publisher, date of publication, and other relevant information. The page you're reading may include a link to the home page. If it doesn't, you can find it by editing the URL in the Address or Location field of your browser. Working backward, delete the end of the URL up to the last slash and hit Enter. Repeat this step until you reach the home page. There you may also find a menu option, often labeled "About," that will lead you to a description of the site's author or publisher.

> ## Questions for evaluating Web sites
>
> - **What type of site are you viewing**—for example, is it scholarly, informational, or commercial?
> - **Who is the author or publisher?** How credible is the person or group responsible for the site?
> - **What is the purpose of the site?** What does the site's author or publisher intend to achieve? Are there ads on the site, signaling that the site is trying to make money from its content?
> - **What is the bias of the site?** Does the site advocate for one side or another of a particular issue?
> - **What does context tell you?** What do you already know about the site's subject that can inform your evaluation? What kinds of support or other information do the site's links provide?
> - **What does presentation tell you?** Is the site's design well thought out and effective? Is the writing clear and error-free?
> - **How worthwhile is the content?** Are the site's claims well supported by evidence from reliable sources? When was the site posted or last updated?

Determine the type of site.

When you search the Web, you're likely to encounter various types of sites. Although they sometimes overlap, the types can usually be identified by their content and purposes. Here are the main types of Web sites you will find using a search engine:

- **Scholarly sites:** These sites have a knowledge-building interest, and they are likely to be reliable. They may include research reports with supporting data and extensive documentation of scholarly sources. For such sites originating in the United States, the URLs generally end in *edu* (originating from a college or university), *org* (a nonprofit organization), or *gov* (a government department or agency). Sites originating in other countries will end differently, usually with a country code such as *uk* (United Kingdom), *de* (Germany), or *kr* (South Korea).
- **Informational sites:** Individuals, nonprofit organizations, corporations, schools, and government bodies all produce sites intended to centralize information on subjects as diverse as

astronomy, hip-hop music, and zoo design. The sites' URLs may end in *edu*, *org*, *gov*, or *com* (originating from a commercial organization). Such sites generally do not have the knowledge-building focus of scholarly sites and may omit supporting data and documentation, but they can provide useful information and sometimes include links to scholarly and other sources.

- **Advocacy sites:** Many sites present the views of individuals or organizations that promote certain policies or actions, such as the National Rifle Association or People for the Ethical Treatment of Animals. Their URLs usually end in *org*, but they may end in *edu* or *com*. Most advocacy sites have a strong bias. Some sites include serious, well-documented research to support their positions, but others select or distort evidence.
- **Commercial sites:** Corporations and other businesses such as automakers, electronics manufacturers, and booksellers maintain Web sites to explain themselves, promote themselves, or sell goods and services. URLs of commercial sites usually end in *com*; however, some end in *biz*, and those of businesses based outside the United States often end in the country code. Although business sites intend to further the publishers' profit-making purposes, they can include reliable data.
- **Personal sites:** The sites maintained by individuals range from diaries of a family's travels to opinions on political issues to reports on evolving scholarship. Those sites' URLs usually end in *com* or *edu*. Personal sites are only as reliable as their authors, but some do provide valuable eyewitness accounts, links to worthy sources, and other usable information.

Identify the author and publisher.

A reputable site lists its authors, names the group responsible for the site, and provides information or a link for contacting the author and the publisher. If none of this information is provided, you should not use the source. If you have only the author's or the publisher's name, you may be able to discover more in a biographical dictionary, through a keyword search, or in your other sources. Make sure the author and the publisher have expertise on the subject they're presenting: if an author is a doctor, for instance, what is he or she a doctor of?

Gauge purpose and bias.

A Web site's purpose determines what ideas and information it offers. Inferring that purpose tells you how to interpret what you see on the site. If a site is intended to sell a product or advocate a particular position, it may emphasize favorable ideas and information while ignoring or even distorting unfavorable information or opposing views. In contrast, if a site is intended to build knowledge—for instance, a scholarly project or journal—it will likely acknowledge diverse views and evidence.

Determining the purpose and bias of a site often requires looking beyond the first page and beneath the surface of words and images. To start, read critically what the site says about itself, usually on a page labeled "About." Be suspicious of any site that doesn't provide information about itself and its goals.

Consider context.

Your evaluation of a Web site should be informed by considerations outside the site itself. Chief among these considerations is your own knowledge. What do you already know about the site's subject and the prevailing views of it? Where does this site seem to fit into that picture? What can you learn from this site that you don't already know?

In addition, you can follow some of the site's links to see how they support, or don't support, the site's credibility. For instance, links to scholarly sources lend authority to a site—but *only* if the scholarly sources actually relate to and back up the site's claims.

Look at presentation.

Considering both the look of a site and the way it's written can illuminate its intentions and reliability. Do the site's elements all support its purpose, or is the site cluttered with irrelevant material and graphics? Is the text clearly written and focused on the purpose? Is it relatively error-free, or does it contain typos and grammatical errors? Does the site seem carefully constructed and well maintained, or is it sloppy? How intrusive are any pop-up advertisements?

Analyze content.

With information about a site's author, purpose, and context, you're in a position to evaluate its content. Are the ideas and information current, or are they dated? (Check the publication date.) Are they slanted and, if so, in what direction? Are the views and data authoritative, or do you need to balance them—or even reject them? Are claims made on the site supported by evidence drawn from reliable sources? These questions require close reading of both the text and its sources.

src 7.3

Evaluating Web sites

Following are screen shots from two Web sites that Brandon Sele consulted for his paper on sustainable agriculture.

American Council on Renewable Energy, "ACORE Leadership Council"

Center for Climate and Energy Solutions, "Scenarios for US Electricity in 2030"

Author and publisher
Author of the page is not given. Web site is sponsored by a nonprofit organization devoted to lobbying and education on behalf of the renewable energy industry.

Author is an expert on energy and public policy. (His biography can be found online.) Publisher is the Center for Climate and Energy Solutions, a nonprofit group specializing in energy and climate change.

Purpose and bias
Informational page with no stated or obvious bias.

Informational site with the stated purpose of "working to promote sound policy on the challenges of energy and climate change." Report expresses bias toward sustainable electricity production.

Context
A nonprofit organization Web site dedicated to promoting the renewable energy industry.

Nonprofit organization's site dedicated to publishing current research on energy and climate issues.

Presentation
Clean, professional-looking page with mostly error-free writing.

Clean, professionally designed site with error-free writing.

Content
Article gives basic information about the leadership council and its role in solving renewable energy problems.

Report is current (date below the author's name); it describes scenarios for meeting future electricity needs, and it cites scholarly sources.

Assessment
Unreliable for academic research: The page has no listed author and few scholarly citations. Possibly suitable for background information but not reliable as a source for an academic paper.

Reliable for academic research: The report has a bias toward sustainable electricity production, but the publisher is reputable and the author is an expert and cites scholarly sources.

Web sites 87

src 7.3

Unreliable source for academic research: A page from the *American Council of Renewable Energy* Web site.

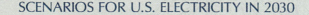

Reliable source for academic research: A report published on the Web site *Center for Climate Change and Energy Solutions*.

Source: Copyright 2014 Center for Climate and Energy Solutions (C2ES). All rights reserved. Reprinted by Permission.

7.4 Other Online Sources

7.4 Evaluate other online sources.

Social media and multimedia require the same critical scrutiny as Web sites do. Social media—including e-mail, blogs, *Twitter*, discussion groups, *Facebook* pages, and wikis—can be sources of reliable data and opinions, but they can also contain wrong or misleading data and skewed opinions. Multimedia—visuals, audio, and video—can provide valuable support for your ideas, but they can also mislead or distort. For example, a *YouTube* search using "I have a dream" brings up videos of Martin Luther King, Jr., delivering his famous speech as well as videos of people speaking hatefully about King and the speech.

> ### Questions for evaluating social media and multimedia
> - **Who is the author or creator?** How credible is he or she?
> - **What is the author's or creator's purpose?** What can you tell about why the author or creator is publishing the work?
> - **What does the context reveal?** What do reasonable responses to the work, such as comments on a blog or a news site, indicate about the source's balance and reliability?
> - **How worthwhile is the content?** Are the claims made by the author or creator supported by evidence? Is the evidence from reliable sources?
> - **How does the source compare with other sources?** Do the claims made by the author or creator seem accurate and fair given what you've seen in sources you know to be reliable?

Identify the author or creator.

Checking out the author or creator of a potential source can help you judge its reliability. The author may be identified on the source—for instance, the blog posting in Figure 7.1 includes a biographical note at the end saying that the author is a professor writing on behalf of the American Anthropological Association's Task Force on Global Climate Change. You may also be able to learn about the author with a keyword search of the Web. If you can't identify the author or creator at all, you can't use the source.

You can also get a sense of the interests and biases of an author or creator by tracking down his or her other work. For instance, you might check whether a blog author cites or links to other publications, look for other postings by the same author in a discussion-group archive, or try to gain an overview of a photographer's work.

Figure 7.1 Evaluating a blog

Source: Richard Wilk, American Anthropological Association. Courtesy of the American Anthropological Association. www.aaanet.org.

Analyze the author's or creator's purpose.

What can you tell about *why* the author or creator is publishing the work? The blog posting in Figure 7.1 provides a quick answer in the title, which indicates the author's negative view of green products. You can also dig to discover purpose, looking for claims, the use (or lack) of evidence, and the treatment of opposing views. All these factors convey the person's stand on the subject and general fairness, and they will help you position the source among your other sources.

Consider the context.

Social media and multimedia are often difficult to evaluate in isolation. Looking beyond a contribution to the responses of others can give you a sense of context by indicating how the author or creator is regarded. On a *Facebook* page or a blog, look at the comments others have posted. If you discover negative or angry responses, try to understand why: sometimes online anonymity encourages hateful responses to even quite reasonable postings.

Analyze content.

A reliable source will offer evidence for claims and will list the sources of its evidence. The blog posting, for example, links to information about carbon dioxide emissions. If you don't see such support, then you probably shouldn't use the source. However, when the source is important to you and biographical information or context indicates that the author or creator is serious and reliable, you might ask him or her to direct you to supporting information.

The tone of writing can also be a clue to its purpose and reliability. In most social media, the writing tends to be more informal and may be more heated than in other kinds of sources; but look askance at any writing that's contemptuous, dismissive, or shrill.

Compare with other sources.

Always consider social-media and multimedia sources in comparison to other sources so that you can distinguish singular, untested views from more mainstream views that have been subject to verification. Don't assume that a blog author's information and opinions are mainstream just because you see them on other blogs. Technology allows content to be picked up instantly by other blogs, so widespread distribution indicates only popular interest, not reliability.

Be wary of blogs that reproduce periodical articles, reports, or other publications. Try to locate the original version of the publication to be sure it has been reproduced fully and accurately, not quoted selectively or distorted. If you can't locate the original version, don't use the publication as a source.

Chapter 8
Synthesizing and Summarizing Sources

Learning Objectives

- **8.1** Gather information from sources.
- **8.2** Synthesize sources.
- **8.3** Summarize, paraphrase, and quote sources.

8.1 Interacting with Sources

8.1 Gather information from sources.

Research writing is much more than finding sources and reporting their contents. The challenge and interest come from interacting with and synthesizing sources: reading them critically to discover their meanings, judge their relevance and reliability, and create relationships among them, and using them to extend and support your own ideas so that you make your subject your own.

You can collect and store source information in a number of ways: handwrite notes, type notes into a file, copy and paste chunks of text from online articles into a file, annotate print or electronic documents such as PDF files, or scan or photocopy pages from books and other print sources.

Whatever method you use to gather information, you have four main goals:

- **Keep accurate records of what sources say.** Accuracy helps prevent misrepresentation and plagiarism. If you write notes by hand or type them into a file, do so carefully to avoid introducing errors.
- **Keep track of others' words and ideas.** Put quotation marks around any words you take from a source, and always include a source citation that ties the quotation to the publication information you have recorded. Also include a source citation for any idea you summarize or paraphrase so that you know the idea is not your own but came from a specific source. For more on summarizing, paraphrasing, and quoting sources, see the next section.
- **Keep accurate records of how to find sources.** Whether you handwrite notes or work with an electronic file, always link the source material to its complete publication information. These records are essential for retracing steps and for citing sources in your drafts and in the final paper. If you have the complete information in your working bibliography, you can use a shorthand reference to it on the source material, such as the author's name and any page or other reference number.
- **Synthesize sources.** Information gathering is a critical process in which you learn from sources, understand the relationships among them, and develop your own ideas about your subject and your sources. Analyze and interact with your sources by highlighting key information and commenting on what they say.

Culture and Language

Making a subject your own requires thinking critically about sources and developing independent ideas. These goals may at first be uncomfortable if your native culture emphasizes understanding and respecting established authority more than questioning and enlarging it. The information here will help you work with sources so that you can become an expert in your own right and convincingly convey your expertise to others.

8.2 Synthesizing Sources

8.2   **Synthesize sources.**

When you begin to see the differences and similarities among sources, you move into the most significant part of research writing: forging relationships for your own purpose. This **synthesis** is an essential step in reading sources critically. As you infer connections—say, between one writer's opinions and another's, or between two works by the same author—you shape your own perspective on your subject and create new knowledge.

Your synthesis of sources will grow more detailed and sophisticated as you proceed through the process of working with sources: gathering information; deciding whether to summarize, paraphrase, or quote sources; and integrating sources into your sentences. Unless you are analyzing primary sources such as the works of a poet, at first read your sources quickly and selectively for an overview of your subject and a sense of how the sources approach it. Don't get bogged down in gathering detailed information, but *do* record your ideas about sources in your research journal or your annotated bibliography.

Respond to sources.

One way to find your own perspective on a topic is to write down what your sources make you think. Do you agree or disagree with the author? Do you find his or her views narrow, or do they open up new approaches for you? Is there anything in the source that you need to research further before you can understand it? Does the source prompt questions that you should keep in mind while reading other sources?

Connect sources.

When you notice a link between sources, write about it. Do two sources differ in their theories or their interpretations of facts? Does one source illuminate another—perhaps commenting or clarifying or supplying additional data? Do two or more sources report studies that support a theory you've read about or an idea of your own?

Heed your insights.

Apart from ideas prompted by your sources, you are sure to come up with independent thoughts: a conviction, a point of confusion that suddenly becomes clear, a question you haven't seen anyone else ask. These insights may occur at unexpected times, so it's good practice to keep a notebook or computer handy to record them.

Draw your own conclusions.

As your research proceeds, the responses, connections, and insights you form through synthesis will lead you to answer your starting research question with a statement of your thesis. They will also lead you to the main ideas supporting your thesis—conclusions you have drawn from your synthesis of sources, forming the main divisions of your paper. Be sure to write them down as they occur to you.

Use sources to support your conclusions.

Effective synthesis requires careful handling of evidence from sources so that it meshes smoothly into your sentences and yet is clearly distinct from your own ideas. When drafting your paper, make sure that each paragraph focuses on an idea of your own, with the support for the idea coming from your sources. Generally, open each paragraph with your idea, provide evidence from a source or sources with appropriate citations, and close with an interpretation of the evidence. (Avoid ending a paragraph with a source citation; instead, end with your own idea.) In this way, your paper will synthesize others' work into something wholly your own.

8.3 Summary, Paraphrase, and Quotation

8.3   Summarize, paraphrase, and quote sources.

Deciding whether to summarize, paraphrase, or quote a source is an important step in synthesizing the source's ideas and your own. You synthesize when you use your own words to summarize an author's argument or paraphrase a significant example, or when you select a significant passage to quote. Choosing between a summary, paraphrase, or quotation should depend on why you are using the source.

Summaries, paraphrases, and quotations all require source citations. A summary or paraphrase without a source citation or a quotation without quotation marks and a source citation is plagiarism.

8.3.1 Summary

When you **summarize,** you condense an extended idea or argument into a sentence or more in your own words. Summary is most useful when you want to record the gist of an author's idea without the background or supporting evidence. Following is a passage from an essay by Jason Lusk published in *The New York Times*. Then a sample note shows a summary of the passage (Figure 8.1).

> **Original quotation**
> Large farmers—who are responsible for 80 percent of the food sales in the United States, though they make up fewer than 8 percent of all farms, according to 2012 data from the Department of Agriculture—are among the most progressive, technologically savvy growers on the planet. Their technology has helped make them far gentler on the environment than at any time in history. And a new wave of innovation makes them more sustainable still.

Figure 8.1 Summary of source

Socioeconomic Impact of Industrial Agriculture

Lusk, par. 2

Large farming operations, aided by progressive and innovative technologies, have become more environmentally friendly and sustainable.

8.3.2 Paraphrase

When you **paraphrase,** you follow much more closely the author's original presentation, but you restate it using your own words and sentence structures. Paraphrase is most useful when you want to present or examine an author's line of reasoning but you don't feel the original words merit direct quotation. The note in Figure 8.2 shows a paraphrase of the quotation in 8.3.1.

Figure 8.2 Paraphrase of source

Socioeconomic Impact of Industrial Agriculture

Lusk, par. 2

By using progressive technologies, large farming operations have reduced their impact on the environment while still providing 80 percent of the American food supply. Additional innovations could improve the sustainability of large farming operations even more.

Part 2

Writing with Sources

- **9** Planning and Drafting *99*
- **10** Organizing and Developing Arguments *114*
- **11** Paragraphs *131*
- **12** Integrating and Using Sources Ethically *146*
- **13** Revising and Editing *158*
- **14** Designing Documents *171*
- **15** Oral Presentations *186*

Part 2
Writing with Sources

9 Planning and Drafting 99
- **9.1** The writing situation 99
- **9.2** Purpose 101
- **9.3** Subject 102
- **9.4** Genre and medium 103
- **9.5** Thesis 104
- **9.6** Organization 107
- **9.7** First draft 111
- **9.8** Sample draft 112

10 Organizing and Developing Arguments 114
- **10.1** The elements of argument 115
- **10.2** Engaging readers 117
- **10.3** Organization 122
- **10.4** Visual arguments 123
- **10.5** Sample argument 127

11 Paragraphs 131
- **11.1** Flow 131
- **11.2** Unity 132
- **11.3** Coherence 133
- **11.4** Development 138
- **11.5** Introductions and conclusions 142

12 Integrating and Using Sources Ethically 146
- **12.1** Integrating sources 146
- **12.2** Defining plagiarism 151
- **12.3** Information you do not need to cite 153
- **12.4** Information you must cite 154
- **12.5** Documenting sources 156

13 Revising and Editing 158
- **13.1** Revision plans 158
- **13.2** Peer review 161
- **13.3** Sample revision 163
- **13.4** Editing 165
- **13.5** Final draft 169

14 Designing Documents 171
- **14.1** Academic writing 171
- **14.2** Visuals and media 174
- **14.3** Writing online 180
- **14.4** Portfolios 185

15 Oral Presentations 186
- **15.1** Organization 186
- **15.2** Delivery 187

Notice that the paraphrase follows the original but uses different words and different sentence structures. In contrast, an unsuccessful paraphrase—one that plagiarizes—copies the author's words or sentence structures or both *without quotation marks*.

Paraphrasing a source

- **Read the relevant material several times to be sure you understand it.**
- **Restate the source's ideas in your own words and sentence structures.** You need not put down in new words the whole passage or all the details. Select what is relevant to your topic, and restate only that. If complete sentences seem too detailed or cumbersome, use phrases.
- **Be careful not to distort meaning.** Don't change the source's emphasis or omit connecting words, qualifiers, or other material whose absence will confuse you later or cause you to misrepresent the source.
- **Be careful not to plagiarize the source.** Use your own words and sentence structures, and always record a citation in your notes. Especially if your source is difficult or complex, you may be tempted to change just a few words or to modify the sentence structure just a bit. But that is plagiarism, not paraphrase.

Culture and Language

If English is not your native language and you have difficulty paraphrasing the ideas in sources, try this. Before attempting a paraphrase, read the original passage several times. Then, instead of "translating" line by line, try to state the gist of the passage without looking at it. Check your effort against the original to be sure you have captured the source author's meaning and emphasis without using his or her words and sentence structures. If you need a synonym for a word, look it up in a dictionary.

8.3.3 Direct quotation

Your notes from sources may include many quotations, especially if you rely on photocopies, printouts, or downloads. Whether to use a quotation in your draft, instead of a summary or paraphrase, depends on how important the exact words are and on whether the source is primary or secondary:

- **Quote extensively when you are analyzing primary sources**—these include firsthand accounts such as works of literature, eyewitness reports, and historical documents. The quotations will

generally be both the target of your analysis and the chief support for your ideas.
- **Quote selectively when you are drawing on secondary sources**—these include reports or analyses of other sources, such as a critic's view of a poem or a historian's synthesis of several eyewitness reports. Favor summaries and paraphrases over quotations, and put every quotation to both tests in the "Tests for direct quotations from secondary sources" box. Most papers of ten or so pages should not need more than two or three quotations that are longer than a few lines each.

Tests for direct quotations from secondary sources

The author's original satisfies one of these requirements:
- The language is unusually vivid, bold, or inventive.
- The quotation cannot be paraphrased without distortion or loss of meaning.
- The words themselves are at issue in your interpretation.
- The quotation represents and emphasizes a body of opinion or the view of an important expert.
- The quotation emphatically reinforces your own idea.
  The quotation is an illustration, such as a graph, diagram, or table.

The quotation is as short as possible:
- It includes only material relevant to your point.
- It is edited to eliminate examples and other unneeded material, using ellipsis marks and brackets.

When you quote a source, either in your notes or in your draft, take precautions to avoid plagiarism or misrepresentation of the source:

- **Copy the material carefully.** Take down the author's exact wording, spelling, capitalization, and punctuation.
- **Proofread every direct quotation at least twice.**
- **Use quotation marks around the quotation** so that later you won't confuse it with a paraphrase or summary. Be sure to transfer the quotation marks into your draft as well, unless the quotation is long and is set off from your text.
- **Use brackets** to add words for clarity or to change the capitalization of letters.
- **Use ellipsis marks** to omit material that is irrelevant to your point.
- **Cite the source of the quotation in your draft.**

Chapter 9
Planning and Drafting

Learning Objectives

9.1 Analyze the writing situation.
9.2 Define your purpose.
9.3 Choose and narrow a subject.
9.4 Identify your genre and medium.
9.5 Develop a thesis statement.
9.6 Organize your ideas.
9.7 Compose a first draft.
9.8 Analyze a sample first draft.

9.1 The Writing Situation

9.1 Analyze the writing situation.

As a writer, you compose a project in response to some situation. In college and academic settings, you will usually compose projects in response to specific assignments. You may be asked to write a rhetorical analysis in an English class, a case study in a business class, or a lab report in a chemistry class, for example. In each case, your writing responds to the needs of a specific **writing situation** (sometimes also called the **rhetorical situation**), and learning how to analyze a writing situation is an important skill.

Audience
- **Who will read your writing?** Will your readers be interested in your writing or not? If not, how can you make your writing interesting to them?
- **What do your readers already know and think about your subject?** In college, you are often writing for readers who know more about the subject than you do. Sometimes you are writing for a mixed audience of non-experts (your peers) and experts (your instructors).
- **Where and when will your audience encounter your writing?** In academic settings, readers encounter your writing in the context of ongoing discussions taking place within a discipline or research community.

Figure 9.1 The elements of the writing situation

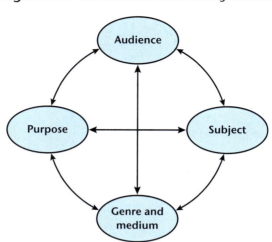

- **How should you project yourself in your writing?** What role should you play in relation to your readers, and what information should you provide? How informal or formal should your writing be?
- **What do you want readers to do or think after they read your writing?** How will you know if your writing has successfully connected with your audience?

Purpose
- **What aim does your assignment specify?** For instance, does it ask you to explain a process or argue a position?
- **Why are you writing?** What do you need to achieve in your writing? Are you writing to fulfill an assignment, to learn, to respond to a reading, to provide information, to argue a case, or to propose a solution?
- **What do you want your work to accomplish?** What effect do you intend it to have on readers?

Subject
- **What does your writing assignment require you to write about?** If you don't have a specific assignment, what subjects might be appropriate for the situation?
- **What interests you about the subject?** What do you already know about it? What questions do you have about it?
- **What kinds of evidence will best suit your subject, purpose, audience, and genre?** What combination of facts, examples, and expert opinions will support your ideas?

- **Does your assignment require research?** Will you need to consult sources or conduct interviews, surveys, or experiments?
- **Even if research is not required, what information do you need to develop your subject?** How will you obtain it?

Genre and medium

- **What genre, or type of writing, does the assignment call for?** Are you to write an analysis, a report, a proposal, or some other type? Or are you free to choose a genre in which to write?
- **What are the conventions of the genre you are using?** For example, readers might expect a claim supported by evidence, a solution to a defined problem, clear description, or easy-to-find information.
- **What medium will you use to present your writing?** Will you deliver it on paper, online, or orally? What does the presentation method require in terms of preparation time, special skills, and use of technology?
- **What are the basic requirements of the writing task?** Consider requirements for length, deadline, subject, purpose, audience, and genre. What leeway do you have with each requirement?
- **What format or method of presentation does the assignment specify or imply?** Does the situation call for a written essay, or can you use a slide presentation or other visual presentation?
- **How might you use illustrations, video, and other media to achieve your purpose?**
- **What documentation style should you use to cite your sources?**

9.2 Purpose

9.2 Define your purpose.

Your **purpose** in writing is your chief reason for communicating something about your subject to a particular audience of readers. It is your answer to a potential reader's question, "So what?"

Many college writing assignments narrow the purpose by using a signal word, such as the following:

- **Report:** Survey, organize, and objectively present the available evidence on the subject.
- **Summarize:** Concisely state the main points in a text, argument, theory, or other work.
- **Discuss:** Examine the main points, competing views, or implications of the subject.
- **Compare and contrast:** Explain the similarities and differences between two subjects.
- **Define:** Specify the meaning of a term or a concept—distinctive characteristics, boundaries, and so on.

- **Analyze:** Identify the elements of the subject, and discuss how they work together.
- **Interpret:** Infer the subject's meaning or implications.
- **Evaluate:** Judge the quality or significance of the subject, considering pros and cons.
- **Argue:** Take a position on the subject, and support your position with evidence.

You can conceive of your purpose more specifically, too, in a way that incorporates your particular subject and the outcome you intend. For example:

- To explain the methods and results of an engineering experiment so that readers understand and accept your conclusions;
- To explain the reasons for a new policy on technology use in classrooms so that students understand why the guidelines are needed; or
- To persuade readers to support the college administration's plan for more required courses.

9.3 Subject

9.3   Choose and narrow a subject.

A subject for writing has several basic requirements:

- **It should be suitable for the assignment.**
- **It should be neither too general nor too limited for the assigned deadline and paper length.**
- **It should be something that interests you and that you are willing to learn more about.**

When you receive an assignment, study its wording and its implications about your writing situation to guide your choice of subject:

- **What's wanted from you?** Many writing assignments contain words such as *discuss, describe, analyze, report, interpret, explain, define, argue,* or *evaluate.* These words specify the approach to take with your subject, the kind of thinking expected, the general purpose, and even the form your writing should take.
- **For whom are you writing?** Many assignments will specify or imply your readers, but sometimes you will have to figure out for yourself who your audience is and what they expect of you.
- **What kind of research is required?** An assignment may specify the kinds of sources you are expected to consult, and you can use such information to choose your subject. (If you are unsure whether research is required, check with your instructor.)

- **Does the subject need to be narrowed?** To do the subject justice in the length and time required, you'll often need to limit it.

Answering questions about your assignment will help set some boundaries for your choice of subject. Then you can explore your own interests and experiences to narrow the subject so that you can cover it adequately within the space and time assigned. Federal aid to college students could be the subject of a book; the kinds of aid available or why the government should increase aid would be a more appropriate subject for a four-page paper due in a week. Here are some guidelines for narrowing broad subjects:

- **Break your broad subject into as many specific subjects as you can think of.** Make a list.
- **For each specific subject that interests you and fits the requirements of the assignment, roughly sketch out the main ideas.** Consider how many paragraphs or pages of specific facts, examples, and other details you would need to pin those ideas down. This thinking should give you at least a vague idea of how much work you will have to do and how long the resulting paper might be.
- **Break a too-broad subject down further,** repeating the previous steps.

9.4 Genre and Medium

9.4 Identify your genre and medium.

Writers use familiar **genres**, or types of writing, to express their ideas. You can recognize many genres: the poems and novels of literature, the résumé in business writing, the news article about a sports event. In college you will be asked to write in a wide range of genres, such as analyses, lab reports, reviews, proposals, oral presentations, even blog posts.

When you receive a writing assignment, be sure to understand any requirements relating to its genre:

- **Is a particular genre being assigned?** An assignment that asks you to write, say, an analysis, an argument, or a report has specified the genre for you to use.
- **What are the conventions of the genre?** Your instructor and/or your textbook will probably outline the requirements for you. You can also learn about a genre by reading samples of it.
- **What flexibility do you have?** Within their conventions, most genres still allow plenty of room for your own approach and voice. Again, reading samples will help you understand more about your options.

Closely related to genre is the concept of **medium**. Medium refers to the technology or platform you might use to present a specific genre. For example, a proposal (genre) might be presented in the form of a written essay, a slide presentation, or an online video. Your choice of medium should be determined by the needs of the audience and by the other elements in the writing situation.

- **Is a medium being assigned?** Sometimes an assignment will specify that you deliver a project in a medium. You may be asked, for example, to deliver a proposal in the medium of a slide presentation.
- **What does your audience expect?** If your audience expects a formal written report, you may not want to deliver your project in the medium of a comic video. In other situations, your audience may welcome a more casual or innovative use of medium.
- **What flexibility do you have?** In some writing situations, you may have a choice of medium. You might decide, for example, that a process explanation showing nursing students how to insert an IV line would be better delivered as a video than as a detailed set of written instructions.

9.5 Thesis

9.5   Develop a thesis statement.

Your readers will expect your essay to be focused on and controlled by a main idea, or **thesis**. The thesis is the intellectual position you are taking on your topic. Often you will express the thesis in a one- or two-sentence **thesis statement** toward the beginning of your paper.

As an expression of the thesis, the thesis statement serves five important functions.

Functions of the thesis statement
- **The thesis statement narrows your subject to a single, central idea.**
- **It claims something specific and significant about your subject.**
- **It conveys your purpose for writing.**
- **It establishes your voice and stance toward your readers.**
- **It previews the arrangement of ideas in your essay.** (Not all thesis statements work as a preview, but many do.)

9.5.1 Formulating a thesis question

A thesis statement probably will not leap fully formed into your head. You can start on it by posing a **thesis question** to help you figure out your position, organize your ideas, start drafting, and stay on track.

In a composition course, Erica Vela's instructor distributed "Is *Google* Making Us Stupid?" in which Nicholas Carr analyzes the effects of the Internet on reading and the human mind. The instructor's assignment calls for a response to the reading.

> As a college student, how do you respond to Carr's argument? How does the Internet affect the way you read? How does the Internet also affect your learning process and your interactions with other people?

Responding to the assignment, Vela first rephrased it as two questions:

> To what extent do I agree or disagree with Carr's argument that the Internet is changing the way we read and process information?
>
> How have my learning process and personal interactions changed?

9.5.2 Drafting a thesis statement

Drafting a thesis statement can occur at almost any time in the writing process. Some instructors suggest that students develop a thesis statement when they have a good stock of ideas, to give a definite sense of direction. Other instructors suggest that students work with their thesis question at least through drafting, to keep their options open. And no matter when it's drafted, a thesis statement can change during the writing process, as the writer discovers ideas and expresses them in sentences.

Erica Vela chose to try writing her thesis statement before drafting. Working from her thesis question, she wrote a sentence that named a topic and made a claim about it:

> The ability to shrink the globe and bring information and education to my fingertips proves that Nicholas Carr's reservations about the Internet are shortsighted.

Vela's topic is the influence of the Internet on reading and learning, and her claim is that Carr's argument is too pessimistic. Although Vela later revised her thesis statement, this draft statement gave her direction, and she used it in the first draft of her paper.

Following are more examples of thesis questions and answering thesis statements. Each statement consists of a topic and a claim. Notice how each statement also expresses purpose. Statements 1–2 are **explanatory**: the writers mainly want to explain something to readers. Statements 3–4 are **argumentative**: the authors mainly want to convince readers of something. Most of the thesis statements you write in college papers will be either explanatory or argumentative.

thesis 9.5

Thesis question	Explanatory thesis statement
1. Why did Abraham Lincoln delay in emancipating the slaves?	Lincoln delayed emancipating any slaves until 1863 because his primary goal was to restore and preserve the Union, with or without slavery. [**Topic:** Lincoln's delay. **Claim:** was caused by his goal of preserving the Union.]
2. What steps can prevent juvenile crime?	Juveniles can be diverted from crime by active learning programs, full-time sports, frequent contact with positive role models, and intervention by consistent mentors. [**Topic:** juvenile crime. **Claim:** can be prevented in four ways.]

Thesis question	Argumentative thesis statement
3. Why should drivers' use of cell phones be banned?	Drivers' use of cell phones should be banned because people who talk and drive at the same time cause accidents. [**Topic:** drivers' use of cell phones. **Claim:** should be banned because it causes accidents.]
4. Which college students should be entitled to federal aid?	As an investment in its own economy, the federal government should provide a tuition grant to any college student who qualifies academically. [**Topic:** federal aid. **Claim:** should be provided to any college student who qualifies academically.]

Note that Statement 2 previews the organization of the essay. Readers often appreciate such a preview, and students often prefer it because it helps them organize their main points during drafting.

Thesis statement
Juveniles can be diverted from crime by active learning programs, full-time sports, frequent contact with positive role models, and intervention by consistent mentors.

Organization of essay
Discussion one by one of four ways to reduce juvenile crime.

Culture and language

In some cultures it is considered rude or unnecessary for a writer to state his or her main idea outright. When writing in standard American English for school or work, you can assume that readers expect a clear and early idea of what you think.

9.5.3 Revising the thesis statement

You may have to write and rewrite a thesis statement before you come to a conclusion about your position. Erica Vela used her draft thesis statement in the first draft of her paper, but it didn't work well at that stage. She saw that it put too little emphasis on her actual topic (*the benefits of online reading*) and overstated her disagreement with Carr (*proves . . . is shortsighted*). After several revisions, Vela responded to a peer reviewer's suggestion that she state her disagreement with Carr more clearly:

> My experience of online education offers a benefit that Nicholas Carr overlooks: the Internet provides more opportunities for learning in areas where there are no well-stocked libraries or centers of higher education, while offering more ways to access information from across the globe.

As you draft and revise your thesis statement, ask the following questions:

Checklist for revising the thesis statement

- **How well does the subject of your statement capture the subject of your writing?**
- **What claim does your statement make about your subject?**
- **What is the significance of the claim?** How does it answer "So what?" and convey your purpose?
- **How can the claim be limited or made more specific?** Does it state a single idea and clarify the boundaries of the idea?
- **How unified is the statement?** How does each word and phrase contribute to a single idea?
- **How well does the statement preview the organization of your writing?**

9.6 Organization

9.6   Organize your ideas.

Most essays share a basic pattern of introduction (states the subject), body (develops the subject), and conclusion (pulls the essay's ideas together). Introductions and conclusions are discussed in Chapter 11. Within the body, every paragraph develops some aspect of the essay's main idea, or thesis. See 9.8 for Erica Vela's essay, with annotations highlighting the body's pattern of support for the thesis statement.

> ## Culture and language
> If you are not used to reading and writing American academic prose, its pattern of introduction–body–conclusion and the organization schemes discussed below may seem unfamiliar. For instance, instead of introductions that focus quickly on the topic and thesis, you may be used to openings that establish personal connections with readers. And instead of body paragraphs that stress general points and support for those points with evidence, you may be used to general statements without support (because writers can assume that readers will supply the evidence themselves) or to evidence without explanation (because writers can assume that readers will infer the general points). When writing American academic prose, you need to take into account readers' expectations for directness and for the statement and support of general points.

9.6.1 The general and the specific

To organize material for an essay, you need to distinguish general and specific ideas and see the relations between ideas. General and specific refer to the number of instances or objects included in a group signified by a word. The following "ladder" illustrates a general-to-specific hierarchy:

Most general
↑ life form
plant
rose
↓ Uncle Dan's prize-winning American Beauty rose
Most specific

As you arrange your material, pick out the general ideas and then the specific points that support them. Set aside points that seem irrelevant to your key ideas. On a computer you can easily experiment with various arrangements of general ideas and supporting information: save your master list of ideas to a new file, and then move material around.

9.6.2 Schemes for organizing essays

An essay's body paragraphs may be arranged in many ways that are familiar to readers. The choice depends on your subject, purpose, and audience.

- **Spatial:** In describing a person, place, or thing, move through space systematically from a starting point to other features—for instance, top to bottom, near to far, left to right.
- **Chronological:** In recounting a sequence of events, arrange the events as they actually occurred in time, first to last.

- **General to specific:** Begin with an overall discussion of the subject; then fill in details, facts, examples, and other support.
- **Specific to general:** First provide the support; then draw a conclusion from it.
- **Climactic:** Arrange ideas in order of increasing importance to your thesis or increasing interest to the reader.
- **Problem–solution:** First outline a problem that needs solving; then propose a solution.

9.6.3 Outlines

It's not essential to craft a detailed outline before you begin drafting an essay; in fact, too detailed a plan could prevent you from discovering ideas while you draft. Still, even a rough scheme can show you patterns of general and specific ideas, suggest proportions, and highlight gaps or overlaps in coverage.

There are several kinds of outlines, some more flexible than others.

Scratch or informal outline

A **scratch outline** lists the key points of the paper in the order they will be covered. Here are Erica Vela's thesis statement and scratch outline for her essay on reading and learning online:

Thesis statement

My experience of online education offers a benefit that Nicholas Carr overlooks: the Internet provides more opportunities for learning in areas where there are no well-stocked libraries or centers of higher education while offering more ways to access information from across the globe.

Scratch outline

Changes in how we process information
    Carr's reservations
    My experiences
My educational experience
    Long-distance research
    Online student
    Personal interactions

Tree diagram

In a **tree diagram**, ideas and details branch out in increasing specificity. Like any outline, the diagram can warn of gaps, overlaps, and digressions. But unlike more linear outlines, it can be supplemented and extended indefinitely, so it is easy to alter for new ideas and arrangements discovered during drafting and revision.

Following are a thesis statement and tree diagram by student Joyanna Logan, based on her brainstorming about a summer job.

Thesis statement

Spending eight weeks in an internship saved me thousands of dollars and gave me a head start on my career.

Figure 9.2 A sample tree diagram

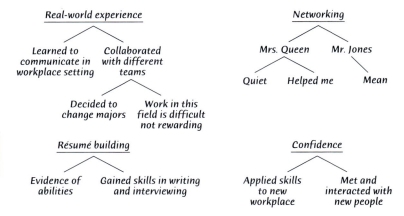

Formal outline

A formal outline not only lays out main ideas and their support but also shows the relative importance of all the essay's elements and how they connect with one another. Erica Vela created this formal outline on the basis of her scratch outline in 9.6.3.

Thesis statement

My experience of online education offers a benefit that Nicholas Carr overlooks: the Internet provides more opportunities for learning in areas where there are no well-stocked libraries or centers of higher education while offering more ways to access information from across the globe.

Formal outline

I. Summary of Carr's article
  A. Reasons for concern
    1. Damaging attention and concentration
    2. Removing the human element in thinking process
  B. Contexts for Carr's article
    1. Carr's age and personal experience
    2. Transition from print to digital reading
II. My online learning experiences
  A. Rural access to information
    1. Online libraries and databases
      a. Distance from campus and public libraries
      b. Access to full text sources through online databases and archives
    2. Online stores
  B. Online post-secondary education
    1. Online classes
    2. Online interaction with professors/peers
III. Comparisons with other technological advancements
  A. Plato's *Phaedrus* and the development of writing
  B. The printing press and the development of the publishing industry

This example illustrates several principles of outlining that can help ensure completeness, balance, and clear relationships. (These principles largely depend on distinguishing between the general and the specific.)

All the outline's parts are systematically indented and labeled. Roman numerals (I, II) label primary divisions of the essay, followed by capital letters (A, B) for secondary divisions, Arabic numerals (1, 2) for principal supporting points, and small letters (a, b) for supporting details, as needed. Each succeeding level contains more specific information than the one before it.

The outline divides the material into several groups.

Within each part of the outline, distinct topics of equal generality appear in parallel headings.

- **All subdivided headings in the outline break into at least two parts** because a topic cannot logically be divided into only one part. Any single subdivision should be matched with another subdivision, combined with the heading above it, or rechecked for its relevance to the heading above it.
- **All headings are expressed in parallel grammatical form.** Vela's is a **topic outline**, in which the headings consist of a noun with modifiers. In a **sentence outline** all headings are expressed as full sentences.
- **The outline covers only the body of the essay, omitting the introduction and the conclusion.** The beginning and the ending are important in the essay itself, but you need not include them in the outline unless you are required to do so or you anticipate special problems with their organization.

9.7 First Draft

9.7 Compose a first draft.

Drafting is an occasion for exploration. Don't expect to transcribe solid thoughts into polished prose: solidity and polish will come with revision and editing. Instead, while drafting let the very act of writing help you find and form your meaning.

9.7.1 Starting a draft

Beginning a draft sometimes takes courage, even for professionals. Procrastination may actually help if you let ideas for writing simmer at the same time. At some point, though, you'll have to face the blank paper or screen. The following techniques can help you begin:

- **Read over what you've already written**—notes, outlines, and so on. Immediately start your draft with whatever comes to mind.
- **Skip the opening and start in the middle.** Or write the conclusion.

- **Write a paragraph.** Explain what you think your essay will be about when you finish it.
- **Start writing the part that you understand best.** Using your outline, divide your work into chunks—say, one for the introduction, another for the first point, and so on. One of these chunks may call out to be written.

9.7.2 Maintaining momentum

Drafting requires momentum: the forward movement opens you to fresh ideas and connections. To keep moving while drafting, try one or more of these techniques:

- **Set aside enough time.** For a brief essay, a first draft is likely to take at least an hour or two.
- **Work in a quiet place.**
- **If you must stop working, write down what you plan to do next.** Then you can pick up where you stopped with minimal disruption.
- **Be as fluid as possible.** Spontaneity will allow your attitudes toward your subject to surface naturally in your sentences.
- **Keep going.** Skip over sticky spots; leave a blank if you can't find the right word; put alternative ideas or phrasings in brackets so that you can reconsider them later. If an idea pops out of nowhere but doesn't seem to fit in, quickly jot it down, or write it into the draft and bracket or boldface it for later attention.
- **Resist self-criticism.** Don't worry about your grammar, spelling, and the like. Don't worry about what your readers will think. These are very important matters, but save them for revision.
- **Use your thesis statement and outline.** They can remind you of your planned purpose, organization, and content. However, if your writing leads you in a more interesting direction, follow.

If you write on a computer, frequently save the text you're drafting—at least every five or ten minutes and every time you leave the computer.

9.8 Sample Draft

9.8 Analyze a sample first draft.

Following is Erica Vela's first-draft response to Nicholas Carr's "Is *Google* Making Us Stupid?" As part of her assignment, Vela showed the draft to four classmates, whose suggestions for revision appear in the margin of the draft. They used the Comment function of *Microsoft Word*, which allows users to add comments without inserting words into the document's text. Notice that her classmates ignore errors in grammar and punctuation, concentrating instead on larger issues such as thesis, clarity of ideas, and unity.

Sample draft

Responding to Carr

In "Is *Google* Making Us Stupid?" Nicholas Carr argues that the Internet is changing our minds at a fundamental level, possibly creating more problems than it solves. He states that the Internet is damaging the way we process information, creating minds that struggle to remain focused on a given task for an extended time. The ability to shrink the globe and bring information and education to my fingertips proves that Nicholas Carr's reservations about the Internet are shortsighted.

Carr describes his experience as "an uncomfortable sense that someone, or something, has been tinkering with [his] brain, remapping the neural circuitry, reprogramming the memory" (para. 2). He laments his inability to focus on extended tasks. He worries that this focus on the Internet and technology is removing the human element from our thinking processes and replacing it with computerization.

Like Carr, I remember what life was like before the Internet. I remember driving to the local library and poring over their card catalog, looking for books that held the information that I needed. If the library did not have the appropriate books, I would have to begin the extended process of interlibrary loan or travel hundreds of miles to a college or university library. But now, I can search a library's database, *Amazon*, or *Google* and find dozens (or even hundreds) of books, journal articles, or Web sites. Some I can read immediately. Others I can order and have shipped to my house within two days. The sharing of knowledge across the globe cannot be a bad thing.

Moreover, the Internet provides other opportunities for learning. Colleges and universities in the United States are building classrooms and degree programs online, allowing students from across the globe to obtain post-secondary educations in a world that increasingly demands them. In my degree program, all classes meet online. It allows me to work full-time while living nearly two hundred miles away from the main campus. I also get personal interaction with my professors and classmates through online discussion boards and video conferencing applications. Without the Internet, I would not be a student today.

Comment [Jason]: Your title doesn't really say what your essay is about, other than being a response to Carr.

Comment [Philip]: I think you need to add a citation for this source.

Comment [Makaila]: There almost seems to be something missing here. This sentence jumps to your thesis about the good things about the Internet but the intro does not lead in to that thesis.

Comment [Jason]: So your personal experience proves Carr is wrong? Your thesis statement is confusing to me. What does shortsighted mean here?

Comment [Davida]: Does Carr give any evidence of this besides his own personal experiences?

Comment [Makaila]: How does your own experience relate to your thesis? Can you explain that better?

Comment [Philip]: This paragraph goes from your personal experience to this broad statement very fast. How do we know that your experience really supports this idea?

Comment [Davida]: This is a strong statement. Make sure you explain how it relates to your main thesis.

Like Carr, I believe the Internet is changing how we think, but I believe that these changes will be a benefit in the future. As Carr notes, Socrates worried about the development of writing in Plato's *Phaedrus*. He believed that our ability to remember things would be permanently destroyed, but he couldn't foresee how writing would spread ideas, ultimately expanding human knowledge. A similar situation arose after the development of the printing press. Critics argued that "cheaply printed books . . . would undermine religious authority, demean the work of scholars and scribes, and spread sedition and debauchery" (para. 31). Can you imagine the world without books? It's a ridiculous thought today.

> Comment [Jason]: I got lost in this paragraph. How did we get from changes being a benefit to talking about books?

We know that the world of the future will look much different than it does today, and the development of the Internet will have much influence on its development. However, we must not fear technological advancement and the spread of new knowledge while clinging to older technologies with the tips of our fingers. As humans, we have learned human speech, developed writing, invented printing, and now we are creating digital spaces and information. We can appreciate what we have while embracing what is to come. Our future depends on it.

> Comment [Makaila]: This is very broad. Maybe focus more on Carr and restate your main idea?

> Comment [Philip]: How does this conclusion relate to Carr and your main point? It seems like a lot of big ideas but I don't see how they exactly support your thesis.

Chapter 10
Organizing and Developing Arguments

Learning Objectives

- 10.1 Define the elements of argument.
- 10.2 Develop your argument to engage readers.
- 10.3 Organize your argument.
- 10.4 Use visual arguments.
- 10.5 Examine a sample argument.

10.1 The Elements of Argument

10.1   Define the elements of argument.

Argument is writing that attempts to solve a problem, open readers' minds to an opinion, change readers' opinions, or move readers to action. Using various techniques, you engage readers to find common ground and narrow the distance between your views and theirs.

> ### Culture and language
> Argument as described here may be initially uncomfortable for you if your native culture approaches such writing differently. In some cultures, for example, a writer is expected to avoid asserting his or her opinion outright, to rely for evidence on appeals to tradition, or to establish a compromise rather than argue a position. In American academic and business settings, writers aim for a well-articulated opinion, evidence gathered from many sources, and a direct and concise argument for the opinion.

An argument has four main elements: subject, claims, evidence, and assumptions. (The last three are adapted from the work of the British philosopher Stephen Toulmin.)

10.1.1   The subject

An argument starts with a subject and often with a view of the subject as well—that is, an idea that makes you want to write about the subject. Your subject should meet several requirements:

- **It can be disputed:** reasonable people can disagree over it.
- **It *will* be disputed:** it is controversial.
- **It is narrow enough to research and argue in the space and time available.**

In contrast, several kinds of subjects will not work as the starting place of argument: indisputable facts, such as the functions of the human liver; personal preferences or beliefs, such as a moral commitment to vegetarianism; and ideas that few would disagree with, such as the value of a secure home.

10.1.2   Claims

Claims are statements that require support. In an argument, you develop your subject into a central claim or thesis, asserted outright in a thesis statement. This central claim is what the argument is about.

A thesis statement is always an **opinion**—that is, a judgment based on facts and arguable on the basis of facts. It may be one of the following:

- **A claim about past or present reality:**

  In both its space and its equipment, the college's chemistry lab is outdated.

  Academic cheating increases with students' economic insecurity.

- **A claim of value:**

  The new room fees are unjustified given the condition of the dormitories.

  Music streaming services undermine the system that encourages the very creation of music.

- **A recommendation for a course of action** (often a solution to a perceived problem):

  The college's outdated chemistry lab should be replaced incrementally over the next five years.

  Schools and businesses can help to resolve the region's traffic congestion by implementing car pools and rewarding participants.

The backbone of an argument consists of specific claims that support the thesis statement. These claims may also be statements of opinion, or they may fall into one of two other categories:

- **Statements of *fact*,** including facts that are generally known or are verifiable (such as the cost of tuition at your school) and those that can be inferred from verifiable facts (such as the monetary value of a college education).
- **Statements of *belief*,** or convictions based on personal faith or values, such as *The primary goal of government should be to provide equality of opportunity for all*. Although seemingly arguable, a statement of belief is not based on facts and so cannot be contested on the basis of facts.

10.1.3 Evidence

Evidence demonstrates the validity of your claims. The evidence to support the claim that the school needs a new chemistry lab might include the present lab's age, an inventory of facilities and equipment, and the testimony of chemistry professors.

There are several kinds of evidence:

- **Facts,** statements whose truth can be verified or inferred: *Poland is slightly smaller than New Mexico.*
- **Statistics,** facts expressed as numbers: *Of those polled, 22% prefer a flat tax.*
- **Examples,** specific instances of the point being made: *Many groups, such as the elderly and people with disabilities, would benefit from this policy.*

- **Expert opinions,** the judgments formed by authorities on the basis of their own examination of the facts: *Affirmative action is necessary to right past injustices, a point argued by Howard Glickstein, a past director of the US Commission on Civil Rights.*
- **Appeals to readers' beliefs or needs,** statements that ask readers to accept a claim in part because it states something they already accept as true without evidence: *The shabby, antiquated chemistry lab shames the school, making it seem a second-rate institution.*

Evidence must be reliable to be convincing. Ask these questions about your evidence:

- **Is it accurate**—trustworthy, exact, and undistorted?
- **Is it relevant**—authoritative, pertinent, and current?
- **Is it representative**—true to its context, neither under- nor over-representing any element of the sample it's drawn from?
- **Is it adequate**—plentiful and specific?

10.1.4 Assumptions

An **assumption** is an opinion, a principle, or a belief that ties evidence to claims: the assumption explains why a particular piece of evidence is relevant to a particular claim. For instance:

Claim: The college needs a new chemistry laboratory.

Evidence (in part): The testimony of chemistry professors.

Assumption: Chemistry professors are the most capable of evaluating the present lab's quality.

Assumptions are not flaws in arguments but necessities: we all acquire beliefs and opinions that shape our views of the world. Interpreting a work's assumptions is a significant part of critical reading and viewing, and recognizing your own assumptions is a significant part of argument. If your readers do not share your assumptions or if they perceive that you are not forthright about your biases, they will be less receptive to your argument.

10.2 Engaging Readers

10.2 Develop your argument to engage readers.

Reasonableness is essential if an argument is to establish common ground between you and your readers. Readers expect logical thinking, appropriate appeals, fairness toward the opposition, and, combining all of these, writing that is free of fallacies.

10.2.1 Logical thinking

The thesis of your argument is a conclusion you reach by reasoning about evidence. Two processes of reasoning, induction and deduction, are familiar to you even if you don't know their names.

Induction

When you're about to buy a used car, you consult friends, relatives, and consumer guides before deciding what kind of car to buy. Using **induction**, or **inductive reasoning**, you make specific observations about cars (your evidence) and you induce, or infer, a **generalization** that Car X is most reliable. The generalization is a claim supported by your observations.

You might also use inductive reasoning in a term paper on print advertising:

> **Evidence:** Advertisements in newspapers and magazines.
>
> **Evidence:** Comments by advertisers and publishers.
>
> **Evidence:** Data on the effectiveness of advertising.
>
> **Generalization or claim:** Print is the most cost-effective medium for advertising.

Reasoning inductively, you connect your evidence to your generalization by assuming that what is true in one set of circumstances (the evidence you examine) is also true in a similar set of circumstances (evidence you do not examine). With induction you create new knowledge out of old.

The more evidence you accumulate, the more probable it is that your generalization is true. Note, however, that absolute certainty is not possible. At some point you must *assume* that your evidence justifies your generalization, for yourself and your readers. Most errors in inductive reasoning involve oversimplifying either the evidence or the generalization.

Deduction

You use **deduction**, or **deductive reasoning**, when you proceed from your generalization that Car X is the most reliable used car to your own specific circumstances (you want to buy a used car) to the conclusion that you should buy Car X. In deduction your assumption is a generalization, principle, or belief that you think is true. It links the evidence (new information) to the claim (the conclusion you draw). With deduction you apply old information to new.

Say that you want the school administration to postpone new room fees for one dormitory. You can base your argument on a deductive **syllogism**:

> **Premise:** The administration should not raise fees on dorm rooms in poor condition. [A generalization or belief that you assume to be true.]
>
> **Premise:** The rooms in Polk Hall are in poor condition. [New information: a specific case of the first premise.]
>
> **Conclusion:** The administration should not raise fees on the rooms in Polk Hall. [Your claim.]

As long as the premises of a syllogism are true, the conclusion derives logically and certainly from them.

10.2.2 Rational, emotional, and ethical appeals

In most arguments you will combine **rational appeals** to readers' capacities for logical reasoning with **emotional appeals** to readers' beliefs and feelings. The following example illustrates both: the second sentence makes a rational appeal (to the logic of financial gain), and the third sentence makes an emotional appeal (to the sense of fairness and open-mindedness).

> Advertising should show more people who are physically challenged. The millions of Americans with disabilities have considerable buying power, yet so far advertisers have made no attempt to tap that power. Further, by keeping people with disabilities out of the mainstream depicted in ads, advertisers encourage widespread prejudice against disability, prejudice that frightens and demeans those who hold it.

For an emotional appeal to be successful, it must be appropriate for the audience and the argument:

- It must not misjudge readers' actual feelings.
- It must not raise emotional issues that are irrelevant to the claims and the evidence.

A third kind of approach to readers, the **ethical appeal**, is the sense you give of being a competent, fair person who is worth heeding. A rational appeal and an appropriate emotional appeal contribute to your ethical appeal, as does your acknowledgment of opposing views. An argument that is concisely written and correct in grammar, spelling, and other matters will underscore your competence. In addition, a sincere and even tone will assure readers that you are a balanced person who wants to reason with them.

A sincere and even tone need not exclude language with emotional appeal—words such as *frightens* and *demeans* at the end of the example above about advertising. But avoid certain forms of expression that will mark you as unfair:

- **Insulting words,** such as *idiotic* or *fascist*.
- **Biased language,** such as *fags* or *broads*.
- **Sarcasm,** such as the phrase *What a brilliant idea* to indicate contempt for the idea and its originator.
- **Exclamation points!** They make you sound shrill!

10.2.3 Acknowledgment of opposing views

A good test of your fairness in argument is how you handle possible objections. Assuming your thesis is indeed arguable, others can marshal their own evidence to support a different view or views.

By dealing squarely with those opposing views, you show yourself to be honest and fair. You strengthen your ethical appeal and thus your entire argument.

Before or while you draft your essay, list for yourself all the opposing views you can think of. You'll find them in your research, by talking to friends and classmates, and by critically thinking about your own ideas. You can also look for a range of views in an online discussion that deals with your subject.

A common way to handle opposing views is to state them, refute those you can, grant the validity of others, and demonstrate why, despite their validity, the opposing views are less compelling than your own. A somewhat different approach, developed by psychologist Carl Rogers, emphasizes the search for common ground. In a **Rogerian argument**, you start by showing that you understand readers' views and by establishing points on which you and readers agree and disagree. Creating a connection in this way can be especially helpful when you expect readers to resist your argument, because the connection encourages them to hear you out as you develop your claims.

10.2.4 Fallacies

Fallacies—errors in argument—either evade the issue of the argument or treat the argument as if it were much simpler than it is.

Evasions

An effective argument squarely faces the central issue or question it addresses. An ineffective argument may dodge the issue in one of the following ways:

- **Begging the question:** treating an opinion that is open to question as if it were already proved or disproved.

  The college library's expenses should be reduced by cutting subscriptions to useless periodicals. [Begged questions: Are some of the library's periodicals useless? Useless to whom?]

- **Non sequitur** (Latin: "It does not follow"): linking two or more ideas that in fact have no logical connection. Usually the problem is an unstated assumption that supposedly links the ideas but is false.

  She uses a wheelchair, so she must be unhappy. [Unstated assumption: People who use wheelchairs are unhappy.]

- **Red herring:** introducing an irrelevant issue intended to distract readers from the relevant issues.

  A campus speech code is essential to protect students, who already have enough problems coping with rising tuition. [Tuition costs and speech codes are different subjects. What protections do students need that a speech code will provide?]

- **Appeal to readers' fear or pity:** substituting emotions for reasoning.

    She should not have to pay taxes because she is an aged widow with no friends or relatives. [Appeals to people's pity. Should age and loneliness, rather than income, determine a person's tax obligation?]

- **Bandwagon:** inviting readers to accept a claim because everyone else does.

    As everyone knows, marijuana use leads to heroin addiction. [What is the evidence?]

- **Ad hominem** (Latin: "to the man"): attacking the qualities of the people holding an opposing view rather than the substance of the view itself.

    One of the scientists has been treated for emotional problems, so his pessimism about nuclear waste merits no attention. [Do the scientist's previous emotional problems invalidate his current views?]

Oversimplifications

In a vain attempt to create something neatly convincing, an ineffective argument may conceal or ignore complexities in one of the following ways:

- **Hasty generalization:** making a claim on the basis of inadequate evidence.

    It is disturbing that several of the youths who shot up schools were users of violent video games. Obviously, these games can breed violence, and they should be banned. [A few cases do not establish the relationship between the games and violent behavior. Most youths who play violent video games do not behave violently.]

- **Sweeping generalization:** making an insupportable statement. Many sweeping generalizations are **absolute statements** involving words such as *all, always, never,* and *no one* that allow no exceptions. Others are **stereotypes**, conventional and oversimplified characterizations of a group of people:

    People who live in cities are unfriendly.
    Californians are fad-crazy.
    Women are emotional.
    Men can't express their feelings.

- **Reductive fallacy:** oversimplifying (reducing) the relationship between causes and effects.

    Poverty causes crime. [If so, then why do people who are not poor commit crimes? And why aren't all poor people criminals?]

- **Post hoc fallacy** (from Latin, *post hoc, ergo propter hoc:* "after this, therefore because of this"): assuming that because *A* preceded *B*, then *A* must have caused *B*.

  The town council erred in permitting the adult bookstore to open, for shortly afterward two women were assaulted. [It cannot be assumed without evidence that the women's assailants visited or were influenced by the bookstore.]

- **Either/or fallacy:** assuming that a complicated question has only two answers, one good and one bad, both good, or both bad.

  Either we permit mandatory drug testing in the workplace or productivity will continue to decline. [Productivity is not necessarily dependent on drug testing.]

10.3 Organization

10.3   Organize your argument.

All arguments include the same parts:

- **The *introduction* establishes the significance of the subject and provides background.** The introduction may run a paragraph or two, and it generally includes the thesis statement. However, if you think your readers may have difficulty accepting your thesis statement before they see at least some support for it, then it may come later in the paper.
- **The *body* states and develops the claims supporting the thesis.** In one or more paragraphs, the body develops each claim with clearly relevant evidence. See below for more on organizing the body.
- **The *response to opposing views* details and addresses those views,** either demonstrating your argument's greater strengths or conceding the opponents' points. See below on organizing this response.
- **The *conclusion* completes the argument,** restating the thesis, summarizing the supporting claims, and making a final appeal to readers.

The structure of the body and the response to opposing views depends on your subject, purpose, audience, and form of reasoning. Here are several possible arrangements:

A common scheme	The Rogerian scheme
Claim 1 and evidence	Common ground and concession to opposing views
Claim 2 and evidence	Claim 1 and evidence
Claim X and evidence	Claim 2 and evidence
Response to opposing views	Claim X and evidence

A variation
Claim 1 and evidence
Response to opposing views
Claim 2 and evidence
Response to opposing views
Claim X and evidence
Response to opposing views

The problem-solution scheme
The problem: claims and evidence
The solution: claims and evidence
Response to opposing views

10.4 Visual Arguments

10.4 Use visual arguments.

Arguments can be visual as well as verbal. Advertisements often provide the most vivid and memorable examples of visual arguments, but writers in almost every field—from medicine to music, from physics to physical education—support their claims with images. The main elements of written arguments—claims, evidence, and assumptions—appear also in visual arguments.

10.4.1 Claims

The claims in a visual may be made by composition as well as by content, with or without accompanying words. For instance:

Visual A photograph framing hundreds of chickens crammed into small cages, resembling familiar images of World War II concentration camps.
Claim Commercial poultry-raising practices are cruel and unethical.

Visual A chart with dramatically contrasting bars that represent the optimism, stress, and heart disease reported by people before and after they participated in a program of daily walking.
Claim Daily exercise leads to a healthier and happier life.

The advertisement in Figure 10.1 is one in the "Army Strong" series that the United States Army runs for recruitment. As noted in the annotations, the ad makes several claims both in the photograph and in the text.

10.4.2 Evidence

The kinds of evidence offered by visuals parallel those found in written arguments:

- **Facts:** You might provide facts in the form of data, as in a graph showing a five-year rise in oil prices or in the text of the US Army advertisement promising "one of over 150 career opportunities." Or you might draw an inference from data, as the army ad does by stating that the army provides "money for college."

124 Organizing and developing arguments

Figure 10.1 Claims in a visual

Advertisement by the United States Army

- **Examples:** Most often, you'll use examples to focus on an instance of your argument's claims. In the army ad, the soldier using technical equipment is an example supporting the claim that the army gives soldiers technical training.
- **Expert opinions:** You might present a chart from an expert showing a trend in unemployment among high school graduates.
- **Appeals to beliefs or needs:** You might depict how things clearly ought to be (an antidrug brochure featuring a teenager who is confidently refusing peer pressure) or, in contrast, show how things clearly should not be (a Web site for an antihunger campaign featuring images of emaciated children).

To make a visual work effectively as evidence, be sure it relates directly to a point in your argument and that it accurately represents the subject. The first graph (Figure 10.2) seems to provide good visual evidence for this claim: *The rising birthrate of US teens is an issue that must be addressed.* The data come from the Centers for

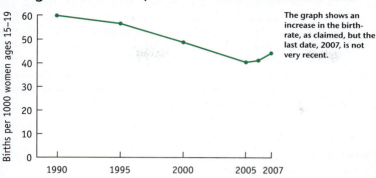

Figure 10.2 Incomplete and unreliable evidence in a visual

The graph shows an increase in the birthrate, as claimed, but the last date, 2007, is not very recent.

Disease Control and Prevention (CDC), a US agency and a reputable source. But the data are incomplete, so the claim is inaccurate and the graph is misleading.

In fact, later data show that the birthrate resumed its downward trend in 2008. The second graph (Figure 10.3) uses more recent data to support a modified claim: *Although the birthrate of US teens has fallen almost every year since 1990, teen pregnancy remains an issue that must be addressed.*

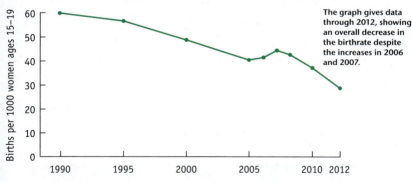

Figure 10.3 Complete and reliable evidence in a visual

The graph gives data through 2012, showing an overall decrease in the birthrate despite the increases in 2006 and 2007.

10.4.3 Assumptions

Like a written argument, a visual argument is based on assumptions—your ideas about the relationship between evidence and claims. Look again at the US Army ad. The advertiser seems to have assumed that a strictly factual claim about the benefits of joining the army would not attract as many recruits as a photograph and text that together claim opportunities for training, education, and life change. With the photograph of the soldier, comfortable among technical equipment, the advertiser seems also to be appealing to young men and women who are interested in technical training.

As in written arguments, the assumptions in a visual argument must be appropriate for your readers if the argument is to succeed with them. The army ad originally appeared in magazines with young adult readers, an audience that might be interested in the possibility of training and life change. But to readers uninterested in technical training, the photograph's emphasis on using equipment might actually undermine the ad's effectiveness.

10.4.4 Appeals

Visuals can help to strengthen the rational, emotional, and ethical appeals of your written argument:

- **Visuals can contribute evidence,** as long as they come from reliable sources, present information accurately and fairly, and relate clearly to the argument's claims.
- **Visuals can appeal to a host of ideas and emotions,** including patriotism, curiosity, moral values, sympathy, and anger. Any such appeal should correctly gauge readers' beliefs and feelings, and it should be clearly relevant to the argument.
- **Visuals can show that you are a competent, fair, and trustworthy source of information,** largely through their relevance, reliability, and sensitivity to readers' needs and feelings.

To see how appeals can work in visuals, look at the billboard from the Ad Council (Figure 10.4). The visual illustrates this claim: *Public-service advertisers try to discourage young drivers from drinking by addressing them directly and depicting the risks.*

Figure 10.4 Appeals in a visual

Rational appeal: Backs up the writer's claim with text that uses slang to address young drivers and a photograph that shows the results of drunk driving.

Emotional appeal: Dramatically illustrates the attempt to discourage young drivers from drinking.

Ethical appeal: Conveys the writer's competence through the appropriateness of the visual for the point being made.

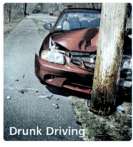

10.4.5 Recognizing fallacies

When making a visual argument, you'll need to guard against fallacies. Here we'll focus on specific visual examples. The first, which appears in the army ad, is snob appeal: inviting readers to be like someone they admire. The soldier is clearly comfortable and competent with the equipment, and the ad appeals to the reader's wish to be someone who is equally capable and fulfilled. If you join the US Army, the ad says subtly, you too may become strong. The ad does have some substance in its specific and verifiable claim of "over 150 career opportunities" and "money for college," but the soldier in quiet command of his equipment makes a stronger claim.

Another example of a visual fallacy is the hasty generalization, a claim that is based on too little evidence or that misrepresents the facts. Figure 10.2 illustrates this fallacy: in omitting recent data that undercut the writer's claim, the graph misrepresents the facts.

10.5 Sample Argument

10.5 Examine a sample argument.

The following essay by student Amalia Berger is a proposal argument that illustrates the principles discussed in this chapter. As you read the essay, notice especially the organization, the relationship of claims and supporting evidence (including illustrations), the kinds of appeals Berger makes, and the ways she responds to opposing views.

Access and Opportunity for Students: A Proposal to
Increase Online Course Offerings

Online college classes are popular with nontraditional students for many reasons. Some students must work off-campus to support themselves and their families, and they are unable to attend an on-campus class. Some students live in remote areas, making trips to campus difficult. Other students may be dealing with disabilities that hinder their ability to attend and participate in traditional classes. At registration, these students are competing against each other for the small number of openings in online classes. In their major fields, closed online sections are unlikely, but in first-year composition—a class required across the curriculum—closed online sections are common because these classes fill quickly. When students who depend on the availability of online classes are unable to enroll, they may have

Introduction: identification and definition of the problem

Thesis statement: proposed solution to the problem	to delay their graduation by a semester or more. Worse yet, they may not persist with their education, leaving college without a degree. To increase student retention and on-time graduation rates, colleges and universities should increase online courses offerings in the core requirements so that half of the total sections are offered online.
Historical background and context used to further define the proposed solution	Online, or distance, learning was introduced in the early 1990s to support students in remote, rural areas who would not otherwise have access to higher education. Since then, online classes have become mainstream. According to the Online Learning Consortium, 5.8 million students enrolled in at least one online course in 2016 (2). As with any new technology, online learning has encountered resistance among students and educators, but research and an increasing amount of student experience confirm that the advantages of online learning outweigh the disadvantages.
First main point in support of the proposed solution	First, online classes offer more interaction and greater ability to concentrate. Web-based classes offer shy or introverted students the opportunity to participate in class discussions. Students can take their time and consider their responses; they are not confined to a fifty-minute class where they must make their voices heard over twenty other students. In addition, students with concentration problems often find that online classes offer a better education experience because they are not distracted by other students or by classroom activity.
Evidence for first point: personal experience and student's own research	
Second main point in support of the proposed solution	Online classes meet the needs of a changing college and university demographic. According to a 2002 report by the National Center for Education Statistics, the number of nontraditional students at American colleges and universities is growing. More than 73 percent of college students today are considered nontraditional in some way (Choy 1). Traditional students—teenagers who enroll immediately after high school, depend on a parent's financial support, and work fewer than 20 hours per week—are the exception on today's college campuses rather than the rule. A 2015 study completed by the Georgetown University Center on Education and the Workforce found that "about 40 percent of undergraduates and 76 percent of graduate students work at least 30 hours a week; 25 percent of all working learners are simultaneously employed full-time and enrolled in college full-time; and 19 percent of all working learners have children" (23, see fig. 1). Ultimately, online classes offer greater access to all students—traditional and nontraditional. Greater access increases student persistence and retention through graduation—the goal of all colleges and universities.
Evidence for second point: published research	

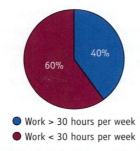

- Work > 30 hours per week
- Work < 30 hours per week

Fig. 1. Proportion of undergraduate students working 30 hours per week or more, as of 2015.

Online classes motivate students to improve their skills in technology and collaboration. Students must learn to navigate the course technology, either a course-management system or other type of course Web site as well as collaboration tools like *Google Drive* for creating and sharing documents and *Skype* for video conferencing. Not only valuable in the online classroom, these improved technology skills prepare the student for the increased emphasis on technology in the modern workplace.

If greater access, student persistence, and degree completion are the goals, why have colleges and universities failed to adapt to their changing demographic and continued to insist on traditional modes of education, particularly in core classes like first-year composition that are in such high demand?

Some college and university administrators point to instructor training and support as a roadblock to greater numbers of online courses. Online instructors face different challenges in the online classroom. All materials must be presented through a course-management system or Web site, which makes online instruction more writing intensive than a traditional face-to-face class. Dr. Beth Hewett, president of the Global Society of Online Literacy Educators, suggests that "teaching one class of 11 online is really teaching 11 classes of one," meaning that most of the actual instruction happens in individualized responses to students. Increasing the number of online classes without preparing instructors for the challenges involved in online teaching would be counterproductive. The instructors would become frustrated and reluctant to repeat the experience while students would fail to learn the material. Therefore, any proposal to increase the number of online classes must also call for additional training and support for online instructors.

Second objection to proposed solution

Some professors object to online courses, arguing that online courses are not rigorous or challenging enough for students. In fact, online classes often have a higher reading and writing workload because there is no traditional lecture component to the class. One recent study concluded that the "literacy load" (combined reading and writing workload for students) was nearly three times greater in an online course than in a similar face-to-face course (Griffin and Minter 153). In some courses, the online nature of the class requires that the material be presented in a different way or that student knowledge on the course objectives be evaluated in a different manner. In most cases, this issue can be addressed by additional training for online instructors. As in most things—including both on-campus and online classrooms—students receive an education equal to their effort to learn the materials.

Response to second objection: information from published research

Conclusion summarizes main points and restates the proposed solution

Considering the increasing numbers of nontraditional students, colleges and universities must address the diverse needs of these student populations. These students depend on the availability of online classes for completing their degrees. Without the flexibility of online classes, these students would likely leave the university setting without their degrees or spend more time than necessary earning their degrees. However, simply adding more online sections will not solve the problem. Colleges and universities must make a commitment to increase the availability of courses, the training of online instructors, and the quality of their online curriculum to offer students the expanded course selection and valuable education they deserve.

[New page.]

Works Cited

Works cited in MLA style

Choy, Susan. *Findings from the Condition of Education 2002: Nontraditional Undergraduates*. National Center for Education Statistics, Aug. 2002, nces.ed.gov/pubs2002/2002012.pdf.

Georgetown University Center on Education and the Workforce. *Seventy Percent of College Students Work While Enrolled, New Georgetown University Research Finds*. Georgetown University, 28 Oct. 2015, cew.georgetown.edu/wp-content/uploads/Press-release-WorkingLearners_FINAL.pdf.

Griffin, June, and Deborah Minter. "The Rise of the Online Writing Classroom: Reflecting on the Material Conditions of College Composition Teaching." *College Composition and Communication*, vol. 65, no. 1, 2013, pp. 140–61.

Works cited entry for a personal e-mail sent to the author

Hewett, Beth L. "Assignment 2.1." Received by Amalia Berger, 2 Apr. 2017.

Online Learning Consortium. *2016: A Year of Acceleration and Growth in Online Learning*. 2017, http://info2.onlinelearningconsortium.org/rs/897-CSM-305/images/2016%20OLC%20Year%20in%20Review.pdf.

—Amalia Berger (student)

Chapter 11
Paragraphs

Learning Objectives

- **11.1** Relate each paragraph to the essay as a whole.
- **11.2** Maintain the unity of each paragraph.
- **11.3** Make each paragraph coherent.
- **11.4** Develop the central idea of each paragraph.
- **11.5** Write effective introductory and concluding paragraphs.

11.1 Flow

11.1 Relate each paragraph to the essay as a whole.

Paragraphs develop the main ideas that support the thesis of a piece of writing, and they break these supporting ideas into manageable chunks. For readers, paragraphs signal the movement between ideas and provide a breather from long stretches of text.

Culture and language

Not all cultures share the paragraphing conventions of American academic writing. In some other languages, writing moves differently from English on the page—not from left to right, but from right to left or down rows from top to bottom. Even in languages that move as English does on the page, writers may not use paragraphs at all, or they may use paragraphs but not state their central ideas. If your native language is not English and you have difficulty writing paragraphs, don't worry about paragraphing during drafting. Instead, during a separate step of revision, divide your text into parts that develop your main points, and mark those parts with indentions. Then you can make sure that each paragraph has a clear central idea supported by evidence such as facts and examples.

Checklist for revising paragraphs

- **Does each paragraph contribute to the essay as a whole?** Does each paragraph support the essay's central idea, or thesis? Does each paragraph relate to the ones that come before and after it?

- **Is each paragraph unified?** Does it adhere to one general idea that is either stated in a topic sentence or is otherwise apparent?
- **Is each paragraph coherent?** Do the sentences follow a clear sequence? Are the sentences linked as needed by parallelism, repetition or restatement, pronouns, consistency, and transitional expressions?
- **Is each paragraph developed?** Is the general idea of each paragraph well supported with specific evidence such as details, facts, examples, and reasons?

¶ un
11.2

Paragraphs do not stand alone: they are key units of a larger piece of writing. Even if you draft a paragraph separately, it needs to connect to your central idea, or thesis—explaining it and deepening it. Together, paragraphs need to flow from one to the other so that readers easily grasp the points you are making and how each point contributes to the whole essay.

To see how effective body paragraphs work to help both writer and reader, look at a paragraph from student Erica Vela's essay "*Google* Opens Our Minds—and Our Worlds." Responding to an article by Nicholas Carr, Vela is supporting her thesis that Carr overlooks the benefits of Internet reading and online learning.

The Internet also provides other opportunities for learning. Colleges and universities in the United States are building virtual classrooms and online degree programs, allowing students from around the globe to obtain postsecondary educations in a world that increasingly demands them.	New main idea linking to previous paragraph ("also") and linking to thesis
In my degree program, all classes meet online. Online courses allow me to work full-time while living nearly two hundred miles away from the main campus. Online courses also provide personal interaction with my professors and classmates through discussion boards and video conferencing applications.	Details to support main idea of paragraph
Without the Internet, I would not have access to a postsecondary education and I would not be a student today.	Concluding sentence sums up paragraph and links to previous paragraph and thesis

11.2 Unity

11.2   Maintain the unity of each paragraph.

Just as readers expect paragraphs to relate clearly to an essay's thesis, they also generally expect each paragraph to be **unified**—that is, to develop a single idea. Often this idea is expressed in a **topic sentence**. For example, look again at the paragraph by Erica Vela in 11.1: the opening statement conveys Vela's promise that she will explain other learning opportunities made possible by the Internet, and the next sentences keep the promise. But what if Vela had written this paragraph instead?

> <u>The Internet also provides other opportunities for learning.</u> [Topic sentence: general statement] Colleges and universities in the United States are building virtual classrooms and online degree programs, allowing students from around the globe to obtain postsecondary educations in a world that increasingly demands them. In my degree program, all classes meet online. [Details supporting topic sentence] Some students may question whether online courses are as good as in-person learning. My friends argue that online courses are not as challenging as their face-to-face classes. But I know that I spend more time on my studies than they do, because I do not have to commute to campus. [Digression]

By wandering from the topic of opportunities for learning, the paragraph fails to deliver on the commitment of its topic sentence.

A topic sentence need not always come first in the paragraph. For instance, it may come last, presenting your idea only after you have provided the evidence for it. Or it may not be stated at all, especially in narrative or descriptive writing in which the point becomes clear in the details. But the idea should always govern the paragraph's content as if it were standing guard at the opening.

11.3 Coherence

11.3 Make each paragraph coherent.

When a paragraph is **coherent**, readers can see how it holds together: the sentences seem to flow logically and smoothly into one another. Exactly the opposite happens with this paragraph:

> Supernatural beliefs influenced every aspect of life for the Mayan civilization. [Topic sentence] Mayans performed ceremonies and rituals for their gods. These rituals included feasting, bloodletting, dance, music, and human sacrifice. The Mayans had a divine king who controlled their religious and political lives. The Mayans buried their dead under their homes. The Mayan hierarchy had a closed priesthood. The supernatural influenced the lives of the Mayan people in many ways. [Sentences related to topic sentence but disconnected from each other]

The paragraph as it was actually written begins below. It is much clearer because the writer arranged information differently and built links into her sentences so that they would flow smoothly:

- After stating the central idea in a topic sentence, the writer moves to two more specific explanations and illustrates the second with two sentences of examples.
- Words in green repeat or restate key terms or concepts.
- Words in pink link sentences and clarify relationships.
- Underlined phrases are in parallel grammatical form to reflect their parallel content.

> Supernatural beliefs influenced every aspect of life for the Mayan civilization. The Mayans believed that the supernatural world was filled with powerful gods that could only be placated with frequent ceremonies and elaborate rituals that included feasting, bloodletting, dance, music, and in some cases, human sacrifice. Moreover, the Mayans believed that their deceased ancestors could gain them favor with the gods so they buried their dead under the floors of their homes. These all-consuming beliefs and rituals evolved over time, creating religious cults with a closed priesthood. Eventually, the power of the priesthood surpassed the power of politicians, consolidating religious and political power in a divine king.
>
> —Molly Avenir (student), "Organized Religion in the Mayan Civilization"

11.3.1 Paragraph organization

A coherent paragraph organizes information so that readers can easily follow along. These are common paragraph schemes:

- **General to specific:** Sentences downshift from more general statements to more specific ones.
- **Climactic:** Sentences increase in drama or interest, ending in a climax.
- **Spatial:** Sentences scan a person, place, or object from top to bottom or in some other way that approximates the way people look at things.
- **Chronological:** Sentences present events as they occurred in time, earlier to later.

11.3.2 Parallelism

One way to achieve coherence is through **parallelism**, the use of similar grammatical structures for similar elements of meaning within a sentence or among sentences. In the following paragraph, the underlined parallel structures link all sentences after the first one, and parallelism also appears within many of the sentences.

> Samuel Langhorne Clemens, better known as Mark Twain, was a particularly interesting man—an American writer and humorist as well as a publisher and well-known lecturer. Born in Hannibal, Missouri, in 1835, Twain served as a printer's apprentice before working as a typesetter. <u>He wrote</u> articles for a newspaper before working as a riverboat pilot. In 1861, <u>he moved</u> to Nevada where he worked as a journalist. Twain received his big break in 1865 when <u>he gained</u> international attention for his short story "The Celebrated Jumping Frog of Calaveras County." <u>He continued</u> to write, earning praise for his wit and satire. His book *Adventures of Huckleberry Finn* is often called "The Great American Novel," and he is considered by some as "the father of American literature." Throughout his life, Twain remained outspoken on issues of importance. <u>He argued</u> against American imperialistic policies and supported the abolition of slavery and the emancipation of slaves. <u>He</u> also <u>criticized</u> organized religion and commended labor unions.
> —Tonya Mayer (student), "Mark Twain: A Legendary Life"

11.3.3 Repetition and restatement

Repeating or restating the important words in a paragraph binds the sentences together and keeps the paragraph's topic uppermost in readers' minds. In the next example, notice how the shaded words relate the sentences and stress the important ideas of the paragraph:

> The Green Dot organization aims to mobilize our ==campus community== into a ==community== of engaged and ==proactive bystanders== when confronted with power-based personal ==violence==. They believe that individual safety is the ==responsibility== of the entire ==campus community==, shifting the focus of personal ==violence== from the victims and perpetrators to the ==proactive bystanders==. Through the training, ==community== members will build the skills and knowledge necessary for effective persuasive communication as a means of preventing ==violence==. We have a choice to tolerate and perpetuate personal ==violence==, or we can stop it. We should choose to join the hundreds of colleges and universities, public schools, military, national, state, and ==community== organizations who have successfully completed the Green Dot training and take personal ==responsibility== for the safety of our ==campus community==.
> —Willow Armigan (student), "Building a Safer Campus Community Through Personal Engagement"

11.3.4 Pronouns

Pronouns such as *she, he, it, they,* and *who* refer to and function as nouns. Thus pronouns naturally help relate sentences to each other.

In Tonya Mayer's paragraph (11.3.2), for example, *he* works in this way by substituting for *Mark Twain*.

11.3.5 Consistency

Consistency (or the lack of it) occurs primarily in the **person** and **number** of nouns and pronouns and in the **tense** of verbs. Any inconsistencies not required by meaning will interfere with a reader's ability to follow the development of ideas.

Note the underlined inconsistencies in the next paragraphs:

Shifts in tense

In the Hopi religion, water is the driving force. Since the Hopi lived in the Arizona desert, they needed water urgently for drinking, cooking, and irrigating crops. Their complex beliefs are focused in part on gaining the assistance of supernatural forces in obtaining water. Many of the Hopi kachinas, or spirit essences, were directly concerned with clouds, rain, and snow.

Shifts in number

Kachinas represent the things and events of the real world, such as clouds, mischief, cornmeal, and even death. A kachina is not worshiped as a god but regarded as an interested friend. They visit the Hopi from December through July in the form of men who dress in kachina costumes and perform dances and other rituals.

Shifts in person

Unlike the man, the Hopi woman does not keep contact with kachinas through costumes and dancing. Instead, one receives a small likeness of a kachina, called a *tihu*, from the man impersonating the kachina. You are more likely to receive a tihu as a girl approaching marriage, though a child or older woman may receive one, too.

11.3.6 Transitional expressions

Transitional expressions such as *therefore, in contrast,* and *meanwhile* can forge specific connections between sentences, as do the highlighted expressions in this paragraph:

Hundreds of bills are introduced in the United States Congress each year, but only some become laws. Members of Congress introduce legislation. Once introduced, a committee reviews the bill. As soon as the bill receives a committee hearing, a vote is held. After committee approval, the bill is immediately placed on the Legislative Calendar. Members debate the bill before voting takes place. Once it passes, the bill moves to the other chamber. Eventually, the other chamber will also debate and vote on the bill. If the bill passes both chambers of Congress, it will be sent to the president. However, the bill still might not become law. The president may choose to sign the bill or veto it. If he vetoes it, the bill will soon return to Congress for review. Then, congressional members may attempt to override the veto by obtaining a supermajority of congressional votes. If a supermajority is attained, the bill becomes law. As you can see, congressional action requires many complicated steps. Therefore, it is easy to understand why so few bills become law.

—Tonisha Jones (student), "Navigating Congress: Turning Ideas into Legislation"

The following box lists many transitional expressions by the functions they perform.

Transitional expressions

To add or show sequence
again, also, and, and then, besides, equally important, finally, first, further, furthermore, in addition, in the first place, last, moreover, next, second, still, too

To compare
also, in the same way, likewise, similarly

To contrast
although, and yet, but, but at the same time, despite, even so, even though, for all that, however, in contrast, in spite of, nevertheless, notwithstanding, on the contrary, on the other hand, regardless, still, though, yet

To give examples or intensify
after all, an illustration of, even, for example, for instance, indeed, in fact, it is true, of course, specifically, that is, to illustrate, truly

To indicate place
above, adjacent to, below, elsewhere, farther on, here, near, nearby, on the other side, opposite to, there, to the east, to the left

To indicate time
after a while, afterward, as long as, as soon as, at last, at length, at that time, before, earlier, eventually, formerly, immediately, in the meantime, in the past, later, meanwhile, now, shortly, simultaneously, since, so far, soon, subsequently, suddenly, then, thereafter, until, until now, when

To repeat, summarize, or conclude
all in all, altogether, as has been said, in brief, in conclusion, in other words, in particular, in short, in simpler terms, in summary, on the whole, that is, therefore, to put it differently, to summarize

To show cause or effect
accordingly, as a result, because, consequently, for this purpose, hence, otherwise, since, then, therefore, thereupon, thus, to this end

> **Culture and language**
>
> If transitional expressions are not common in your native language, you may be tempted to compensate when writing in English by adding them to the beginnings of most sentences. But such explicit transitions aren't needed everywhere, and in fact, too many can be intrusive and awkward. When inserting transitional expressions, consider the reader's need for a signal: often the connection from sentence to sentence is already clear from the context, or it can be made clear by relating the content of sentences more closely. When you do need transitional expressions, try varying their positions in your sentences.

11.4 Development

11.4 Develop the central idea of each paragraph.

An effective, well-developed paragraph always provides the specific information that readers need and expect in order to understand you and to stay interested in what you say. Paragraph length can be a rough gauge of development: anything much shorter than 100 to 150 words may leave readers with a sense of incompleteness.

To develop or shape an idea in a paragraph, try one or more of the following patterns.

11.4.1 Narration

Narration retells a significant sequence of events, usually in the order of their occurrence (that is, chronologically). A narrator is concerned not just with the sequence of events but also with their consequence, their importance to the whole.

> I was so nervous. Would anyone know? Would anyone be able to tell that my hands were sweating, and my stomach was in knots? I stood in the shadows and listened while a voice spoke softly in the distance. I could feel my heart racing, and I just knew that I was going to be sick. I glanced around the area, looking for a wastebasket or a restroom. As I began to move, the sound of applause shocked me, and I staggered slightly in my heels. A woman waved at me, begging me to come closer. She stood on a lighted stage behind a podium. I realized that I had two choices: I could run away and hide, hopefully in an empty restroom, or I could walk toward the woman. I took a moment to wonder if these people would be upset if the guest speaker took a run for the exit. One internal sigh later, I took a step toward her and that blasted podium.
> —Per Daarsgsar (student), "The Introvert at the Podium"

11.4.2 Description

Description details the sensory qualities of a person, scene, thing, or feeling, using concrete and specific words to convey a dominant mood, illustrate an idea, or achieve some other purpose.

> The sun struck straight upon the house, making the white walls glare between the dark windows. Their panes, woven thickly with green branches, held circles of impenetrable darkness. Sharp-edged wedges of light lay upon the window-sill and showed inside the room plates with blue rings, cups with curved handles, the bulge of a great bowl, the crisscross pattern in the rug, and the formidable corners and lines of cabinets and bookcases. Behind their conglomeration hung a zone of shadow in which might be a further shape to be disencumbered of shadow or still denser depths of darkness.
> —Virginia Woolf, *The Waves*, Harcourt, 1931

11.4.3 Illustration or support

An idea may be developed with several specific examples or with a single extended example, as in the next paragraph:

> Chronic migraine headaches can affect nearly every part of a patient's life. Ellen, a 30-year-old married mother of two, suffers them in clusters that can last for weeks. While experiencing a migraine, her head throbs behind her eyes and near the base of her skull. She deals with constant nausea and sensitivities to light and sound which prevent her from working or caring for her family. Ellen's treatment doesn't stop and start with the clusters. Even pain free, she still makes decisions based on her chronic condition. She eats a restricted diet, eliminating any food thought to trigger migraines. She also takes preventative medications which cause mood changes and weight gain.
> —Carmela Vasquez (student), "Living with Migraines"

Sometimes you can develop a paragraph by providing your reasons for stating a general idea. For instance:

> There are three reasons, quite apart from scientific considerations, that mankind needs to travel in space. The first reason is the need for garbage disposal: we need to transfer industrial processes into space, so that the earth may remain a green and pleasant place for our grandchildren to live in. The second reason is the need to escape material impoverishment: the resources of this planet are finite, and we shall not forgo forever the abundant solar energy and minerals and living space that are spread out all around us. The third reason is our spiritual need for an open frontier: the ultimate purpose of space travel is to bring to humanity not only scientific discoveries and an occasional spectacular show on television but a real expansion of our spirit.
> —Freeman Dyson, "Disturbing the Universe"

11.4.4 Definition

Defining a complicated, abstract, or controversial term often requires extended explanation. The following definition of the professional middle class comes from a book about changes in the American middle class:

> Before this story [of changes in America's middle class] can be told, I must first introduce its central character, the professional middle class. This class can be defined, somewhat abstractly, as all those people whose economic and social status is based on education, rather than on ownership of capital or property. Most professionals are included, and so are white-collar managers, whose positions require at least a college degree, and increasingly also a graduate degree. Not all white-collar people are included, though; some of these are entrepreneurs who are better classified as "workers." But the professional middle class is still extremely broad, and includes such diverse types as schoolteachers, anchorpersons, engineers, professors, government bureaucrats, corporate executives (at least up through the middle levels of management), scientists, advertising people, therapists, financial managers, architects, and, I should add, myself.
> —Barbara Ehrenreich, *Fear of Falling: The Inner Life of the Middle Class*, HarperCollins, 1989

11.4.5 Division or analysis

Division and analysis both involve separating something into its elements—for instance, you might divide a newspaper into its sections. You may also approach the elements critically, interpreting their meaning and significance:

> *The New York Times* Web site looks very similar to the print edition. The most prominent feature of the Web site is the traditional logo, centered at the top of the page. Under the logo is a small menu that contains the date, a link to today's paper, a link to video clips, a link to the weather forecast, and a link to the stock exchange. In some ways, it's like the folio line of a print edition. Ads fill the spaces on either side of the logo with search functionality and subscriber information above it. Under this pseudo-folio line is a longer menu, offering links to additional Web pages containing world and U.S. news, politics, opinion, technology, science, health, sports, arts, style, food, travel, and *The New York Times Magazine*.
> —Pam Rizzoli (student), "Dissecting *The New York Times* Web site"

11.4.6 Classification

When you classify items, you sort them into groups. The classification allows you to see and explain the relationships among items. The following paragraph identifies three groups, or classes, of parents:

> In my experience, the parents who hire daytime sitters for their school-age children tend to fall into one of three groups. The first group

includes parents who work and want someone to be at home when the children return from school. These parents are looking for an extension of themselves, someone who will give the care they would give if they were at home. The second group includes parents who may be home all day themselves but are too disorganized or too frazzled by their children's demands to handle child care alone. They are looking for an organizer and helpmate. The third and final group includes parents who do not want to be bothered by their children, whether they are home all day or not. Unlike the parents in the first two groups, who care for their children however they can, these parents seek a permanent substitute for themselves.   —Nancy Whittle (student), "Modern Parenting"

11.4.7   Comparison and contrast

Comparison and contrast may be used separately or together to develop an idea. The following paragraph illustrates one of two common ways of organizing a paragraph of comparison and contrast: **subject by subject**, first one subject and then the other.

> Consider the differences between *Facebook* and *Twitter*. *Facebook* offers long-form posts, image and video posts, instant messaging, phone calls, video chats, and an assortment of games—all from their Web site or applications. *Facebook* has a higher net worth and more than double the number of users. It also has more advertising. Advertising takes many shapes on *Facebook*, including banner ads, sponsored feed content, referral ads, paid-content games, and video ads. In contrast, *Twitter*'s advertising remains confined to promoted tweets and promoted accounts. Perhaps the largest difference between the two social-media platforms is content. *Twitter* allows users to post images and videos, but any textual content is limited to 140 characters. A character limit might work if you can communicate in short concise statements, but if you prefer extended discussions, you may prefer a platform like *Facebook*.
> —Rod Bennis (student), "Social-Media Platforms"

The next paragraph illustrates the other common organization: **point by point**, with the two subjects discussed side by side and matched feature for feature.

> Criticism is often equated with negative feelings, but in some instances, criticism can be constructive and beneficial. A person offering negative criticism is often mean-spirited while a person offering constructive criticism is generally kind and sympathetic to your feelings. A person offering negative criticism makes personal comments about you—not comments about your work or actions. On the other hand, a person offering constructive criticism makes comments about your work or actions without making judgments about you as a person. A person offering negative criticism does not care if anything improves; they undermine you. A person offering constructive criticism encourages improvement and supports your better efforts.
> —Peggy Chou (student), "Constructive Criticism"

11.4.8 Cause-and-effect analysis

When you use analysis to explain why something happened or what did or may happen, then you are determining causes or effects. In the following paragraph the author looks at the cause of an effect—Japanese collectivism:

> The *shinkansen* or "bullet train" speeds across the rural areas of Japan giving a quick view of cluster after cluster of farmhouses surrounded by rice paddies. This particular pattern did not develop purely by chance, but as a consequence of the technology peculiar to the growing of rice, the staple of the Japanese diet. The growing of rice requires the construction and maintenance of an irrigation system, something that takes many hands to build. More importantly, the planting and the harvesting of rice can only be done efficiently with the cooperation of twenty or more people. The "bottom line" is that a single family working alone cannot produce enough rice to survive, but a dozen families working together can produce a surplus. Thus the Japanese have had to develop the capacity to work together in harmony, no matter what the forces of disagreement or social disintegration, in order to survive.
> —William Ouchi, *Theory Z*, Reading: Addison-Wesley, 1981. Print.

11.4.9 Process analysis

When you analyze how to do something or how something works, you explain a process. The following example identifies a process, describes the ingredients needed, and details the steps in the process:

> Nothing tastes as good as homemade cheesecake. It is not difficult to make, even if you are not an expert in the kitchen. All you need is graham cracker crumbs, cinnamon, butter, cream cheese, sugar, sour cream, vanilla extract, and eggs. First, preheat the oven and prepare a pan for the water bath. Then, make the crust by combining the graham cracker crumbs with the cinnamon and the butter. Place the crust in the freezer until ready to fill. Make the filling by mixing the cream cheese, sugar, sour cream, and vanilla. Once it is blended smooth and creamy, add the eggs. Pour the cream cheese mixture into the crust and place the cheesecake into the water bath. Bake for an hour. Place on a wire rack to cool.
> —April Ammons (student), "Cheesecake"

11.5 Introductions and Conclusions

11.5 Write effective introductory and concluding paragraphs.

11.5.1 Introductions

An introduction draws readers from their world into yours.

- It focuses readers' attention on the topic and arouses curiosity about what you have to say.
- It specifies your subject and implies your attitude.

- Often it includes your thesis statement.
- **It is concise and sincere.**

The box below gives options for focusing readers' attention.

Some strategies for introductions

- Ask a question.
- Relate an incident.
- Use a vivid quotation.
- Create a visual image that represents your subject.
- Offer a surprising statistic or other fact.
- Provide background.
- State an opinion related to your thesis.
- Outline the argument your thesis refutes.
- Make a historical comparison or contrast.
- Outline a problem or dilemma.
- Define a word central to your subject.
- In some business or technical writing, simply state your main idea.

Culture and language

These options for an introduction may not be what you are used to if your native language is not English. In other cultures, readers may seek familiarity or reassurance from an author's introduction, or they may prefer an indirect approach to the subject. In academic and business English, however, writers and readers prefer concise, direct expression.

Effective openings

A very common introduction opens with a statement of the essay's general subject, clarifies or limits the subject in one or more sentences, and then asserts the point of the essay in the thesis statement (underlined in the following examples):

> Playing video games is addictive and promotes social isolation, obesity, and violence. Some research and a lot of anecdotal evidence supports these opinions. However, video games have been found to have long-lasting positive effects as well. <u>Basic mental processes like perception, memory, attention, and decision-making show marked improvement in recent studies, as well as logical, social, and literary skills.</u>
>
> —Barry Oppen (student), "The Power of Gaming"

> The Constitution of the United States is so widely revered as the document that codified American ideals and values into law that its origins tend to be overlooked. Between 1777 and 1789, the United States of America was organized under the Articles of Confederation, a wartime document created to unite the states under a central government.

Unfortunately, that central government was weak. Congress could print money but had no way to give it value. It could borrow money but could not repay the debts to foreign governments. It could not force the states to pay their taxes. Domestically, Congress was unable to pay the army, which put the security of the United States at risk. Moreover, states were violating treaties negotiated by Congress. They were independently placing tariffs and embargoes, negotiating with foreign governments, raising armies, and waging wars. As these problems spread, some Revolutionary heroes began to fear that the American Experiment would be over as soon as it began. <u>The Constitution may not be the embodiment of the government imagined when the United States declared its independence, but it became a political necessity.</u>

—Jeffrey Thomason (student), "Reframing the United States Government"

In much public writing, it's more important to tell readers immediately what your point is than to try to engage them. This introduction to a brief memo quickly outlines a problem and (in the thesis statement) suggests a way to solve it:

> Starting next month, the holiday rush and staff vacations will leave our department short-handed. <u>We need to hire two or perhaps three temporary keyboarders to maintain our schedules for the month.</u>

Openings to avoid

When writing and revising your introduction, avoid approaches that are likely to bore or confuse readers:

- **A vague generality or truth.** Don't extend your reach too far with a line such as *Throughout human history . . .* or *In today's world . . .* You may have needed a warm-up paragraph to start drafting, but your readers can do without it.
- **A flat announcement.** Don't start with *The purpose of this essay is . . . , In this essay I will . . . ,* or any similar presentation of your intention or topic.
- **A reference to the essay's title.** Don't refer to the title of the essay in the first sentence—for example, *This is a big problem* or *This book is about the history of the guitar.*
- ***According to Webster. . . .*** Don't start by citing a dictionary definition. A definition can be an effective springboard to an essay, but this kind of lead-in has become dull with overuse.
- **An apology.** Don't fault your opinion or your knowledge with *I'm not sure if I'm right, but I think . . . , I don't know much about this, but . . . ,* or a similar line.

11.5.2 Conclusions

Your conclusion finishes off your essay and tells readers where you think you have brought them. It answers the question "So what?"

Effective conclusions

Usually set off in its own paragraph, the conclusion may consist of a single sentence or a group of sentences. It may take one or more of the approaches listed in the following box.

> ## Some strategies for conclusions
> - Recommend a course of action.
> - Summarize the paper.
> - Echo the approach of the introduction.
> - Restate your thesis and reflect on its implications.
> - Strike a note of hope or despair.
> - Give a symbolic or powerful fact or other detail.
> - Give an especially compelling example.
> - Create an image that represents your subject.
> - Use a quotation.

The following paragraph concludes the essay on the Constitution (the introduction appears in 11.5.1):

> The Constitution has become one of the most revered documents in American history, creating a strong federal government based on American ideals and the rule of law, but that was not its intended purpose in 1789. The flailing central government of the United States could not continue under the Articles of Confederation. As a matter of survival and expediency, the Constitution built a stronger federal government to ensure the nation's future.
>
> —Jeffrey Thomason (student), "Reframing the United States Government"

In the next paragraph, the author concludes an essay on environmental protection with a call for action:

> Until we get the answers, I think we had better keep on building power plants and growing food with the help of fertilizers and such insect-controlling chemicals as we now have. The risks are well known, thanks to the environmentalists. If they had not created a widespread public awareness of the ecological crisis, we wouldn't stand a chance. But such awareness by itself is not enough. Flaming manifestos and prophecies of doom are no longer much help, and a search for scapegoats can only make matters worse. The time for sensations and manifestos is about over. Now we need rigorous analysis, united effort and very hard work.
>
> —Peter F. Drucker, "How Best to Protect the Environment," *Reader's Digest,* March 1972. P. 86. From *Toward the Next Economics: And Other Essays.* By Peter Ferdinand Drucker, *Saving the Crusade: The High Cost of Our Environmental Future,* page 35.

Conclusions to avoid

Several kinds of conclusions rarely work well:

- **A repeat of the introduction.** Don't simply replay your introduction. The conclusion should capture what the body paragraphs have added to the introduction.
- **A new direction.** Don't introduce a subject that is different from the one your essay has been about.
- **A sweeping generalization.** Don't conclude more than you reasonably can from your evidence. If your essay is about your frustrating experience trying to clear a parking ticket, you cannot reasonably conclude that *all* local police forces are too tied up in red tape to be of service to the people.
- **An apology.** Don't cast doubt on your essay. Don't say *Even though I'm no expert* or *This may not be convincing, but I believe it's true* or anything similar. Rather, to win your readers' confidence, display confidence.

Chapter 12
Integrating and Using Sources Ethically

⌄ Learning Objectives

- **12.1** Integrate sources into your text.
- **12.2** Distinguish between deliberate and careless plagiarism.
- **12.3** Describe types of information you do not need to cite.
- **12.4** Describe types of information that require citations.
- **12.5** Describe the elements of source citations.

12.1 Integrating Sources

12.1 Integrate sources into your text.

Integrating source material into your sentences is key to synthesizing others' ideas and information with your own. Evidence drawn from sources should *back up* your conclusions, not *be* your conclusions: you don't want to let your evidence overwhelm your own point of view. To keep your ideas in the forefront, you do more than merely present borrowed material; you introduce and interpret it as well.

The examples in this section use the MLA style of source documentation and also present-tense verbs (such as *disagrees* and *claims*).

12.1.1 Introduction of borrowed material

Always introduce a summary, a paraphrase, or a quotation by identifying it and by providing a smooth transition between your words and ideas and those of your source. In the passage below, the writer has not meshed the structures of her own and her source's sentences:

> **Awkward** One editor disagrees with this view and "a good reporter does not fail to separate opinions from facts" (Lyman 52).

In the following revision, the writer adds words to integrate the quotation into her sentence:

> **Revised** One editor disagrees with this view, <u>maintaining that</u> "a good reporter does not fail to separate opinions from facts" (Lyman 52).

To mesh your own and your source's words, you may sometimes need to make a substitution or addition to the quotation, signaling your change with brackets:

> **Words added** "The tabloids [of England] are a journalistic case study in bad reporting," claims Lyman (52).
>
> **Verb form changed** A bad reporter, Lyman implies, is one who "[fails] to separate opinions from facts" (52). [The bracketed verb replaces *fail* in the original.]
>
> **Capitalization changed** "[T]o separate opinions from facts" is the work of a good reporter (Lyman 52). [In the original, *to* is not capitalized.]
>
> **Noun supplied for pronoun** The reliability of a news organization "depends on [reporters'] trustworthiness," says Lyman (52). [The bracketed noun replaces *their* in the original.]

12.1.2 Interpretation of borrowed material

You need to work borrowed material into your sentences so that readers see without effort how it contributes to the points you are making. If you merely dump source material into your paper without explaining how you intend it to be interpreted, readers will have to struggle to understand your sentences and the relationships you are trying to establish. For example, the following passage forces us to figure out for ourselves that the writer's sentence and the quotation state opposite points of view:

Dumped Many news editors and reporters maintain that it is impossible to keep personal opinions from influencing the selection and presentation of facts. "True, news reporters, like everyone else, form impressions of what they see and hear. However, a good reporter does not fail to separate opinions from facts" (Lyman 52).

In the revision, the underlined additions tell us how to interpret the quotation:

Revised Many news editors and reporters maintain that it is impossible to keep personal opinions from influencing the selection and presentation of facts. <u>Yet not all authorities agree with this view. One editor grants that</u> "news reporters, like everyone else, form impressions of what they see and hear." <u>But, he insists,</u> "a good reporter does not fail to separate opinions from facts" (Lyman 52).

Signal phrases

The words *One editor grants* and *he insists* in the revised passage above are **signal phrases**: they tell readers who the source is and what to expect in the quotations that follow. Signal phrases usually contain (1) the source author's name (or a substitute for it, such as *One editor* and *he*) and (2) a verb that indicates the source author's attitude or approach to what he or she says.

Some verbs for signal phrases appear in the following list. These verbs are in the present tense, which is typical of writing in the humanities. In the social and natural sciences, the past tense (*noted*) or present perfect tense (*has noted*) is more common.

Author is neutral	Author infers or suggests	Author argues	Author is uneasy or disparaging
comments	analyzes	claims	belittles
describes	asks	contends	bemoans
explains	assesses	defends	complains
illustrates	concludes	holds	condemns
notes	considers	insists	deplores
observes	finds	maintains	deprecates
points out	predicts		derides
records	proposes	**Author agrees**	disagrees
relates	reveals	admits	laments
reports	shows	agrees	warns
says	speculates	concedes	
sees	suggests	concurs	
thinks	supposes	grants	
writes			

Vary your signal phrases to suit your interpretation of borrowed material and also to keep readers' interest. A signal phrase may precede, interrupt, or follow the borrowed material:

Precedes	Lyman insists that "a good reporter does not fail to separate opinions from facts" (52).
Interrupts	"However," Lyman insists, "a good reporter does not fail to separate opinions from facts" (52).
Follows	"[A] good reporter does not fail to separate opinions from facts," Lyman insists (52).

Background information

You can add information to a quotation to integrate it into your text and to inform readers why you are using it. In most cases, provide the author's name in the text, especially if the author is an expert or if readers will recognize the name:

Author named	Harold Lyman grants that "news reporters, like everyone else, form impressions of what they see and hear." But, Lyman insists, "a good reporter does not fail to separate opinions from facts" (52).

If the source title contributes information about the author or the context of the quotation, you can provide it in the text:

Title given	Harold Lyman, in his recent book *The Conscience of Journalism*, grants that "news reporters, like everyone else, form impressions of what they see and hear." But, Lyman insists, "a good reporter does not fail to separate opinions from facts" (52).

If the quoted author's background and experience reinforce or clarify the quotation, you can provide those credentials in the text:

Credentials given	Harold Lyman, a newspaper editor for more than forty years, grants that "news reporters, like everyone else, form impressions of what they see and hear." But, Lyman insists, "a good reporter does not fail to separate opinions from facts" (52).

You need not name the author, source, or credentials in your text when you are simply establishing facts or weaving together facts and opinions from varied sources. In the following passage, the information is more important than the source, so the name of the source is confined to a parenthetical acknowledgment:

> To end the abuses of the British, many colonists were urging three actions: forming a united front, seceding from Britain, and taking control of their own international relations (Wills 325–36).

12.1.3 Discipline styles for integrating sources

The preceding guidelines for introducing and interpreting borrowed material apply generally across academic disciplines, but the disciplines do differ in their verb tenses and documentation styles.

English and some other humanities

Writers in English, foreign languages, and related disciplines use MLA style for documenting sources and generally use the present tense of verbs in signal phrases. In discussing sources other than works of literature, the present perfect tense is also sometimes appropriate:

> Lyman insists . . . [present]
> Lyman has insisted . . . [present perfect]

In discussing works of literature, use only the present tense to describe both the work of the author and the action in the work:

> Kate Chopin builds irony into every turn of "The Story of an Hour." For example, Mrs. Mallard, the central character, finds joy in the death of her husband, whom she loves, because she anticipates "the long procession of years that would belong to her absolutely" (23).

Avoid shifting tenses in writing about literature. You can, for instance, shorten quotations to avoid their past-tense verbs.

> **Shift** Her freedom elevates her, so that "she carried herself unwittingly like a goddess of victory" (24).
>
> **No shift** Her freedom elevates her, so that she walks "unwittingly like a goddess of victory" (24).

History and other humanities

Writers in history, art history, philosophy, and related disciplines generally use the present perfect tense or present tense of verbs in signal phrases.

> Lincoln persisted, as Haworth has noted, in "feeling that events controlled him."[3]
>
> What Miller calls Lincoln's "severe self-doubt"[6] undermined his effectiveness on at least two occasions.

The raised numbers after the quotations are part of the Chicago documentation style, used in history and other disciplines.

Social and natural sciences

Writers in the sciences generally use a verb's present tense just for reporting the results of a study (*The data suggest* . . .). Otherwise, they use a verb's past tense or present perfect tense in a signal phrase, as when introducing an explanation, interpretation, or other commentary. (Thus, when you are writing for the sciences, generally convert the list of signal-phrase verbs in 12.1.2 from the present to the present perfect tense or past tense.)

> Lin (1999) has suggested that preschooling may significantly affect children's academic performance through high school (pp. 22–23).

In an exhaustive survey of the literature published between 1990 and 2000, Walker (2001) found "no proof, merely a weak correlation, linking place of residence and rate of illness" (p. 121).

These passages conform to APA documentation style. APA style is also used in sociology, education, nursing, biology, and many other sciences.

12.2 Defining Plagiarism

12.2   Distinguish between deliberate and careless plagiarism.

The knowledge building that is the focus of academic writing rests on the integrity of everyone who participates, including students, in using and crediting sources. The work of a writer or creator is his or her intellectual property. You and others may borrow the work's ideas and even its words or an image, but you *must* acknowledge that what you borrowed came from someone else.

When you acknowledge sources in your writing, you are doing more than giving credit to the writer or creator of the work you consulted. You are also showing what your own writing is based on, which in turn adds to your integrity as a researcher and writer. Acknowledging sources creates the trust among scholars, students, writers, and readers that knowledge building requires.

Plagiarism (from a Latin word for "kidnapper") is the presentation of someone else's work as your own. Whether deliberate or careless, plagiarism is a serious offense. It breaks trust, and it undermines or even destroys your credibility as a researcher and writer. In most colleges, a code of academic honesty calls for severe consequences for plagiarism: a reduced or failing grade, suspension from school, or expulsion. The way to avoid plagiarism is to acknowledge your sources: keep track of the ones you consult for each paper you write, and document them within the paper and in a list of works cited.

Culture and Language

The concepts of originality, intellectual property, and plagiarism are not universal. In some other cultures, for instance, students may be encouraged to copy the words of scholars without acknowledgment, in order to demonstrate their mastery of or respect for the scholars' work. In the United States, however, using an author's work without a source citation is a serious offense, whether it is accidental or intentional. When in doubt about the guidelines in this chapter, ask your instructor for advice.

Instructors usually distinguish between deliberate plagiarism, which is cheating, and careless plagiarism, which often stems from a writer's inexperience with managing sources.

12.2.1 Deliberate plagiarism

Deliberate plagiarism is intentional: the writer chooses to cheat by turning in someone else's work as his or her own. Students who deliberately plagiarize deprive themselves of an education in honest research. When their cheating is detected, the students often face stiff penalties, including expulsion.

Following are examples of deliberate plagiarism:

- Copying a phrase, a sentence, or a longer passage from a source and passing it off as your own by not adding quotation marks and a source citation.
- Summarizing or paraphrasing someone else's ideas without acknowledging the source in a citation.
- Handing in as your own work a paper you have copied off the Web, had a friend write, or accepted from another student.
- Handing in as your own work a paper you have purchased from a paper-writing service. **Paying for research or a paper does not make it your work.**

Checklist for avoiding plagiarism

Know your source.
Are you using

- your own experience,
- common knowledge, or
- someone else's material?

You must acknowledge someone else's material.

Quote carefully.

- Check that every quotation exactly matches its source.
- Insert quotation marks around every quotation that you run into your text.
- Indicate any omission from a quotation with an ellipsis mark and any addition with brackets.
- Acknowledge the source of every quotation.

Paraphrase and summarize carefully.

- Use your own words and sentence structures for every paraphrase and summary. If you have used the author's words, add quotation marks around them.
- Acknowledge the source of the idea(s) in every paraphrase or summary.

Cite sources responsibly.

- Acknowledge every use of someone else's material in each place you use it.
- Include all your sources in your list of works cited. See **MLA** Chapter 51, **APA** Chapter 52, **Chicago** Chapter 53, and **CSE** Chapter 54 for citing sources in the most common documentation styles.

12.2.2 Careless plagiarism

Careless plagiarism is unintentional: grappling with complicated information and ideas in sources, the writer neglects to put quotation marks around a source's exact words or neglects to include a source citation for a quotation, paraphrase, or summary. Most instructors and schools do not permit careless plagiarism, but they treat it less harshly than deliberate plagiarism—at least the first time it occurs.

Here are examples of careless plagiarism:

- Reading sources without taking notes on them and then not distinguishing what you recently learned from what you already knew.
- Copying and pasting material from a source into your document without placing quotation marks around the other writer's work.
- Forgetting to add a source citation for a paraphrase. Even though a paraphrase casts another person's idea in your own words, you still need to cite the source of the idea.
- Omitting a source citation for another's idea because you are unaware of the need to acknowledge the idea.

Plagiarism and the Internet

The Internet has made it easier to plagiarize than ever before: with just a few clicks, you can copy and paste passages or whole documents into your own files. If you do so without quoting and acknowledging your source, you plagiarize.

The Internet has also made plagiarism easier to detect. Instructors can use search engines to find specific phrases or sentences anywhere on the Web, including among scholarly publications, all kinds of Web sites, and term-paper collections. They can search term-paper sites as easily as students can, looking for similarities with papers they've received. They can also use detection software—such as *Turnitin*, *PlagiServe*, and *Glatt Plagiarism Services*—which compares students' work with other work anywhere on the Internet, seeking matches as short as a few words.

Some instructors suggest that their students use plagiarism-detection programs to verify that their own work does not include careless plagiarism, at least not from the Internet.

12.3 Information You Do Not Need to Cite

12.3 Describe types of information you do not need to cite.

12.3.1 Your independent material

Your own observations, thoughts, compilations of facts, or experimental results—expressed in your words and format—do not require acknowledgment. You should describe the basis for your conclusions so that readers can evaluate your thinking, but you need not cite sources for them.

12.3.2 Common knowledge

Common knowledge consists of the standard information on a subject as well as folk literature and commonsense observations.

- **Standard information** includes the major facts of history, such as the dates during which Charlemagne ruled as emperor of Rome (800–814). It does *not* include interpretations of facts, such as a historian's opinion that Charlemagne was sometimes needlessly cruel in extending his power.
- **Folk literature,** such as the fairy tale "Snow White," is popularly known and cannot be traced to a particular writer. Literature traceable to a writer is *not* folk literature, even if it is very familiar.
- **Commonsense observations** are things most people know, such as that inflation is most troublesome for people with low and fixed incomes. However, a particular economist's argument about the effects of inflation on Chinese immigrants is *not* a commonsense observation.

If you do not know a subject well enough to determine whether a piece of information is common knowledge, make a record of the source as you would for any other quotation, paraphrase, or summary. As you read more about the subject, the information may come up repeatedly without acknowledgment, in which case it is probably common knowledge. But if you are still in doubt when you finish your research, always acknowledge the source.

12.4 Information You Must Cite

12.4 Describe types of information that require citations.

You must always acknowledge other people's independent material—that is, any facts, ideas, or opinions that are not common knowledge or your own. The source may be a formal publication or release, such as a book, an article, a movie, an interview, an artwork, a comic strip, a map, a Web page, or a blog. The source may also be informal, such as a tweet, a posting on *Facebook*, an opinion you heard on the radio, or a comment by your instructor or a classmate that substantially shaped your argument. You must acknowledge summaries or paraphrases of ideas or facts as well as quotations of the language and format in which ideas or facts appear: wording, sentence structures, arrangement, and special graphics (such as a diagram). You must acknowledge another's material no matter how you use it, how much of it you use, or how often you use it.

12.4.1 Copied language: Quotation marks and a source citation

The following example baldly plagiarizes the original quotation from Jessica Mitford's *Kind and Usual Punishment*, p. 9. Without quotation marks or a source citation, the example matches Mitford's wording (underlined) and closely parallels her sentence structure:

Original quotation	"The character and mentality of the keepers may be of more importance in understanding prisons than the character and mentality of the kept."
Plagiarism	But the character of prison officials (the keepers) is of more importance in understanding prisons than the character of prisoners (the kept).

To avoid plagiarism, the writer can paraphrase and cite the source (see the examples on the next page) or use Mitford's actual words *in quotation marks* and *with a source citation* (here, in MLA style):

Revision (quotation)	According to Mitford, a critic of the penal system, "The character and mentality of the keepers may be of more importance in understanding prisons than the character and mentality of the kept" (9).

Even with a source citation and with a different sentence structure, the next example is still plagiarism because it uses some of Mitford's words (underlined) without quotation marks:

Plagiarism	According to Mitford, a critic of the penal system, the psychology of the kept may say less about prisons than the psychology of the keepers (9).
Revision (quotation)	According to Mitford, a critic of the penal system, the psychology of "the kept" may say less about prisons than the psychology of "the keepers" (9).

12.4.2 Paraphrase or summary: Your own words and sentence structure and a source citation

The example below changes the sentence structure of the original Mitford quotation above, but it still uses Mitford's words (underlined) without quotation marks and without a source citation:

Plagiarism	In understanding prisons, we should know more about the character and mentality of the keepers than of the kept.

To avoid plagiarism, the writer can use quotation marks and cite the source (see examples above) or *use his or her own words* and still *cite the source* (because the idea is Mitford's, not the writer's):

Revision (paraphrase)	Mitford holds that we may be able to learn more about prisons from the psychology of the prison officials than from that of the prisoners (9).

Revision (paraphrase)		We may understand prisons better if we focus on the personalities and attitudes of the prison workers rather than those of the inmates (Mitford 9).

In the next example, the writer cites Mitford and does not use her words but still plagiarizes her sentence structure. The revision changes the sentence structure as well as the words.

Plagiarism	Mitford, a critic of the penal system, maintains that the psychology of prison officials may be more informative about prisons than the psychology of prisoners (9).
Revision (paraphrase)	Mitford, a critic of the penal system, maintains that we may learn less from the psychology of prisoners than from the psychology of prison officials (9).

12.4.3 Using online sources

Online sources are so accessible and so easy to copy into your own documents that it may seem they are freely available, exempting you from the obligation to acknowledge them. They are not. Acknowledging online sources is somewhat trickier than acknowledging print sources, but it is no less essential: when you use someone else's independent material from an online source, you must acknowledge the source.

Citing online sources is easier when you keep track of them as you work:

- **Record complete publication information each time you consult an online source.** Online sources may change from one day to the next or even disappear entirely. Without the proper information, you may *not* use the source.
- **Immediately put quotation marks around any text that you copy and paste into your document.** If you don't add quotation marks right away, you risk forgetting which words belong to the source and which are yours. If you don't know whose words you are using, recheck the source or do *not* use them.
- **Acknowledge linked sites.** If you use not only a Web site but also one or more of its linked sites, you must acknowledge the linked sites as well. The fact that one person has used a second person's work does not release you from the responsibility to cite the second work.

12.5 Documenting Sources

12.5 Describe the elements of source citations.

Every time you borrow the words, facts, or ideas of others, you must **document** the source—that is, supply a reference (or document) telling readers that you borrowed the material and where you borrowed it from.

Editors and instructors in most academic disciplines require special documentation formats (or styles) in their scholarly journals and in students' papers. All the styles share two features described in the following box.

> ## Key features of source documentation
>
> - **Citations in the text signal that material is borrowed and refer readers to detailed information about the sources.** The following text citation, in MLA style, gives the source author's last name and the page number in the source. Other styles add a publication date. Some styles use raised numerals to refer to numbered source information.
>
>   > Veterans are more likely to complete college degrees if they have not only professional support but also a community of peers (Dao A16).
>
> - **Detailed source information, either in footnotes or at the end of the paper, tells how to locate sources.** The following source listing, also in MLA style, provides detailed publication information for the source summarized above. Most styles provide the same information, but they may organize and punctuate it differently.
>
>   > Dao, James. "Getting Them Through: Helping Veterans Graduate." *The New York Times*, 5 Feb. 2013, pp. A16+.

12.5.1 Using discipline styles for documentation

Aside from the similarities of citations in the text and detailed source information, the disciplines' documentation styles vary markedly in citation form, arrangement of source information, and other particulars. Each discipline's style reflects the needs of its practitioners for certain kinds of information presented in certain ways. For instance, the currency of a source is important in the social sciences, where studies build on and correct each other; thus, in-text citations in the social sciences include a source's year of publication. In the humanities, however, currency is less important, so in-text citations do not include the date of publication.

This text discusses and illustrates four common documentation styles:

- MLA style, used in English, foreign languages, and some other humanities (**MLA** Chapter 51).
- APA style, used in psychology and some other social sciences (**APA** Chapter 52).
- Chicago style, used in history, art history, philosophy, religion, and some other humanities (**Chicago** Chapter 53).
- CSE style, used in the biological and some other sciences (**CSE** Chapter 54).

Always ask your instructor which documentation style you should use. If your instructor does not specify a particular style, use the one in this text that's most appropriate for the discipline in which you're writing. Do follow a single system for citing sources so that you provide all the necessary information in a consistent format.

12.5.2 Using bibliography software

Bibliography software can help you format your source citations in the style of your choice, and some programs can help you keep track of sources as you research. Your library may offer one or more bibliography programs, such as *RefWorks* or *Endnote*, or you can find free options on the Web, such as *Zotero*, *Bibme*, and *EasyBib*.

The programs vary in what they can do. Some simply prompt you for needed information (author's name, book title, and so on) and then format the information into a bibliography following the format of your documentation style. Others go beyond formatting to help you organize your sources, export citations from databases, and insert in-text citations as you write.

As helpful as bibliography programs can be, they don't always work the way they're advertised, and they can't substitute for your own care and attention in giving your sources accurate and complete acknowledgment. Always ask your instructors if you may use such software for your papers, and always review the citations compiled by any software to ensure that they meet your instructors' requirements.

Chapter 13
Revising and Editing

Learning Objectives

- **13.1** Read your work critically and plan your revision.
- **13.2** Give and receive feedback to guide revision.
- **13.3** Analyze a revised draft.
- **13.4** Edit for clarity and correctness.
- **13.5** Format and proofread your final draft.

13.1 Revision Plans

13.1 Read your work critically and plan your revision.

Revising is an essential task in creating an effective piece of writing. During revision—literally, "re-seeing"—you shift your focus outward from yourself and your subject toward your readers, concentrating on what will help them respond as you want. Many writers revise in two stages: first they view the work as a whole, evaluating and improving its overall meaning and structure; then they edit sentences for wording, grammar, punctuation, spelling, and so on.

In revising your writing, you may work alone or you may receive input from your instructor and/or other students in a collaborative group. Whether you are responding to your own evaluation or that of readers, you may need to rethink your thesis, move or delete whole paragraphs, clarify how ideas relate to the thesis, or support ideas with details or further research. Knowing that you will edit later gives you the freedom to look beyond the confines of the page or screen to see the paper as a whole.

To revise your writing, you have to read it critically, and that means you have to create some distance between your draft and yourself. These techniques may help you to see your work objectively:

- **Take a break after finishing the draft.** A few hours may be enough; a whole night or day is preferable.
- **Ask someone to respond to your draft.** A roommate, family member, or tutor in the writing center can call attention to what needs revising.
- **Read your draft in a new medium.** Typing a handwritten draft or printing out a word-processed draft can reveal weaknesses that you didn't see in the original.
- **Outline your draft.** Highlight the main points supporting the thesis, and convert these sentences to outline form. Then examine the outline you've made for logical order, gaps, and digressions. A formal outline can be especially illuminating because of its careful structure.
- **Listen to your draft.** Read the draft out loud to yourself or to a friend or classmate, record and listen to it, or have someone read the draft to you.
- **Use a revision checklist.** Don't try to re-see everything in your draft at once. Use the "Checklist for revision," making a separate pass through the draft for each item.

Checklist for revision

Assignment
How have you responded to the assignment for this writing? Verify that your subject, purpose, and genre are appropriate for the requirements of the assignment.

Purpose
What is the purpose of your writing? Does it conform to the assignment? Is it consistent throughout the paper?

(continued)

> ## Checklist for revision
> *(continued)*
>
> ### Audience
> How does the writing address the intended audience? How does it meet readers' likely expectations for your subject? Where might readers need more information?
>
> ### Genre
> How does your writing conform to the conventions of the genre you're writing in—features such as organization, kinds of evidence, language, and format?
>
> ### Thesis
> What is the thesis of your writing? Where does it become clear? How well do the thesis and the paper match: Does any part of the paper stray from the thesis? Does the paper fulfill the commitment of the thesis?
>
> ### Organization
> What are the main points of the paper? (List them.) How well does each support the thesis? How effective is their arrangement for the paper's purpose?
>
> ### Development
> How well do details, examples, and other evidence support each main point? Where, if at all, might readers find support skimpy or have trouble understanding the content?
>
> ### Unity
> What does each sentence and paragraph contribute to the thesis? Where, if at all, do digressions occur? Should they be cut, or can they be rewritten to support the thesis?
>
> ### Coherence
> How clearly and smoothly does the paper flow? Where does it seem rough or awkward? Can any transitions be improved?
>
> ### Title, introduction, conclusion
> How accurately and interestingly does the title reflect the essay's content? How well does the introduction engage and focus readers' attention? How effective is the conclusion in providing a sense of completion?

13.1.1 Writing a title

The revision stage is a good time to consider a title because summing up your essay in a phrase focuses your attention sharply on your topic, purpose, and audience. The title should tell the reader what your paper is about, but it should not restate the assignment or the thesis. Most titles fall into one of these categories:

- A *descriptive title* announces the subject clearly and accurately. Such a title is almost always appropriate, and it is usually expected

for academic writing. Erica Vela chose to title her essay "*Google Opens Our Minds—and Our Worlds*," for example.
- **A *suggestive title* hints at the subject to arouse curiosity.** Such a title is common in popular magazines and may be appropriate for writing that is somewhat informal. Vela could have used a suggestive metaphor in her response to Carr: "Jet-Skiing into the Future," for example.

13.2 Peer Review

13.2 Give and receive feedback to guide revision.

Peer review is a common practice in many college writing courses. Learning to give and receive helpful feedback is an important skill, and working in a collaborative environment builds skills that will help you in your career, too. Collaborative peer review may occur face to face in small groups, on paper via drafts and comments, or online, either through a course-management system such as *Blackboard* or *Canvas*, or through a class blog, e-mail list, or wiki.

Whatever the medium of collaboration, following a few guidelines will help you gain more from others' comments and become a more constructive reader yourself.

Benefiting from comments on your writing

- **Think of your readers as counselors or coaches.** They can help you see the virtues and flaws in your work and sharpen your awareness of readers' needs.
- **Read or listen to comments closely.**
- **Know what the critic is saying.** If you need more information, ask for it, or consult the appropriate section of this handbook.
- **Don't become defensive.** Letting comments offend you will only erect a barrier to improvement in your writing. As one writing teacher advises, "Leave your ego at the door."
- **Revise your work in response to appropriate comments.** You will learn more from the act of revision than from just thinking about changes.
- **Remember that you are the final authority on your work.** You should be open to suggestions, but you are free to decline advice when you think it is inappropriate.
- **Keep track of both the strengths and the weaknesses others identify.** Then in later assignments you can build on your successes and give special attention to problem areas.

Commenting on others' writing

- **Be sure you know what the writer is saying.** If necessary, summarize the paper to understand its content.

- **Address only your most significant concerns with the work.** Focus on the deep issues in other writers' drafts, especially early drafts: thesis, purpose, audience, organization, and support for the thesis. Use the revision checklist as a guide to what is significant. Unless you have other instructions, ignore mistakes in grammar, punctuation, spelling, and the like. (The temptation to focus on such errors may be especially strong if the writer is less experienced than you are with standard American English.) Emphasizing mistakes will contribute little to the writer's revision.
- **Remember that you are the reader, not the writer.** Don't edit sentences, add details, or otherwise assume responsibility for the paper.
- **Phrase your comments carefully.** Avoid misunderstandings by making sure comments are both clear and respectful. If you are responding on paper or online, not face to face with the writer, remember that the writer has nothing but your written words to go on. He or she can't ask you for immediate clarification and can't infer your attitudes from gestures, facial expressions, and tone of voice.
- **Be specific.** If something confuses you, say *why*. If you disagree with a conclusion, say *why*.
- **Be supportive as well as honest.** Tell the writer what you like about the paper. Phrase your comments positively: instead of *This paragraph doesn't interest me*, say *You have an interesting detail here that I almost missed*. Question the writer in a way that emphasizes the effect of the work on you, the reader: *This paragraph confuses me because....* And avoid measuring the work against a set of external standards: *This essay is poorly organized. Your thesis statement is inadequate.*
- **While reading, make your comments in writing.** Even if you will be delivering your comments in person later on, the written record will help you recall what you thought.
- **Link comments to specific parts of a paper.** Especially if you are reading the paper on a computer, be clear about what in the paper each comment relates to. You can use a word processor's Comment function, which annotates documents.

Culture and language

In some cultures writers do not expect criticism from readers, or readers do not expect to think and speak critically about what they read. If critical responses are uncommon in your native culture, collaboration may at first be uncomfortable for you. As a writer, think of a draft or even a final paper more as an exploration of ideas than as the last word on your subject; then you may be more receptive to readers' suggestions. As a reader, know that your tactful questions and suggestions about focus, content, and organization will usually be considered appropriate.

13.3 Sample Revision

13.3 Analyze a revised draft.

Erica Vela was satisfied with her first draft: she had her ideas down, and the arrangement seemed logical. Still, from the revision checklist she knew the draft needed work, and her classmates' comments highlighted what she needed to focus on. The following revised draft shows Vela's changes in response to these comments. She used the Track Changes function on her word processor, so that deletions are crossed out and additions are in blue.

Google Opens Our Minds—and Our Worlds

In "Is *Google* Making Us Stupid?" Nicholas Carr laments that he was once "a scuba diver in the sea of words," but now he "zip[s] along the surface like a guy on a jet ski" (par. 4). He believes ~~argues~~ that the Internet is changing our minds at a fundamental level, ~~possibly creating more problems than it solves. He states that the Internet is~~ damaging the way we process information and~~,~~ creating minds that struggle to remain focused on a given task for an extended time. Yet the Internet is changing more than how we process information. It is changing how we access and share information as well as how we interact with people across the globe. My experience of online education offers a benefit that Nicholas Carr overlooks: the Internet provides more opportunities for learning in areas where there are no well-stocked libraries or centers of higher education while offering more ways to access information from across the globe. ~~The ability to shrink the globe and bring information and education to my fingertips proves that Nicholas Carr's reservations about the Internet are shortsighted.~~

Carr describes his experience as "an uncomfortable sense that someone, or something, has been tinkering with [his] brain, remapping the neural circuitry, reprogramming the memory" (par. 2). He laments his inability to focus on extended tasks. He worries that this focus on the Internet and technology is removing the human element from our thinking processes and, as sociologist Daniel Bell might suggest, replacing it with computerization (par. 14).

Like Carr, I remember what life was like before the Internet. I live in a remote area, hundreds of miles from any college, university, or center of learning. I remember driving to the small local library and poring over their ancient card catalog, looking for books that held the information that I needed. If the library did not have the ~~appropriate~~ needed books, I would have to begin the extended process of interlibrary loan or travel hundreds of miles to ~~a college or~~ the closest university library. But now I can search a library's database, *Amazon*, or *Google* and find dozens (or even hundreds) of books, journal articles, or Web sites. Some I can read immediately. Others

New, descriptive title names topic and previews approach.

Expanded introduction moves from an overview of Carr's argument to Vela's disagreement with it, building to a thesis statement at the end of the paragraph.

Expanded and clarified response to Carr, ending in a revised thesis.

Expanded summary of Carr's essay, including quotations cited in MLA style.

> **New sentences expand on Vela's claims and connect back to her thesis.**

I can order and have shipped to my house within two days. In this way and others, the Internet makes knowledge accessible across the globe. In most cases, you no longer need access to the physical source; you only need an access to the World Wide Web. Surely, Carr would agree that more equal and open access to information is a good thing. ~~The sharing of knowledge across the globe cannot be a bad thing.~~

Moreover, the Internet provides other opportunities for learning. Colleges and universities in the United States are building classrooms and degree programs online, allowing students from across the globe to obtain post-secondary educations in a world that increasingly demands them. In my degree program, all classes meet online. It allows me to work full-time while living nearly two hundred miles away from the main campus. I also get personal interaction with my professors and classmates through online discussion boards and video conferencing applications. Without the Internet, I would not have access to a post-secondary education and would not be a student today.

> **rev 13.3**
>
> **Revised wording here sharpens Vela's claim about the importance of the Internet to her own education.**

Like Carr, I believe the Internet is changing how we think, but I believe that these changes will be a benefit in the future. As Carr notes, Socrates worried about the development of writing in Plato's *Phaedrus*. He believed that our ability to remember things would be permanently destroyed, but he couldn't foresee how writing would spread ideas, ultimately expanding human knowledge. A similar situation arose after the development of the printing press. Critics argued that "cheaply printed books . . . would undermine religious authority, demean the work of scholars and scribes, and spread sedition and debauchery" (par. 31). Despite these concerns, I doubt you would find many people who would argue against the development of writing or the printing press. Writing and printed books have changed the world in ways that have been considered more beneficial than detrimental. Surely future generations will look back at the development of the Internet in the same way. ~~Can you imagine the world without books? It's a ridiculous thought today.~~

> **New sentences expand on Vela's response to Carr. The paragraph moves from points of agreement to a clearer statement of her thesis.**

We know that the world of the future will look much different than it does today, and the development of the Internet will have much influence on how information is accessed, processed, and shared, likely shaping societies for generations. I understand Carr's concerns and even share some of them. ~~its development.~~ However, ~~we~~ I believe that the benefits greatly outweigh the disadvantages. We must not fear technological advancement and the spread of new knowledge while clinging to older technologies with the tips of our fingers. As humans, we have learned speech, developed writing, invented printing, and are now creating digital spaces and information. ~~We can~~

~~appreciate what we have while embracing what is to come.~~ I wonder what the next advancement in technology will be and how it will change our lives and our minds. ~~Our future depends on it.~~

Work Cited

Carr, Nicholas. "Is *Google* Making Us Stupid? What the Internet Is Doing to Our Brains." *The Atlantic,* July-Aug. 2008, www.theatlantic.com/magazine/archive/2008/07/is-google-making-us-stupid/306868.

New citation for the Carr article, in MLA documentation format (see Chapter 51).

13.4 Editing

13.4 Edit for clarity and correctness.

After you have revised your essay so that you are satisfied with the content, turn to the work of editing your sentences to correct them and clarify your ideas. In your editing, work first for clear and effective sentences that flow smoothly from one to the next. Then check your sentences for correctness. Use the questions in the "Checklist for editing" box below to guide your editing, making several passes through your draft.

Checklist for editing

Are my sentences clear?

Do my words and sentences mean what I intend them to mean? Is anything confusing? Check especially for these:

Exact language
Parallelism
Clear modifiers
Clear reference of pronouns
Complete sentences
Sentences separated correctly

Are my sentences effective?

How well do words and sentences engage and hold readers' attention? Where does the writing seem wordy, choppy, or dull? Check especially for these:

Emphasis of main ideas
Smooth and informative transitions
Variety in sentence length and structure
Appropriate language
Concise sentences

(continued)

> ## Checklist for editing
> *(continued)*
>
> ### Do my sentences contain errors?
> **Where do surface errors interfere with the clarity and effectiveness of my sentences?** Check especially for these:
>
> - **Spelling errors**
> - **Sentence fragments**
> - **Comma splices**
> - **Verb errors**
>
>   Verb forms, especially *-s* and *-ed* endings, correct forms of irregular verbs, and appropriate helping verbs
>   Verb tenses, especially consistency
>   Agreement between subjects and verbs, especially when words come between them or the subject is *each, everyone,* or a similar word
>
> - **Pronoun errors**
>
>   Pronoun forms, especially subjective (*he, she, they, who*) vs. objective (*him, her, them, whom*)
>   Agreement between pronouns and antecedents, especially when the antecedent contains *or* or the antecedent is *each, everyone, person,* or a similar word
>
> - **Punctuation errors**
>
>   Commas, especially with comma splices and with *and* or *but,* with introductory elements, with nonessential elements, and with series
>   Apostrophes in possessives but not plural nouns (*Dave's/witches*) and in contractions but not possessive personal pronouns (*it's/its*)

13.4.1 Discovering what needs editing

Try these approaches to gain distance from your work:

- **Take a break.** Even fifteen minutes can clear your head.
- **Read the draft slowly, and read what you actually see.** Otherwise, you're likely to read what you intended to write but didn't. (If you have trouble slowing down, try reading your draft from back to front, sentence by sentence.)
- **Read as if you are encountering the draft for the first time.** Put yourself in the reader's place.
- **Have a classmate, friend, or relative read your work.** Make sure you understand and consider the reader's suggestions, even if you eventually decide not to take them.
- **Read the draft aloud or, even better, record it.** Listen for awkward rhythms, repetitive sentence patterns, and missing or clumsy transitions.

- **Learn from your own experience.** Keep a record of the problems that others have pointed out in your writing. When editing, check your work against this record.

13.4.2 A sample edited paragraph

In the following example of editing, Erica Vela tightens wording, improves parallelism (with *online courses* . . . as sentence opener), and improves coherence by repeating key words and phrases.

> ~~Moreover, the~~ The Internet also provides other opportunities for learning. Colleges and universities in the United States are building virtual classrooms and online degree programs ~~online~~, allowing students from ~~across~~ around the globe to obtain postsecondary ~~post-secondary~~ educations in a world that increasingly demands them. In my degree program, all classes meet online. ~~It~~ Online courses allow~~s~~ me to work full-time while living nearly two hundred miles away from the main campus. Online courses also provide personal interaction with my professors and classmates through ~~online~~ discussion boards and video conferencing applications. Without the Internet, I would not have access to a postsecondary education and I would not be a student today.

13.4.3 Working with spelling and grammar/style checkers

A spelling checker and grammar/style checker can be helpful *if* you work within their limitations. The programs miss many problems and may flag items that are actually correct. Further, they know nothing of your purpose and your audience, so they cannot make important decisions about your writing. Always use these tools critically:

- **Read your work yourself to ensure that it's clear and error-free.**
- **Consider a checker's suggestions carefully against your intentions.** If you aren't sure whether to accept a checker's suggestion, consult a dictionary, writing handbook, or other source. Your version may be fine.

Using a spelling checker

Your word processor's spelling checker can be a great ally: it will flag words that are spelled incorrectly and will usually suggest alternative spellings that resemble what you've typed. However, this ally can also undermine you because of its limitations:

- **The checker may flag a word that you've spelled correctly** just because the word does not appear in its dictionary.

rev 13.4

- **The checker may suggest incorrect alternatives.** In providing a list of alternative spellings for your word, the checker may highlight the one it considers most likely to be correct. For example, if you misspell *definitely* by typing *definately*, your checker may highlight *defiantly* as the correct option. You need to verify that the alternative suggested by the checker is actually what you intend before selecting it. Consult an online or printed dictionary when you aren't sure about the checker's recommendations.
- **Most important, a spelling checker will not flag words that appear in its dictionary but that you have misused.** The paragraph in the screen shot below contains eleven errors that a spelling checker overlooked. Can you spot them?

Spelling checker

The whether effects all of us, though it's affects are different for different people. Some people love a fare day with warm temperatures and sunshine. They revel in spending a hole day outside. Other people enjoy dark, rainy daze. They like to slow down and here they're inner thoughts. Most people agree, however, that to much of one kind of weather makes them board.

A spelling checke[r failed] to catch any of th[e] errors in this para[graph.]

Using a grammar/style checker

Grammar/style checkers can flag incorrect grammar or punctuation and wordy or awkward sentences. However, these programs can call your attention only to passages that *may* be faulty. They miss many errors because they are not yet capable of analyzing language in all its complexity. (For instance, they can't accurately distinguish a word's part of speech when there are different possibilities, as *light* can be a noun, a verb, or an adjective.) And they often question passages that don't need editing, such as an appropriate passive verb or a deliberate and emphatic use of repetition.

You can customize a grammar/style checker to suit your needs and habits as a writer. Most checkers allow you to specify whether to check grammar only or grammar and style. Some style checkers can be set to the level of writing you intend, such as formal, standard, and informal. (For academic writing, choose formal.) You can also instruct the checker to flag specific grammar and style problems that tend to occur in your writing, such as mismatched subjects and verbs, overused passive voice, or a confusion between *its* and *it's*.

13.5 Final Draft

13.5 Format and proofread your final draft.

After editing your essay, format and proofread it before you submit it to your instructor. Follow any required format for your paper, such as MLA (Chapter 51) and APA (Chapter 52).

Be sure to proofread the final essay several times to spot and correct errors. To increase the accuracy of your proofreading, you may need to experiment with ways to keep yourself from relaxing into the rhythm and the content of your prose. Here are a few tricks, including some used by professional proofreaders:

- **Read printed copy,** even if you will eventually submit the paper electronically. Most people proofread more accurately when reading type on paper than when reading it on a computer screen. (At the same time, don't view the printed copy as error-free just because it's clean. Clean-looking copy may still harbor errors.)
- **Read the paper aloud,** very slowly, and distinctly pronounce exactly what you see.
- **Place a ruler under each line as you read it.**
- **Read "against copy,"** comparing your final draft one sentence at a time against the edited draft.
- **Ignore content.** To keep the content of your writing from distracting you, read the essay backward sentence by sentence. Or use your word processor to isolate each paragraph from its context by printing it on a separate page. (Of course, reassemble the paragraphs before submitting the paper.)

13.5.1 Examining a sample final draft

Erica Vela's final essay begins below, presented in MLA format except for page breaks and page numbers. Comments in the margins point out key features of the essay's content.

Google Opens Our Minds—and Our Worlds

  In "Is *Google* Making Us Stupid?" Nicholas Carr laments that he was once "a scuba diver in the sea of words," but now he "zip[s] along the surface like a guy on a jet ski" (par. 4). He believes that the Internet is changing our minds at a fundamental level, damaging the way we process information and creating minds that struggle to remain focused on a given task for an extended time. Yet the Internet is changing more than how we process information. It is changing how we access and share information as well as how we interact with people across the globe. My experience of online education offers a benefit that Nicholas Carr overlooks: the Internet provides more opportunities for learning in areas where there are no well-stocked libraries or centers of higher education while offering more ways to access information from across the globe.

Descriptive title

Summary of Carr, with quotations cited parenthetically in MLA style (Chapter 51)

Thesis statement: basic difference with and response to Carr

Carr describes his experience as "an uncomfortable sense that someone, or something, has been tinkering with [his] brain, remapping the neural circuitry, reprogramming the memory" (par. 2). He laments his inability to focus on extended tasks. He worries that this focus on the Internet and technology is removing the human element from our thinking processes and, as sociologist Daniel Bell might suggest, replacing it with computerization (par. 14).

> Continued summary of Carr

Like Carr, I remember what life was like before the Internet. I live in a remote area, hundreds of miles from any college, university, or center of learning. I remember driving to the small local library and poring over their ancient card catalog, looking for books that held the information that I needed. If the library did not have the needed books, I would have to begin the extended process of interlibrary loan or travel hundreds of miles to the closest university library. But now I can search a library's database, *Amazon,* or *Google* and find dozens (or even hundreds) of books, journal articles, or Web sites. Some I can read immediately. Others I can order and have shipped to my house within two days. In this way and others, the Internet makes knowledge accessible across the globe. In most cases, you no longer need access to the physical source; you only need an access to the World Wide Web. Surely, Carr would agree that more equal and open access to information is a good thing.

> Transition to personal experience, beginning by noting points of agreement with Carr

> Final sentence in this paragraph previews the argument against Carr to follow

The Internet also provides other opportunities for learning. Colleges and universities in the United States are building virtual classrooms and online degree programs, allowing students from around the globe to obtain postsecondary educations in a world that increasingly demands them. In my degree program, all classes meet online. Online courses allow me to work full-time while living nearly two hundred miles away from the main campus. Online courses also provide personal interaction with my professors and classmates through discussion boards and video conferencing applications. Without the Internet, I would not have access to a postsecondary education and I would not be a student today.

> Examples to support disagreement with Carr

Like Carr, I believe the Internet is changing how we think, but I believe that these changes will be a benefit in the future. As Carr notes, Socrates worried about the development of writing in Plato's *Phaedrus*. He believed that our ability to remember things would be permanently destroyed, but he couldn't foresee how writing would spread ideas, ultimately expanding human knowledge. A similar situation arose after the development of the printing press. Critics argued that "cheaply printed books . . . would undermine religious authority, demean the work of scholars and scribes, and spread sedition and debauchery" (par. 31). Despite these concerns, I doubt you would find many people who would argue against the development of writing or the printing press. Writing and printed books have changed the world in ways that have been considered more beneficial than detrimental.

> Second main point of disagreement with Carr

> Elaboration and supporting examples to clarify second point of disagreement

> Final point reinforces Vela's second disagreement with Carr and provides additional context

Surely future generations will look back at the development of the Internet in the same way.

We know that the world of the future will look much different than it does today, and the development of the Internet will have much influence on how information is accessed, processed, and shared, likely shaping societies for generations. I understand Carr's concerns and even share some of them. However, I believe that the benefits greatly outweigh the disadvantages. We must not fear technological advancement and the spread of new knowledge while clinging to older technologies with the tips of our fingers. As humans, we have learned human speech, developed writing, invented printing, and now we are creating digital spaces and information. I wonder what the next advancement in technology will be and how it will change our lives and our minds.

Conclusion returns to summarize Vela's main points of agreement and disagreement with Carr, but does not merely restate the thesis

[New page.]

Work Cited

Carr, Nicholas. "Is *Google* Making Us Stupid? What the Internet Is Doing to Our Brains." *The Atlantic,* July-Aug. 2008, www.theatlantic.com/magazine/archive/2008/07/is-google-making-us-stupid/306868/.

Work cited in MLA style (see Chapter 51)

Chapter 14
Designing Documents

Learning Objectives

14.1 Format writing for academic audiences.
14.2 Use visuals and other media in multimodal writing.
14.3 Design and present writing for online audiences.
14.4 Prepare a writing portfolio.

14.1 Academic Writing

14.1 Format writing for academic audiences.

Many of the assignments you receive in college will require you to submit a written text either on paper or electronically—for instance, attached to an e-mail or uploaded to a course Web site.

Erica Vela
Professor Towns
Rhetoric 1311
16 March 2018

Google Opens Our Minds—and Our Worlds

In "Is *Google* Making Us Stupid?" Nicholas Carr laments that he was once "a scuba diver in the sea of words," but now he "zip[s] along the surface like a guy on a jet ski" (par. 4). He believes that the Internet is changing our minds at a fundamental level, damaging the way we process information and creating minds that struggle to remain focused on a given task for an extended time. Yet the Internet is changing more than how we process information. It is changing how we access and share information as well as how we interact with people across the globe (see Fig. 1). My experience of online education offers a benefit that Nicholas Carr overlooks: the Internet provides more opportunities for learning in areas where there are no well-stocked libraries or centers of higher education while offering more ways to access information from across the globe.

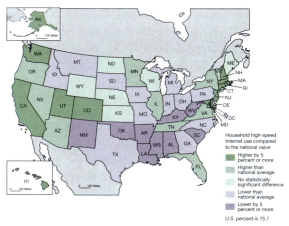

Fig. 1. States in the West and Northeast have higher rates of Internet use than states in the South.

United States Census Bureau. "A Digital Nation." 23 Mar. 2016, www.census.gov/library/visualizations/2016/comm/digital_nation.html.

> Vela 2
>
> Carr describes his experience as "an uncomfortable sense that someone, or something, has been tinkering with [his] brain, remapping the neural circuitry, reprogramming the memory" (par. 2). He laments his inability to focus on extended tasks. He worries that this focus on the Internet and technology is removing the human element from our thinking processes and, as sociologist Daniel Bell might suggest, replacing it with computerization (par. 14).

Indentations (one-half inch) marking paragraph breaks

Quotation cited in MLA style

des 14.1

For most print papers and files of papers, the preceding example shows a basic format that will help make your writing attractive and readable.

Many academic style guides recommend specific formats. This book details two such formats:

- **MLA style,** used in English, foreign languages, and some other humanities (Chapter 51).
- **APA style,** used in the social sciences (Chapter 52).

Considering readers with vision loss

If your audience may include readers who have low vision, problems with color perception, or difficulties processing visual information, adapt your design to meet these readers' needs:

- **Use large type fonts.** Most guidelines call for 14 points or larger.
- **Use standard type fonts.** Many people with low vision find it easier to read sans serif fonts such as Arial than serif fonts. Avoid decorative fonts with unusual flourishes, even in headings.
- **Avoid words in all-capital letters.**
- **Avoid relying on color alone to distinguish elements.** Label elements, and distinguish them by position or size.
- **Use red and green selectively.** To readers who are red-green color-blind, these colors will appear in shades of gray, yellow, or blue.
- **Use contrasting colors.** To make colors distinct, choose them from opposite sides of the color spectrum—violet and yellow, for instance, or orange and blue.
- **Use only light colors for tints behind type.** Make the type itself black or a very dark color.

Although they do vary, most academic formats share preferences for the design of standard elements:

- **Margins:** minimum one inch on all sides.
- **Line spacing:** double-spaced throughout.
- **Type fonts and sizes:** standard 10- or 12-point fonts such as Times New Roman and Cambria (serif fonts, with small lines finishing the letters) or Arial and Calibri (sans serif fonts, lacking the small lines). Serif fonts are generally easier to read on paper, while sans serif fonts are easier to read on a screen.
- **Highlighting:** underlining, *italics,* or **boldface** to mark headings and emphasize text elements such as terms being defined.
- **Headings:** one or two levels as needed to direct readers' attention to significant ideas and transitions. Word headings consistently—for instance, all questions (*What Is Sustainability?*) or all phrases with *-ing* words (*Understanding Sustainability*). Indicate the relative importance of headings with highlighting and position—perhaps bold for first-level headings and lightface italic for second-level headings. (Document format in psychology and some other social sciences requires a particular treatment of headings. See Chapter 52.)
- **Lists:** numbered or bulleted (as in the list you're reading), to show the relationship of like items, such as the elements of a document or the steps in a process or proposal.
- **Color:** mainly for illustrations, occasionally for headings, bullets, and other elements. Always use black for the text of a paper, and make sure that any other colors are dark enough to be legible.

14.2 Visuals and Media

14.2 Use visuals and other media in multimodal writing.

Academic writing is often **multimodal**—that is, it includes more than one medium, whether text, charts, photographs, video, or audio. A simple multimodal paper involves just two media—mainly text with some illustrations embedded in the text. A paper submitted online might add links to audio or video files as well. This section provides tips for selecting and using such media in your writing. The next section treats media in Web compositions, blogs, and wikis.

Any visual or digital media you include or link to in your writing needs to be cited to provide information about the source for your readers. Treat visual media just like text: If you did not compose it yourself, you need to cite the source.

14.2.1 Selecting visuals and other media

Depending on your writing situation, you might use anything from a table to a bar chart to a video to support your writing. The "Selecting visuals" box describes and illustrates the options.

You can find many visuals via online searches (see Chapter 5). You can also use programs like *Adobe Photoshop* or Web-based services like *Canva* to design your own illustrations. Use *PowerPoint, Google Slides, Prezi,* or a similar program for visuals in oral presentations (see Chapter 15).

Selecting visuals

Visuals can be placed in print or electronic documents. They include tables, pie charts, bar charts, line graphs, infographics, diagrams, flowcharts, and images such as photographs, maps, fine art, advertisements, and cartoons.

Selecting video and audio

You can use video or audio files to emphasize or support points in digital writing, such as Web pages or blogs, and in oral presentations. For example, you might explain a process with a video of how something works, support an interpretation of a play with a video of a scene from a performance, or illustrate a profile of a person by linking to a podcast interview. The screen shot in Figure 14.1 shows a passage of text from an online paper that links to video of the poet Rita Dove reading her poem "American Smooth."

14.2.2 Using visuals and other media effectively

An image or a video clip can attract readers' attention, but if it does no more it will amount to mere decoration or, worse, it will detract from the substance of your writing. Before using any type of media, consider whether it meets the requirements of your assignment, serves a purpose, and is appropriate for your audience.

Figure 14.1 Link to video file

Often a reading by the poet reinforces both the sound and the meaning of the poem. In Rita Dove's "American Smooth," two people move self-consciously through an intricate dance, smiling and holding their bodies just so, when suddenly they experience a moment of perfection: they nearly float. When Dove reads the poem aloud, she builds to that moment, allowing listeners to feel the same magic (http://www.poetryfoundation.org/features/video/267).

Selecting visuals

Tables

Tables present raw data to show how variables relate to one another or how two or more groups contrast. Place a descriptive title above the table, and use headings to label rows and columns.

Table 1
Public- and private-school enrollment of US students, 2013

	Number of students (in thousands)	Percentage in public school	Percentage in private school
All students	74,603	85	15
Kindergarten through grade 8	39,179	88	12
Grades 9-12	16,332	92	8

Source: Data from *Digest of Education Statistics: 2013*; National Center for Education Statistics, Apr. 2014, nces.ed.gov/tables/dt13_205.10.asp.

Diagrams and flowcharts

Diagrams show concepts visually, such as the structure of an organization or the way something works or looks.

Fig. 4. *MyPlate*, a graphic representation of daily food portions recommended for a healthy diet.

From *ChooseMyPlate.gov*; United States Department of Agriculture, 2011, www.choosemyplate.gov.

Images

Photographs, maps, paintings, advertisements, and cartoons can be the focus of critical analysis or can support points you make.

Fig. 5. View from the *Cassini* spacecraft, showing Saturn and its rings.

From *Cassini-Huygens: Mission to Saturn and Titan*; NASA, Jet Propulsion Laboratory, 24 Feb. 2015, nasa.gov/multimedia/imagegallery/137.html.

Pie charts

Pie charts show the relations among the parts of a whole, adding up to 100%. Use a pie chart to show shares of data. Label each pie slice, and make it proportional to its share of the whole.

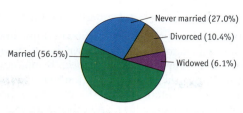

Fig. 1. Marital status in 2013 of adults age eighteen and over.

Data from *2013 Statistical Abstract*; US Census Bureau, Jan. 2014, www.census.gov/library/publications/time-series/statistical_abstracts.html.

Bar charts

Bar charts compare groups or time periods. Use a bar chart when relative size is important. On the vertical scale, start with a zero point in the lower left and label the values being measured. On the horizontal scale, label the groups being compared.

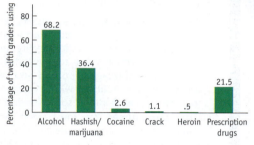

Fig. 2. Lifetime prevalence of use of alcohol, compared with other drugs, among twelfth graders in 2013.

Data from *Monitoring the Future: A Continuing Study of American Youth*; U of Michigan, 3 Feb. 2013, www.icpsr.umich.edu/icpsrweb/NAHDAP/studies/36407.

Line graphs

Line graphs compare many points of data to show change over time. On the vertical scale, start with a zero point in the lower left and label the values being measured. On the horizontal scale, label the range of dates. Label the lines, and distinguish them with color, dots, or dashes.

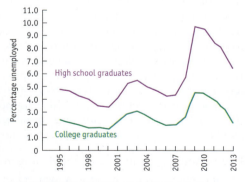

Fig. 3. Unemployment rates of high school graduates and college graduates, 1995–2013.

Data from *Economics News Release*; United States Department of Labor, Bureau of Labor Statistics, 7 Oct. 2013, www.bls.gov/newsrelease/empsite/nr0.htm.

Considering the requirements and limits of your writing situation

What do the type of writing you're doing and its format allow? Look through examples of similar writing to gauge the kinds of media, if any, that your readers will expect. It matters, too, how you will present your work: a short animation sequence might be terrific in a *PowerPoint* presentation or on the Web, but a printed document requires photographs, drawings, and other static means of explanation.

des 14.2

Using visuals and other media responsibly

Visuals and other media require special care to avoid distortion and to ensure honest use of others' material.

- **Create and evaluate tables, charts, and graphs carefully.** Verify that the data you use are accurate and that the highlighted changes, relationships, or trends reflect reality. In a line graph, for instance, starting the vertical axis at zero puts the lines in context.
- **Be skeptical of images you find on the Web.** Altered photographs are posted and circulated widely on the Web. If a photograph seems inauthentic, check into its source or don't use it.
- **Cite your sources.** You must credit the source whenever you use someone else's data to create a visual, embed someone else's visual in your document, or link to someone else's media file.
- **Obtain permission if it is required.** For projects that will reside on the Web, you may need to clear permission from the copyright holder of a visual or a media file.

Making sure visuals and other media support your writing

Ensure that any visual you use relates directly to a point in your writing, adds to that point, and gives your audience something to think about. In an evaluation of an advertisement, the ad itself would support the claim you make about it. In a paper arguing for earthquake preparedness, a photograph could show earthquake damage and a chart could show levels of current preparedness.

The two images in Figure 14.2 supported a paper with this thesis: *While earthquakes cannot be prevented, homeowners can take practical, inexpensive steps to prepare their homes and reduce damage.*

Integrating visuals and other media into your writing

Readers should understand why you are including visuals or other media in your writing and how they relate to the overall project:

- **In projects with embedded visuals, connect the visuals to your text.** Refer to the visuals at the point(s) where readers will benefit from consulting them—for instance, "See Fig. 2" or "See table 1." Number figures and tables separately (Fig. 1, Fig. 2, and so on;

Figure 14.2 Visuals as support

Visual examples support the thesis about earthquake preparedness.

Caption explains the visuals, tying them to the text of the paper and providing source information.

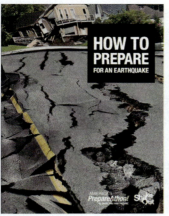

The cover (left) and interior page (right) of a brochure illustrating practical steps homeowners can take to reduce earthquake damage.

How to Prepare for an Earthquake. United States Department of Homeland Security, Federal Emergency Management Agency.

Table 1, Table 2, and so on), and always include a title above a table and a caption under a visual (see below).

- **In online projects using audio or video, work the files or links into your text.** Your audience should know what you intend the media to show, whether you link to a photograph from a mainly text document or integrate text, sound, still images, and video into a complex Web project.

Writing captions and source notes

For a figure such as a chart, graph, or diagram, always provide a caption that performs two functions: (1) it ties a visual to your text so that readers don't have to puzzle out your intention; and (2) it cites the source of the data or the entire visual. Many discipline styles have distinctive formats for captions and source information.

Figure caption (MLA style)

Fig. 1. Marital status in 2017 of adults age eighteen and over. Data from *2017 Statistical Abstract*; United States Census Bureau, Jan. 2018, www.census.gov/library/publications/2018/131ed.html.

For a table, provide a title on top that tells readers what the content shows, and then give a note at the bottom that cites the source.

Table title (MLA style)

Public- and private-school enrollment of US students, 2017

Table source note (MLA style)

Source: Data from *Digest of Education Statistics: 2017*; National Center for Education Statistics, Apr. 2018, nces.ed.gov/tables/dt13_205.10.asp.

14.3 Writing Online

14.3 Design and present writing for online audiences.

You may already be experienced in creating online writing projects—perhaps a *Tumblr* site, a blog, a video, or a digital collage posted on *YouTube*. You know that the purposes and audiences for such multimodal writing vary widely, and so do readers' expectations for design.

Many creators of online projects upload files into existing templates that make design relatively easy. Even with such software, you will still have to make choices about elements such as fonts, colors, and layout. The design guidelines for academic writing can help you with such decisions, as can the following discussion of online academic compositions such as a Web site or a multimodal project posted on a blog or wiki.

14.3.1 Conceiving a Web composition

Whether you are developing a Web site or preparing a digital composition to be posted on the Web, the following general guidelines will help you plan your project:

- **Consider how design can reflect your purpose for writing and your sense of audience.** Unlike a conventional academic paper, a Web text often allows considerable design freedom. Think about how type fonts and sizes, headings, visuals and other media, background colors, and other design elements can connect with readers and further the purpose of your writing.
- **Anticipate how readers will move within your composition.** A digital document with links to other pages, posts, Web sites, and media can disorient readers as they scroll up and down and pursue various links. Page length, links, menus, and other cues should work to keep readers oriented.
- **Imagine what readers may see on their screens.** Each reader's screen frames and organizes the experience of reading online. Screen space is limited, and it varies widely. Design for small screens first.
- **Integrate visuals, audio, and video into the text.** Web compositions will likely include visuals such as charts and photographs as well as video (such as animation or film clips) and audio (such as music or excerpts from interviews). Any visual or sound

element should add essential information that can't be provided otherwise, and it should be well integrated with the rest of your composition. Avoid using visuals and sound merely as attention grabbers.
- **Acknowledge your sources.** It's easy to incorporate text, visuals, audio, and video from other sources into a Web composition, but you have the same obligation to cite your sources as you do in a printed document. Your Web composition is a form of publication, like a magazine or a book. Unless the material you are using explicitly allows copying without permission, you may need to seek the copyright holder's permission, just as print publishers do.

If you anticipate that some of your readers may have visual, hearing, or reading disabilities, you'll need to consider their needs while designing writing that will appear on a screen. Some of these considerations are covered above, and others are fundamental to any effective Web-based design, as discussed in this section. In addition, avoid any content that relies exclusively on visuals or sound, instead supplementing such elements with text descriptions. At the same time, try to provide key concepts in words as well as in visuals and sound. For more on Web design for readers with disabilities, visit the World Wide Web Consortium at *www.w3.org*.

14.3.2 Creating a Web site

Traditional printed documents are intended to be read page by page in sequence. In contrast, Web sites are intended to be examined in whatever order readers choose as they follow links to pages within a site and to other sites. The diagram in Figure 14.3 shows a

Figure 14.3 Web site organization

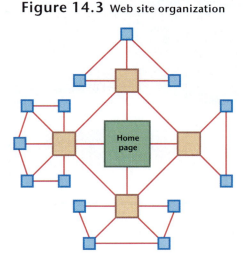

schematic Web site, with pages at different levels (orange and then blue squares) interconnecting with the home page and with one another.

While reading Web sites, readers generally alternate between skimming pages for highlights and focusing intently on one section of text. To facilitate this kind of reading, you'll want to consider the following guidelines.

Structure and content

Organize a Web site so that it efficiently arranges your content and also orients readers:

- **Sketch possible site plans before getting started.** A diagram like the one above can help you develop the major components of your project and create a logical space for each component.
- **Consider how menus can provide overviews of the organization as well as direct access to the linked content.** The sample Web site *ChooseMyPlate.gov* (Fig. 14.4) includes a menu near the top of the page.
- **Treat the first few sentences of any page as a get-acquainted space for you and your readers.** In the sample Web site, the text hooks readers with visuals and orients them with general information.

Figure 14.4 Web site home page

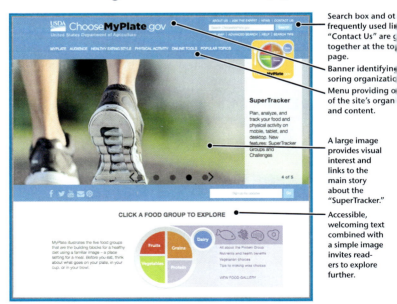

Source: Choose my plate, homepage retrieved from https://www.choosemyplate.gov

- **Distill your text so that it includes only essential information.** Concise prose is essential in any writing situation, of course, but readers of Web sites expect to scan text quickly.

Flow

Take advantage of the Web's visual nature by thinking about how information will flow on each page:

- **Standardize elements of your design to create and fulfill expectations in readers.** For instance, develop a uniform style for the main headings of pages, for headings within pages, and for menus.
- **Make scanning easy for readers.** Focus readers on crucial text by adding space around it. Add headings to break up text and to highlight content. Use lists to reinforce the parallel importance of items.

Navigation

Provide a menu so that readers can navigate your Web site. Like the table of contents in a book, a menu lists the features of a site, showing its plan at a glance.

You can embed a menu at the top, side, or bottom of a page—or use more than one position. Menus at the top or side allow readers to move around the site without having to read the full home page. Menus at the bottom prevent readers from dead-ending—that is, reaching a point where they can't easily move forward or backward.

In designing a menu, keep it simple: many different type fonts and colors will overwhelm readers instead of orienting them. Also, make your menus look the same from one page to the next so that readers recognize them easily.

14.3.3 Posting to a blog or a wiki

Blogs and wikis are Web sites that allow users to post text and media such as images and video. Unlike other Web sites, which are generally designed to advocate a position or provide information, blogs and wikis encourage interaction: readers can comment on blog posts or, on a wiki, contribute to posts and collaborate on documents.

You may create a blog or a wiki as an academic assignment, in which case you will need to make decisions about the appearance of the site as a whole. For most academic blog or wiki writing, however, you will post drafts of your projects and comment on your classmates' work. You can compose and edit your text in your word processor and paste the text into the blog or wiki. At that point, you'll have the opportunity to write a descriptive title for your post, upload images and other media, and add links to other Web sites. You can also preview the post before making it public.

The following illustration shows a student's draft of a personal essay, which she posted to her class blog.

---

des 14.3

The writing situation: Literacy narrative

- **Subject:** Reading *Charlotte's Web*; student's choice for an assignment in a first-year writing course
- **Purpose:** To tell a story that explains the significance of reading and writing in the writer's childhood
- **Audience:** Classmates, instructor, and readers of the student's blog
- **Genre:** Literacy narrative—a personal essay about the writer's experience with learning to read and/or write
- **Sources:** Personal experience

Literacy narrative posted to a blog

Monday, March 27, 2017

Embracing Family Traditions[1]

Descriptive title hints at the theme of the essay

Vivid descriptive detail opens the essay

A solid wood bookshelf dominated the living room of my childhood home that I shared with my grandparents, aunt, and mother. It covered an entire wall—nearly six feet wide and over seven feet tall. It was a family heirloom, built by my great-grandfather and grandfather. It was beautiful, but it wasn't merely a showcase. No knick-knacks graced its shelves; every flat surface was covered by a hardcover book. From horror fiction and true crime to Buddhist spiritualism and the classics, my family read every book on the shelves, and they always encouraged me to do the same. In fact, my family gave me the bottom shelf and filled it with dozens of books.

Key sentence capturing the main theme of the essay

Transitional sentence that shifts focus to the emotional event at the heart of the essay

Books were sprinkled throughout our home as well. We were always reading. Don't get me wrong—we weren't one of those families that didn't own a television. I have very vivid memories of watching television with my grandfather—he loved *M*A*S*H* and *Happy Days*. More though, I remember sharing his recliner, reading my book while he read one of his own. He listened as I excitedly described my newest Dr. Seuss book, and he hugged me as I cried after reading *Charlotte's Web*.

Short paragraph emphasizing the emotional impact of reading Charlotte's Web

Unfortunately for my grandfather, *Charlotte's Web* crushed me. With my mother and aunt at work, he turned to my grandmother for help. It was a decision that still impacts my life to this day.

My grandmother was a writer. It wasn't her job; it was her passion. She would occasionally send submissions in to women's magazines, but mostly she wrote short stories and poetry because she felt compelled to put pen to

---

[1] Sample student papers and extracts, Heather Anne Tolliver

paper. "If you're not happy with how the story ends," she said, "let's change it." I sat at the dining room table and wrote. I don't remember my revised ending for *Charlotte's Web*, but I know that it was my first piece of creative writing. Writing became my escape, and I've been writing fiction and nonfiction stories ever since.

> Direct quotation of grandmother's words

My grandparents are gone now, but I continue to embrace my family traditions—reading and writing a little each day.

> Conclusion points out the significance of the story

Posted by Emily Everett at 7:42 pm.

14.4 Portfolios

14.4 Prepare a writing portfolio.

A portfolio is a showcase of your best work in a course or degree program. A portfolio gives you a chance to consider all your writing over time and to choose the work that best represents your growth as a writer.

The purposes and requirements for portfolios vary. As you consider what work to include in your portfolio, answer the following questions:

- **What is the purpose of the portfolio?** A portfolio may be intended to showcase your best work, demonstrate progress you have made, or provide examples of your versatility as a writer.
- **What are the requirements of the portfolio?** You may be asked to submit final drafts of your best work; journal entries, notes, early drafts, and a final draft of one or more essays; or projects representing different types of writing—say, one narrative, one critical analysis, one argument, and so on.
- **Is a reflective essay or letter required as part of the portfolio?** Many teachers require an opening essay or letter in which you discuss the selections in the portfolio. Explain why you chose each one, and perhaps evaluate your development as a writer. If a reflective essay is required, be sure you understand its purpose and scope.
- **Should the portfolio be print or electronic, or can you choose the medium?** Many students use free services like *Google Sites* or *Weebly* to set up an online portfolio that can be viewed by instructors as well as potential employers. Design your site, upload files, proofread, and test your site before making it public.
- **How will the portfolio be evaluated?** Will it be read by peers, your instructor, or a committee of teachers? Will it be graded?

Unless the guidelines specify otherwise, provide error-free copies of your final drafts and label all your samples with your name before you place them in a folder or upload them as files.

Chapter 15
Oral Presentations

Learning Objectives

15.1 Organize your presentation.
15.2 Deliver your presentation.

15.1 Organization

15.1 **Organize your presentation.**

Give your oral presentation a recognizable shape so that listeners can see how ideas and details relate to each other.

The introduction

The beginning of an oral presentation should try to accomplish three goals:

- **Gain the audience's attention and interest.** Begin with a question, an unusual example or statistic, or a short, relevant story.
- **Put yourself in the speech.** Demonstrate your expertise, experience, or concern to gain the interest and trust of your audience.
- **Introduce and preview your topic and purpose.** By the time your introduction is over, listeners should know what your subject is and the direction you'll take to develop your ideas.

Your introduction should prepare your audience for your main points but not give them away. Think of it as a sneak preview of your speech, not the place for an apology such as *I wish I'd had more time to prepare. . .*, or a dull statement such as *My speech is about. . . .*

Supporting material

Just as you do when writing, you should use facts, statistics, examples, and expert opinions to support the main points of your oral presentation. In addition, you can make your points more memorable with vivid description, well-chosen quotations, true or fictional stories, and analogies.

The conclusion

You want your conclusion to be clear, of course, but you also want it to be memorable. Remind listeners of how your topic and main idea connect to their needs and interests. If your speech was motivational, tap an emotion that matches your message. If your speech was informational, give some tips on how to remember important details.

15.2 Delivery

15.2 Deliver your presentation.

Methods of delivery

You can deliver an oral presentation in several ways:

- **Impromptu, without preparation:** Make a presentation without planning what you will say. Impromptu speaking requires confidence and excellent general preparation.
- **Extemporaneously:** Prepare notes to glance at, but not to read from. This method allows you to look and sound natural while ensuring that you don't forget anything.
- **Speaking from a text:** Read aloud from a written presentation. You won't lose your way, but you may lose your audience. Avoid reading for an entire presentation.
- **Speaking from memory:** Deliver a prepared presentation without notes. You can look at your audience every minute, but the stress of retrieving the next words may make you seem tense and unresponsive.

Vocal delivery

The sound of your voice will influence how listeners receive you. Rehearse your presentation several times until you are confident that you are speaking loudly, slowly, and clearly enough for your audience to understand you.

Physical delivery

You are more than your spoken words when you make an oral presentation. If you are able, stand up to deliver your presentation, turning your body toward one side of the room and then the other, stepping out from behind any lectern or desk, and gesturing as appropriate. Above all, make eye contact with your audience as you speak. Looking directly into your listeners' eyes conveys your honesty, your confidence, and your control of the material.

Culture and language

Eye contact is customary in the United States, both in conversation and in oral presentation. Listeners expect it and may perceive a speaker who doesn't make eye contact as evasive or insincere.

Visual aids

You can supplement an oral presentation with visual aids such as posters, models, slides, or videos.

- **Use visual aids to underscore your points.** Short lists of key ideas, illustrations such as graphs or photographs, and objects such as models can make your presentation more interesting and memorable. But use visual aids judiciously: a constant flow of illustrations or objects will bury your message.
- **Match visual aids and setting.** An audience of five people may be able to see a photograph and share a chart; a classroom or an audience of a hundred will need projected images.
- **Coordinate visual aids with your message.** Time each visual to reinforce a point you're making. Tell listeners what they're looking at. Give them enough viewing time so that they don't mind turning their attention back to you.
- **Show visual aids only while they're needed.** To regain your audience's attention, remove or turn off any aid as soon as you have finished with it.

Many speakers use *PowerPoint*, *Prezi*, or other software to project main points, key images, video, or other elements. To use such software effectively, follow the guidelines with the sample presentation slides (Fig. 15.1) and also these tips:

- **Don't put your whole presentation on-screen.** Select key points and distill them to as few words as possible. Use slides as quick, easy-to-remember summaries or ways to present examples. For a twenty-minute presentation, plan to use approximately ten slides.
- **Use a simple design.** Avoid turning your presentation into a show about the software's many capabilities and special effects.
- **Make text readable.** The type should be easy to see for viewers in the back of the room, whether the lights are on or not.
- **Use a consistent design.** For optimal flow through the presentation, each slide should be formatted similarly.
- **Add relevant images and media.** Presentation software allows you to play images, audio, and video as part of your speech. Before you add them, however, be sure each has a point so that you don't overload the presentation. Include citations for images and media used in your presentation (unless they are your own original work).
- **Review all your slides before the presentation.** Go through the slides to be sure they are complete, consistent, and easy to read. Proofread each slide.
- **Don't talk to the computer or the projection during the presentation.** Move away from both and face the audience.

Figure 15.1 Presentation slides

- **Pace your presentation and your slides.** If a section of your presentation doesn't have a slide keyed to it, insert a blank slide to project during that section.

Practice

Take time to rehearse your presentation out loud, with the notes you will be using. Gauge your performance by making an audio- or videotape of yourself or by practicing in front of a mirror. Practicing out loud will also tell you if your presentation is running too long or too short.

If you plan to use visual aids, you'll need to practice with them, too. Your goal is to eliminate glitches (slides in the wrong order, missing charts) and to weave the visuals seamlessly into your presentation.

Stage fright

Many people report that speaking in front of an audience is their number-one fear. Even many experienced and polished speakers have some anxiety about delivering an oral presentation, but they use this nervous energy to their advantage, letting it propel them into working hard on each presentation. Several techniques can help you reduce anxiety:

- **Use simple relaxation exercises.** Deep breathing or tensing and relaxing your stomach muscles can ease some of the physical symptoms of speech anxiety—stomachache, rapid heartbeat, and shaky hands, legs, and voice.
- **Think positively.** Instead of worrying about the mistakes you might make, concentrate on how well you've prepared and practiced your presentation and how significant your ideas are.
- **Don't avoid opportunities to speak in public.** Practice and experience build your presentation skills and offer the best insurance for success.

Part 3

Clarity and Style

16 Emphasis *193*
17 Parallelism *200*
18 Variety and Details *202*
19 Appropriate and Exact Language *206*
20 Completeness *220*
21 Conciseness *221*

Part 3
Clarity and Style

16 Emphasis *193*
    16.1 Subjects and verbs *193*
    16.2 Sentence beginnings and endings *194*
    16.3 Coordination *196*
    16.4 Subordination *198*

17 Parallelism *200*
    17.1 Understanding parallelism *200*
    17.2 Equal elements *200*

18 Variety and Details *202*
    18.1 Sentence length and structure *202*
    18.2 Details *205*

19 Appropriate and Exact Language *206*
    19.1 Standard English *206*
    19.2 Sexist and biased language *209*
    19.3 Exact language *213*

20 Completeness *220*
    20.1 Compounds *220*
    20.2 Adding needed words *220*

21 Conciseness *221*
    21.1 Subjects and verbs *221*
    21.2 Empty words *223*
    21.3 Unnecessary repetition *224*
    21.4 Other strategies *224*

Chapter 16
Emphasis

⌄ Learning Objectives

16.1 Use subjects and verbs effectively.
16.2 Create emphasis using sentence beginnings and endings.
16.3 Relate equal ideas using coordination.
16.4 Use subordination to distinguish main ideas.

16.1 Subjects and Verbs

16.1 Use subjects and verbs effectively.

The heart of every sentence is its **subject**, which usually names the actor, and its predicate **verb**, which usually specifies the subject's action: *Children* [subject] *grow* [verb]. When these elements do not identify the key actor and action in the sentence, readers must find that information elsewhere and the sentence may be wordy and unemphatic.

In the following sentences, the subjects and verbs are underlined:

> **Unemphatic** The <u>intention</u> of the company <u>was</u> to expand its workforce. A <u>proposal</u> <u>was</u> also <u>made</u> to allow flexible work hours and telework.

These sentences are unemphatic because their key ideas do not appear in their subjects and verbs. In the revision below, the sentences are not only clearer but also more concise:

> **Revised** The <u>company</u> <u>intended</u> to expand its workforce. It also <u>proposed</u> to allow flexible work hours and telework.

The following constructions usually drain meaning from a sentence's subject and verb.

Nouns made from verbs

Nouns made from verbs can obscure the key actions of sentences and add words. These nouns include *intention* (from *intend*), *proposal* (from *propose*), *decision* (from *decide*), *expectation* (from *expect*), and *inclusion* (from *include*).

emph
16.1

Unemphatic	After the company made a decision to permit telework, its next step was the development of virtual conference rooms.
Revised	After the company decided to permit telework, it next developed virtual conference rooms.

Weak verbs

Weak verbs, such as *made* and *was* in the unemphatic sentence above, tend to stall sentences just where they should be moving, and often bury key actions:

Unemphatic	The company is now the leader among businesses in supporting work-from-home and virtual teleconferencing. Its officers make frequent speeches on the initiative to business groups.
Revised	The company now leads other businesses in supporting work-from-home and virtual teleconferencing. Its officers frequently speak on the initiative to business groups.

Forms of *be, have,* and *make* are often weak, but don't try to eliminate every use of them: *be* and *have* are essential as **helping verbs** (*is going, has written*); *be* links subjects and the words describing them (*Planes are noisy*); and *have* and *make* have independent meanings (among them "possess" and "force," respectively). But do consider replacing a form of *be, have,* or *make* when a word after it could be made into a strong verb itself, as in the following examples:

Unemphatic	Emphatic
was influential	influenced
have a preference	prefer
had the appearance	appeared, seemed
made a claim	claimed

Passive voice

Verbs in the **passive voice** state actions received by, not performed by, their subjects. Thus the passive de-emphasizes the true actor of the sentence, sometimes omitting it entirely. Generally, prefer the **active voice**, in which the subject performs the action.

Unemphatic	The 2018 law is seen by most businesses as fair, but the costs of complying have sometimes been objected to.
Revised	Most businesses see the 2018 law as fair, but some have objected to the costs of complying.

16.2 Sentence Beginnings and Endings

16.2   Create emphasis using sentence beginnings and endings.

Readers automatically seek a writer's principal meaning in the **main clause** of a sentence—that is, in the subject that names the actor and

Old and new information

Generally, readers expect the beginning of a sentence to contain information that they already know or that you have already introduced. They then look to the sentence ending for new information. In the unemphatic passage below, the second and third sentences both begin with new topics, while the old topics appear at the ends of the sentences. The pattern of the unemphatic passage is A→B, C→B, and D→A.

> Unemphatic [A] Education often means [B] controversy these days, with rising costs and constant complaints about its inadequacies. But the [C] value of schooling should not be obscured by the [B] controversy. The single best [D] means of economic advancement, despite its shortcomings, remains [A] education.

In the more emphatic revision, the old information begins each sentence and new information ends the sentence. The passage follows the pattern A→B, B→C, and then A→D.

emph
16.2

> Revised [A] Education often means [B] controversy these days, with rising costs and constant complaints about its inadequacies. But the [B] controversy should not obscure the [C] value of schooling. [A] Education, despite its shortcomings, remains the single best [D] means of economic advancement.

Cumulative and periodic sentences

You can call attention to information by placing it first or last in a sentence, reserving the middle for incidentals:

> Unemphatic Education remains the single best means of economic advancement, despite its shortcomings. [Emphasizes shortcomings.]
>
> Revised Despite its shortcomings, education remains the single best means of economic advancement. [Emphasizes advancement more than shortcomings.]
>
> Revised Education, despite its shortcomings, remains the single best means of economic advancement. [De-emphasizes shortcomings.]

A sentence that adds **modifiers** to the main clause is called **cumulative** because it accumulates information as it proceeds:

Cumulative   Education has no equal in opening minds, instilling values, and creating opportunities.

Cumulative   Most of the Great American Desert is made up of bare rock, rugged cliffs, mesas, canyons, mountains, separated from one another by broad flat basins covered with sun-baked mud and alkali, supporting a sparse and measured growth of sagebrush or creosote or saltbush, depending on location and elevation.

—Edward Abbey

The opposite kind of sentence, called **periodic**, saves the main clause until just before the end (the period) of the sentence. Everything before the main clause points toward it:

Periodic   In opening minds, instilling values, and creating opportunities, education has no equal.

Periodic   With people from all over the world—Korean doctors, Jamaican cricket players, Vietnamese engineers, Haitian cabdrivers, Chinese grocers, Indian restaurant owners—the American mosaic is continually changing.

coord 16.3

The periodic sentence creates suspense by reserving important information for the end. But readers should already have an idea of the sentence's subject—because it was mentioned in the preceding sentence—so that they know what the opening modifiers describe.

16.3 Coordination

16.3   Relate equal ideas using coordination.

Use **coordination** to show that two or more elements in a sentence are equally important in meaning and to clarify the relationship between them:

Ways to coordinate information in sentences

- **Link main clauses with a comma and a coordinating conjunction:** *and, but, or, nor, for, so, yet.*

  Independence Hall in Philadelphia is faithfully restored, but many years ago it was in bad shape.

- **Relate main clauses with a semicolon alone or with a semicolon and a conjunctive adverb:** *however, indeed, therefore, thus,* etc.

  The building was standing; however, it suffered from neglect.

- **Within clauses, link words and phrases with a coordinating conjunction:** *and, but, or, nor.*

  The people and officials of the nation were indifferent to Independence Hall or took it for granted.

- **Link main clauses, words, or phrases with a correlative conjunction:** *both . . . and, not only . . . but also,* etc.

  People not only took the building for granted but also neglected it.

16.3.1 Coordinating to relate equal ideas

Coordination shows the equality between elements, as illustrated by the examples in the preceding box. At the same time that it clarifies meaning, it can also help smooth choppy sentences:

Choppy sentences We should not rely so heavily on oil. Coal and natural gas are also overused. We have a substantial energy resource in the moving waters of our rivers. Smaller streams add to the total volume of water. The resource renews itself. Oil and coal are irreplaceable. Gas is also irreplaceable. The cost of water does not increase much over time. The costs of coal, oil, and gas fluctuate dramatically.

The following revision groups coal, oil, and uranium and clearly opposes them to water (the connecting words are underlined):

Ideas coordinated We should not rely so heavily on oil, coal, and natural gas, for we have a substantial energy resource in the moving waters of our rivers and streams. Oil, coal, and gas are irreplaceable and thus subject to dramatic cost fluctuations; water, however, is self-renewing and more stable in cost.

16.3.2 Coordinating effectively

Use coordination only to express the *equality* of ideas or details. A string of coordinated elements—especially main clauses—implies that all points are equally important:

Excessive coordination The weeks leading up to the resignation of President Nixon were eventful, and the Supreme Court and the Congress closed in on him, and the Senate Judiciary Committee voted to begin impeachment proceedings, and finally the president resigned on August 9, 1974.

Such a passage needs editing to stress the important points (underlined below) and to de-emphasize the less important information:

Revised The weeks leading up to the resignation of President Nixon were eventful, as the Supreme Court and the Congress closed in on him and the Senate Judiciary Committee voted to begin impeachment proceedings. Finally, the president resigned on August 9, 1974.

Even within a single sentence, coordination should express a logical equality between ideas:

> **Faulty** John Stuart Mill was a nineteenth-century utilitarian, and he believed that actions should be judged by their usefulness or by the happiness they cause.

The two clauses are not separate and equal: the second expands on the first by explaining what a utilitarian such as Mill believed.

> **Revised** John Stuart Mill, a nineteenth-century utilitarian, believed that actions should be judged by their usefulness or by the happiness they cause.

16.4 Subordination

16.4 Use subordination to distinguish main ideas.

Use **subordination** to indicate that some elements in a sentence are less important than others for your meaning. Usually, the main idea appears in the main clause, and supporting details appear in subordinate structures:

Ways to subordinate information in sentences

- Use a subordinate clause beginning with a subordinating word: *who* (*whom*), *that, which, although, because, however, if, therefore, unless, whereas,* etc.

  Although some citizens had tried to rescue Independence Hall, they had not gained substantial public support.

  The first strong step was taken by the federal government, which made the building a national monument.

- **Use a phrase.**

  Like most national monuments, Independence Hall is protected by the National Park Service.

  Protecting many popular tourist sites, the service is a highly visible government agency.

- **Use a short modifier.**

  At the red brick Independence Hall, park rangers give guided tours, answer visitors' questions, and protect the irreplaceable building from vandalism.

16.4.1 Subordinating to emphasize main ideas

A string of main clauses can make everything in a passage seem equally important:

Subordination

String of main clauses	Computer prices have dropped, and production costs have dropped more slowly, and computer manufacturers have had to struggle, for their profits have been shrinking.

Emphasis comes from keeping the truly important information in the main clause (underlined) and subordinating the less important details:

Revised	Because production costs have dropped more slowly than prices, <u>computer manufacturers have struggled with shrinking profits</u>.

16.4.2 Subordinating effectively

Use subordination only for the less important information in a sentence.

Faulty	Ms. Angelo was in her first year of teaching, although she was a better instructor than others with many years of experience.

The preceding sentence suggests that Angelo's inexperience is the main idea, whereas the writer intended to stress her skill *despite* her inexperience. Reducing the inexperience to a subordinate clause and elevating the skill to the main clause (underlined) gives appropriate emphasis:

Revised	Although Ms. Angelo was in her first year of teaching, <u>she was a better instructor than others with many years of experience</u>.

Subordination loses its power to emphasize when too much loosely related detail crowds into one long, meandering sentence:

Overloaded	The boats that were moored at the dock when the hurricane, which was one of the worst in three decades, struck were ripped from their moorings, because the owners had not been adequately prepared, since the weather service had predicted that the storm would blow out to sea, which they do at this time of year.

The revision stresses important information in the main clauses (underlined):

Revised	Struck by one of the worst hurricanes in three decades, <u>the boats at the dock were ripped from their moorings</u>. <u>The owners were unprepared</u> because the weather service had said that hurricanes at this time of year blow out to sea.

Chapter 17
Parallelism

Learning Objectives

17.1 Define parallelism.
17.2 Use parallelism for equal elements.

17.1 Understanding Parallelism

17.1 Define parallelism.

Parallelism gives similar grammatical form to sentence elements that have similar function and importance.

> The air is dirtied by ‖ factories belching smoke
> and ‖ cars spewing exhaust.

In the preceding example the two underlined **phrases** have the same function and importance (both specify sources of air pollution), so they also have the same grammatical construction. Parallelism makes form follow meaning.

17.2 Equal Elements

17.2 Use parallelism for equal elements.

The **coordinating conjunctions** *and, but, or, nor,* and *yet* always signal a need for parallelism.

> The industrial base was shifting and shrinking. [Parallel words.]
>
> Politicians rarely acknowledged the problem or proposed alternatives. [Parallel phrases.]
>
> Industrial workers were understandably disturbed that they were losing their jobs but that no one seemed to care. [Parallel clauses.]

When sentence elements linked by coordinating conjunctions are not parallel in structure, the sentence is awkward and distracting:

> Nonparallel   The reasons steel companies kept losing money were that their plants were inefficient, high labor costs, and foreign competition was increasing.
>
> Revised   The reasons steel companies kept losing money were inefficient plants, high labor costs, and increasing foreign competition.

Nonparallel	Success was difficult even for efficient companies because of the shift away from all manufacturing in the United States and the fact that steel production was shifting toward emerging nations.
Revised	Success was difficult even for efficient companies because of the shift away from all manufacturing in the United States and toward steel production in emerging nations.

All the words required by idiom or grammar must be stated in **compound constructions**:

Faulty	Given training, workers can acquire the skills and interest in other jobs. [Idiom dictates different prepositions with *skills* and *interest*.]
Revised	Given training, workers can acquire the skills for and interest in other jobs.

17.2.1 Using parallelism with *both . . . and, not . . . but,* or another correlative conjunction

Correlative conjunctions stress equality and balance between elements. Parallelism confirms the equality.

> It is not a tax bill but a tax relief bill, providing relief not for the needy but for the greedy. —Franklin Delano Roosevelt

With correlative conjunctions, the element after the second connector must match the element after the first connector:

Nonparallel	Huck Finn learns not only that human beings have an enormous capacity for folly but also enormous dignity. [The first element includes *that human beings have;* the second element does not.]
Revised	Huck Finn learns that human beings have not only an enormous capacity for folly but also enormous dignity. [Repositioning *that human beings have* makes the two elements parallel.]

17.2.2 Using parallelism in comparisons

Parallelism confirms the likeness or difference between two elements being compared using *than* or *as*:

Nonparallel	Huck Finn proves less a bad boy than to be an independent spirit. In the end he is every bit as determined in rejecting help as he is to leave for "the territory."
Revised	Huck Finn proves less a bad boy than an independent spirit. In the end he is every bit as determined to reject help as he is to leave for "the territory."

17.2.3 Using parallelism with lists, headings, and outlines

The items in a list or outline are coordinate and should be parallel. Parallelism is essential in a formal topic outline and in the headings that divide a paper into sections.

Nonparallel	Revised
Changes in Renaissance England	Changes in Renaissance England
1. Extension of trade routes	1. Extension of trade routes
2. Merchant class became more powerful	2. Increased power of the merchant class
3. The death of feudalism	3. Death of feudalism
4. Upsurging of the arts	4. Upsurge of the arts
5. Religious quarrels began	5. Rise of religious quarrels

Chapter 18
Variety and Details

Learning Objectives

18.1 Vary sentence length and structure.
18.2 Create variety by adding details.

18.1 Sentence Length and Structure

18.1 Vary sentence length and structure.

Writing that's interesting as well as clear has at least two features: the sentences vary in length and structure, and they are well textured with details.

18.1.1 Varying sentence length

Sentences generally vary from about ten to about forty words. When sentences are all at one extreme or the other, readers may have difficulty focusing on main ideas and seeing the relationships among them.

- **Long sentences.** If most of your sentences contain thirty-five words or more, your main ideas may not stand out from the details that support them. Break some of the long sentences into shorter, simpler ones.
- **Short sentences.** If most of your sentences contain fewer than ten or fifteen words, all your ideas may seem equally important and the links between them may not be clear. Try combining sentences with coordination and subordination to show relationships and stress main ideas over supporting information.

18.1.2 Varying sentence structure

A passage will be monotonous if all its sentences follow the same pattern, like soldiers marching in a parade. Try the following techniques for varying structure.

Subordination

A string of **main clauses** can make all ideas seem equally important and be especially plodding.

Monotonous   The moon is now drifting away from the earth. It moves away at the rate of about one inch a year. This movement is lengthening our days. They increase a thousandth of a second every century. Forty-seven of our present days will someday make up a month. We might eventually lose the moon altogether. Such great planetary movement rightly concerns astronomers, but it need not worry us. It will take 50 million years.

Enliven such writing—and make the main ideas stand out—by expressing the less important information in **subordinate clauses** and **phrases**. In the revision below, underlining indicates subordinate structures that used to be main clauses:

Revised   The moon is now drifting away from the earth <u>about one inch a year</u>. <u>At a thousandth of a second every century</u>, this movement is lengthening our days. Forty-seven of our present days will someday make up a month, <u>if we don't eventually lose the moon altogether</u>. Such great planetary movement rightly concerns astronomers, but it need not worry us. It will take 50 million years.

Sentence combining

As the preceding example shows, subordinating to achieve variety often involves combining short, choppy sentences into longer units that link related information and stress main ideas. Here is another unvaried passage:

> **Monotonous** Astronomy may seem a remote science. It may seem to have little to do with people's daily lives. However, many astronomers find otherwise. They see their science as soothing. It gives perspective to everyday routines and problems.

Combining five sentences into one, the following revision is both clearer and easier to read. Underlining highlights the changes.

> **Revised** Astronomy may seem a remote science <u>having</u> little to do with people's daily lives, <u>but</u> many astronomers <u>find their science soothing because</u> it gives perspective to everyday routines and problems.

Varied sentence beginnings

An English sentence often begins with its **subject**, which generally captures old information from a preceding sentence:

> The defendant's <u>lawyer</u> was determined to break the prosecution's witness. <u>He</u> relentlessly cross-examined the stubborn witness for more than a week.

However, an unbroken sequence of sentences beginning with the subject quickly becomes monotonous:

> **Monotonous** The defendant's lawyer was determined to break the prosecution's witness. He relentlessly cross-examined the witness for more than a week. The witness had expected to be dismissed within an hour and was visibly irritated. She did not cooperate. She was reprimanded by the judge.

Beginning some of these sentences with other expressions improves readability and clarity:

> **Revised** The defendant's lawyer was determined to break the prosecution's witness. <u>For more than a week</u> he relentlessly cross-examined the witness. <u>Expecting to be dismissed within an hour</u>, the witness was visibly irritated. She did not cooperate. <u>Indeed</u>, she was reprimanded by the judge.

The underlined expressions represent the most common choices for varying sentence beginnings:

- **Adverb modifiers,** such as *For more than a week* (modifies the verb *cross-examined*).
- **Adjective modifiers,** such as *Expecting to be dismissed within an hour* (modifies *witness*).
- **Transitional expressions,** such as *Indeed*.

Culture and language

In standard American English, placing some negative adverb modifiers at the beginning of a sentence requires you to use the word order of a question, in which the verb or a part of it precedes the subject. These modifiers include *never, rarely, seldom,* and adverb phrases beginning with *no, not since,* and *not until.*

                                           verb
                    adverb   subject   phrase
Faulty   Seldom a witness has held the stand so long.

                         helping   main
                adverb   verb   subject   verb
Revised Seldom has a witness held the stand so long.

Varied word order

Occasionally you can vary a sentence and emphasize it at the same time by inverting the usual order of parts:

> A dozen witnesses testified for the prosecution, and the defense attorney barely questioned eleven of them. The twelfth, however, he grilled. [Normal word order: *He grilled the twelfth, however.*]

Inverted sentences used without need are artificial. Use them only when emphasis demands.

18.2 Details

18.2 Create variety by adding details.

Relevant details such as facts and examples create the texture and life that keep readers awake and helps them to grasp your meaning. For instance:

> **Flat**   Constructed after World War II, Levittown, New York, consisted of thousands of houses in two basic styles. Over the decades, residents have altered the houses so dramatically that the original styles are often unrecognizable.
>
> **Detailed**   Constructed on potato fields after World War II, Levittown, New York, consisted of more than seventeen thousand houses in Cape Cod and ranch styles. Over the decades, residents have added expansive front porches, punched dormer windows through roofs, converted garages to sun porches, and otherwise altered the houses so dramatically that the original styles are often unrecognizable.

The details in the revised passage are effective because they relate to the writer's point and make that point clearer. Details that don't support and clarify your point will likely distract or annoy readers.

Chapter 19
Appropriate and Exact Language

> **Learning Objectives**

19.1 Choose appropriate language.
19.2 Eliminate sexist and other biased language.
19.3 Choose exact language.

19.1 Standard English

19.1 **Choose appropriate language.**

Appropriate language suits your writing situation—your subject, purpose, and audience. In most college and career writing you should rely on what's called **standard American English**, the dialect of English normally expected and used in school, business, the professions, government, and the communications media.

The vocabulary of written standard English is huge, allowing you to express an infinite range of ideas and feelings. However, it does exclude words that are too imprecise for writing and that only some groups of people use, understand, or find inoffensive. The types of excluded words are discussed in this section. Whenever you doubt a word's status, consult a dictionary. A label such as *nonstandard, slang,* or *colloquial* tells you that the word is not generally appropriate in academic or business writing.

Remember that language is in a state of constant change; social media and many community and workplace settings now employ fast-paced, casual forms of written English. Study the conventions of the medium in which you are writing and adjust your language to match the expectations of your audience.

> **Culture and language**
>
> Like many countries, the United States includes scores of regional, social, and ethnic groups with their own distinct **dialects**, or versions of English. Standard American English is one of those dialects, and so are African American Vernacular English, Appalachian English, Creole, and the English of coastal Maine. All the dialects of English share many features, but each also has its own vocabulary, pronunciation, and grammar.

If you speak a dialect other than standard English, you are probably already adept at moving between your dialect and standard English in speech and writing. Dialects are not wrong in themselves, but forms imported from one dialect into another may still be perceived as unclear or incorrect. When standard English is expected, such as in academic and public writing, edit your work to revise expressions that you know (or have been told) differ from standard English. These expressions may include *theirselves, hisn, them books,* and others labeled *nonstandard* by a dictionary.

Your participation in the community of standard English does not require you to abandon your own dialect. You may want to use it in writing you do for yourself, such as journals, notes, and drafts, which should be composed as freely as possible. You may want to quote it in an academic paper, as when analyzing or reporting conversation in dialect. And, of course, you will want to use it with others who speak it.

19.1.1 Shortcuts of texting and other electronic communication

Rapid communication by e-mail and text or instant messaging encourages some informalities that are inappropriate for academic writing. If you use these media frequently, you may need to proofread your academic papers especially to identify and revise errors such as the following:

- **Sentence fragments.** Make sure every sentence has a subject and a predicate.

  Not Observed the results.
  But Researchers observed the results.

- **Missing punctuation.** Between and within sentences, use standard punctuation marks. Check especially for missing commas within sentences and missing apostrophes in possessives and contractions.

  Not The dogs bony ribs visible through its fur were evidence of neglect.
  But The dog's bony ribs, visible through its fur, were evidence of neglect.

- **Missing capital letters.** Use capital letters at the beginnings of sentences, for proper nouns and adjectives, and in titles.

  Not scholars have written about abraham lincoln more than any other american.
  But Scholars have written about Abraham Lincoln more than any other American.

- **Nonstandard abbreviations and spellings.** Write out most words, avoiding forms such as *2* for *to* or *too, b4* for *before, bc* for *because, ur* for *you are* or *you're,* and + or & for *and.*

Not	Students + tutors need to meet b4 the third week of the semester.
But	Students and tutors need to meet before the third week of the semester.

19.1.2 Slang

Slang is the language used by a group, such as musicians or computer programmers, to reflect common experiences and to make technical references efficient. The following example is from an essay on the slang of "skaters" (skateboarders):

> Curtis slashed ultra-punk crunchers on his longboard, while the Rube-man flailed his usual Gumbyness on tweaked frontsides and lofty fakie ollies.
> —Miles Orkin, "Mucho Slingage by the Pool"

Among those who understand it, slang may be vivid and forceful. It often occurs in dialog, and an occasional slang expression can enliven an informal essay. But most slang is too flippant and imprecise for effective communication, and it is generally inappropriate for college or business writing:

Slang	Many students start out pretty together but then get weird.
Revised	Many students start out with clear goals but then lose their direction.

19.1.3 Colloquial language

Colloquial language is the everyday spoken language, including expressions such as *chill out, go nuts,* and *get off on.*

When you write informally, colloquial language may be appropriate to achieve the casual, relaxed effect of conversation. But colloquial language generally is not precise enough for college, public, and professional writing. In these more formal writing situations, avoid any words and expressions labeled *informal* or *colloquial* in your dictionary.

Colloquial	According to a Native American myth, the Great Creator had a dog hanging around with him when he created the earth.
Revised	According to a Native American myth, the Great Creator was accompanied by a dog when he created the earth.

19.1.4 Technical words and jargon

All disciplines and professions rely on specialized language that allows the members to communicate precisely and efficiently with each other. Chemists, for instance, have their *phosphatides,* and literary critics have their *motifs* and *subtexts*. Without explanation, technical words are meaningless to nonspecialists. When you are writing for nonspecialists, avoid unnecessary technical terms and carefully define terms you must use.

19.1.5 Indirect and pretentious writing

In most writing, small, plain, and direct words are preferable to evasive or showy words.

- **Euphemisms** are presumably inoffensive words that substitute for words deemed potentially offensive or too direct, such as *passed away* for "died." Euphemisms can soften the truth, but they are appropriate only when blunt, truthful words would needlessly hurt or offend your audience.
- **Double talk** (also called *doublespeak* or *weasel words*) is language intended to confuse or be misunderstood. It is unfortunately common in politics and advertising—the *revenue enhancement* that is really a tax, for example. Double talk has no place in honest writing.
- **Pretentious writing** is excessively showy. Such writing is more fancy than its subject requires. Choose your words for their exactness and economy. The big, ornate word may be tempting, but pass it up. Your readers will be grateful.

Pretentious   Hardly a day goes by without a new revelation about the devastation of the natural world, and to a significant extent our dependence on the internal combustion engine is the culprit. Respected scientific minds coalesce around the argument that carbon dioxide emissions, such as those from automobiles imbibing gasoline, are responsible for a gradual escalation in temperatures on the planet earth.

Revised   Much of the frequent bad news about the environment can be blamed on the internal combustion engine. Respected scientists argue that carbon dioxide emissions, such as those from gas-powered cars, are warming the earth.

19.2 Sexist and Biased Language

19.2   Eliminate sexist and other biased language.

Even when we do not mean it to, our language can reflect and perpetuate hurtful prejudices toward groups of people, especially racial, ethnic, religious, age, and sexual groups. Such biased language can be obvious; we all recognize words that are intended to be hurtful and dismissive of others. But it can also be subtle, generalizing about groups in ways that may be familiar but that are also inaccurate or unfair. For instance, people with physical disabilities are as varied a group as any other: the only thing they have in common is some form of physical impairment. To assume that people with disabilities share certain attitudes (shyness, helplessness, victimization) is to disregard the uniqueness of each person.

Biased language reflects poorly on the user, not on the person or persons whom it mischaracterizes or insults. Unbiased language does not submit to false generalizations. It treats people as individuals and labels groups as they wish to be labeled.

19.2.1 Stereotypes of race, ethnicity, religion, age, and other characteristics

A **stereotype** is a generalization based on poor evidence, a kind of formula for understanding and judging people simply because of their membership in a group:

> Men are uncommunicative.
> Women are emotional.
> Liberals want to raise taxes.
> Conservatives are affluent.

At best, stereotypes betray a noncritical writer, one who is not thinking beyond notions received from others. In your writing, be alert for statements that characterize whole groups of people:

Stereotype	Elderly drivers should have their licenses limited to daytime driving only. [Asserts that all elderly people are poor night drivers.]
Revised	Drivers with impaired night vision should have their licenses limited to daytime driving only.

Some stereotypes have become part of the language, but they are still potentially offensive:

Stereotype	The administrators are too blind to see the need for a new gymnasium. [Equates vision loss and lack of understanding.]
Revised	The administrators do not understand the need for a new gymnasium.

19.2.2 Sexist language

Among the most subtle and persistent biased language is that expressing narrow ideas about men's and women's roles, position, and value in society. Like other stereotypes, this **sexist language** can wound or irritate readers, and it indicates the writer's thoughtlessness or unfairness.

Eliminating sexist language

- **Avoid demeaning and patronizing language:**

  Sexist   Dr. Keith Kim and Lydia Hawkins coauthored the article.
  Revised   Dr. Keith Kim and Dr. Lydia Hawkins coauthored the article.
  Revised   Keith Kim and Lydia Hawkins coauthored the article.

  Sexist   Ladies are entering almost every occupation formerly filled by men.
  Revised   Women are entering almost every occupation formerly filled by men.

- **Avoid occupational or social stereotypes:**

  Sexist   The considerate doctor commends a nurse when she provides his patients with good care.
  Revised   The considerate doctor commends a nurse who provides good care for patients.

  Sexist   The grocery shopper should save her coupons.
  Revised   Grocery shoppers should save their coupons.

- **Avoid referring needlessly to gender:**

  Sexist   Marie Curie, a woman chemist, discovered radium.
  Revised   Marie Curie, a chemist, discovered radium.

  Sexist   The patients were tended by a male nurse.
  Revised   The patients were tended by a nurse.

  However, don't overcorrect by avoiding appropriate references to gender: *Pregnant women* [not *people*] *should avoid drinking alcohol.*

- **Avoid using *man* or words containing *man* to refer to all human beings.** Here are a few alternatives:

businessman	businessperson
chairman	chair, chairperson
congressman	congressperson, legislator
craftsman	craftsperson, artisan
layman	layperson
mailman	letter carrier, mail carrier
mankind	humankind, humanity, human beings, humans
manmade	handmade, manufactured, synthetic, artificial
manpower	personnel, human resources
policeman	police officer
salesman	salesperson

  Sexist   Man has not reached the limits of social justice.
  Revised   Humankind [or Humanity] has not reached the limits of social justice.

  Sexist   The furniture consists of manmade materials.
  Revised   The furniture consists of synthetic materials.

  (continued)

Eliminating sexist language

(continued)

- **Avoid the generic *he*,** the male pronoun used to refer to both genders.

Sexist	The newborn child explores his world.
Revised	Newborn children explore their world. [Use the plural for the pronoun and the word it refers to.]
Revised	The newborn child explores the world. [Avoid the pronoun altogether.]
Revised	The newborn child explores his or her world. [Substitute male and female pronouns.]

  Use the last option sparingly—only once in a group of sentences and only to stress the singular individual.

- **Use singular *they* when that is the preferred choice of a gender-nonconforming person.**

  They as a singular pronoun is now commonly accepted as a pronoun of choice for individuals who do not identify as specifically male or female.

Culture and language

Forms of address vary widely from culture to culture. In some cultures, for instance, one shows respect by referring to all older women as if they were married, using the equivalent of *Mrs.* Usage in the United States is changing toward making no assumptions about marital status, rank, or other characteristics—for instance, addressing a woman as *Ms.* unless she is known to prefer *Mrs.* or *Miss.*

19.2.3 Appropriate labels

We often need to label groups: *swimmers, politicians, mothers, Christians, Westerners, students.* But labels can be shorthand stereotypes, slighting the person labeled and ignoring the preferences of the group members themselves. Although sometimes dismissed as "political correctness," showing sensitivity about labels hurts no one and helps gain your readers' trust and respect.

- **Avoid labels that (intentionally or not) insult the person or group you refer to.** A person with emotional problems is not a *mental patient.* A person with cancer is not a *cancer victim.* A person using a wheelchair is not *wheelchair-bound.*
- **Use names for racial, ethnic, and other groups that reflect the preferences of each group's members,** or at least of many of them. Examples of current preferences include *African American* or *black* and *people with disabilities* (rather than *the disabled* or *the*

handicapped). But labels change often. To learn how a group's members wish to be labeled, ask them directly, attend to usage in reputable periodicals, or check a recent dictionary.

- **Identify a person's group only when it is relevant to the point you're making.** Consider the context of the label: Is it a necessary piece of information? If not, don't use it.

19.3 Exact Language

19.3 Choose exact language.

To write clearly and effectively, you will want to find the words that fit your meaning exactly and convey your attitude precisely.

19.3.1 Word meanings and synonyms

For writing exactly, a dictionary is essential and a thesaurus can be helpful.

Dictionaries

A dictionary defines words and provides pronunciation, grammatical functions, etymology (word history), and other information. The sample in Figure 19.1 is from the print version of *Merriam-Webster's Collegiate Dictionary*.

Besides *Merriam-Webster,* other good print dictionaries include *American Heritage College Dictionary, Random House Webster's College Dictionary,* and *Webster's New World College Dictionary*.

Most dictionary publishers offer online dictionaries that give the same information in less abbreviated form and also allow you to hear how a word is pronounced. Figure 19.2 shows part of the entry for *reckon* from *Merriam-Webster Online*.

Figure 19.1 Print dictionary entry

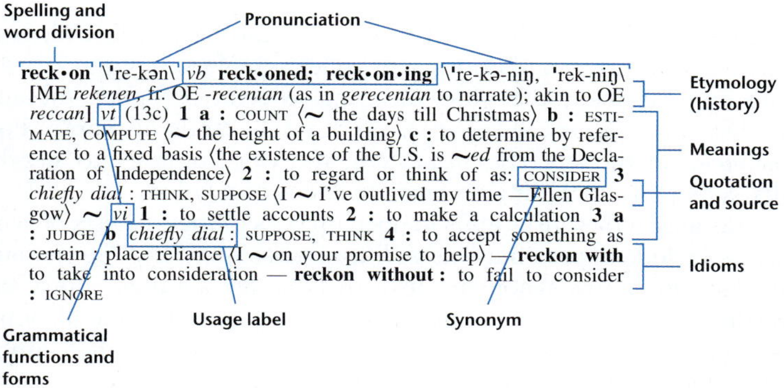

Spelling and word division — reck•on
Pronunciation — \'re-kən\
Grammatical functions and forms — *vb* reck•oned; reck•on•ing \'re-kə-niŋ, 'rek-niŋ\
Etymology (history) — [ME *rekenen*, fr. OE *-recenian* (as in *gerecenian* to narrate); akin to OE *reccan*] *vt* (13c)
Meanings — 1 a : COUNT ⟨~ the days till Christmas⟩ b : ESTIMATE, COMPUTE ⟨~ the height of a building⟩ c : to determine by reference to a fixed basis ⟨the existence of the U.S. is ~ed from the Declaration of Independence⟩ 2 : to regard or think of as: **Synonym** CONSIDER 3 **Usage label** *chiefly dial* : THINK, SUPPOSE ⟨I ~ I've outlived my time — **Quotation and source** Ellen Glasgow⟩ ~ *vi* 1 : to settle accounts 2 : to make a calculation 3 a : JUDGE b *chiefly dial* : SUPPOSE, THINK 4 : to accept something as certain : place reliance ⟨I ~ on your promise to help⟩ — **Idioms** **reckon with** to take into consideration — **reckon without** : to fail to consider : IGNORE

Figure 19.2 Partial online dictionary entry

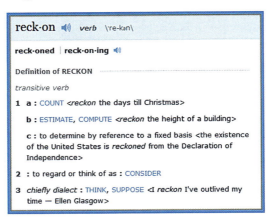

Other useful online resources are *Dictionary.com* and *The Free Dictionary*, which provide entries from several dictionaries at once.

exact 19.3 Culture and language

If English is not your native language, you probably should have a dictionary prepared especially for students using English as a second language (ESL). Such a dictionary contains special information on prepositions, count versus noncount nouns (22.1), and many other matters. The following are reliable print ESL dictionaries, each with an online version: *Longman Dictionary of Contemporary English, Oxford Advanced Learner's Dictionary,* and *Merriam-Webster Advanced Learner's English Dictionary*.

Thesauruses

To find a word with the exact shade of meaning you intend, you may want to consult a thesaurus, or collection of **synonyms**—words with approximately the same meaning. A print or online thesaurus lists most imaginable synonyms for thousands of words. For instance, on the site *Thesaurus.com,* the word *reckon* has nearly fifty synonyms, including *account, evaluate,* and *judge*.

Because a thesaurus aims to open up possibilities, its lists of synonyms include approximate as well as precise matches. The thesaurus does not define synonyms or distinguish among them, however, so you need a dictionary to discover exact meanings. In general, don't use a word from a thesaurus—even one you like the sound of—until you are sure of its appropriateness for your meaning.

Spelling checkers

Before you select a word suggested by a spelling checker, make sure it's the one you mean.

Incorrect   The results were defiant: the experiment was a failure.
Revised   The results were definite: the experiment was a failure.

In addition to tools for checking spelling, most word-processing software today includes an integrated dictionary, thesaurus, and Web search tools. In *Microsoft Word*, for example, you can highlight a specific word and use Smart Lookup to access online dictionary and research sources related to that word. If you are unsure about the meaning or use of a word, these digital tools provide a quick reference to help you make decisions about word choice.

19.3.2 The right word for your meaning

All words have one or more basic meanings, called **denotations**—the meanings listed in the dictionary, without reference to emotional associations. If readers are to understand you, you must use words according to their established meanings.

- Consult a dictionary whenever you are unsure of a word's meaning.
- Distinguish between similar-sounding words that have widely different denotations:

    Inexact   Older people often suffer infirmaries [places for the sick].
    Exact   Older people often suffer infirmities [disabilities].

    Some words, called **homonyms**, sound exactly alike but differ in meaning: for example, *principal/principle* and *rain/reign/rein*.

- Distinguish between words with related but distinct meanings:

    Inexact   Television commercials continuously [unceasingly] interrupt programming.
    Exact   Television commercials continually [regularly] interrupt programming.

In addition to their emotion-free meanings, many words carry related meanings that evoke specific feelings. These **connotations** can shape readers' responses and are thus a powerful tool for writers. The following word pairs have related denotations but very different connotations:

pride: sense of self-worth
vanity: excessive regard for oneself

firm: steady, unchanging, unyielding
stubborn: unreasonable, bullheaded

enthusiasm: excitement
mania: excessive interest or desire

A dictionary can help you track down words with the exact connotations you want. Besides providing meanings, your dictionary may also list and distinguish synonyms to guide your choices. A thesaurus can also help if you use it carefully.

19.3.3 Concrete and specific words

Clear, exact writing balances abstract and general words, which outline ideas and objects, with concrete and specific words, which sharpen and solidify.

- **Abstract words** name ideas: *beauty, inflation, management, culture, liberal.* **Concrete words** name qualities and things we can know by our five senses, sight, hearing, touch, taste, and smell: *sleek, humming, rough, salty, musty.*
- **General words** name classes or groups of things, such as *birds, weather,* and *buildings,* and include all the varieties of the class. **Specific words** limit a general class, such as *buildings,* by naming a variety, such as *skyscraper, Victorian courthouse,* or *hut.*

Abstract and general words are useful in the broad statements that set the course for your writing.

> The wild horse in America has a romantic history.
>
> Relationships between the sexes today are more relaxed than they were in the past.

But such statements need development with concrete and specific detail. Detail can turn a vague sentence into an exact one:

> Vague   The workspace was well designed and encouraged collaboration. [How was this visible? What about it encouraged collaboration?]
>
> Exact   The workspace had a large central room with desks clustered in four groups, surrounded by three smaller conference rooms designed for group meetings.

You can use your computer's Find function to help you find and revise abstract and general words that you tend to overuse. Examples of such words include *nice, interesting, things, very, good, a lot, a little,* and *some.*

19.3.4 Idioms with prepositions

Idioms are expressions in any language that do not fit the rules for meaning or grammar—for instance, *put up with, plug away at, make off with.*

Idioms that involve prepositions can be especially confusing for both native and nonnative speakers of English.

Idioms with prepositions

abide by a rule
    in a place or state
according to
accords with
accuse of a crime
accustomed to
adapt from a source
    to a situation
afraid of
agree on a plan as a group
    to someone else's plan
    with a person
angry with
aware of
based on
belong in or on a place
    to a group
capable of
certain of
charge for a purchase
    with a crime
concur in an opinion
    with a person
contend for a principle
    with a person
dependent on
differ about or over a question
    from in some quality
    with a person
disappointed by or in a person
        in or with a thing
familiar with

identical with or to
impatient for a raise
    with a person
independent of
infer from
inferior to
involved in a task
    with a person
oblivious of or to surroundings
    of something forgotten
occupied by a person
    in study
    with a thing
opposed to
part from a person
    with a possession
prior to
proud of
related to
rewarded by the judge
    for something done
    with a gift
similar to
sorry about an error
    for a person
superior to
wait at, beside, by, under a place or thing
    for a train, a person
    in a room
    on a customer

Culture and language

If you are learning standard American English, you may find its prepositions difficult; their meanings can shift depending on context, and they have many idiomatic uses. In mastering the prepositions of standard English, you probably can't avoid memorization. But you can help yourself by memorizing related groups, such as *at/in/on* and *for/since*.

At, *in*, or *on* in expressions of time

- Use *at* before actual clock time: *at* 8:30.
- Use *in* before a month, year, century, or period: *in* April, *in* 2018, *in* the twenty-first century, *in* the next month.
- Use *on* before a day or date: *on* Tuesday, *on* August 3, *on* Labor Day.

(continued)

Culture and language

(continued)

At, in, or *on* in expressions of place

- **Use *at* before a specific place or address:** <u>at</u> the school, <u>at</u> 511 Iris Street.
- **Use *in* before a place with limits or before a city, state, country, or continent:** <u>in</u> the house, <u>in</u> a box, <u>in</u> Oklahoma City, <u>in</u> Ohio, <u>in</u> China, <u>in</u> Asia.
- **Use *on* to mean "supported by" or "touching the surface of":** <u>on</u> the table, <u>on</u> Iris Street, <u>on</u> page 150.

For or *since* in expressions of time

- **Use *for* before a period of time:** <u>for</u> an hour, <u>for</u> two years.
- **Use *since* before a specific point in time:** <u>since</u> 1999, <u>since</u> Friday.

A dictionary of English as a second language is the best source for the meanings of prepositions.

19.3.5 Figurative language

Figurative language (or a **figure of speech**) departs from the literal meanings of words, usually by comparing very different ideas or objects:

| Literal | As I try to write, I can think of nothing to say. |
| Figurative | As I try to write, <u>my mind is a slab of black slate</u>. |

Imaginatively and carefully used, figurative language can capture meaning more precisely and emotionally than literal language. Here is a figure of speech at work in technical writing (paraphrasing the physicist Edward Andrade):

> The molecules in a liquid move continuously like couples on an overcrowded dance floor, jostling each other.

The two most common figures of speech are the simile and the metaphor. Both compare two things of different classes, often one abstract and the other concrete.

- **A *simile* makes the comparison explicit and usually begins with *like* or *as*:**

> Whenever we grow, we tend to feel it, <u>as</u> a young seed must feel the weight and inertia of the earth when it seeks to break out of its shell on its way to becoming a plant.

- **A *metaphor* claims that the two things are identical, omitting such words as *like* and *as*:**

> A school is a hopper into which children are heaved while they are young and tender; therein they are pressed into certain standard shapes and covered from head to heels with official rubber stamps.

To be successful, figurative language must be not only fresh but also unstrained, calling attention not to itself but to the writer's meaning. Be especially wary of mixed metaphors, which combine two or more incompatible figures:

Mixed Various thorny problems that we try to sweep under the rug continue to bob up all the same.

Improved Various thorny problems that we try to weed out continue to thrive all the same.

19.3.6 Trite expressions

Trite expressions, or **clichés**, are phrases so old and so often repeated that they have become stale. They include the following:

- acid test
- add insult to injury
- better late than never
- cold, hard facts
- crushing blow
- easier said than done
- face the music
- few and far between
- flat as a pancake
- green with envy
- hard as a rock
- heavy as lead
- hit the nail on the head
- hour of need
- ladder of success
- moving experience
- needle in a haystack
- point with pride
- pride and joy
- ripe old age
- rude awakening
- shoulder the burden
- shoulder to cry on
- sneaking suspicion
- sober as a judge
- stand in awe
- strong as an ox
- thin as a rail
- tired but happy
- tried and true
- untimely death
- wise as an owl

To edit clichés, listen to your writing for any expressions that you have heard or used before. You can also supplement your efforts with a style checker available on your computer or online, which may also include a cliché detector. When you find a cliché, substitute fresh words of your own or restate the idea in plain language.

Chapter 20
Completeness

Learning Objectives

20.1 Write complete compounds.
20.2 Revise incomplete sentences by adding needed words.

20.1 Compounds

20.1 Write complete compounds.

Sentences are incomplete when they omit one or more words needed for clarity.

You may omit words from a **compound construction** when the omission will not confuse readers, as in the following examples:

> Environmentalists have hopes for alternative fuels and [for] public transportation.
> Some cars will run on electricity and some [will run] on hydrogen.

Such omissions are possible only when the words omitted are common to all the parts of a compound construction. When the parts differ in any way, all words must be included in all parts.

> One new car gets eighty miles per gallon; some old cars get as little as five miles per gallon. [One verb is singular, the other plural.]
> Environmentalists believe in and work for fuel conservation. [Idiom requires different prepositions with *believe* and *work*.]

20.2 Adding Needed Words

20.2 Revise incomplete sentences by adding needed words.

In haste or carelessness, do not omit small words that are needed for clarity:

> **Incomplete** Regular payroll deductions are a type painless savings. You hardly notice missing amounts, and after period of years the contributions can add a large total.
>
> **Revised** Regular payroll deductions are a type of painless savings. You hardly notice the missing amounts, and after a period of years the contributions can add up to a large total.

Attentive proofreading is the only insurance against this kind of omission. *Proofread all your papers carefully.*

Culture and language

If your native language or dialect is not standard American English, you may have difficulty knowing when to use the English articles *a, an,* and *the*. For guidelines, see 34.5.

Chapter 21
Conciseness

  Learning Objectives

21.1 Focus on subjects and verbs to revise for conciseness.
21.2 Eliminate empty words.
21.3 Eliminate unnecessary repetition.
21.4 Use other strategies to achieve conciseness.

21.1 Subjects and Verbs

21.1 Focus on subjects and verbs to revise for conciseness.

Concise writing makes every word count. Conciseness is not the same as mere brevity: detail and originality should not be cut along with needless words. Rather, the length of an expression should be appropriate to the thought.

You may find yourself writing wordily when you are unsure of your subject or when your thoughts are tangled. It's fine, even necessary, to grope while drafting. But you should straighten out your ideas and eliminate wordiness during revision and editing.

Culture and language

Wordiness is not a problem of incorrect grammar. A sentence may be perfectly grammatical but still contain unneeded words that make it unclear or awkward.

Using the **subjects** and **verbs** of your sentences for the key actors and actions will reduce words and emphasize important ideas.

Wordy The reason why most of the country shifts to daylight time is that summer days are much longer than winter days.

Concise Most of the country shifts to daylight time because summer days are much longer than winter days.

Focusing on subjects and verbs will also help you avoid several other causes of wordiness:

Nouns made from verbs

Wordy The occurrence of the shortest day of the year is about December 22.

Concise The shortest day of the year occurs about December 22.

Ways to achieve conciseness

Wordy (87 words)

The highly pressured nature of critical-care nursing is due to the fact that the patients have life-threatening illnesses. Critical-care nurses must have possession of steady nerves to care for patients who are critically ill and very sick. The nurses must also have possession of interpersonal skills. They must also have medical skills. It is considered by most health-care professionals that these nurses are essential if there is to be improvement of patients who are now in critical care from that status to the status of intermediate care.

- Focus on subject and verb, and cut or shorten empty words and phrases.
- Avoid nouns made from verbs.
- Cut unneeded repetition.
- Combine sentences.
- Change passive voice to active voice.
- Revise *there is* constructions.
- Cut unneeded repetition, and tighten modifiers.

Concise (37 words)

Critical-care nursing is highly pressured because the patients have life-threatening illnesses. Critical-care nurses must possess steady nerves and interpersonal and medical skills. Most health-care professionals consider these nurses essential if patients are to improve to intermediate care.

Weak verbs

Wordy The earth's axis has a tilt as the planet is in orbit around the sun so that the northern and southern hemispheres are alternately in alignment toward the sun.

Concise The earth's axis tilts as the planet orbits the sun so that the northern and southern hemispheres alternately align toward the sun.

Passive voice

Wordy During its winter the northern hemisphere is tilted farthest away from the sun, so the nights are made longer and the days are made shorter.

Concise During its winter the northern hemisphere tilts away from the sun, which makes the nights longer and the days shorter.

21.2 Empty Words

21.2 Eliminate empty words.

Empty words walk in place, gaining little or nothing in meaning. Many can be cut entirely. The following are just a few examples:

all things considered	in a manner of speaking
as far as I'm concerned	in my opinion
for all intents and purposes	last but not least
for the most part	more or less

Other empty words can also be cut, usually along with some of the words around them:

area	element	kind	situation
aspect	factor	manner	thing
case	field	nature	type

Still others can be reduced from several words to a single word:

For	Substitute
at all times	always
at the present time	now, yet
because of the fact that	because
due to the fact that	because
for the purpose of	for
in the event that	if
in the final analysis	finally

Cutting or reducing such words and phrases will make your writing move faster and work harder:

> **Wordy** In my opinion, the council's proposal to improve the nature of the city center is inadequate for the reason that it ignores pedestrians.
>
> **Concise** The council's proposal to improve the city center is inadequate because it ignores pedestrians.

21.3 Unnecessary Repetition

21.3 Eliminate unnecessary repetition.

Unnecessary repetition weakens sentences:

> **Wordy** Many unskilled workers without training in a particular job are unemployed and do not have any work.
>
> **Concise** Many unskilled workers are unemployed.

Be especially alert to phrases that say the same thing twice. In the examples below, the unneeded words are underlined:

circle around
consensus of opinion
cooperate together
final completion
frank and honest exchange
the future to come

important [basic] essentials
puzzling in nature
repeat again
return again
square [round] in shape
surrounding circumstances

Culture and language

The preceding phrases are redundant because the main word already implies the underlined word or words. A dictionary will tell you what meanings a word implies. *Assassinate,* for instance, means "murder someone well known," so the following sentence is redundant: *Julius Caesar was assassinated and killed.*

21.4 Other Strategies

21.4 Use other strategies to achieve conciseness.

21.4.1 Tightening modifiers

Modifiers can be expanded or contracted depending on the emphasis you want to achieve. When editing your sentences, consider whether any modifiers can be tightened without loss of emphasis or clarity.

Wordy	The weight-loss industry faces new competition from lipolysis, which is a cosmetic procedure that is relatively noninvasive.
Concise	The weight-loss industry faces new competition from lipolysis, a relatively noninvasive cosmetic procedure.

21.4.2 Revising *there is* and *it is* constructions

You can postpone the sentence subject with the words *there* and *it*: *There are three points made in the text. It was not fair that only seniors could vote.* These **expletive constructions** can be useful to emphasize the subject (as when introducing it for the first time) or to indicate a change in direction. But often they just add words and weaken sentences:

Wordy	There is a completely noninvasive laser treatment that makes people thinner by rupturing fat cells and releasing the fat into the spaces between cells. It is the expectation of some doctors that the procedure will replace liposuction.
Concise	A completely noninvasive laser treatment makes people thinner by rupturing fat cells and releasing the fat into the spaces between cells. Some doctors expect that the procedure will replace liposuction.

Culture and language

When you must use an expletive construction, be careful to include *there* or *it*. Only commands and some questions can begin with verbs.

21.4.3 Combining sentences

Often the information in two or more sentences can be combined into one tight sentence.

Wordy	People who receive fat-releasing laser treatments can lose inches from their waists. They can also lose inches from their hips and thighs. They do not lose weight. The released fat remains in their bodies.
Concise	People who receive fat-releasing laser treatments can lose inches from their waists, hips, and thighs; but they do not lose weight because the released fat remains in their bodies.

21.4.4 Rewriting jargon

Jargon can refer to the special vocabulary of any discipline or profession. But it has also come to describe vague, inflated language that is overcomplicated, even incomprehensible. When it comes from government or business, we call it bureaucratese.

Jargon The necessity for individuals to become separate entities in their own right may impel children to engage in open rebelliousness against parental authority or against sibling influence, with resultant bewilderment of those being rebelled against.

Translation Children's natural desire to become themselves may make them rebel against bewildered parents or siblings.

Part 4

Sentence Parts and Patterns

Basic Grammar *229*

Verbs *246*

Pronouns *272*

Modifiers *284*

Sentence Faults *297*

Part 4
Sentence Parts and Patterns

Basic Grammar

22 Parts of Speech *229*
  22.1 Nouns, pronouns, and verbs *230*
  22.2 Adjectives and adverbs *232*
  22.3 Prepositions, conjunctions, and interjections *233*

23 The Sentence *235*
  23.1 Subjects and predicates *235*
  23.2 Sentence patterns *237*

24 Phrases and Subordinate Clauses *240*
  24.1 Phrases *241*
  24.2 Subordinate clauses *243*

25 Sentence Types *244*
  25.1 Types of sentences *244*

Verbs

26 Forms *246*
  26.1 Verb forms *246*
  26.2 Easily confused verb forms *248*
  26.3 Verb endings *249*
  26.4 Helping verbs *250*
  26.5 Verbs with gerunds and infinitives *254*
  26.6 Verbs with particles *255*

27 Tenses *257*
  27.1 Verb tenses *257*
  27.2 Sequence of tenses *260*

28 Mood *262*
  28.1 Subjunctive mood *262*
  28.2 Consistency *263*

29 Voice *264*
  29.1 Active and passive voice *264*
  29.2 Consistency *266*

30 Agreement of Subject and Verb *266*
  30.1 Subject-verb agreement *266*
  30.2 Unusual word order *268*
  30.3 Subjects joined by conjunctions *269*
  30.4 Indefinite and relative pronouns *269*
  30.5 Collective and plural nouns *270*

Pronouns

31 Case *272*
  31.1 Subjective, objective, and possessive cases *272*
  31.2 Compound subjects and objects *273*
  31.3 *Who* or *whom* *274*
  31.4 Common questions about case *276*

32 Agreement of Pronoun and Antecedent *277*
  32.1 Agreement in person, number, and gender *277*
  32.2 Antecedents with *and, or,* or *nor* *278*
  32.3 Indefinite pronouns *279*
  32.4 Collective nouns *280*

33 Reference of Pronoun to Antecedent *281*
  33.1 Clear reference *281*
  33.2 Specific reference *282*
  33.3 Appropriate *you* *283*

Modifiers

34 Adjectives and Adverbs *284*
  34.1 Functions of adjectives and adverbs *284*
  34.2 Comparative and superlative forms *286*
  34.3 Double negatives *288*
  34.4 Participles as adjectives *288*
  34.5 Determiners *289*

35 Misplaced and Dangling Modifiers *292*
  35.1 Misplaced modifiers *293*
  35.2 Dangling modifiers *296*

Sentence Faults

36 Sentence Fragments *297*
  36.1 Identifying fragments *297*
  36.2 Correcting fragments *300*
  36.3 Acceptable fragments *301*

37 Comma Splices and Fused Sentences *301*
  37.1 Identifying comma splices and fused sentences *301*
  37.2 Correcting comma splices and fused sentences *303*

38 Mixed Sentences *305*
  38.1 Mixed meaning *305*
  38.2 Mixed grammar *306*
  38.3 Repeated elements *307*

Chapter 22
Parts of Speech

 Learning Objectives

22.1 Identify nouns, pronouns, and verbs.
22.2 Identify adjectives and adverbs.
22.3 Identify prepositions, conjunctions, and interjections.

22.1 Nouns, Pronouns, and Verbs

22.1 Identify nouns, pronouns, and verbs.

22.1.1 Recognizing nouns

Nouns name. They may name a person (*Lupita Nyong'o, Chadwick Boseman, actor*), a thing (*chair, book, Mt. Rainier*), a quality (*pain, mystery, simplicity*), a place (*city, Washington, ocean, Red Sea*), or an idea (*reality, peace, success*).

The forms of nouns depend partly on where they fit in certain groups. As the following examples indicate, the same noun may appear in more than one group:

- A *common noun* names a general class of things and does not begin with a capital letter: *earthquake, citizen, earth, fortitude, army.*
- A *proper noun* names a specific person, place, or thing and begins with a capital letter: *Saoirse Ronan, El Paso, Washington Monument, US Congress.*
- A *count noun* names a thing considered countable in English. Most count nouns add *-s* or *-es* to distinguish between singular (one) and plural (more than one): *citizen, citizens; city, cities*. Some count nouns form irregular plurals: *woman, women; child, children.*
- A *noncount noun* names things or qualities that aren't considered countable in English: *earth, sugar, chaos, fortitude*. Noncount nouns do not form plurals.
- A *collective noun* is singular in form but names a group: *army, family, herd, US Congress.*

In addition, most nouns form the **possessive** by adding *-'s* to show ownership (*Nadia's books, citizen's rights*), source (*Auden's poems*), and some other relationships.

22.1.2 Recognizing pronouns

Most **pronouns** substitute for nouns and function in sentences as nouns do: *Susanne Ling enlisted in the Air Force when she graduated.*

Pronouns fall into groups depending on their form or function:

- A *personal pronoun* refers to a specific individual or to individuals: *I, you, he, she, it, we,* and *they.*
- An *indefinite pronoun* does not refer to a specific noun: *anyone, everything, no one, somebody,* and so on. *No one came. Nothing moves. Everybody speaks.*
- A *relative pronoun* relates a group of words to a noun or another pronoun: *who, whoever, which, that. Everyone who attended received a prize. The book that won is a novel.*
- An *interrogative pronoun* introduces a question: *who, whom, whose, which, what. What song is that? Who will contribute?*

- A *demonstrative pronoun* identifies or points to a noun: *this, these, that, those,* and so on. <u>Those</u> berries are ripe. <u>This</u> is the site.
- An *intensive pronoun* emphasizes a noun or another pronoun: *myself, himself, itself, themselves,* and so on. *I <u>myself</u> asked that question. The price <u>itself</u> is in doubt.*
- A *reflexive pronoun* indicates that the sentence subject also receives the action of the verb: *myself, himself, itself, themselves,* and so on. *He perjured <u>himself</u>. They injured <u>themselves</u>.*

The personal pronouns *I, he, she, we,* and *they* and the relative pronouns *who* and *whoever* change form depending on their function in the sentence.

22.1.3 Recognizing verbs

Verbs express an action (*bring, change, grow, consider*), an occurrence (*become, happen, occur*), or a state of being (*be, seem, remain*).

Forms of verbs

Verbs have five distinctive forms. If a word's form can change as described here, the word is a verb:

- **The *plain form* is the dictionary form of the verb.** When the subject is a plural noun or the pronoun *I, we, you,* or *they,* the plain form indicates action that occurs in the present, occurs habitually, or is generally true.

   A few artists <u>live</u> in town today.
   They <u>hold</u> classes downtown.

- **The *-s form* ends in *-s* or *-es*.** When the subject is a singular noun, a pronoun such as *everyone,* or the personal pronoun *he, she,* or *it,* the *-s* form indicates action that occurs in the present, occurs habitually, or is generally true.

   The artist <u>lives</u> in town today.
   She <u>holds</u> classes downtown.

- **The *past-tense form* indicates that the action of the verb occurred before now.** It usually adds *-d* or *-ed* to the plain form, although most irregular verbs create it in different ways.

   Many artists <u>lived</u> in town before this year.
   They <u>held</u> classes downtown. [Irregular verb.]

- **The *past participle* is usually the same as the past-tense form, except in most irregular verbs.** It combines with forms of *have* or *be* (*has <u>climbed</u>, was <u>created</u>*), or by itself it modifies nouns and pronouns (*the <u>sliced</u> apples*).

   Artists have <u>lived</u> in town for decades.
   They have <u>held</u> classes downtown. [Irregular verb.]

- **The *present participle* adds *-ing* to the verb's plain form.** It combines with forms of *be* (*is buying*), modifies nouns and pronouns (*the boiling water*), or functions as a noun (*running exhausts me*).

  A few artists are living in town today.
  They are holding classes downtown.

The verb *be* has eight forms rather than the five forms of most other verbs:

Plain form	be		
Present participle	being		
Past participle	been		
	I	*he, she, it*	*we, you, they*
Present tense	am	is	are
Past tense	was	was	were

Helping verbs

Some verb forms combine with **helping verbs** to indicate time, possibility, obligation, necessity, and other kinds of meaning: *can run, was sleeping, had been working*. In these **verb phrases** *run, sleeping,* and *working* are **main verbs**—they carry the principal meaning.

	Verb phrase	
	Helping	*Main*
Artists	can	train others to draw.
The techniques	have	changed little.

Common helping verbs

Forms of *be*: be, am, is, are, was, were, been, being
Forms of *have*: have, has, had, having
Forms of *do*: do, does, did

be able to	could	may	ought to	used to
be supposed to	had better	might	shall	will
can	have to	must	should	would

22.2 Adjectives and Adverbs

22.2 Identify adjectives and adverbs.

Adjectives describe or modify nouns and pronouns. They specify which one, what quality, or how many.

old	city	generous	one	two	pears
adjective	noun	adjective	pronoun	adjective	noun

Adverbs describe or modify verbs, adjectives, other adverbs, and whole groups of words. They specify when, where, how, and to what extent.

nearly destroyed   too quickly
adverb   verb   adverb adverb

very   generous   Unfortunately, taxes will rise.
adverb adjective   adverb   word group

An *-ly* ending often signals an adverb, but not always: *friendly* is an adjective; *never* and *not* are adverbs. The only way to tell whether a word is an adjective or an adverb is to determine what it modifies.

Adjectives and adverbs appear in three forms: **positive** (*green, angrily*), **comparative** (*greener, more angrily*), and **superlative** (*greenest, most angrily*).

See Chapter 34 for more on adjectives and adverbs.

22.3 Prepositions, Conjunctions, and Interjections

22.3 Identify prepositions, conjunctions, and interjections.

Connecting words are mostly small words that link parts of sentences. They never change form.

22.3.1 Prepositions

Prepositions form nouns or pronouns (plus any modifiers) into word groups called **prepositional phrases**: *about love, down the stairs*. These phrases usually serve as **modifiers** in sentences, as in *The plants trailed down the stairs*.

Common prepositions

about	before	except for	of	throughout
above	behind	excepting	off	till
according to	below	for	on	to
across	beneath	from	onto	toward
after	beside	in	on top of	under
against	between	in addition to	out	underneath
along	beyond	inside	out of	unlike
along with	by	inside of	outside	until
among	concerning	in spite of	over	up
around	despite	instead of	past	upon
as	down	into	regarding	up to
aside from	due to	like	round	with
at	during	near	since	within
because of	except	next to	through	without

22.3.2 Subordinating conjunctions

Subordinating conjunctions form sentences into word groups called **subordinate clauses**, such as *when the meeting ended* or *that she knew*. These clauses serve as parts of sentences: *Everyone was relieved when the meeting ended. She said that she knew.*

Common subordinating conjunctions

after	even if	rather than	until
although	even though	since	when
as	if	so that	whenever
as if	if only	than	where
as long as	in order that	that	whereas
as though	now that	though	wherever
because	once	till	whether
before	provided	unless	while

Culture and language

Learning the meanings of subordinating conjunctions can help you to express your ideas clearly. Note that each one conveys its meaning on its own. It does not need help from another function word, such as the coordinating conjunction *and, but, for,* or *so*:

Faulty Even though the parents cannot read, but their children may read well. [*Even though* and *but* have the same meaning, so both are not needed.]

Revised Even though the parents cannot read, their children may read well.

22.3.3 Coordinating and correlative conjunctions

Coordinating and correlative conjunctions connect words or word groups of the same kind, such as nouns or sentences.

Coordinating conjunctions consist of a single word:

Coordinating conjunctions

and	nor	for	yet
but	or	so	

Dieting or exercise alone is not enough for most people to maintain a healthy weight.

Dieting takes discipline, but exercise takes discipline and time.

Correlative conjunctions are combinations of coordinating conjunctions and other words:

> ## Common correlative conjunctions
>
> both . . . and   neither . . . nor
> not only . . . but also whether . . . or
> not . . . but   as . . . as
> either . . . or

<u>Both</u> a balanced diet <u>and</u> regular exercise are necessary to maintain a healthy weight.
<u>Neither</u> diet <u>nor</u> exercise alone will substantially improve a person's health.

22.3.4   Interjections

Interjections express feeling or command attention. They are rarely used in academic or business writing.

<u>Oh</u>, the meeting went fine.
They won seven thousand dollars! <u>Wow!</u>

Chapter 23
The Sentence

Learning Objectives

23.1   Identify the parts of basic sentences.
23.2   Form sentences using basic patterns.

23.1   Subjects and Predicates

23.1   Identify the parts of basic sentences.

The **sentence** is the basic unit of expression, forming a complete thought. Its subject and predicate usually name an actor and an action. Most sentences make statements. First the **subject** names something; then the **predicate** makes an assertion about the subject or describes an action by the subject.

<table>
<tr><th>Subject</th><th>Predicate</th></tr>
<tr><td>Art</td><td>thrives.</td></tr>
</table>

The **simple subject** consists of one or more **nouns** or **pronouns**, whereas the **complete subject** also includes any **modifiers**. The **simple predicate** consists of one or more **verbs**, whereas the **complete predicate** adds any words needed to complete the meaning of the verb plus any modifiers.

Sometimes, as in the short example *Art thrives*, the simple and complete subject and predicate are the same. More often, they are different:

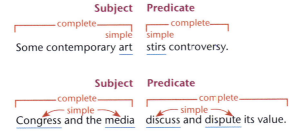

In the second example, the simple subject and simple predicate are both **compound:** in each, two words joined by a coordinating conjunction (*and*) serve the same function. If a sentence contains a word group such as *that makes it into museums* or *because viewers agree about its quality*, you may be tempted to mark the subject and verb in the word group as the subject and verb of the sentence. But these word groups are subordinate clauses, made into modifiers by the words they begin with: *that* and *because*.

gram
23.1

Culture and language

The subject of a sentence in standard American English may be a noun (*art*) or a pronoun that refers to the noun (*it*), but not both.

Faulty	Art it can stir controversy.
Revised	Art can stir controversy.
Revised	It can stir controversy.

When identifying the subject and the predicate of a sentence, be aware that some English words can serve as both nouns and verbs. For example, *visits* below functions as a verb and as a noun:

She visits the museum every Saturday. [Verb.]
Her visits are enjoyable. [Noun.]

Tests to find subjects and predicates

The tests below use the following example:

Art that makes it into museums has often survived controversy.

Identify the subject.

- Ask *who* or *what* is acting or being described in the sentence.

  Complete subject   art that makes it into museums

- Isolate the simple subject by deleting modifiers—words or word groups that don't name the actor of the sentence but give information about it. In the example, the word group *that makes it into museums* does not name the actor but modifies it.

  Simple subject   art

Identify the predicate.

- Ask what the sentence asserts about the subject. What is its action, or what state is it in? In the example, the assertion about *art* is that it *has often survived controversy*.

  Complete predicate   has often survived controversy

- Isolate the verb, the simple predicate, by changing the time of the subject's action. The simple predicate is the word or words that change as a result.

Example	Art . . . has often survived controversy.
Present	Art . . . often survives controversy.
Future	Art . . . will often survive controversy.
Simple predicate	has survived

23.2 Sentence Patterns

23.2   Form sentences using basic patterns.

All English sentences are based on five patterns, each differing in the complete predicate (the verb and any words following it).

The five basic sentence patterns

Subject — **Predicate**

1. Subject → Verb (intransitive)
   The earth — trembled.

2. Subject → Verb (transitive) → Direct object
   The earthquake — destroyed — the city.

3. Subject ⟷ Verb (linking) ⟷ Subject complement: noun or adjective
   The result — was — chaos.

4. Subject → Verb (transitive) → Indirect object → Direct object
   The government — sent — the city — aid.

5. Subject → Verb (transitive) → Direct object ← Object complement: noun or adjective
   The citizens — considered — the earthquake — a disaster.

gram 23.2

Culture and language

Word order in English sentences may not correspond to word order in the sentences of your native language or dialect. For instance, some other languages prefer the verb first in the sentence, whereas English strongly prefers the subject first.

Pattern 1: The earth trembled.

In the simplest pattern the predicate consists only of an **intransitive verb**, a verb that does not require a following word to complete its meaning.

Subject	Predicate
	Intransitive verb
The earth	trembled.
The hospital	may close.

Pattern 2: The earthquake destroyed the city.

In pattern 2 the verb is followed by a **direct object**, a noun or pronoun that identifies who or what receives the action of the verb. A verb that requires a direct object to complete its meaning is called **transitive**.

Subject	Predicate	
	Transitive verb	*Direct object*
The earthquake	destroyed	the city.
Education	opens	doors.

Culture and language

Only transitive verbs may be used in the **passive voice:** *The city was destroyed by the earthquake.* Your dictionary says whether a verb is transitive or intransitive, often with an abbreviation such as *tr.* or *intr.* Some verbs (*begin, learn, read, write,* and others) can be either transitive or intransitive.

Pattern 3: The result was chaos.

In pattern 3 the verb is followed by a **subject complement**, a word that renames or describes the subject. A verb in this pattern is called a **linking verb** because it links its subject to the description following. The linking verbs include *be, seem, appear, become, grow, remain, stay, prove, feel, look, smell, sound,* and *taste.* Subject complements are usually nouns or adjectives.

Subject	Predicate	
	Linking verb	*Subject complement*
The result	was	chaos. [Noun.]
The man	became	an accountant. [Noun.]
The car	seems	expensive. [Adjective.]

Pattern 4: The government sent the city aid.

In pattern 4 the verb is followed by a direct object and an **indirect object**, a word identifying to or for whom the action of the verb is performed. The direct object and indirect object refer to different things, people, or places.

Subject	Predicate		
	Transitive verb	*Indirect object*	*Direct object*
The government	sent	the city	aid.
One company	offered	its employees	bonuses.

A number of verbs can take indirect objects, including *send* and *offer* (preceding examples) and *allow, bring, buy, deny, find, get, give, leave, make, pay, read, sell, show, teach,* and *write*.

Culture and language

With some verbs that express action done to or for someone, the indirect object must be turned into a phrase beginning with *to* or *for*. In addition, the phrase must come after the direct object. The verbs that require these changes include *admit, announce, demonstrate, explain, introduce, mention, prove, recommend, say,* and *suggest*.

Faulty The manual explains [indirect object] workers the new [direct object] procedure.
Revised The manual explains the new [direct object] procedure [to phrase] to workers.

Pattern 5: The citizens considered the earthquake a disaster.

In pattern 5 the verb is followed by a direct object and an **object complement**, a word that renames or describes the direct object. Object complements may be nouns or adjectives.

Subject	Predicate		
	Transitive verb	*Direct object*	*Object complement*
The citizens	considered	the earthquake	a disaster.
Success	makes	some people	nervous.

Chapter 24
Phrases and Subordinate Clauses

Learning Objectives

24.1 Expand basic sentences with phrases.
24.2 Expand basic sentences with subordinate clauses.

24.1 Phrases

24.1 Expand basic sentences with phrases.

Most sentences contain word groups that serve as adjectives, adverbs, or nouns and thus cannot stand alone as sentences.

- A *phrase* lacks either a subject or a predicate or both: *fearing an accident*; *in a panic*.
- A *subordinate clause* contains a subject and a predicate but begins with a subordinating word: *when prices rise*; *whoever laughs*.

24.1.1 Prepositional phrases

A **prepositional phrase** consists of a preposition plus a noun, a pronoun, or a word group serving as a noun, called the object of the preposition.

Preposition	Object
of	spaghetti
on	the surface
with	great satisfaction
upon	entering the room
from	where you are standing

Prepositional phrases usually function as adjectives or adverbs.

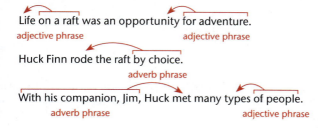

Life on a raft was an opportunity for adventure.
    adjective phrase   adjective phrase

Huck Finn rode the raft by choice.
                        adverb phrase

With his companion, Jim, Huck met many types of people.
    adverb phrase   adjective phrase

24.1.2 Verbal phrases

Certain forms of verbs, called **verbals**, can serve as modifiers or nouns. Often these verbals appear with their own modifiers and objects in **verbal phrases**. A verbal is not a verb: it cannot serve as the complete verb of a sentence. *The sun rises over the dump* is a sentence; *The sun rising over the dump* is a sentence fragment.

Participial phrases

Present participles end in *-ing*: *living, walking*. **Past participles** usually end in *-d* or *-ed*: *lived, walked*. **Participial phrases** are made from participles plus modifiers and objects. Participles and participial phrases usually serve as adjectives.

Strolling shoppers fill the malls.
participle

They make selections determined by personal taste.
participial phrase

With irregular verbs, the past participle may have a different ending—for instance, *hidden funds*.

> ### Culture and language
> The present and past participles of verbs that express feelings have different meanings. The present participle modifies the thing that causes the feeling: *It was a boring lecture*. The past participle modifies the thing that experiences the feeling: *The bored students slept*.

Gerund phrases

A **gerund** is the *-ing* form of a verb when it serves as a noun. Gerunds and gerund phrases can do whatever nouns can do.

sentence subject
Shopping satisfies personal needs.
noun

object of preposition
Malls are good at creating such needs.
noun phrase

Infinitive phrases

An **infinitive** is the plain form of a verb plus *to*: *to hide*. Infinitives and infinitive phrases serve as adjectives, adverbs, or nouns.

sentence
subject   *subject complement*
To design a mall is to create an artificial environment.
noun phrase   *noun phrase*

Malls are designed to make shoppers feel safe.
adverb phrase

The environment supports the impulse to shop.
adjective

> ### Culture and language
> Infinitives and gerunds may follow some verbs and not others and may differ in meaning after a verb: *The cowboy stopped to sing* (he stopped to do the activity). *The cowboy stopped singing* (he finished the activity).

24.1.3 Absolute phrases

An **absolute phrase** consists of a noun or pronoun and a participle, plus any modifiers. It modifies the entire rest of the sentence it appears in.

[absolute phrase] Their own place established, many ethnic groups are making way for new arrivals.

Unlike a participial phrase, an absolute phrase always contains a noun that serves as a subject.

[participial phrase] Learning English, many immigrants discover American culture.

[absolute phrase] Immigrants having learned English, their opportunities widen.

24.1.4 Appositive phrases

An **appositive** is usually a noun that renames another noun. An appositive phrase includes modifiers as well.

[appositive phrase] Bizen ware, a dark stoneware, is produced in Japan.

Appositives and appositive phrases sometimes begin with *that is, such as, for example,* or *in other words.*

Bizen ware is used in the Japanese tea ceremony, that is, the Zen Buddhist observance that links meditation and art. [appositive phrase]

24.2 Subordinate Clauses

24.2 Expand basic sentences with subordinate clauses.

A **clause** is any group of words that contains both a subject and a predicate. There are two kinds of clauses, and the distinction between them is important:

- A *main clause* makes a complete statement and can stand alone as a sentence: *The sky darkened.*
- A *subordinate clause* is just like a main clause *except* that it begins with a subordinating word: *when the sky darkened; whoever calls.* The subordinating word reduces the clause from a complete statement to a single part of speech: an adjective, adverb, or noun. Use subordinate clauses to support the ideas in main clauses.

Adjective clauses

An **adjective clause** modifies a noun or pronoun. It usually begins with the relative pronoun *who, whom, whose, which,* or *that.* The relative pronoun is the subject or object of the clause it begins. The clause ordinarily falls immediately after the word it modifies.

                    —adjective clause—
Parents who cannot read may have bad memories of school.

               ———adjective clause———
One school, which is open year-round, helps parents learn to read.

Adverb clauses

An **adverb clause** modifies a verb, an adjective, another adverb, or a whole word group. It always begins with a **subordinating conjunction**, such as *although, because, if,* or *when*.

                                             ———adverb clause———
The school began teaching parents when adult illiteracy gained national attention.

       ———adverb clause———   *—main clause—*
Because it was directed at people who could not read, advertising had to be inventive.

Noun clauses

A **noun clause** replaces a noun in a sentence and serves as a subject, object, or **complement**. It begins with *that, what, whatever, who, whom, whoever, whomever, when, where, whether, why,* or *how*.

      ———sentence subject———
Whether the program would succeed depended on door-to-door advertising.
         noun clause

                               ———object of verb———
Teachers explained in person how the program would work.
                                         noun clause

Chapter 25
Sentence Types

Learning Objectives

25.1 Identify different types of sentence structures.

25.1 Types of Sentences

25.1 Identify different types of sentence structures.

The four basic sentence structures vary in the number of **main clauses** and **subordinate clauses**. Each structure gives different emphasis to the main and supporting information in a sentence.

25.1.1 Recognizing simple sentences

A **simple sentence** consists of a single main clause and no subordinate clause.

⎯⎯ main clause ⎯⎯
Last summer was unusually hot.

⎯⎯⎯⎯⎯⎯⎯⎯⎯⎯⎯⎯ main clause ⎯⎯⎯⎯⎯⎯⎯⎯⎯⎯⎯⎯
The summer made many farmers leave the area for good or reduced them to bare existence.

25.1.2 Recognizing compound sentences

A **compound sentence** consists of two or more main clauses and no subordinate clause.

⎯ main clause ⎯   ⎯⎯ main clause ⎯⎯
Last July was hot, but August was even hotter.

⎯⎯⎯ main clause ⎯⎯⎯   ⎯⎯⎯⎯ main clause ⎯⎯⎯⎯
The hot sun scorched the earth, and the lack of rain killed many crops.

25.1.3 Recognizing complex sentences

A **complex sentence** consists of one main clause and one or more subordinate clauses.

⎯ main clause ⎯   ⎯⎯⎯⎯ subordinate clause ⎯⎯⎯⎯
Rain finally came, although many had left the area by then.

⎯⎯⎯⎯⎯ main clause ⎯⎯⎯⎯⎯   ⎯ subordinate clause ⎯
Those who remained were able to start anew because the government
⎯ subordinate clause ⎯
came to their aid.

25.1.4 Recognizing compound-complex sentences

A **compound-complex sentence** has the characteristics of both the compound sentence (two or more main clauses) and the complex sentence (at least one subordinate clause).

⎯⎯⎯ subordinate clause ⎯⎯⎯   ⎯⎯⎯ main clause ⎯⎯⎯
When government aid finally came, many people had already been reduced
                                ⎯⎯ main clause ⎯⎯
to poverty and others had been forced to move.

Chapter 26
Verb Forms

> ## Learning Objectives
>
> **26.1** Use the correct forms of irregular verbs.
> **26.2** Distinguish between *sit* and *set*, *lie* and *lay*, and *rise* and *raise*.
> **26.3** Use the *-s* and *-ed* forms of the verb when they are required.
> **26.4** Use helping verbs with main verbs appropriately.
> **26.5** Use a gerund or an infinitive after a verb as appropriate.
> **26.6** Use the appropriate particles with two-word verbs.

26.1 Verb Forms

26.1 Use the correct forms of irregular verbs.

Most verbs are **regular**: they form their past tense and past participle by adding *-d* or *-ed* to the plain form.

Plain form	Past tense	Past participle
live	lived	lived
act	acted	acted

About two hundred English verbs are **irregular**: they form their past tense and past participle in some irregular way. A dictionary lists the forms of irregular verbs: **plain form**, past tense, and past participle in that order (*go, went, gone*). If the dictionary gives only two forms (as in *think, thought*), then the past tense and the past participle are the same.

vb
26.1

Common irregular verbs

Plain form	Past tense	Past participle
be	was, were	been
become	became	become
begin	began	begun
bid	bid	bid
bite	bit	bitten, bit
blow	blew	blown
break	broke	broken
bring	brought	brought

Verb forms

Plain form	Past tense	Past participle
burst	burst	burst
buy	bought	bought
catch	caught	caught
choose	chose	chosen
come	came	come
cut	cut	cut
dive	dived, dove	dived
do	did	done
dream	dreamed, dreamt	dreamed, dreamt
drink	drank	drunk
drive	drove	driven
eat	ate	eaten
fall	fell	fallen
find	found	found
flee	fled	fled
fly	flew	flown
forget	forgot	forgotten, forgot
freeze	froze	frozen
get	got	got, gotten
give	gave	given
go	went	gone
grow	grew	grown
hang (suspend)	hung	hung
have	had	had
hear	heard	heard
hide	hid	hidden
hold	held	held
keep	kept	kept
know	knew	known
lead	led	led
leave	left	left
lend	lent	lent
let	let	let
lose	lost	lost
pay	paid	paid
ride	rode	ridden
ring	rang	rung
run	ran	run
say	said	said
see	saw	seen
shake	shook	shaken
sing	sang, sung	sung
sink	sank, sunk	sunk
sleep	slept	slept
slide	slid	slid
speak	spoke	spoken
spring	sprang, sprung	sprung
stand	stood	stood
steal	stole	stolen
swim	swam	swum

(continued)

Common irregular verbs

(continued)

Plain form	Past tense	Past participle
swing	swung	swung
take	took	taken
tear	tore	torn
throw	threw	thrown
wear	wore	worn
write	wrote	written

Culture and language

Some English dialects use verb forms that differ from those of standard American English: for instance, *drug* for *dragged*, *growed* for *grew*, *come* for *came*, or *went* for *gone*. In situations requiring standard English, use the forms in the preceding list or in a dictionary.

Faulty	They have went to the movies.
Revised	They have gone to the movies.

26.2 Easily Confused Verb Forms

26.2 Distinguish between *sit* and *set*, *lie* and *lay*, and *rise* and *raise*.

The forms of *sit* and *set*, *lie* and *lay*, and *rise* and *raise* are easy to confuse.

Plain form	Past tense	Past participle
sit	sat	sat
set	set	set
lie	lay	lain
lay	laid	laid
rise	rose	risen
raise	raised	raised

In each of these confusing pairs, one verb is **intransitive** (it does not take an object) and one is **transitive** (it does take an object).

Intransitive

The patients lie in their beds. [*Lie* means "recline" and takes no object.]

Visitors sit with them. [*Sit* means "be seated" or "be located" and takes no object.]

Patients' temperatures rise. [*Rise* means "increase" or "get up" and takes no object.]

Transitive

Nursing aides lay the dinner trays on tables. [*Lay* means "place" and takes an object, here *trays*.]

The aides set the trays down. [*Set* means "place" and takes an object, here *trays*.]

The aides raise the shades. [*Raise* means "lift" or "bring up" and takes an object, here *shades*.]

The verb *lie* meaning "to tell an untruth" is a regular verb. Its past tense and past participle forms are *lied*: *Nikki lied to us. She has lied to us for many years.*

26.3 Verb Endings

26.3 Use the *-s* and *-ed* forms of the verb when they are required.

Speakers of some English dialects and nonnative speakers of English sometimes omit the *-s* and *-ed* verb endings when they are required in standard American English. If you tend to omit these endings in writing, practice pronouncing them when speaking or when reading correct verbs aloud, such as those in the examples here. The spoken practice can help you remember the endings when writing.

26.3.1 Required *-s* ending

Use the *-s* form of a verb when **both** of these situations hold:

- **The subject is a singular noun (*woman*), an indefinite pronoun (*everyone*), or *he*, *she*, or *it*.** These subjects are **third person**, used when someone or something is being spoken about.
- **The verb's action occurs in the present.**

The letter asks [not ask] for a quick response.
Delay costs [not cost] money.
It wastes [not waste] time.
Everyone hopes [not hope] for a good outcome.

Be especially careful with the *-s* forms of *be* (*is*), *have* (*has*), and *do* (*does, doesn't*). These forms should always be used to indicate present time with third-person singular subjects:

The company is [not be] late in responding.
It has [not have] problems.
It doesn't [not don't] have the needed data.
The contract does [not do] depend on the response.

In addition, *be* has the *-s* form *was* in the past tense with *I* and third-person singular subjects:

The company was [not were] in trouble before.

Except for the past tense *I was,* the pronouns *I* and *you* and all plural subjects do *not* take the *-s* form of verbs:

I am [not is] a student.
You are [not is] also a student.
They are [not is] students, too.

26.3.2 Required *-ed* or *-d* ending

The *-ed* or *-d* verb form is required in *any* of these situations:

- **The verb's action occurred in the past.**

    The company asked [not ask] for more time.

- **The verb form functions as a modifier.**

    The data concerned [not concern] should be retrievable.

- **The verb form combines with a form of *be* or *have*.**

    The company is supposed [not suppose] to be the best.
    It has developed [not develop] an excellent reputation.

Watch especially for a needed *-ed* or *-d* ending when it isn't pronounced clearly in speech, as in *asked, discussed, mixed, supposed, walked,* and *used.*

26.4 Helping Verbs

26.4 Use helping verbs with main verbs appropriately.

Helping verbs combine with main verbs in verb phrases: *The line should have been cut. Who was calling?*

26.4.1 Required helping verbs

Standard American English requires helping verbs in certain situations:

- **The main verb ends in *-ing.***

    Researchers are conducting fieldwork all over the world. [Not Researchers conducting. . . .]

- **The main verb is *been* or *be.***

    Many have been fortunate in their discoveries. [Not Many been. . . .]
    Some could be real-life Indiana Joneses. [Not Some be. . . .]

- **The main verb is a past participle,** such as *talked, thrown,* or *begun.*

    Their discoveries were covered in newspapers and magazines. [Not Their discoveries covered. . . .]

    The researchers have given interviews on TV. [Not The researchers given. . . .]

Helping verbs 251

The omission of a helping verb may create an incomplete sentence, or sentence fragment, because a present participle (*conducting*), an irregular past participle (*been*), or the plain form *be* cannot stand alone as the only verb in a sentence. To work as sentence verbs, these verb forms need helping verbs.

26.4.2 Combination of helping verb + main verb

Helping verbs and main verbs combine into verb phrases in specific ways. The main verb in a verb phrase (the one carrying the main meaning) does not change to show a change in subject or time: *she has sung, you had sung*. Only the helping verb may change.

Form of *be* + present participle

The **progressive tenses** indicate action in progress. Create them with *be, am, is, are, was, were,* or *been* followed by the main verb's present participle, the *-ing* form:

> She is working on a new book.

Be and *been* always require additional helping verbs to form progressive tenses:

can	might	should		have	
could	must	will	} be working	has	} been working
may	shall	would		had	

When forming the progressive tenses, be sure to use the *-ing* form of the main verb.

> Faulty   Her ideas are grow more complex. She is developed a new approach to ethics.
>
> Revised   Her ideas are growing more complex. She is developing a new approach to ethics.

Form of *be* + past participle

The **passive voice** of the verb indicates that the subject *receives* the action of the verb. Create the passive voice with a form of *be* (*be, am, is, are, was, were, being,* or *been*) followed by the main verb's past participle.

> Her latest book was completed in four months.

Be, being, and *been* always require additional helping verbs to form the passive voice.

have		am	was	
has	} been completed	is	were	} being completed
had		are		
will be completed				

vb
26.4

Always use the main verb's past participle for the passive voice:

Faulty   Her next book will be <u>publish</u> soon.
Revised Her next book will be <u>published</u> soon.

Only transitive verbs may form the passive voice:

Faulty   A philosophy conference <u>will be occurred</u> in the same week. [*Occur* is not a transitive verb.]
Revised A philosophy conference <u>will occur</u> in the same week.

See Chapter 29 for advice on when to use and when to avoid the passive voice.

Forms of *have*

Four forms of *have* serve as helping verbs: *have, has, had, having.* One of these forms plus the main verb's past participle creates one of the **perfect tenses**, those expressing action completed before another specific time or action:

> Some students <u>have complained</u> about the laboratory.
> Others <u>had complained</u> before.

Will and other helping verbs sometimes accompany forms of *have* in the perfect tenses:

> Several more students <u>will have complained</u> by the end of the week.

Forms of *do*

Do, does, and *did* have three uses as helping verbs, always with the plain form of the main verb:

- **To pose a question:** *How <u>did</u> the trial <u>end</u>?*
- **To emphasize the main verb:** *It <u>did end</u> eventually.*
- **To negate the main verb, along with *not* or *never*:** *The judge <u>did not withdraw</u>.*

Be sure to use the main verb's plain form with any form of *do*:

Faulty   The judge did <u>remained</u> in court.
Revised The judge did <u>remain</u> in court.

Modals

The modal helping verbs include *can, may, should, would,* and several two- and three-word combinations, such as *have to* and *be able to.* Use the plain form of the main verb with a modal unless the modal combines with another helping verb (usually *have*).

Faulty   The equipment <u>can detects</u> small vibrations. It <u>should have detect</u> the change.
Revised The equipment <u>can detect</u> small vibrations. It <u>should have detected</u> the change.

Modals convey various meanings, with these being most common:

- **Ability:** *can, could, be able to*

    The equipment can detect small vibrations. [Present.]
    The equipment could detect small vibrations. [Past.]
    The equipment is able to detect small vibrations. [Present. Past: *was able to*. Future: *will be able to*.]

- **Possibility:** *could, may, might; could/may/might have* + past participle

    The equipment could fail. [Present or future.]
    The equipment may fail. [Present or future.]
    The equipment might fail. [Present or future.]
    The equipment may have failed. [Past.]

- **Necessity or obligation:** *must, have to, be supposed to*

    The lab must purchase a backup. [Present or future.]
    The lab has to purchase a backup. [Present or future. Past: *had to*.]
    The lab will have to purchase a backup. [Future.]
    The lab is supposed to purchase a backup. [Present. Past: *was supposed to*.]

- **Permission:** *may, can, could*

    The lab may spend the money. [Present or future.]
    The lab can spend the money. [Present or future.]
    The lab could spend the money. [Present or future, more tentative.]
    The lab could have spent the money. [Past.]

- **Intention:** *will, shall, would*

    The lab will spend the money. [Future.]
    Shall we offer advice? [Future. Use *shall* for questions requesting opinion or consent.]
    We would have offered advice. [Past.]

- **Request:** *could, can, would*

    Could [or Can or Would] you please obtain a bid? [Present or future.]

- **Advisability:** *should, had better, ought to; should have* + past participle

    You should obtain three bids. [Present or future.]
    You had better obtain three bids. [Present or future.]
    You ought to obtain three bids. [Present or future.]
    You should have obtained three bids. [Past.]

- **Past habit:** *would, used to*

    In years past we would obtain five bids.
    We used to obtain five bids.

26.5 Verbs with Gerunds and Infinitives

26.5 Use a gerund or an infinitive after a verb as appropriate.

A **gerund** is the *-ing* form of a verb used as a noun: <u>Smoking</u> is *unhealthful*. An **infinitive** is the plain form of a verb preceded by *to*: *Try not <u>to smoke</u>*. Gerunds and infinitives may follow certain verbs but not others. Sometimes the use of a gerund or an infinitive with the same verb changes the meaning.

26.5.1 Either gerund or infinitive

A gerund or an infinitive may come after the following verbs with no significant difference in meaning:

begin	continue	intend	prefer
can't bear	hate	like	start
can't stand	hesitate	love	

The pump began <u>working</u>.
The pump began <u>to work</u>.

I can't stand <u>waiting</u> in line.
I can't stand <u>to wait</u> in line.

26.5.2 Meaning change with gerund or infinitive

With four verbs, a gerund has quite a different meaning from an infinitive:

forget	stop
remember	try

The man stopped <u>eating</u>. [He no longer ate.]
The man stopped <u>to eat</u>. [He stopped in order to eat.]

26.5.3 Gerund, not infinitive

Do not use an infinitive after these verbs:

admit	discuss	mind	recollect
adore	dislike	miss	resent
appreciate	enjoy	postpone	resist
avoid	escape	practice	risk
consider	finish	put off	suggest
deny	imagine	quit	tolerate
detest	keep	recall	understand

Faulty   He finished <u>to eat</u> lunch.
Revised   He finished <u>eating</u> lunch.

26.5.4 Infinitive, not gerund

Do not use a gerund after these verbs:

agree	claim	manage	promise
appear	consent	mean	refuse
arrange	decide	offer	say
ask	expect	plan	wait
assent	have	prepare	want
beg	hope	pretend	wish

Faulty   He decided <u>checking</u> the meter.
Revised He decided <u>to check</u> the meter.

26.5.5 Noun or pronoun + infinitive

Some verbs may be followed by an infinitive alone or by a noun or pronoun and an infinitive. The presence of a noun or pronoun changes the meaning.

ask	dare	need	wish
beg	expect	promise	would like
choose	help	want	

He expected <u>to wait</u>.
He expected <u>his friends</u> <u>to wait</u>.

Some verbs *must* be followed by a noun or pronoun before an infinitive:

advise	encourage	oblige	require
allow	forbid	order	teach
cause	force	permit	tell
challenge	hire	persuade	train
command	instruct	remind	urge
convince	invite	request	warn

He told <u>his friends to wait</u>.

Do not use *to* before the infinitive when it follows one of these verbs and a noun or pronoun:

feel	hear	make ("force")	watch
have	let	see	

He watched his friends <u>leave</u> without him.

26.6 Verbs with Particles

26.6   Use the appropriate particles with two-word verbs.

Standard American English includes some verbs that consist of two (and occasionally three) words: the verb itself and a **particle**, a preposition or adverb that affects the meaning of the verb.

<u>Look up</u> the answer. [Research the answer.]
<u>Look over</u> the answer. [Examine the answer.]

Culture and language

The meanings of these two-word verbs are often quite different from the meanings of the individual words that make them up. A dictionary of English as a second language will define two-word verbs and say whether the verbs may be separated in a sentence, as explained below. Many two-word verbs are more common in speech than in academic or business writing. For formal writing, consider using *research* instead of *look up,* and *examine* instead of *look over.*

26.6.1 Inseparable two- and three-word verbs

Verbs and particles that may not be separated by any other words include the ones below:

catch on	go over	play around	stay away
come across	grow up	run into	stay up
get along	keep on	run out of	take care of
give in	look into	speak up	turn up at

Faulty Children grow quickly up.
Revised Children grow up quickly.

26.6.2 Separable two-word verbs

Most two-word verbs that take **direct objects** may be separated by the object.

> Parents help out their children.
> Parents help their children out.

If the direct object is a **pronoun**, the pronoun *must* separate the verb from the particle.

> **Faulty** Parents help out them.
> **Revised** Parents help them out.

The separable two-word verbs include the following:

call off	give away	look over	take out
call up	give back	look up	take over
drop off	hand in	make up	try out
fill out	hand out	point out	turn on
fill up	help out	put off	wrap up

Chapter 27
Verb Tenses

 Learning Objectives

27.1 Use the appropriate tense to express your meaning.
27.2 Use the appropriate sequence of verb tenses.

27.1 Verb Tenses

27.1 **Use the appropriate tense to express your meaning.**

Tense shows the time of a verb's action.

Tenses of a regular verb (active voice)

Present Action that is occurring now, occurs habitually, or is generally true

Simple present Plain form or -s form
I walk.
You/we/they walk.
He/she/it walks.

Present progressive *Am*, *is*, or *are* plus *-ing* form
I am walking.
You/we/they are walking.
He/she/it is walking.

Past Action that occurred before now

Simple past Past-tense form (*-d* or *-ed*)
I/he/she/it walked.
You/we/they walked.

Past progressive *Was* or *were* plus *-ing* form
I/he/she/it was walking.
You/we/they were walking.

Future Action that will occur in the future

Simple future *Will* plus plain form
I/you/he/she/it/we/they will walk.

Future progressive *Will be* plus *-ing* form
I/you/he/she/it/we/they will be walking.

Present perfect Action that began in the past and is linked to the present

Present perfect *Have* or *has* plus past participle (*-d* or *-ed*)
I/you/we/they have walked.
He/she/it has walked.

Present perfect progressive *Have been* or *has been* plus *-ing* form
I/you/we/they have been walking.
He/she/it has been walking.

(continued)

Tenses of a regular verb (active voice)

(continued)

Past perfect Action that was completed before another past action

Past perfect *Had* plus past participle (*-d* or *-ed*)
I/you/he/she/it/we/they had walked.

Past perfect progressive *Had been* plus *-ing* form
I/you/he/she/it/we/they had been walking.

Future perfect Action that will be completed before another future action

Future perfect *Will have* plus past participle (*-d* or *–ed*)
I/you/he/she/it/we/they will have walked.

Future perfect progressive *Will have been* plus *–ing* form
I/you/he/she/it/we/they will have been walking.

Culture and language

In standard American English, a verb conveys time through its form. In some other languages and English dialects, various markers besides verb form may indicate the time of a verb. For instance, in African American Vernacular English, *I be attending class on Tuesday* means that the speaker attends class every Tuesday. But to someone who doesn't know the dialect, the sentence could mean last Tuesday, this Tuesday, or every Tuesday. In standard English, the intended meaning is indicated by verb tense:

I attended class on Tuesday. [Past tense indicates *last* Tuesday.]
I will attend class on Tuesday. [Future tense indicates *next* Tuesday.]
I attend class on Tuesday. [Present tense indicates habitual action, *every* Tuesday.]

27.1.1 Observe the special uses of the present tense.

The present tense has several distinctive uses:

Action occurring now
She understands the problem.
We define the problem differently.

Habitual or recurring action
Banks regularly undergo audits.
The audits monitor the banks' activities.

A general truth
The mills of the gods grind slowly.
The earth is round.

Discussion of literature, film, and so on
Huckleberry Finn <u>has</u> adventures we all envy.
In that article the author <u>examines</u> several causes of crime.

Future time
Next week we <u>draft</u> a new budget.
Funding <u>ends</u> in less than a year.

(The present tense shows future time with expressions like those in the examples above: *next week, in less than a year.*)

27.1.2 Observe the uses of the perfect tenses.

The **perfect tenses** consist of a form of *have* plus the verb's **past participle** (*closed, hidden*). They indicate an action completed before another specific time or action. The present perfect tense also indicates action begun in the past and continued into the present.

present perfect
The dancer <u>has performed</u> here only once. [The action is completed at the time of the statement.]

present perfect
Critics <u>have written</u> about the performance ever since. [The action began in the past and continues now.]

past perfect
The dancer <u>had trained</u> in Asia before his performance. [The action was completed before another past action.]

future perfect
He <u>will have danced</u> here again by the end of the year. [The action begins now or in the future and will be completed by a specific time in the future.]

Culture and language

With the present perfect tense, the words *since* and *for* are followed by different information. After *since*, give a specific point in time: *The play has run <u>since 1989</u>.* After *for*, give a span of time: *It has run <u>for decades</u>.*

27.1.3 Observe the uses of the progressive tenses.

The **progressive tenses** indicate continuing (therefore progressive) action. In standard American English the progressive tenses consist of a form of *be* plus the verb's *-ing* form. (The words *be* and *been* must be combined with other helping verbs.)

present progressive
The team <u>is improving</u>.

past progressive
Last year the team <u>was losing</u>.

future progressive
The owners will be watching for signs of improvement.

present perfect progressive
Sports writers have been expecting an upturn.

past perfect progressive
New players had been performing well.

future perfect progressive
If the season goes badly, fans will have been watching their team lose for ten straight years.

Verbs that express unchanging conditions (especially mental states) rather than physical actions do not usually appear in the progressive tenses. These verbs include *adore, appear, believe, belong, care, hate, have, hear, know, like, love, mean, need, own, prefer, remember, see, sound, taste, think, understand,* and *want.*

Faulty She is wanting to study ethics.
Revised She wants to study ethics.

27.1.4 Keep tenses consistent.

Within a sentence, the tenses of verbs and verb forms need not be identical as long as they reflect actual changes in time: *Ramon will graduate from college thirty years after his father arrived in America.* But needless shifts in tense will confuse or distract readers:

Inconsistent tense Immediately after Booth shot Lincoln, Major Rathbone threw himself upon the assassin. But Booth pulls a knife and plunges it into the major's arm.

Revised Immediately after Booth shot Lincoln, Major Rathbone threw himself upon the assassin. But Booth pulled a knife and plunged it into the major's arm.

Inconsistent tense The main character in the novel suffers psychologically because he has a clubfoot, but he eventually triumphed over his disability.

Revised The main character in the novel suffers psychologically because he has a clubfoot, but he eventually triumphs over his disability. [Use the present tense to discuss the content of literature, film, and so on.]

27.2 Sequence of Tenses

27.2 Use the appropriate sequence of verb tenses.

The **sequence of tenses** is the relationship between the verb tense in a **main clause** and the verb tense in a **subordinate clause**. The tenses should change when necessary to reflect changes in actual or relative time.

27.2.1 Past or past perfect tense in main clause

When the verb in the main clause is in the past or past perfect tense, the verb in the subordinate clause must also be past or past perfect:

    main clause: past   *subordinate clause: past*
The researchers <u>discovered</u> that people <u>varied</u> widely in their knowledge of public events.

    main clause: past   *subordinate clause: past perfect*
The variation <u>occurred</u> because respondents <u>had been born</u> in different decades.

    main clause: past perfect   *subordinate clause: past*
None of them <u>had been born</u> when Dwight Eisenhower <u>was</u> president.

Always use the present tense for a general truth, such as *The earth is round*:

    main clause: past   *subordinate clause: present*
Most <u>understood</u> that popular presidents <u>are</u> not necessarily good presidents.

27.2.2 Conditional sentences

A **conditional sentence** states a factual relationship between cause and effect, makes a prediction, or speculates about what might happen. Such a sentence usually contains a subordinate clause beginning with *if, when,* or *unless* and a main clause stating the result. The three kinds of conditional sentences use distinctive verbs.

Factual relationship

Statements linking factual causes and effects use matched tenses in the subordinate and main clauses:

    subordinate clause: present   *main clause: present*
When a voter <u>casts</u> a ballot, he or she <u>has</u> complete privacy.

    subordinate clause: past   *main clause: past*
When voters <u>registered</u> in some states, they <u>had</u> to pay a poll tax.

Prediction

Predictions generally use the present tense in the subordinate clause and the future tense in the main clause:

    subordinate clause: present   *main clause: future*
Unless citizens <u>regain</u> faith in politics, they <u>will</u> not <u>vote</u>.

Sometimes the verb in the main clause consists of *may, can, should,* or *might* plus the verb's **plain form**: *If citizens <u>regain</u> faith, they <u>may vote</u>.*

Speculation

The verbs in speculations depend on whether the linked events are possible or impossible. For possible events in the present, use the past tense in the subordinate clause and *would, could,* or *might* plus the verb's plain form in the main clause:

<pre>
    subordinate clause: main clause:
         past   would + verb
</pre>
If voters had more confidence, they would vote more often.

Use *were* instead of *was* in the subordinate clause, even when the subject is *I, he, she, it,* or a singular noun.

<pre>
    subordinate clause: main clause:
         past   would + verb
</pre>
If the voter were more confident, he or she would vote more often.

For impossible events in the present—events that are contrary to fact—use the same forms as above (including the distinctive *were* when applicable):

<pre>
    subordinate clause: main clause:
         past   might + verb
</pre>
If Lincoln were alive, he might inspire confidence.

For impossible events in the past, use the past perfect tense in the subordinate clause and *would, could,* or *might* plus the present perfect tense in the main clause:

<pre>
    subordinate clause: main clause:
       past perfect   might + present perfect
</pre>
If Lincoln had lived past the Civil War, he might have helped stabilize the country.

Chapter 28

Verb Mood

Learning Objectives

28.1 Use subjunctive verb forms appropriately.
28.2 Avoid confusing shifts in mood.

28.1 Subjunctive Mood

28.1 **Use subjunctive verb forms appropriately.**

Mood in grammar is a verb form that indicates the writer's attitude:

- The *indicative mood* states a fact or opinion or asks a question: *The theater needs support.*
- The *imperative mood* expresses a command or gives direction: *Support the theater.*
- The *subjunctive mood* expresses wishes, suggestions, requirements, and other attitudes,* using *he were* and other distinctive verb forms described below.

The subjunctive mood expresses a wish or desire, a suggestion, a requirement, or a request, or it states a condition that is contrary to fact (that is, imaginary or hypothetical).

- **Verbs such as *ask, insist, urge, require, recommend,* and *suggest* indicate request or requirement.** They often precede a subordinate clause beginning with *that* and containing the substance of the request or requirement. For all subjects, the verb in the *that* clause is the **plain form**:

  plain form
  Rules require that every donation be mailed.

- **Contrary-to-fact clauses state imaginary or hypothetical conditions. They usually begin with *if* or *unless,* or they follow *wish*.** For present contrary-to-fact clauses, use the verb's **past-tense form** (for *be,* use the past-tense form *were* for all subjects):

  past *past*
  If the theater were in better shape and had more money, its future would be assured.

  past
  I wish I were able to donate money.

For past contrary-to-fact clauses, use *had* plus the verb's past participle:

  past perfect
  The theater would be better funded if it had been better managed.

Do not use the **helping verb** *would* or *could* in a contrary-to-fact clause beginning with *if*:

Not   Many people would have helped if they would have known.
But   Many people would have helped if they had known.

28.2 Consistency

28.2 Avoid confusing shifts in mood.

Shifts in mood within a sentence or among related sentences can be confusing. Such shifts occur most frequently in directions.

Inconsistent mood   Cook the mixture slowly, and you should stir it until the sugar is dissolved. [Mood shifts from imperative to indicative.]
Revised   Cook the mixture slowly, and stir it until the sugar is dissolved. [Consistently imperative.]

Chapter 29
Verb Voice

Learning Objectives

29.1 Distinguish between active and passive voice.
29.2 Avoid confusing shifts in voice.

29.1 Active and Passive Voice

29.1 Distinguish between active and passive voice.

The voice of a verb tells whether the subject of the sentence performs the action (active) or is acted upon (passive).

Active voice

She wrote the book. [The subject performs the action.]
subject verb

Passive voice

The book was written by her. [The subject receives the action.]
   subject   verb

Culture and language

A passive verb always consists of a form of *be* plus the **past participle** of the main verb: *Rents are controlled*. *People were inspired*. Other **helping verbs** must also be used with the words *be, being,* and *been*: *Rents will be controlled*. *Rents are being controlled*. *Rents have been controlled*. *People would have been inspired*. Only a **transitive verb** (one that takes an object) may be used in the passive voice.

Active and passive voice

Active voice   The subject acts.

Active and passive voice **265**

Passive voice The subject is acted upon.

29.1.1   Use active voice in most situations.

The active voice is usually clearer, more concise, and more forthright than the passive voice.

Weak passive The library is used by both students and teachers, and the plan to expand it has been praised by many.
Strong active Both students and teachers use the library, and many have praised the plan to expand it.

29.1.2   Use the passive voice when the actor is unknown or unimportant or when naming the actor might be offensive.

The passive voice can be useful when naming the actor is not possible or desirable.

- **The actor is unknown, unimportant, or less important than the object of the action.** In the following sentences, the writer wishes to stress the Internet rather than the actors.

  The Internet was established in 1969 by the US Department of Defense. The network has been extended internationally to governments, universities, corporations, and private individuals.

  In the next example, the person who performed the experiment, perhaps the writer, is less important than the procedure. Passive sentences are common in scientific writing.

  After the solution had been cooled to 10°C, the acid was added.

- **The actor should be secondary to the action.** Particularly in sensitive correspondence, this use of the passive can avoid offending readers. In the next example, not naming the person who turned away the shelter residents focuses on the action without accusing anyone specifically.

  The residents of the shelter were turned away from your coffee shop.

29.2 Consistency

29.2 Avoid confusing shifts in voice.

Shifts in voice that involve shifts in subject are usually unnecessary and confusing.

Inconsistent subject and voice	Blogs cover an enormous range of topics. Opportunities for people to discuss their interests are provided on these sites.
Revised	Blogs cover an enormous range of topics and provide opportunities for people to discuss their interests.

A shift in voice is appropriate when it helps focus the reader's attention on a single subject, as in *The candidate campaigned vigorously and was nominated on the first ballot.*

Chapter 30
Agreement of Subject and Verb

Learning Objectives

30.1 Make subjects and verbs agree in number.
30.2 Make subjects and verbs agree in sentences with unusual word order.
30.3 Make subjects and verbs agree when subjects are joined by *and*, *or*, or *nor*.
30.4 Make indefinite and relative pronouns agree with verbs.
30.5 Make collective and plural nouns agree with verbs.

30.1 Subject-Verb Agreement

30.1 Make subjects and verbs agree in number.

A subject and its verb should agree in number and person:

Daniel Inouye was the first Japanese American in Congress.
    subject   verb

More Japanese Americans live in Hawaii and California than elsewhere.
           subject   verb

	Number	
Person	*Singular*	*Plural*
First	I eat.	We eat.
Second	You eat.	You eat.
Third	He/she/it eats.	They eat.
	The bird eats.	Birds eat.

Most problems of subject-verb agreement arise when endings are omitted from subjects or verbs or when the relationship between sentence parts is uncertain.

An *-s* or *-es* ending does opposite things to nouns and verbs: it usually makes a noun *plural*, but it always makes a present-tense verb *singular*. Thus a singular-noun subject will not end in *-s*, but its verb will. A plural-noun subject will end in *-s*, but its verb will not. Between them, subject and verb use only one *-s* ending.

Singular subject	**Plural subject**
The boy plays.	The boys play.
The bird soars.	The birds soar.

The only exception involves the nouns that form irregular plurals, such as *child/children, woman/women*. The irregular plural still requires a plural verb: *The children play. The women sing.*

Culture and language

If your first language or dialect is not standard American English, subject-verb agreement may be difficult, especially for the following reasons:

- **Some English dialects omit the *-s* ending for singular verbs or use the *-s* ending for plural verbs.**

Nonstandard	The voter resist change.
Standard	The voter resists change.
Standard	The voters resist change.

The verb *be* changes spelling for singular and plural in both present and past tense.

Nonstandard	Taxes is high. They was raised just last year.
Standard	Taxes are high. They were raised just last year.

Have also has a distinctive *-s* form, *has*:

Nonstandard	The new tax have little chance of passing.
Standard	The new tax has little chance of passing.

- **Some other languages change all parts of verb phrases to match their subjects.** In English verb phrases, however, only the

(continued)

Culture and language

(continued)

helping verbs *be, have,* and *do* change for different subjects. The **modal** helping verbs—*can, may, should, will*, and others—do not change:

Nonstandard   The tax mays pass next year.
Standard   The tax may pass next year.

The **main verb** in a verb phrase also does not change for different subjects:

Nonstandard   The tax may passes next year.
Standard   The tax may pass next year.

30.2 Unusual Word Order

30.2 Make subjects and verbs agree in sentences with unusual word order.

30.2.1 Subject and verb should agree even when other words come between them.

The survival of hibernating frogs in freezing temperatures is [not are] fascinating.

A chemical reaction inside the cells of the frogs stops [not stop] the formation of ice crystals.

Phrases beginning with *as well as, together with, along with,* and *in addition to* do not change a singular subject to plural:

The president, together with the deans, has [not have] agreed.

30.2.2 The verb agrees with the subject even when it precedes the subject.

The verb precedes the subject mainly in questions and in constructions beginning with *there* or *here* and a form of *be*:

Is voting a right or a privilege?

Are a right and a privilege the same thing?

There are differences between them.

30.2.3 *Is, are,* and other linking verbs agree with their subjects, not subject complements.

Make a **linking verb** agree with its subject, usually the first element in the sentence, not with the noun or pronoun serving as a **subject complement**.

The child's sole support is her court-appointed guardians.

Her court-appointed guardians are the child's sole support.

30.3 Subjects Joined by Conjunctions

30.3 Make subjects and verbs agree when subjects are joined by *and*, *or*, or *nor*.

30.3.1 Subjects joined by *and* usually take plural verbs.

Frost and Roethke were contemporaries.

When the parts of the subject form a single idea or refer to a single person or thing, they take a singular verb:

Avocado and bean sprouts is a California sandwich.

When a compound subject is preceded by the adjective *each* or *every*, the verb is usually singular:

Each man, woman, and child has a right to be heard.

30.3.2 When parts of a subject are joined by *or* or *nor*, the verb agrees with the nearer part.

Either the painter or the carpenter knows the cost.

The cabinets or the bookcases are too costly.

When one part of the subject is singular and the other plural, avoid awkwardness by placing the plural part closer to the verb so that the verb is plural:

Awkward   Neither the owners nor the contractor agrees.

Revised   Neither the contractor nor the owners agree.

30.4 Indefinite and Relative Pronouns

30.4 Make indefinite and relative pronouns agree with verbs.

30.4.1 With *everyone* and other indefinite pronouns, use a singular or plural verb as appropriate.

Indefinite pronouns include *anyone, anybody, each, everyone, everybody, nobody, no one, nothing,* and *someone.* Most indefinite pronouns are singular in meaning (they refer to a single unspecified person or thing), and they take a singular verb:

Something smells.   Neither is right.

Four indefinite pronouns are always plural in meaning: *both, few, many, several.*

Both are correct.   Several were invited.

Six indefinite pronouns may be either singular or plural in meaning: *all, any, more, most, none, some.* The verb with one of these pronouns depends on what the pronoun refers to:

All of the money is reserved for emergencies. [*All* refers to *money.*]

All of the funds are reserved for emergencies. [*All* refers to *funds.*]

None may be singular even when referring to a plural word, especially to emphasize the meaning "not one": *None* [*Not one*] *of the animals has a home.*

30.4.2 *Who, which,* and *that* take verbs that agree with their antecedents.

When used as subjects, *who, which,* and *that* refer to another word in the sentence, called the **antecedent**. The verb agrees with the antecedent:

Mayor Garber ought to listen to the people who work for her.

Bardini is the only aide who has her ear.

Agreement problems often occur with *who* and *that* when the sentence includes *one of the* or *the only one of the*:

Bardini is one of the aides who work unpaid. [Of the aides who work unpaid, Bardini is one.]

Bardini is the only one of the aides who knows the community. [Of the aides, only one, Bardini, knows the community.]

In phrases beginning with *one of the,* be sure the noun is plural: *Bardini is one of the aides* [not *aide*] *who work unpaid.*

30.5 Collective and Plural Nouns

30.5   Make collective and plural nouns agree with verbs.

30.5.1 Collective nouns such as *team* take singular or plural verbs depending on meaning.

A collective noun has singular form and names a group of persons or things: *army, audience, committee, crowd, family, group, team.*

Use a singular verb with a collective noun when the group acts as a unit.

> The team has won five of the last six meets.

But when the group's members act separately, not together, use a plural verb.

> The old team have gone to various colleges.

If a combination such as *team have* seems awkward, reword the sentence: *The members of the old team have gone to various colleges.*

The collective noun *number* may be singular or plural. Preceded by *a*, it is plural; preceded by *the*, it is singular:

> A number of people are in debt.

> The number of people in debt is very large.

Culture and language

Some **noncount nouns** (nouns that don't form plurals) are collective nouns because they name groups: for instance, *furniture, clothing, mail, machinery, equipment, military, police*. These noncount nouns usually take singular verbs: *Mail arrives daily*. But some of these nouns take plural verbs, including *clergy, military, people, police*, and any collective noun that comes from an adjective, such as *the poor, the rich, the young, the elderly*. If you mean one representative of the group, use a singular noun such as *police officer* or *poor person*.

30.5.2 *News* and other singular nouns ending in *-s* take singular verbs.

Singular nouns ending in *-s* include *athletics, economics, mathematics, measles, mumps, news, physics, politics*, and *statistics*, as well as place names such as *Athens, Wales*, and *United States*:

> After so long a wait, the news has to be good.

> Statistics is required of psychology majors.

> The United States is a diverse nation.

A few of these words also take plural verbs, but only when they describe individual items rather than whole bodies of activity or knowledge: *The statistics prove him wrong. The mayor's politics make compromise difficult.*

Measurements and figures ending in *-s* may also be singular when the quantity they refer to is a unit:

Three years is a long time to wait.

Three-fourths of the library consists of reference books.

30.5.3 Use singular verbs with titles and with words being defined.

Hakada Associates is a new firm.

Dream Days remains a favorite book.

Folks is a down-home word for *people*.

Chapter 31
Pronoun Case

Learning Objectives

- **31.1** Define subjective, objective, and possessive cases.
- **31.2** Use the appropriate case for compound subjects, compound objects, and subject complements.
- **31.3** Use *who* or *whom* depending on the pronoun's function.
- **31.4** Use the appropriate case in other constructions.

31.1 Subjective, Objective, and Possessive Cases

31.1 Define subjective, objective, and possessive cases.

Case is the form of a **noun** or **pronoun** that shows the reader how it functions in a sentence.

- **The subjective case** indicates that the word is a **subject** or **subject complement**.
- **The objective case** indicates that the word is an **object** of a verb or preposition.
- **The possessive case** indicates that the word owns or is the source of a noun in the sentence.

Nouns change form only to show possession: *teacher's*. Most of the pronouns listed below change more often.

Subjective	Objective	Possessive
I	me	my, mine
you	you	your, yours
he	him	his
she	her	her, hers
it	it	its
we	us	our, ours
you	you	your, yours
they	them	their, theirs
who	whom	whose
whoever	whomever	—

Culture and language

In standard American English, *-self* pronouns do not change form to show function. Their only forms are *myself, yourself, himself, herself, itself, ourselves, yourselves, themselves*. Avoid nonstandard forms such as *hisself, ourself,* and *theirselves*.

> Nonstandard   He bought hisself a new laptop.
> Revised   He bought himself a new laptop.

31.2 Compound Subjects and Objects

31.2 Use the appropriate case for compound subjects, compound objects, and subject complements.

Compound subjects or **compound objects**—those consisting of two or more nouns or pronouns—have the same case forms as they would if one noun or pronoun stood alone:

compound subject
She and Novick discussed the proposal.

compound object
The proposal disappointed her and him.

If you are in doubt about the correct form, try this test:

A test for case forms in compound subjects or objects

1. **Identify a compound construction** (one connected by *and, but, or, nor*).

   [He, Him] and [I, me] won the prize.
   The prize went to [he, him] and [I, me].

(continued)

> ### A test for case forms in compound subjects or objects
> *(continued)*
>
> 2. **Write a separate sentence for each part of the compound:**
>
>   [He, Him] won the prize. [I, Me] won the prize.
>   The prize went to [he, him]. The prize went to [I, me].
>
> 3. **Choose the pronouns that sound correct.**
>
>   He won the prize. I won the prize. [Subjective.]
>   The prize went to him. The prize went to me. [Objective.]
>
> 4. **Put the separate sentences back together.**
>
>   He and I won the prize.
>   The prize went to him and me.

Avoid using the pronoun *myself* in place of the personal pronoun *I* or *me*: *Stephen and I* [not *myself*] *trained. Everyone went except me* [not *myself*].

After a **linking verb**, a pronoun renaming the subject (a subject complement) should be in the subjective case.

                 subject complement
The delegates are she and Novick.

  subject
complement
It was they whom the mayor appointed.

If this construction sounds odd to you, use the more natural order: *She and Novick are the delegates. The mayor appointed them.*

31.3 *Who* or *Whom*

31.3 Use *who* or *whom* depending on the pronoun's function.

Use *who* where you would use *he* or *she*—all ending in vowels. Use *whom* where you would use *him* or *her*—all ending in consonants.

31.3.1 Questions

At the beginning of a question, use *who* for a subject and *whom* for an object:

   subject
Who wrote the policy?   
Whom does it affect?

To find the correct case of *who* in a question, use the following test:

1. **Pose the question:**

    [Who, Whom] makes that decision?
    [Who, Whom] does one ask?

2. **Answer the question, using a personal pronoun.** Choose the pronoun that sounds correct, and note its case:

    [She, Her] makes that decision. She makes that decision. [Subjective.]
    One asks [she, her]. One asks her. [Objective.]

3. **Use the same case (*who* or *whom*) in the question:**

    Who makes that decision? [Subjective.]
    Whom does one ask? [Objective.]

31.3.2 Subordinate clauses

In a **subordinate clause**, use *who* or *whoever* for a subject, *whom* or *whomever* for an object.

Give old clothes to whoever needs them. [subject]

I don't know whom the mayor appointed. [object]

To determine which form to use, try the following test:

1. **Locate the subordinate clause:**

    Few people know [who, whom] they should ask.
    They are unsure [who, whom] makes the decision.

2. **Rewrite the subordinate clause as a separate sentence, substituting a personal pronoun for *who, whom*.** Choose the pronoun that sounds correct, and note its case:

    They should ask [she, her]. They should ask her. [Objective.]
    [She, her] makes the decision. She makes the decision. [Subjective.]

3. **Use the same case (*who* or *whom*) in the subordinate clause:**

    Few people know whom they should ask. [Objective.]
    They are unsure who makes the decision. [Subjective.]

Don't let expressions such as *I think* and *she says* mislead you into using *whom* rather than *who* for the subject of a clause.

He is the one who I think is best qualified. [subject]

To choose between *who* and *whom* in such constructions, delete the interrupting phrase so that you can see the true relationship between parts: *He is the one who is best qualified.*

31.4 Common Questions about Case

31.4 Use the appropriate case in other constructions.

31.4.1 *We* or *us* with a noun

The choice of *we* or *us* before a noun depends on the use of the noun:

Freezing weather is welcomed by us skaters.
(us — object of preposition)

We skaters welcome freezing weather.
(We — subject)

31.4.2 Pronoun in an appositive

In an **appositive**, the case of a pronoun depends on the function of the word the appositive describes or identifies:

The class elected two representatives, DeShawn and me.
(DeShawn and me — appositive identifies object)

Two representatives, DeShawn and I, were elected.
(DeShawn and I — appositive identifies subject)

31.4.3 Pronoun after *than* or *as*

When a pronoun follows *than* or *as* in a comparison, the case of the pronoun indicates what words may have been omitted. A subjective pronoun must be the subject of the omitted verb:

Some critics like Glass more than he [does].
(he — subject)

An objective pronoun must be the object of the omitted verb:

Some critics like Glass more than [they like] him.
(him — object)

31.4.4 Subject and object of infinitive

An infinitive is the **plain form** of the verb plus *to* (*to swim*). Both the object *and* the subject of an infinitive are in the objective case of the pronoun.

The school asked him to speak.
(him — subject of infinitive)

Students chose to invite him.
(him — object of infinitive)

Agreement in person, number, and gender 277

31.4.5 Case before a gerund

A gerund is the *-ing* form of the verb used as a noun (*a runner's breathing*). Generally, use the possessive form of a pronoun or noun immediately before a gerund:

The coach disapproved of their lifting weights.

The coach's disapproving was a surprise.

Chapter 32
Agreement of Pronoun and Antecedent

Learning Objectives

32.1 Make pronouns and their antecedents agree in person, number, and gender.

32.2 Make pronouns joined by *and, or,* or *nor* agree with their antecedents.

32.3 Make indefinite pronouns agree with their antecedents.

32.4 Make collective nouns take singular or plural pronouns depending on meaning.

32.1 Agreement in Person, Number, and Gender

32.1 Make pronouns and their antecedents agree in person, number, and gender.

The **antecedent** of a **pronoun** is the **noun** or other pronoun to which the pronoun refers:

Students fret over their tuition bills.
antecedent   pronoun

Its yearly increases make the tuition bill a dreaded document.
pronoun   antecedent

Agreement of pronoun and antecedent

For clarity, a pronoun should agree with its antecedent in person and number as well as in gender (masculine, feminine, neuter).

	Number	
Person	*Singular*	*Plural*
First	I	we
Second	you	you
Third	he, she, it	they
	indefinite pronouns	plural nouns
	singular nouns	

Culture and language

The gender of a pronoun should match its antecedent, not a noun that the pronoun may modify: *Sara Young invited her* [not *his*] *son*. Also, English nouns have only neuter gender unless they specifically refer to males or females. Thus nouns such as *book*, *table*, *sun*, and *earth* take the neuter pronoun *it*: *I am reading a new book. It is inspiring*.

32.2 Antecedents with *and, or,* or *nor*

32.2 Make pronouns joined by *and, or,* or *nor* agree with their antecedents.

32.2.1 Antecedents joined by *and* usually take plural pronouns.

Mr. Bartos and I cannot settle our dispute.

The dean and my adviser have offered their help.

When the compound antecedent refers to a single idea, person, or thing, then the pronoun is singular.

My friend and adviser offered her help.

When the compound antecedent follows *each* or *every*, the pronoun is singular:

Every girl and woman took her seat.

32.2.2 When parts of an antecedent are joined by *or* or *nor*, the pronoun agrees with the nearer part.

Tenants or owners must present their grievances.

Either the tenant or the owner will have her way.

When one subject is plural and the other singular, the sentence will be awkward unless you put the plural subject second.

Awkward Neither the tenants nor the owner has yet made her case.

Revised Neither the owner nor the tenants have yet made their case.

32.3 Indefinite Pronouns

32.3 Make indefinite pronouns agree with their antecedents.

Indefinite words do not refer to a specific person or thing. **Indefinite pronouns** include *anyone, each, everybody, nobody, no one, nothing, somebody,* and *someone*. **Generic nouns** include *person, individual,* and *student*. Most indefinite pronouns and all generic nouns are singular in meaning. When they serve as antecedents, they take singular pronouns:

Each of the animal shelters in the region has its population of homeless pets.
indefinite pronoun

Every worker in our shelter cares for his or her favorite animal.
generic noun

Four indefinite pronouns are plural in meaning: *both, few, many, several*. As antecedents, they take plural pronouns:

Many of the animals show affection for their caretakers.

Six indefinite pronouns may be singular or plural in meaning: *all, any, more, most, none, some*. As antecedents, they take singular pronouns if they refer to singular words, plural pronouns if they refer to plural words:

Most of the shelter's equipment was donated by its original owner. [*Most* refers to *equipment*.]

Most of the veterinarians donate their time. [*Most* refers to *veterinarians*.]

None may be singular even when referring to a plural word, especially to emphasize the meaning "not one": *None* [*Not one*] *of the shelters has increased its capacity*.

Most agreement problems arise with the singular indefinite words. We often use these words to mean "many" or "all" rather than "one" and then refer to them with plural pronouns, as in *Everyone has their own locker*. Often, too, we mean indefinite words to include both masculine and feminine genders and thus resort to *they* instead of the **generic *he*** — the masculine pronoun referring to both genders, as in *Everyone deserves his privacy*. To achieve agreement in such cases, you have the options listed in the following box.

Ways to correct agreement with indefinite words

- **Change the indefinite word to a plural, and use a plural pronoun to match:**

  Faulty   Every athlete deserves their privacy.
  Revised Athletes deserve their privacy.

- **Rewrite the sentence to omit the pronoun:**

  Faulty   Everyone is entitled to their own locker.
  Revised Everyone is entitled to a locker.

- **Use *he or she* (*him or her, his or her*) to refer to the indefinite word:**

  Faulty   Now everyone has their private space.
  Revised Now everyone has his or her private space.

  However, used more than once in several sentences, *he or she* quickly becomes awkward. (Some academic readers do not accept the alternative *he/she*.) Using the plural or omitting the pronoun will usually correct agreement problems and create more readable sentences.

32.4 Collective Nouns

32.4 Make collective nouns take singular or plural pronouns depending on meaning.

A **collective noun** has singular form and names a group of persons or things: *army, audience, family, group, team*. Use a singular pronoun with a collective noun when referring to the group as a unit:

> The committee voted to disband itself.

When referring to the individual members of the group, use a plural pronoun:

> The old team have gone their separate ways.

If a combination such as *team have . . . their* seems awkward, reword the sentence: *The members of the old team have gone their separate ways*.

Culture and language

In standard American English, collective nouns that are noncount nouns (they don't form plurals) usually take singular pronouns: *The mail sits in its own basket.* A few noncount nouns take plural pronouns, including *clergy, military, police, the rich,* and *the poor*: *The police support their unions.*

Chapter 33
Reference of Pronoun to Antecedent

Learning Objectives

33.1 Make a pronoun refer clearly to one antecedent.
33.2 Make a pronoun refer to a specific antecedent, not an implied one.
33.3 Use *you* and other pronouns consistently.

33.1 Clear Reference

33.1 **Make a pronoun refer clearly to one antecedent.**

A **pronoun** should refer clearly to its **antecedent**, the noun it substitutes for. Otherwise, readers will have difficulty grasping the pronoun's meaning.

Culture and language

In standard American English, a pronoun needs a clear antecedent nearby, but don't use both a pronoun and its antecedent as the **subject** of the same sentence: *James* [not *James he*] *told Victor to go alone.*

When either of two nouns can be a pronoun's antecedent, the reference will not be clear.

> **Confusing**   Emily Dickinson is sometimes compared with Jane Austen, but she led a more reclusive life.

Revise such a sentence in one of two ways:

- **Replace the pronoun with the appropriate noun.**

    > **Clear**   Emily Dickinson is sometimes compared with Jane Austen, but Dickinson led a more reclusive life.

- **Avoid repetition by rewriting the sentence.** If you use the pronoun, make sure it has only one possible antecedent.

    > **Clear**   Despite occasional comparison of their lives, Emily Dickinson was more reclusive than Jane Austen.
    >
    > **Clear**   Though sometimes compared with her, Emily Dickinson was more reclusive than Jane Austen.

A **clause** beginning with *who, which,* or *that* should generally fall immediately after the word to which it refers.

> **Confusing**   Jody found a lamp in the attic that her aunt had used.
>
> **Clear**   In the attic Jody found a lamp that her aunt had used.

33.2 Specific Reference

33.2   Make a pronoun refer to a specific antecedent, not an implied one.

A pronoun should refer to a specific noun or other pronoun. A reader can only guess at the meaning of a pronoun when its antecedent is implied by the context, not stated outright.

33.2.1 Vague *this, that, which,* or *it*

This, that, which, or *it* should refer to a specific noun, not to a whole word group expressing an idea or situation.

> **Confusing**   The British knew little of the American countryside, and they had no experience with the colonists' guerrilla tactics. This gave the colonists an advantage.
>
> **Clear**   The British knew little of the American countryside, and they had no experience with the colonists' guerrilla tactics. This ignorance and inexperience gave the colonists an advantage.

33.2.2 Indefinite antecedents with *it* and *they*

It and *they* should have definite noun antecedents. Rewrite the sentence if the antecedent is missing.

Confusing	In Chapter 4 of this book it describes the early flights of the Wright brothers.
Clear	Chapter 4 of this book describes the early flights of the Wright brothers.
Confusing	Even in reality TV shows, they present a false picture of life.
Clear	Even reality TV shows present a false picture of life.
Clear	Even in reality TV shows, the producers present a false picture of life.

33.2.3 Implied nouns

A noun may be implied in some other word or phrase, as *happiness* is implied in *happy*, *driver* is implied in *drive*, and *mother* is implied in *mother's*. But a pronoun cannot refer clearly to an implied noun, only to a specific, stated one.

Confusing	In Cohen's report she made claims that led to a lawsuit.
Clear	In her report Cohen made claims that led to a lawsuit.
Confusing	Her reports on psychological development generally go unnoticed outside it.
Clear	Her reports on psychological development generally go unnoticed outside the field.

33.3 Appropriate *you*

33.3 Use *you* and other pronouns consistently.

You should clearly mean "you, the reader." The context must be appropriate for such a meaning:

Inappropriate	In the fourteenth century you had to struggle simply to survive.
Revised	In the fourteenth century one [or a person] had to struggle simply to survive.

Writers sometimes drift into *you* because *one*, *a person*, or a similar word can be difficult to sustain. Sentence after sentence, the indefinite word may sound stuffy, and it requires *he* or *he or she* for pronoun-antecedent agreement. To avoid these problems, try using plural nouns and pronouns:

Original	In the fourteenth century one had to struggle simply to survive.
Revised	In the fourteenth century people had to struggle simply to survive.

Within a sentence or a group of related sentences, pronouns should be consistent. Partly, consistency comes from making pronouns and their antecedents agree (see Chapter 32). In addition, the pronouns within a passage should match each other.

Inconsistent pronouns	One finds when reading that your concentration improves with practice, so that I now comprehend more in less time.
Revised	I find when reading that my concentration improves with practice, so that I now comprehend more in less time.

Chapter 34
Adjectives and Adverbs

Learning Objectives

- **34.1** Use adjectives and adverbs as modifiers.
- **34.2** Use the comparative and superlative forms of adjectives and adverbs.
- **34.3** Watch for double negatives.
- **34.4** Distinguish between present and past participles as adjectives.
- **34.5** Use *a, an, the,* and other determiners appropriately.

34.1 Functions of Adjectives and Adverbs

34.1 Use adjectives and adverbs as modifiers.

Adjectives modify **nouns** (*happy child*) and **pronouns** (*special someone*). **Adverbs** modify **verbs** (*almost see*), adjectives (*very happy*), other adverbs (*not very*), and whole word groups (*Otherwise, I'll go*). The only way to tell whether a modifier should be an adjective or an adverb is to determine its function in the sentence.

Culture and language

In standard American English, an adjective does not change along with the noun it modifies to show plural number: *square* [not *squares*] *spaces*. Only nouns form plurals.

Do not use adjectives instead of adverbs to modify verbs, adverbs, or other adjectives:

Faulty Educating children good should be everyone's focus.

Revised Educating children well should be everyone's focus.

Faulty Some children suffer bad.

Revised Some children suffer badly.

Culture and language

Choosing between *not* and *no* can be a challenge. *Not* is an adverb, so it makes a verb or an adjective negative:

They do not learn. They are not happy. They have not been in class.

No is an adjective, so it makes a noun negative:

No child likes to fail. No good school fails children.

Place *no* before the noun or any other modifier.

Use adjectives and adverbs with linking verbs.

A **linking verb** connects the subject and a word that describes the subject—for instance, *seem, become, look,* and forms of *be*. Some verbs may or may not be linking verbs, depending on their meaning in the sentence. When the word after the verb modifies the subject, the verb is linking and the word should be an adjective: *He looked happy*. When the word modifies the verb, however, it should be an adverb: *He looked carefully*.

Two word pairs are especially troublesome in this context. One is *bad* and *badly*:

The weather grew bad. She felt bad.
  linking adjective   linking adjective
  verb   verb

Flowers grow badly in such soil.
  verb adverb

Adjectives and adverbs

The other pair is *good* and *well*. *Good* serves only as an adjective. *Well* may serve as an adverb with a host of meanings or as an adjective meaning only "fit" or "healthy."

Decker trained well.
    verb   adverb

She felt well.
linking adjective
verb

Her health was good.
linking adjective
verb

34.2 Comparative and Superlative Forms

34.2 Use the comparative and superlative forms of adjectives and adverbs.

Adjectives and adverbs can show degrees of quality or amount with the endings *-er* and *-est* or with the words *more* and *most* or *less* and *least*. Most modifiers have the three forms, as shown in the following chart:

Positive	Comparative	Superlative
The basic form listed in the dictionary	A greater or lesser degree of the quality	The greatest or least degree of the quality
Adjectives		
red	redder	reddest
awful	more/less awful	most/least awful
Adverbs		
soon	sooner	soonest
quickly	more/less quickly	most/least quickly

If sound alone does not tell you whether to use *-er/-est* or *more/most,* consult a dictionary. If the endings can be used, the dictionary will list them. Otherwise, use *more* or *most*.

34.2.1 Irregular adjectives and adverbs

Irregular modifiers change the spelling of their positive form to show comparative and superlative degrees.

Positive	Comparative	Superlative
Adjectives		
good	better	best
bad	worse	worst
little	littler, less	littlest, least
many, some, much	more	most
Adverbs		
well	better	best
badly	worse	worst

34.2.2 Double comparisons

A double comparative or double superlative combines the *-er* or *-est* ending with the word *more* or *most*. It is redundant.

> Chang was the wisest [not most wisest] person in town.
> He was smarter [not more smarter] than anyone else.

34.2.3 Logical comparisons

Absolute modifiers

Some adjectives and adverbs cannot logically be compared—for instance, *perfect, unique, dead, impossible, infinite*. These absolute words can be preceded by adverbs like *nearly* or *almost* that mean "approaching," but they cannot logically be modified by *more* or *most* (as in *most perfect*).

Not	He was the most unique teacher we had.
But	He was a unique teacher.

Completeness

To be logical, a comparison must also be complete in the following ways:

- **The comparison must state a relationship fully enough for clarity.**

Unclear	Carmakers worry about their industry more than environmentalists.
Clear	Carmakers worry about their industry more than environmentalists do.
Clear	Carmakers worry about their industry more than they worry about environmentalists.

- **The items being compared should in fact be comparable.**

Illogical	The cost of a hybrid car can be greater than a gasoline-powered car. [Illogically compares a cost and a car.]
Revised	The cost of a hybrid car can be greater than the cost of [or that of] a gasoline-powered car.

Any versus *any other*

Use *any other* when comparing something with others in the same group. Use *any* when comparing something with others in a different group.

Illogical	Los Angeles is larger than any city in California. [Since Los Angeles is itself a city in California, the sentence seems to say that Los Angeles is larger than itself.]
Revised	Los Angeles is larger than any other city in California.

Illogical	Los Angeles is larger than any other city in Canada. [The cities in Canada constitute a group to which Los Angeles does not belong.]
Revised	Los Angeles is larger than any city in Canada.

34.3 Double Negatives

34.3 Watch for double negatives.

In a **double negative** two negative words such as *no, not, none, neither, barely, hardly,* or *scarcely* cancel each other out. Some double negatives are intentional: for instance, *She was not unhappy* indicates with understatement that she was indeed happy. But most double negatives say the opposite of what is intended: *Nadia did not feel nothing* asserts that Nadia felt other than nothing, or something. For the opposite meaning, one of the negatives must be eliminated (*She felt nothing*) or one of them must be changed to a positive (*She did not feel anything*).

Faulty	The IRS cannot hardly audit all tax returns. None of its audits never touch many cheaters.
Revised	The IRS cannot audit all tax returns. Its audits never touch many cheaters.

34.4 Participles as Adjectives

34.4 Distinguish between present and past participles as adjectives.

Both **present participles** and **past participles** may serve as adjectives: *a burning building, a burned building*. As in the examples, the two participles usually differ in the time they indicate, present (*burning*) or past (*burned*).

But some present and past participles—those derived from verbs expressing feeling—can have altogether different meanings. The present participle modifies something that causes the feeling: *That was a frightening storm* (the storm frightens). The past participle modifies something that experiences the feeling: *They quieted the frightened horses* (the horses feel fright).

The following participles are among those likely to be confused:

amazing/amazed
amusing/amused
annoying/annoyed
astonishing/astonished
boring/bored
confusing/confused
depressing/depressed
embarrassing/embarrassed
exciting/excited
exhausting/exhausted

fascinating/fascinated
frightening/frightened
frustrating/frustrated
interesting/interested
pleasing/pleased
satisfying/satisfied
shocking/shocked
surprising/surprised
tiring/tired
worrying/worried

34.5 Determiners

34.5 Use *a, an, the,* and other determiners appropriately.

Determiners are special kinds of adjectives that mark nouns because they always precede nouns. Some common determiners are *a, an,* and *the* (called **articles**) and *my, their, whose, this, these, those, one, some,* and *any.*

Culture and language

Native speakers of standard American English can rely on their intuition when using determiners, but speakers of other languages and dialects often have difficulty with them. In standard American English, the use of determiners depends on the context they appear in and the kind of noun they precede:

- A *proper noun* names a particular person, place, or thing and begins with a capital letter: *February, Joe Allen, Red River.* Most proper nouns are not preceded by determiners.
- A *count noun* names something that is countable in English and can form a plural: *girl/girls, apple/apples, child/children.* A singular count noun is always preceded by a determiner; a plural count noun sometimes is.
- A *noncount noun* names something not usually considered countable in English, so it does not form a plural. A noncount noun is sometimes preceded by a determiner. Here is a sample of noncount nouns, sorted into groups by meaning:

  Abstractions: confidence, democracy, education, equality, evidence, health, information, intelligence, knowledge, luxury, peace, pollution, research, success, supervision, truth, wealth, work

  Food and drink: bread, candy, cereal, flour, meat, milk, salt, water, wine

  Emotions: anger, courage, happiness, hate, joy, love, respect, satisfaction

  Natural events and substances: air, blood, dirt, gasoline, gold, hair, heat, ice, oil, oxygen, rain, silver, smoke, weather, wood

  Groups: clergy, clothing, equipment, furniture, garbage, jewelry, junk, legislation, machinery, mail, military, money, police, vocabulary

  Fields of study: architecture, accounting, biology, business, chemistry, engineering, literature, psychology, science

A dictionary of English as a second language will tell you whether a noun is a count noun, a noncount noun, or both. Many nouns are sometimes count nouns and sometimes noncount nouns:

> The library has a room for readers. [*Room* is a count noun meaning "walled area."]
>
> The library has room for reading. [*Room* is a noncount noun meaning "space."]

34.5.1 A, an, and the

With singular count nouns

A or *an* precedes a singular count noun when the reader does not already know its identity, usually because you have not mentioned it before:

> A scientist in our chemistry department developed a process to strengthen metals. [*Scientist* and *process* are being mentioned for the first time.]

The precedes a singular count noun that has a specific identity for the reader, for one of the following reasons:

- **You have mentioned the noun before:**

    > A scientist in our chemistry department developed a process to strengthen metals. The scientist patented the process. [*Scientist* and *process* were identified in the preceding sentence.]

- **You identify the noun immediately before or after you state it:**

    > The most productive laboratory is the research center in the chemistry department. [*Most productive* identifies *laboratory*. *In the chemistry department* identifies *research center*. And *chemistry department* is a shared facility—see below.]

- **The noun names something unique—the only one in existence:**

    > The sun rises in the east. [*Sun* and *east* are unique.]

- **The noun names an institution or facility that is shared by the community of readers:**

    > Many men and women aspire to the presidency. [*Presidency* is a shared institution.]
    > The cell phone has changed business communication. [*Cell phone* is a shared facility.]

The is not used before a singular noun that names a general category:

> Wordsworth's poetry shows his love of nature [not the nature].
> General Sherman said that war is hell. [*War* names a general category.]
> The war in Iraq left many wounded. [*War* names a specific war.]

With plural count nouns

A or *an* never precedes a plural noun. *The* does not precede a plural noun that names a general category. *The* does precede a plural noun that names specific representatives of a category.

> Men and women are different. [*Men* and *women* name general categories.]
> The women formed a team. [*Women* refers to specific people.]

With noncount nouns

A or *an* never precedes a noncount noun. *The* does precede a noncount noun that names specific representatives of a general category.

Vegetation suffers from drought. [*Vegetation* names a general category.]
The vegetation in the park withered and died. [*Vegetation* refers to specific plants.]

With proper nouns

A or *an* never precedes a proper noun. *The* generally does not precede proper nouns.

> Garcia lives in Boulder.

There are exceptions, however. For instance, we generally use *the* before plural proper nouns (*the Murphys, the Boston Celtics*) and before the names of groups and organizations (*the Department of Justice, the Sierra Club*), ships (*the Lusitania*), oceans and seas (*the Pacific, the Caribbean*), mountain ranges (*the Alps, the Rockies*), regions (*the Middle East*), rivers (*the Mississippi*), and some countries (*the United States, the Netherlands*).

34.5.2 Other determiners

The uses of English determiners besides articles also depend on context and kind of noun. The following determiners may be used as indicated with singular count nouns, plural count nouns, or noncount nouns.

With any kind of noun (singular count, plural count, noncount)

> *my, our, your, his, her, its, their,* possessive nouns (*boy's, boys'*)
> *whose, which*(*ever*), *what*(*ever*)
> *some, any, the other*
> *no*

> Their account is overdrawn. [Singular count.]
> Their funds are low. [Plural count.]
> Their money is running out. [Noncount.]

Only with singular nouns (count and noncount)

> *this, that*

> This account has some money. [Count.]
> That information may help. [Noncount.]

Only with noncount nouns and plural count nouns

> *most, enough, other, such, all, all of the, a lot of*

> Most funds are committed. [Plural count.]
> Most money is needed elsewhere. [Noncount.]

Only with singular count nouns

> *one, every, each, either, neither, another*

> One car must be sold. [Singular count.]

Only with plural count nouns

these, those
both, many, few, a few, fewer, fewest, several
two, three, and so forth

Two cars are unnecessary. [Plural count.]

Few means "not many" or "not enough." *A few* means "some" or "a small but sufficient quantity."

Few committee members came to the meeting.
A few members can keep the committee going.

Do not use *much* with a plural count noun.

Many [not Much] members want to help.

Only with noncount nouns

much, more, little, a little, less, least, a large amount of

Less luxury is in order. [Noncount.]

Little means "not many" or "not enough." *A little* means "some" or "a small but sufficient quantity."

Little time remains before the conference.
The members need a little help from their colleagues.

Do not use *many* with a noncount noun.

Much [not Many] work remains.

Chapter 35
Misplaced and Dangling Modifiers

> **Learning Objectives**
>
> **35.1** Reposition misplaced modifiers.
> **35.2** Connect dangling modifiers to their sentences.

35.1 Misplaced Modifiers

35.1 Reposition misplaced modifiers.

A **misplaced modifier** falls in the wrong place in a sentence. It is usually awkward or confusing. It may even be unintentionally funny.

35.1.1 Clear placement

Readers tend to link a modifier to the nearest word it could modify. Any other placement can link the modifier to the wrong word.

Confusing He served steak to the men on paper plates.

Clear He served the men steak on paper plates.

Confusing According to the police, many dogs are killed by automobiles and trucks roaming unleashed.

Clear According to the police, many dogs roaming unleashed are killed by automobiles and trucks.

35.1.2 *Only* and other limiting modifiers

Limiting modifiers include *almost, even, exactly, hardly, just, merely, nearly, only, scarcely,* and *simply.* For clarity, place such a modifier immediately before the word or word group you intend it to limit.

Unclear The archaeologist only found the skull on her last dig.

Clear The archaeologist found only the skull on her last dig.

Clear The archaeologist found the skull only on her last dig.

35.1.3 Adverbs with grammatical units

Adverbs can often move around in sentences, but some will be awkward if they interrupt certain grammatical units:

- **A long adverb stops the flow from subject to verb.**

                subject   adverb   verb
  Awkward The city, after the hurricane, began massive rebuilding.

                adverb   subject   verb
  Revised After the hurricane, the city began massive rebuilding.

- **Any adverb is awkward between a verb and its direct object.**

                    verb   adverb   object
  Awkward The hurricane had damaged badly many homes in the city.

                    verb   object
  Revised The hurricane had badly damaged many homes in the city.
                              adverb

- A *split infinitive*—an adverb placed between *to* and the verb—annoys many readers.

  Awkward   The weather service expected temperatures to not rise.

  Revised   The weather service expected temperatures not to rise.

  A split infinitive may sometimes be natural and preferable, though it may still bother some readers.

  Several US industries expect to more than triple their use of robots.

  Here the split infinitive is more economical than the alternatives, such as *Several US industries expect to increase their use of robots by more than three times*.

- A long adverb is usually awkward inside a verb phrase.

  Awkward   People with osteoporosis can, by increasing their daily intake of calcium and vitamin D, improve their bone density.

  Revised   By increasing their daily intake of calcium and vitamin D, people with osteoporosis can improve their bone density.

Culture and language

In a question, place a one-word adverb immediately after the subject:

Will spacecraft ever be able to leave the solar system?

35.1

Other adverb positions

Placements of a few adverbs can be difficult for nonnative speakers of English:

- **Adverbs of frequency** include *always, never, often, rarely, seldom,* and *sometimes*. They generally appear at the beginning of a sentence, before a one-word verb, or after a **helping verb**.

  Robots have sometimes put humans out of work.

  Sometimes robots have put humans out of work.

Adverbs of frequency always follow the verb *be*.

verb adverb
Robots are often helpful to workers.

verb adverb
Robots are seldom useful around the house.

When *rarely, seldom,* or another negative adverb of frequency begins a sentence, the normal subject-verb order changes.

adverb verb subject
Rarely are robots simple machines.

- **Adverbs of degree** include *absolutely, almost, certainly, completely, definitely, especially, extremely, hardly,* and *only.* They fall just before the word modified (an adjective, another adverb, sometimes a verb).

  adverb adjective
  Robots have been especially useful in making cars.

- **Adverbs of manner** include *badly, beautifully, openly, sweetly, tightly, well,* and others that describe how something is done. They usually fall after the verb.

  verb   adverb
  Robots work smoothly on assembly lines.

- **The adverb *not*** changes position depending on what it modifies. When it modifies a verb, place it after the helping verb (or the first helping verb if more than one).

  helping   main
verb   verb
  Robots do not think.

  When *not* modifies another adverb or an adjective, place it before the other modifier.

  adjective
  Robots are not sleek machines.

Culture and language

English follows distinctive rules for arranging two or three adjectives before a noun. (A string of more than three adjectives before a noun is rare.) The rules arrange adjectives by type and by meaning, as shown in the following chart:

(continued)

Culture and language
(continued)

Determiner	Opinion	Size or shape	Color	Origin	Material	Noun used as adjective	Noun
many						state	laws
	lovely		green	Thai			birds
a	fine			German			camera
this		square			wooden		table
all						business	reports
the			blue		litmus		paper

35.2 Dangling Modifiers

35.2 Connect dangling modifiers to their sentences.

A **dangling modifier** does not sensibly modify anything in its sentence.

Dangling Passing the building, the vandalism became visible.

Dangling modifiers usually introduce sentences, contain a **verb** form, and imply but do not name a **subject**. In the example above, the implied subject is the someone or something passing the building. Readers assume that this implied subject is the same as the subject of the sentence (*vandalism* in the example), but vandalism does not pass buildings. The modifier "dangles" because it does not connect sensibly to the rest of the sentence.

Identifying and revising dangling modifiers

- **Find a subject.** If the modifier lacks a subject of its own (e.g., *when in diapers*), identify what it describes.
- **Connect the subject and modifier.** Verify that what the modifier describes is in fact the subject of the main clause. If it is not, the modifier is probably dangling:

       modifier   subject
  Dangling When in diapers, my mother remarried.

- **Revise as needed.** Revise a dangling modifier (*a*) by recasting it with a subject of its own or (*b*) by changing the subject of the main clause:

  Revision *a* When I was in diapers, my mother remarried.
  Revision *b* When in diapers, I attended my mother's second wedding.

Here is another example:

Dangling Although intact, graffiti covered every inch of the walls and windows. [The walls and windows, not the graffiti, were intact.]

To revise a dangling modifier, you have to recast the sentence it appears in. (Revising just by moving the modifier will leave it dangling: *The vandalism became visible passing the building.*) Choose a revision method depending on what you want to emphasize in the sentence.

- **Rewrite the dangling modifier as a complete clause with its own stated subject and verb.** Readers can accept that the new subject and the sentence subject are different.

  Dangling Passing the building, the vandalism became visible.

  Revised As we passed the building, the vandalism became visible.

- **Change the subject of the sentence to a word the modifier properly describes.**

  Dangling Trying to understand the causes, vandalism has been extensively studied.

  Revised Trying to understand the causes, researchers have extensively studied vandalism.

Chapter 36
Sentence Fragments

> **Learning Objectives**
>
> 36.1 Test your sentences and identify sentence fragments.
> 36.2 Revise sentence fragments.
> 36.3 Recognize acceptable uses of incomplete sentences.

36.1 Identifying Fragments

36.1 Test your sentences and identify sentence fragments.

A **sentence fragment** is part of a sentence that is presented as if it were a whole sentence by an initial capital letter and a final period or other end punctuation. Readers perceive most fragments as serious errors.

A word group that is punctuated as a sentence should contain a predicate verb and a subject and should not be a subordinate clause. It should pass *all three* of the following tests. If it does not, it is a fragment and needs revision.

Tests for sentence fragments

1. Does the word group have a predicate verb?

Example	Answer	Revision
Millions of devices on cellular networks.	No →	Add a verb.
Millions of devices use cellular networks.	Yes	—

2. Does the word group have a subject?

Example	Answer	Revision
Cell phones are convenient. But annoy many people.	No →	Add a subject.
Cell phones are convenient. But they annoy many people.	Yes	—

3. Is the word group a freestanding subordinate clause?

Example	Answer	Revision
Phones ring everywhere. Because users forget to silence them.	Yes →	Make it a main clause or attach it to a main clause.
Phones ring everywhere. Users forget to silence them.	No (because removed)	—
Phones ring everywhere because users forget to silence them.	No (clause attached)	—

frag
36.1

Test 1: Find the predicate verb.

Look for a **verb** that can serve as the predicate of a sentence. Some fragments lack any verb at all.

> Fragment   Millions of sites on the Web.
> Revised   Millions of sites make up the Web.

Other sentence fragments contain a verb form, but it is not a predicate verb. Instead, it is often the *-ing* or *to* form (for instance, *walking*, *to walk*):

> Fragment   The Web growing with new sites and users every day.
> Revised   The Web grows with new sites and users every day.

Identifying fragments

> ## Culture and language
>
> Some languages allow forms of *be* to be omitted as helping verbs or linking verbs. But English requires stating forms of *be*, as shown in the following revised example.
>
> **Fragments** The network growing. It much larger than anticipated.
> **Revised** The network is growing. It is much larger than anticipated.

Test 2: Find the subject.

The **subject** of the sentence will usually come before the verb. If there is no subject, the word group is probably a fragment:

Fragment The Web continues to grow. And shows no sign of slowing down.
Revised The Web continues to grow. And it shows no sign of slowing down.

In one kind of complete sentence, a command, the subject *you* is understood: [*You*] *Try this recipe.*

> ## Culture and language
>
> Some languages allow the omission of the sentence subject, especially when it is a **pronoun**. But in English, except in commands, the subject is always stated:
>
> **Fragment** Web shopping has exploded. Has hurt traditional stores.
> **Revised** Web shopping has exploded. It has hurt traditional stores.

Test 3: Make sure the clause is not subordinate.

A **subordinate clause** usually begins with a subordinating word, such as one of the following:

Subordinating conjunctions			Relative pronouns	
after	once	until	that	who/whom
although	since	when	which	whoever/whomever
as	than	where		whose
because	that	whereas		
if	unless	while		

Subordinate clauses serve as parts of sentences (as nouns or modifiers), not as whole sentences:

Fragment	When the government devised the Internet.
Revised	The government devised the Internet.
Revised	When the government devised the Internet, no expansive computer network existed.
Fragment	The reason that the government devised the Internet.
Revised	The reason that the government devised the Internet was to link departments and defense contractors.

Questions beginning with *how, what, when, where, which, who, whom, whose,* and *why* are not sentence fragments: *Who was responsible? When did it happen?*

36.2 Correcting Fragments

36.2 Revise sentence fragments.

Almost all sentence fragments can be corrected in one of two ways. The choice depends on the importance of the information in the fragment and how much you want to stress it.

- **Rewrite the fragment as a complete sentence.** Add a predicate verb or a subject as needed, or make a subordinate clause into a complete sentence. Any of these revisions gives the information in the fragment the same importance as that in other complete sentences.

Fragment	A major improvement in public health occurred with the widespread use of vaccines. Which protected children against life-threatening diseases.
Revised	A major improvement in public health occurred with the widespread use of vaccines. They protected children against life-threatening diseases.

    Two main clauses may be separated by a semicolon instead of a period.

- **Attach the fragment to a main clause.** This revision subordinates the information in the fragment to the information in the main clause.

Fragment	The polio vaccine eradicated the disease from most of the globe. The first vaccine to be used widely.
Revised	The polio vaccine, the first to be used widely, eradicated the disease from most of the globe.

36.3 Acceptable Fragments

36.3 Recognize acceptable uses of incomplete sentences.

A few word groups lacking the usual subject-predicate combination are incomplete sentences, but they are not fragments because they conform to the expectations of most readers. They include commands (*Move along. Shut the window.*); exclamations (*Oh no!*); questions and answers (*Where next? To Kansas.*); and descriptions in employment résumés (*Weekly volunteer in soup kitchen.*)

Experienced writers sometimes use sentence fragments when they want to achieve a special effect. Such fragments appear more in informal than in formal writing. Unless you are experienced and thoroughly secure in your own writing, you should avoid all fragments and concentrate on writing clear, well-formed sentences.

Chapter 37
Comma Splices and Fused Sentences

 Learning Objectives

37.1 Identify comma splices and fused sentences.
37.2 Revise comma splices and fused sentences.

37.1 Identifying Comma Splices and Fused Sentences

37.1 Identify comma splices and fused sentences.

When two **main clauses** appear in a row, readers need a signal that one main clause is ending and another is beginning. The four ways to provide this signal appear in the box below.

Punctuation of two or more main clauses

- **Separate main clauses with periods.**

  Main clause . Main clause .

  Hybrid cars are popular with consumers. Automakers are releasing new models.

- **Link main clauses with a comma and a coordinating conjunction.**

  Main clause , *for and or so but nor yet* main clause .

  Hybrid cars are popular with consumers , and automakers are releasing new models.

- **Link main clauses with a semicolon.**

  Main clause ; main clause .

  Hybrid cars are popular with consumers ; automakers are releasing new models.

- **Relate main clauses with a semicolon and a conjunctive adverb or transitional expression.**

  Main clause ; *however for example, etc.* , main clause .

  Hybrid cars are popular with consumers ; as a result , automakers are releasing new models.

Two problems in punctuating main clauses fail to signal the break between the clauses. One is the **comma splice**, in which the clauses are joined (or spliced) *only* with a comma:

> **Comma splice**   The ship was huge, its mast stood eighty feet high.

The other is the **fused sentence** (or **run-on sentence**), in which no punctuation or conjunction appears between the clauses.

> **Fused sentence**   The ship was huge its mast stood eighty feet high.

Culture and language

In standard American English, a sentence may not include more than one main clause unless the clauses are separated by a comma and a **coordinating conjunction** or by a semicolon. If your native language does not have such a rule or has accustomed you to writing long sentences, you may need to edit your English writing especially for comma splices and fused sentences.

37.2 Correcting Comma Splices and Fused Sentences

37.2 Revise comma splices and fused sentences.

If your readers point out comma splices or fused sentences in your writing, you're not creating enough separation between main clauses in your sentences. Separate main clauses in the following ways.

37.2.1 Separate main clauses.

Separate sentences

Make the clauses into separate sentences when the ideas expressed are only loosely related.

Comma splice	Chemistry has contributed much to our understanding of foods, many foods such as wheat and beans can be produced in the laboratory.
Revised	Chemistry has contributed much to our understanding of foods. Many foods such as wheat and beans can be produced in the laboratory.

Coordinating conjunction

Insert a **coordinating conjunction** such as *and* or *but* in a comma splice when the ideas in the main clauses are closely related and equally important:

Comma splice	Some laboratory-grown foods taste good, they are nutritious.
Revised	Some laboratory-grown foods taste good, and they are nutritious.

In a fused sentence, insert a comma and a coordinating conjunction:

Fused sentence	Chemists have made much progress they still have a way to go.
Revised	Chemists have made much progress, but they still have a way to go.

Semicolon

Insert a semicolon between clauses if the relationship between the ideas is very close and obvious without a conjunction:

> **Comma splice** Good taste is rare in laboratory-grown vegetables, they are usually bland.
>
> **Revised** Good taste is rare in laboratory-grown vegetables; they are usually bland.

Subordination

When one idea is less important than the other, express the less important idea in a **subordinate clause**:

> **Comma splice** The vitamins are adequate, the flavor is poor.
>
> **Revised** Although the vitamins are adequate, the flavor is poor.

37.2.2 Revise comma splices and fused sentences using *however* and other transitional expressions.

Two groups of words describe how one main clause relates to another: **conjunctive adverbs** and other **transitional expressions**. See the list of these words in the following box.

Common conjunctive adverbs and transitional expressions

accordingly	for instance	instead	otherwise
anyway	further	in the meantime	similarly
as a result	furthermore	in the past	still
at last	hence	likewise	that is
besides	however	meanwhile	then
certainly	incidentally	moreover	thereafter
consequently	in contrast	nevertheless	therefore
even so	indeed	nonetheless	thus
finally	in fact	now	undoubtedly
for all that	in other words	of course	until now
for example	in short	on the contrary	

When two main clauses are related by a conjunctive adverb or another transitional expression, they must be separated by a period or by a semicolon. The adverb or expression is also generally set off by a comma or commas.

> **Comma splice** Healthcare costs are higher in the United States than in many other countries, consequently health insurance is also more costly.

Revised	Healthcare costs are higher in the United States than in many other countries. Consequently, health insurance is also more costly.
Revised	Healthcare costs are higher in the United States than in many other countries; consequently, health insurance is also more costly.

Conjunctive adverbs and transitional expressions are different from **coordinating conjunctions** (*and, but,* and so on) and **subordinating conjunctions** (*although, because,* and so on):

- **Unlike conjunctions, conjunctive adverbs and transitional expressions do not join two clauses into a grammatical unit.** They merely describe the way two clauses relate in meaning.
- **Unlike conjunctions, conjunctive adverbs and transitional expressions can be moved within a clause.** No matter where in the clause an adverb or expression falls, though, the clause must be separated from another main clause by a period or semicolon:

Healthcare costs are higher in the United States than in many other countries; health insurance, consequently, is also more costly.

Chapter 38
Mixed Sentences

Learning Objectives

- **38.1** Revise sentences that are mixed in meaning.
- **38.2** Revise sentences that are mixed in grammar.
- **38.3** Revise sentences with repeated subjects and other parts.

38.1 Mixed Meaning

38.1 Revise sentences that are mixed in meaning.

A **mixed sentence** contains parts that do not fit together. The misfit may be in meaning or in grammar.

In a sentence with mixed meaning, the **subject** is said to do or be something illogical. Such a mixture is sometimes called **faulty predication** because the **predicate** conflicts with the subject.

38.1.1 Illogical equation with *be*

When a form of *be* connects a subject and a word that describes the subject (a **complement**), the subject and complement must be logically related.

> Mixed   A compromise between the city and the country would be the ideal place to live.
>
> Revised   A community that offered the best qualities of both city and country would be the ideal place to live.

38.1.2 *Is when, is where*

Definitions require **nouns** on both sides of *be*. **Clauses** that define and begin with *when* or *where* are common in speech but should be avoided in writing:

> Mixed   An examination is when you are tested on what you know.
>
> Revised   An examination is a test of what you know.

38.1.3 *Reason is because*

The commonly heard construction *reason is because* is redundant since *because* means "for the reason that":

> Mixed   The reason the temple requests donations is because the school needs expansion.
>
> Revised   The reason the temple requests donations is that the school needs expansion.
>
> Revised   The temple requests donations because the school needs expansion.

38.1.4 Other mixed meanings

Faulty predications are not confined to sentences with *be*:

> Mixed   The use of emission controls was created to reduce air pollution.
>
> Revised   Emission controls were created to reduce air pollution.

38.2 Mixed Grammar

38.2   **Revise sentences that are mixed in grammar.**

Many mixed sentences start with one grammatical plan or construction but end with a different one:

> Mixed   By paying more attention to impressions than facts causes us to misjudge others.
>
> *(modifier (prepositional phrase) — predicate)*

| | modifier (prepositional phrase) | subject |
Revised By paying more attention to impressions than facts, we
predicate
misjudge others.

Constructions that use *Just because* clauses as subjects are common in speech but should be avoided in writing.

Mixed modifier (subordinate clause) — predicate
Just because no one is watching does not mean we have license to break the law.

Revised modifier (subordinate clause) — subject + predicate
Even when no one is watching, we do not have license to break the law.

A mixed sentence is especially likely when you are working on a computer and connect parts of two sentences or rewrite half a sentence but not the other half. A mixed sentence may also occur when you don't make the subject and predicate verb carry the principal meaning.

38.3 Repeated Elements

38.3 Revise sentences with repeated subjects and other parts.

Culture and language

In some languages other than English, certain parts of sentences may be repeated. These include the subject in any kind of clause or an object or adverb in an adjective clause. In English, however, these parts are stated only once in a clause.

38.3.1 Repetition of subject

You may be tempted to restate a subject as a pronoun before the verb. But the subject needs stating only once in its clause:

Faulty   The liquid it boiled.
Revised   The liquid boiled.

Faulty   Gases in the liquid they escaped.
Revised   Gases in the liquid escaped.

38.3.2 Repetition in an adjective clause

Adjective clauses begin with *who, whom, whose, which, that, where,* and *when*. The beginning word replaces another word: the subject (*He is the person who called*), an **object** (*He is the person whom I* *mentioned*), or a phrase such as *in which, at which,* or *on which.* (*He knows the office where [in which] the conference will occur*).

Do not state the word being replaced in an adjective clause:

Faulty   The technician whom the test depended on her was burned. [*Whom* should replace *her.*]

Revised   The technician whom the test depended on was burned.

Adjective clauses beginning with *where* or *when* do not need an adverb such as *there* or *then*:

Faulty   Gases escaped at a moment when the technician was unprepared then.

Revised   Gases escaped at a moment when the technician was unprepared.

Whom, which, and similar words are sometimes omitted but are still understood by the reader. Thus the word being replaced should not be stated.

Faulty   Accidents rarely happen to technicians the lab has trained them. [*Whom* is understood: . . . *technicians whom the lab has trained.*]

Revised   Accidents rarely happen to technicians the lab has trained.

mixed
38.3

Part 5

Punctuation

39 End Punctuation *311*
40 The Comma *313*
41 The Semicolon *324*
42 The Colon *326*
43 The Apostrophe *328*
44 Quotation Marks *332*
45 Other Marks *336*

Part 5
Punctuation

- **39 End Punctuation** *311*
  - **39.1** Period *311*
  - **39.2** Question mark *312*
  - **39.3** Exclamation point *312*
- **40 The Comma** *313*
  - **40.1** Uses of the comma *313*
  - **40.2** Main clauses linked by conjunctions *313*
  - **40.3** Introductory elements *315*
  - **40.4** Nonessential elements *315*
  - **40.5** Series and coordinate adjectives *319*
  - **40.6** Quotations and other conventional uses *320*
  - **40.7** Unnecessary commas *321*
- **41 The Semicolon** *324*
  - **41.1** Main clauses without coordinating conjunctions *324*
  - **41.2** Main clauses with transitional words *324*
  - **41.3** Main clauses that are long or contain commas *325*
  - **41.4** Unnecessary semicolons *326*
- **42 The Colon** *326*
  - **42.1** To introduce and separate *326*
- **43 The Apostrophe** *328*
  - **43.1** Possession *328*
  - **43.2** Contractions and abbreviations *331*
- **44 Quotation Marks** *332*
  - **44.1** Direct quotations *332*
  - **44.2** Titles of works *333*
  - **44.3** Words used in a special sense *334*
  - **44.4** With other punctuation *335*
- **45 Other Marks** *336*
  - **45.1** Dash *336*
  - **45.2** Parentheses *337*
  - **45.3** Ellipsis mark *338*
  - **45.4** Brackets *340*
  - **45.5** Slash *340*

Chapter 39
End Punctuation

Learning Objectives

39.1 Use periods to end sentences and to indicate abbreviations.
39.2 Use question marks to end direct questions and to indicate doubt.
39.3 Use an exclamation point after an emphatic statement, interjection, or command.

39.1 Period

39.1 Use periods to end sentences and to indicate abbreviations.

39.1.1 Statements, mild commands, and indirect questions

Statement
The airline went bankrupt.   It no longer flies.

Mild command
Think of the possibilities.   Please consider others.

An **indirect question** reports what someone asked but not in the exact form or words of the original question:

Indirect question
The judge asked why I had been driving with my lights off.
No one asked how we got home.

> ### Culture and language
> In standard American English, the reporting verb in an indirect question (for example, *asked* or *said*) usually precedes a clause that contains a subject and verb in normal order, not question order: *The reporter asked why the negotiations failed* [not *why did the negotiations fail*].

39.1.2 Abbreviations

Use periods with abbreviations that consist of or end in small letters. Otherwise, omit periods from abbreviations.

Dr.	Mr., Mrs.	e.g.	Feb.	ft.
St.	Ms.	i.e.	p.	a.m., p.m.
PhD	BC, BCE	USA	IBM	AM, PM
BA	AD, CE	US	USMC	AIDS

When a sentence ends in an abbreviation with a period, don't add a second period: *My first class is at 8 a.m.*

39.2 Question Mark

39.2 Use question marks to end direct questions and to indicate doubt.

39.2.1 Direct questions

Who will follow her?
What is the difference between these two people?

After indirect questions, use a period: *We wondered who would follow her.*

Questions in a series are each followed by a question mark:

The officer asked how many times the suspect had been arrested. Three times? Four times? More than that?

Do not combine question marks with other question marks, periods, commas, or other punctuation.

39.2.2 Doubt

A question mark within parentheses can indicate doubt about a number or date.

The Greek philosopher Socrates was born in 470 (?) BC and died in 399 BC from drinking poison. [The date of Socrates's birth is not known for sure.]

Use sentence structure and words, not a question mark, to express sarcasm or irony.

Not Stern's friendliness (?) bothered Crane.
But Stern's insincerity bothered Crane.

39.3 Exclamation Point

39.3 Use an exclamation point after an emphatic statement, interjection, or command.

No! We must not lose this election!
Come here immediately!

Follow mild **interjections** and commands with commas or periods, as appropriate: *Oh, call whenever you can.*

Do not combine exclamation points with periods, commas, or other punctuation marks. And use exclamation points sparingly, even in informal writing. Overused, they'll fail to impress readers, and they may make you sound overwrought.

Chapter 40
The Comma

> **Learning Objectives**
>
> 40.1 Identify the principal uses of the comma.
> 40.2 Use a comma before *and*, *but*, or another coordinating conjunction linking main clauses.
> 40.3 Use a comma to set off most introductory elements.
> 40.4 Use commas to set off nonessential elements.
> 40.5 Use commas between items in a series and between coordinate adjectives.
> 40.6 Use commas to set off quotations and for other conventional purposes.
> 40.7 Delete unnecessary commas.

40.1 Uses of the Comma

40.1 Identify the principal uses of the comma.

The comma (,) is the most common punctuation mark inside sentences.

40.2 Main Clauses Linked by Conjunctions

40.2 Use a comma before *and*, *but*, or another coordinating conjunction linking main clauses.

When a **coordinating conjunction** links words or phrases, do not use a comma: *Dugain plays and sings Irish and English folk songs*. However, *do* use a comma when a coordinating conjunction joins **main clauses**, as in the next examples.

> Caffeine can help coffee drinkers stay alert, and it may elevate their mood.
>
> Caffeine was once thought to be safe, but now researchers warn of harmful effects.
>
> Coffee drinkers may suffer sleeplessness, for the drug acts as a stimulant to the nervous system.

The comma goes *before,* not after, a coordinating conjunction that links main clauses: *Caffeine increases heart rate, and it* [not *and, it*] *constricts blood vessels.*

Principal uses of the comma

- Separate main clauses linked by a coordinating conjunction:

  Main clause , [for and or / so but nor / yet] main clause .

  The building is finished, but it has no tenants.

- Set off most introductory elements:

  Introductory element , main clause .

  Unfortunately, the only tenant pulled out.

- Set off nonessential elements:

  Main clause , nonessential element .

  The empty building symbolizes a weak local economy, which affects everyone.

  Beginning of main clause , nonessential element , end of main clause .

  The primary cause, the decline of local industry, is not news.

- Separate items in a series:

  ... item 1 , item 2 , [and / or] item 3 ...

  The city needs more jobs, new schools, and better housing.

- Separate coordinate adjectives:

  ... first adjective , second adjective word modified ...

  A tall, sleek skyscraper is not needed.

Other uses of the comma:
Set off absolute phrases.
Set off phrases expressing contrast.
Separate parts of dates, addresses, place names, and long numbers.
Separate quotations and signal phrases.
Prevent misreading.

Some writers omit the comma between main clauses that are very short and closely related in meaning: *Caffeine helps but it also hurts.* If you are in doubt about whether to use the comma in such a sentence, use it. It will always be correct.

40.3 Introductory Elements

> 40.3 Use a comma to set off most introductory elements.

An **introductory element** begins a sentence and modifies a word or words in the main clause. It is usually followed by a comma.

Subordinate clause
<u>Even when identical twins are raised apart</u>, they grow up very like each other.

Verbal or verbal phrase
<u>Explaining the similarity</u>, some researchers claim that one's genes are one's destiny.
<u>Concerned</u>, other researchers deny the claim.

Prepositional phrase
<u>In a debate that has lasted centuries</u>, scientists use identical twins to argue for or against genetic destiny.

Transitional expression
<u>Of course</u>, scientists can now look directly at the genes themselves to answer questions.

You may omit the comma after a short subordinate clause or prepositional phrase if its omission does not create confusion: *<u>When snow falls</u> the city collapses. <u>By the year 2000</u> the world population had topped 6 billion.* You may also omit the comma after some transitional expressions, when they start sentences: *<u>Thus</u> the debate ended.* However, in both situations the comma is never wrong.

Take care to distinguish *-ing* words used as modifiers from *-ing* words used as subjects. The former almost always take a comma; the latter never do.

    ⌈——— modifier ———⌉   subject   verb
<u>Studying identical twins</u>, geneticists learn about inheritance.

    ⌈——— subject ———⌉   verb
<u>Studying identical twins</u> helps geneticists learn about inheritance.

40.4 Nonessential Elements

> 40.4 Use commas to set off nonessential elements.

Commas around part of a sentence often signal that the element is not necessary to the meaning. This **nonessential element** may modify or rename the word it refers to, but it does not limit the word to a particular individual or group. The meaning of the word would still be clear if the element were deleted:

Nonessential element
The company, which is located in Oklahoma, has a good reputation.

(Because it does not restrict meaning, a nonessential element is also called a **nonrestrictive element**.)

In contrast, an **essential** (or **restrictive**) element *does* limit the word it refers to: the element cannot be omitted without leaving the meaning too general. Because it is essential, such an element is *not* set off with a comma or commas.

Essential element
The company rewards employees who work hard.

Omitting *who work hard* would distort the meaning: the company doesn't necessarily reward *all* employees, only the hardworking ones.

The same element in the same sentence may be essential or nonessential depending on your meaning and the context:

Essential
Not all the bands were equally well received, however. The band playing old music held the audience's attention. The other groups created much less excitement. [*Playing old music* identifies a particular band.]

Nonessential
A new band called Fats made its debut on Saturday night. The band, playing old music, held the audience's attention. If this performance is typical, the group has a bright future. [*Playing old music* adds information about a band already named.]

When a nonessential element falls in the middle of a sentence, be sure to set it off with a pair of commas, one *before* and one *after* the element.

A test for nonessential and essential elements

1. **Identify the element:**
   Hai Nguyen who emigrated from Vietnam lives in Dallas.
   Those who emigrated with him live elsewhere.

2. **Remove the element.** Does the fundamental meaning of the sentence change?
   Hai Nguyen lives in Dallas. ***No.***
   Those live elsewhere. ***Yes.*** [Who are *Those*?]

3. **If *no*, the element is *nonessential* and *should* be set off with punctuation:**

   Hai Nguyen, who emigrated from Vietnam, lives in Dallas.

   If *yes*, the element is *essential* and should *not* be set off with punctuation:

   Those who emigrated with him live elsewhere.

40.4.1 Nonessential phrases and clauses

Nonessential phrases and **subordinate clauses** function as **adjectives** or, less commonly, as **adverbs**. In each of the following examples, the underlined words could be omitted with no loss of clarity.

> Elizabeth Blackwell was the first woman to graduate from an American medical school, in 1849. [Adverb phrase.]
>
> She was a medical pioneer, helping to found the first medical college for women. [Adjective phrase.]
>
> She taught at the school, which was affiliated with the New York Infirmary. [Adjective clause.]
>
> Blackwell, who published books and papers on medicine, practiced pediatrics and gynecology. [Adjective clause.]
>
> She moved to England in 1869, when she was forty-eight. [Adverb clause.]

Use *that* only in an essential clause, never in a nonessential clause. Many writers reserve *which* for nonessential clauses.

> **Faulty** The tree, that is 120 years old, shades the house.
>
> **Revised** The tree, which is 120 years old, shades the house.

40.4.2 Nonessential appositives

A **nonessential appositive** merely adds information about the word it refers to.

> Toni Morrison's fifth novel, *Beloved*, won the Pulitzer Prize in 1988. [The word *fifth* identifies the novel, while the title adds a detail.]

In contrast, an essential appositive limits or defines the word it refers to:

> Morrison's novel *The Bluest Eye* is about an African American girl who longs for blue eyes. [Morrison has written more than one novel, so the title is essential to identify the intended one.]

40.4.3 Other nonessential elements

Many other elements contribute to texture, tone, or overall clarity but are not essential to the meaning. Unlike nonessential modifiers or appositives, these other nonessential elements generally do not refer to any specific word in the sentence. Use a pair of commas—one before, one after—when any of these elements falls in the middle of a sentence.

Absolute phrases

Household recycling having succeeded, the city now wants to extend the program to businesses.

Many businesses, their profits already squeezed, resist recycling.

Parenthetical and transitional expressions

Generally, set off **parenthetical expressions** and **transitional expressions** with commas:

The world's most celebrated holiday is, perhaps surprisingly, New Year's Day. [Parenthetical expression.]

Interestingly, Americans have relatively few holidays. [Parenthetical expression.]

US workers, for example, receive fewer holidays than European workers do. [Transitional expression.]

When a transitional expression links **main clauses**, precede it with a semicolon and follow it with a comma:

European workers often have long paid vacations; indeed, they may receive a full month after just a few years with a company.

The conjunctions *and* and *but,* sometimes used as transitional expressions, are never followed by commas. Usage varies with some other transitional expressions, depending on the expression and the writer's judgment. Many writers omit commas with expressions that we read without pauses, such as *also, hence, next, now, then,* and *thus.* The same applies to *therefore* and *instead* when they fall inside or at the ends of clauses.

US workers therefore put in more work days. But the days themselves may be shorter.

Then the total hours worked would come out roughly the same.

Phrases of contrast

The substance, not the style, is important.

Substance, unlike style, cannot be faked.

Tag questions

They don't stop to consider others, do they?

Jones should be allowed to vote, shouldn't he?

Yes and *no*

Yes, the writer did have a point.

No, that can never be.

Words of direct address
Cody, please bring me the newspaper.
With all due respect, sir, I will not.

Mild interjections
Well, you will never know who did it.
Oh, they forgot all about the baby.

40.5 Series and Coordinate Adjectives

40.5 Use commas between items in a series and between coordinate adjectives.

40.5.1 Use commas between items in a series.

A **series** consists of three or more items of equal importance. The items may be words, phrases, or clauses.

> Anna Spingle married at the age of seventeen, had three children by twenty-one, and divorced at twenty-two.
>
> She worked as a cook, a babysitter, and a crossing guard.

Some writers omit the comma before the last item in a series (*Breakfast consisted of coffee, eggs and kippers*). But the final comma is never wrong, and it always helps the reader see the last two items as separate.

40.5.2 Use commas between two or more adjectives that equally modify the same word.

Adjectives that equally modify the same word—**coordinate adjectives**—may be separated either by *and* or by a comma.

> Spingle's scratched and dented car is old, but it gets her to work.
>
> She dreams of buying a sleek, shiny car.

Adjectives are not coordinate—and should not be separated by commas—when the adjective nearer the modified word is more closely related to the word in meaning.

> Spingle's children work at various part-time jobs.
>
> They all expect to go to a nearby community college.

Tests for commas with adjectives

1. **Identify the adjectives.**
   She was a faithful sincere friend.
   They are dedicated medical students.

(continued)

> ### Tests for commas with adjectives
> *(continued)*
>
> 2. **Can the adjectives be reversed without changing meaning?**
>   She was a sincere faithful friend. *Yes.*
>   They are medical dedicated students. *No.*
>
> 3. **Can the word *and* be sensibly inserted between the adjectives?**
>   She was a faithful and sincere friend. *Yes.*
>   They are dedicated and medical students. *No.*
>
> 4. **If *yes* to both questions, the adjectives *are* coordinate and *should* be separated by a comma.**
>   She was a faithful, sincere friend.
>
>   **If *no* to both questions, the adjectives are *not* coordinate and should *not* be separated by a comma.**
>   They are dedicated medical students.

40.6 Quotations and Other Conventional Uses

40.6 Use commas to set off quotations and for other conventional purposes.

40.6.1 Use commas in dates, addresses, place names, and long numbers.

Within a sentence, any date, address, or place name that contains a comma should also end with a comma.

Dates

July 4, 1776, is the date the Declaration was signed.

The bombing of Pearl Harbor on Sunday, December 7, 1941, prompted American entry into World War II.

Do not use commas between the parts of a date in inverted order (*15 December 1992*) or in dates consisting of a month or season and a year (*December 1941*).

Addresses and place names

Use the address 220 Cornell Road, Woodside, California 94062, for all correspondence. [Do not use a comma between a state name and a zip code.]

Columbus, Ohio, is the location of Ohio State University.

Long numbers

Use the comma to separate the figures in long numbers into groups of three, counting from the right. With numbers of four digits, the comma is optional.

The new assembly plant cost $7,525,000.

A kilometer is 3,281 feet [*or* 3281 feet].

40.6.2 Use commas with quotations according to standard practice.

The words *she said, he writes,* and so on identify the source of a quotation. These **signal phrases** should be separated from the quotation by punctuation, usually a comma or commas.

> "Knowledge is power," writes Francis Bacon.
>
> "The shore has a dual nature," observes Rachel Carson, "changing with the swing of the tides." [The signal phrase interrupts the quotation at a comma and thus ends with a comma.]

Do not use commas with signal phrases in some situations:

- **Use a semicolon or a period after a signal phrase that interrupts a quotation between main clauses.** The choice depends on the punctuation of the original:

    Not "That door was closed," she wrote, "his words had sealed it shut."

    But "That door was closed," she wrote. "His words had sealed it shut." [*She wrote* interrupts the quotation at a period.]

    Or "That door was closed," she wrote; "his words had sealed it shut." [*She wrote* interrupts the quotation at a semicolon.]

- **Omit a comma when a signal phrase follows a quotation ending in an exclamation point or a question mark:**

    "Claude!" Mrs. Harrison called.

    "Why must I come home?" he asked.

- **Use a colon when a complete sentence introduces a quotation:**

    Her statement was clear: "I will not resign."

- **Omit commas when a quotation is integrated into your sentence structure,** including a quotation introduced by *that*:

    James Baldwin insists that "one must never, in one's life, accept . . . injustices as commonplace."

    Baldwin thought that the violence of a riot "had been devised as a corrective" to his own violence.

- **Omit commas with a quoted title unless it is a nonessential appositive:**

    The Beatles recorded "She Loves You" in 1963.

    The Beatles' first huge US hit, "She Loves You," appeared in 1963.

40.7 Unnecessary Commas

40.7 Delete unnecessary commas.

Commas can make sentences choppy and even confusing if they are used more often than needed.

40.7.1 No comma between subject and verb, verb and object, or preposition and object

Not The returning soldiers, received a warm welcome. [Separated subject and verb.]

But The returning soldiers received a warm welcome.

Not They had chosen, to fight for their country despite, the risks. [Separated verb *chosen* and its object; separated preposition *despite* and its object.]

But They had chosen to fight for their country despite the risks.

40.7.2 No comma in most compound constructions

Compound constructions consisting of two elements almost never require a comma. The only exception is the sentence consisting of two main clauses linked by a coordinating conjunction: *The network failed, but employees kept working.*

Not Banks, and other financial institutions [compound subject] have helped older people with money management, and investment. [compound object]

But Banks and other financial institutions have helped older people with money management and investment.

Not One bank created special accounts for older people, and held [compound predicate] classes, and workshops. [compound object]

But One bank created special accounts for older people and held classes and workshops.

40.7.3 No comma after a conjunction

Not Parents of adolescents notice increased conflict at puberty, and, they complain of bickering.

But Parents of adolescents notice increased conflict at puberty, and they complain of bickering.

Not Although, other primates leave the family at adolescence, humans do not.

But Although other primates leave the family at adolescence, humans do not.

40.7.4 No commas around essential elements

Not Hawthorne's work, *The Scarlet Letter*, was the first major American novel. [The title is essential to distinguish the novel from the rest of Hawthorne's work.]

But   Hawthorne's work *The Scarlet Letter* was the first major American novel.

Not   The symbols, that Hawthorne uses, have influenced many other novelists. [The clause identifies which symbols have been influential.]

But   The symbols that Hawthorne uses have influenced many other novelists.

Not   Published in 1850, *The Scarlet Letter* is still popular, because its theme of secret sin resonates with contemporary readers. [The clause is essential to explain why the novel is popular.]

But   Published in 1850, *The Scarlet Letter* is still popular because its theme of secret sin resonates with contemporary readers.

Like the *because* clause in the preceding example, most adverb clauses are essential because they describe conditions necessary to the main clause.

40.7.5   No commas around a series

Commas separate the items *within* a series but do not separate the series from the rest of the sentence.

Not   The skills of, hunting, herding, and agriculture, sustained the Native Americans.

But   The skills of hunting, herding, and agriculture sustained the Native Americans.

40.7.6   No comma before an indirect quotation

Not   The report concluded, that dieting could be more dangerous than overeating.

But   The report concluded that dieting could be more dangerous than overeating.

Chapter 41
The Semicolon

Learning Objectives

41.1 Use a semicolon between main clauses not joined by a coordinating conjunction.

41.2 Use a semicolon between main clauses related by *however, for example,* and other transitional expressions.

41.3 Use semicolons between main clauses or series items containing commas.

41.4 Delete or replace unneeded semicolons.

41.1 Main Clauses without Coordinating Conjunctions

41.1 Use a semicolon between main clauses not joined by a coordinating conjunction.

The semicolon (;) separates equal and balanced sentence elements. When no **coordinating conjunction** links two **main clauses**, the clauses should be separated by a semicolon.

> A new ulcer drug arrived on the market with a mixed reputation**;** doctors find that the drug works but worry about its side effects.
>
> The side effects are not minor**;** some leave the patient quite uncomfortable or even ill.

This rule prevents the errors known as comma splices and fused sentences.

41.2 Main Clauses with Transitional Words

41.2 Use a semicolon between main clauses related by *however, for example,* and other transitional expressions.

When a **conjunctive adverb** or another **transitional expression** relates two main clauses in a single sentence, the clauses should be separated with a semicolon:

> An American immigrant, Levi Strauss, invented blue jeans in the 1860s**;** eventually, his product clothed working men throughout the West.

The position of the semicolon between main clauses never changes, but the conjunctive adverb or transitional expression may move around in the second clause. Wherever the adverb or expression falls, it is usually set off with a comma or commas.

> Blue jeans have become fashionable all over the world; however, the American originators still wear more jeans than anyone else.
>
> Blue jeans have become fashionable all over the world; the American originators, however, still wear more jeans than anyone else.
>
> Blue jeans have become fashionable all over the world; the American originators still wear more jeans than anyone else, however.

The semicolon in such sentences prevents the error known as a comma splice.

Distinguishing the semicolon and the colon

Semicolon

The semicolon separates elements of *equal* importance, almost always complete main clauses.

> Few enrolling students know exactly what they want from the school; most hope generally for a managerial career.

Colon

The colon separates elements of *unequal* importance, such as statements and explanations. The first element must be a complete main clause; the second element need not be.

> The business school caters to working students: it offers special evening courses in business writing, finance, and management.
>
> The school has one goal: to train students to be responsible, competent businesspeople.

41.3 Main Clauses that Are Long or Contain Commas

41.3 Use semicolons between main clauses or series items containing commas.

Normally, commas separate main clauses linked by **coordinating conjunctions** (*and, but, or, nor*) and separate items in a series. But when the clauses or series items contain commas, a semicolon between them makes the sentence easier to read.

> Lewis and Clark led the men of their party with consummate skill, inspiring and encouraging them, doctoring and caring for them; and they kept voluminous journals.
> —Page Smith

> The custody case involved Amy Dalton, the child; Ellen and Mark Dalton, the parents; and Ruth and Hal Blum, the grandparents.

41.4 Unnecessary Semicolons

41.4 Delete or replace unneeded semicolons.

Semicolons are often misused in certain constructions that call for other punctuation or no punctuation.

41.4.1 No semicolon between a main clause and a subordinate clause or phrase

The semicolon does not separate unequal parts, such as main clauses and **subordinate clauses** or phrases.

- **Not** Pygmies are in danger of extinction; because of encroaching development.
- **But** Pygmies are in danger of extinction because of encroaching development.
- **Not** According to African authorities; about 35,000 Pygmies exist today.
- **But** According to African authorities, about 35,000 Pygmies exist today.

41.4.2 No semicolon before a series or explanation

Colons and dashes, not semicolons, introduce series, explanations, and so forth.

- **Not** Teachers have heard many reasons why students do poorly; psychological problems, family illness, too much work, too little time.
- **But** Teachers have heard many reasons why students do poorly: psychological problems, family illness, too much work, too little time.

Chapter 42
The Colon

Learning Objective

42.1 Use the colon to introduce and to separate.

42.1 To Introduce and Separate

42.1 Use the colon to introduce and to separate.

The colon (:) is mainly a mark of introduction: it signals that the words following will explain or amplify. The colon also has several conventional uses, such as in expressions of time.

42.1.1 Use a colon to introduce a concluding explanation, a series, an appositive, and some quotations.

As an introducer, a colon is always preceded by a complete **main clause**. It may or may not be followed by a main clause. This is one way the colon differs from the semicolon, which generally separates main clauses only.

Explanation
Soul food has a deceptively simple definition: the ethnic cooking done by African Americans.

Sometimes a concluding explanation is preceded by *the following* or *as follows* and a colon:

> A more precise definition might be the following: soul food draws on ingredients, cooking methods, and dishes that originated in Africa, were brought to the New World by slaves, and were modified or supplemented in the Caribbean and the American South.

A complete sentence *after* a colon may begin with a capital letter or a small letter (as in the preceding example). Just be consistent throughout an essay.

Series
At least three soul food dishes are familiar to most Americans: fried chicken, barbecued spareribs, and sweet potatoes.

Appositive
Soul food has only one disadvantage: fat.

Namely, that is, and other expressions that introduce appositives follow the colon: *Soul food has only one disadvantage: namely, fat.*

Quotation
One soul food chef has a solution: "Soul food doesn't have to be greasy to taste good. Instead of using ham hocks to flavor beans, I use smoked turkey wings. The soulful, smoky taste remains, but without all the fat of pork."

Use a colon before a quotation when the introduction is a complete sentence.

42.1.2 Use a colon after the salutation of a business letter, between a title and subtitle, and between divisions of time.

Salutation of a business letter
Dear Ms. Burak:

Title and subtitle
Charles Dickens: An Introduction to His Novels

Time
12:26 AM   6:00 PM

42.1.3 Delete or replace unneeded colons.

Use the colon only at the end of a **main clause**, not in the following situations:

- **Delete a colon after a verb.**

  Not   The best-known soul food dish is: fried chicken.
  But   The best-known soul food dish is fried chicken.

- **Delete a colon after a preposition.**

  Not   Soul food recipes can be found in: mainstream cookbooks as well as specialized references.
  But   Soul food recipes can be found in mainstream cookbooks as well as specialized references.

- **Delete a colon after** *such as* **or** *including*.

  Not   Many Americans have not tasted delicacies such as: chitlins and black-eyed peas.
  But   Many Americans have not tasted delicacies such as chitlins and black-eyed peas.

Chapter 43
The Apostrophe

Learning Objectives

43.1 Use apostrophes to show possession.
43.2 Use apostrophes in contractions or abbreviations.

43.1 Possession

43.1   Use apostrophes to show possession.

A noun or **indefinite pronoun** shows possession with an apostrophe and, usually, an *-s*: *the dog's hair, everyone's hope*. Only certain pronouns do not use apostrophes for possession: *mine, yours, his, hers, its, ours, theirs,* and *whose*.

Apostrophes are easy to misuse. Always check your drafts to be sure that all words ending in *-s* neither omit needed apostrophes nor add unneeded ones. Also, remember that the apostrophe or apostrophe-plus-*s* is an *addition*. Before this addition, always spell the name of the owner or owners without dropping or adding letters.

Uses and misuses of the apostrophe

Uses of the apostrophe

- **Use an apostrophe to form the possessives of nouns and indefinite pronouns.**

Singular	Plural
Ms. Park's	the Parks'
lawyer's	lawyers'
everyone's	two weeks'

- **Use an apostrophe to form contractions.**

it's a girl	shouldn't
you're	won't

- **The apostrophe is optional for plurals of abbreviations, dates, and words or characters named as words.**

MAs or MA's	Cs or C's
1960s or 1960's	ifs or if's

Misuses of the apostrophe

- **Do not use an apostrophe plus -s to form the possessives of plural nouns.** Instead, first form the plural with -s and *then* add an apostrophe.

Not	But
the Kim's car	the Kims' car
boy's father	boys' fathers
baby's care	babies' care

- **Do not use an apostrophe to form plurals of nouns.**

Not	But
book's are	books are
the Freed's	the Freeds

- **Do not use an apostrophe with verbs ending in -s.**

Not	But
swim's	swims

(continued)

> ## Uses and misuses of the apostrophe
> *(continued)*
>
> - Do not use an apostrophe to form the possessives of personal and relative pronouns.
>
> | Not | But |
> |---|---|
> | it's toes | its toes |
> | your's | yours |
> | who's car | whose car |

43.1.1 Singular words: Add -'s.

Bill Boughton's skillful card tricks amaze children.
Some of the earth's forests are regenerating.
Everyone's fitness can be improved through exercise.

The -'s ending for singular words pertains also to singular words ending in -s, as the next examples show.

Henry James's novels reward the patient reader.
The business's customers filed suit.

An apostrophe alone may be added to a singular word ending in -s when another s would make the word difficult to say: *Moses' mother, Joan Rivers' jokes*. But the added -s is never wrong (*Moses's, Rivers's*).

43.1.2 Plural words ending in -s: Add -' only.

Workers' incomes have fallen slightly over the past year.
Many students benefit from several years' work after high school.
The Jameses' talents are extraordinary.

Note the difference in the possessives of singular and plural words ending in -s. The singular form usually takes the apostrophe plus -s: *James's*. The plural takes only the apostrophe: *Jameses'*.

43.1.3 Plural words not ending in -s: Add -'s.

Children's educations are at stake.
We need to attract the media's attention.

The plurals of nouns are generally formed by adding -s or -es, never with an apostrophe: *boys, families, Joneses, Murphys*.

Not The Jones' controlled the firm's until 2010.
But The Joneses controlled the firms until 2010.

43.1.4 Compound words: Add -'s only to the last word.

The brother-in-law's business failed.
Taxes are always somebody else's fault.

43.1.5 Two or more owners: Add -'s depending on possession.

Individual possession
Zimbale's and Mason's comedy techniques are similar. [Each comedian has his own technique.]

Joint possession
The children recovered despite their mother and father's neglect. [The mother and father were jointly neglectful.]

43.1.6 No apostrophe with a singular verb

Verbs ending in -s never take an apostrophe:

Not The subway break's down less often now.
But The subway breaks down less often now.

43.1.7 No apostrophe with a possessive personal pronoun or relative pronoun

His, hers, its, ours, yours, theirs, and *whose* are possessive forms of the pronouns *he, she, it, we, you, they,* and *who.* They do not take apostrophes:

Not The house is her's. It's roof leaks.
But The house is hers. Its roof leaks.

Don't confuse possessive pronouns with contractions.

43.2 Contractions and Abbreviations

43.2 Use apostrophes in contractions or abbreviations.

A **contraction** replaces one or more letters, numbers, or words with an apostrophe, as in the following examples:

Standard contractions

it is, it has	it's	cannot	can't
they are	they're	does not	doesn't
you are	you're	were not	weren't
who is, who has	who's	class of 2018	class of '18

Contractions vs. possessive pronouns

Don't confuse contractions with possessive pronouns:

Contractions	Possessive pronouns
It**'s** a book.	It**s** cover is green.
They**'re** coming.	Th**eir** car broke down.
You**'re** right.	You**r** idea is good.
Who**'s** coming?	Who**se** party is it?

Abbreviations, dates, and words or characters named as words

You'll sometimes see apostrophes used to form the plurals of abbreviations (BA's), dates (1900's), and words or characters named as words (*but*'s). However, most current style guides recommend against the apostrophe in these cases.

BAs   PhDs
1990s   2000s

Italicize or underline a word or character named as a word, but not the added *-s*.

The sentence has too many *but*s.
Two 3s end the zip code.

Chapter 44
Quotation Marks

Learning Objectives

44.1 Use quotation marks to indicate direct quotations.
44.2 Put quotation marks around the titles of works that are parts of other works.
44.3 Use quotation marks to enclose words used in a special sense.
44.4 Place other punctuation marks inside or outside quotation marks according to standard practice.

44.1 Direct Quotations

44.1 Use quotation marks to indicate direct quotations.

Quotation marks—either double (" ") or single (' ')—mainly enclose direct quotations and certain titles. Always use quotation marks in pairs, one at the beginning of a quotation and one at the end.

44.1.1 Use double quotation marks to enclose direct quotations.

A **direct quotation** reports what someone said or wrote, in the exact words of the original:

> "Life," said the psychoanalyst Karen Horney, "remains a very efficient therapist."

Do not use quotation marks with a direct quotation that is set off from your text. Also do not use quotation marks with an **indirect quotation**, which reports what someone said or wrote but not in the exact words.

> The psychoanalyst Karen Horney claimed that life is a good therapist.

44.1.2 Use single quotation marks to enclose a quotation within a quotation.

"In so doing," Maryanne Wolf writes, "both artist and novelist are examples of Emily Dickinson's enigmatic charge to 'tell all the truth, but tell it slant.'"

Notice that two different quotation marks appear at the end of the sentence—one single (to finish the interior quotation) and one double (to finish the main quotation).

44.1.3 Set off quotations of dialog according to standard practice.

When quoting conversations, begin a new paragraph for each speaker.

> "What shall I call you? Your name?" Andrews whispered rapidly, as with a high squeak the latch of the door rose.
> "Elizabeth," she said. "Elizabeth."
> —Graham Greene, *The Man Within*

When you quote a single speaker for more than one paragraph, put quotation marks at the beginning of each paragraph but at the end of only the last paragraph.

Quotation marks are optional for quoting unspoken thoughts or imagined dialog:

> I asked myself, "How can we solve this?"
> I asked myself, How can we solve this?

44.2 Titles of Works

44.2 Use quotation marks around the titles of works that are parts of other works.

Use quotation marks to enclose the titles of works that are published or released within larger works. (See the following box.) Use single quotation marks for a quotation within a quoted title, as in the article title and essay title in the box. And enclose all punctuation in the title within the quotation marks, as with the question mark in the article title.

Don't use quotation marks in the titles of your papers unless they contain or are themselves direct quotations:

No	"The Death Wish in One Poem by Robert Frost"
But	The Death Wish in One Poem by Robert Frost
Or	The Death Wish in "Stopping by Woods on a Snowy Evening"

Titles to be enclosed in quotation marks
Other titles should be italicized or underlined.

Song
"Lucy in the Sky with Diamonds"

Short poem
"Stopping by Woods on a Snowy Evening"

Short story
"The Gift of the Magi"

Article in a periodical
"Does 'Scaring' Work?"

Essay
"Joey: A 'Mechanical Boy'"

Unpublished speech
"Horses and Healing"

Page or work on a Web site
"Readers' Page" (on the site *Friends of Prufrock*)

Episode of a television or radio program
"The Mexican Connection" (on *60 Minutes*)

Subdivision of a book
"The Mast Head" (Chapter 35 of *Moby-Dick*)

44.3 Words Used in a Special Sense

44.3 Use quotation marks to enclose words used in a special sense.

On film sets, movable "wild walls" make a one-walled room seem four-walled on film.

Use italics or underlining for words you are defining.

The *codex* is a stack of printed paper bound along one edge.

Common nickname

Not	As President, "Jimmy" Carter preferred to use his nickname.
But	As President, Jimmy Carter preferred to use his nickname.

Slang or trite expression

Quotation marks will not excuse slang or a trite expression that is inappropriate to your writing. If slang is appropriate, use it without quotation marks.

> Not   We should support the professor in her "hour of need" rather than "wimp out" on her.
>
> But   We should give the professor the support she needs rather than turn away like cowards.

44.4 With Other Punctuation

44.4 Place other punctuation marks inside or outside quotation marks according to standard practice.

44.4.1 Commas and periods: Inside quotation marks

> Swift uses irony in his essay "A Modest Proposal."
> Many readers are shocked to see infants described as "delicious."
> "'A Modest Proposal,'" writes one critic, "is so outrageous that it cannot be believed."

When a parenthetical source citation immediately follows a quotation, place any period or comma *after* the citation:

> One critic calls the essay "outrageous" (Olms 26).
> Partly because of "the cool calculation of its delivery" (Olms 27), Swift's satire still chills a modern reader.

44.4.2 Colons and semicolons: Outside quotation marks

> A few years ago the slogan in elementary education was "learning by playing"; now educators are concerned with basic skills.
> We all know what is meant by "inflation": more money buys less.

44.4.3 Dashes, question marks, and exclamation points: Inside quotation marks only if part of the quotation

When a dash, question mark, or exclamation point is part of the quotation, place it *inside* quotation marks. Don't use any other punctuation, such as a period or comma:

> "But must you—" Marcia hesitated, afraid of the answer.
> "Go away!" I yelled.
> Did you say, "Who is she?" [When both your sentence and the quotation would end in a question mark or exclamation point, use only the mark in the quotation.]

When a dash, question mark, or exclamation point applies only to the larger sentence, not to the quotation, place it *outside* quotation marks—again, with no other punctuation:

> One evocative line in English poetry—"After many a summer dies the swan"—comes from Alfred, Lord Tennyson.
> Who said, "Now cracks a noble heart"?
> The woman called me "stupid"!

Chapter 45
Other Marks

Learning Objectives

- **45.1** Use the dash or dashes to indicate shifts or interruptions.
- **45.2** Use parentheses to enclose expressions and labels for lists.
- **45.3** Use the ellipsis mark to indicate omissions.
- **45.4** Use brackets to indicate changes in quotations.
- **45.5** Use the slash between options and between lines of poetry.

45.1 Dash

45.1 **Use the dash or dashes to indicate shifts or interruptions.**

The dash (—) is mainly a mark of interruption: it signals a shift, insertion, or break. In your papers, form a dash with two hyphens (--) or use the character called an em dash on your word processor. Do not add extra space around or between the hyphens or around the em dash. When an interrupting element starting with a dash falls in the middle of a sentence, be sure to add the closing dash to signal the end of the interruption. See the first example below.

45.1.1 Shifts in tone or thought

> The novel—if one can call it that—appeared in 2010.
> If the book had a plot—but a plot would be conventional.

45.1.2 Nonessential elements

Dashes may be used instead of commas to set off and emphasize **modifiers**, **parenthetical expressions**, and other **nonessential elements**, especially when these elements are internally punctuated:

The qualities Monet painted—sunlight, rich shadows, deep colors—abounded near the rivers and gardens he used as subjects.

Though they are close together—separated by only a few blocks—the two neighborhoods could be in different countries.

45.1.3 Introductory series and concluding series and explanations

Shortness of breath, skin discoloration or the sudden appearance of moles, persistent indigestion, the presence of small lumps—all these may signify cancer. [Introductory series.]

The patient undergoes a battery of tests—imaging, blood work, perhaps even biopsy. [Concluding series.]

Many patients are disturbed by MRI imaging—by the need to keep still for long periods in an exceedingly small space. [Concluding explanation.]

A colon could be used instead of a dash in the last two examples. The dash is more informal.

45.1.4 Overuse

Too many dashes can make writing jumpy or breathy.

Not In all his life—eighty-seven years—my great-grandfather never allowed his picture to be taken—not even once. He claimed the "black box"—the camera—would steal his soul.

But In all his eighty-seven years, my great-grandfather did not allow his picture to be taken even once. He claimed the "black box"—the camera—would steal his soul.

45.2 Parentheses

45.2 Use parentheses to enclose expressions and labels for lists.

Parentheses *always* come in pairs, one before and one after the punctuated material.

45.2.1 Parenthetical expressions

Parenthetical expressions include explanations, facts, digressions, and examples that may be helpful or interesting but are not essential to meaning. Parentheses de-emphasize parenthetical expressions. (Commas emphasize them more than parentheses do, and dashes emphasize them still more.)

The population of Philadelphia (now about 1.5 million) has declined since 1950.

Don't put a comma before a parenthetical expression enclosed in parentheses. Punctuation that comes after the parenthetical expression should be placed outside the closing parenthesis.

> **Not** The population of Philadelphia compares with that of Phoenix, (about 1.5 million.)
>
> **But** The population of Philadelphia compares with that of Phoenix (about 1.5 million).

If you enclose a complete sentence in parentheses, capitalize the sentence and place the closing period *inside* the closing parenthesis:

> In general, coaches will tell you that scouts are just guys who can't coach. (But then, so are brain surgeons.) —Roy Blount Jr.

45.2.2 Labels for lists within sentences

> Outside the Middle East, the countries with the largest oil reserves are **(1)** Venezuela (297 billion barrels), **(2)** Canada (197 billion barrels), and **(3)** Russia (116 billion barrels).

When you set a list off from your text, do not enclose such labels in parentheses.

45.3 Ellipsis Mark

45.3 Use the ellipsis mark to indicate omissions.

The ellipsis mark, consisting of three periods separated by space (. . .), generally indicates an omission from a quotation. All the examples quote from the following passage about environmentalism:

> **Original quotation**
> "At the heart of the environmentalist world view is the conviction that human physical and spiritual health depends on sustaining the planet in a relatively unaltered state. Earth is our home in the full, genetic sense, where humanity and its ancestors existed for all the millions of years of their evolution. Natural ecosystems—forests, coral reefs, marine blue waters—maintain the world exactly as we would wish it to be maintained. When we debase the global environment and extinguish the variety of life, we are dismantling a support system that is too complex to understand, let alone replace, in the foreseeable future."
> —Edward O. Wilson, "Is Humanity Suicidal?"
>
> **1. Omission of the middle of a sentence**
> "Natural ecosystems . . . maintain the world exactly as we would wish it to be maintained."
>
> **2. Omission of the end of a sentence, without source citation**
> "Earth is our home. . . ." [The sentence period, closed up to the last word, precedes the ellipsis mark.]
>
> **3. Omission of the end of a sentence, with source citation**
> "Earth is our home . . . " (Wilson 27). [The sentence period follows the source citation.]

4. Omission of parts of two or more sentences

Wilson writes, "At the heart of the environmentalist world view is the conviction that human physical and spiritual health depends on sustaining the planet . . . where humanity and its ancestors existed for all the millions of years of their evolution."

5. Omission of one or more sentences

As Wilson puts it, "At the heart of the environmentalist world view is the conviction that human physical and spiritual health depends on sustaining the planet in a relatively unaltered state. . . . When we debase the global environment and extinguish the variety of life, we are dismantling a support system that is too complex to understand, let alone replace, in the foreseeable future."

6. Omission from the middle of a sentence through the end of another sentence

"Earth is our home. . . . When we debase the global environment and extinguish the variety of life, we are dismantling a support system that is too complex to understand, let alone replace, in the foreseeable future."

7. Omission of the beginning of a sentence, leaving a complete sentence

a. Bracketed capital letter
"[H]uman physical and spiritual health," Wilson writes, "depends on sustaining the planet in a relatively unaltered state." [No ellipsis mark is needed because the brackets around the *H* indicate that the letter was not capitalized originally and thus that the beginning of the sentence has been omitted.]

b. Small letter
According to Wilson, "human physical and spiritual health depends on sustaining the planet in a relatively unaltered state." [No ellipsis mark is needed because the small *h* indicates that the beginning of the sentence has been omitted.]

c. Capital letter from the original
One reviewer comments, " . . . Wilson argues eloquently for the environmentalist world view" (Hami 28). [An ellipsis mark *is* needed because the quoted part of the sentence begins with a capital letter and it is otherwise not clear that the beginning of the original sentence has been omitted.]

8. Use of a word or phrase

Wilson describes the earth as "our home." [No ellipsis mark needed.]

Note these features of the examples:

- **Use an ellipsis mark when it is not otherwise clear that you have left out material from the source,** as when you omit one or more sentences (examples 5 and 6) or when the words you quote form a complete sentence that is different in the original (examples 1–4 and 7c).
- **You don't need an ellipsis mark when it is obvious that you have omitted something,** such as when a bracketed capital letter or a

small letter indicates omission (examples 7a and 7b) or when a phrase clearly comes from a larger sentence (example 8).
- **Place an ellipsis mark after any sentence period *except* when a parenthetical source citation follows the quotation,** as in examples 3 and 7c. Then the sentence period falls after the citation.

If you omit one or more lines of poetry or paragraphs of prose from a quotation, use a separate line of ellipsis marks across the full width of the quotation to show the omission.

> In "Song: Love Armed" from 1676, Aphra Behn contrasts two lovers' experiences of a romance:
>
> > Love in fantastic triumph sate,
> > > Whilst bleeding hearts around him flowed,
> > ....
> > But my poor heart alone is harmed,
> > > Whilst thine the victor is, and free. (lines 1-2, 15-16)

45.4 Brackets

45.4 Use brackets to indicate changes in quotations.

Brackets have specialized uses in mathematical equations, but their main use for all kinds of writing is to indicate that you have altered a quotation to explain, clarify, or correct it.

> "That Chevron station **[just outside Dallas]** is one of the busiest in the nation," said a company spokesperson.

The word *sic* (Latin for "in this manner") in brackets indicates that an error in the quotation appeared in the original and was not made by you. Do not underline or italicize *sic* in brackets.

> According to the newspaper report, "The car slammed thru **[sic]** the railing and into oncoming traffic."

Do not use *sic* to make fun of a writer or to note errors in a passage that is clearly nonstandard.

45.5 Slash

45.5 Use the slash between options and between lines of poetry.

Option
Some teachers oppose pass/fail courses.

Poetry
Many readers have sensed a reluctant turn away from death in Frost's lines "The woods are lovely, dark and deep, / But I have promises to keep" (13–14).

When separating lines of poetry in this way, leave a space before and after the slash.

Part 6

Spelling and Mechanics

46 Spelling and the Hyphen *343*
47 Capital Letters *348*
48 Italics or Underlining *352*
49 Abbreviations *354*
50 Numbers *357*

Part 6
Spelling and Mechanics

46 Spelling and the Hyphen *343*
   46.1 Common spelling problems *343*
   46.2 Spelling rules *345*
   46.3 Hyphenating words *347*

47 Capital Letters *348*
   47.1 Conventions *349*
   47.2 First word of sentence *349*
   47.3 Title and subtitles *350*
   47.4 Proper nouns and proper adjectives *350*

48 Italics or Underlining *352*
   48.1 Titles of works *352*
   48.2 Foreign words and for emphasis *353*

49 Abbreviations *354*
   49.1 Abbreviations in nontechnical writing *355*
   49.2 Misuses of abbreviations *356*

50 Numbers *357*
   50.1 Numerals and words *357*
   50.2 Dates and addresses *358*

Chapter 46
Spelling and the Hyphen

sp 46.1

Learning Objectives

46.1 Recognize common spelling problems.
46.2 Follow spelling rules.
46.3 Use hyphens to form or divide words.

46.1 Common Spelling Problems

46.1 Recognize common spelling problems.

Certain situations, such as misleading pronunciation, commonly lead to misspelling.

46.1.1 Pronunciation

In English, pronunciation of words is an unreliable guide to how they are spelled. Pronunciation is especially misleading with **homonyms**, words pronounced the same but spelled differently. Some homonyms and near-homonyms appear in the following box.

> ### Words commonly confused
>
> accept (to receive)
> except (other than)
>
> affect (to have an influence on)
> effect (a result)
>
> all ready (prepared)
> already (by this time)
>
> allusion (an indirect reference)
> illusion (an erroneous belief or perception)
>
> ascent (a movement up)
> assent (to agree, or an agreement)
>
> bare (unclothed)
> bear (to carry, or an animal)
>
> board (a plane of wood)
> bored (uninterested)
>
> brake (to stop)
> break (to smash)
>
> buy (to purchase)
> by (next to)
>
> cite (to quote an authority)
> sight (the ability to see)
> site (a place)
>
> desert (to abandon)
> dessert (after-dinner course)
>
> discreet (reserved, respectful)
> discrete (individual, distinct)
>
> *(continued)*

Words commonly confused

(continued)

fair (average, or lovely)
fare (a fee for transportation)

forth (forward)
fourth (after *third*)

hear (to perceive by ear)
here (in this place)

heard (past tense of *hear*)
herd (a group of animals)

hole (an opening)
whole (complete)

its (possessive of *it*)
it's (contraction of *it is* or *it has*)

know (to be certain)
no (the opposite of *yes*)

loose (not attached)
lose (to misplace)

meat (flesh)
meet (to encounter, or a competition)

passed (past tense of *pass*)
past (after, or a time gone by)

patience (forbearance)
patients (people under medical care)

peace (the absence of war)
piece (a portion of something)

plain (clear)
plane (a carpenter's tool, or an airborne vehicle)

presence (the state of being at hand)
presents (gifts)

principal (most important, or the head of a school)
principle (a basic truth or law)

rain (precipitation)
reign (to rule)
rein (a strap for controlling an animal)

right (correct)
rite (a religious ceremony)
write (to make letters)

road (a surface for driving)
rode (past tense of *ride*)

scene (where an action occurs)
seen (past participle of *see*)

stationary (unmoving)
stationery (writing paper)

their (possessive of *they*)
there (opposite of *here*)
they're (contraction of *they are*)

to (toward)
too (also)
two (following *one*)

waist (the middle of the body)
waste (discarded material)

weak (not strong)
week (Sunday through Saturday)

weather (climate)
whether (*if*, or introducing a choice)

which (one of a group)
witch (a sorcerer)

who's (contraction of *who is* or *who has*)
whose (possessive of *who*)

your (possessive of you)
you're (contraction of *you are*)

46.1.2 Different forms of the same word

Often, the noun form and the verb form of the same word are spelled differently: for example, *advice* (noun) and *advise* (verb). Sometimes the noun and the adjective forms of the same word differ: *height* and *high*. Similar changes occur in the parts of some irregular verbs (*know, knew, known*) and the plurals of irregular nouns (*man, men*).

46.1.3 American vs. British spellings

> ### Culture and language
>
> When writing for American readers, use American spellings instead of their British equivalents. An American dictionary will show a British spelling as a variant or give it a label such as *chiefly British*.
>
> | American | British |
> |---|---|
> | color, humor | colour, humour |
> | theater, center | theatre, centre |
> | canceled, traveled | cancelled, travelled |
> | judgment | judgement |
> | realize, civilize | realise, civilise |
> | connection | connexion |

46.2 Spelling Rules

46.2 Follow spelling rules.

46.2.1 *ie* vs. *ei*

To distinguish between *ie* and *ei*, use the familiar jingle:

I before *e*, except after *c*, or when pronounced "ay" as in *neighbor* and *weigh*.

i before *e*	believe	thief	hygiene
	grief	bier	friend
ei after *c*	ceiling	conceive	perceive
	deceit	receive	conceit
ei sounded as "ay"	sleigh	eight	beige
	vein	freight	neighbor

For some exceptions, remember this sentence:

The weird foreigner neither seizes leisure nor forfeits height.

46.2.2 Final *e*

When adding an ending to a word with a final *e*, drop the *e* if the ending begins with a vowel:

advise + able = advisable   surprise + ing = surprising

Keep the *e* if the ending begins with a consonant:

care + ful = careful   like + ly = likely

Retain the *e* after a soft *c* or *g*, to keep the sound of the consonant soft rather than hard: *courageous, changeable*. And drop the *e* before a consonant when the *e* is preceded by another vowel: *argue + ment = argument, true + ly = truly*.

46.2.3 Final *y*

When adding an ending to a word with a final *y*, change the *y* to *i* if it follows a consonant:

    beauty, beauties   worry, worried   supply, supplies

But keep the *y* if it follows a vowel, if it ends a proper name, or if the added ending is *ing*:

    day, days   Minsky, Minskys   cry, crying

46.2.4 Final consonants

When adding an ending to a one-syllable word ending in a consonant, double the final consonant when it follows a single vowel. Otherwise, don't double the consonant.

    slap, slapping   park, parking   pair, paired

In words of more than one syllable, double the final consonant when it follows a single vowel *and* when it ends a stressed syllable once the new ending is added. Otherwise, don't double the consonant.

    refer, referring   refer, reference   relent, relented

46.2.5 Prefixes

When adding a prefix, do not drop a letter from or add a letter to the original word:

    unnecessary   disappoint   misspell

46.2.6 Plurals

Most nouns form plurals by adding *s* to the singular form. Add *es* for the plural of nouns ending in *s*, *sh*, *ch*, or *x*.

    boy, boys   kiss, kisses   church, churches

Nouns ending in *o* preceded by a vowel usually form the plural with *s*. Those ending in *o* preceded by a consonant usually form the plural with *es*.

    ratio, ratios   hero, heroes

Some very common nouns form irregular plurals.

    child, children   woman, women   mouse, mice

Some English nouns that were originally Italian, Greek, Latin, or French form the plural according to their original language:

    analysis, analyses   criterion, criteria   piano, pianos
    basis, bases   datum, data   thesis, theses
    crisis, crises   medium, media

A few such nouns may form irregular *or* regular plurals: for instance, *index, indices, indexes; curriculum, curricula, curriculums*. The regular plural is more contemporary.

With compound nouns, add *s* to the main word of the compound. Sometimes this main word is not the last word.

city-states   fathers-in-law   passersby

Culture and language

Noncount nouns do not form plurals, either regularly (with an added *s*) or irregularly. Examples of noncount nouns include *equipment, intelligence,* and *wealth*.

46.3 Hyphenating Words

46.3   Use hyphens to form or divide words.

The hyphen is used either to form compound words or to divide words at the ends of lines.

46.3.1   Compound adjectives

When two or more words serve together as a single adjective before a noun, a hyphen forms the modifying words clearly into a unit.

> She is a well-known actor.
> Some Spanish-speaking students work as translators.

When such a compound adjective follows the noun, the hyphen is unnecessary.

> The actor is well known.
> Many students are Spanish speaking.

The hyphen is also unnecessary in a compound adjective containing an *-ly* **adverb**, even before the noun: *clearly defined terms*.

When part of a compound adjective appears only once in two or more parallel compounds, hyphens indicate which words the reader should mentally join with the missing part.

> School-age children should have eight- or nine-o'clock bedtimes.

46.3.2   Fractions and compound numbers

Hyphens join the numerator and denominator of fractions: *one-half, three-fourths*. Hyphens also join the parts of the whole numbers *twenty-one* to *ninety-nine*.

When a hyphenated number is part of a compound adjective before a noun, join all parts of the modifier with hyphens: *sixty-three-foot wall*.

46.3.3 Prefixes and suffixes

Do not use hyphens with prefixes except as follows:

- **With the prefixes** *self-, all-,* **and** *ex-*: *self-control, all-inclusive, ex-student.*
- **With a prefix before a capitalized word:** *un-American.*
- **With a capital letter before a word:** *T-shirt.*
- **To prevent misreading:** *de-emphasize, re-create a story.*

The only suffix that regularly requires a hyphen is *-elect,* as in *president-elect.*

46.3.4 Words at the ends of lines

You can avoid occasional short lines in your documents by setting your word processor to divide words automatically at appropriate breaks. To divide words manually, follow these guidelines:

- **Divide words only between syllables**—for instance, *win-dows,* not *wi-ndows.* Check a dictionary for correct syllable breaks.
- **Never divide a one-syllable word.**
- **Leave at least two letters on the first line and three on the second line.** If a word cannot be divided to follow this rule (for instance, *a-bus-er*), don't divide it.
- **Do not use a hyphen in breaking a URL** because readers may perceive any added hyphens as part of the electronic address. The documentation styles differ in where they allow breaks in URLs. For example, MLA style allows a break after a slash or a hyphen, while APA style allows a break before most punctuation marks.

Chapter 47
Capital Letters

Learning Objectives

47.1 Follow conventions when capitalizing words.
47.2 Capitalize the first word of every sentence.
47.3 Capitalize most words in titles and subtitles of works.
47.4 Capitalize proper nouns and proper adjectives.

47.1 Conventions

47.1 Follow conventions when capitalizing words.

Generally, capitalize a word only when a dictionary or conventional use says you must.

Avoid using all capitals or all small letters in electronic communication. Online messages written in all-capital letters or with no capital letters are difficult to read. Further, messages in all-capital letters may be considered rude.

> **Culture and language**
>
> Conventions of capitalization vary from language to language. English, for instance, is the only language to capitalize the first-person singular pronoun (*I*), and its practice of capitalizing proper nouns but not most common nouns also distinguishes it from some other languages.
>
> My **f**riend **N**athaniel and **I** both play the **d**rums.
>
> (common noun, proper noun, pronoun, common noun)

47.2 First Word of Sentence

47.2 Capitalize the first word of every sentence.

No one expected the outcome.

When quoting other writers, you should reproduce the capital letters beginning their sentences or indicate that you have altered the source's capitalization. Whenever possible, integrate the quotation into your own sentence so that its capitalization coincides with yours:

> "**P**sychotherapists often overlook the benefits of self-deception," the author argues (122).
>
> The author argues that "the benefits of self-deception" are not always recognized by psychotherapists (122).

If you need to alter the capitalization in the source, indicate the change with brackets:

> "**[T]**he benefits of self-deception" are not always recognized by psychotherapists, the author argues (122).
>
> The author argues that "**[p]**sychotherapists often overlook the benefits of self-deception" (122).

Capitalization of questions in a series is optional. Both of the following examples are correct:

> **I**s the population a hundred? **T**wo hundred? **M**ore?
>
> **I**s the population a hundred? two hundred? more?

Also optional is capitalization of the first word in a complete sentence after a colon.

47.3 Title and Subtitles

47.3 Capitalize most words in titles and subtitles of works.

Within your text, capitalize all the words in a title *except* the following: **articles** (*a, an, the*), *to* in **infinitives**, **coordinating conjunctions** (*and, but,* etc.), and **prepositions** (*with, between,* etc.). Capitalize even these words when they are the first or last word in a title or when they fall after a colon or semicolon.

"Courtship through the Ages"	*Management: A New Theory*
A Diamond Is Forever	"Once More to the Lake"
"Knowing Whom to Ask"	*An End to Live For*
Learning from Las Vegas	*File under Architecture*

The style guides of the academic disciplines have their own rules for capitals in titles. For instance, the preceding guidelines reflect MLA style for English and some other humanities. In contrast, APA style for the social sciences and CSE style for the sciences capitalize only the first word and proper names in the titles of books and articles within source citations.

47.4 Proper Nouns and Proper Adjectives

47.4 Capitalize proper nouns and proper adjectives.

47.4.1 Proper nouns and proper adjectives

Proper nouns name specific persons, places, and things: *Shakespeare, California, World War I.* **Proper adjectives** are formed from some proper nouns: *Shakespearean, Californian.* Capitalize all proper nouns and proper adjectives but not the articles (*a, an, the*) that precede them.

Proper nouns and adjectives to be capitalized

Specific persons and things
Isabel Allende
Napoleon Bonaparte
Boulder Dam
the Empire State Building

Specific places and geographical regions
New York City
China
the Mediterranean Sea
the Northeast, the South
But: northeast of the city, going south, northern

Days of the week, months, holidays
Monday
May
Yom Kippur
Christmas

Historical events, documents, periods, movements
Vietnam War Renaissance
Constitution Romantic Movement

Government offices, departments, and institutions
House of Representatives Polk Municipal Court
Department of Defense Sequoia Hospital

Academic institutions and departments
University of Kansas Department of Nursing
Santa Monica College Haven High School
But: the university, college course, high school diploma

Political, social, athletic, and other organizations and associations and their members
Democratic Party, Democrats League of Women Voters
Sierra Club Boston Celtics
B'nai B'rith Chicago Symphony Orchestra

Races, nationalities, and their languages
Native American Germans
African American Swahili
Caucasian Italian
But: blacks, whites

Religions, their followers, and terms for the sacred
Christianity, Christians God
Catholicism, Catholics Allah
Judaism, Orthodox Jews Bible [*but:* biblical]
Islam, Muslims Koran, Qur'an

47.4.2 Common nouns used as essential parts of proper nouns

Capitalize the common nouns *street, avenue, park, river, ocean, lake, company, college, county,* and *memorial* when they are part of proper nouns naming specific places or institutions:

Main Street Lake Superior
Central Park Ford Motor Company
Mississippi River Madison College
Pacific Ocean George Washington Memorial

47.4.3 Relationships

Capitalize the names of relationships only when they precede or replace proper names:

Our aunt scolded us for disrespecting Father and Uncle Jake.

47.4.4 Titles with persons' names

Before a person's name, capitalize his or her title. After or apart from the name, do not capitalize the title.

> **P**rofessor Otto Osborne   Otto Osborne, a **p**rofessor
> **D**octor Jane Covington   Jane Covington, a **d**octor
> **G**overnor Ella Moore   Ella Moore, the **g**overnor

Many writers capitalize a title denoting very high rank even when it follows a name or is used alone: *Ronald Reagan, past President of the United States.*

Chapter 48
Italics or Underlining

Learning Objectives

48.1 Italicize or underline the titles of works that appear independently.
48.2 Use italics or underlining for foreign words or for emphasis.

48.1 Titles of Works

48.1 Italicize or underline the titles of works that appear independently.

Italic type and underlining indicate the same thing: the word or words are being distinguished or emphasized. Always use one or the other consistently throughout a document in both text and source citations:

> **Text**
> The importance of play is one of several themes Steven Johnson explores in *Wonderland*.
>
> **Source citation (MLA style)**
> Johnson, Steven. *Wonderland: How Play Made the Modern World*. Riverhead Books, 2016.

Some forms of online communication do not allow italics or underlining for the purposes described in this chapter. On Web sites, for instance, underlining often indicates a link to another site. If you can't use italics or underlining for highlighting, type an underscore before and after the element: _Measurements coincide with those in _Joule's Handbook_. You can also emphasize words with asterisks: *I *will not* be able to attend.* Avoid using all-capital letters for emphasis.

Within your text, underline or italicize the titles of works that are published, released, or produced separately from other works. Use quotation marks for all other titles.

Titles to be italicized or underlined

Books
War and Peace
And the Band Played On

Plays
Hamlet
The Phantom of the Opera

Periodicals
Time
Philadelphia Inquirer

Television and radio programs
This American Life
Radio Lab

Movies, DVDs, and videos
Schindler's List
How to Relax

Long poems
Beowulf
Paradise Lost

Long musical works
Tchaikovsky's *Swan Lake*
But: Symphony in C

Pamphlets
The Truth about Alcoholism

Works of visual art
Michelangelo's *David*
Picasso's *Guernica*

Computer software
Microsoft Word
Google Chrome

Web sites
YouTube
Friends of Prufrock

Published speeches
Lincoln's *Gettysburg Address*

Legal documents, the Bible, the Koran, and their parts are generally not italicized or underlined:

Not We studied the *Book of Revelation* in the *Bible*.
But We studied the Book of Revelation in the Bible.

48.2 Foreign Words and for Emphasis

48.2 Use italics or underlining for foreign words or for emphasis.

48.2.1 Italicize or underline foreign words that are not part of the English language.

Italicize or underline a foreign expression that has not been absorbed into English. A dictionary will say whether a word is still considered foreign to English.

The scientific name for the brown trout is *Salmo trutta*. [The Latin scientific names for plants and animals are always italicized or underlined.]

The Latin *De gustibus non est disputandum* translates roughly as "There's no accounting for taste."

48.2.2 Italicize or underline words or characters named as words.

Use italics or underlining to indicate that you are citing a character or word as a word rather than using it for its meaning. Words you are defining fall under this convention.

The word *syzygy* refers to a straight line formed by three celestial bodies, as in the alignment of the earth, sun, and moon.

Some people say *th*, as in *thought*, with a faint *s* or *f* sound.

48.2.3 Italicize or underline the names of ships, aircraft, spacecraft, and trains.

Challenger	*Montrealer*
Apollo XI	*Queen Mary 2*
Orient Express	*Spirit of St. Louis*

48.2.4 Occasionally, italics or underlining may be used for emphasis.

Italics or underlining can stress an important word or phrase, especially in reporting how someone said something:

"Why on earth would *you* do that?" she cried.

But use such emphasis very rarely. Excessive underlining or italics will make your writing sound immature or hysterical:

The settlers had *no* firewood and *no* food. Many of them *starved* or *froze to death* that first winter.

Chapter 49
Abbreviations

Learning Objectives

49.1 Use abbreviations sparingly in nontechnical writing.

49.2 Spell out most units of measurement and names of places, calendar designations, people, and courses.

49.1 Abbreviations in Nontechnical Writing

49.1 Use abbreviations sparingly in nontechnical writing.

The following guidelines on abbreviations pertain to the text of a nontechnical document. All academic disciplines use abbreviations in source citations, and much technical writing, such as in the sciences and engineering, uses many abbreviations in the document text. For the in-text requirements of the discipline you are writing in, consult an appropriate style guide.

Usage varies, but writers increasingly omit periods from abbreviations that consist of or end in capital letters: *US, BA, USMC, PhD*.

49.1.1 Use standard abbreviations for titles immediately before and after proper names.

Before the name	After the name
Dr. James Hsu	James Hsu, MD
Mr., Mrs., Ms., Hon.,	DDS, DVM, PhD,
St., Rev., Msgr., Gen.	EdD, OSB, SJ, Sr., Jr.

Do not use abbreviations such as *Rev., Hon., Prof., Rep., Sen., Dr.,* and *St.* (for *Saint*) unless they appear before a proper name.

49.1.2 Familiar abbreviations and acronyms are acceptable in most writing.

An **acronym** is an abbreviation that spells a pronounceable word, such as NATO and AIDS. These and other abbreviations using initials are acceptable in most writing as long as they are familiar to readers.

Institutions	LSU, UCLA, TCU
Organizations	CIA, FBI, YMCA, AFL-CIO
Corporations	IBM, CBS, ITT
People	JFK, LBJ, FDR
Countries	US, USA

If a name or term (such as *operating room*) appears often in a piece of writing, then its abbreviation (*OR*) can cut down on extra words. Spell out the full term at its first appearance, indicate its abbreviation in parentheses, and then use the abbreviation thereafter.

49.1.3 Use *BC, BCE, AD, CE, AM, PM, no.,* and *$* only with specific dates and numbers.

| 44 BC | AD 1492 | 11:26 AM (*or* a.m.) | no. 36 (*or* No. 36) |
| 44 BCE | 1492 CE | 8:05 PM (*or* p.m.) | $7.41 |

The abbreviations BC ("before Christ"), BCE ("before the common era"), and CE ("common era") always follow a date. In contrast, AD (*anno Domini,* Latin for "in the year of the Lord") precedes a date.

49.1.4 Generally reserve Latin abbreviations for source citations and comments in parentheses.

Latin abbreviations are generally not italicized or underlined.

i.e.	*id est:*	that is
cf.	*confer:*	compare
e.g.	*exempli gratia:*	for example
et al.	*et alii:*	and others
etc.	*et cetera:*	and so forth
NB	*nota bene:*	note well

He said he would be gone a fortnight (i.e., two weeks).
Bloom et al., editors, *Anthology of Light Verse*
Trees, too, are susceptible to disease (e.g., Dutch elm disease).

Some writers avoid these abbreviations in formal writing, even within parentheses.

49.1.5 Use *Inc., Bros., Co.*, or & (for *and*) only in official names of business firms.

Not	The Santini bros. operate a large moving firm in New York City & environs.
But	The Santini brothers operate a large moving firm in New York City and environs.
Or	Santini Bros. is a large moving firm in New York City and environs.

49.2 Misuses of Abbreviations

49.2 Spell out most units of measurement and names of places, calendar designations, people, and courses.

In most academic, general, and business writing, the following types of words should always be spelled out (in source citations and technical writing, however, these words are more often abbreviated):

Units of measurement
The dog is thirty inches [not in.] high.

Geographical names
The publisher is in Massachusetts [not Mass. or MA].

Names of days, months, and holidays
The truce was signed on Tuesday [not Tues.], April [not Apr.] 16.

Names of people
Robert [not Robt.] Frost wrote accessible poems.

Courses of instruction
I'm majoring in political science [not poli. sci.].

Chapter 50
Numbers

Learning Objectives

50.1 Use numerals according to standard practice in the field you are writing in.

50.2 Use numerals according to convention for dates, addresses, and other information.

50.1 Numerals and Words

50.1 **Use numerals according to standard practice in the field you are writing in.**

Expressing numbers in numerals (*28*) or in words (*twenty-eight*) is often a matter of style in a discipline: the technical disciplines more often prefer numerals, and the nontechnical disciplines more often prefer words. All disciplines use many more numerals in source citations than in the document text.

Always use numerals for numbers that require more than two words to spell out:

> The leap year has 366 days.
> The population of Minot, North Dakota, is about 32,800.

In nontechnical academic writing, spell out numbers of one or two words. A hyphenated number may be considered one word.

> The waiting period is eighteen to twenty-four days.
> The ball game drew forty-two thousand people.

In much business writing, use numerals for all numbers over ten: *five reasons, 11 participants*. In technical academic and business writing, such as in science and engineering, use numerals for all numbers over ten, and use numerals for zero through nine when they refer to exact measurements: *2 liters, 1 hour*.

Use a combination of numerals and words for round numbers over a million: *26 million, 2.45 billion*. Use either all numerals or all words when several numbers appear together in a passage, even if convention would require a mixture. And avoid using two numbers in a row, which can be confusing:

> **Confusing** Out of 530, 101 children caught the virus.
> **Clear** Out of 530 children, 101 caught the virus.

For clarity, spell out any number that begins a sentence. If the number requires more than two words, reword the sentence so that the number falls later and can be expressed as a numeral.

Not   3.9 billion people live in Asia.
But   The population of Asia is 3.9 billion.

Culture and language

In standard American English, a comma separates the numerals in long numbers (26**,**000), and a period functions as a decimal point (2**.**06).

50.2 Dates and Addresses

50.2 Use numerals according to convention for dates, addresses, and other information.

Days and years
June 18, 1985   AD 12
456 BCE   2010

The time of day
9:00 AM   3:45 PM

Addresses
355 Clinton Avenue
Washington, DC 20036

Exact amounts of money
$3.5 million $4.50

Decimals, percentages, and fractions
22.5   3½
48% (*or* 48 percent)

Scores and statistics
21 to 7   a ratio of 8 to 1
a mean of 26

Pages, chapters, volumes, acts, scenes, lines
Chapter 9, page 123
Hamlet, act 5, scene 3

Round dollar or cent amounts of only a few words may be expressed in words: *seventeen dollars*; *sixty cents*. When the word *o'clock* is used for the time of day, also express the number in words: *two o'clock* (not *2 o'clock*).

Part 7

Writing in the Disciplines

51 MLA Documentation and Format *365*
52 APA Documentation and Format *422*
53 Chicago Documentation *456*
54 CSE Documentation *470*

Part 7
Writing in the Disciplines

51 MLA Documentation and Format *365*
- 51.1 In-text citations *365*
- 51.2 List of works cited *373*
- 51.3 MLA paper format *405*
- 51.4 Sample MLA paper *407*

52 APA Documentation and Format *422*
- 52.1 In-text citations *422*
- 52.2 Reference list *425*
- 52.3 APA paper format *441*
- 52.4 Sample research report *443*

53 Chicago Documentation *456*
- 53.1 Notes and bibliography *456*
- 53.2 Models of Chicago notes and bibliography entries *458*

54 CSE Documentation *470*
- 54.1 Name-year citations *470*
- 54.2 Numbered text citations *470*
- 54.3 Reference list *471*

MLA Documentation and Format

MLA Documentation and Format

51 MLA Documentation and Format *365*
   51.1 In-text citations *365*
   51.2 List of works cited *373*
   51.3 MLA paper format *405*
   51.4 Sample MLA paper *407*

MLA in-text citations

1. Author not named in your text *366*
2. Author named in your text *366*
3. Work with two authors *366*
4. Work with more than two authors *366*
5. Work by an author of two or more cited works *367*
6. Anonymous work *367*
7. Work with a corporate author *367*
8. Electronic or other nonprint source *367*
   a. Work with a named author and stable page numbers *368*
   b. Work with a named author and no page numbers *368*
   c. Work with a named author on an e-reader or other device *368*
   d. Work with a named author and numbered paragraphs or sections *368*
   e. Work with no named author *368*
   f. Audio or video *368*
9. One-page work or entire work *369*
10. Work with no page or other reference numbers *369*
11. Multivolume work *369*
12. Source referred to by another source (indirect source) *369*
13. Literary work *370*
14. The Bible *370*
15. Two or more works in the same citation *371*

MLA works-cited entries

1. Authors
1. One author 378
2. Two authors 378
3. More than two authors 378
4. Same author(s) for two or more works 378
5. Corporate author 379
   a. Cited by author 379
   b. Cited by title 379
6. Author not named (anonymous) 379

2. Articles in journals, newspapers, and magazines

Articles in scholarly journals
Visual Journal articles: Print and database 380–381
7. Article in a journal with volume and issue numbers 382
   a. Print 382
   b. Database 382
   c. Web 382
8. Article in a journal with only issue numbers 382

Articles in newspapers
Visual Newspaper article: Database 383
9. Article in a national newspaper 384
   a. Print 384
   b. Database 384
   c. Web 384
10. Article in a local newspaper 384

Articles in magazines
11. Article in a weekly or biweekly magazine 385
    a. Print 385
    b. Database 385
    c. Web 385
12. Article in a monthly or bimonthly magazine 385

3. Books and government publications

Complete books
Visual Books: Print and database 386–387
13. Basic format for a complete book 388
    a. Print or e-reader 388
    b. Database 388
    c. Web 388
14. Second or subsequent edition 388
15. Book with an editor 388
16. Book with an author and an editor 389
17. Book with a translator 389
18. Anthology 389
19. Illustrated book or graphic narrative 389
20. Multivolume work 390
21. Series 390
22. Book published before 1900 390
23. Republished book 390
24. Sacred works 390
25. Book with a title in its title 390
26. Book lacking publication information or pagination 391

Parts of books
27. Selection from an anthology 391
28. Two or more selections from the same anthology 391
29. Work from a collection of scholarly articles 392
30. Article in a reference work 392
    a. Print 392
    b. Web 392
    c. CD-ROM or DVD-ROM 392
31. Introduction, preface, foreword, or afterword 392
32. Published letter 393

(continued)

MLA works-cited entries

(continued)

Government publications
33. Government publication *393*
    a. Cited by author *393*
    b. Cited by title *394*

4. Web sources and social media

Web sites and parts of Web sites

Visual Page or work on a Web site *394*

34. Page or work on a Web site *394*
    a. With an author and a title *394*
    b. Without an author *396*
    c. Without a title *396*
    d. With print publication information *396*
35. Entire Web site *396*
    a. With an author or an editor *396*
    b. Without an author or an editor *396*
36. Wiki *396*
37. Undated Web source *397*

Social media
38. Post on a blog *397*
39. Post on a social-networking site *397*
40. Comment *397*
41. Tweet *397*
42. Post to a discussion group *398*
43. E-mail or text message *398*

5. Visual, audio, and other media sources

44. Painting, photograph, or other work of visual art *398*
    a. Original *398*
    b. Reproduction *398*
    c. Web *398*
    d. Digital file *399*
45. Advertisement *399*
    a. Untitled *399*
    b. Titled *399*
46. Comic strip or cartoon *399*
    a. Titled comic strip *399*
    b. Individual cartoon *399*
47. Map, chart, or diagram *400*
    a. Print *400*
    b. Web *400*
48. Television episode or series *400*
    a. Broadcast *400*
    b. Web *400*
    c. DVD, Blu-ray, or videocassette *400*
    d. Series *401*
49. Radio program *401*
    a. Broadcast *401*
    b. Web *401*
50. Interview *401*
    a. Broadcast *401*
    b. Web *402*
51. Film or video *402*
    a. Film *402*
    b. DVD, Blu-ray, or videocassette *402*
    c. Web *402*
52. Sound recording *402*
    a. Song *402*
    b. Album *403*
    c. Spoken word *403*
53. Podcast *403*
54. Live performance *403*
55. Lecture, speech, address, or reading *404*
56. Video game, computer software, or app *404*

6. Other sources
57. Personal interview *404*
58. Unpublished or personal letter *404*
    a. Unpublished letter *404*
    b. Personal letter *405*
59. Dissertation *405*
60. Pamphlet or brochure *405*

Chapter 51
MLA Documentation and Format

Learning Objectives

51.1 Use MLA in-text citations.
51.2 Write an MLA list of works cited.
51.3 Use MLA paper format.
51.4 Examine a sample paper in MLA style.

51.1 In-text Citations

51.1 Use MLA in-text citations.

English, foreign languages, and some other humanities use the documentation style of the Modern Language Association, described in the *MLA Handbook* (8th ed., 2016).

In MLA style, you acknowledge the sources of borrowed material in two places:

- **In your text, a brief citation adjacent to the borrowed material directs readers to a complete list of all the works you cite.** The citation consists of the author's last name and usually the page number in the source where the borrowed material appears. If the author's name is not mentioned in your sentence, it appears in parentheses with the page number:

    In-text citation

    Many readers assume that humans have always dreamed of transporting themselves across time, but one historian of science describes time travel as "a fantasy of the modern era" (Gleick 5).

- **At the end of your paper, the list of works cited includes complete bibliographical information for every source.**

    Works-cited entry

    Gleick, James. *Time Travel: A History*, Pantheon Books, 2016.

51.1.1 Writing in-text citations

In-text citations of sources must include just enough information for the reader to locate both of the following:

- The *source* in your list of works cited.
- The *place* in the source where the borrowed material appears.

For any kind of source, you can usually meet both these requirements by providing the author's last name and (if the source uses them) the page numbers where the material appears. The reader can find the source in your list of works cited and can find the borrowed material in the source itself.

1. Author not named in your text

When you have not already named the author in your sentence, provide the author's last name and the page number(s), with no punctuation between them, in parentheses.

> One researcher concludes that "women impose a distinctive construction on moral problems, seeing moral dilemmas in terms of conflicting responsibilities" (Gilligan 105-06).

See models 6 and 8–10 for the forms to use when the source does not list an author or provide page numbers.

2. Author named in your text

When you have already given the author's name with the material you're citing, do not repeat it in the parenthetical citation. Give just the page number(s).

> Carol Gilligan concludes that "women impose a distinctive construction on moral problems, seeing moral dilemmas in terms of conflicting responsibilities" (105-06).

See models 6 and 8–10 for the forms to use when the source does not list an author or provide page numbers.

3. Work with two authors

If the source has two authors, give both of their last names in the text or in the citation. Separate the names with and.

> As Frieden and Sagalyn observe, "The poor and the minorities were the leading victims of highway and renewal programs" (29).

> According to one study, "The poor and the minorities were the leading victims of highway and renewal programs" (Frieden and Sagalyn 29).

4. Work with more than two authors

If the source has more than two authors, give only the first author's name followed by et al. (the abbreviation for the Latin *et alii*, "and others").

> Increased competition means that employees of public relations firms may find their loyalty stretched in more than one direction (Wilcox et al. 417).

5. Work by an author of two or more cited works

If your list of works cited includes two or more works by the same author, then your citation must tell the reader which of the author's works you are referring to. Give the title either in the text or in a parenthetical citation. In a parenthetical citation, omit any *A*, *An*, or *The* and shorten the title if it is longer than a noun preceded by its modifiers, if any. For instance, *Time's Arrow, Time's Cycle* shortens to *Time's Arrow*. In the following example, *Arts* is short for Gardner's full title, *The Arts and Human Development*.

> At about age seven, children begin to use appropriate gestures with their stories (Gardner, *Arts* 144-45).

If the title does not start with a noun or a noun preceded by modifiers, shorten the title to the first word (again excluding *A*, *An*, or *The*): for instance, shorten *As the Eye Moves* to *As*.

6. Anonymous work

For a work with no named author or editor (whether an individual or an organization), use a full or shortened version of the title, as explained with the previous model. In your list of works cited, you alphabetize an anonymous work by the first word of the title excluding *A*, *An*, or *The*, and the first word of a shortened title will be the same. The following citations refer to an unsigned source titled "The Right to Die." The title appears in quotation marks because the source is a periodical article.

> One article notes that a death-row inmate may demand his own execution to achieve a fleeting notoriety ("Right" 16).

> "The Right to Die" notes that a death-row inmate may demand execution to achieve a fleeting notoriety (16).

If two or more anonymous works have the same title, distinguish them with additional information in the text citation, such as the publication date.

7. Work with a corporate author

Some works list as author a government body, association, committee, company, or other group. Cite such a work by the organization's name except when it and the publisher are the same. When the organization and publisher have the same name, omit the author and cite the work by the title (see model 6 above).

If the organization's name is long, work it into the text to avoid an intrusive parenthetical citation.

> A 2014 report by the Nevada Department of Education provides evidence of an increase in graduation rates (12).

8. Electronic or other nonprint source

Electronic or other nonprint sources vary widely, including articles in databases, e-books, Web pages, *Facebook* posts, films or videos, and tweets. If possible, cite such a source as you would any other source, giving author and page number; but often these elements and others are lacking. The following models give a range of possibilities.

a. Work with a named author and stable page numbers

Brannon observes that students respond readily to some poets (53).

If the work you cite has stable page numbers, like those in a PDF file, give them in your citation.

b. Work with a named author and no page numbers

Smith reports that almost 20% of commercial banks have been audited in recent years.

When you cite a passage from a work with no page or other reference numbers, such as a Web source or an article in HTML format, try to give the author's name in your text. You will not need a parenthetical citation then, but you must list the source in your works cited.

If the author's name does not appear in your text, give it in a parenthetical citation.

Clean cars are defined as vehicles with low pollution emissions and high fuel economy (Hagedorn).

c. Work with a named author on an e-reader or other device

Writing about post-Saddam Iraq, the journalist George Packer describes the tense relationship that existed between Kurdistan and the rest of the country (ch. 1).

Page numbers are not always the same on Kindles, iPads, and other e-readers and tablets. For a book you read on such a device, give the chapter number, not the device's page numbers.

d. Work with a named author and numbered paragraphs or sections

Twins reared apart report similar feelings (Palfrey, pars. 6-7).

If the work gives numbered paragraphs or sections, use the abbreviation par., pars., sec., or secs. to tell readers that you are citing one or more paragraphs or sections rather than page numbers.

e. Work with no named author

Many decades after its release, Citizen Kane is still remarkable for its rich black-and-white photography.

When your works-cited entry lists the work under its title, cite the work by title in your text, as explained in model 6. This example, a film, gives the title in the text, so it omits a parenthetical citation (see model 9).

f. Audio or video

In an episode of *Master of None*, the characters recognize how little they know about the lives of their fathers in their native countries of India and China ("Parents" 14:02-27).

You may view or listen to a video or audio source on a device that displays the time span of the recording you are citing. Give the start and stop times of your source in hours (if any), minutes, and seconds, separated by colons. The numbers above cite 14 minutes, 2 to 27 seconds.

9. One-page work or entire work

When you cite a work that's a single page long or cite an entire work—for instance, a one-page article, a tweet, a Web site, a book, or a film—you may omit any page or other reference number. If the work you cite has an author, try to give the name in the text. If the work does not have an author, give the title.

> Boyd deals with the need to acknowledge and come to terms with our fear of nuclear technology.

10. Work with no page or other reference numbers

When the work you cite, print or nonprint, has no page or other reference numbers, give the author's name, if available, in your text or in a parenthetical citation. (If no author is listed, give the title.)

> In the children's classic picture book *The Very Busy Spider,* hard work and patience are rewarded when the spider catches a fly in her web (Carle).

11. Multivolume work

If you consulted only one volume of a multivolume work, your list of works cited will say so (see model 20), and you can treat the volume as you would any book.

If you consulted more than one volume of a multivolume work, give the appropriate volume before the page number (here volume 5).

> After issuing the Emancipation Proclamation, Lincoln said, "What I did, I did after very full deliberations, and under a very heavy and solemn sense of responsibility" (5: 438).

The number 5 indicates the volume from which the quotation was taken; the number 438 indicates the page number in that volume. When the author's name appears in such a citation, place it before the volume number with no punctuation: (Lincoln 5: 438).

If you are referring generally to an entire volume of a multivolume work and are not citing specific page numbers, add the abbreviation vol. before the volume number, as in (vol. 5) or (Lincoln, vol. 5) (note the comma after the author's name). Then readers will not misinterpret the volume number as a page number.

12. Source referred to by another source (indirect source)

When you want to use a quotation that is already in quotation marks—indicating that the author you are reading is quoting someone else—try to find the original source and quote directly from it. If you can't find the original source, then your citation must indicate that your quotation of it is indirect. In the following citation, qtd. in ("quoted in") says that Davino was quoted by Boyd.

George Davino maintains that "even small children have vivid ideas about nuclear energy" (qtd. in Boyd 22).

The list of works cited then includes only Boyd (the work consulted), not Davino.

13. Literary work

Novels, plays, and poems are often available in many editions, so your instructor may ask you to provide information that will help readers find the passage you cite no matter what edition they consult.

a. Novel

Toward the end of James's novel, Maggie suddenly feels "the thick breath of the definite—which was the intimate, the immediate, the familiar, as she hadn't had them for so long" (535; pt. 6, ch. 41).

Give the page number first, followed by a semicolon and then information on the appropriate part or chapter of the work.

b. Poem not divided into parts

In Shakespeare's Sonnet 73 the speaker identifies with the trees of late autumn, "Bare ruined choirs, where late the sweet birds sang" (line 4). "In me," Shakespeare writes, "thou seest the glowing of such fire / That on the ashes of his youth doth lie . . ." (9-10).

You may omit the page number and supply the line number(s) for the quotation. To prevent confusion with page numbers, precede the numbers with line or lines in the first citation; then use just the numbers.

c. Verse play or poem divided into parts

Later in Shakespeare's *King Lear* the disguised Edgar says, "The prince of darkness is a gentleman" (3.4.147).

Omit a page number and cite the appropriate part—act (and scene, if any), canto, book, and so on—plus the line number(s). Use Arabic numerals for parts, including acts and scenes (3.4), unless your instructor specifies Roman numerals (III.iv).

d. Prose play

In Miller's *Death of a Salesman*, Willie Loman's wife, Linda, acknowledges her husband's failings but also the need for him to be treated with dignity: "He's not the finest character that ever lived. But he's a human being, and a terrible thing is happening to him" (56; act 1).

Provide the page number followed by the act and scene, if any.

14. The Bible

When you cite passages of the Bible in parentheses, abbreviate the title of any book longer than four letters—for instance, Gen. (Genesis), 1 Sam. (1 Samuel), Ps. (Psalms), Prov. (Proverbs), Matt.

(Matthew), Rom. (Romans), 2 Cor. (2 Corinthians). Then give the chapter and verse(s) in Arabic numerals.

> According to the Bible, at Babel God "did . . . confound the language of all the earth" (Gen. 11.9).

15. Two or more works in the same citation

When you refer to more than one work in a single parenthetical citation, separate the references with a semicolon.

> Two recent articles point out that a computer badly used can be less efficient than no computer at all (Gough and Hall 201; Richards 162).

Since long citations in the text can distract the reader, you may choose to cite several or more works in an endnote or footnote rather than in the text.

51.1.2 Positioning and punctuating parenthetical citations

The following guidelines will help you place and punctuate text citations to distinguish between your own and your sources' ideas and to make your own text readable.

Where to place citations

Position text citations to accomplish two goals:

- **Make it clear exactly where your borrowing begins and ends.**
- **Keep the citation as unobtrusive as possible.**

You can accomplish both goals by placing the parenthetical citation at the end of the sentence element containing the borrowed material. This sentence element may be a phrase or a clause, and it may begin, interrupt, or conclude the sentence. Usually, as in the following examples, the element ends with a punctuation mark.

> The inflation rate might climb as high as 30 percent (Kim 164), an increase that could threaten the small nation's stability.

> The inflation rate, which might climb as high as 30 percent (Kim 164), could threaten the small nation's stability.

> The small nation's stability could be threatened by its inflation rate, which, one source predicts, might climb as high as 30 percent (Kim 164).

In the last example, the addition of one source predicts clarifies that Kim is responsible only for the inflation-rate prediction, not for the statement about stability.

When your paraphrase or summary of a source runs longer than a sentence, clarify the boundaries by using the author's name in the first sentence and placing the parenthetical citation at the end of the last sentence.

> Juliette Kim studied the effects of acutely high inflation in several South American and African countries since World War II. She discovered that a major change in government accompanied or followed the inflationary period in 56% of cases (22-23).

When you cite two or more sources in the same paragraph, position authors' names and parenthetical citations so that readers can see who said what. In the following example, the beginnings and ends of sentences clearly mark the different sources.

> Schools use computers extensively for drill-and-practice exercises, in which students repeat specific skills such as spelling words, using the multiplication facts, or, at a higher level, doing chemistry problems. But many education experts criticize such exercises for boring students and failing to engage their critical thinking and creativity. Jane M. Healy, a noted educational psychologist and teacher, takes issue with "interactive" software for children as well as drill-and-practice software, arguing that "some of the most popular 'educational' software . . . may be damaging to independent thinking, attention, and motivation" (20). Another education expert, Harold Wenglinsky of the Educational Testing Service, found in a well-regarded study that fourth and eighth graders who used computers frequently, including for drill and practice, actually did worse on tests than their peers who used computers less often (*Does* 21). In a later article, Wenglinsky concludes that "the quantity of use matters far less than the quality of use." In schools, he says, high-quality computer work, involving critical thinking, is still rare ("In" 17).

How to punctuate citations

Generally, place a parenthetical citation *before* any punctuation required by your sentence. If the borrowed material is a quotation, place the citation *between* the closing quotation mark and the punctuation.

> Spelling argues that during the 1970s American automobile manufacturers met consumer needs "as well as could be expected" (26), but not everyone agrees with him.

The exception is a quotation ending in a question mark or exclamation point. Then, use the appropriate punctuation inside the closing quotation mark, and follow the quotation with the text citation and a period.

> "Of what use is genius," Emerson asks, "if the organ . . . cannot find a focal distance within the actual horizon of human life?" ("Experience" 60). Mad genius is no genius.

When a citation appears at the end of a quotation set off from the text, place it one space *after* the punctuation ending the quotation. Do not use additional punctuation with the citation or quotation marks around the quotation.

> In Charles Dickens's *A Christmas Carol*, Scrooge and the Ghost of Christmas Past visit Scrooge's childhood boarding school. They watch as the schoolmaster offers young Ebenezer and his sister some unappealing food and drink:

> Here he produced a decanter of curiously light wine, and a block of curiously heavy cake, and administered installments of those dainties to the young people: at the same time, sending out a meager servant to offer a glass of the "something" to the postboy, who answered that he thanked the gentleman, but if it was the same tap as he had tasted before, he had rather not. (34)

See the sample research paper (51.4) for further examples of placing in-text citations in relation to summaries, paraphrases, and quotations.

51.1.3 Using footnotes or endnotes in special circumstances

Occasionally you may want to use footnotes or endnotes in place of parenthetical citations. If you need to refer to several sources at once, listing them in a long parenthetical citation could be intrusive. In that case, you use a note for the information, following the style described here.

Signal the citation with a numeral raised above the appropriate line of text and write a note beginning with the same numeral to cite the sources.

Text At least five studies have confirmed these results.[1]

Note 1. Abbott and Winger 266-68; Casner 27; Hoyenga 78-79; Marino 36; Tripp et al. 179-83.

You may also use a footnote or endnote to comment on a source or to provide information that does not fit easily in the text.

Text So far, no one has confirmed these results.[2]

Note 2. Manter tried repeatedly to replicate the experiment, but he was never able to produce the high temperatures (616).

For a footnote or an endnote, type the numeral on the text line, followed by a period, a space, and the text of the note. If the note appears as a footnote, use the footnote feature of your word processor to set it at the bottom of the page on which the citation appears. Double-space the note. If the note appears as an endnote, place it in numerical order with the other endnotes on a page between the text and the list of works cited. Double-space all the endnotes.

51.2 List of Works Cited

51.2 Write an MLA list of works cited.

In MLA documentation style, your in-text citations (51.1) refer the reader to complete information on your sources in a list you title Works Cited and place at the end of your paper. The list should include all the sources you quoted, paraphrased, or summarized in your

Figure 51.1 MLA works-cited page

paper. (If your instructor asks you to include sources you examined but did not cite, title the list Works Consulted.)

Format of the list of works cited

To format the list of works cited, use Figure 51.1 and the following guidelines. For complete lists of works cited, see the paper by Brandon Sele (51.4).

Arrangement
Arrange sources alphabetically by the author's last name. If there is no author, alphabetize by the first main word of the title (excluding *A*, *An*, or *The*).

Spacing
Double-space everything in the list, as shown in the sample.

Indention
As shown in the sample, begin each entry at the left margin, and indent the second and subsequent lines one-half inch. Your word processor can create this so-called hanging indent automatically.

Elements of works-cited entries

The eighth edition of the *MLA Handbook* simplifies writing works-cited entries by building them on the core, visible elements in sources. In the following description and the box below, these core elements are listed in order of their appearance in a works-cited entry. Few sources include all of the listed elements: as you build works-cited entries, give the elements that you find in your sources. For more information from MLA, go to *style.mla.org*.

Building MLA works-cited entries

Following are the core elements and their order in works-cited entries. Most sources will not contain every element. The colors correspond to the highlight colors in the models in this chapter.

Author's last name, First name.
"Title of Shorter Work." or *Title of Longer Work.*

Container 1
Give these elements in this order if they are available. Skip "Title of Container" for self-contained works.

Title of Container 1,
Other contributors,
Version,
Number,
Publisher,
Publication date,
Location.

Container 2
Give these elements in this order if they are available.

Title of Container 2,
Other contributors,
Version,
Number,
Publisher,
Publication date,
Location.

Author

Begin each entry with the author's last name, a comma, and the author's first name and middle name or initial, if any—for instance, Hohulin, John D. End the author's name with a period. See models 1–6 for how to cite various numbers and kinds of authors.

Title of source

After the author, give the full title and any subtitle of the source, separating them with a colon. End the title with a period.

- **Quotation marks for shorter works:** Use quotation marks around titles of works that are part of larger works, such as articles, pages on Web sites, and selections from anthologies: "A Rose for Emily."
- **Italics for longer works:** Use italics for the titles of longer, independent works such as books and films: *Do the Right Thing*. Containers (next item) also have italicized titles.
- **Descriptions for untitled works:** For works that do not have titles, such as interviews, give a description of the work after the name of the author. (See models 32, 34, and 50 for examples of descriptions of untitled works.)

Title of container

Many sources used in research are shorter works, such as articles and Web pages, that are published in larger works, such as journals and Web sites. In MLA style, the larger publication is called the **container**. In your works-cited entry, give the title of the container in italics, followed by a comma.

- **Container 1:** Some works fall in one container. For example, if you are citing an article on a Web site, the container is the Web site (see model 34). If you are citing a short story or a chapter from a print anthology, the container is the anthology (see models 27 and 28).
- **Container 2:** Many sources have more than one container—in essence, the source is inside container 1, which is inside container 2. For example, if you are citing an article from a journal that you found in a database, container 1 is the journal and container 2 is the database. If your source is an episode of a television series that you watched on *Netflix*, container 1 is the television series and container 2 is *Netflix* (see model 48b).
- **Self-contained works:** Note that some sources are self-contained. These include books such as novels, manuals, works of nonfiction, and the like.

The models on the following pages give examples of many short works in containers such as books, journals, databases, and Web sites, as well as longer, self-contained works such as books, films, Web sites, music albums, and so on.

Other contributors

Some sources and some containers, such as anthologies and edited collections, may include the work of people besides the author. If a person's contribution to a work is important to your research, add the contributor's name to your works-cited entry preceded by a description such as adapted by, directed by, edited by, illustrated by, introduction by, narrated by, performance by, or translated by. Follow the name of a contributor with a comma. For examples of works-cited entries showing contributors, see models 16, 17, 19 (books), 48 (television episodes and series), 49 (radio programs), 51 (films and videos), 52 (sound recordings), and 54 (live performances).

Version

Books, films, and computer software such as games and apps often appear in updated or revised editions and versions. If your source or its container gives a version or edition, add it to your works-cited entry, followed by a comma—for instance, version 8.1, or 3rd ed., (ed. stands for "edition"). For examples of works-cited entries showing editions and versions, see models 14 (book) and 56 (app).

Number in a sequence

Some sources and containers are published in a numbered sequence. Examples include academic journals, which often have volume and issue numbers (models 7 and 8). Some books are published in sets consisting of multiple volumes (model 20). Television series and episodes are typically numbered by season and by episode (model 48). In your works-cited entry, follow a sequence number with a comma—for example, season 1, episode 6, or vol. 32, no. 6, (vol. and no. stand for "volume" and "number," respectively).

Publisher

Give the publisher followed by a comma. For instance, the publisher of a book is the company that issued the book, the publisher of a Web site is the organization that sponsors the site, and the publisher of a TV series is generally the main studio that produced the series (see model 48). If the source has more than one publisher, separate the names with a forward slash: Vertigo / DC Comics.

You do not need to list a publisher for some kinds of sources or containers, including periodicals (journals, newspapers, and magazines), databases, self-published works, and Web sites whose titles and publishers are the same.

Publication date

Give the date of publication followed by a comma. Publication dates vary considerably depending on the type of source you are citing. To identify and cite the publication date, see the index at the **MLA** divider to locate a model that most closely matches your source. See also model 37 to cite an undated source you find on the Web.

Location

Give a location telling where you found the source or its container so that other researchers can find the source, too. Follow the location with a period.

- **Page numbers:** For a source within a container with page numbers, such as a chapter of a book or an article in a periodical, provide the page numbers. Use the abbreviation p. or pp. before the page numbers: p. 72 or pp. 210-13.
- **Digital Object Identifier (DOI):** Many journal articles, books, and other documents have a DOI attached to them, a permanent URL that links to the text and functions as a unique identifier. When a DOI is available, include it at the end of your works-cited entry and follow it with a period: doi:10.1682/ JRRD.2010.03.0024. Usually a DOI will follow the title of a container such as a database or a Web site.
- **URL:** If a DOI is not available for a source you found in a database or on the Web, copy and paste the URL from your browser into your works-cited entry, deleting "http://"—for instance, harpers.org/archive/2012/10/contest-of-words/. If your source gives a stable URL, such as a *permalink*, give it instead.
- **Name and city:** If you viewed an object in a museum or an archive or attended a performance or lecture, give the name of the institution or venue and the city in which it is located—for instance, DeYoung Museum, San Francisco. For examples, see models 44, 54, and 58.

Models of MLA works-cited entries

Unlike earlier editions of the *MLA Handbook*, which gave numerous examples of works-cited entries organized by the type of source, the eighth edition emphasizes building entries based on the elements described in the preceding section. This chapter blends the two approaches, applying the new guidelines to a wide variety of sources you may encounter during your research. (See the index at the MLA divider.) The models here are extensive but not exhaustive, and you will surely come across sources that do not match exactly. For such sources, refer to the list of core elements and give whatever information you can find in the source.

51.2.1 Authors

The models below show how to handle authors' names in citing any kind of source.

1. One author

Ehrenreich, Barbara. *Dancing in the Streets: A History of Collective Joy.* Henry Holt, 2006.

Give the author's full name—last name first, a comma, first name, and any middle name or initial. Omit any title, such as *Dr.* or *PhD*. End the name with a period. If your source lists an editor as author, see model 15.

2. Two authors

Lifton, Robert Jay, and Greg Mitchell. *Who Owns Death: Capital Punishment, the American Conscience, and the End of Executions.* William Morrow, 2000.

Give the authors' names in the order provided on the title page. Reverse the first and last names of the first author *only*, not of the other author. Separate the authors' names with a comma and *and*. If your source lists two editors as authors, see model 15.

3. More than two authors

Wilcox, Dennis L., et al. *Think Public Relations.* 2nd ed., Allyn & Bacon, 2013.

Give the name of the first author only, and follow the name with a comma and the abbreviation et al. (for the Latin *et alii*, meaning "and others"). If your source lists more than two editors as authors, see model 15.

4. The same author(s) for two or more works

Gardner, Howard. *The Arts and Human Development.* John Wiley & Sons, 1973.

---. *Five Minds for the Future.* Harvard Business School P, 2007.

Give the author's name only in the first entry. For the second and any subsequent works by the same author, substitute three hyphens for the author's name, followed by a period. Note that the three hyphens may substitute only for *exactly* the same name or names. If the second Gardner source were by Gardner and somebody else, both names would have to be given in full.

Place an entry or entries using three hyphens immediately after the entry that names the author. Within the set of entries by the same author, arrange the sources alphabetically by the first main word of the title, as in the Gardner examples (*Arts*, then *Five*).

If you cite two or more sources that list as author(s) exactly the same editor(s), follow the hyphens with a comma and editor or editors as appropriate. (See model 15.)

5. A corporate author

Corporate authors include associations, committees, institutions, government bodies, companies, and other groups. When a source gives only the name of the organization as author and not an individual's name, the source has a corporate author.

a. Source cited by author

Vault Technologies. *Turnkey Parking Solutions*. Mills, 2014.

When the corporate author and the publisher are different, start with the name of the author.

b. Source cited by title

"Thailand's Campaign for Tobacco Control." *Center for Global Development*, 2015, millionssaved.cgdev.org/case-studies/thailands-campaign-for-tobacco-control.

When the corporate author and the publisher are the same, omit the author and start with the title. Omit the publisher as well when its name is the Web site title, as in the preceding example. (For examples of government documents cited in this way, see model 33b.)

6. Author not named (anonymous)

The Dorling Kindersley World Atlas. DK Publishing, 2013.

List a work that names no author—neither an individual nor a group—by its full title. If the work is a book, italicize the title. If the work is a periodical article or other short work, enclose the title in quotation marks.

"Drilling in the Wilderness." *The Economist,* 24 Apr. 2014, p. 32.

Alphabetize the work by the title's first main word, excluding *A*, *An*, or *The* (*Dorling* in the first example and Drilling in the second).

51.2.2 Articles in journals, newspapers, and magazines

Articles in scholarly journals, in newspapers, and in magazines appear in print periodicals, in online databases available through your library, and on the Web.

Articles in scholarly journals

To cite an article in a scholarly journal, give the author and the title of the article. (See "Citing journal articles" box.) Enclose the title in quotation marks. Then give information about the container(s), depending on what is available. In container 1, give the title of the journal, any volume and issue numbers, the publication date (abbreviate all months except May, June, and July), and the location of the

(continued on p. 382)

Citing journal articles: Print and database

Print journal article

First page of article

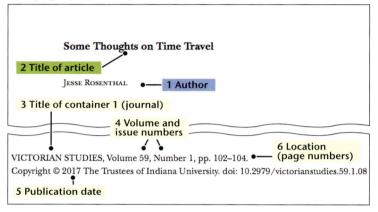

Database journal article

Detailed record

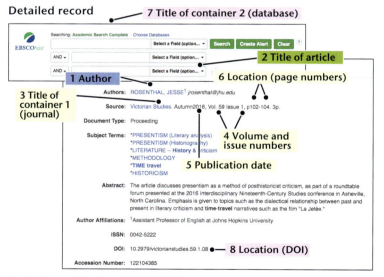

Used with permission from EBSCO Publishing.

Works-cited entry: Print journal article

Rosenthal, Jesse. "Some Thoughts on Time Travel."
    Victorian Studies, vol. 59, no. 1, Autumn 2016,
    pp. 102-04.

Works-cited entry: Database journal article

Rosenthal, Jesse. "Some Thoughts on Time Travel." *Victorian
    Studies,* vol. 59, no. 1, Autumn 2016, pp. 102-04. *Academic
    Search Complete,* doi:10.2979/victorianstudies.59.1.08.

1. **Author.** Give the full name—last name first, a comma, first name, and any middle name or initial. Omit *Dr.*, *PhD*, or any other title. End the name with a period.

2. **Title of article,** in quotation marks. Give the full title and any subtitle, separating them with a colon. End the title with a period inside the final quotation mark.

3. **Title of container 1 (journal),** in italics. End with a comma.

4. **Volume and issue numbers,** in Arabic numerals, preceded by *vol.* and *no.*, respectively, and followed by commas.

5. **Publication date,** preceded by the month or season, if available. Abbreviate all months except May, June, and July. End with a comma.

6. **Location (page numbers of the article),** preceded by *pp.* and ending with a period. Provide only as many digits in the last number as needed for clarity, usually two.

7. **Title of container 2 (database),** in italics. End with a comma.

8. **Location.** If available, give a Digital Object Identifier (DOI), preceded by *doi:*. End with a period. If no DOI is available, give the URL without "http://."

source, such as page numbers of the article or possibly a URL. Add a container 2 if you reached the source electronically—for instance, through a library database—and give the source's location, such as a Digital Object Identifier (DOI) or a URL.

You do not need to give a publisher for articles in academic journals in print, in online databases such as *Academic Search Complete* or *ProQuest*, or on Web sites.

7. Article in a scholarly journal with volume and issue numbers
a. Print journal article

Mattingly, Carol. "Telling Evidence: Rethinking What Counts in Rhetoric." *Rhetoric Society Quarterly,* vol. 32, no. 1, Winter 2002, pp. 99-108.

b. Database journal article

Neves, Joshua. "Cinematic Encounters in Beijing." *Film Quarterly,* vol. 67, no. 1, Fall 2013, pp. 27-40. *Academic Search Complete,* doi:10.1525/FQ.2.13.67.1.27.

Basically, start with the information for a print article (previous model), and add the information for container 2—the title of the database and the DOI or URL.

c. Web journal article

Aulisio, George J. "Green Libraries Are More Than Just Buildings." *Electronic Green Journal,* vol. 35, no. 1, 2013, escholarship.org/uc/item/3x11862z#page-1.

For a scholarly article you find in a Web journal, begin with the author and title. Then give available information about the container: the title of the journal, the volume and issue numbers, the publication date, and a URL, as here, or a DOI. If the journal article does not have page numbers, omit them from the works-cited entry.

8. Article in a journal with only issue numbers

Dobozy, Tomas. "The Writing of Trespass." *Canadian Literature,* no. 218, Autumn 2013, pp. 11-28. *Academic Search Premier,* web.a.ebscohost.com/ehost/detail/AN=94425037&db=aph.

If a scholarly journal numbers only issues, not volumes, give the issue alone after the journal title.

Articles in newspapers

To cite an article in a newspaper, give the author and the title of the article. Enclose the title in quotation marks. Then give information about the container(s), depending on what is available. In container 1, give the title of the newspaper, the publication date (abbreviate all months except May, June, and July), and the location of the article (generally page numbers or a URL). Add information for a container 2 if you used another source, such as a library database, to reach the article.

List of works cited 383

Citing a newspaper article: Database

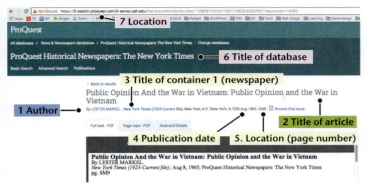

Used with permission from ProQuest LLC.

Markel, Lester. "Public Opinion and the War in Vietnam." *The New York Times,* 8 Aug. 1965, p. SM9. *ProQuest Historical Newspapers: The New York Times,* 0-search.proquest.com.iii-server.ualr.edu/hnpnewyorktimes/docview/116969740/63156C1C6E3E4D30PQ/.

1. **Author.** Give the full name—last name first, a comma, first name, and any middle name or initial. End the name with a period.

2. **Title of article,** in quotation marks. Give the full title and any subtitle, separating them with a colon. End the title with a period inside the final quotation mark.

3. **Title of container 1 (newspaper),** in italics. End with a comma.

4. **Publication date,** giving day, month, and year. Abbreviate all months except May, June, and July. End with a comma.

5. **Location (page number),** preceded by p. and ending with a period. (Use pp. if the article runs on more than one page.) Include a section designation before the page number, as in SM9 here, if the newspaper does.

6. **Title of container 2 (database),** in italics. End with a comma.

7. **Location.** Give the URL without "http://." End with a period.

MLA
51.2

You do not need to give a publisher for newspaper articles that appear in print, in online databases such *LexisNexis*, or on Web sites.

9. Article in a national newspaper

a. Print newspaper article

Lowery, Annie. "Cities Advancing Inequality Fight." *The New York Times,* 7 Apr. 2014, pp. A1+.

If the newspaper is divided into lettered sections, provide the section designation before the page number when the newspaper does the same: A1+ above. The plus sign indicates that the article continues on a later page.

b. Database newspaper article

Stein, Rob. "Obesity May Stall Trend of Increasing Longevity." *The Washington Post,* 15 Mar. 2015, p. A2. *LexisNexis Academic,* www.lexisnexis.com/lnacademic/HEADLINE(Obesity+may+stall%2C+trend+of+increasing%2C+longevity)%2BDATE%2B2015.

See "Citing a newspaper article: Database" for an explanation of this format and where to find the required information in a database. Basically, start with the information for a print article (previous model), and add the information for container 2—the title of the database and the URL or DOI.

c. Web news article

Jarvie, Jenny. "What Life Is Like on $7.25 Per Hour." *Los Angeles Times*, 6 Apr. 2016, www.latimes.com/nation/la-na-minimum-wage-life-20160405-story.html.

To cite a newspaper article that you find on the open Web, follow the author and title with the information for the container: the title of the newspaper, the publication date (day, month, year), and the URL. To cite a reader's comment on an article, see model 40.

10. Article in a local newspaper

Beckett, Lois. "The Ignored PTSD Crisis: Americans Wounded in Their Own Neighborhoods." *The Louisiana Weekly* [New Orleans], 17 Feb. 2014, pp. 12-13.

If the city of publication does not appear in the title of a local newspaper, follow the title with the city name in brackets, not italicized.

Articles in magazines

To cite an article in a magazine, give the author and the title of the article. Enclose the title in quotation marks. Then give information about the container(s), depending on what is available. For container 1, give the title of the magazine, the publication date (abbreviate all months except May, June, and July), and the location of the article (page numbers, a URL, or a DOI). Add information for a container 2 if you used another source, such as a library database, to reach the article.

You do not need to give a publisher for magazine articles that appear in print, in online databases such as *Academic Search Complete*, or on Web sites.

11. Article in a weekly or biweekly magazine

a. Print magazine article

Toobin, Jeffrey. "This Is My Jail." *The New Yorker,* 14 Apr. 2014, pp. 26-32.

Following the author and title, give information for the container: the title of the magazine, the publication date (day, month, year), and the page numbers.

b. Database magazine article

Barras, Colin. "Right on Target." *New Scientist,* 25 Jan. 2014, pp. 40-43. *Academic Search Complete,* web.a.ebscohost.com/ehost/detail/AN=93983067&db=aph.

To cite a magazine article you found in an online database, start with the information for a print article (model 11a). Then add the information for the second container—the title of the database and the DOI or URL.

c. Web magazine article

Stampler, Laura. "These Cities Have the Most Open-Minded Daters." *Time,* 14 Apr. 2014, time.com/61947/these-cities-have-the-most-open-minded-daters/.

To cite a magazine article you find on the open Web, follow the author and title with information for the container: the title of the magazine, the publication date (day, month, year), and the URL. To cite a reader's comment on an article, see model 40.

12. Article in a monthly or bimonthly magazine

Wong, Kate. "Rise of the Human Predator." *Scientific American,* Apr. 2014, pp. 46-51.

Follow the magazine title with the month and the year of publication. If the date on the magazine spans two months, give both months: Jan.-Feb. 2016.

51.2.3 Books and government publications

Complete books

A complete, stand-alone book is self-contained, so the title of a book is followed by the names of other contributors (if any) and publication information. If you found the book in a library database or on the Web, provide the name of the database or Web site and a DOI or URL after the publication information.

(continued on p. 388)

Citing books: Print and database

Print book
Title Page

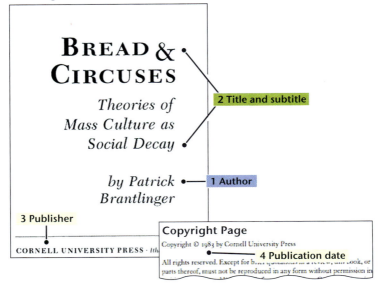

Screenshot of Title page and Copyright page, "Bread and Circuses." *Bread & Circuses: Theories of Mass Culture as Social Decay* (1983), Cornell University Press. Used with permission from Cornell University Press.

Database book
Detailed record

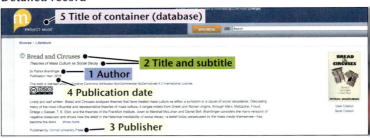

Works-cited entry: Print book

Brantlinger, Patrick.[1] *Bread and Circuses: Theories of Mass Culture as Social Decay.*[2] Cornell UP, 1983.

Works-cited entry: Database book

Brantlinger, Patrick.[1] *Bread and Circuses: Theories of Mass Culture as Social Decay.*[2] Cornell UP,[3] 1983.[4] *Project Muse,*[5] 0-muse.jhu.edu.iii-server.ualr.edu/book/47564.[6]

1. **Author.** Give the full name—last name first, a comma, first name, and any middle name or initial. Omit *Dr.*, *PhD*, or any other title. End the name with a period.

2. **Title,** in italics. Give the full title and subtitle, separating them with a colon. Capitalize all significant words of the title even if the book does not. End the title with a period.

3. **Publisher.** Give the name as it appears on the title page or copyright page, followed by a comma. Shorten "University Press" to UP and omit "Company," "Co.," and "Inc." from other publishers' names. If two publisher names are listed on the title or copyright page, determine their relationship: If they are both independent entities, list them both with a forward slash between the names (see model 19). If one is a division of the other (for instance, Scribner is a division of Simon & Schuster), cite only the division.

4. **Publication date.** If the date does not appear on the title page, look for it on the copyright page. End with a period.

5. **Title of container (database),** in italics. End with a comma.

6. **Location.** Give the URL without "http://," ending with a period. If the database record gives a DOI, provide it instead.

13. Basic format for a complete book

To cite a book, give the author, the title, the publisher, and the date. When other information is present, give it between the author's name and the title, between the title and the publication information, or at the end of the entry, as in models 14–23.

a. Print book or book on an e-reader

Shteir, Rachel. *The Steal: A Cultural History of Shoplifting.* The Penguin Press, 2011.

See "Citing books: Print and Database" for an explanation of this format and where to find the required information in a print book or an e-book with print publication information.

If an e-book has no print publication information, give the e-book publication instead. Your in-text citations will vary depending on whether you are citing a print or digital version: for a print version you will cite page numbers; for an e-book version you will cite chapters.

b. Database book

Levine, Daniel. *Bayard Rustin and the Civil Rights Movement.* Rutgers UP, 2000. *eBook Collection,* web.a.ebscohost.com/ehost/ebookviewer/ebook/ e6967d23-394e-41d9-ab54-d292ebd6287b=2.

To cite a book that you find in a database, give any print publication information before information about the container—the name of the database and a DOI or URL. See "Citing books: Print and Database" for an explanation of this format and where to find the required information in a database.

c. Web book

Cather, Willa. *One of Ours.* Alfred A. Knopf, 1922. *Bartleby.com,* 2000, www.bartleby.com/1006/1.html.

Providing print publication information for a book on the Web is not required, but it can be helpful to readers. This example gives the original publisher and publication date followed by information for the container: the title of the Web site and the URL. (The title of the Web site and the name of the publisher are the same, so only the Web site is given.)

14. Second or subsequent edition

Bolinger, Dwight L. *Aspects of Language.* 3rd ed., Harcourt Brace Jovanovich, 1981.

Books are often revised and published in new editions. For any edition after the first, place the edition number after the title. Use the designation given in the source, such as Expanded ed., Updated ed., or 3rd ed., as in the example.

15. Book with an editor

Holland, Merlin, and Rupert Hart-Davis, editors. *The Complete Letters of Oscar Wilde.* Henry Holt, 2000.

Handle editors' names like authors' names (models 1–4), but add a comma and editor or editors after the last editor's name.

16. Book with an author and an editor

Mumford, Lewis. *The City in History.* Edited by Donald L. Miller, Pantheon, 1986.

When citing the work of the author, give the author's name first. After the title, give the editor's name (another contributor) preceded by Edited by. When citing the work of the editor, use model 15 for a book with an editor, adding By and the author's name after the title.

Miller, Donald L., editor. *The City in History.* By Lewis Mumford, Mariner Books, 1968.

17. Book with a translator

Alighieri, Dante. *The Inferno.* Translated by John Ciardi, New American Library, 1971.

When citing the work of an author, shown above, give his or her name first, and give the translator's name (another contributor) after the title, preceded by Translated by.

When citing the work of the translator, give his or her name first, followed by a comma and translator. Follow the title with By and the author's name.

Ciardi, John, translator. *The Inferno.* By Dante Alighieri, New American Library, 1971.

When a book you cite by the author's name has a translator *and* an editor, give the translator's and the editor's names in the order used on the book's title page.

18. Anthology

Kennedy, X. J., and Dana Gioia, editors. *Literature: An Introduction to Fiction, Poetry, Drama, and Writing.* 13th ed., Pearson, 2016.

Cite an entire anthology only when citing the work of the editor or editors or when your instructor permits cross-referencing like that shown in model 28. Give the name of the editor or editors (followed by editor or editors) and then the title of the anthology.

19. Illustrated book or graphic narrative

Wilson, G. Willow. *Cairo.* Illustrated by M. K. Perker, Vertigo / DC Comics, 2005.

When citing the work of the writer of a graphic narrative or illustrated book, follow the example above: the author's name, the title, Illustrated by, and the illustrator's name (another contributor). This book's two publishers, Vertigo and DC Comics, are separated by a forward slash.

When citing the work of an illustrator, list his or her name first, followed by a comma and illustrator. After the title and By, list the author's name.

Williams, Garth, illustrator. *Charlotte's Web.* By E. B. White, Harper & Brothers, 1952.

20. Multivolume work

Lincoln, Abraham. *The Collected Works of Abraham Lincoln*. Edited by Roy P. Basler, vol. 5, Rutgers UP, 1953. 8 vols.

When the work you cite is one volume in a set of numbered volumes, give the volume number before the publication information (vol. 5 in the example). The total number of volumes at the end of the entry is optional (8 vols. in the example).

If you use two or more volumes of a multivolume work, give the work's total number of volumes before the publication information (8 vols. in the following example). Your in-text citation will indicate which volume you are citing.

Lincoln, Abraham. *The Collected Works of Abraham Lincoln*. Edited by Roy P. Basler, 8 vols., Rutgers UP, 1953.

21. Book in a series

Bergman, Ingmar. *The Seventh Seal*. Simon and Schuster, 1960. Modern Film Scripts Series 12.

When the work you cite is part of a series, you may give the name of the series, not italicized or in quotation marks, at the end of the entry.

22. Book published before 1900

James, Henry. *The Bostonians*. London, 1886.

Although the city of publication is not required in most works-cited entries, MLA recommends giving the city rather than the publisher for books published before 1900 because such books are usually associated with the cities in which they were published.

23. Republished book

Achebe, Chinua. *Things Fall Apart*. 1958. Anchor Books, 1994.

Many books, especially classic literary works, are republished and reissued by publishers. If the original publication date of a book is important to your use of it, give the date after the title. Then provide the publication information for the source you are using.

24. Sacred works

The Bible: Authorized King James Version with Apocrypha. Edited by Robert Carroll and Stephen Prickett, Oxford UP, 2008.

The Koran. Translated by N. J. Dawood, rev. ed., Penguin, 2015.

When citing a sacred work, give the edition you consulted, beginning with the title unless you are citing the work of an editor or translator.

25. Book with a title in its title

Eco, Umberto. *Postscript to* The Name of the Rose. Translated by William Weaver, Harcourt Brace Jovanovich, 1983.

When a book's title contains another book title (here *The Name of the Rose*), do not italicize the second title. When a book's title contains a quotation or the title of a work normally placed in quotation marks, keep the quotation marks and italicize both titles: *Critical Response to Henry James's "The Beast in the Jungle."*

26. Book lacking publication information or pagination

Carle, Eric. *The Very Busy Spider*. Philomel Books, 1984, n. pag.

Some books are not paginated or do not list a publisher or date of publication. Although MLA style no longer requires you to indicate missing information, your instructor may ask you to do so for clarity. These abbreviations are conventional: n.p. if no publisher, n.d. if no publication date, and n. pag. if no page numbers.

Parts of books

Parts of books include selections from anthologies, articles and chapters in scholarly collections and reference works, and the like. Works-cited entries for these short works include the author and title as well as information about the container in which they appear: the title, any other contributors, publication information, and page numbers, if available.

27. Selection from an anthology

Munro, Alice. "How I Met My Husband." *Literature: An Introduction to Fiction, Poetry, Drama, and Writing*, edited by X. J. Kennedy and Dana Gioia, 13th ed., Pearson, 2016, pp. 189-201.

This listing adds to the anthology entry in model 18: author of selection, title of selection (in quotation marks), and inclusive page numbers for the selection. If you wish, you may also supply the original date of publication for the work you are citing, after its title. See model 23.

If the work you cite comes from a collection of works by one author that has no editor, use the following form:

Hempel, Amy. "San Francisco." *The Collected Stories of Amy Hempel*, Scribner, 2006, pp. 27-28.

28. Two or more selections from the same anthology

Bradstreet, Anne. "The Author to Her Book." Kennedy and Gioia, pp. 657-58.
Kennedy, X. J., and Dana Gioia, editors. *Literature: An Introduction to Fiction, Poetry, Drama, and Writing*. 13th ed., Pearson, 2016.
Merwin, W. S. "For the Anniversary of My Death." Kennedy and Gioia, p. 828.
Stevens, Wallace. "Thirteen Ways of Looking at a Blackbird." Kennedy and Gioia, pp. 831-33.

When you are citing more than one selection from the same anthology, your instructor may allow you to avoid repetition by giving the anthology information in full (the Kennedy and Gioia entry) and then simply cross-referencing it in entries for the works you used. Thus, the Bradstreet, Merwin, and Stevens examples replace full publication information with Kennedy and Gioia and the appropriate pages in that book. Note that each entry appears in its proper alphabetical place among other works cited.

29. Work from a collection of scholarly articles

Molloy, Francis C. "The Suburban Vision in John O'Hara's Short Stories." *Short Story Criticism: Excerpts from Criticism of the Works of Short Fiction Writers,* edited by David Segal, Gale, 1989, pp. 287-92. Originally published in *Critique: Studies in Modern Fiction,* vol. 25, no. 2, 1984, pp. 101-13.

Scholarly articles may be in collections like the one in the preceding example, *Short Story Criticism*. If the articles were written for the collection, you can follow model 27 for a selection from an anthology. However, if the articles were previously printed elsewhere—for instance, in scholarly journals—your instructor may ask you to provide the information for the earlier publication of articles you cite. Add Originally published in to the end of the entry and then give information for the earlier publication.

30. Article in a reference work

List an article in a reference work by the title if no author is given (models a and b) or by the author (model c). Then give the information for the container.

a. Print reference work

"Fortune." *Encyclopedia of Indo-European Culture,* edited by J. P. Malloy and D. Q. Adams, Fitzroy, 1997, pp. 211-12.

b. Web reference work

"Ming Dynasty." *Encyclopaedia Britannica,* 14 Dec. 2015, www.britannica.com/topic/Ming-dynasty-Chinese-history.

c. CD-ROM or DVD-ROM reference work

Nunberg, Geoffrey. "Usage in the Dictionary." *The American Heritage Dictionary of the English Language,* 4th ed., Houghton Mifflin, 2000.

Single-issue CD-ROMs may be encyclopedias, dictionaries, books, and other resources that are published just once. Cite such sources like print books.

31. Introduction, preface, foreword, or afterword

Quindlen, Anna. Foreword. *A Tree Grows in Brooklyn,* by Betty Smith, HarperCollins, 2011, pp. vii-xv.

An introduction, foreword, or afterword is often written by someone other than the book's author. When citing such a piece, give its name without quotation marks or italics, as with Foreword in the example. (If the piece has a title of its own, provide it, in quotation marks, between the name of the author and the title of the book.) Give the inclusive page numbers of the part you cite. (In the preceding example, the small Roman numerals refer to the front matter of the book, before page 1.)

When the author of a preface or introduction is the same as the author of the book, give only the last name after the title.

> Gould, Stephen Jay. Prologue. *The Flamingo's Smile: Reflections in Natural History,* by Gould, W. W. Norton, 1985, pp. 13-20.

32. Published letter

> Buttolph, Mrs. Laura E. Letter to Reverend and Mrs. C. C. Jones. 20 June 1857. *The Children of Pride: A True Story of Georgia and the Civil War,* edited by Robert Manson Myers, Yale UP, 1972, pp. 334-35.

List a published letter under the writer's name. Give it a descriptive label, specifying that the source is a letter and to whom it was addressed, and give the date on which it was written. Do not put this description in quotation marks or italics. Treat the rest of the information like a selection from an anthology (model 27), giving the title of the collection, the editor, publication information, and any page numbers.

Government publications

33. Government publication

a. Publication cited by author

> Gray, Colin S. *Defense Planning for National Security: Navigation Aids for the Mystery Tour.* United States Army War College Press, 2014.

> United States, Dept. of Defense, Office of Civil Defense. *Fallout Protection: What to Know and Do about Nuclear Attack.* US Government Printing Office, 1961.

If a government publication lists a person as author or editor, treat the source as an authored or edited book (first example). If a publication does not list an author or editor, give the government and the agency as author (second example).

For a congressional publication, give the house and committee involved before the title. Then give the title (in italics) and information for the container: the title of the Web site, the date, and the URL.

> United States, Congress, Senate, Committee on Veterans' Affairs. *Post-9/11 Veterans Educational Assistance Improvements Act of 2010.* US Government Printing Office, 2010, www.gpo.gov/fdsys/pkg/BILLS-111s3447.

If you like, after the URL you may include the number and session of Congress, the chamber (House of Representatives or Senate), and the type and number of the publication—for instance, 111th Congress, 2nd session, Senate Bill 3447.

b. Publication cited by title

"Autism Spectrum Disorder." *National Institute of Mental Health,* Sept. 2015, www.nimh.nih.gov/health/publications/autism-spectrum-disorder-qf-15-5511/index.shtml.

"A Comprehensive Approach to Bullying Prevention." *Wisconsin Dept. of Public Instruction,* 24 Feb. 2016, dpi.wi.gov/sspw/safe-schools/bullying-prevention.

MLA style recommends omitting a corporate author when it is the same as the publisher and omitting the publisher when it has the same name as its Web site. The preceding examples begin with the title and then give information for the container: the title of the Web site, the date, and the URL. (For more on corporate authors, see model 5.)

51.2.4 Web sources and social media
Web sites and parts of Web sites

The following models encompass pages, essays, articles, stories, poems, plays, and other works that you find on larger Web sites. To cite journal, newspaper, and magazine articles that you find on the open Web, see, respectively, models 7c, 9c, and 11c. To cite books that you find on the open Web, see model 13c. To cite a government document on a Web site, see model 33. To cite a complete Web site, see model 35.

34. Page or work on a Web site

When you cite a page or work that you find on a Web site, treat the Web site as the container of the source. After the author and title, give the title of the Web site (in italics), any other contributors (such as an editor of the site), the publisher (if different from the site title), the publication date, and the location of the source (the URL).

a. Work with an author and a title

Murray, Amanda. "Invention Hot Spot: Birth of Hip-Hop in the Bronx, New York, in the 1970s." *Lemelson Center for the Study of Invention and Innovation,* Smithsonian Institution, 15 Oct. 2010, invention.si.edu/invention-hot-spot-birth-hip-hop-bronx-new-york-1970s.

See "Citing a page or work on a Web site" for an explanation of this format and where to find the required information on a Web site.

Most works on Web sites are brief, and their titles should be placed in quotation marks. However, some works, such as books and plays, are longer, and their titles should be italicized. The work cited below is a collection of poems:

Wheatley, Phillis. *Poems on Various Subjects, Religious and Moral.* London, 1773. Bartleby.com, www.bartleby.com/150/.

Citing a page or work on a Web site

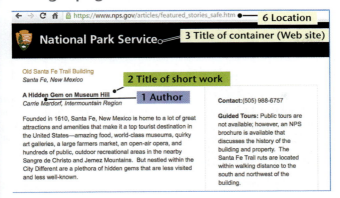

Bottom of page

Screenshot of article "Old Santa Fe Trial Building" by Carrie Mardorf; National Park Service

Mardorf, Carrie. "A Hidden Gem on Museum Hill." *National Park Service,* US Department of the Interior, 3 July 2012, www.nps.gov/articles/featured_stories_safe.htm.

1. **Author.** Give the full name—last name first, a comma, first name, and any middle name or initial. Omit *Dr., PhD,* or any other title. End the name with a period. If no author is listed, begin with the title of the short work.

2. **Title of the short work,** in quotation marks. End the title with a period inside the final quotation mark.

3. **Title of container (Web site),** in italics. End with a comma.

4. **Publisher,** followed by a comma. The publisher of a Web site may be at the top of the home page, at the bottom of the home page, or on a page that provides information about the site. If the site title and the publisher are the same, omit the publisher.

5. **Publication date.** For dates that include day and month, give the day first, then month, then year. Abbreviate all months except May, June, and July. End with a comma.

6. **Location.** Give the URL without "http://." End with a period.

b. Work without an author

"Eliminating Polio in Haiti." *Center for Global Development,* 2015, millionssaved
.cgdev.org/case-studies/eliminating-polio-in-haiti.

If the work lacks an author, start with the title.

c. Work without a title

Cyberbullying Research Center. Home page. 2016, cyberbullying.org/.

If you are citing an untitled work from a Web site, such as the home page or an untitled blog posting, give the name of the site followed by Home page, Online posting, or another descriptive label. Do not use quotation marks or italics for this label.

d. Work with print publication information

Herodotus. *The Histories.* Translated by A. D. Godley, Harvard UP, 1920. *Perseus
Digital Library,* Tufts U, Dept. of Classics, www.perseus.tufts.edu/hopper/
text?doc=Perseus:text:1999.01.0126.

If the print information for a source is relevant to your research, give it after the title of the work. In this example, the name of the translator and the publication information identify a specific version of the work. The title of the Web site, the publisher, and the URL follow. For more examples of digital books, see model 13.

35. Entire Web site

a. Web site with an author or an editor

Crane, Gregory, editor. *The Perseus Digital Library.* Tufts U, Dept. of Classics,
1985-2016, www.perseus.tufts.edu/hopper/.

When citing an entire Web site—for instance, a scholarly project or a foundation site—include the name of the editor or author (if available), followed by the title of the site, the publisher, the publication date, and the URL.

b. Web site without an author or an editor

Center for Financial Security. U of Wisconsin, 2016, cfs.wisc.edu/.

If a Web site lacks an author or an editor (as many do), begin with the title of the site.

36. Wiki

"Podcast." *Wikipedia.* Wikimedia Foundation, 6 Apr. 2016, en.wikipedia.org/
wiki/Podcast.

To cite an entry from a wiki, give the entry title, the site title, the publisher (if different from the title of the Web site), the publication date, and the URL.

37. Undated Web source

"Clean Cars 101." *Union of Concerned Scientists,* www.ucsusa.org/our-work/
clean-vehicles/clean-cars-101#.Vwa-KfkrKM8. Accessed 7 Apr. 2016.

MLA style no longer requires access dates for all online sources. However, if the work you cite is undated, or if your instructor requires an access date, give it at the end of the entry preceded by Accessed.

Social Media

38. Post on a blog

Minogue, Kristin. "Diverse Forests Are Stronger against Deer."
Smithsonian Insider, 8 Apr. 2014, insider.si.edu/2014/04/
diverse-forests-resist-deer-better/2014.

Cite a blog post like a work on a Web site, giving the author, the title of the post, and information about the container. The example gives the title of the blog, the publication date, and the URL. It does not give the name of the publisher because the name is clear from the title of the blog.

Cite an entire blog as you would cite an entire Web site (see model 35).

39. Post on a social-networking site

Literacy Network. Status update. *Facebook,* 5 Apr. 2016, www.facebook.com/
LiteracyNetwork/?fref=ts.

Give the name of the author (a person or an organization, as here), the type of post, the title of the site, the publisher (if different from the site title), the date of the post, and the URL.

40. Comment

Teka. Comment on "When a Feminist Pledges a Sorority." By Jessica Bennett,
The New York Times, 9 Apr. 2016, www.nytimes.com/2016/04/10/fashion/
sorority-ivy-league-feminists.

List the author's name or user name if the author uses a pseudonym (as here). Then give Comment on followed by the title of the article or post the comment responds to and the information for the container. This example includes the author of the article the comment responds to, the title of the site, the article's publication date, and the URL.

41. Tweet

Bittman, Mark. "Eating Less Meat Could Save up to $31 Trillion (and Many Lives)
bit.ly/1UyYxyp." *Twitter,* 21 Mar. 2016, 2:21 p.m., twitter.com/bittman/
status/712026468738404352?lang=en.

Give the author's name or user name if the author uses a pseudonym. Give the tweet in its entirety, using the author's capitalization, in quotation marks. Then give the information for the container: the name of the site (*Twitter*), the date and time of the tweet, and the URL.

42. Post to a discussion group

Williams, Frederick. "Circles as Primitive." *The Math Forum @ Drexel,* Drexel U, 28 Feb. 2012, mathforum.org/kb/thread.jspa?threadID=2583537.

If a discussion-group post does not have a title, say Online posting instead. Then give the information for the container: the title of the discussion group, the publisher, the date, and the URL of the discussion thread.

43. E-mail or text message

Green, Reginald. "Re: College Applications." Received by the author, 2 May 2016.

For an e-mail message, use the subject heading as the title, in quotation marks, with standard capitalization. Then name the recipient, whether yourself (the author) or someone else. Cite a text message like an e-mail message but without a subject title.

Soo, Makenna. Text message to the author. 16 Apr. 2016.

51.2.5 Visual, audio, and other media sources

44. Painting, photograph, or other work of visual art

a. Original artwork

Abbott, Berenice. *Soap Bubbles.* 1946, Museum of Modern Art, New York.

To cite a work of visual art that you see in person, such as in a museum, name the artist and give the title (in italics). Then give the date of creation and the name and location of the place where you saw the work. You may omit the city if the name of the place includes the city.

b. Reproduction of an artwork in a print publication

Graham, David. *Bob's Java Jive, Tacoma, Washington, 1989. Only in America: Some Unexpected Scenery,* Alfred A. Knopf, 1991, p. 93.

To cite a reproduction of a work of visual art, give the artist and title of the work followed by information for the container in which you found it. In the example, the container is a print book with title, publisher, publication date, and location (a page number).

c. Work of art on the Web

O'Keefe, Georgia. *It Was Red and Pink.* 1959, *Milwaukee Art Museum,* collection.mam.org/details.php?id=6725.

List of works cited

To cite a work of art that you view on the Web, give the name of the artist or creator, the title of the work, and the date of the work (if any). Then give information for the container: the title of the Web site, the publisher of the Web site (if different from the title), and the location of the work (here, a URL).

d. Artwork in a digital file

Girls on the playground. Personal photograph by the author, 10 Aug. 2015.

To cite an unpublished artwork in a digital file that you are reproducing, such as personal photograph or work of art, give a description of it, the photographer, and the date.

45. Advertisement

a. Advertisement without a title

Apple iPhone SE. Advertisement. *Vogue,* May 2016, p. 3.

To cite an advertisement without a title, start with the name of the company and/or product followed by Advertisement. Then give information for the container of the source, in this case a print magazine: title, date, and location (page number).

b. Advertisement with a title

Honey Maid. "This Is Wholesome." *YouTube,* 10 Mar. 2016, youtu.be/2xeanX6xnRU.

Many companies post titled advertisements on their Web sites and on *YouTube*. To cite such an ad, give the company's name and/or product followed by the title of the ad in quotation marks. Then give information for the container: the site where you viewed the ad, the date, and the URL.

46. Comic strip or cartoon

a. Titled comic strip

Johnston, Lynn. "For Better or Worse." *San Francisco Chronicle,* 22 Aug. 2014, p. E6.

Cite a titled comic strip with the artist's name, the title of the strip (in quotation marks), and the information for the container—here, the title of the newspaper, the date, and the page number.

b. Individual cartoon

Sipress, David. Cartoon. *The New Yorker,* 7 Apr. 2016, www.newyorker.com/cartoons/daily-cartoon/daily-cartoon-thursday-april-7th/.

To cite a cartoon that is not part of a comic strip, start with the name of the artist. If the cartoon has a title, give it in quotation marks. If it does not have a title, provide the description Cartoon (as in the example), without quotation marks or italics. Then give information for the container of the work—here, the title of the Web site, the date, and the URL.

47. Map, chart, or diagram

Unless the creator of an illustration is given on the source, list the illustration by its title. Put the title in quotation marks if it is contained in another publication or in italics if it is published independently. If the illustration does not have a title, provide a description in place of the title, without quotation marks or italics (for instance, Diagram). End with publication information for the source.

a. Print map, chart, or diagram

"The Sonoran Desert." *Sonoran Desert: An American Deserts Handbook,* by Rose Houk, Western National Parks Association, 2000, p. 12.

b. Web map, chart, or diagram

"Water Cycle Diagram." *Earthguide,* Scripps Institution of Oceanography, 2013, earthguide.ucsd.edu/earthguide/diagrams/watercycle/index.html.

48. Television episode or series

To cite a television series or episode, start with the title (first example) unless you are citing the work of a person or persons (second example). Give the names of contributors if they are important to your project. The models in this section show various contributors and their roles. To cite contributors to specific episodes, give the name(s) after the episode title (second example). To cite contributors to an entire series, give the names(s) after the series title (third and fourth examples).

a. Broadcast TV episode

"Sink or Swim." *Nurse Jackie,* season 6, episode 1, Showtime, 2014.

This example gives the episode title and information for the container: the series title, the season and episode numbers, the name of the network, and the date.

b. Web TV episode

Peretz, Jesse, director. "Sink or Swim." By Clyde Phillips. *Nurse Jackie,* season 6, episode 1, Showtime, 2014. *Netflix,* www.netflix.com/watch/80065552.

This example gives the director and title of the episode. The writer is given next because he wrote this episode, not the entire series. Container 1 includes the name of the series, the season, and the episode number. Container 2 gives the streaming service, *Netflix,* and the URL.

c. TV episode on DVD, Blu-ray, or videocassette

"Sink or Swim." *Nurse Jackie Complete Collection,* created by Liz Brixius, Linda Wallem, and Evan Dunsky, performance by Edie Falco, season 6, episode 1, Lion's Gate, 2016, disc 7.

This example gives the episode title followed by the information for the container, a DVD set. The creators of the series and the actor who played the central character are named, followed by the season and episode numbers and publication information about the DVD.

d. TV series

Nurse Jackie. Created by Liz Brixius, Linda Wallem, and Evan Dunsky, Showtime, 2009-15.

This example gives information on the series as a whole: the title, the creators, the network, and the years during which the series aired.

49. Radio program

To cite a radio program, start with the title of the program (first example) unless you are citing the work of a person or persons (second example). Then give information about the container: the title of the radio show, any contributors you wish to include (first example), and broadcast or Web publication information (second example). (To cite a podcast, see model 53.)

a. Broadcast radio program

On the Media. Hosted by Brooke Gladstone and Bob Garfield, WNYC, New York, 5 Feb. 2016.

This example gives the name of the radio program, the main contributors, the station that produces the show, and the date.

b. Web radio program

McEvers, Kelly. "Opioid Epidemic Sparks HIV Outbreak in Tiny Indiana Town." *All Things Considered,* National Public Radio, 31 Mar. 2016, www.npr.org/2016/03/31/472577254/opioid-epidemic-sparks-hiv-outbreak-in-tiny-indiana-town.

Radio content streamed from a Web site may give the names of reporters and titles of stories. This example gives the name of the reporter, the title of the story, and information about the container: the name of the program, the publisher (because it is different from the title of the site), the date, and the URL. If instead of listening to the story you consulted the written transcript, add Transcript at the end of the entry, followed by a period.

50. Interview

This section provides models for interviews you heard or saw. See model 57 to cite an interview you conducted yourself.

a. Broadcast interview

Schumer, Amy. Interview by Terry Gross. *Fresh Air,* National Public Radio, WHYY, Philadelphia, 18 Apr. 2014.

For an interview broadcast on radio or television, begin with the name of the person interviewed, followed by a description (not italicized or in quotation marks) in place of a title, such as Interview by and the name of the interviewer. Then give information for the container: the title of the program and broadcast information.

b. Web interview

Gates, Henry Louis, Jr. Interview by Tavis Smiley. *Tavis Smiley,* Public Broadcasting Service, 31 Oct. 2013, pbs.org/video/2365708336/.

For a video or audio interview on the Web, follow the interviewer's name with information about the container: the title of the Web site, the publisher (if different from the site title), the date, and the URL.

51. Film or video

Start with the title (model a) unless you are citing the work of a person or a corporation (models b and c). Generally, list the director. You may also cite other contributors and their roles after the title (model b).

a. Film

Chi-Raq. Directed by Spike Lee, Amazon Studios, 2015.

For a film you see in a theater, end with the distributor and the date.

b. DVD, Blu-ray, or videocassette

Balanchine, George. *Serenade.* 1991. Directed by Hilary Bean, performance by the San Francisco Ballet, PBS Video, 1999.

For a DVD, Blu-ray disc, or videocassette, include the original release date after the title (as here) if it is relevant to your use of the source.

c. Video on the Web

CBS News. "1968 King Assassination Report." 4 Apr. 1968. *YouTube,* 3 Apr. 2008, youtube/cm0BbxgxKvo.

For a film or video on the Web, give a creator, if available, and a title or a description. Then give information for the container: the title of the Web site, the date (if available), and the URL. If the video's original publication date is significant, give it after the title, as here.

52. Sound recording

Sound recordings include music on vinyl LPs, CDs, the Web, and other devices. They also include spoken-word recordings.

a. Song

Springsteen, Bruce. "This Life." *Working on a Dream,* Columbia, 2009.

Start with the name of the artist and the title of the song. Treat the album like a container, giving the title, publisher, and date.

For a song you stream on the Web, treat the service like a second container:

> Jackson, Michael. "Billie Jean." *Thriller,* MJJ Productions, 1982. *Spotify,* play.spotify.com/track/5ORmAhIMRTcisVlB6jShJl.

b. Album

> Shocked, Michelle. *Short, Sharp, Shocked.* PolyGram Records, 1988.

Give the name of the artist and the title of the album. Then give information about the container: other contributors if relevant, the recording company (as in the example), and the date of release. For an album on the Web, add the name of the streaming service and a URL, as in the Jackson example above.

If you are citing a musical work identified by form, number, and key, see model 54.

c. Spoken word

> Dunbar, Paul Laurence. "We Wear the Mask." Narrated by Rita Dove. *Poetry Out Loud,* Poetry Foundation / National Endowment for the Arts, 2014, www.poetryoutloud.org/poems-and-performance/listen-to-poetry.

Spoken-word performances include readings, recitations, monologues, and the like. This example, of a poem read aloud, gives the author of the poem, the title, the narrator, and the container information: the Web site, the publishers (separated by a slash), the date, and the URL.

53. Podcast

> Sedaris, David. "Now We Are Five." *This American Life,* Chicago Public Media, 31 Jan. 2014, www.thisamericanlife.org/podcast/episode/517/day-at-the-beach?act=4.

This podcast from a radio program lists the author of a story on the program, the title of the story (in quotation marks), and information about the container: the title of the program, the publisher, the date of the broadcast, and the URL. If a podcast does not list an author or other creator, begin with the title.

54. Live performance

> Beethoven, Ludwig van. *Symphony no. 9 in D-minor.* Performance by Ricardo Muti and the Chicago Symphony Orchestra, 8 May 2015, Symphony Center, Chicago.
>
> *The New Century.* By Paul Rudnick, directed by Nicholas Martin, 6 May 2013, Mitzi E. Newhouse Theater, New York.

For a live performance, place the title first (second example) unless you are citing the work of an individual (first example). After the title, provide relevant information about contributors as well as the date of the performance, the performance venue, and the city (if it is not part of the venue's name).

If you are citing a work of classical music identified by form, number, and key (first example), do not use quotation marks or italics for the title.

55. Lecture, speech, address, or reading

Fontaine, Claire. "Economics and Education." 7 June 2014, Museum of Contemporary Art, North Miami. Address.

Give the speaker's name and the title of the talk (if any), the date of the presentation, the name of the venue, and the city (if it is not part of the venue's name). If the presentation occurred at a sponsored meeting, add the title of the meeting and the sponsor's name before the date. You can also give the type of presentation (Lecture, Speech, Address, Reading) if doing so will help readers understand what you are citing.

To cite a classroom lecture in a course you are taking, adapt the preceding format by giving a description in place of the title:

Cavanaugh, Carol. Class lecture on teaching mentors. Lesley U, 4 Apr. 2018. Lecture.

To cite a video of a lecture or other presentation that you view on the Web, see model 51c.

56. Video game, computer software, or app

Notch Development. *Minecraft: Pocket Edition.* Version 0.14.1, Mojang, 6 Apr. 2016, minecraft.net.

For a video game, computer program, or app, give the name of the developer or author, the title, the version, the publisher, the publication date, and the URL.

51.2.6 Other sources

57. Personal interview

Greene, Matthew. Personal interview. 7 May 2018.

Begin with the name of the person interviewed. For an interview you conducted, give a description of the interview—Personal interview, Telephone interview, or E-mail interview—and then give the date.

See also model 50 to cite a broadcast interview or a video of an interview on the Web.

58. Unpublished or personal letter

a. Unpublished letter

James, Jonathan E. Letter to his sister. 16 Apr. 1970. Jonathan E. James papers, South Dakota State Archive, Pierre.

For an unpublished letter in the collection of a library or archive, give the writer, a description in place of a title, and the date (if the letter is dated). Then give the information for the container: the title of the archive and the location.

See also model 32 to cite a published letter.

b. Personal letter

Murray, Elizabeth. Letter to the author. 6 Apr. 2018.

For a letter you received, give a description in place of the title and the date. To cite an e-mail message, see model 43.

59. Dissertation

McFaddin, Marie Oliver. *Adaptive Reuse: An Architectural Solution for Poverty and Homelessness.* Dissertation, U of Maryland, 2007. UMI, 2007.

Treat a published dissertation like a book, but after the title insert Dissertation, the name of the degree-granting institution, and the year.

60. Pamphlet or brochure

Understanding Childhood Obesity. Obesity Action Network, 2013.

Most pamphlets and brochures can be treated as books. In this example, the pamphlet has no listed author, so the title comes first. If your source has an author, give the name first, followed by the title and publication information.

51.3 MLA Paper Format

51.3 Use MLA paper format.

The MLA's Web site (*style.mla.org*) provides guidelines for the format of a paper, with just a few elements. For guidelines on type fonts, headings, lists, illustrations, and other features that MLA style does not specify, see Chapter 14.

Figures 51.2 and 51.3 show the formats for the first page and a later page of a paper. For the format of the list of works cited, see 51.2.

Margins

Use one-inch margins on all sides of every page.

Spacing and indentions

Double-space throughout. Indent the first lines of paragraphs one-half inch. (See below for treatment of poetry and long prose quotations.)

Paging

Begin numbering on the first page, and number consecutively through the end (including the list of works cited). Use Arabic numerals (1, 2, 3) positioned in the upper right, about one-half inch from the top. Place your last name before the page number in case the pages later become separated.

Figure 51.2 First page of MLA paper

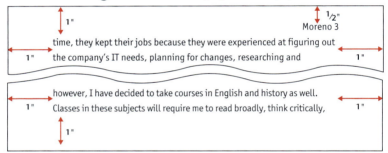

Figure 51.3 Later page of MLA paper

Identification and title

A title page is not required. Instead, give your name, your instructor's name, the course title, and the date on separate lines. Place this identification an inch from the top of the page, aligned with the left margin and double-spaced.

Double-space again, and center the title. Do not highlight the title with italics, underlining, boldface, larger type, or quotation marks. Capitalize the words in the title according to the guidelines in 47.3. Double-space the lines of the title and between the title and the text.

Poetry and long prose quotations

Treat a single line of poetry like any other quotation, running it into your text and enclosing it in quotation marks. You may run in two or three lines of poetry as well, separating the lines with a slash surrounded by space.

> An example of Robert Frost's incisiveness is in two lines from "Death of the Hired Man": "Home is the place where, when you have to go there / They have to take you in" (119-20).

Always set off from your text a poetry quotation of more than three lines. Use double spacing above and below the quotation and for the quotation itself. Indent the quotation one-half inch from the left margin. *Do not add quotation marks.*

> In "The Author to Her Book," written in 1678, Anne Bradstreet characterizes her book as a child. In these lines from the poem, she captures a parent's and a writer's frustration with the imperfections of her offspring:
>> I washed thy face, but more defects I saw,
>> and rubbing off a spot, still made a flaw.
>> I stretched thy joints to make thee even feet,
>> Yet still thou run'st more hobbling than is meet. (13-16)

Also set off a prose quotation of more than four typed lines. Double-space and indent as with the preceding poetry example. *Do not add quotation marks.*

> In the influential *Talley's Corner* from 1967, Elliot Liebow observes that "unskilled" construction work requires more skill than is generally assumed:
>> A healthy, sturdy, active man of good intelligence requires from two to four weeks to break in on a construction job.... It frequently happens that his foreman or the craftsman he services is not willing to wait that long for him to get into condition or to learn at a glance the difference in size between a rough 2 × 8 and a finished 2 × 10. (62)

Do not use a paragraph indention for a quotation of a single complete paragraph or a part of a paragraph. If the quotation contains more than one paragraph, indent the first lines of the second and any subsequent paragraphs.

51.4 Sample MLA Paper

51.4 Examine a sample paper in MLA style.

The sample paper below follows the eighth edition of the *MLA Handbook* for overall format, in-text citations, and the list of works cited. Annotations in the margins highlight features of the paper: some address format and documentation; the others address content.

Because the sample paper addresses a current topic, many of its sources come from the Internet and do not use page or other reference numbers. Thus, the in-text citations of these sources do not give reference numbers. In a paper relying solely on printed sources, most if not all in-text citations would include page numbers.

A note on outlines

Some instructors ask students to submit an outline of the final paper. For advice on constructing a formal or topic outline, see 9.6.3. Below is an outline of the sample paper following, written in complete sentences. Note that the thesis statement precedes a formal topic or sentence outline.

Outline

Thesis Statement: While sustainable agriculture offers some solutions for the environmental damages of industrial agriculture, it also creates new problems. It seems that agriculture itself remains the root of some of the biggest ecological problems facing our society. To make a real difference, humans must become more mindful of their food and resource consumption.

I. Industrial agriculture damages the environment.
    a. The Dust Bowl remains the largest ecological disaster in U.S. history.
    b. Water pollution is the biggest problem caused by industrial agriculture.
    c. Chemical pollution can have an impact on food supplies and other animal populations.
    d. Crop irrigation is required for sizable farming operations in arid areas—areas not naturally intended for farming purposes.

II. Sustainable agriculture resolves some of the damaging aspects of industrial agriculture.
    a. Preferred crops are drought-resistant with reduced dependence on irrigation.
    b. Innovative field designs reduce water runoff and soil erosion.
    c. Fertilizer alternatives provide uses for animal wastes and crop residues.

III. Sustainable agriculture creates its own problems that might surpass those created by industrial agriculture.
    a. Free-grazing animal agriculture would require additional land area to sustain equal production.
    b. Increased overall costs will lead to consumer price increases or a return to industrial methods.
    c. Only large farming operations can afford to implement technological advances.

IV. Only reduction in food and resource consumption will effectively reduce the impact of agriculture on the environment.

Sele 1

Brandon Sele
Prof. Borgman
English 1301
27 April 2018

The Dream of Sustainable Agriculture

Since the country's founding, the United States has cultivated an agricultural ethos where the farmer and his family represent the best of American society. Throughout the nineteenth and early twentieth centuries, ranchers and farmers pushed west, mastering the land and producing greater amounts of food. Unfortunately, this unchecked agricultural expansion into the Great Plains created the Dust Bowl, a devastating humanmade ecological disaster that covered more than 150,000 square miles and lasted more than a decade.[1]

Grazing livestock were pushed aside when grain prices rose during World War I. Agricultural innovations allowed farmers to cultivate more land and grow more wheat. Unfortunately, when a drought struck between 1934 and 1937, the topsoil had no root systems—no anchors. The winds "easily picked up loose topsoil and swirled it into dense dust clouds, called 'black blizzards' . . . recurrent dust storms wreaked havoc, choking cattle and pasture lands and driving 60 percent of the population from the region" (*Dust Bowl*). Despite the governmental response and soil conservation practices, farmers flirted with disaster again

Fig. 1. Rothstein, Arthur. *Dust storm. Amarillo, Texas*. Apr. 1936. Library of Congress, Farm Security Administration, Office of War Information Photograph Collection, www.loc.gov/pictures/item/fsa1998018986/PP/.

Sele 2

in the 1950s when another drought threatened, prompting the question—could it happen again?

> Question poses a key issue that leads into the body of the essay.

Critics of industrial farming suggest that unchecked agricultural practices can cause or exacerbate several environmental issues, including climate change, water pollution, soil degradation, and deforestation (Nistor 112). Most agree that sustainable farming practices should be employed. Sustainable agriculture is agriculture that uses a system of plant and animal production practices that provide food security for human populations while improving environmental resources, conserving nonrenewable resources, maintaining reasonable profitability for farming operations, and providing an improved quality of life for all. Unfortunately, sustainable agriculture has its critics as well, with some of the same environmental concerns; so the question becomes: Can sustainable agriculture solve the environmental, socioeconomic, and public health problems caused by industrial agriculture while reducing concerns over food security, affordability, and its own environmental impact?

> Citation form: Author and page number reference for the paraphrase from the source.

> Definition of the term *sustainable agriculture*. Because the term is important to the paper's thesis, a definition is used to clarify the meaning and use of the term in this context.

> Thesis of the paper, expressed in the form of a question. The body of the paper presents a detailed answer, supported with evidence from sources.

Industrial agricultural practices are based primarily on increased economic growth with demonstrable increases in production (Nistor 116). However, these practices have measurable negative effects on the environment through losses in plant species and animal habitats, soil degradation, and water pollution. As a concept, sustainable agriculture focuses on the use of renewable resources with an emphasis on protecting existing ecological systems. To protect air, soil, and water quality and wildlife habitats, sustainable farmers and ranchers select crops and livestock based on an area's topography, soil characteristics, and climate (Horrigan et al. 446). Well-chosen plants and livestock should thrive without extensive use of chemical enhancements.

> Citation form: Author and page number; author not named in text. Provides source for paraphrase.

> Background on the differences between industrial and sustainable agriculture, drawing on evidence from two different sources.

Some might wonder about the need for such practices—how severe is the damage caused by industrial agriculture?

> One-sentence paragraph uses a question to provide a transition into the next section of the paper.

By most measures, water pollution is the biggest problem caused by industrial agriculture. Chemical and waste runoff from industrial farms cause more than half of all sediment damage to natural waterways, costing billions of dollars

> First main point, supported with evidence from two sources.

(most in taxpayer dollars) per year to clean (Pimentel et al. 573). Moreover, nitrogen fertilizers, insecticides, and herbicides increase the risk of groundwater contamination. In fact, more than half of U.S. states have detectable amounts of pesticides in the groundwater (Pimentel et al. 573). So why do farmers generally rely so heavily on insecticides and fertilizers? Monocultural farming practices—the growing of a single crop on an area of land—forces farmers to rely on chemicals to replace the depleted nutrients in the topsoil (Nistor 116).

Unfortunately, water is not the only victim of chemically enhanced farming practices. Many of the traditional chemicals found in fertilizers and pesticides have found their way into the food supply (Horrigan et al. 445-46, 450-51). It is believed that these chemicals can be harmful to humans in small doses with prolonged exposure (Horrigan et al. 445-46, 450-51). Moreover, these chemicals can damage other animal populations—most notably, bees and other pollinating insects (Horrigan et al. 446). Unsurprisingly, continued reliance on chemicals like pesticides often result in pest populations that have developed resistance to pesticides, creating even more problems.

Yet chemical dependence isn't the only environmental problem faced by industrial farmers. In some areas of the country, particularly the western United States, crop irrigation is required for any sizable agricultural practice. The limited supply of surface water has caused a depletion of groundwater, resulting in salt water intrusions into aquifers (Horrigan et al. 447). Moreover, this depletion of surface water contributes to soil erosion—an environmental problem that costs more than $45 billion annually (Pimentel et al. 573).

So how can sustainable agriculture improve the problems created by industrial agriculture?

To improve water conservation and storage, sustainable farmers select drought-resistant crop species, adopt reduced-volume irrigation systems (drip and trickle irrigation methods), and manage selected crops to reduce water usage and loss. Improved irrigation systems also reduce salt water intrusions

Sele 4

into aquifers. Sustainable farmers can use temporary processes like tile drainage to remove water and salt as well as pesticides, nitrates, and other chemical contaminants from the soil. Long-term solutions include drought-tolerant forages and restoring wildlife habitats.

> *Second main point: Sustainable agriculture aids in soil conservation.*

Perhaps the most valuable aspect of sustainable agriculture is soil conservation. To prevent erosion, sustainable farmers might leave strips of grass in the field's waterways to capture soil that had eroded from the plowed field. Farmers might also use contour plowing, the method of plowing across a hill instead of up and down the hill, allowing for the capture of eroded soil and water runoff. Last, farmers might use terracing, the method of shaping the land into shelves to retain water and soil. Terracing is cost-prohibitive, but it allows farmers to use steep hillsides that might otherwise be left unused.

> *Third main point about sustainable agriculture, supported by evidence from a source.*

While livestock and other farm animals can cause water pollution through the improper disposal of their waste by farmers, free-range livestock can contribute to sustainable farming practices. Sustainable farmers can rotate livestock fields and crop fields, improving soil quality and naturally fertilizing the fields, or they can grow row crops on level soil and raise livestock on steeper slopes of pastureland, reducing soil erosion overall (Horrigan et al. 452).

> *Citation form: Author and page number, source with more than two authors; author not named in text.*

Sustainable farmers can also use green manure—crops specifically raised to be plowed under to provide nutrients to the soil. Moreover, farmers can leave crop residue—parts of the crops that are not harvested for sale—on the fields between plantings to prevent soil erosion (Horrigan et al. 452).

> *Citation form: Author and page number, source with more than two authors; author not named in text.*

Crop rotation remains an important aspect of sustainable agriculture since planting the same crop every year in the same field results in depleted soil (Horrigan et al. 445; Lawrence and Walker 452; Mason 37). Farmers can repair the soil by rotating nitrogen-depleting crops (corn, tomatoes, cotton) with nitrogen-increasing crops (legumes) (Pimentel et al. 574; Mason 37). Crop rotation improves the condition of the soil by providing nutrients for the more-marketable crops as well as preventing soil erosion.

> *Citation form: Citing multiple sources in support of one main idea.*

Still, sustainable agriculture is not confined to traditional farms. For some people, sustainable agriculture involves learning how to grow crops in urban areas—a practice called restoration ecology by some (Handel 1). The restoration ecology movement grew from "a need to bring locally grown fresh and affordable food into our cities . . . add[ing] additional economic and social vitality to our cities that had been lacking" while addressing an increased need for food security in urban populations (Handel 1; Feenstra 100-03). Urban agriculture is not restricted to plots of undeveloped land; it is tied closely to the theories of landscape ecology—"green roofs, backyards . . . fire escapes . . . vertical greenhouses, glass walled high rises . . . floriculture and vegetable greenhouses . . . nurseries and small orchards" (Handel 1). Urban agriculture also improves the environment through reduction of urban heat, redirection of storm water, improvement of air quality, and reduction of urban noise.

While some believe that sustainable agriculture practices can reduce the damage created by industrial farming, others argue that sustainable agriculture would likely fail environmentally and economically in widespread practice. James E. McWilliams, author of *Just Food: Where Locavores Get It Wrong and How We Can Truly Eat Responsibly*, asserts that these alternatives are "ultimately a poor substitute for industrial production," particularly in the production of meat (A31).

McWilliams argues that free-range or grass-grazing farming practices are a greater danger to the environment than the current standard of factory farms, citing a study on grass-grazing practices. If all cattle ranchers used grass-grazing practices, nearly half of the country's land would be needed for grazing, and that land would not include space for pigs or chickens (McWilliams). Deforestation for free-grazing farming is already an environmental concern in South American countries (FAO 122).

Moreover, McWilliams claims that "the economics of alternative animal systems are similarly problematic." Grass-grazing or free-range practices raise the overhead for ranchers and farmers; reduced profits bring increased consumer prices (and the

Sele 6

beginning of food insecurity for families with lower incomes), or the farmers and ranchers will "gradually seek a larger market share, [cut] corners, [increase] stocking density, and [aim] to fatten animals faster than competitors could" (McWilliams). Ultimately, McWilliams concludes that it would take little time before production systems to revert to the current practices.

Jayson Lusk, professor of agricultural economics at Oklahoma State University, agrees with McWilliams. He admits that "there is much to like about small, local farms and their influence . . . but if we are to sustainably deal with the problems presented by population growth and climate change, we need to look to the farmers who grow a majority of the country's food and fiber"—the large farmers (SR4). He believes that large farm owners are "among the most progressive, technologically savvy growers on the planet," and he contends that farmers, not environmentalists, are more concerned with issues like fertilizer use and soil runoff (SR4).

By using progressive technologies, large farming operations have reduced their impact on the environment while still providing 80 percent of the American food supply. These technologies allow farmers to "watch the evolution of crop prices and track thunderstorms on their smartphones . . . use livestock waste to create electricity using anaerobic digesters, which convert manure to methane . . . [and use] [d]rones [to] monitor crop yields, insect infestations and the location and health of cattle" (Lusk SR4).

Lusk contends that these environmentally safe technologies are generally cost-prohibitive for smaller farming operations, so large industrial farms are necessary for environmental improvements through increased technology.

Moreover, sustainable agriculture relies on the willingness of the consumers to eat certain types of produce only in season as well as produce that can be grown locally. Some environmentally conscious consumers relish the idea that they "can walk through [their] pantry and tell you the first name of the farmer who grew everything there" (Kemple 17). However, other consumers demand fresh pineapples, bananas, and avocados in areas where they cannot be grown naturally. Ultimately, consumers will drive the agricultural markets with their food dollars.

While sustainable agriculture offers some solutions for the environmental damages of industrial agriculture, it also creates new problems. It seems that agriculture itself remains the root of some of the biggest ecological problems facing our society. All agriculture consumes natural resources, and all too often, we buy more food than we need. To make a real difference, humans must become more mindful of their food and resource consumption. Small sacrifices can make a large difference, preserving our natural resources for future generations.

> **Concluding paragraph restates the opening question and provides a detailed answer that reinforces the thesis question posed in the introduction.**

Sele 8

Notes

> Endnote provides a commentary note and source information about a documentary film on the Dust Bowl.

1. More information on the ecological and socioeconomic impact of the Dust Bowl can be found in Ken Burns's PBS documentary *The Dust Bowl* (2012).

Works Cited

Dust Bowl. 2009. A+E Networks. 15 May 2017. http://www.history.com/topics/dust-bowl/.

FAO. *State of the World's Forests 2016: Forests and Agriculture: Land-Use Challenges and Opportunities.* Food and Agriculture Organization of the United Nations, 2016.

Feenstra, Gail. "Creating Space for Sustainable Food Systems: Lessons from the Field." *Agriculture and Human Values,* vol. 19, no. 2, June 2002, p. 99. *EBSCOhost,* 0-search.ebscohost.com.iii-server.ualr.edu/login.aspx?direct=true&db=edo&AN=ejs37704535&site=eds-live.

Handel, Steven N. "Greens and Greening: Agriculture and Restoration Ecology in the City." *Ecological Restoration,* no. 1, 2016, p. 1. *EBSCOhost,* 0-search.ebscohost.com.iii-server.ualr.edu/login.aspx?direct=true&db=edspmu&AN=edspmu.S154340791610000X&site=eds-live.

Horrigan, Leo, et al. "How Sustainable Agriculture Can Address the Environmental and Human Health Harms of Industrial Agriculture." *Environmental Health Perspectives,* no. 5, 2002, p. 445. *EBSCOhost,* 0-search.ebscohost.com.iii-server.ualr.edu/login.aspx?direct=true&db=edsjsr&AN=edsjsr.3455330&site=eds-live.

Kemple, Megan. "Why I'm a Locavore." *Communities,* no. 167, Summer 2015, p. 17. *EBSCOhost,* 0-search.ebscohost.com.iii-server.ualr.edu/login.aspx?direct=true&db=a9h&AN=103147851&site=eds-live.

Lusk, Jayson. "Why Industrial Farms Are Good for the Environment." *The New York Times,* 25 Sept. 2016: SR4.

Mason, John. *Sustainable Agriculture.* 2nd ed. Collingwood: Landlinks Press, 2003.

McWilliams, James E. "The Myth of Sustainable Meat." *The New York Times,* 13 Apr. 2012: A31.

Article in a scholarly journal that numbers volumes and issues, accessed from a database.

Nistor, Cornelia. "Green Agriculture: Features and Agricultural Policy Measures for the Transition to a Sustainable Agriculture." *Manager*, vol. 22, no. 1, 2015, pp. 112-27. *EBSCOhost*, 0-search.ebscohost.com.iii-server.ualr.edu/login.aspx?direct=true&db=edsdoj&AN=edsdoj.1ad5b51289d54711a6e306499e67c27c&site=eds-live.

Article in a scholarly journal that numbers only issues, accessed from a database.

Pimentel, David, et al. "Environmental, Energetic, and Economic Comparisons of Organic and Conventional Farming Systems." *Bioscience*, no. 7, 2005, p. 573. *EBSCOhost*, doi:10.1641/0006-3568.

APA Documentation and Format

APA Documentation and Format

52 APA Documentation and Format *422*
    52.1 In-text citations *422*
    52.2 List of references *425*
    52.3 Format of paper *441*
    52.4 Sample research report *443*

APA in-text citations

1. Author not named in your text *422*
2. Author named in your text *423*
3. Work with two authors *423*
4. Work with three to five authors *423*
5. Work with six or more authors *424*
6. Work with a group author *424*
7. Work with no author or an anonymous work *424*
8. One of two or more works by the same author(s) *424*
9. Two or more works by different authors *425*
10. Indirect source *425*
11. Electronic or Web source *425*

APA references

Finding the right model for a source

1. What type of source is it? Locate the type in the index beginning opposite.

Article, models 7–13
Complete book or part of book, models 14–20
Government publication, model 21
Report, model 22
Dissertation, model 23
Web or social media, models 24–30
Visual, audio, other media, models 31–37

2. What is the medium of the source? From within each type of source, choose the right model for the medium. Common media:

Print
Web
Database
E-book

Tweet
Television; radio
Film; video recording
Computer software; app

3. Who is the author? Choose the right model for the number and type of author(s).

How many authors? models 1–3
Corporation, agency, or other group author? model 4
No named author? model 5
Author(s) of two or more of your sources? model 6

Authors
1. One author *428*
2. Two to seven authors *428*
3. Eight or more authors *429*
4. Group author *429*
5. Author not named (anonymous) *429*
6. Two or more works by the same author(s) published in the same year *429*

Articles in journals, magazines, and newspapers
7. Article in a scholarly journal *432*
   a. Print, database, or Web with a DOI *432*
   b. Print without a DOI *432*
   c. Database or Web without a DOI *432*
8. Article in a magazine *432*
   a. Print *433*
   b. Database or Web *433*
9. Article in a newspaper *433*
   a. Print *433*
   b. Database or Web *433*
10. Review *433*
11. Interview *433*
12. Supplemental content that appears only online *434*
13. Abstract *434*

Books, government publications, and other independent works
14. Basic format for a book *434*
    a. Print *434*
    b. Web or database *434*
    c. E-book *434*
15. Book with an editor *435*
16. Book with a translator *435*
17. Later edition *435*
18. Work in more than one volume *435*
19. Article or chapter in an edited book *435*
20. Article in a reference work *435*
21. Government publication *436*
    a. Print *436*
    b. Web *436*
22. Report *436*
    a. Print *436*
    b. Web *436*
23. Dissertation *437*

Web sources and social media
24. Part or all of a Web site *437*
25. Post to a blog or discussion group *438*
26. Blog comment *438*
27. Social-networking post *438*
28. Tweet *438*
29. Wiki *438*
30. E-mail or other personal communication *438*

Video, audio, and other media sources
31. Film or video recording *439*
    a. Motion picture or DVD *439*
    b. Web *439*
32. Recorded interview *439*
33. Television series or episode *439*
    a. Entire series *439*
    b. Broadcast episode *440*
    c. Web episode *440*
34. Musical recording *440*
35. Podcast *440*
36. Visual *440*
37. Video game, computer software, or app *440*

Chapter 52
APA Documentation and Format

⌄ Learning Objectives

52.1 Write APA in-text citations.
52.2 Prepare the APA reference list.
52.3 Use APA paper format.
52.4 Examine a sample research report in APA style.

52.1 In-text Citations

52.1 **Write APA in-text citations.**

The style guide for psychology and some other social sciences is the *Publication Manual of the American Psychological Association* (6th ed., 2010). The APA provides answers to frequently asked questions at *www.apastyle.org/learn/faqs*.

In APA documentation style, you acknowledge each of your sources twice:

- In your text, a brief citation adjacent to the borrowed material directs readers to a complete list of all the works you refer to.
- At the end of your paper, the list of references includes complete bibliographical information for every source.

Every entry in the list of references has at least one corresponding citation in the text, and every in-text citation has a corresponding entry in the list of references.

In APA documentation style, citations within the body of the text refer the reader to a list of sources at the end of the text. When you cite the same source more than once in a paragraph, APA style does not require you to repeat the date beyond the first citation as long as it's clear what source you refer to. Do give the date in every citation if your source list includes more than one work by the same author(s).

1. Author not named in your text

One critic of Milgram's experiments questioned whether the researchers behaved morally toward their subjects (Baumrind, 1988).

When you do not name the author in your text, place in parentheses the author's last name, the date of the source, and sometimes the page number, as explained below. Separate the elements with commas. Position the reference so that it is clear what material is being documented *and* so that the reference fits as smoothly as possible into your sentence structure.

Unless none is available, the APA requires a page or other identifying number for a direct quotation and recommends an identifying number for a paraphrase:

> In the view of one critic of Milgram's experiments (Baumrind, 1988), the subjects "should have been fully informed of the possible effects on them" (p. 34).

Use an appropriate abbreviation before the number—for instance, p. for *page* and para. for *paragraph*. The identifying number may fall by itself in parentheses, as in the preceding example, or it may fall with the author and date: (Baumrind, 1988, p. 34). See also model 11.

2. Author named in your text

> Baumrind (1988) insisted that the subjects in Milgram's study "should have been fully informed of the possible effects on them" (p. 34).

When you use the author's name in the text, do not repeat it in parentheses. Place the date of the source in parentheses after the author's name. Place any page or paragraph reference either after the borrowed material (as in the example) or with the date: (1988, p. 34).

3. Work with two authors

> Bunning and Ellis (2013) revealed significant communication differences between teachers and students.
>
> One study (Bunning & Ellis, 2013) revealed significant communication differences between teachers and students.

When given in the text, two authors' names are connected by *and*. In a parenthetical citation, they are connected by an ampersand, &.

4. Work with three to five authors

> Pepinsky, Dunn, Rentl, and Corson (2010) demonstrated the biases evident in gestures.

In the first citation of a work with three to five authors, name all the authors.

In the second and subsequent references to a work with three to five authors, generally give only the first author's name, followed by et al. (Latin abbreviation for "and others"):

> In the work of Pepinsky et al. (2010), the loaded gestures included head shakes and eye contact.

However, two or more sources published in the same year could shorten to the same form—for instance, two references shortening to Pepinsky et al., 2010. In that case, cite the last names of as many authors as you need to distinguish the sources, and then give et al.: for instance, (Pepinsky, Dunn, et al., 2010) and (Pepinsky, Bradley, et al., 2010).

5. Work with six or more authors

One study (McCormack et al., 2012) explored children's day-to-day experience of living with a speech impairment.

For six or more authors, even in the first citation of the work, give only the first author's name, followed by et al. If two or more sources published in the same year shorten to the same form, give additional names as explained in model 4.

6. Work with a group author

The students' later work improved significantly (Lenschow Research, 2013).

For a work that lists an institution, agency, corporation, or other group as author, treat the name of the group as if it were one person's name. If the name is long and has a familiar abbreviation, you may use the abbreviation in the second and subsequent citations. For example, you might abbreviate American Psychological Association as APA.

7. Work with no author or an anonymous work

One article ("Leaping the Wall," 2013) examines Internet freedom and censorship in China.

For a work with no named author, use the first two or three words of the title in place of an author's name, excluding an initial *The*, *A*, or *An*. Italicize book and journal titles, place quotation marks around article titles, and capitalize the significant words in all titles cited in the text. (In the reference list, however, do not use quotation marks for article titles, and capitalize only the first word in all but periodical titles.)

For a work that lists "Anonymous" as the author, use that word in the citation: (Anonymous, 2014).

8. One of two or more works by the same author(s)

At about age seven, most children begin to use appropriate gestures to reinforce their stories (Gardner, 1973a).

When you cite one of two or more works by the same author(s), the date will tell readers which source you mean—as long as your reference list includes only one source published by the author(s) in that year. If your reference list includes two or more works published by the same author(s) *in the same year,* the works should be lettered in the reference list. Then your text citation should include the appropriate letter with the date: 1973a above.

9. Two or more works by different authors

Two studies (Marconi & Hamblen, 1999; Torrence, 2011) found that monthly safety meetings can dramatically reduce workplace injuries.

List the sources in alphabetical order by their authors' names. Insert a semicolon between sources.

10. Indirect source

Supporting data appeared in a study by Wong (as cited in Gallivan, 2013).

The phrase *as cited in* indicates that the reference to Wong's study was found in Gallivan. Only Gallivan then appears in the list of references.

11. Electronic or Web source

Ferguson and Hawkins (2012) did not anticipate the "evident hostility" of the participants (para. 6).

Many electronic and Web sources can be cited like printed sources, with the author's last name, the publication date, and page numbers. Others are missing one or more pieces of information:

- **No page numbers:** When quoting or paraphrasing a source that numbers paragraphs instead of pages, provide the paragraph number preceded by para., as in the preceding example. If the source does not number pages or paragraphs but does include headings, list the heading under which the quotation appears and then (counting paragraphs yourself) the number of the paragraph in which the quotation appears—for example, (Endter & Decker, 2013, Method section, para. 3). When the source does not number pages or paragraphs or provide frequent headings, omit any reference number.
- **No author:** For a source with no listed author, follow model 7.
- **No date:** For a source that is undated, use n.d. ("no date") in place of the date.

52.2 Reference List

52.2 **Prepare the APA reference list.**

In APA style, the in-text citations refer readers to the list of sources at the end of the text. Title this list References and include in it the full publication information for every source you cited in your paper. Place the list at the end of the paper, and number its page(s) in sequence with the preceding pages.

The sample in Figure 52.1 shows the format of the first page of the APA reference list:

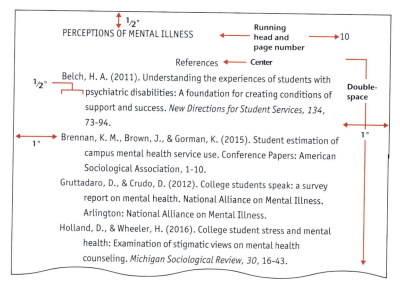

Figure 52.1 APA reference list

Arrangement

Arrange sources alphabetically by the author's last name. If there is no author, alphabetize by the first main word of the title.

Spacing

Double-space everything in the references, as shown in the sample, unless your instructor requests single spacing. (If you do single-space the entries themselves, always double-space *between* them.)

Indention

As illustrated in the sample, begin each entry at the left margin, and indent the second and subsequent lines one-half inch. Your word processor can create this so-called hanging indent automatically.

Punctuation

Separate the parts of the reference (author, date, title, and publication information) with a period and one space. Do not use a final period in references that conclude with a DOI or URL.

Authors

For works with up to seven authors, list all authors with last name first, separating names and parts of names with commas. Use initials for first and middle names even when names are listed fully on the source itself. Use an ampersand (&) before the last author's name. See model 3 for the treatment of eight or more authors.

Publication date

Place the publication date in parentheses after the author's or authors' names, followed by a period. Generally, this date is the year only, though for some sources (such as magazine and newspaper articles) it includes the month and sometimes the day as well.

Titles

In titles of books and articles, capitalize only the first word of the title, the first word of the subtitle, and proper nouns; all other words begin with small letters. In titles of journals, capitalize all significant words. Italicize the titles of books and journals. Do not italicize or use quotation marks around the titles of articles.

City and state of publication

For sources that are not periodicals (such as books or government publications), give the city of publication, a comma, the two-letter postal abbreviation of the state, and a colon. Omit the state if the publisher is a university whose name includes the state name, such as University of Arizona.

Publisher's name

Also for nonperiodical sources, give the publisher's name after the place of publication and a colon. Shorten names of many publishers (such as Morrow for William Morrow), and omit *Co., Inc.,* and *Publishers.* However, give full names for associations, corporations, and university presses (such as Harvard University Press), and do not omit *Books* or *Press* from a publisher's name.

Page numbers

Use the abbreviation p. or pp. before page numbers in books and in newspapers. Do *not* use the abbreviation for journals and magazines. For inclusive page numbers, include all figures: 667–668.

Digital Object Identifier (DOI) or retrieval statement

At the end of each entry in the reference list, APA style requires a DOI for print and electronic sources (if one is available) or a retrieval statement for electronic sources.

- **DOI:** Many publishers assign a DOI to journal articles, books, and other documents. A DOI is a permanent URL that links to the text and functions as a unique identifier. When a DOI is available, include it in your citation of any print or electronic source. DOIs appear in one of two formats, as shown in models 7a and 10. Use the format given in the source.
- **Retrieval statement:** If a DOI is not available for a source you found in a database or on the Web, provide a statement beginning with Retrieved from and then give the URL of the periodical's or Web site's home page (model 7c). You need not include the date you retrieved the source unless it is undated (model 22b) or is likely to change (model 29). If the source is difficult to find from the home page, you may give the complete URL. If you have questions about whether to include a home-page URL or a complete URL, ask your instructor.

Do not add a period after a DOI or a URL. Break a DOI or URL from one line to the next only before punctuation, such as a period or a slash, and do not hyphenate.

An index to the following models appears at the APA divider. If you don't see a model for the kind of source you used, try to find one that comes close, and provide ample information so that readers can trace the source. Often you will have to combine models to cite a source accurately.

52.2.1 Authors

1. One author

Rodriguez, R. (1982). *A hunger of memory: The education of Richard Rodriguez.* Boston, MA: Godine.

The initial R. appears instead of the author's first name, even though the author's full first name appears on the source. In this book title, only the first words of the title and subtitle and the proper name are capitalized.

2. Two to seven authors

Nesselroade, J. R., & Baltes, P. B. (1999). *Longitudinal research in behavioral studies.* New York, NY: Academic Press.

With two to seven authors, separate authors' names with commas and use an ampersand (&) before the last author's name.

3. Eight or more authors

Wimple, P. B., Van Eijk, M., Potts, C. A., Hayes, J., Obergau, W. R., Smith, H., . . . Zimmer, S. (2001). *Case studies in moral decision making among adolescents.* San Francisco, CA: Jossey-Bass.

For a work by eight or more authors, list the first six authors' names, insert an ellipsis mark (three spaced periods), and then give the last author's name.

4. A group author

Lenschow Research. (2013). *Trends in secondary curriculum.* Baltimore, MD: Arrow Books.

For a work with a group author—such as a research group, a committee, a government agency, an association, or a corporation—begin the entry with the group name. In the reference list, alphabetize the work as if the first main word (excluding any *The*, *A*, or *An*) were an author's last name.

5. Author not named (anonymous)

Merriam-Webster's collegiate dictionary (11th ed.). (2008). Springfield, MA: Merriam-Webster.

Resistance is not futile. (2014, April 5). *New Scientist, 221*(15), 5.

When no author is named, list the work under its title and alphabetize it by the first main word (excluding any *The, A, An*).

For a work whose author is actually given as "Anonymous," use that word in place of the author's name and alphabetize it as if it were a name:

Anonymous. (2014). *Teaching research, researching teaching.* New York, NY: Alpine Press.

6. Two or more works by the same author(s) published in the same year

Gardner, H. (1973a). *The arts and human development.* New York, NY: Wiley.

Gardner, H. (1973b). *The quest for mind: Piaget, Lévi-Strauss, and the structuralist movement.* New York, NY: Knopf.

When citing two or more works by exactly the same author(s), published in the same year, arrange them alphabetically by the first main word of the title and distinguish the sources by adding a letter to the date. Both the date and the letter are used in citing the source in your text.

When citing two or more works by exactly the same author(s) but *not* published in the same year, arrange the sources in order of their publication dates, earliest first.

(continued on p. 432)

52.2.2 Articles in journals, magazines, and newspapers

Citing journal articles: Print, database, or Web with DOI

Print journal article

5 Volume number — Volume 47, Number 9, **2 Year of publication** — Department of Veterans Affairs

JRRD
Pages 863–876 — **6 Page numbers**
Journal of Rehabilitation Research & Development — **4 Title of journal**

3 Title of article
Symptom burden in individuals with cerebral palsy

1 Authors
Adam T. Hirsh, PhD;[1*] Juan C. Gallegos, BA;[1] Kevin J. Gertz, BA;[1] Joyce M. Engel, PhD;[2] Mark P. Jensen, PhD[1]
[1]*Department of Rehabilitation Medicine, University of Washington School of Medicine, Seattle, WA;* [2]*Department of Occupational Science and Technology, University of Wisconsin-Milwaukee, Milwaukee, WI*

Abstract—The current study sought to (1) determine the relative frequency and severity of eight symptoms in adults with cerebral palsy (CP), (2) examine the perceived course of these

gressive disorder, research over the past several years has highlighted a number of health conditions and functional declines experienced by individuals with CP as they age

INTRODUCTION

Cerebral palsy (CP) is a neurodevelopmental disorder of movement and posture [1]. The onset of CP occurs very early in life, and although it is described as a nonpro-

*Address all correspondence to Adam T. Hirsh, PhD; Department of Psychology, Indiana University-Purdue University Indianapolis, 402 N Blackford St, LD 124, Indianapolis, IN 46202; 317-274-6942; fax: 317-274-6756. Email: athirsh@iupui.edu
DOI:10.1682/JRRD.2010.03.0074

7 Retrieval information

Database or Web journal article

4 Title of journal
Journal of Rehabilitation Research & Development (*JRRD*)
5 Volume number
Volume 47 Number 9, 2010 — **2 Year of publication**
Pages 863 — 876 — **6 Page numbers**
3 Title of article
Symptom burden in individuals with cerebral palsy

Adam T. Hirsh, PhD;[1*] Juan C. Gallegos, BA;[1] Kevin J. Gertz, BA;[1] Joyce M. Engel, PhD;[2] Mark P. Jensen, PhD[1] — **1 Authors**

[1]*Department of Rehabilitation Medicine, University of Washington School of Medicine, Seattle, WA;*
[2]*Department of Occupational Science and Technology, University of Wisconsin-Milwaukee, Milwaukee, WI*

Abstract — The current study sought to (1) determine the relative frequency and severity of eight symptoms in adults with cerebral palsy (CP), (2) examine the perceived course of these eight symptoms over time, and (3) determine the associations between the severity of these symptoms and psychosocial functioning. Eighty-three adults with CP completed a measure assessing the frequency, severity, and perceived course of eight symptoms (pain, weakness, fatigue, imbalance, numbness, memory loss, vision loss, and shortness of breath). This study highlighted several common and problematic symptoms experienced by adults with CP. Additional research is needed to identify the most effective treatments for those symptoms that affect community integration and psychological functioning as a way to improve the quality of life of individuals with CP.

Key words: cerebral palsy, community integration, fatigue, imbalance, pain, psychological functioning, quality of life, rehabilitation, signs and symptoms, weakness.

Abbreviations: CIQ = Community Integration Questionnaire, CP = cerebral palsy, MHS = Mental Health Scale (of the SF-36), MMSE = Modified Mini-Mental Status Examination, SCI = spinal cord injury, SD = standard deviation, SF-36 = Medical Outcomes Study 36-Item Short Form Health Survey.
*Address all correspondence to Adam T. Hirsh, PhD; Department of Psychology, Indiana University-Purdue University Indianapolis, 402 N Blackford St, LD 124, Indianapolis, IN 46202; 317-274-6942; fax: 317-274-6756. Email: athirsh@iupui.edu
DOI:10.1682/JRRD.2010.03.0024

7 Retrieval information

References entry: Print, database, or Web journal article with DOI

Hirsh, A. T., Gallegos, J. C., Gertz, K. J., Engel, J. M., & Jensen, M. P. (2010). Symptom burden in individuals with cerebral palsy. *Journal of Rehabilitation Research & Development, 47*, 860-876. doi:10.1682/JRRD.2010.03.0024

1. **Authors.** Give each author's last name, first initial, and any middle initial. Separate names from initials with commas, and use & before the last author's name. Omit *Dr., PhD,* or any other title. See models 1–6 for how to cite various numbers and kinds of authors.

2. **Year of publication,** in parentheses and followed by a period.

3. **Title of article.** Give the full article title and any subtitle, separating them with a colon. Capitalize only the first words of the title and subtitle, and do not place the title in quotation marks.

4. **Title of journal,** in italics. Capitalize all significant words and end with a comma.

5. **Volume number,** italicized and followed by a comma. Include just the volume number when all the issues in each annual volume are paginated in one sequence. Include the issue number only when the issues are paginated separately.

6. **Inclusive page numbers of article,** without "pp." Do not omit any numerals.

7. **Retrieval information.** If the article has a DOI, give it using the format here or as shown in model 10. Do not end with a period. If the article does not have a DOI, see models 7b and 7c.

7. Article in a scholarly journal

Some journals number the pages of issues consecutively during a year, so that each issue after the first begins numbering where the previous issue left off—say, at page 132 or 416. For this kind of journal, give the volume number after the title (models a, b, c). Other journals as well as most magazines start each issue with page 1. For these journals and magazines, place the issue number in parentheses and not italicized immediately after the volume number (model 8). See "Citing journal articles" for an illustrated example.

a. Print, database, or Web journal article with a DOI

Hirsh, A. T., Gallegos, J. C., Gertz, K. J., Engel, J. M., & Jensen, M. P. (2010). Symptom burden in individuals with cerebral palsy. *Journal of Rehabilitation Research & Development, 47,* 860–876. doi:10.1682/JRRD.2010.03.0024

See above for an explanation of this format and the location of the required information on a source. The format is the same for any journal article that has a DOI—print, database, or Web.

DOIs appear in one of two formats, as shown above and in model 10. Use the format given in the source.

b. Print journal article without a DOI

Atkinson, N. S. (2011). Newsreels as domestic propaganda: Visual rhetoric at the dawn of the cold war. *Rhetoric and Public Affairs, 14,* 69–105.

If a print journal article does not have a DOI, simply end with the page numbers of the article.

c. Database or Web journal article without a DOI

Rosen, I. M., Maurer, D. M., & Darnall, C. R. (2008). Reducing tobacco use in adolescents. *American Family Physician, 77,* 483-490. Retrieved from http://www.aafp.org/online/en/home/publications/journals/afp.html

If a journal article you found in a database or on the Web does not have a DOI, use a search engine to find the home page of the journal and give the home-page URL, as above. Generally, do not give the name of a database in which you found an article because readers may not be able to find the source the same way you did. However, do give the database name if you cannot find the home page of the journal on the Web, as in this example:

Smith, E. M. (1926, March). Equal rights—internationally! *Life and Labor Bulletin, 4,* 1–2. Retrieved from Women and Social Movements in the United States, 1600–2000, database.

8. Article in a magazine

For magazine articles, give the month of publication as well as any day along with the year. If the magazine gives volume and issue numbers, list them after the title of the magazine. Italicize the volume number and place the issue number, not italicized, in parentheses.

a. Print magazine article

Newton-Small, J. (2013, February 18). Blood for oil. *Time, 181*(6), 22.

b. Database or Web magazine article

Weir, K. (2014, March 22). Your cheating brain. *New Scientist, 221*(12), 35–37. Retrieved from http://www.newscientist.com

If a magazine article includes a DOI, give it after the page numbers. Otherwise, give the URL of the magazine's home page in a retrieval statement. If you do not find the home page, give the name of the database in which you found the article (see the Smith example in model 7c above).

9. Article in a newspaper

For newspaper articles, give the month and day of publication along with the year. Use *The* in the newspaper name if the paper itself does.

a. Print newspaper article

Zimmer, C. (2014, May 4). Young blood may hold key to reversing aging. *The New York Times*, p. C1.

Precede the page number(s) with p. or pp.

b. Database or Web newspaper article

Angier, N. (2013, November 26). The changing American family. *The New York Times*. Retrieved from http://www.nytimes.com

Give the URL of the newspaper's home page in the retrieval statement. If you do not find the home page, give the name of the database in which you found the article (see the Smith example in model 7c above).

10. Review

Bond, M. (2008, December 18). Does genius breed success? [Review of the book *Outliers: The story of success*, by M. Gladwell]. *Nature, 456*, 785. http://dx.doi.org/10.1038/456874a

If a review has no title, use the bracketed information in its place, keeping the brackets.

11. Interview

Shaffir, S. (2013). It's our generation's responsibility to bring a genuine feeling of hope [Interview by H. Schenker]. *Palestine-Israeli Journal of Politics, Economics, and Culture, 18*(4). Retrieved from http://pij.org

List an interview under the interviewee's name and give the title, if any. If there is no title, or if the title does not indicate that the source is an interview, add a bracketed explanation, as above. End with publication information for the kind of source the interview appears in—here a journal on the Web, which requires retrieval information.

See model 32 to cite a recorded interview. See model 30 to cite an interview you conduct, which should be treated like a personal communication and cited only in the text, not in the list of references.

12. Supplemental periodical content that appears only online

Anderson, J. L. (2014, May 2). Revolutionary relics [Supplemental material]. *The New Yorker*. Retrieved from http://www.newyorker.com

If you cite material from a periodical's Web site that is not included in the print version of the publication, add [Supplemental material] after the title and give the URL of the publication's home page.

13. Abstract of a journal article

Polletta, F. (2008). Just talk: Public deliberation after 9/11. *Journal of Public Deliberation*, 4(1). Abstract retrieved from http://services.bepress.com/jpd

When you cite the abstract of an article, give the full publication information for the article, followed by Abstract and information about where you found the abstract.

52.2.3 Books, government publications, and other independent works

14. Basic format for a book

a. Print book

Ehrenreich, B. (2007). *Dancing in the streets: A history of collective joy*. New York, NY: Holt.

Give the author's or authors' names, following models 1–4. Then give the complete title, including any subtitle. Italicize the title, and capitalize only the first words of the title and subtitle. End the entry with the city and state of publication and the publisher's name.

b. Web or database book

Reuter, P. (Ed.). (2010). *Understanding the demand for illegal drugs*. Retrieved from http://books.nap.edu

For a book available on the Web or in an online library or database, replace any print publication information with a DOI if one is available (see model 7a) or with a retrieval statement, as above.

c. E-book

Waltz, M. (2013). *Autism: A social and medical history* [Kindle version]. Retrieved from http://www.amazon.com

For an e-book, give the format in brackets and a retrieval statement.

15. Book with an editor

Dohrenwend, B. S., & Dohrenwend, B. P. (Eds.). (1999). *Stressful life events: Their nature and effects*. New York, NY: Wiley.

List the names of the editors as if they were authors, but follow the last name with (Eds.).—or (Ed.). with only one editor. Note the periods inside and outside the final parenthesis.

16. Book with a translator

Trajan, P. D. (1927). *Psychology of animals* (H. Simone, Trans.). Washington, DC: Halperin.

17. Later edition

Bolinger, D. L. (1981). *Aspects of language* (3rd ed.). New York, NY: Harcourt Brace Jovanovich.

18. Work in more than one volume

Lincoln, A. (1953). *The collected works of Abraham Lincoln* (R. P. Basler, Ed.). (Vol. 5). New Brunswick, NJ: Rutgers University Press.

Lincoln, A. (1953). *The collected works of Abraham Lincoln* (R. P. Basler, Ed.). (Vols. 1–8). New Brunswick, NJ: Rutgers University Press.

The first entry cites a single volume (5) in the eight-volume set. The second entry cites all eight volumes. Use Vol. or Vols. in parentheses and follow the closing parenthesis with a period. In the absence of an editor's name, this description would follow the title directly: *The collected works of Abraham Lincoln* (Vol. 5).

19. Article or chapter in an edited book

Paykel, E. S. (1999). Life stress and psychiatric disorder: Applications of the clinical approach. In B. S. Dohrenwend & B. P. Dohrenwend (Eds.), *Stressful life events: Their nature and effects* (pp. 239–264). New York, NY: Wiley.

Give the publication date of the collection (1999 here) as the publication date of the article or chapter. After the article or chapter title and a period, say In and then provide the editors' names (in normal order), (Eds.) and a comma, the title of the collection, and the page numbers of the article in parentheses.

20. Article in a reference work

Wood, R. (1998). Community organization. In W. A. Swados, Jr. (Ed.), *Encyclopedia of religion and society*. Retrieved from http://hirr.hartsem.edu/ency/commorg.htm

If the entry you cite has no named author, begin with the title of the entry and then the date. Use a DOI instead of a URL if the source has one.

21. Government publication

a. Print publication

Hawaii. Department of Education. (2014). *Kauai district schools, profile 2013-14*.
   Honolulu, HI: Author.

Stiller, A. (2012). *Historic preservation and tax incentives*. Washington, DC: U.S.
   Department of the Interior.

If no person is named as the author, list the publication under the name of the sponsoring agency. When the agency is both the author and the publisher, use Author in place of the publisher's name, as in the first example.

For legal materials such as court decisions, laws, and testimony at hearings, the APA recommends formats that correspond to conventional legal citations. The following example of a congressional hearing includes the full title, the number of the Congress, the page number where the hearing transcript starts in the official publication, and the date of the hearing.

> *Medicare payment for outpatient physical and occupational therapy services: Hearing before the Committee on Ways and Means, House of Representatives*, 110th Cong. 3 (2007).

b. Web publication

National Institute on Alcohol Abuse and Alcoholism. (2013, July). *Underage
   drinking* [Fact sheet]. Retrieved from http://pubs.niaaa.nih.gov/publications
   /UnderageDrinking/Underage_Fact.pdf

For a government publication on the Web, add a retrieval statement.

22. Report

a. Print report

Gerald, K. (2003). *Medico-moral problems in obstetric care* (Report No. NP-71).
   St. Louis, MO: Catholic Hospital Association.

Treat a printed report like a book, but provide any report number in parentheses after the title, with no punctuation between them.

b. Web report

Anderson, J. A., & Rainie, L. (2014, March 11). *Digital life in 2025*. Retrieved
   from Pew Research Internet Project Web site: http://www.pewinternet.org

For a report on the Web, give the name of the publisher in the retrieval statement if the publisher is not the author of the report. Generally, provide the URL of the Web site's home page.

If the work you cite is undated, use the abbreviation n.d. in place of the publication date and give the date of your access in the retrieval statement:

> U.S. Census Bureau. (n.d.). *Men's marital status: 1950-2013*. Retrieved April 23, 2014, from https://www.census.gov/hhes/families/files/graphics/MS-1a.pdf

23. Dissertation

a. Dissertation in a commercial database

> McFaddin, M. O. (2007). *Adaptive reuse: An architectural solution for poverty and homelessness* (Doctoral dissertation). Available from ProQuest Dissertations and Theses database. (ATT 1378764)

If a dissertation is from a commercial database, give the name of the database in the retrieval statement, followed by the accession or order number in parentheses.

b. Dissertation in an institutional database

> Chang, J. K. (2003). *Therapeutic intervention in treatment of injuries to the hand and wrist* (Doctoral dissertation). Retrieved from http://medsci.archive.liasu.edu/61724

If a dissertation is from an institution's database, give the URL in the retrieval statement.

52.2.4 Web sources and social media

Specific types of Web sources are covered under their respective categories, such as articles in periodicals (models 7a, 7c, 8b, 9b), books (model 14b), and reports (model 22b). When citing URLs, APA recommends giving the home-page URL unless the source is difficult to find from the home page. In such a case, provide the complete URL.

24. Part or all of a Web site

> American Psychological Association. (2014). Information for students with disabilities [Web page]. Retrieved from http://www.apa.org

To cite a page or document on a Web site, give the author (if any), the date (or n.d. if the page or site is undated), the title of the page or document, a description in brackets, and a retrieval statement.

Cite an entire Web site just in the text of your paper, giving the name of the site in your text and the URL in parentheses:

> The Web site of the Cyberbullying Research Center provides information on the causes and nature of cyberbullying among teenagers (http://cyberbullying.us).

Although APA does not require you to include entire Web sites in your list of references, some instructors ask for such references. Then you can use the format shown in the first example, substituting the title of the Web site for the title of the Web page or document.

25. Post to a blog or discussion group

Kristof, N. (2014, March 22). Confronting the netherworld of child pornography [Blog post]. Retrieved from http://kristof.blogs.nytimes.com

Include postings to blogs and discussion groups in your list of references only if they are retrievable by others. (The source above is retrievable by a search of the home page URL.) Follow the message title with [Blog post], [Electronic mailing list message], or [Online forum comment]. Include the name of the blog or discussion group in the retrieval statement if it isn't part of the URL.

26. Blog comment

Peter. (2014, March 23). Re: Confronting the netherworld of child pornography [Blog comment]. Retrieved from http://kristof.blogs.nytimes.com

27. Post to a social-networking site

Environmental Defense Fund. (2014, May 1). Extreme weather = extreme consequences [Facebook status update]. Retrieved from https://www.facebook.com/EnvDefenseFund?fref=ts

28. Tweet

Bittman, M. [bittman]. (2014, April 1). Almost 90% of fast food workers say they've experienced wage theft: buff.ly/1i18eTb [Tweet]. Retrieved from http://twitter.com/bittman

29. Wiki

Clinical neuropsychology. (2013, November 12). Retrieved April 15, 2014, from Wikipedia: http://en.wikipedia.org/wiki/Clinical_neuropsychology

Give your date of retrieval for sources that are likely to change, such as this wiki.

30. E-mail or other personal communication (text citation)

At least one member of the research team has expressed reservations about the design of the study (L. Kogod, personal communication, February 6, 2014).

Personal e-mail, personal letters, interviews that you conduct yourself, and other communication that is not retrievable by others should be cited only in the text, not in the list of references.

52.2.5 Video, audio, and other media sources

31. Film or video recording

If you cite a film or video as a whole, begin with the producer's name as in the first example below. Otherwise, cite the name or names of the creator, director, or other contributor, followed by the function in parentheses. Add the medium in brackets after the title: [Motion picture] for film, [DVD], [Videocassette], or [Video file].

a. Motion picture or DVD

American Psychological Association (Producer). (2001). *Ethnocultural psychotherapy* [DVD]. Available from http://www.apa.org/videos

Tyrrell, C. (Director). (2010). *The Joneses* [Motion picture]. United States: Bjort Productions.

For a work in wide circulation (second example), give the country of origin and the studio that released the picture. For a work that is not widely circulated (first example), give the distributor's address or URL.

b. Video on the Web

CBS News (Producer). (1968, April 4). *1968 King assassination report* [Videofile]. Retrieved from http://www.youtube.com/watch?v=cmOBbxgxKvo

In the retrieval statement, give the home-page URL unless the video you cite is difficult to locate from the home page. In that case, give the complete URL, as in the example.

32. Recorded interview

Ambar, S. (2014, April 1). Interview by T. Smiley [Video file]. Retrieved from http://www.pbs.org/wnet/tavissmiley

For an interview you view or listen to on the Web, give the name of the interviewee, the date, and the title of the interview, if any. Then give the interviewer's name if you wish, the type of file [Video file] or [Audio file], and a retrieval statement.

For an interview you see on television or hear in a podcast, adapt the preceding example using model 33b or 35.

33. Television series or episode

a. Television series

Rhimes, S. (Executive producer). (2014). *Grey's anatomy* [Television series]. New York, NY: ABC.

For a television series, begin with the producer's name and function. Add [Television series] after the title, and give either the city and name of the network or a Web retrieval statement.

b. Broadcast episode of television program

McKee, S. (Writer), & Wilson, C. (Director). (2014). Do you know? [Television series episode]. In S. Rhimes (Executive producer), *Grey's anatomy*. New York, NY: ABC.

For a TV episode, begin with the writer and then the director, identifying the function of each in parentheses, and add [Television series episode] after the episode title. Then provide the series information, beginning with In and the producer's name and function, giving the series title, and ending with the city and name of the network.

c. Web episode of a television program

Randall, T. (Writer & Director). (2012). How smart can we get? [Television series episode]. In J. Cort (Executive producer), *Nova*. Retrieved from http://www.pbs.org/wgbh/nova

Cite a TV episode you view on the Web as you would a broadcast episode, giving a retrieval statement rather than the city and name of the network.

34. Musical recording

Springsteen, B. (2002). Empty sky. On *The rising* [CD]. New York, NY: Columbia.

Begin with the name of the writer or composer. (If you cite another artist's recording of the work, provide this information after the title of the work—for example, [Recorded by E. Davila].) Give the medium in brackets ([CD], [LP], [mp3 file], and so on). Finish with the city, state, and name of the recording label or a retrieval statement.

35. Podcast

Glass, I. (Producer). (2014, April 11). The hounds of Blairsville [Audio podcast]. *This American life*. Retrieved from http://www.thisamericanlife.org

36. Visual

Southern Illinois University School of Medicine. (n.d.). Reporting child abuse and neglect [Diagram]. Retrieved from http://www.siumed.edu/oec/Year4/how_to_report_child_abuse.pdf

United Nations Population Fund (Cartographer). (2014). *Percent of population living on less than $1/day* [Demographic map]. Retrieved from http://www.unfpa.org

37. Video game, computer software, or app

Mojang. (2014). Minecraft: Pocket Edition (Version 0.8.1) [Mobile application software]. Retrieved May 7, 2014, from https://minecraft.net

For a video game, computer program, or app, give the following: the name of the developer or author, the publication date, the title, the version, a bracketed description of the program (such as [Video game], [Computer software], or [Mobile application software], as here), and a retrieval statement.

52.3 APA Paper Format

52.3 Use APA paper format.

Use the following guidelines and samples to prepare papers in APA format. Check with your instructor for any modifications to this format.

Margins

Use one-inch margins on the top, bottom, and both sides.

Spacing and indentions

Double-space everywhere. (The only exception is in tables and figures, where related data, labels, and other elements may be single-spaced.) Indent paragraphs and displayed quotations one-half inch.

Paging

Begin numbering on the title page, and number consecutively through the end (including the reference list). Provide a header about one-half inch from the top of every page, as shown in the samples in Figures 52.2 and 52.3. The header consists of the page number on the far right and your full or shortened title on the far left. Type the title in all-capital letters. On the title page only, precede the title with the label Running head and a colon. Omit this label on all other pages.

Title page

Include the full title, your name, the course title, the instructor's name, and the date. Type the title on the top half of the page, followed by the identifying information, all centered horizontally and double-spaced.

Abstract

Summarize (in a maximum of 120 words) your subject, research method, findings, and conclusions. Put the abstract on a page by itself.

Body

Begin with a restatement of the paper's title and then an introduction (not labeled). The introduction presents the problem you researched, your method, the relevant background, and the purpose of your research.

Figure 52.2 APA title page

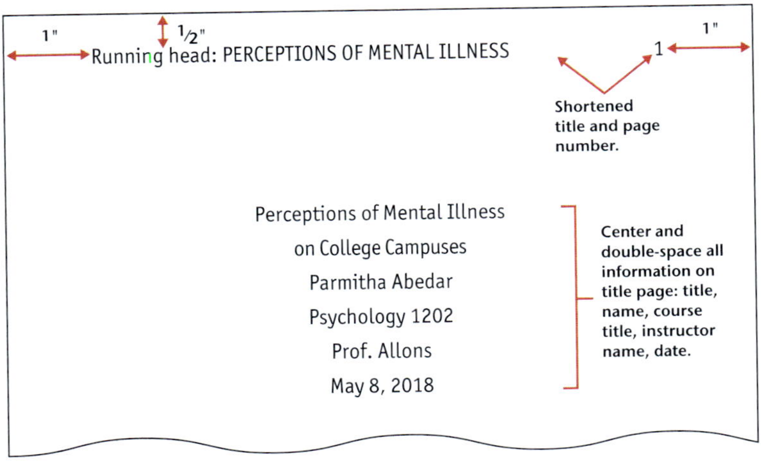

Running head: PERCEPTIONS OF MENTAL ILLNESS   1

Shortened title and page number.

Perceptions of Mental Illness
on College Campuses
Parmitha Abedar
Psychology 1202
Prof. Allons
May 8, 2018

Center and double-space all information on title page: title, name, course title, instructor name, date.

Figure 52.3 APA abstract

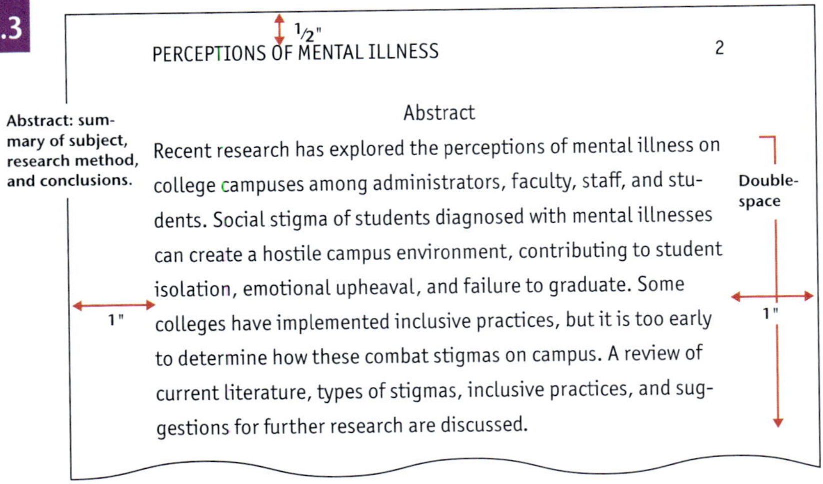

PERCEPTIONS OF MENTAL ILLNESS   2

Abstract

Recent research has explored the perceptions of mental illness on college campuses among administrators, faculty, staff, and students. Social stigma of students diagnosed with mental illnesses can create a hostile campus environment, contributing to student isolation, emotional upheaval, and failure to graduate. Some colleges have implemented inclusive practices, but it is too early to determine how these combat stigmas on campus. A review of current literature, types of stigmas, inclusive practices, and suggestions for further research are discussed.

Abstract: summary of subject, research method, and conclusions.

Double-space

After the introduction, a section labeled **Method** provides a detailed discussion of how you conducted your research, including a description of the research subjects, any materials or tools you used (such as questionnaires), and the procedure you followed.

Format headings (including a third level, if needed) as follows:

First-Level Heading

Second-Level Heading

Third-level heading.
Run this heading into the text paragraph with a standard paragraph indention.

The **Results** section (labeled with a first-level heading) summarizes the data you collected, explains how you analyzed them, and presents them in detail, often in tables, graphs, or charts.

The **Discussion** section (labeled with a first-level heading) interprets the data and presents your conclusions. (When the discussion is brief, you may combine it with the previous section under the heading **Results and Discussion**.)

The **References** section, beginning a new page, includes all your sources.

Long quotations

Run into your text all quotations of forty words or fewer, and enclose them in quotation marks. For quotations of more than forty words, set them off from your text by indenting all lines one-half inch, double-spacing throughout.

> Echoing the opinions of other Europeans at the time, Freud (1961) had a poor view of Americans:
>
> > The Americans are really too bad. . . . Competition is much more pungent with them, not succeeding means civil death to every one, and they have no private resources apart from their profession, no hobby, games, love or other interests of a cultured person. And success means money. (p. 86)

Do not use quotation marks around a quotation displayed in this way.

Illustrations

Present data in tables, graphs, or charts, as appropriate. Begin each illustration on a separate page. Number each kind of illustration consecutively and separately from the other (Table 1, Table 2, etc., and Figure 1, Figure 2, etc.). Refer to all illustrations in your text—for instance, (see Figure 3). Generally, place illustrations immediately after the text references to them.

52.4 Sample Research Report

52.4 Examine a sample research report in APA style.

The paper below illustrates APA structure and documentation for a report of original research.

PERCEPTIONS OF MENTAL ILLNESS 3

Perceptions of Mental Illness
on College Campuses

    Psychiatric disabilities like depression, social anxiety, bipolar disorder, and assorted personality disorders have become the fastest-growing category of disability reported on college campuses (Belch, 2011; Kampsen, 2009). Despite the increased numbers of afflicted students, these disabilities remain "the least understood and least academically supported on campus" by administrators, faculty, staff, and other students (Belch, 2011, p. 74). A recent survey conducted by the Substance Abuse and Mental Health Services Administration concluded that more than 18 percent of all American adults and more than 20 percent of American adults aged 18–25 have a diagnosed mental illness (see Figure 1). While the nontraditional student enrollment is expanding, adults aged 18–25 remain the largest demographic of college students in the campus community.

    The college experience often presents new challenges to students with mental illness. Studies suggest that more than 70% of afflicted students have experienced a mental health crisis while in college (Gruttadaro & Crudo, 2012).

    These crises are often triggered by

- "extreme feelings of anxiety, panic, and depression about school and life";
- "difficulty adjusting to a new routine and environment";
- "feelings of homesickness, loneliness, and isolation";
- "stressed or overwhelmed about course load";
- "posttraumatic stress disorder episode triggered by class content"; or
- "medications stopped working" (Gruttadaro & Crudo, 2012, p. 17).

PERCEPTIONS OF MENTAL ILLNESS 4

[New page]

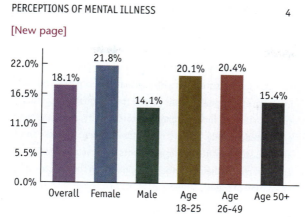

Figure 1.
Prevalence of mental illness among U.S. adults. Adapted from "Results from the 2014 National Survey on Drug Use and Health: Mental Health Detailed Tables" by Substance Abuse and Mental Health Services Administration, 2015.

[New page]

Therefore, assessing perceptions of mental illness on college campuses is the first step in creating an inclusive community that supports students with psychiatric disabilities. These inclusion efforts must extend beyond the designated disability support staff and include administrators, faculty, staff, and the entire student body. Positive perceptions of mental illness and afflicted students allows those students to "develop their talents and realize their potential, culminating in their successful navigation of college" (Belch, 2011, p. 74).

Method

Definition and Types of Mental Illness

According to National Alliance on Mental Illness (n.d.), mental illnesses are conditions that affect a person's thoughts, feelings, or moods, impairing a person's ability to function normally. There is no one cause for mental illness. Causes include genetics, biochemical processes, environment, and lifestyle.

The most common types of mental illness on college campuses include depression, bipolar disorder, anxiety, post-traumatic stress disorder, schizophrenia, and attention-deficit/hyperactivity disorder (Gruttadaro & Crudo, 2012). Despite the common diagnoses, each person experiences mental illness differently, so considerations must be individually made.

Student Self-Stigmatization

While physical disabilities have become more accepted and commonplace on college campuses, psychological disabilities are still often denigrated as invisible disorders. So there is little surprise that stigma is the most common reason given by students with mental illness for not disclosing their condition to others on campus (Belch, 2011; Brennan, Brown, & Gorman, 2015; Gruttadaro & Crudo, 2012; Holland & Wheeler, 2016).

The stigmatization of mental illnesses has far-reaching implications. Afflicted students may isolate themselves from their instructors and their peers, resulting in alienation from the campus community and a higher instance of leaving the college without a degree. In fact, some studies suggest that nearly 86% of students with mental illness leave college before receiving a degree, compared to 37% of students in the general population (Kessler, Foster, Saunders, & Stang, 1995). Moreover, estimates suggest that 4.29 million people failed to receive college degrees due to mental illness (Kitzrow, 2009).

Stigma can also prevent students from seeking treatment through campus counseling and mental health services. Students often avoid mental health centers in high traffic areas because they fear being seen by their peers (Gruttadaro & Crudo, 2012). Moreover, some mental health centers utilize work-study students, which only creates more problems. Students worry about being seen by their peers but also worry about the confidentiality of their records (Gruttadaro & Crudo, 2012).

Peer Stigmatization

Some studies suggest that one of the continuing barriers to public acceptance of mental illness is the "conflation of dangerousness and 'mental illness'" (Martin, Pescosolido, Olafsdottir, & McLeod, 2007, p. 63). Other studies suggest a gender division where male college students hold more negative perceptions of mental illness than their female counterparts (Ionta & Scherman, 2007). Researchers conclude that women are less likely to stigmatize the psychologically disabled because they are more likely to be afflicted themselves. Moreover, men are more likely to consider mental illness a weakness and refuse to seek treatment (Ionta & Scherman, 2007).

> This paragraph and the following discuss implications and effects of student self-stigma.

However, the greatest indicator of stigmatization might be social proximity. Brennan, Brown, and Gorman (2015) and Belch (2011) suggest that students who interact with afflicted students and the mental health services on campus hold less stigma for those diagnosed with a mental illness. The opposite seems to hold true as well. Students who consider their mental health as superior to other students often lack significant interaction with afflicted students. Therefore, their views are consistently more negative (Brennan, Brown, & Gorman, 2015).

Faculty and Staff Stigmatization

Psychiatric disabilities can impede student success in the classroom by creating problems with concentration, memory, motivation, decision making, and interactions (Belch, 2011). Ultimately, students may have no choice but to disclose their mental illness to a professor. Studies show that students who disclosed their illness to faculty received "an array of responses that included negative reactions, such as faculty who believed the students were faking an illness or faculty and [others] who expressed resentment about the accommodations" (Belch, 2011, p. 83; Collins & Mowbray, 2005). While some faculty were willing to accommodate students, others expressed anger, viewing these students as less able and unwelcome on campus (Belch, 2011; Collins & Mowbray, 2005).

Students often find that administration has not educated faculty and staff on mental health, allowing stigmas to remain among the faculty and a reluctance to follow suggested accommodations (Gruttadaro & Crudo, 2012). Moreover, in some cases, the college does not publicly support mental health initiatives or fails to welcome afflicted students into campus housing (Gruttadaro & Crudo, 2012). These issues perpetuate stigma on campus.

Some students complain that on-campus disability resource centers fail to help adequately. They claim that staff members focus primarily on physical disabilities. Moreover, staff members rarely communicate with afflicted students, failing to ensure appropriate accommodations or proactively inform students about additional resources (Gruttadaro & Crudo, 2012).

Second main point: Students who interact with other students with mental illness are less likely to stigmatize mental illness.

Third main point: Faculty attitudes and awareness of mental illness often contributes to problems experienced by students with mental illness.

Discussion

While these perceptions seem grim, stigmatization of mental illness is declining. Some colleges actively work toward the goal of inclusivity for all students. Gruttadaro and Crudo (2012) suggest that colleges expand their outreach by

- training advocates who will explain the rights and services provided to afflicted students;
- educating faculty and staff on mental health and the college experience;
- offering off-campus referrals for mental health care if campus resources are unavailable;
- requiring mental health training or wellness course for students;
- increasing visibility of mental health issues and resources; and
- providing unlimited counseling and support for students.

Others recommend that the disability resource center, faculty, and administrative staff discuss possible accommodations like reduced course loads for full-time students, designated quiet rooms for study, or dedicated dormitories where alcohol is prohibited in advance of accommodation requests (Otto et al., 2011).

Survey responses suggest that afflicted students want their peers to understand that mental illness is more prevalent than expected, and many people suffer in silence when it's unnecessary (Gruttadaro & Crudo, 2012). Moreover, they would like their peers to consider mental health as important as physical health (Gruttadaro & Crudo, 2012). These considerations would make college campuses more inviting destinations.

Other survey responses recommend mental health education for all faculty and staff that would provide information on warning signs, symptoms, and treatment of mental health issues as well as training on supporting students in crisis (Gruttadaro & Crudo, 2012). Like their peers, afflicted students would like faculty and staff to consider mental health as imperative as physical health.

Most current research fails to measure changes in perceptions of mental illness on college campuses over time. Therefore, it is difficult to determine the precise steps to take to reduce stigmatization. However, if a college or university implemented some of the above suggestions, additional studies could be launched to determine the efficacy of the changes.

References

Belch, H. A. (2011). Understanding the experiences of students with psychiatric disabilities: A foundation for creating conditions of support and success. *New Directions for Student Services, 134,* 73–94.

Brennan, K. M., Brown, J., & Gorman, K. (2015). Student estimation of campus mental health service use. Conference Papers: American Sociological Association, 1–10.

Gruttadaro, D., & Crudo, D. (2012). College students speak: A survey report on mental health. National Alliance on Mental Illness. Arlington: National Alliance on Mental Illness.

Holland, D., & Wheeler, H. (2016). College student stress and mental health: Examination of stigmatic views on mental health counseling. *Michigan Sociological Review, 30,* 16–43.

Ionta, J. R., & Scherman, C. D. (2007). An examination of college students' perceptions of people diagnosed with mental illness. *College of St. Elizabeth Journal of the Behavioral Sciences, 1,* 1–10.

Kampsen, A. (2009). *Personal, social, and institutional factors influencing college transition and adaptation experiences for students with psychiatric disabilities* (Order No. 3389330). Available from ProQuest Dissertations & Theses Global. (304954362). Retrieved from http://74.217.196.173/docview/304954362?accountid=14482

Kessler, R. C., Foster, C. L., Saunders, W. B., & Stang, P. E. (1995). Social consequences of psychiatric disorders, I: Educational attainment. *The American Journal of Psychiatry, 152*(7), 1026–1032.

Kitzrow, M. A. (2009). The mental health needs of today's college students: Challenges and recommendations. *NASPA Journal (National Association of Student Personnel Administrators, Inc.), 46*(4), 646–660.

PERCEPTIONS OF MENTAL ILLNESS

Martin, J. K., Pescosolido, B. A., Olafsdottir, S., & McLeod, J. D. (2007). The construction of fear: Americans' preferences for social distance from children and adolescents with mental health problems. *Journal of Health and Social Behavior, 48*(1), 50–67.

Source with no author listed; published by an organization.

Mental health conditions. (2017, January 1). National Alliance on Mental Illness. Retrieved from http://www.nami.org/Learn-More/Mental-Health-Conditions

Printed book.

Otto, M. W., Reilly-Harrington, N. A., Knauz, R. O., Henin, A., Kogan, J. N., & Sachs, G. S. (2011). *Living with bipolar disorder.* New York, NY: Oxford University Press.

Source by a corporate (government) author.

Substance Abuse and Mental Health Services Administration. (2014, September 9). *Results from the 2014 National Survey on Drug Use and Health: Mental health detailed tables.* Retrieved January 2, 2017, from Substance Abuse and Mental Health Services Administration: https://www.samhsa.gov/data/population-data-nsduh/reports?tab=38

Chicago Documentation

Chicago Documentation

53 Chicago Documentation *456*
  53.1 Notes and bibliography *456*
  53.2 Models *458*

Finding the right model for a source

1. **What type of source is it?** Locate the type in the Chicago index. Common types: periodical article, book, government publication, Web or social media, visual or audio.

2. **What is the medium of the source?** From within each type of source, choose the right model for the medium. Common media: print, Web, database, e-book, DVD, video.

3. **Who is the author?** Choose the right model for the number and type of author(s).

Chicago notes and bibliography entries

Authors
1. One, two, or three authors *459*
2. More than three authors *459*
3. Author not named *459*

Articles in journals, newspapers, and magazines
4. Article in a scholarly journal *459*
   a. Print *459*
   b. Database or Web with a DOI *459*
   c. Database without a DOI *460*
   d. Web without a DOI *460*
5. Article in a newspaper *460*
   a. Print *460*
   b. Database *460*
   c. Web *460*
6. Article in a magazine *461*
   a. Print *461*
   b. Database *461*
   c. Web *461*
7. Review *461*

Books and government publications
8. Basic format for a book *461*
   a. Print *461*
   b. Database *461*
   c. E-book *461*
   d. Web *462*

9. Book with an editor *462*
10. Book with an author and an editor *462*
11. Translation *462*
12. Later edition *462*
13. Work in more than one volume *462*
14. Selection from an anthology *462*
15. Work in a series *463*
16. Article in a reference work *463*
    a. Print *463*
    b. Web *463*
17. Government publication *463*

Web sites and social media

18. Page or work on a Web site *463*
19. Post on a blog or discussion group *464*
20. Comment *464*
21. E-mail, text, or direct message *464*

Video, audio, and other media sources

22. Work of art *464*
    a. Original *464*
    b. Print reproduction *464*
    c. Web reproduction *464*
23. Film or video *465*
    a. Film, DVD, Blu-ray, or video recording *465*
    b. Web *465*
24. Published or broadcast interview *465*
25. Sound recording *465*
    a. LP or CD *465*
    b. Web *465*
26. Podcast *465*

Other sources

27. Letter *465*
    a. Published *465*
    b. Personal *466*
28. Personal interview *466*
29. Work on CD-ROM or DVD-ROM *466*

Shortened notes

Chapter 53
Chicago Documentation

Learning Objectives

53.1 Use Chicago notes and bibliography entries.
53.2 Document sources using Chicago style.

53.1 Notes and Bibliography

53.1 Use Chicago notes and bibliography entries.

History, art history, philosophy, and some other humanities use endnotes or footnotes to document sources, following one style recommended by *The Chicago Manual of Style* (17th ed., 2017) and the student guide adapted from it, Kate L. Turabian's *A Manual for Writers of Research Papers, Theses, and Dissertations* (8th ed., revised by Wayne C. Booth, Gregory G. Colomb, and Joseph M. Williams, 2013).

In the Chicago note style, raised numerals in the text refer to footnotes (bottoms of pages) or endnotes (end of paper). These notes contain complete source information. A separate bibliography is optional: ask your instructor for his or her preference.

For both footnotes and endnotes, use single spacing for each note and double spacing between notes, as shown in Figure 53.1 and Figure 53.2. (This is the spacing recommended by *A Manual for*

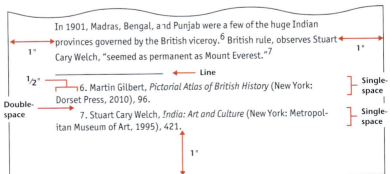

Figure 53.1 Chicago footnotes

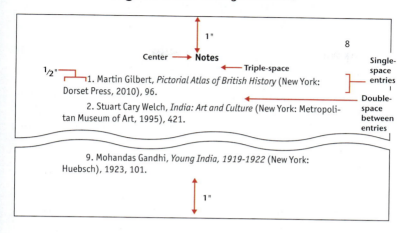

Figure 53.2 Chicago endnotes

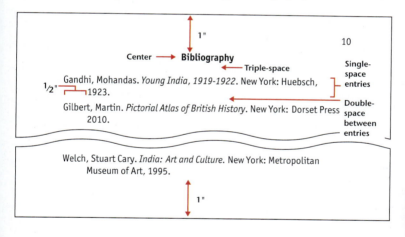

Figure 53.3 Chicago bibliography

Writers, the student guide. For manuscripts that will be published, *The Chicago Manual* recommends double spacing throughout.) Separate footnotes from the text with a short line. Place endnotes directly after the text, beginning on a new page. For a bibliography at the end of the paper, use the format shown in Figure 53.3. Arrange the sources alphabetically by the authors' last names.

The examples below illustrate the essentials of a note and a bibliography entry.

Note

6. Martin Gilbert, *Pictorial Atlas of British History* (New York: Dorset Press, 2010), 96.

Bibliography entry

Gilbert, Martin. *Pictorial Atlas of British History.* New York: Dorset Press, 2010.

Treat some features of notes and bibliography entries the same:

- Unless your instructor requests otherwise, single-space each note or entry, and double-space between them.
- Italicize the titles of books and periodicals.
- Enclose in quotation marks the titles of parts of books or articles in periodicals.
- Do not abbreviate publishers' names, but omit "Inc.," "Co.," and similar abbreviations.
- Do not use "p." or "pp." before page numbers.

Treat other features of notes and bibliography entries differently:

Note	Bibliography entry
Start with a number that corresponds to the note number in the text.	Do not begin with a number.
Indent the first line one-half inch.	Indent the second and subsequent lines one-half inch.
Give the author's name in normal order.	Begin with the author's last name.
Use commas between elements such as author's name and title.	Use periods between elements.
Enclose a book's publication information in parentheses, with no preceding punctuation.	Precede a book's publication information with a period, and don't use parentheses.
Include the specific page number(s) you borrowed from, omitting "p." or "pp."	Omit page numbers except for parts of books or articles in periodicals.

You can instruct your computer to position footnotes at the bottoms of appropriate pages. It will also automatically number notes and renumber them if you add or delete one or more.

53.2 Models of Chicago Notes and Bibliography Entries

53.2 Document sources using Chicago style.

An index to the following Chicago models appears on the Chicago divider. The models themselves show notes and bibliography entries together for easy reference. Be sure to use the numbered note form for notes and the unnumbered bibliography form for bibliography entries. Chicago style generally recommends notes only, not bibliography entries, for personal communication such as e-mail, personal letters, and interviews you conduct yourself. Bibliography entries are shown here in case your instructor requires such entries.

53.2.1 Authors

1. One, two, or three authors

1. Carol Gilligan, *In a Different Voice: Psychological Theory and Women's Development* (Cambridge: Harvard University Press, 1982), 27.

Gilligan, Carol. *In a Different Voice: Psychological Theory and Women's Development*. Cambridge: Harvard University Press, 1982.

1. Dennis L. Wilcox, Phillip H. Ault, and Warren K. Agee, *Public Relations: Strategies and Tactics,* 10th ed. (New York: Pearson, 2011), 182.

Wilcox, Dennis L., Phillip H. Ault, and Warren K. Agee. *Public Relations: Strategies and Tactics*. 10th ed. New York: Pearson, 2011.

2. More than three authors

2. Geraldo Lopez et al., *China and the West* (Boston: Little, Brown, 2004), 461.

Lopez, Geraldo, Judith P. Salt, Anne Ming, and Henry Reisen. *China and the West*. Boston: Little, Brown, 2004.

The Latin abbreviation et al. in the note means "and others."

3. Author not named (anonymous)

3. *The Dorling Kindersley World Atlas* (London: Dorling Kindersley, 2013), 150–51.

The Dorling Kindersley World Atlas. London: Dorling Kindersley, 2013.

53.2.2 Articles in journals, newspapers, and magazines

4. Article in a scholarly journal

For journals that are paginated continuously through an annual volume, include at least the volume number—or, for greater clarity, add the issue number, if any, or the month or season of publication, as in models a and b below. The month or season precedes the year of publication in parentheses. The issue number is required if the journal paginates issues separately (no. 1 in models c and d).

a. Print journal article

4. Janet Lever, "Sex Differences in the Games Children Play," *Social Problems* 23 (Spring 1996): 482.

Lever, Janet. "Sex Differences in the Games Children Play." *Social Problems* 23 (Spring 1996): 478–87.

b. Database or Web journal article with DOI

4. Jonathan Dickens, "Social Policy Approaches to Intercountry Adoption," *International Social Work* 52 (September 2009): 600, doi:10.1177/0020872809337678.

Dickens, Jonathan. "Social Policy Approaches to Intercountry Adoption." *International Social Work* 52 (September 2009): 595–607. doi:10.1177/0020872809337678.

A DOI, or Digital Object Identifier, is a unique identifier that many publishers assign to journal articles and other documents. (See APA

Chapter 52 for more on DOIs.) If the article you cite has a DOI, give it in the format shown in the source: preceded by doi, as above, or preceded by http://dx.doi.org/.

c. Database journal article without DOI

> 4. Nathan S. Atkinson, "Newsreels as Domestic Propaganda: Visual Rhetoric at the Dawn of the Cold War," *Rhetoric and Public Affairs* 14, no. 1 (Spring 2011): 72, Academic Search Complete (60502112).

> Atkinson, Nathan S. "Newsreels as Domestic Propaganda: Visual Rhetoric at the Dawn of the Cold War." *Rhetoric and Public Affairs* 14, no. 1 (Spring 2011): 69–100. Academic Search Complete (60502112).

If no DOI is available for an article in a database, give the name of the database and the accession number.

d. Web journal article without DOI

> 4. Rebecca Butler, "The Rise and Fall of Union Classification," *Theological Librarianship* 6, no. 1 (2013): 21, https://journal.atla.com/ojs/index.php/theolib/article/view/254.

> Butler, Rebecca. "The Rise and Fall of Union Classification." *Theological Librarianship* 6, no. 1 (2013): 21–28. https://journal.atla.com/ojs/index.php/theolib/article/view/254.

If no DOI is available for an article you find on the open Web, give the URL.

5. Article in a newspaper

a. Print newspaper article

> 5. Annie Lowery, "Cities Advancing Inequality Fight," *New York Times*, April 7, 2014, national edition, A1.

> Lowery, Annie. "Cities Advancing Inequality Fight." *New York Times*, April 7, 2014, national edition, A1.

b. Database newspaper article

> 5. Rob Stein, "Obesity May Stall Trend of Increasing Longevity," *Washington Post*, March 15, 2014, final edition, A2, LexisNexis Academic.

> Stein, Rob. "Obesity May Stall Trend of Increasing Longevity." *Washington Post*, March 15, 2014, final edition, A2, LexisNexis Academic.

If an accession number is available, give it after the database name, as in model 6b below.

c. Web newspaper article

> 5. Marcia Dunn, "Vast Ocean Found beneath Ice of Saturn Moon," *Detroit News*, April 3, 2014, http://www.detroitnews.com/article/20140403/SCIENCE/304030081.

> Dunn, Marcia. "Vast Ocean Found beneath Ice of Saturn Moon." *Detroit News*, April 3, 2014. http://www.detroitnews.com/article/20140403/SCIENCE/304030081.

6. Article in a magazine

a. Print magazine article

6. Jeffrey Toobin, "This Is My Jail," *New Yorker,* April 14, 2014, 28.

Toobin, Jeffrey. "This Is My Jail." *New Yorker,* April 14, 2014, 26–32.

b. Database magazine article

6. Colin Barras, "Right on Target," *New Scientist,* January 25, 2014, 42, Academic Search Complete (93983067).

Barras, Colin. "Right on Target." *New Scientist,* January 25, 2014, 40-43. Academic Search Complete (93983067).

If no accession number is available, give just the database name, as in model 5b.

c. Web magazine article

6. Laura Stampler, "These Cities Have the Most Open-Minded Daters," *Time,* April 14, 2014, http://time.com/61947/these-cities-have-the-most-open-minded-daters.

Stampler, Laura. "These Cities Have the Most Open-Minded Daters." *Time,* April 14, 2014. http://time.com/61947/these-cities-have-the-most-open-minded-daters.

7. Review

7. John Gregory Dunne, "The Secret of Danny Santiago," review of *Famous All over Town,* by Danny Santiago, *New York Review of Books,* August 16, 1994, 25.

Dunne, John Gregory. "The Secret of Danny Santiago." Review of *Famous All over Town,* by Danny Santiago. *New York Review of Books,* August 16, 1994, 17–27.

53.2.3 Books and government publications

8. Basic format for a book

a. Print book

8. Barbara Ehrenreich, *Dancing in the Streets: A History of Collective Joy* (New York: Henry Holt, 2006), 97-117.

Ehrenreich, Barbara. *Dancing in the Streets: A History of Collective Joy.* New York: Henry Holt, 2006.

b. Database book

8. Daniel Levine, *Bayard Rustin and the Civil Rights Movement* (New Brunswick: Rutgers University Press, 1999), 21-45, eBook Collection (44403).

Levine, Daniel. *Bayard Rustin and the Civil Rights Movement.* New Brunswick: Rutgers University Press, 1999. eBook Collection (44403).

c. E-book

8. Marilyn Booth, *May Her Likes Be Multiplied: Biography and Gender Politics in Egypt* (Oakland: University of California Press, 2001), Kindle.

Booth, Marilyn. *May Her Likes Be Multiplied: Biography and Gender Politics in Egypt.* Oakland: University of California Press, 2001. Kindle.

d. Web book

8. Jane Austen, *Emma*, ed. R. W. Chapman (1816; Oxford: Clarendon, 1926; Oxford Text Archive, 2014), Chap. 1, http://ota.ahds.ac.uk/Austen/Emma.1519.

Austen, Jane. *Emma*. Edited by R. W. Chapman. 1816. Oxford: Clarendon, 1926. Oxford Text Archive, 2014. http://ota.ahds.ac.uk/Austen/Emma.1519.

Provide print publication information, if any.

9. Book with an editor

9. Patricia Rushton, ed., *Vietnam War Nurses: Personal Accounts of Eighteen Americans* (Jefferson, NC: McFarland, 2013), 70–72.

Rushton, Patricia, ed. *Vietnam War Nurses: Personal Accounts of Eighteen Americans*. Jefferson, NC: McFarland, 2013.

10. Book with an author and an editor

10. Lewis Mumford, *The City in History*, ed. Donald L. Miller (New York: Pantheon, 1986), 216–17.

Mumford, Lewis. *The City in History*. Edited by Donald L. Miller. New York: Pantheon, 1986.

11. Translation

11. Dante Alighieri, *The Inferno*, trans. John Ciardi (New York: New American Library, 1971), 51.

Alighieri, Dante. *The Inferno*. Translated by John Ciardi. New York: New American Library, 1971.

12. Later edition

12. Dwight L. Bolinger, *Aspects of Language*, 3rd ed. (New York: Harcourt Brace Jovanovich, 1981), 20.

Bolinger, Dwight L. *Aspects of Language*. 3rd ed. New York: Harcourt Brace Jovanovich, 1981.

13. Work in more than one volume

a. One volume without a title

13. Abraham Lincoln, *The Collected Works of Abraham Lincoln*, ed. Roy P. Basler (New Brunswick: Rutgers University Press, 1953), 5:426–28.

Lincoln, Abraham. *The Collected Works of Abraham Lincoln*. Edited by Roy P. Basler. Vol. 5. New Brunswick: Rutgers University Press, 1953.

b. One volume with a title

13. Linda B. Welkin, *The Age of Balanchine*, vol. 3 of *The History of Ballet* (New York: Columbia University Press, 1999), 56.

Welkin, Linda B. *The Age of Balanchine*. Vol. 3 of *The History of Ballet*. New York: Columbia University Press, 1999.

14. Selection from an anthology

14. Rosetta Brooks, "Streetwise," in *The New Urban Landscape*, ed. Richard Martin (New York: Rizzoli, 2005), 38–39.

Brooks, Rosetta. "Streetwise." In *The New Urban Landscape,* edited by Richard Martin, 37–60. New York: Rizzoli, 2005.

15. Work in a series

15. Ingmar Bergman, *The Seventh Seal,* Modern Film Scripts 12 (New York: Simon and Schuster, 1995), 27.

Bergman, Ingmar. *The Seventh Seal*. Modern Film Scripts 12. New York: Simon and Schuster, 1995.

16. Article in a reference work

As shown in the following examples, use the abbreviation s.v. (Latin *sub verbo*, "under the word") for reference works that are alphabetically arranged. Well-known works (model a) do not need publication information except for the edition number. Chicago style generally recommends notes only, not bibliography entries, for reference works; bibliography models are given here in case your instructor requires such entries.

a. Print reference work

16. *Merriam-Webster's Collegiate Dictionary,* 11th ed., s.v. "reckon."

Merriam-Webster's Collegiate Dictionary. 11th ed. S.v. "reckon."

b. Web reference work

16. *Wikipedia,* s.v. "Wuhan," last modified May 9, 2014, http://en.wikipedia.org/wiki/Wuhan.

Wikipedia. S.v. "Wuhan." Last modified May 9, 2014. http://en.wikipedia.org/wiki/Wuhan.

17. Government publication

17. House Comm. on Agriculture, Nutrition, and Forestry, *Food and Energy Act of 2008,* 110th Cong., 2nd Sess., H.R. Doc. No. 884, at 21-22 (2008).

House Comm. on Agriculture, Nutrition, and Forestry. *Food and Energy Act of 2008*. 110th Cong. 2nd Sess. H.R. Doc. No. 884 (2008).

17. Hawaii Department of Education, *Kauai District Schools, Profile 2013–14* (Honolulu, 2014), 38.

Hawaii Department of Education. *Kauai District Schools, Profile 2013–14*. Honolulu, 2014.

53.2.4 Web sites and social media

18. Page or work on a Web site

18. Justin W. Patchin, "Ban School, Open Facebook," Cyberbullying Research Center, accessed May 10, 2018, http://cyberbullying.us/021649.

Patchin, Justin W. "Ban School, Open Facebook." Cyberbullying Research Center. Accessed May 10, 2018. http://cyberbullying.us/021649.

For Web pages and works that are not dated or are likely to change, *The Chicago Manual* suggests giving the date of your access, as here, or a statement beginning with last modified (model 16).

19. Post on a blog or discussion group

19. Bettina Smith, "No Such Animal," *Smithsonian Collections Blog,* April 29, 2014, http://si-siris.blogspot.com.

Smith, Bettina. "No Such Animal." *Smithsonian Collections Blog.* April 29, 2014. http://si-siris.blogspot.com.

20. Comment

20. Tony Drees, April 15, 2014, comment on Nicholas Kristof, "Standing by Our Veterans," *On the Ground* (blog), *New York Times,* April 12, 2014, http://kristof.blogs.nytimes.com.

Kristof, Nicholas. *On the Ground* (blog). *New York Times.* http://kristof.blogs.nytimes.com.

In a note, cite a reader's comment on a blog by the reader's name (Drees above). However, in the bibliography, cite the entire blog by the blog author's name (Kristof above).

21. E-mail, text, or direct message

Personal communications including email, text messages, or other private messages on social media are usually cited in a note but not included in the bibliography.

21. Naomi Lee, e-mail message to author, May 16, 2018.

21. Facebook direct message to author, May 16, 2018.

53.2.5 Video, audio, and other media sources

22. Work of art

a. Original artwork

22. John Singer Sargent, *In Switzerland,* 1908, Metropolitan Museum of Art, New York.

Sargent, John Singer. *In Switzerland.* 1908. Metropolitan Museum of Art, New York.

b. Print reproduction of an artwork

22. David Graham, *Bob's Java Jive, Tacoma, Washington, 1989,* photograph, in *Only in America: Some Unexpected Scenery* (New York: Knopf, 1991), 93.

Graham, David. *Bob's Java Jive, Tacoma, Washington, 1989.* Photograph. In *Only in America: Some Unexpected Scenery.* New York: Knopf, 1991.

c. Web reproduction of an artwork

22. Jackson Pollock, *Shimmering Substance,* 1946, Museum of Modern Art, New York, http://moma.org/collection/conservation/pollock/shimmering_substance.html.

Pollock, Jackson. *Shimmering Substance.* 1946. Museum of Modern Art, New York. http://moma.org/collection/conservation/pollock/shimmering_substance.html.

23. Film or video

a. Film, DVD, Blu-ray, or video recording

23. George Balanchine, *Serenade,* San Francisco Ballet, performed February 2, 2000 (New York: PBS Video, 2006), DVD.

Balanchine, George. *Serenade.* San Francisco Ballet. Performed February 2, 2000. New York: PBS Video, 2006. DVD.

b. Video on the Web

23. Leslie J. Stewart, *96 Ranch Rodeo and Barbecue* (1951); 16mm, from Library of Congress, *Buckaroos in Paradise: Ranching Culture in Northern Nevada, 1945-1982,* MPEG, http://memory.loc.gov/cgi-bin/query.

Stewart, Leslie J. *96 Ranch Rodeo and Barbecue.* 1951. 16 mm. From Library of Congress, *Buckaroos in Paradise: Ranching Culture in Northern Nevada, 1945-1982.* MPEG. http://memory.loc.gov/cgi-bin/query.

24. Published or broadcast interview

24. Dexter Filkins, interview by Terry Gross, *Fresh Air,* NPR, April 29, 2014.

Filkins, Dexter. Interview by Terry Gross. *Fresh Air*. NPR. April 29, 2014.

25. Sound recording

a. LP or CD

25. Philip Glass, *String Quartet no. 5,* with Kronos Quartet, recorded 1991, Nonesuch 79356-2, 1995, compact disc.

Glass, Philip. *String Quartet no. 5.* Kronos Quartet. Recorded 1991. Nonesuch 79356-2. 1995. Compact disc.

b. Web recording

25. Ronald W. Reagan, "State of the Union Address," January 26, 1982, Vincent Voice Library, Digital and Multimedia Center, Michigan State University, http://www.lib.msu.edu/vincent/presidents/reagan.html.

Reagan, Ronald W. "State of the Union Address." January 26, 1982. Vincent Voice Library. Digital and Multimedia Center, Michigan State University. http://www.lib.msu.edu/vincent/presidents/reagan.html.

26. Podcast

26. Stephanie Foo, "The Hounds of Blairsville," *This American Life,* podcast audio, April 11, 2014, http://www.thisamericanlife.org/radio-archives/episode/522/tarred-and-feathered?act=1.

Foo, Stephanie. "The Hounds of Blairsville." *This American Life.* Podcast audio. April 11, 2014. http://www.thisamericanlife.org/radio-archives/episode/522/tarred-and-feathered?act=1.

53.2.6 Other sources

27. Letter

a. Published letter

27. Mrs. Laura E. Buttolph to Rev. and Mrs. C. C. Jones, June 20, 1857, in *The Children of Pride: A True Story of Georgia and the Civil War,* ed. Robert Manson Myers (New Haven, CT: Yale University Press, 1972), 334.

Buttolph, Laura E. Mrs. Laura E. Buttolph to Rev. and Mrs. C. C. Jones, June 20, 1857. In *The Children of Pride: A True Story of Georgia and the Civil War,* edited by Robert Manson Myers. New Haven, CT: Yale University Press, 1972.

b. Personal letter

27. Ann E. Packer, letter to author, June 15, 2011.

Packer, Ann E. Letter to author. June 15, 2011.

28. Personal interview

28. Janelle White, interview by author, December 19, 2013.

White, Janelle. Interview by author. December 19, 2013.

29. Work on CD-ROM or DVD-ROM

29. *The American Heritage Dictionary of the English Language,* 4th ed. (Boston: Houghton Mifflin, 2006), CD-ROM.

The American Heritage Dictionary of the English Language. 4th ed. Boston: Houghton Mifflin, 2006. CD-ROM.

53.2.7 Shortened notes

To streamline documentation, Chicago style recommends shortened notes for sources that are fully cited elsewhere, either in a bibliography or in previous notes. Ask your instructor whether your paper should include a bibliography and, if so, whether you may use shortened notes for first references to sources as well as for subsequent references.

A shortened note contains the author's last name, the work's title (minus any initial *A*, *An*, or *The*), and the page number. Reduce long titles to four or fewer key words.

Complete note

4. Janet Lever, "Sex Differences in the Games Children Play," *Social Problems* 23 (Spring 1996): 482.

Complete bibliography entry

Lever, Janet. "Sex Differences in the Games Children Play." *Social Problems* 23 (Spring 1996): 478–87.

Shortened note

12. Lever, "Sex Differences," 483.

Chicago style allows for in-text parenthetical citations when you cite one or more works repeatedly. In the following example, the raised number 2 refers to the source information in a note; the number in parentheses is a page number in the same source.

British rule, observes Stuart Cary Welch, "seemed as permanent as Mount Everest."[2] Most Indians submitted, willingly or not, to British influence in every facet of life (42).

CSE Documentation

CSE Documentation

54 CSE Documentation *470*
    54.1 Name-year citations *470*
    54.2 Numbered text citations *470*
    54.3 Reference list *471*

Finding the right model for a source

1. **What type of source is it?** Locate the type in the CSE index. Common types: periodical article, book, government publication, Web or social media, visual or audio.

2. **What is the medium of the source?** From within each type of source, choose the right model for the medium. Common media: print, Web, database, e-book, DVD, video.

3. **Who is the author?** Choose the right model for the number and type of author(s).

CSE references

Authors
1. One author *472*
2. Two to ten authors *473*
3. More than ten authors *473*
4. Author not named *473*
5. Two or more cited works by the same author(s) published in the same year *473*

Articles in journals, newspapers, and magazines
6. Article in a journal *473*
   a. Print *473*
   b. Database or Web *473*
7. Article in a newspaper *474*
8. Article in a magazine *474*

Books
9. Basic format for a book *474*
   a. Print *474*
   b. Web *474*
10. Book with an editor *474*
11. Selection from a book *474*

Web sites and social media
12. Web site *474*
13. Blog post *475*
14. Personal communication *475*

Other sources
15. Report written and published by the same organization *475*
16. Report written and published by different organizations *475*
17. Audio or visual recording *475*
18. Document on CD-ROM or DVD-ROM *475*

Chapter 54
CSE Documentation

Learning Objectives

54.1 Write CSE name-year text citations.
54.2 Write CSE numbered text citations.
54.3 Prepare a CSE reference list.

54.1 Name-Year Citations

54.1 Write CSE name-year text citations.

Writers in the life sciences, physical sciences, and mathematics rely for documentation style on *Scientific Style and Format: The CSE Manual for Authors, Editors, and Publishers* (8th ed., 2014), published by the Council of Science Editors.

Scientific Style and Format details two styles of scientific documentation: one using author and date and one using numbers. Both types of text citation refer to a list of references at the end of the paper. Ask your instructor which style you should use.

In the CSE name-year style, in-text citations provide the last name of the author being cited and the source's year of publication. At the end of the paper, a list of references, arranged alphabetically by authors' last names, provides complete information on each source (see 54.3).

The CSE name-year style closely resembles the APA name-year style detailed in APA Chapter 52. You can follow the APA examples for in-text citations, making several notable changes for CSE:

- **Do not use a comma to separate the author's name and the date:** (Baumrind 1968).
- **Separate two authors' names with** and **(not "&"):** (Pepinsky and DeStefano 1997).
- **For sources with three or more authors, use** et al. **(Latin abbreviation for "and others") after the first author's name:** (Singh et al. 2014).

54.2 Numbered Text Citations

54.2 Write CSE numbered text citations.

In the CSE number style, raised numbers in the text refer to a numbered list of references at the end of the paper.

Two standard references[1,2] use this term.
These forms of immunity have been extensively researched.[3]
Hepburn and Tatin[2] do not discuss this project.

Assignment of numbers

The number for each source is based on the order in which you cite the source in the text: the first cited source is 1, the second is 2, and so on.

Reuse of numbers

When you cite a source you have already cited and numbered, use the original number again (see the last example above, which reuses the number 2 from the first example).

This reuse is the key difference between the CSE numbered citations and numbered references to footnotes or endnotes. In the CSE style, each source has only one number, determined by the order in which the source is cited. With notes, in contrast, the numbering proceeds in sequence, so that each source has as many numbers as it has citations in the text.

Citation of two or more sources

When you cite two or more sources at once, arrange their numbers in sequence and separate them with a comma and a space, as in the first example above.

54.3 Reference List

54.3 Prepare a CSE reference list.

For both the name-year and number styles of in-text citation, provide a list, titled References, of all sources you have cited. Center this heading about an inch from the top of the page, and double-space beneath it.

The following examples show the differences and similarities between the name-year and number styles:

Name-year style

Hepburn PX, Tatin JM. 2005. Human physiology. New York (NY): Columbia University Press.

Number style

2. Hepburn PX, Tatin JM. Human physiology. New York (NY): Columbia University Press; 2005.

Spacing

In both styles, single-space each entry and double-space between entries.

Arrangement

In the name-year style, arrange entries alphabetically by authors' last names. In the number style, arrange entries in numerical order—that is, in order of their citation in the text.

Format

In the name-year style, type all lines of entries at the left margin—do not indent. In the number style, begin the first line of each entry at the left margin and indent subsequent lines.

Authors

In both styles, list each author's name with the last name first, followed by initials for first and middle names. Do not use a comma between an author's last name and initials, and do not use periods or spaces with the initials. Do use a comma to separate authors' names.

Placement of dates

In the name-year style, the date follows the author's or authors' names. In the number style, the date follows the publication information (for a book) or the periodical title (for a journal, magazine, or newspaper).

Journal titles

In both styles, do not italicize or underline journal titles. For titles of two or more words, abbreviate words of six or more letters (without periods) and omit most prepositions, articles, and conjunctions. Capitalize each word. For example, *Journal of Chemical and Biochemical Studies* becomes J Chem Biochem Stud, and *Hospital Practice* becomes Hosp Pract.

Book and article titles

In both styles, do not italicize, underline, or use quotation marks around a book or an article title. Capitalize only the first word and any proper nouns.

Publication information for journal articles

The name-year and number styles differ in the placement of the publication date (see above). However, after the journal title both styles give the journal's volume number, any issue number in parentheses, a colon, and the inclusive page numbers of the article, run together without space: 28:329-30 or 62(2):26-40. See model 6.

The following examples show both a name-year reference and a number reference for each type of source. An index to all the models appears opposite the **CSE** divider.

54.3.1 Authors

1. One author

Gould SJ. 1987. Time's arrow, time's cycle. Cambridge (MA): Harvard University Press.

1. Gould SJ. Time's arrow, time's cycle. Cambridge (MA): Harvard University Press; 1987.

2. Two to ten authors

Hepburn PX, Tatin JM, Tatin JP. 2012. Human physiology. New York (NY): Columbia University Press.

2. Hepburn PX, Tatin JM, Tatin JP. Human physiology. New York (NY): Columbia University Press; 2012.

3. More than ten authors

Evans RW, Bowditch L, Dana KL, Drumond A, Wildovitch WP, Young SL, Mills P, Mills RR, Livak SR, Lisi OL, et al. 2011. Organ transplants: ethical issues. Ann Arbor (MI): University of Michigan Press.

3. Evans RW, Bowditch L, Dana KL, Drummond A, Wildovitch WP, Young SL, Mills P, Mills RR, Livak SR, Lisi OL, et al. Organ transplants: ethical issues. Ann Arbor (MI): University of Michigan Press; 2011.

4. Author not named

Health care for children with diabetes. 2014. New York (NY): US Health Care.

4. Health care for children with diabetes. New York (NY): US Health Care; 2014.

5. Two or more cited works by the same author(s) published in the same year

Gardner H. 1973a. The arts and human development. New York (NY): Wiley.

Gardner H. 1973b. The quest for mind: Piaget, Lévi-Strauss, and the structuralist movement. New York (NY): Knopf.

(The number style does not require such forms.)

54.3.2 Articles in journals, newspapers, and magazines

6. Article in a journal

a. Print article

Campos JJ, Walle EA, Dahl A, Main A. 2011. Reconceptualizing emotion regulation. Emotion Rev. 3(1):26-35.

6. Campos JJ, Walle EA, Dahl A, Main A. Reconceptualizing emotion regulation. Emotion Rev. 2011; 3(1):26-35.

b. Database or Web article

Grady GF. 2014. New research on immunizations. Today's Med. [accessed 2014 Dec 10];10(3):45-49. http://www.fmrt.org/todaysmedicine/Grady050389.pdf8. doi:10.1087/262534887.

6. Grady GF. New research on immunizations. Today's Med. 2014 [accessed 2014 Dec 10];10(3):45-49. http://www.fmrt.org/todaysmedicine/Grady050389.pdf8.doi:10.1087/262534887.

Give the date of your access after the journal title (first example) or after the publication date (second example). If the article has no page, paragraph, or other reference numbers, give your calculation of its length in brackets—for instance, [about 15 p.] or [20 paragraphs].

Conclude with the source's URL and the DOI (Digital Object Identifier) if one is available. (See APA Chapter 52 for more on DOIs.)

7. Article in a newspaper

Zimmer C. 2014 May 8. Antibiotic-resistant germs lying in wait everywhere. New York Times (National Ed.). Sect. C:1 (col. 1).

7. Zimmer C. Antibiotic-resistant germs lying in wait everywhere. New York Times (National Ed.). 2014 May 8;Sect. C:1 (col. 1).

8. Article in a magazine

Talbot M. 2013 Mar 18. About a boy. New Yorker. 56-65.

8. Talbot M. About a boy. New Yorker. 2013 Mar 18;56-65.

54.3.3 Books

9. Basic format for a book

a. Print book

Wilson EO. 2004. On human nature. Cambridge (MA): Harvard University Press.

9. Wilson EO. On human nature. Cambridge (MA): Harvard University Press; 2004.

b. Web book

Ruch BJ, Ruch DB. 2013. New research in medicine and homeopathy. New York (NY): Albert Einstein College of Medicine; [accessed 2014 Jan 25]. http://www.einstein.edu/medicine/books/ruch&ruch.pdf.

9. Ruch BJ, Ruch DB. New research in medicine and homeopathy. New York (NY): Albert Einstein College of Medicine; 2013 [accessed 2014 Jan 25]. http://www.einstein.edu/medicine/books/ruch&ruch.pdf.

10. Book with an editor

Jonson P, editor. 2014. Anatomy yearbook 2014. Los Angeles (CA): Anatco.

10. Jonson P, editor. Anatomy yearbook 2014. Los Angeles (CA): Anatco; 2014.

11. Selection from a book

Kriegel R, Laubenstein L, Muggia F. 2005. Kaposi's sarcoma. In: Ebbeson P, Biggar RS, Melbye M, editors. AIDS: a basic guide for clinicians. 2nd ed. Philadelphia (PA): Saunders. p. 100-126.

11. Kriegel R, Laubenstein L, Muggia F. Kaposi's sarcoma. In: Ebbeson P, Biggar RS, Melbye M, editors. AIDS: a basic guide for clinicians. 2nd ed. Philadelphia (PA): Saunders; 2005. p. 100-126.

54.3.4   Web sites and social media

12. Web site

American Medical Association. c1995-2014. Chicago (IL): American Medical Association; [accessed 2014 Nov 22]. http://ama-assn.org/ama.

12. American Medical Association. Chicago (IL): American Medical Association; c1995-2014 [accessed 2014 Nov 22]. http://ama-assn.org/ama.

If you are unable to determine the most recent update to a Web site, give the copyright date, typically found at the bottom of the home page, preceded by c: c1995-2014 in the preceding examples.

13. Blog post

Tenenbaum, LF. 2014 Apr 29. Zombies vs. Goldilocks: the insurrection [blog post]. Earth Right Now. [accessed 2014 May 19]. http://climate.nasa.gov/blog/1075.

13. Tenenbaum, LF. Zombies vs. Goldilocks: the insurrection [blog post]. Earth Right Now. 2014, Apr 29. [accessed 2014 May 19]. http://climate.nasa.gov/blog/1075.

14. Personal communication (text citation)

One member of the research team has expressed reservation about the study design (personal communication from L. Kogod, 2014 Feb 6; unreferenced).

A personal letter or e-mail message should be cited in your text, not in your reference list. The format is the same for both the name-year and the number styles.

54.3.5   Other sources

15. Report written and published by the same organization

Warnock M. 2006. Report of the Committee on Fertilization. Waco (TX): Baylor University Department of Embryology. Report No.: BU/DE.4261.

15. Warnock M. Report of the Committee on Fertilization. Waco (TX): Baylor University Department of Embryology; 2006. Report No.: BU/DE.4261.

16. Report written and published by different organizations

Hackney, JD (Rancho Los Amigos Hospital, Downey, CA). 2012. Effect of atmospheric pollutants on human physiologic function. Washington (DC): Environmental Protection Agency (US). Report No.: R-801396.

16. Hackney, JD (Rancho Los Amigos Hospital, Downey, CA). Effect of atmospheric pollutants on human physiologic function. Washington (DC): Environmental Protection Agency (US); 2012. Report No.: R-801396.

17. Audio or visual recording

Cell mitosis [DVD–ROM]. 2014. White Plains (NY): Teaching Media.

17. Cell mitosis [DVD–ROM]. White Plains (NY): Teaching Media; 2014.

18. Document on CD-ROM or DVD-ROM

Reich WT, editor. c2013. Encyclopedia of bioethics [DVD-ROM]. New York (NY): Co-Health. 1 DVD.

18. Reich WT editor. Encyclopedia of bioethics [DVD-ROM]. New York (NY): Co-Health; c2013. 1 DVD.

Glossary of Usage

This glossary provides notes on words or phrases that often cause problems for writers. The recommendations for standard American English are based on current dictionaries and usage guides. Items labeled **nonstandard** should be avoided in academic and business settings. Those labeled **colloquial** and **slang** occur in speech and in some informal writing but are best avoided in formal college and business writing. (Words and phrases labeled *colloquial* include those labeled by many dictionaries with the equivalent term *informal*.)

a, an Use *a* before words beginning with consonant sounds, including those spelled with an initial pronounced *h* and those spelled with vowels that are sounded as consonants: *a historian, a one-o'clock class, a university*. Use *an* before words that begin with vowel sounds, including those spelled with an initial silent *h*: *an organism, an L, an honor*.

Using *a* or *an* before an abbreviation depends on how the abbreviation is to be read: *She was once an AEC undersecretary* (*AEC* is to be read as three separate letters). *Many Americans opposed a SALT treaty* (*SALT* is to be read as one word, *salt*). (See also 34.5.1 on the uses of *a/an* versus *the*.)

accept, except *Accept* is a verb meaning "receive." *Except* usually means "but for" or "other than"; when it is used as a verb, it means "leave out": *I can accept all your suggestions except the last one. I'm sorry you excepted my last suggestion from your list.*

advice, advise *Advice* is a noun, and *advise* is a verb: *Take my advice; do as I advise you.*

affect, effect Usually *affect* is a verb, meaning "to influence," and *effect* is a noun, meaning "result": *The drug did not affect his driving; in fact, it seemed to have no effect at all.* But *effect* occasionally is used as a verb meaning "to bring about": *Her efforts effected a change.* And *affect* is used in psychology as a noun meaning "feeling or emotion": *One can infer much about affect from behavior.*

agree to, agree with *Agree to* means "consent to," and *agree with* means "be in accord with": *How can they agree to a treaty when they don't agree with each other about the terms?*

all ready, already *All ready* means "completely prepared," and *already* means "by now" or "before now": *We were all ready to go to the movie, but it had already started.*

all right *All right* is always two words. *Alright* is a common error.

all together, altogether *All together* means "in unison" or "gathered in one place." *Altogether* means "entirely": *It's not altogether true that our family never spends vacations all together.*

allusion, illusion An *allusion* is an indirect reference, and an *illusion* is a deceptive appearance: *Paul's constant allusions to Shakespeare created the illusion that he was an intellectual.*

almost, most *Almost* means "nearly"; *most* means "the greater number (or part) of." In formal writing, *most* should not be used as a substitute for *almost*: *We see each other almost* [not *most*] *every day.*

a lot *A lot* is always two words, used informally to mean "many." *Alot* is a common misspelling.

among, between In general, use *among* for relationships involving more than two people or for comparing one thing to a group to which it belongs: *The four of them agreed among themselves that the choice was between New York and Los Angeles.*

amount, number Use *amount* with a singular noun that names something not countable (a noncount noun): *The amount of food varies.* Use *number* with a plural noun that names more than one of something countable (a plural count noun): *The number of calories must stay the same.*

and/or *And/or* indicates three options: one or the other or both. *The decision is made by the mayor and/or the council.* If you mean all three options, *and/or* is appropriate. Otherwise, use *and* if you mean both; use *or* if you mean either.

ante-, anti- The prefix *ante-* means "before" (*antedate, antebellum*); *anti-* means "against" (*antiwar, antinuclear*). Before a capital letter or *i*, *anti-* takes a hyphen: *anti-Freudian, anti-isolationist.*

anxious, eager *Anxious* means "nervous" or "worried" and is usually followed by *about*. *Eager* means "looking forward" and is usually followed by *to*: *I've been anxious about getting blisters. I'm eager* [not *anxious*] *to get new running shoes.*

anybody, any body; anyone, any one *Anybody* and *anyone* are indefinite pronouns; *any body* is a noun modified by *any*; *any one* is a pronoun or adjective modified by *any*: *How can anybody communicate with any body of government? Can anyone help Amy? She has more work than any one person can handle.*

any more, anymore *Any more* means "no more"; *anymore* means "now." Both are used in negative constructions: *He doesn't want any more. She doesn't live here anymore.*

apt, liable, likely *Apt* and *likely* are interchangeable. Strictly speaking, though, *apt* means "having a tendency to": *Horace is apt to forget his lunch in the morning. Likely* means "probably going to": *Horace is leaving so early today that he's likely to catch the first bus.*

Liable normally means "in danger of" and should be confined to situations with undesirable consequences: *Horace is liable to trip over that hose.* Strictly, *liable* means "responsible" or "exposed to": *The owner will be liable for Horace's injuries.*

are, is Use *are* with a plural subject (*books are*), *is* with a singular subject (*a book is*).

as *As* may be unclear when it substitutes for *because, since,* or *while*: *As the researchers asked more questions, their money ran out.* (Does *as* mean "while" or "because"?) *As* should never be used as a substitute for *whether* or *who*: *I'm not sure whether* [not *as*] *we can make it. That's the man who* [not *as*] *gave me directions.*

Glossary of usage

as, like In formal speech and writing, *like* should not introduce a main clause (with a subject and a verb) because it is a preposition. The preferred choice is *as* or *as if*: *The plan succeeded as* [not *like*] *we hoped. It seemed as if* [not *like*] *it might fail. Other plans like it have failed.*

as, than In comparisons, *as* and *than* precede a pronoun when it is a subject: *I love you more than he* [*loves you*]. *As* and *than* precede a pronoun when it is an object: *I love you as much as* [*I love*] *him*. (See also 31.4.3.)

assure, ensure, insure *Assure* means "to promise": *He assured us that we would miss the traffic. Ensure* and *insure* are often used interchangeably to mean "make certain," but some reserve *insure* for matters of legal and financial protection and use *ensure* for more general meanings: *We left early to ensure that we would miss the traffic. It's expensive to insure yourself against floods.*

at The use of *at* after *where* is wordy and should be avoided: *Where are you meeting him?* is preferable to *Where are you meeting him at?*

awful, awfully Strictly speaking, *awful* means "awe-inspiring." As intensifiers meaning "very" or "extremely" (*He tried awfully hard*), *awful* and *awfully* should be avoided in formal speech or writing.

a while, awhile *Awhile* is an adverb; *a while* is an article and a noun: *I will be gone awhile* [not *a while*]. *I will be gone for a while* [not *awhile*].

bad, badly In formal speech and writing, *bad* should be used only as an adjective; the adverb is *badly*: *He felt bad because his tooth ached badly.* In *He felt bad*, the verb *felt* is a linking verb and the adjective *bad* describes the subject. (See also 34.1.)

being as, being that Colloquial for *because*, the preferable word in formal speech or writing: *Because* [not *Being as*] *the world is round, Columbus never did fall off the edge.*

beside, besides *Beside* means "next to," while *besides* means "except," "in addition to," or "in addition": *Besides, several other people besides you want to sit beside Dr. Christensen.*

better, had better In *had better* (meaning "ought to"), the verb *had* is necessary and should not be omitted: *You had better* [not just *better*] *go.*

between, among See *among, between*.

bring, take Use *bring* only for movement from a farther place to a nearer one and *take* for any other movement: *First take these books to the library for renewal; then take them to Mr. Daniels. Bring them back to me when he's finished.*

but, hardly, scarcely These words are negative in their own right; using *not* with any of them produces a double negative (see 34.3): *We have but* [not *haven't got but*] *an hour before our plane leaves. I could hardly* [not *couldn't hardly*] *make out her face.*

but, however, yet Each of these words is adequate to express contrast. Don't combine them: *He had finished, yet* [not *but yet*] *he continued.*

can, may Strictly, *can* indicates capacity or ability, and *may* indicates permission or possibility: *If I may talk with you a moment, I believe I can solve your problem.*

censor, censure To *censor* is to edit or remove from public view on moral or some other grounds; to *censure* is to give a formal scolding: *The lieutenant was censured by Major Taylor for censoring the letters her soldiers wrote home from boot camp.*

center around *Center on* is more logical than, and preferable to, *center around*.

cite, sight, site *Cite* is a verb usually meaning "quote," "commend," or "acknowledge": *You must cite your sources. Sight* is both a noun meaning "the ability to see" or "a view" and a verb meaning "perceive" or "observe": *What a sight you see when you sight Venus through a strong telescope. Site* is a noun meaning "place" or "location" or a verb meaning "situate": *The builder sited the house on an unlikely site.*

climatic, climactic *Climatic* comes from *climate* and refers to the weather: *Recent droughts may indicate a climatic change. Climactic* comes from *climax* and refers to a dramatic high point: *During the climactic duel between Hamlet and Laertes, Gertrude drinks poisoned wine.*

complement, compliment To *complement* something is to add to, complete, or reinforce it: *Her yellow blouse complemented her black hair.* To *compliment* something is to make a flattering remark about it: *He complimented her on her hair. Complimentary* can also mean "free": *complimentary tickets.*

conscience, conscious *Conscience* is a noun meaning "a sense of right and wrong"; *conscious* is an adjective meaning "aware" or "awake": *Though I was barely conscious, my conscience nagged me.*

contact Avoid using *contact* imprecisely as a verb instead of a more exact word such as *consult, talk with, telephone,* or *write to.*

continual, continuous *Continual* means "constantly recurring": *Most movies on television are continually interrupted by commercials. Continuous* means "unceasing": *Some cable channels present movies continuously without commercials.*

could of See *have, of.*

credible, creditable, credulous *Credible* means "believable": *It's a strange story, but it seems credible to me. Creditable* means "deserving of credit" or "worthy": *Steve gave a creditable performance. Credulous* means "gullible": *The credulous Claire believed Tim's lies.* (See also *incredible, incredulous.*)

criteria The plural of *criterion* (meaning "standard for judgment"): *Our criteria are strict. The most important criterion is a sense of humor.*

data The plural of *datum* (meaning "fact"). Though *data* is often used as a singular noun, most careful writers still treat it as plural: *The data fail* [not *fails*] *to support the hypothesis.*

device, devise *Device* is the noun, and *devise* is the verb: *Can you devise some device for getting his attention?*

different from, different than *Different from* is preferred: *His purpose is different from mine.* But *different than* is widely accepted when a construction using *from* would be wordy: *I'm a different person now than I used to be* is preferable to *I'm a different person now from the person I used to be.*

differ from, differ with To *differ from* is to be unlike: *The twins differ from each other only in their hairstyles.* To *differ with* is to disagree with: *I have to differ with you on that point.*

discreet, discrete *Discreet* (noun form *discretion*) means "tactful": *What's a discreet way of telling Maud to be quiet? Discrete* (noun form *discreteness*) means "separate and distinct": *Within a computer's memory are millions of discrete bits of information.*

disinterested, uninterested *Disinterested* means "impartial": *We chose Pete, as a disinterested third party, to decide who was right. Uninterested* means "bored" or "lacking interest": *Unfortunately, Pete was completely uninterested in the question.*

don't, doesn't *Don't* is the contraction for *do not,* not for *does not*: *I don't care, you don't care, and he doesn't* [not *don't*] *care.*

due to the fact that Wordy for *because.*

eager, anxious See *anxious, eager.*

effect See *affect, effect.*

elicit, illicit *Elicit* means "bring out" or "call forth." *Illicit* means "unlawful": *The crime elicited an outcry against illicit drugs.*

emigrate, immigrate *Emigrate* means "to leave one place and move to another": *The Chus emigrated from Korea. Immigrate* means "to move into a place where one was not born": *They immigrated to the United States.*

ensure See *assure, ensure, insure.*

enthused Avoid using *enthused* colloquially to mean "showing enthusiasm." Prefer *enthusiastic*: *The coach was enthusiastic* [not *enthused*] *about the team's prospects.*

et al., etc. Use *et al.,* the Latin abbreviation for "and other people," only in source citations: *Jones et al.* Avoid *etc.,* the Latin abbreviation for "and other things," in formal writing, and do not use it to refer to people or to substitute for precision, as in *The government provides health care, etc.*

everybody, every body; everyone, every one *Everybody* and *everyone* are indefinite pronouns: *Everybody* [*everyone*] *knows Tom steals. Every one* is a pronoun modified by *every,* and *every body* a noun modified by *every.* Both refer to each thing or person of a specific group and are typically followed by *of*: *The commissioner has stocked every body of fresh water with fish, and now every one of the state's rivers is a potential trout stream.*

everyday, every day *Everyday* is an adjective meaning "used daily" or "common"; *every day* is a noun modified by *every*: *Everyday problems tend to arise every day.*

everywheres Nonstandard for *everywhere*.

except See *accept, except*.

except for the fact that Wordy for *except that*.

explicit, implicit *Explicit* means "stated outright": *I left explicit instructions.* *Implicit* means "implied, unstated": *We had an implicit understanding.*

farther, further *Farther* refers to additional distance: *How much farther is it to the beach?* *Further* refers to additional time, amount, or other abstract matters: *I don't want to discuss this any further.*

fewer, less *Fewer* refers to individual countable items (a plural count noun), *less* to general amounts (a noncount noun, always singular): *Skim milk has fewer calories than whole milk. We have less milk left than I thought.*

flaunt, flout *Flaunt* means "show off": *If you have style, flaunt it.* *Flout* means "scorn" or "defy": *Hester Prynne flouted convention and paid the price.*

flunk A colloquial substitute for *fail*.

fun As an adjective, *fun* is colloquial and should be avoided in most writing: *It was a pleasurable* [not *fun*] *evening.*

further See *farther, further*.

get This common verb is used in many slang and colloquial expressions: *get lost, that really gets me, getting on. Get* is easy to overuse: watch out for it in expressions such as *it's getting better* (substitute *improving*) and *we got done* (substitute *finished*).

good, well *Good* is an adjective, and *well* is nearly always an adverb: *Larry's a good dancer. He and Linda dance well together. Well* is properly used as an adjective only to refer to health: *You look well.* (*You look good*, in contrast, means "Your appearance is pleasing.")

good and Colloquial for "very": *I was very* [not *good and*] *tired.*

had better See *better, had better*.

had ought The *had* is unnecessary and should be omitted: *He ought* [not *had ought*] *to listen to his mother.*

hanged, hung Though both are past-tense forms of *hang*, *hanged* is used to refer to executions and *hung* is used for all other meanings: *Tom Dooley was hanged* [not *hung*] *from a white oak tree. I hung* [not *hanged*] *the picture you gave me.*

hardly See *but, hardly, scarcely*.

have, of Use *have*, not *of*, after helping verbs such as *could, should, would, may, must,* and *might*: *You should have* [not *should of*] *told me.*

he, she; he/she Convention has allowed the use of *he* to mean "he or she": *After the infant learns to creep, he progresses to crawling.*

However, many writers today consider this usage inaccurate and unfair because it seems to exclude females. The construction *he/she*, one substitute for *he*, is awkward and objectionable to most readers. The better choice is to make *he* plural, to rephrase, or, sparingly, to use *he or she*. For instance: *After infants learn to creep, they progress to crawling. After learning to creep, the infant progresses to crawling. After the infant learns to creep, he or she progresses to crawling.* (See also 19.2.2 and 32.3.)

herself, himself See *myself, herself, himself, yourself, ourselves, themselves, yourselves.*

hisself Nonstandard for *himself.*

hopefully *Hopefully* means "with hope": *Freddy waited hopefully for a glimpse of Eliza.* The use of *hopefully* to mean "it is to be hoped," "I hope," or "let's hope" is now very common; but try to avoid it in writing because many readers continue to object strongly to the usage. *I hope* [not *Hopefully*] *the law will pass.*

idea, ideal An *idea* is a thought or conception. The noun *ideal* is a model of perfection or a goal. *Ideal* should not be used in place of *idea*: *The idea* [not *ideal*] *of the play is that our ideals often sustain us.*

if, whether For clarity, use *whether* rather than *if* when you are expressing an alternative: *If I laugh hard, people can't tell whether I'm crying.*

illicit See *elicit, illicit.*

illusion See *allusion, illusion.*

immigrate, emigrate See *emigrate, immigrate.*

implicit See *explicit, implicit.*

imply, infer Writers or speakers *imply*, meaning "suggest": *Jim's letter implies he's having a good time.* Readers or listeners *infer*, meaning "conclude": *From Jim's letter I infer he's having a good time.*

incredible, incredulous *Incredible* means "unbelievable," while *incredulous* means "unbelieving": *When Nancy heard Dennis's incredible story, she was frankly incredulous.* (See also *credible, creditable, credulous.*)

individual, person, party *Individual* should refer to a single human being in contrast to a group or should stress uniqueness: *The US Constitution places strong emphasis on the rights of the individual.* For other meanings *person* is preferable: *What person* [not *individual*] *wouldn't want the security promised in that advertisement? Party* means "group" (*Can you seat a party of four for dinner?*) and should not be used to refer to an individual except in legal documents. (See also *people, persons.*)

infer See *imply, infer.*

in regards to Nonstandard for *in regard to, as regards,* or *regarding.*

inside of, outside of The *of* is unnecessary when *inside* and *outside* are used as prepositions: *Stay inside* [not *inside of*] *the house. The decision is outside* [not *outside of*] *my authority. Inside of* may refer colloquially to time, though in formal English *within* is preferred: *The law was passed within* [not *inside of*] *a year.*

insure See *assure, ensure, insure.*

irregardless Nonstandard for *regardless.*

is, are See *are, is.*

is because See *reason is because.*

is when, is where These are faulty constructions in sentences that define: *Adolescence is a stage* [not *is when a person is*] *between childhood and adulthood. Socialism is a system in which* [not *is where*] *government owns the means of production.* (See also 38.1.2.)

its, it's *Its* is the pronoun *it* in the possessive case: *That plant is losing its leaves. It's* is a contraction for *it is* or *it has: It's* [*It is*] *likely to die. It's* [*It has*] *got a fungus.* Many people confuse *it's* and *its* because possessives are most often formed with *-'s;* but the possessive *its,* like *his* and *hers,* never takes an apostrophe.

-ize, -wise The suffix *-ize* forms a verb: *revolutionize, immunize.* The suffix *-wise* forms an adverb: *clockwise, otherwise, likewise.* Avoid the two suffixes except in established words: *I'm highly sensitive* [not *sensitized*] *to that kind of criticism. Financially* [not *Moneywise*], *it's a good time to buy real estate.*

kind of, sort of, type of In formal speech and writing, avoid using *kind of* or *sort of* to mean "somewhat": *He was rather* [not *kind of*] *tall.*

Kind, sort, and *type* are singular and take singular adjectives and verbs: *This kind of dog is easily trained.* Agreement errors often occur when the singular *kind, sort,* or *type* is combined with the plural adjective *these* or *those: These kinds* [not *kind*] *of dogs are easily trained. Kind, sort,* and *type* should be followed by *of* but not by *a: I don't know what type of* [not *type* or *type of a*] *dog that is.*

Use *kind of, sort of,* or *type of* only when the word *kind, sort,* or *type* is important: *That was a strange* [not *strange sort of*] *statement.*

lay, lie *Lay* means "put" or "place" and takes a direct object: *We could lay the tablecloth in the sun.* Its main forms are *lay, laid, laid. Lie* means "recline" or "be situated" and does not take an object: *I lie awake at night. The town lies due east of the river.* Its main forms are *lie, lay, lain.* (See also 26.2.)

leave, let *Leave* and *let* are interchangeable only when followed by *alone: Leave me alone* is the same as *Let me alone.* Otherwise, *leave* means "depart" and *let* means "allow": *Jill would not let Sue leave.*

less See *fewer, less.*

liable See *apt, liable, likely.*

lie, lay See *lay, lie.*

like, as See *as, like.*

like, such as Strictly, *such as* precedes an example that represents a larger subject, whereas *like* indicates that two subjects are comparable: *Steve has recordings of many great saxophonists such as Ben Webster and Lee Konitz. Steve wants to be a great jazz saxophonist like Ben Webster and Lee Konitz.*

likely See *apt, liable, likely.*

literally This word means "actually" or "just as the words say," and it should not be used to qualify or intensify expressions whose words are not to be taken at face value. The sentence *He was literally climbing the walls* describes a person behaving like an insect, not a person who is restless or anxious. For the latter meaning, *literally* should be omitted.

lose, loose *Lose* means "mislay": *Did you lose a brown glove? Loose* means "unrestrained" or "not tight": *Ann's canary got loose. Loose* also can function as a verb meaning "let loose": *They loose the dogs as soon as they spot the bear.*

lots, lots of Avoid these colloquialisms in college or business writing. Use *very many, a great many,* or *much* instead.

may, can See *can, may.*

may be, maybe *May be* is a verb, and *maybe* is an adverb meaning "perhaps": *Tuesday may be a legal holiday. Maybe we won't have classes.*

may of See *have, of.*

media *Media* is the plural of *medium* and takes a plural verb: *All the news media are increasingly visual.* The singular verb is common, even in the media, but many readers prefer the plural verb and it is always correct.

might of See *have, of.*

moral, morale As a noun, *moral* means "ethical conclusion" or "lesson": *The moral of the story escapes me. Morale* means "spirit" or "state of mind": *Victory improved the team's morale.*

most, almost See *almost, most.*

must of See *have, of.*

myself, herself, himself, yourself, ourselves, themselves, yourselves Avoid using the *-self* words in place of personal pronouns: *No one except me* [not *myself*] *saw the accident. Michiko and I* [not *myself*] *planned the ceremony.* The *-self* words have two uses: they emphasize a noun or other pronoun (*Paul did the work himself; he himself said so*), or they indicate that the sentence subject also receives the action of the verb: *I drove myself to the hospital.* (See also 31.1 on the unchanging forms of the *-self* pronouns in standard American English.)

nowheres Nonstandard for *nowhere.*

number See *amount, number.*

of, have See *have, of.*

off of *Of* is unnecessary. Use *off* or *from* rather than *off of*: *He jumped off* [or *from*, not *off of*] *the roof.*

OK, O.K., okay All three spellings are acceptable, but avoid this colloquial term in formal speech and writing.

on account of Wordy for *because of.*

on the other hand This expression of contrast should be preceded by its mate, *on the one hand*: *On the one hand, we hoped for snow. On the other hand, we worried that it would harm the animals.* However, the two combined can be unwieldy, and a simple *but, however, yet,* or *in contrast* often suffices: *We hoped for snow, yet we worried that it would harm the animals.*

outside of See *inside of, outside of.*

owing to the fact that Wordy for *because.*

party See *individual, person, party.*

people, persons In formal usage, *people* refers to a general group: *We the people of the United States. . . . Persons* refers to a collection of individuals: *Will the person or persons who saw the accident please notify. . . .* Except when emphasizing individuals, prefer *people* to *persons.* (See also *individual, person, party.*)

per Except in technical writing, an English equivalent is usually preferable to the Latin *per*: *$10 an* [not *per*] *hour*; *sent by* [not *per*] *parcel post*; *requested in* [not *per* or *as per*] *your letter.*

percent (per cent), percentage Both these terms refer to fractions of one hundred. *Percent* always follows a number (*40 percent of the voters*), and the word is often used instead of the symbol (%) in nontechnical writing. *Percentage* stands alone (*the percentage of voters*) or follows an adjective (*a high percentage*).

person See *individual, person, party.*

persons See *people, persons.*

phenomena *Phenomena* is the plural of *phenomenon* (meaning "perceivable fact" or "unusual occurrence"): *Many phenomena are not recorded. One phenomenon is attracting attention.*

plenty A colloquial substitute for *very*: *The reaction occurred very* [not *plenty*] *fast.*

plus *Plus* is standard to mean "in addition to": *His income plus mine is sufficient.* But *plus* is colloquial when it relates main clauses: *Our organization is larger than theirs; moreover* [not *plus*], *we have more money.*

precede, proceed *Precede* means "come before": *My name precedes yours in the alphabet. Proceed* means "move on": *We were told to proceed to the waiting room.*

prejudice, prejudiced *Prejudice* is a noun; *prejudiced* is an adjective. Do not drop the *-d* from *prejudiced*: *I was fortunate that my parents were not prejudiced* [not *prejudice*].

pretty Overworked as an adverb meaning "rather" or "somewhat": *He was somewhat* [not *pretty*] *irked at the suggestion.*

previous to, prior to Wordy for *before.*

principal, principle *Principal* is an adjective meaning "foremost" or "major," a noun meaning "chief official," or, in finance, a noun meaning "capital sum." *Principle* is a noun only, meaning "rule" or "axiom." *Her principal reasons for confessing were her principles of right and wrong.*

proceed, precede See *precede, proceed.*

question of whether, question as to whether Wordy substitutes for *whether*.

raise, rise *Raise* means "lift" or "bring up" and takes a direct object: *The Kirks raise cattle*. Its main forms are *raise, raised, raised*. *Rise* means "get up" and does not take an object: *They must rise at dawn*. Its main forms are *rise, rose, risen*. (See also 26.2.)

real, really In formal speech and writing, *real* should not be used as an adverb; *really* is the adverb and *real* an adjective: *Popular reaction to the announcement was really* [not *real*] *enthusiastic*.

reason is because Although colloquially common, this expression should be avoided in formal speech and writing. Use a *that* clause after *reason is*: *The reason he is absent is that* [not *is because*] *he is sick*. Or: *He is absent because he is sick*. (See also 38.1.3.)

respectful, respective *Respectful* means "full of (or showing) respect": *Be respectful of other people*. *Respective* means "separate": *The French and the Germans occupied their respective trenches*.

rise, raise See *raise, rise*.

scarcely See *but, hardly, scarcely*.

sensual, sensuous *Sensual* suggests sexuality; *sensuous* means "pleasing to the senses": *Stirred by the sensuous scent of meadow grass and flowers, Cheryl and Paul found their thoughts growing increasingly sensual*.

set, sit *Set* means "put" or "place" and takes a direct object: *He sets the pitcher down*. Its main forms are *set, set, set*. *Sit* means "be seated" and does not take an object: *She sits on the sofa*. Its main forms are *sit, sat, sat*. (See also 26.2.)

shall, will *Will* is a helping verb for all persons: *I will go, you will go, they will go*. The main use of *shall* is for first-person questions requesting an opinion or consent: *Shall I order a pizza? Shall we dance? Shall* can also be used for the first person when a formal effect is desired: *I shall expect you around three*. It is occasionally used with the second or third person to express the speaker's determination: *You shall do as I say*.

should of See *have, of*.

sight, site, cite See *cite, sight, site*.

since *Since* mainly relates to time: *I've been waiting since noon*. But *since* is also often used to mean "because": *Since you asked, I'll tell you*. Revise sentences in which the word could have either meaning, such as *Since I studied physics, I have been planning to major in engineering*.

sit, set See *set, sit*.

site, cite, sight See *cite, sight, site*.

so Avoid using *so* alone or as a vague intensifier: *He was so late*. *So* needs to be followed by *that* and a statement of the result: *He was so late that I left without him*.

somebody, some body; someone, some one *Somebody* and *someone* are indefinite pronouns; *some body* is a noun modified by *some*; and *some one* is a pronoun or an adjective modified by *some*: *Somebody ought to invent a shampoo that will give hair some body. Someone told Janine she should choose some one plan and stick with it.*

sometime, sometimes, some time *Sometime* means "at an indefinite time in the future": *Why don't you come up and see me sometime? Sometimes* means "now and then": *I still see my old friend Joe sometimes. Some time* means "a span of time": *I need some time to make the payments.*

somewheres Nonstandard for *somewhere*.

sort of, sort of a See *kind of, sort of, type of*.

such Avoid using *such* as a vague intensifier: *It was such a cold winter. Such* should be followed by *that* and a statement of the result: *It was such a cold winter that Napoleon's troops had to turn back.*

such as See *like, such as*.

supposed to, used to In both these expressions, the *-d* is essential: *I used to* [not *use to*] *think so. He's supposed to* [not *suppose to*] *meet us.*

sure Colloquial when used as an adverb meaning *surely*: *James Madison sure was right about the need for the Bill of Rights.* If you merely want to be emphatic, use *certainly*: *Madison certainly was right.* If your goal is to convince a possibly reluctant reader, use *surely*: *Madison surely was right.*

sure and, sure to; try and, try to *Sure to* and *try to* are the correct forms: *Be sure to* [not *sure and*] *buy milk. Try to* [not *Try and*] *find some decent tomatoes.*

take, bring See *bring, take*.

than, as See *as, than*.

than, then *Than* is used in comparisons, whereas *then* indicates time: *Holmes knew then that Moriarty was wilier than he had thought.*

that, which *That* introduces an essential element: *We should use the lettuce that Susan bought* (*that Susan bought* limits the lettuce to a particular lettuce). *Which* can introduce both essential elements and nonessential elements, but many writers reserve *which* only for nonessential: *The leftover lettuce, which is in the refrigerator, would make a good salad* (*which is in the refrigerator* simply provides more information about the lettuce we already know of). Essential elements (with *that* or *which*) are not set off by commas; nonessential elements (with *which*) are. (See also 40.4.)

that, which, who Use *that* for animals, things, and sometimes collective or anonymous people: *The rocket that failed cost millions. Infants that walk need constant tending.* Use *which* only for animals and things: *The river, which flows south, divides two countries.* Use *who* only for people and for animals with names: *Dorothy is the girl who visits Oz. Her dog, Toto, who accompanies her, gives her courage.*

their, there, they're *Their* is the possessive form of *they*: *Give them their money. There* indicates place (*I saw her standing there*) or functions as an expletive (*There is a hole behind you*). *They're* is a contraction for *they are*: *They're going fast*.

theirselves Nonstandard for *themselves*.

them In standard American English, *them* does not serve as an adjective: *Those* [not *them*] *people want to know.*

then, than See *than, then*.

these kind, these sort, these type, those kind See *kind of, sort of, type of*.

this, these *This* is singular: *this car* or *This is the reason I left*. *These* is plural: *these cars* or *These are not valid reasons*.

thru A colloquial spelling of *through* that should be avoided in all academic and business writing.

to, too, two *To* is a preposition; *too* is an adverb meaning "also" or "excessively"; and *two* is a number. *I too have been to Europe two times.*

too Avoid using *too* as a vague intensifier: *Monkeys are too mean.* If you do use *too*, explain the consequences of the excessive quality: *Monkeys are too mean to make good pets.*

toward, towards Both are acceptable, though *toward* is preferred. Use one or the other consistently.

try and, try to See *sure and, sure to; try and, try to*.

type of See *kind of, sort of, type of*. Don't use *type* without *of*: *It was a family type of* [not *type*] *restaurant*. Or better: *It was a family restaurant.*

uninterested See *disinterested, uninterested*.

unique *Unique* means "the only one of its kind" and so cannot sensibly be modified with words such as *very* or *most*: *That was a unique* [not *a very unique* or *the most unique*] *movie.*

usage, use *Usage* refers to conventions, most often those of a language: *Is "hadn't ought" proper usage? Usage* is often misused in place of the noun *use*: *Wise use* [not *usage*] *of insulation can save fuel.*

use, utilize *Utilize* can be used to mean "make good use of": *Many teachers utilize computers for instruction.* But for all other senses of "place in service" or "employ," prefer *use*.

used to See *supposed to, used to*.

wait for, wait on In formal speech and writing, *wait for* means "await" (*I'm waiting for Paul*) and *wait on* means "serve" (*The owner of the store herself waited on us*).

ways Colloquial as a substitute for *way*: *We have only a little way* [not *ways*] *to go*.

well See *good, well*.

whether, if See *if, whether*.

which, that See *that, which*.

which, who, that See *that, which, who*.

who's, whose *Who's* is the contraction of *who is* or *who has*: *Who's* [*Who is*] *at the door? Jim is the only one who's* [*who has*] *passed. Whose* is the possessive form of *who*: *Whose book is that?*

will, shall See *shall, will*.

-wise See *-ize, -wise*.

would be *Would be* is often used instead of *is* or *are* to soften statements needlessly: *One example is* [not *would be*] *gun-control laws.* *Would* can combine with other verbs for the same unassertive effect: *would ask, would seem, would suggest,* and so on.

would have Avoid this construction in place of *had* in clauses that begin with *if* and state a condition contrary to fact: *If the tree had* [not *would have*] *withstood the fire, it would have been the oldest in town.* (See also 28.1.)

would of See *have, of*.

you In all but very formal writing, *you* is generally appropriate as long as it means "you, the reader." In all writing, avoid indefinite uses of *you,* such as *In one ancient tribe your first loyalty was to your parents.* (See also 33.3.)

your, you're *Your* is the possessive form of *you*: *Your dinner is ready.* *You're* is the contraction of *you are*: *You're bound to be late.*

yourself See *myself, herself, himself, yourself*.

Glossary of Terms

This section defines the terms and concepts of basic English grammar.

absolute phrase A phrase that consists of a noun or pronoun plus the *-ing* or *-ed* form of a verb (a participle): *Our accommodations arranged, we set out on our trip. They will hire a local person, other things being equal.*

active voice The verb form used when the sentence subject names the performer of the verb's action: *The drillers used a rotary blade.* For more, see *voice*.

adjective A word used to modify a noun or pronoun: *beautiful morning, ordinary one, good spelling*. Contrast *adverb*. Nouns, word groups, and some verb forms may also serve as **adjective modifiers**: *book sale; sale of old books; the sale, which occurs annually; increasing profits.*

adjective clause See *adjective*.

adverb A word used to modify a verb, an adjective, another adverb, or a whole sentence: *warmly greet* (verb), *only three people* (adjective), *quite seriously* (adverb), *Fortunately, she is employed* (sentence). Word groups may also serve as **adverb modifiers**: *drove by a farm, plowed the field when the earth thawed.*

adverb clause See *adverb*.

agreement The correspondence of one word to another in person, number, or gender. Mainly, a verb must agree with its subject (*The chef orders eggs*), and a pronoun must agree with its antecedent (*The chef surveys her breakfast*). (See also Chapter 30 and Chapter 32.)

antecedent The word a pronoun refers to: *Jonah, who is not yet ten, has already chosen the college he will attend.* (*Jonah* is the antecedent of the pronouns *who* and *he*.)

appositive A word or word group appearing next to a noun or pronoun that renames or identifies it and is equivalent to it: *My brother Michael, the best horn player in town, won the state competition.* (*Michael* identifies which brother is being referred to; *the best horn player in town* renames *My brother Michael*.)

article The words *a, an,* and *the*. A kind of determiner, an article always signals that a noun follows. See 34.5 for the rules governing *a/an* and *the*.

auxiliary verb See *helping verb*.

case The form of a pronoun or noun that indicates its function in the sentence. Most pronouns have three cases. The subjective case is for subjects and subject complements: *I, you, he, she, it, we, they, who, whoever*. The objective case is for objects: *me, you, him, her, it, us, them, whom, whomever*. The possessive case is for ownership: *my/mine, your/yours, his, her/hers, its, our/ours, their/theirs, whose*. Nouns use the subjective form (*dog, America*) for all cases except the possessive (*dog's, America's*).

clause A group of words containing a subject and a predicate. A main clause can stand alone as a sentence: *We can go to the movies.* A subordinate clause cannot stand alone as a sentence: *We can go if Bridget gets back on time.* For more, see *subordinate clause*.

collective noun A word with singular form that names a group of individuals or things: *team, army, family, flock, group*. A collective noun generally takes a singular verb and a singular pronoun: *The army is prepared for its role*. (See also 30.5.1 and 32.4.)

comma splice A sentence error in which two sentences (main clauses) are separated by a comma without *and, but, or, nor,* or another coordinating conjunction. Splice: *The book was long, it contained useful information*. Revised: *The book was long; it contained useful information*. Or: *The book was long, and it contained useful information*. See Chapter 37.

comparison The form of an adjective *or* adverb that shows its degree of quality or amount. The positive is the simple, uncompared form: *small, clumsily*. The comparative compares the thing modified to at least one other thing: *smaller, more clumsily*. The superlative indicates that the thing modified exceeds all other things to which it is being compared: *smallest, most clumsily*. The comparative and superlative are formed either with the endings *-er/-est* or with the words *more/most* or *less/least*.

complement See *subject complement*.

complete predicate See *predicate*.

complete subject See *subject*.

complex sentence See *sentence*.

compound adjective See *compound construction*.

compound-complex sentence See *sentence*.

compound construction Two or more words or word groups serving the same function, such as a compound subject (*Harriet and Peter poled their barge down the river*), compound object (*John writes stories and screenplays*), compound predicate (*The scout watched and waited*) or parts of a predicate (*She grew tired and hungry*), and compound sentence (*He smiled, and I laughed*). (See 25.1.) Compound words include nouns (*roommate, strip-mining*) and adjectives (*two-year-old, downtrodden*).

compound object See *compound construction*.

compound sentence See *sentence*.

compound subject See *compound construction*.

conditional statement A statement expressing a condition contrary to fact and using the subjunctive mood of the verb: *If she were mayor, the unions would cooperate*.

conjunction A word that links and relates parts of a sentence. See *coordinating conjunction* (*and, but,* etc.), *correlative conjunction* (*either . . . or, both . . . and,* etc.), and *subordinating conjunction* (*because, if,* etc.).

conjunctive adverb A word such as *besides*, *however*, or *therefore* that can relate two ideas: *We had hoped to own a house by now; however, prices are still too high*. (See 37.2.1 for a list of conjunctive adverbs.) When main clauses are related by a conjunctive adverb, they must be separated by a semicolon or a period to prevent a comma splice or a fused sentence. (See Chapter 37.)

contraction A condensed expression, with an apostrophe replacing the missing letters: *doesn't* (*does not*), *we'll* (*we will*).

coordinating conjunction A word linking words or word groups serving the same function: *The dog and cat sometimes fight, but they usually get along.* The coordinating conjunctions are *and, but, or, nor, for, so, yet.*

coordination The linking of words or word groups that are of equal importance, usually with a coordinating conjunction. *He and I laughed, but she was not amused.* Contrast *subordination.*

correlative conjunction Two or more connecting words that work together to link words or word groups serving the same function: *Both Michiko and June signed up, but neither Stan nor Carlos did.* The correlatives include *both . . . and, just as . . . so, not only . . . but also, not . . . but, either . . . or, neither . . . nor, whether . . . or, as . . . as.*

count noun A word that names a person, place, or thing that can be counted (and so may appear in plural form): *camera/cameras, river/rivers, child/children.*

dangling modifier A modifier that does not sensibly describe anything in its sentence. Dangling: *Having arrived late, the concert had already begun.* Revised: *Having arrived late, we found that the concert had already begun.* See 35.2.

demonstrative pronoun A word such as *this, that, these, those,* or *such* that identifies or points to a noun: *This is the problem.*

determiner A word such as *a, an, the, my,* and *your* that indicates that a noun follows. See also *article.*

direct address A construction in which a word or phrase indicates the person or group spoken to: *Have you finished, John? Farmers, unite.*

direct object A noun or pronoun that identifies who or what receives the action of a verb: *Education opens doors.* For more, see *object* and *predicate.*

direct question A sentence asking a question and concluding with a question mark: *Do they know we are watching?* Contrast *indirect question.*

direct quotation Repetition of what someone has written or said, using the exact words of the original and enclosing them in quotation marks: *Feinberg writes, "The reasons are both obvious and sorry."*

double negative A nonstandard form consisting of two negative words used in the same construction so that they effectively cancel each other: *I don't have no money.* Rephrase as *I have no money* or *I don't have any money.* (See also 34.3.)

ellipsis The omission of a word or words from a quotation, indicated by the three spaced periods of an ellipsis mark: *"all . . . are created equal."* (See also 45.3.)

essential element A word or word group that is necessary to the meaning of the sentence because it limits the word it refers to: removing it would leave the meaning unclear or too general. Essential elements are *not* set off by commas: *Dorothy's companion the Scarecrow lacks a brain. The man who called about the apartment said he'd try again.* Contrast *nonessential element.* (See also 40.4.)

expletive construction A sentence that postpones the subject by beginning with *there* or *it* and a form of *be*: *It is impossible to get a ticket. There are no more seats available.*

first person See *person*.

fused sentence (run-on sentence) A sentence error in which two complete sentences (main clauses) are joined with no punctuation or connecting word between them. Fused: *I heard his lecture it was dull.* Revised: *I heard his lecture; it was dull.* See Chapter 37.

future perfect tense The verb tense expressing an action that will be completed before another future action: *They will have heard by then.* For more, see *tense*.

future tense The verb tense expressing action that will occur in the future: *They will hear soon.* For more, see *tense*.

gender The classification of nouns or pronouns as masculine (*he, boy*), feminine (*she, woman*), or neuter (*it, computer*).

generic he *He* used to mean *he or she.* Avoid *he* when you intend either or both genders. See 19.2.2 and 32.3.

generic noun A noun that does not refer to a specific person or thing: *Any person may come. A student needs good work habits. A school with financial problems may shortchange its students.* A singular generic noun takes a singular pronoun (*he, she,* or *it*). (See also *indefinite pronoun* and 32.3.)

gerund A verb form that ends in *-ing* and functions as a noun: *Running is ideal for getting exercise year round.* For more, see *verbals and verbal phrases*.

gerund phrase See *verbals and verbal phrases*.

helping verb (auxiliary verb) A verb used with another verb to convey time, possibility, obligation, and other meanings: *You should write a letter. You have written other letters.* The modals are *be able to, be supposed to, can, could, had better, had to, may, might, must, ought to, shall, should, used to, will, would.* The other helping verbs are forms of *be, have,* and *do.* (See also 26.4.)

idiom An expression that is peculiar to a language and that may not make sense if taken literally: *bide your time, by and large, put up with.*

imperative See *mood*.

indefinite pronoun A word that stands for a noun and does not refer to a specific person or thing. A few indefinite pronouns are plural (*both, few, many, several*) or may be singular or plural (*all, any, more, most, none, some*). But most are only singular (*anybody, anyone, anything, each, either, everybody, everyone, everything, neither, nobody, no one, nothing, one, somebody, someone, something*). The singular indefinite pronouns take singular verbs and are referred to by singular pronouns: *Something makes its presence felt.* (See also *generic noun* and 30.4 and 32.3.)

indicative See *mood*.

indirect object A noun or pronoun that identifies to whom or what something is done: *Give them the award.* For more, see *object* and *predicate*.

indirect question A sentence reporting a question and ending with a period: *Writers wonder whether their work must always be lonely.* Contrast *direct question*.

indirect quotation A report of what someone has written or said, but not using the exact words of the original and not enclosing the words in quotation marks. Quotation: *"Events have controlled me."* Indirect quotation: *Lincoln said that events had controlled him.*

infinitive A verb form consisting of the verb's dictionary form plus *to*: *to swim, to write.* For more, see *verbals and verbal phrases.*

infinitive phrase See *verbals and verbal phrases.*

intensive pronoun A personal pronoun plus *-self* or *-selves* that emphasizes a noun or other pronoun: *He himself asked that question.*

interjection A word standing by itself or inserted in a construction to exclaim: *Hey! What the heck did you do that for?*

interrogative pronoun A word that begins a question and serves as the subject or object of the sentence. The interrogative pronouns are *who, whom, whose, which,* and *what. Who received the flowers? Whom are they for?*

intransitive verb A verb that does not require a following word (direct object) to complete its meaning: *Mosquitoes buzz. The hospital may close.* For more, see *predicate.*

irregular verb See *verb forms.*

linking verb A verb that links, or connects, a subject and a word that renames or describes the subject (a subject complement): *They are golfers. You seem lucky.* The linking verbs are the forms of *be*, the verbs of the senses (*look, sound, smell, feel, taste*), and a few others (*appear, become, grow, prove, remain, seem, turn*). For more, see *predicate.*

main clause A word group that contains a subject and a predicate, does not begin with a subordinating word, and may stand alone as a sentence: *The president was not overbearing.* For more, see *clause.*

main verb The part of a verb phrase that carries the principal meaning: *had been walking, could happen, was chilled.* Contrast *helping verb.*

misplaced modifier A modifier whose position makes unclear its relation to the rest of the sentence. Misplaced: *The children played with firecrackers that they bought illegally in the field.* Revised: *The children played in the field with firecrackers that they bought illegally.*

modal See *helping verb.*

modifier Any word or word group that limits or qualifies the meaning of another word or word group. Modifiers include adjectives and adverbs as well as words and word groups that act as adjectives and adverbs.

mood The form of a verb that shows how the speaker views the action. The indicative mood, the most common, is used to make statements or ask questions: *The play will be performed Saturday. Did you get tickets?* The imperative mood gives a command: *Please get good seats. Avoid the top balcony.* The subjunctive mood expresses a wish, a condition contrary to fact, a recommendation, or a request: *I wish George were coming with us. If he were here, he'd come. I suggested that he come. The host asked that he be here.*

noncount noun A word that names a person, place, or thing and that is not considered countable in English (and so does not appear in plural form): *confidence, information, silver, work*. See 34.5 for a longer list.

nonessential appositive See *nonessential element*.

nonessential element A word or word group that does not limit the word it refers to and that is not necessary to the meaning of the sentence. Nonessential elements are usually set off by commas: *Sleep, which we all need, occupies a third of our lives. His wife, Patricia, is a chemist.* Contrast *essential element*. (See also 40.4.)

nonessential modifier See *nonessential element*.

nonessential phrase See *nonessential element*.

nonrestrictive element See *nonessential element*.

noun A word that names a person, place, thing, quality, or idea: *Maggie, Alabama, clarinet, satisfaction, socialism.* See also *collective noun, count noun, generic noun, noncount noun,* and *proper noun*.

noun clause See *subordinate clause*.

number The form of a word that indicates whether it is singular or plural. Singular: *I, he, this, child, runs, hides*. Plural: *we, they, these, children, run, hide*.

object A noun or pronoun that receives the action of or is influenced by another word. A direct object receives the action of a verb or verbal and usually follows it: *We watched the stars*. An indirect object tells for or to whom something is done: *Reiner bought us tapes*. An object of a preposition usually follows a preposition: *They went to New Orleans*.

objective case The form of a pronoun when it is the object of a verb (*call him*) or the object of a preposition (*for us*). For more, see *case*.

object of preposition See *object*.

parallelism Similarity of form between two or more coordinated elements: *Rising prices and declining incomes left many people in bad debt and worse despair*. (See also Chapter 17.)

parenthetical expression A word or construction that interrupts a sentence and is not part of its main structure, called *parenthetical* because it could (or does) appear in parentheses: *Mary Cassatt (1845–1926) was an American painter. Her work, incidentally, is in the museum.*

participial phrase See *verbals and verbal phrases*.

participle See *verbals and verbal phrases*.

particle A preposition or adverb in a two-word verb: *catch on, look up*.

parts of speech The classes of words based on their form, function, and meaning: nouns, pronouns, verbs, adjectives, adverbs, conjunctions, prepositions, and interjections. See separate entries for each part of speech.

passive voice The verb form used when the sentence subject names the receiver of the verb's action: *The mixture was stirred*. For more, see *voice*.

past participle The *-ed* form of most verbs: *fished, hopped*. The past participle may be irregular: *begun, written*. For more, see *verbals and verbal phrases* and *verb forms*.

past perfect tense The verb tense expressing an action that was completed before another past action: *No one had heard that before*. For more, see *tense*.

past tense The verb tense expressing action that occurred in the past: *Everyone laughed*. For more, see *tense*.

past-tense form The verb form used to indicate action that occurred in the past, usually created by adding *-d* or *-ed* to the verb's dictionary form (*smiled*) but created differently for most irregular verbs (*began, threw*). For more, see *verb forms*.

perfect tenses The verb tenses indicating action completed before another specific time or action: *have walked, had walked, will have walked*. For more, see *tense*.

person The form of a verb or pronoun that indicates whether the subject is speaking, spoken to, or spoken about. In the first person the subject is speaking: *I am, we are*. In the second person the subject is spoken to: *you are*. In the third person the subject is spoken about: *he/she/it is, they are*.

personal pronoun *I, you, he, she, it, we,* or *they*: a word that substitutes for a specific noun or other pronoun. For more, see *case*.

phrase A group of related words that lacks a subject or a predicate or both: *She ran into the field*. *She tried to jump the fence*. See also *absolute phrase, prepositional phrase, verbals* and *verbal phrases*.

plain form The dictionary form of a verb: *buy, make, run, swivel*. For more, see *verb forms*.

plural More than one. See *number*.

positive form See *comparison*.

possessive case The form of a noun or pronoun that indicates its ownership of something else: *men's attire, your briefcase*. For more, see *case*.

possessive pronoun A word that replaces a noun or other pronoun and shows ownership: *The cat chased its tail*. The possessive pronouns are *my, our, your, his, her, its, their, whose*.

predicate The part of a sentence that makes an assertion about the subject. A predicate must contain a verb and may contain modifiers, objects of the verb, and complements. The simple predicate consists of the verb and its helping verbs: *A wiser person would have made a different decision*. The complete predicate includes the simple predicate and any modifiers, objects, and complements: *A wiser person would have made a different decision*. See also *intransitive verb, linking verb,* and *transitive verb*. (See also 23.1.)

preposition A word that forms a noun or pronoun (plus any modifiers) into a prepositional phrase: *about love, down the steep stairs*. The common prepositions include: *about, before, by, during, for, from, in, on, to, with,* and many others. (See 22.3.1.)

prepositional phrase A word group consisting of a preposition and its object. Prepositional phrases usually serve as adjectives (*We saw a movie about sorrow*) or as adverbs (*We went back for the second show*).

present participle The *-ing* form of a verb: *swimming, flying*. For more, see *verbals and verbal phrases*.

present perfect tense The verb tense expressing action that began in the past and is linked to the present: *Dogs have buried bones here before*. For more, see *tense*.

present tense The verb tense expressing action that is occurring now, occurs habitually, or is generally true: *Dogs bury bones here often*. For more, see *tense*.

principal parts The three forms of a verb from which its various tenses are created: the plain form (*stop, go*), the past-tense form (*stopped, went*), and the past participle (*stopped, gone*). For more, see *tense* and *verb forms*.

progressive tenses The verb tenses that indicate continuing (progressive) action and use the *-ing* form of the verb: *A dog was barking here this morning*. For more, see *tense*.

pronoun A word used in place of a noun, such as *I, he, everyone, who,* and *herself*. See also *demonstrative pronoun, indefinite pronoun, intensive pronoun, interrogative pronoun, personal pronoun, possessive pronoun, reflexive pronoun, relative pronoun*.

proper adjective A word formed from a proper noun and used to modify a noun or pronoun: *Alaskan winter*.

proper noun A word naming a specific person, place, or thing and beginning with a capital letter: *David Letterman, Mt. Rainier, Alaska, US Congress*.

reflexive pronoun A personal pronoun plus *-self* or *-selves* that receives the action of the verb (*He blamed himself for the accident*).

regular verb See *verb forms*.

relative pronoun A word that relates a group of words to a noun or another pronoun. The relative pronouns are *who, whom, whoever, whomever, which,* and *that. Ask the woman who knows all. This may be the question that stumps her*. For more, see *case*.

restrictive element See *essential element*.

run-on sentence See *fused sentence*.

-s form See *verb forms*.

second person See *person*.

sentence A complete unit of thought, consisting of at least a subject and a predicate that are not introduced by a subordinating word. A simple sentence contains one main clause: *I'm leaving*. A compound sentence contains at least two main clauses: *I'd like to stay, but I'm leaving*. A complex sentence contains one main clause and at least one subordinate clause: *If you let me go now, you'll be sorry*.

A compound-complex sentence contains at least two main clauses and at least one subordinate clause: *I'm leaving because you want me to, but I'd rather stay.*

sentence fragment An error in which an incomplete sentence is set off as a complete sentence. Fragment: *She was not in shape for the race. Which she had hoped to win.* Revised: *She was not in shape for the race, which she had hoped to win.* See 36.1.

series Three or more items with the same function: *We gorged on ham, eggs, and potatoes*.

simple sentence See *sentence*.

simple tenses See *tense*.

singular One. See *number*.

split infinitive The usually awkward interruption of an infinitive and its marker *to* by a modifier: *Management decided to not introduce the new product.* See 35.1.3.

squinting modifier A modifier that could modify the words on either side of it: *The plan we considered seriously worries me.*

subject In grammar, the part of a sentence that names something and about which an assertion is made in the predicate. The simple subject consists of the noun alone: *The quick, brown fox jumps over the lazy dog.* The complete subject includes the simple subject and its modifiers: *The quick brown fox jumps over the lazy dog.* See 23.1.

subject complement A word that renames or describes the subject of a sentence, after a linking verb. *The stranger was a man* (noun). *He seemed gigantic* (adjective).

subjective case The form of a pronoun when it is the subject of a sentence (*I called*) or a subject complement (*It was I*). For more, see *case*.

subjunctive See *mood*.

subordinate clause A word group that consists of a subject and a predicate, begins with a subordinating word such as *because* or *who*, and is not a question: *They voted for whoever cared the least because they mistrusted politicians.* Subordinate clauses may serve as adjectives (*The car that hit Edgar was blue*), as adverbs (*The car hit Edgar when it ran a red light*), or as nouns (*Whoever was driving should be arrested*). Subordinate clauses are *not* complete sentences.

subordinating conjunction A word that turns a complete sentence into a word group (a subordinate clause) that can serve as an adverb or a noun. *Everyone was relieved when the meeting ended.* Some common subordinating conjunctions are *because, even though, unless,* and *until.* (For a list, see 22.3.2.)

subordination Deemphasizing one element in a sentence by making it dependent on rather than equal to another element. Through subordination, *I left six messages; the doctor failed to call* becomes *Although I left six messages, the doctor failed to call* or *After six messages, the doctor failed to call.*

superlative See *comparison*.

tag question A question attached to the end of a statement and composed of a pronoun, a helping verb, and sometimes the word *not*: *It isn't raining, is it? It is sunny, isn't it?*

tense The form of a verb that expresses the time of its action, usually indicated by the verb's inflection and by helping verbs.

- The **simple tenses** are the **present** (*I race, you go*), the **past** (*I raced, you went*), and the **future,** formed with the helping verb *will* (*I will race, you will go*).
- The **perfect tenses,** formed with the helping verbs *have* and *had*, indicate completed action. They are the **present perfect** (*I have raced, you have gone*), the **past perfect** (*I had raced, you had gone*), and the **future perfect** (*I will have raced, you will have gone*).
- The **progressive tenses,** formed with the helping verb *be* plus the present participle, indicate continuing action. They include the **present progressive** (*I am racing, you are going*), the **past progressive** (*I was racing, you were going*), and the **future progressive** (*I will be racing, you will be going*).

(See 27.1 for a list of tenses with examples.)

third person See *person*.

transitional expression A word or phrase, such as *thus* or *for example*, that links ideas and shows the relations between them. (See 11.3.6 for a list.) When main clauses are related by a transitional expression, they must be separated by a semicolon or a period to prevent a comma splice or a fused sentence. See Chapter 37.

transitive verb A verb that requires a following word (a direct object) to complete its meaning: *We repaired the roof.* For more, see 23.2.

verb A word that expresses an action (*bring, change*), an occurrence (*happen, become*), or a state of being (*be, seem*). A verb is the essential word in a predicate, the part of a sentence that makes an assertion about the subject. With endings and helping verbs, verbs can indicate tense, mood, voice, number, and person. For more, see separate entries for each of these aspects as well as *verb forms*.

verbals and verbal phrases Verbals are verb forms used as adjectives, adverbs, or nouns. They form verbal phrases with objects and modifiers. A present participle adds *-ing* to the dictionary form of a verb (*living*). A past participle usually adds *-d* or *-ed* to the dictionary form (*lived*), although irregular verbs work differently (*begun, swept*). A participle or participial phrase usually serves as an adjective: *Strolling shoppers fill the malls.* A gerund is the *-ing* form of a verb used as a noun. Gerunds and gerund phrases can do whatever nouns can do: *Shopping satisfies needs.* An infinitive is the verb's dictionary form plus *to*: *to live.* Infinitives and infinitive phrases may serve as nouns (*To design a mall is a challenge*), as adverbs (*Malls are designed to make shoppers feel safe*), or as adjectives (*The mall supports the impulse to shop*).

A verbal *cannot* serve as the only verb in a sentence. For that, it requires a helping verb: *Shoppers were strolling.*

verb forms Verbs have five distinctive forms. The plain form is the dictionary form: *A few artists live in town today.* The *-s* form adds *-s* or *-es* to the plain form: *The artist lives in town today.* The past-tense form usually adds *-d* or *-ed* to the plain form: *Many artists lived in town before this year.* Some verbs' past-tense forms are irregular, such as *began, fell, swam, threw, wrote.* The past participle is usually the same as the past-tense form, although, again, some verbs' past participles are irregular (*begun, fallen, swum, thrown, written*). The present participle adds *-ing* to the plain form: *A few artists are living in town today.*

Regular verbs are those that add *-d* or *-ed* to the plain form for the past-tense form and past participle. **Irregular verbs** create these forms in irregular ways (see above).

verb phrase A verb of more than one word that serves as the predicate of a sentence: *The movie has started.*

voice The form of a verb that tells whether the sentence subject performs the action or is acted upon. In the active voice the subject acts: *The city controls rents.* In the passive voice the subject is acted upon: *Rents are controlled by the city.* (See also Chapter 29.)

Index

A

a, an
   capitalization conventions, 350
   determiner adjectives, 289
   use with count nouns, 290
   use with noncount nouns, 290–291
   use with proper nouns, 291
   when to use, 221
Abbreviations
   for articles in reference works (s.v), 463
   for book citations lacking publication information or pagination (n.p. or n.pag.), 391
   in e-mail and electronic communication, 31, 207
   for long names, 424
   misuses of, 356
   in nontechnical writing, 355–356
   for "and others" (et al.), 366, 378, 423–424, 459, 470
   for page number citations (p. or pp.), 377, 423, 427
   for paragraph citations (par., pars., sec., or secs.), 368, 423
   for states, 427
   for transitive (*tr.*) and intransitive (*intr.*) verbs, 239
   for undated works (n.d.), 437
   in URLs, 56
   uses of, 354
   uses of apostrophe in, 329, 331–332
   uses of periods in, 311–312
   for volume citations (vol.), 369
abide by/in, 217
about, 233
Absolute modifiers, 287
Absolute phrases
   comma with, 318
   overview of, 243
   subjects in, 231–232
Absolute statements, 121
Abstract words (abstraction), 216
Abstracts
   APA guidelines for abstracts of journal articles, 434
   applying APA paper format to, 441–442
   as source material, 67–68
Academic community
   communication with instructors and classmates, 30
   writing for academic audiences, 171–174
Academic integrity
   ethical use of source materials, 26
   plagiarism and, 151
Academic language
   common features of, 29
   formal use, 28–29
   strategies for writing academic genres, 26
   too casual vs. too wordy or awkward, 30
Academic research
   conducting, 60
   evaluating library sources, 80–81
   evaluating Web sites, 82, 86–87
   Web search strategies, 69–72
Academic Search Complete, 66
Academic writing
   abbreviations in source citations, 355–356
   academic language, 28–30
   analyzing the writing situation, 99
   arguments, 24
   avoiding interjections, 235
   avoiding slang and colloquial language, 206–208
   avoiding two-word verbs, 256
   common genres, 23
   communicating in the academic settings, 30–32
   concise, direct expression, 143
   convention for expressing numbers in written form (numerals), 357
   critical analysis, 46
   descriptive titles, 161
   design guidelines for online writing, 180

determining purpose and audience, 22–23
ethical use of source materials, 26–28
evaluating library sources in academic research, 80
grammar/spell checkers, 168
informative essays, 24–25
multimodal use of mediums, 174
overview of, 21
paragraph conventions and, 131
personal essays, 25
plagiarism and, 151
reading response exercise, 23–24
research papers/reports, 25–26
rules for capitalization in titles, 350
source documentation, 157
synthesis in, 47
Acknowledgment of sources. See Citations; Sources
Acronyms, 355
Active voice. See also Verb voice
changing passive to, 222
compared to passive voice, 194, 264
verb tense and, 257
when to use, 265
Actor, active and passive voice and, 265
Acts (of a play), numeric conventions, 358
AD (anno Domini), abbreviation of dates, 355
Ad hominem, fallacies in arguments due to evasion, 121
Address (forms of address to a person)
commas in direct address, 319
culture and language and, 212
use of names, 31
Addresses (electronic), 56, 348
Addresses (lectures)
audience and, 22
MLA style, 404
MLA works-cited guidelines, 404
Addresses (physical location)
commas in, 320
numeric conventions, 358
at, in, or *on* in expressions of place, 218

Adjective clauses
revising sentences with repeated elements, 307–308
types of subordinate clauses, 243–244
Adjective modifiers, 204, 319–320
Adjectives
adverb clauses, 244
adverbs modifying, 232
capitalization conventions, 350–352
comma use in, 314
commas between adjectives modifying same word, 319–320
comparative and superlative forms, 286–288
determiners, 289–292
double negatives, 288
functions of, 284–285
hyphenation with compound adjectives, 347
identifying, 232–233
infinitive phrases as, 242
nonessential phrases and clauses, 317
overview of, 284
participial phrases as, 241–242
participles as, 288, 241–242
prepositional phrases functioning as, 241
rules for arranging two or three adjectives before a noun, 295–296
use with linking verbs, 285–286
Adverb clauses, 244
Adverbs
adding interest by varying sentence beginnings, 204
avoiding awkward placement in sentence, 293–294
comparative and superlative forms, 286–288
double negatives, 288
functions of, 284–285
identifying, 232–233
infinitive phrases as, 242
nonessential phrases and clauses, 317
overview of, 284
placing of frequency, degree, and manner, 294–295

Adverbs (*continued*)
  prepositional phrases functioning as, 241
  revising sentences with repeated elements, 308
  semicolon use with conjunctive adverbs, 324–325
  use with linking verbs, 285–286
  verbs with particles, 255–256
Advertisements
  MLA style, 399
  selecting visuals, 175–176
Advocacy sites, evaluating Web sites, 84
African American Vernacular English, 206
Afterword, MLA style, 392–393
Agreement of pronouns and antecedents
  collective nouns and, 280–281
  indefinite pronouns and, 279–280
  in person, number, and gender, 277
  plural and singular forms, 277–278
Agreement of subject and verbs. See Subject-verb agreement
Aircraft, italics or underlining with names of, 354
Albums, MLA style for sound recording, 403
along with, 268
Alphabetical arrangement
  in APA reference list, 426
  in Chicago documentation, 457
  in CSE reference list, 472
  in MLA works cited list, 374
although, 198
American Psychological Association style. See APA style
Ampersands (&), 356
an. See *a, an*
Analysis. See also Critical analysis
  of content of online sources, 90
  critical response and, 38–39
  discovering and exploring ideas, 18
  of example of first draft, 112–114
  moving from description to analysis to interpretation, 19

patterns for development of central idea in paragraphs, 140
  of Web site content, 85–86
  of writing situation, 99–101
and
  capitalization conventions, 350
  comma use with transitional expressions, 318
  commas in main clauses linked by conjunctions, 313–314
  coordinating conjunctions signaling need for parallelism, 200
  plural pronouns, 278
  semicolon use in main clauses linked by coordinating conjunctions, 325
  subject-verb agreement and, 268–269
  using conjunctions to coordinate information in sentences, 196–197
AND (+), boolean operators in refining keywords, 62–63
AND, in custom searches, 70
Annotated bibliographies, 57–58
Annotation(s)
  of advertisement, 42
  in critical reading, 35–36
  overview of, 34–35
Anonymous works
  APA in-text citation, 424
  APA reference lists, 429
  Chicago documentation, 459
  MLA in-text citations, 367
  MLA works-cited, 379
Antecedents. See also Pronoun antecedents, 270
Anthologies
  Chicago documentation, 462
  MLA works-cited, 375–376, 389, 391–393
any, 287–288
APA style
  capitalization conventions, 350
  documenting source material, 151
  documenting sources, 157
  formatting final draft, 169
  overview of, 420–421
  paper format, 441–443
  research report, 443–452
  writing format for academic audiences, 173

APA style, in-text citations
  author citations, 422–425
  electronic or Web sources, 425
  indirect sources, 425
  writing, 422
APA style, reference lists
  abstracts of journal articles, 434
  articles in journals, 430–432
  articles in magazines, 433
  articles in newspapers, 433–434
  author citations, 428–429
  books, 434–435
  dissertations, 437
  government publications, 436
  preparing, 425–428
  reports, 436–437
  social media, 438
  visuals and media, 439–441
  Web publications, 436
  Web sources, 437–438
Apostrophes
  for contractions and abbreviations, 331–332
  punctuation errors, 166
  for showing possession, 328–331
  uses/misuses, 328–329
Appalachian English, 206
Appeals (to belief or needs)
  evidence in visual argument, 124
  rational, emotional, and ethical appeals in arguments, 119
  strength of visual argument, 126
  types of evidence, 117
Appositive phrases
  colon use, 327
  nonessential, 317
  overview of, 243
  pronoun case in, 276
  when not use commas in signal phrases, 321
Apps
  APA style, 440–441
  MLA style, 404
Argumentative statements, drafting, 105–106
Arguments
  acknowledging opposing views, 119–120
  appeal and strength of visual argument, 126

assumptions in visual argument, 125–126
claims in visual argument, 123
elements of, 115–117
engaging readers, 117
evidence in visual argument, 123–125
example, 127–130
fallacies, 120–122
logical thinking in, 117–119
organizing, 122–123
overview of, 114
rational, emotional, and ethical appeals in, 119
recognizing fallacies in visual argument, 127
types of, 24
visual, 123
Art. See Artwork
Articles (parts of speech)
  avoiding awkward placement of adverbs, 289
  capitalization conventions, 350
  with count nouns, 290
  with noncount nouns, 290–291
  with proper nouns, 291
  when to use, 221
Articles (written sources)
  APA style for abstracts of journal articles, 434
  APA style for articles in edited book, 435
  APA style for journal articles, 430–432
  APA style for magazine articles, 433
  APA style for newspaper articles, 433–434
  Chicago documentation, 459–461
  CSE citations, 473–474
  CSE reference list, 473–474
  CSE style for book and article titles, 472
  MLA paper format, 417–418
  MLA style for articles in journals, 379–382
  MLA style for articles in magazines, 384–385
  MLA style for articles in newspapers, 382–384
  MLA style for articles in reference work, 392

Articles (written sources) (*continued*)
   MLA style for collection of articles, 392
   MLA works-cited style, 363
Artwork. See also Graphics; Illustrations
   APA paper format, 443
   Chicago style, 464
   MLA style, 389, 398–399
   selecting visuals, 175–176
as
   parallelism in comparisons, 201
   pronoun case in comparisons, 276
as well as, 268
Assertions, turning judgment into, 40
Assumptions
   elements of arguments, 117
   interpreting text, 39
   in visual argument, 125–126
at
   in expressions of time, 217
   preposition use in exact language, 217–218
Audience
   academic language and, 29
   analyzing the writing situation, 99–100
   conceiving Web composition, 180
   designing documents for online audiences, 180
   determing for academic participation, 22–23
   elements of rhetoric, 8
   reading visuals, 41
   revision checklist, 160
   writing for academic audiences, 171–174
Audio. See also Visuals and media
   APA style, 368
   conceiving Web composition, 180–181
   CSE style, 475
   finding source material, 73–75
   MLA style, 364
   multimodal use of mediums, 174
   selecting, 175
   sound recordings, 402–403, 465
Authors
   APA in-text citation, 422–425
   APA reference lists, 427
   background information, 149
   Chicago documentation, 459
   CSE citations, 472–473
   CSE reference list, 472–473
   evaluating library sources, 79–80
   evaluating online sources, 88–89
   identifying author bias, 82
   identifying in Web sites, 84
   learning about, 34
   MLA works-cited, 378–379
   MLA works-cited entries, 363, 375
   MLA works-cited for government publications, 393
   MLA works-cited for Web sites, 394–396
   signal phrases and, 148
   source materials and, 56
   synthesizing text, 40
   writing in-text citations, 366–368
Auxiliary verbs. See Helping (auxiliary) verbs

B

Background information, integrating source material into text, 149
Bandwagon fallacy, 121
Bar charts. See also Graphics; Visuals and media
   selecting visuals, 175–177
   using media responsibly, 178
BC ("before Christ"), abbreviation of dates, 355
BCE ("before the common era), abbreviation of dates, 355
be
   adverbs of frequency always follow, 294
   form of, 232
   progressive tenses and, 259
   revising sentences with mixed meaning, 306
   when helping verbs are required, 250–252
because, 198
Begging the question, 120
between, 350
Biases
   evaluating library sources, 80
   identifying author bias, 82

identifying in Web sites, 84–85
in language, 209–210
observations and, 77
source materials and, 56
unfair uses in arguments, 119
Bible
  capitalization, 351
  italicizing or underlining conventions, 353
  MLA in-text citations, 370–371
Bibliographies
  annotations, 57–58
  APA style, 422
  Chicago style, 456–458
  developing working, 56–57
  finding reference works, 63
  information for creating, 58–59
  MLA style, 365
  software for, 158
  source information, 57
Blogs. See also Social media
  APA reference list, 438
  Chicago style, 464
  CSE reference list, 475
  designing for online audiences, 180
  evaluating online sources, 89
  finding source material, 72
  MLA works-cited, 397
  posting to, 183–185
Blu-ray discs
  Chicago style, 455
  finding source material, 75
  MLA style for film or video, 402
  MLA style for TV episodes, 400–401
Body
  APA paper format, 441
  of argument, 122
  introduction-body-conclusion pattern, 108
Boldface type, 174
Book review
  APA style, 433
  Chicago style, 461
Bookmarks, public searches and, 70
Books
  APA reference list, 434–435
  Chicago style, 461–463
  CSE style, 474
  CSE reference list, 472
  finding source material, 64–65, 68–69
  MLA paper format sample, 417
  MLA works-cited style, 363–364
  MLA works-cited style for books published prior to 1900, 390
  MLA works-cited style for complete books, 385–391
  MLA works-cited style for government publications, 393–394
  MLA works-cited style for parts of a book, 391–393
Boolean operators (AND/NOT/OR), refining keywords, 62–63
Borrowed material. See also Sources
  documenting, 156–158
  interpreting, 147–149
  introducing into text, 147
both.and
  correlative conjunctions stressing equality and balance, 201
  ways to coordinate information in sentences, 197
Brackets ([ ])
  conventions for handling quotes, 96
  indicating changes in quotations, 340
  in MLA paper format sample, 413–414
Break, in words, dash marking, 336
Brochures, MLA works-cited style. See also Publications, 405
Bros., uses of abbreviations, 356
Business writing
  avoiding interjections, 235
  avoiding slang and colloquial language, 206–208
  avoiding two-word verbs, 256
  convention for expressing numbers in written form (numerals), 357
  expressing numbers in written form, 357
  misuses of abbreviations, 356
  résumé, 103
but
  capitalization conventions, 350
  comma use with transitional expressions, 318

but (*continued*)
　commas in main clauses linked by conjunctions, 313–314
　coordinating conjunctions signaling need for parallelism, 200
　semicolon use and, 325
　using conjunctions to coordinate information in sentences, 196–197

C

can, 252–253
Capitalization
　considering readers with vision loss, 173
　conventions, 349
　identifying and correcting errors, 207
　overview of, 348
　of proper nouns and proper adjectives, 350–352
　of titles and subtitles, 350
Captions
　MLA style, 179
　writing, 179–180
　writing for academic audiences, 172
Cartoons/comic strips
　MLA style, 399
　selecting visuals, 175–176
Case
　common questions regarding, 276
　gerunds and, 277
　pronoun case. See Pronoun case
Cause-and-effect analysis, 142
CDs/CD-ROMs
　APA style, 440
　Chicago style, 455
　CSE style, 475
　finding source material, 75
　MLA style, 363, 392, 402
CE (common era), 355
Chapters (of a publication)
　APA reference list, 435
　numeric conventions, 358
Characters (in a dramatization), 43
Characters named as words, 332, 354
Charts
　finding visuals, 74
　MLA works-cited guidelines, 400
　multimodal use of mediums, 174
　selecting visuals, 175–177
　using media responsibly, 178
　using responsibly, 178
The Chicago Manual, 150, 457
Chicago style
　articles, 459–461
　authors, 459
　books and government publications, 461–463
　interviews, 466
　letters, 465–466
　notes and bibliographic entries, 456–458
　overview of, 453–455
　shortened notes, 466
　of sources, 157
　visuals and media, 464–465
　Web sources and social media, 463–464
Chronological organization
　of essays, 108
　of paragraphs, 134
Citations. See also Sources
　analyzing a revised draft, 163, 165
　APA. See APA style
　bibliography software and, 158
　checklist for avoiding plagiarism, 152
　Chicago. See Chicago style
　CSE. See CSE style
　documenting sources, 156–158
　examining final draft, 171
　information needs citation, 154–156
　information that does not need citation, 153–154
　Latin abbreviations in, 356
　managing sources, 28
　MLA. See MLA style
　online sources, 156
　placement of, 371–372
　punctuation of, 372
　summarizing text, 37
　using visuals and media responsibly, 178
　writing format for academic audiences, 173
Claims
　assumptions and, 117
　elements of arguments, 115–116

Index 509

evidence demonstrating validity of, 116–117
in visual argument, 123
Clarity and conciseness, editing for, 165
Class discussion. See also Discussion, 19–21
Classification, in paragraph development, 140–141
Classmates, communicating with, 30–31
Clauses. See also by individual type
  adjective, 243–244
  adverb, 244
  clear reference of pronoun to one antecedent, 282
  defined, 243
  main. See Main clauses
  nonessential, 317
  noun, 244
  subordinate. See Subordinate clauses
Clichés, avoiding, 219
Climatic organization, of paragraphs, 134
Co., uses of abbreviations, 356
Coaches
  instructor roles, 23
  readers as, 161
Coherence
  parallelism for achieving in paragraphs, 134–135
  qualities of paragraphs, 133–134
  revision checklist, 160
Collaboration, in development of ideas related to reading, 19–21
Collections, Anthologies
Collective nouns
  agreement with antecedent in person, number, and gender, 280–281
  identifying nouns, 230
  noncount nouns as, 271
Collective pronouns, 270–272
Colloquial language, 208
Colons (:)
  deleting unnecessary, 328
  for introducing and separating, 326–327
  outside quotation marks, 335
  overview of uses, 326
  semicolon compared with, 325

use before series or explanation, 326
when not use commas in signal phrases, 321
Color(s)
  considering readers with vision loss, 173
  writing format for academic audiences, 174
Combining sentences
  for conciseness, 225
  for variety, 203–204
Comic strips/cartoons, MLA style, 399
Comma splices
  correcting, 303–305
  identifying, 301–303
Commands
  imperative mood, 263
  use of exclamation points, 312
  uses of periods, 311
Commas (,)
  between adjectives modifying same word, 319–320
  in dates, addresses, place names, and long numbers, 320, 358
  deleting unnecessary, 321–323
  inside quotation marks, 335
  between items in a series, 319
  in main clauses linked by conjunctions, 313, 315
  overview of uses, 313–314
  parenthetical expressions and, 337–338
  punctuation errors, 166
  in quotations, 321
  semicolon use in clauses containing, 325
  setting off introductory elements, 315
  setting off nonessential elements, 315–319
  ways to coordinate information in sentences, 196
Commercial sites, evaluating Web sites, 84
Comments
  abbreviations for comments in parentheses, 356
  APA style, 438
  Chicago style, 464
  making annotations in critical reading, 35

Comments (*continued*)
  MLA style, 397
  on other's writing, 161–162
Common knowledge, 154
Common nouns
  capitalization, 351
  identifying, 230
Communication, CSE style for personal communication, 475
Communication, in academic settings, 30–32
Community
  academic, 30, 171–174
  audience and, 23, 99
Comparative form, adjectives and adverbs, 233, 286–288
Comparison and contrast
  cause-and-effect analysis, 142
  in introduction, 143
  overview of, 141
  process analysis, 142
Comparisons
  double, 287
  logical, 287–288
  in paragraph development, 141
  parallelism in, 201
  social media to other sources, 90
Complements
  correcting illogical equation using *be*, 306
  noun clauses as, 244
  object complement, 240
  subject complement, 239, 268–269, 273
Completeness
  adding needed words, 220
  logical comparisons, 287
  writing complete compounds, 220
Complex sentences, 245
Compound adjectives, 347–348
Compound antecedents, 278
Compound constructions
  deleting unnecessary commas, 322
  joining compound elements in sentence structure, 236
  prepositions in, 201
  writing complete compounds, 220
Compound numbers, uses of hyphenation, 347
Compound objects
  deleting unnecessary commas, 322
  pronoun case and, 273–274
Compound predicates, in sentence structure, 236
Compound sentences, 245
Compound subjects
  deleting unnecessary commas, 322
  pronoun case and, 273–274
  in sentence structure, 236
Compound words
  hyphenation and, 347
  uses/misuses of apostrophe, 331
Compound-complex sentences, 245
Computer apps. See Apps
Computer software. See Software
Computers
  keeping research journal, 52
  organizing ideas on, 108
  positioning footnotes, 458
  recording observations and insights, 77, 93
  style checker on, 219
  technical slang, 208
Conciseness
  avoiding unnecessary repetition, 224
  combining sentences, 225
  editing for, 165
  eliminating empty words, 223–224
  focusing on subjects and verbs, 221–222
  nouns made from verbs, 222–223
  overview of, 221
  of prose, 183
  revising modifier use, 224–225
  revising *there is* and *it is* contractions, 225
  rewriting jargon, 226
  ways to achieve, 222
Concluding elements, dashes with, 337
Conclusions
  colon use to introduce concluding explanation, 327
  conclusions to avoid, 146
  effective conclusions, 145
  examining final draft, 171
  introduction-body-conclusion pattern, 108

Index **511**

in literacy narrative example, 185
in MLA paper format sample, 415
oral presentations, 186–187
organizing arguments, 122
overview of, 144
revision checklist, 160
strategies for, 145
Concrete words, 216
Conditional sentences, 261–262
Conjunctions
 commas in main clauses linked by, 313, 315
 coordinating, 200, 234–235
 correlative, 201, 234–235
 deleting unnecessary commas, 322
 subject-verb agreement and, 269
 subordinating, 234, 244
 testing for sentence fragments, 299
 ways to coordinate information in sentences, 196–197
Conjunctive adverbs
 correcting comma splices and fused sentences, 304–305
 semicolon use with, 324–325
Connotation, 215
Consistency
 in paragraphs, 136
 pronoun use, 284
 of verb mood, 263
 of verb tenses, 260
 of verb voice, 266
Consonants, final, 346
Content
 considering and analyzing Web sites, 85–86
 evaluating online sources, 89, 90
 organizing Web sites, 182
 previewing for content cues, 33
Context
 elements of rhetoric, 8
 evaluating online sources, 88–89
 evaluating Web sites, 85–86
Contractions
 apostrophe uses, 331–332
 punctuation errors, 166
 revising *there is* and *it is* contractions, 225
 uses/misuses of apostrophe, 329
Contrary-to-fact clauses, 263

Contrast. See also Comparison and contrast
 patterns for development of central idea in paragraphs, 141
 phrases of, 318
Contributors, MLA style, 376
Coordinate adjectives
 commas between adjectives modifying same word, 319–320
 uses of commas, 314
Coordinating conjunctions
 capitalization conventions, 350
 commas in main clauses linked by conjunctions, 313–314
 correcting comma splices and fused sentences, 305
 guideline for combining main clauses, 303
 joining compound elements in sentence structure, 236
 list of, 234
 semicolon use in clauses containing commas, 325
 semicolons in main clauses not joined by, 324
 using parallelism for equal elements, 200
Coordination
 effective use of, 197–198
 of information in sentences, 196–197
 relating equal ideas, 197
Copied language, information that does need citation, 155
Copyrights
 information on copyright page, 387
 seeking permission to use source materials, 74, 181
 seeking permission to use visuals, 178
 Web sites, 475
Corporate (group) authors
 APA in-text citations, 424
 APA reference lists, 429
 MLA in-text citations, 367
 MLA list of works cited, 379, 394
Correlative conjunctions
 list of, 235
 for parallelism, 201
 ways to coordinate information in sentences, 197

could, 262
Council of Science Editors. See CSE style
Count nouns
  article use with, 290
  determiner adjectives and, 289
  determiner use with, 291–292
  identifying nouns, 230
Creator. See Publisher (creator)
Creole dialect, 206
Critical analysis
  critical response and, 38–39
  deciding how to respond, 46
  emphasizing synthesis, 47–48
  example, 48–50
  shaping, 46–47
  of text or visual, 24
  writing, 46
  writing to learn and, 13
Critical reading
  analysis key to, 18
  example, 35–36
  first read, reread, annotate, 34–35
  previewing, 33–34
  summarizing, 36–38
  techniques, 32–33
  writing to learn and, 13
Critical response
  analyzing, 38–39
  evaluating, 40
  interpreting, 39
  overview of, 38
  synthesizing, 39–40
Critiques. See Critical analysis
CSE style
  article citations, 473–474
  author citations, 472–473
  book citations, 474
  documenting sources, 157
  name-year citations, 470
  numbered text citations, 470–471
  overview of, 467–469
  reference lists, 471–472
  reports, 475
  visuals and media, 475
  Web and social media, 474–475
Culture and language issues
  adverb modifiers, 205
  adverb placement, 294
  arguments and, 115
  article use, 221
  attitudes towards criticism, 162
  capitalization conventions, 349
  choosing between *no* and *not*, 285
  clear reference of pronoun to one antecedent, 281–282
  collective nouns and plural form, 281
  combining main clauses, 303
  comma use in long numbers, 358
  conventions for organizing ideas, 108
  critical thinking and, 92
  determiner adjectives, 289
  dialects, 206–207
  English as a second language, 34
  ESL (English as a second language), 214
  expletive construction, 225
  eye contact and, 187
  forms of address, 212
  indirect questions, 311
  indirect objects, 240
  infinitives and gerunds, 242
  introductions, 143
  multilingual individuals, 30
  noncount nouns, 271, 347
  paragraph conventions, 131
  paraphrasing, 95
  plagiarism and, 151
  plurality of adjectives, 285
  prepositions, 217–218
  present and past participles, 242
  pronoun case, 273
  pronoun gender, 278
  proper use of subject in American English, 236
  reading critically, 33
  redundancy and, 224
  revising sentences with repeated elements, 307
  rules for arranging two or three adjectives before a noun, 295–296
  sentence subject, 299
  subject-verb agreement, 267–268
  synthesizing text, 40
  thesis statements, 106
  transitional expressions, 138
  transitive verbs in passive voice, 239
  two-word verbs, 256

Index 513

verb forms, 248
verb tense, 258–259
verb voice, 264
wordiness, 221
Cumulative sentences, 195–196

D

Dangling modifiers, identifying and correcting, 296–297
Dashes (--)
  punctuation inside quotation marks, 335–336
  use before series or explanation, 326
  uses of, 336–337
Data
  charting, 177–178, 443–444
  citing, 179
  as evidence, 123–125
  online sources, 88
  publication data, 58–59
  research papers/reports, 25
  Web site, 83–85
Databases
  abstracts, 67–68
  APA reference list, 434, 437
  article citations, 430–431
  Chicago documentation, 460–461
  CSE reference list, 473
  finding source material, 60–61
  image databases, 74
  list of helpful, 68
  periodical databases, 65–66
  searching, 66–67
  selecting, 66
Dates
  abbreviations, 355
  apostrophe uses, 331–332
  citing undated Web sources, 397
  commas in, 320
  CSE reference list, 472
  name-year style, 470
  numeric conventions, 358
  publication date, 377, 427
  uses of commas, 314
  uses/misuses of apostrophe, 329
Days of the week
  misuses of abbreviations, 356
  numeric conventions, 358
Decimal point, use in numbers, 358

Decimals, numeric conventions, 358
Deduction (deductive reasoning), 118–119
Definitions
  patterns for development of central idea in paragraphs, 140
  revising sentences with mixed meaning, 306
  singular verbs with definition of plural term, 272
Delivery, oral presentations
  practice and stage fright, 190
  visual aids, 188–189
  vocal and physical methods, 187
Demonstrative pronouns, 231
Denotation, 215
Dependent clauses. See Subordinate clauses
Description. See also Summary, 139
Descriptive titles, 160–161
Descriptors. See Keywords
Designing documents
  considering readers with vision loss, 173
  considering requirements and limits of writing situation, 178
  creating Web site, 181–183
  format writing for academic audiences, 171–174
  integrating visuals and media, 178–179
  making sure visuals and media support document, 178
  for online audiences, 180
  overview of, 171
  planning Web composition, 180–181
  posting to blogs or wikis, 183–185
  preparing portfolio of writings, 185
  selecting visuals and media, 174–177
  using visuals and media, 175–176
  writing captions and source notes, 179–180
Designing visual aids, for oral presentations, 188

Detail, creating variety by adding, 205
Determiners
  as adjectives, 289–292
  use with noun types, 291–292
Development
  of central idea in paragraph, 138–142
  of ideas related to reading, 19–21
  of reading processes, 11
  revision checklist, 160
Diagrams. See also Charts; Maps
  MLA works-cited guidelines, 400
  organizing Web sites, 182
  outlines and tree diagrams, 109–111
  selecting visuals, 176
Dialects
  ethnic groups, 206–207
  subject-verb agreement, 267–268
  verb forms, 248
  verb tense, 258
Dialog, format for, 333
Dictionaries
  American vs. British usage, 345, 353
  bibliographic, 84
  capitalization, 349
  choosing appropriate language, 206–208
  comparative and superlative forms and, 286
  denotations, 215–216
  ESL (English as a second language), 218
  for exact language, 213–215
  finding synonyms, 95
  looking up word meaning, 35, 224
  nouns and count nouns, 289
  openings to avoid, 144
  as reference work, 63
  spell checking with, 167–168
  syllable breaks, 348
  two-word verbs and, 256
  verb forms, 246, 248
Dictionary form. See Plain form
Digital artwork, MLA style, 399
Digital Object Identifier (DOI)
  APA reference lists, 427–428, 430–433
  Chicago style, 459–460
  f MLA works-cited, 377

Direct address, comma use in, 319
Direct messaging, Chicago documentation, 464
Direct objects
  active and passive voice and, 264
  basic sentence patterns, 238–240
  two-word verbs and, 256
Direct questions, punctuation of, 312
Direct quotations
  APA style, 423
  paraphrasing compared with, 94
  primary sources, 95–96
  quotation marks indicating, 332–334
  research, 52
  tests for, 96
Directories, public images, 74–75
Discussion
  in development of ideas related to reading, 19–21
  sharing responses to what you read, 11–12
Discussion groups
  APA reference list, 438
  Chicago documentation, 464
  MLA works-cited guidelines for social media, 398
Discussion lists (listserv/list), 72–73
Dissertations
  APA style, 437
  MLA style, 405
Division (analysis). See also Analysis, 140
do, 252
Documentation of sources
  APA. See APA style
  Chicago. See Chicago style
  CSE. See CSE style
  MLA. See MLA style
  overview of, 156–158
Documentation strategies, for writing academic genres, 26
Documents
  APA formats and design styles. See APA style
  Chicago formats and design styles. See Chicago style
  CSE formats and design styles. See MLA style

Index

designing. See Designing documents
MLA formats and design styles. See MLA style
visuals and media supporting, 178
DOI. See Digital Object Identifier (DOI)
Double comparatives or superlatives, 287
Double negatives, avoiding, 288
Double talk (doublespeak/weasel words), avoiding, 209
Double-space, MLA style, 374
Doubt, indicated by question mark within a parenthesis, 312
Drafts. See also Planning and drafting
analyzing first draft, 112–114
analyzing revised draft, 163–165
discovering what needs editing, 166
examining final draft, 169–171
final draft, 169–171
first draft, 111–112
making drafts of text summary, 37–38
revisions and, 159
DVDs
APA style, 439
Chicago style, 455, 466
CSE style, 475
finding source material, 75
MLA works-cited, 400–402

E

-e, spelling rules regarding final *e*, 345
each, 166
E-books, 461
Economics, synthesizing text, 40
-ed or *-d*, verb endings, 249–250
Editing. See also Revisions
checklist for, 165–166
for clarity and conciseness, 165
discovering what needs editing, 166–167
example of edited paragraph, 167
final draft and, 169–171
using grammar/style checkers, 168

using spell checkers, 167–168
Editions
Chicago style, 462
of literary works, 370
MLA style, 376, 388
Editors
APA style for books with editor, 435
Chicago style for books with editor, 462
CSE style for books with an editor, 474
MLA style for books with an editor, 388–389
ei vs. *ie*, spelling rules, 345
Either/or fallacy, 122
Electronic addresses. See URLs
Electronic communication
avoiding shortcuts, 207–208
E-books, 461
E-mail. See E-mail
Electronic sources
APA style, 425
MLA style, 367
Ellipsis marks(.)
conventions for handling quotes, 96
overview of uses, 338–340
Em dash, 336
E-mail
APA style, 438
Chicago style, 464
communicating in the academic settings, 31
finding source material, 72
MLA works-cited guidelines, 398
Emotional appeals
in arguments, 119
strength of visual argument, 126
Emphasis
coordination of information in sentences, 196–198
elements of visuals, 42
overview of, 193
sentence beginnings and endings, 194–196
subjects and verbs and, 193–194
subordination to distinguish main ideas, 198–199
Encyclopedias, reference works, 63–64, 392

End punctuation
  exclamation points, 312
  overview of, 311
  periods, 311–312
Endings, verb forms, 249–250
Endnotes, 373, 416
English
  culture and language. See Culture and Language issues
  styles for integrating source material into text, 150
English, standard American
  appropriate use of labels, 212–213
  biased language, 209–210
  choosing appropriate language, 206–207
  colloquial language, 208
  sexist language, 210–212
  slang, 208
  technical words and jargon, 208–209
  texting and electronic communication shortcuts, 207–208
English as a second language (ESL). See also Culture and language issues, 214, 218
Entertainment, reading for, 6
Episodes
  APA style for TV episodes, 439–440
  MLA style for TV episodes, 376, 400–401
Equal elements, parallelism for, 200–201
Error checking
  checklist for editing, 166
  identifying and correcting errors, 207
-*es* ending. See also -s ending
ESL (English as a second language). See also Culture and language issues, 214, 218
Essays. See also Research; Writing
  informative, 24–25
  paragraphs relating to whole, 131
  personal, 25
  in portfolio, 185
  schemes for organizing, 108–109
Essence, 3
Essential elements, 322–323

Ethical appeals
  in arguments, 119
  strength of visual argument, 126
Ethical use, of sources. See Sources, ethical use
Ethnicity
  dialects, 206–207
  using appropriate labels, 212
Euphemisms, 209
Evaluation
  critical response and, 40
  of source materials. See Sources, evaluating
  types of arguments, 24
  of visuals, 46
Evasions, fallacies in arguments due to, 120–121
everyone, 166, 269–270
Evidence
  appeals contributing to, 126
  assumptions and, 117
  in example argument, 128
  strategies for writing academic genres, 26
  supporting assertions, 40
  use of sources and, 146–147
  validity of claims, 116–117
  in visual argument, 123–125
Exact language
  concrete and specific words, 216
  dictionaries, 213–214
  expressing meaning and, 215–216
  figurative language, 218–219
  idioms with prepositions, 216–217
  overview of, 213
  spell checkers, 215
  thesauruses, 214
  trite expressions, 219
Examples
  evidence in visual argument, 124
  types of evidence, 116
Exclamation points (!)
  punctuation inside quotation marks, 335–336
  unfair uses in arguments, 119
Exclamation points, 312
Expert opinion
  evidence in visual argument, 124
  types of evidence, 117

Explanations
  colon use to introduce concluding explanation, 327
  dash uses, 337
  deleting unnecessary semicolons, 326
Explanatory statements, drafting thesis statement, 105–106
Expletive construction, 225
Extemporaneous, presentation delivery methods, 187
Eye contact, culture and language, 187

F

Fact checking, publications, 33
Facts
  distinguishing facts and opinions in critical reading, 35
  evidence in visual argument, 123
  types of evidence, 116
Factual relationships, conditional sentences, 261
Fallacies
  in arguments, 120–122
  errors in arguments, 120
  evasions, 120–121
  oversimplification, 121–122
  reductive fallacy, 121
  in visual argument, 127
Faulty predication, revising sentences with mixed meaning, 305–306
Favorites, public searches and, 70
Feedback, peer review and, 161–162
Figurative language (figures of speech), 218–219
Figure captions. See also Captions, 179, 409
Films
  APA style, 439
  Chicago style, 455, 465
  MLA style, 402, 417
Final draft
  example, 169–171
  formatting and proofreading, 169
First draft
  analyzing example of, 112–114
  maintaining momentum, 111–112
  starting, 111–112

First read, 34
Flow, creating Web sites, 183
Flowcharts, selecting visuals, 176
Folk literature, 154
Fonts. See Type fonts
Footnotes
  Chicago style, 456–458, 466
  MLA style, 373
for, 196
Foreign words
  for emphasis, 353–354
  italics or underlining conventions, 352–353
  MLA style, 157, 173, 365
  spelling rules, 345
Forewords, MLA style, 392
Formal outline, 110–111
Formal vs. informal usage, academic language, 28–29
Formats
  APA, APA style
  Chicago. See Chicago style
  CSE. See CSE style
  MLA. See MLA style
  writing for academic audiences, 171–174
Formatting, final draft, 169
Fractions
  numeric conventions, 358
  uses of hyphenation, 347
French, spelling rules for English words derived from, 346
Functional reading, 6
Fused sentences (run-on)
  correcting, 303–305
  identifying, 301–303
Future perfect tense, of regular verb, 258
Future progressive tense, 257, 260
Future tense, of regular verb, 257

G

Gender
  avoiding sexist language, 211–212
  pronoun and antecedent agreement, 277
General
  organizing via general and specific ideas, 108–109
  paragraph organization by general and specific, 134
General words, 216

Generalizations
  inductive thinking and, 118
  oversimplification due to, 121
  recognizing fallacies in visual argument, 127
Generic nouns, 279
Genres
  academic, 23
  analyzing the writing situation, 101
  identifying in planning and drafting phase, 103–104
  revision checklist, 160
  strategies for writing academic genres, 26
  of text, 8
Geographical names, 356
Gerunds
  case, 277
  gerund phrases, 242
  verbs with, 254–255
Google, 69, 71
Google Scholar, 61
Government publications
  APA style, 436
  Chicago style, 463
  finding source material, 73
  MLA style, 363–364, 393–394
Grammar
  academic language and, 29
  revising sentences with mixed grammar, 306–307
Grammar/style checkers, 168
Graphic works, MLA style, 389
Graphics
  charts. See Charts
  diagrams. See Diagrams
  illustrations. See Illustrations
  maps. See Maps
Graphs
  finding visuals, 74
  selecting visuals, 175–176, 177
  using media responsibly, 178
  using responsibly, 178
Greek, spelling rules for English words derived from, 346
Group authors. See Corporate (group) authors

H

Hanging indents
  APA style, 426
  word processor handling, 374
Hasty generalization
  oversimplification due to, 121
  recognizing fallacies in visual argument, 127
have
  modal helping verbs, 252–253
  when helping verbs are required, 252
he
  avoiding generic use for both genders, 212
  conventions of academic language, 29
  pronoun errors, 166
  pronoun use in paragraphs, 135–136
Headings
  APA paper format, 443
  parallelism used with, 201
  writing format for academic audiences, 174
Helping (auxiliary) verbs
  combining with main verb, 251–252
  list of, 232
  modals, 252–253
  passive verbs and, 264
  progressive tenses and, 259
  required, 250–251
  subject-verb agreement and, 268
  verb forms, 250–253
here, 268
Highlighting, writing format for academic audiences, 174
History
  styles for integrating source material into text, 150
  synthesizing text, 40
History, 70
Holidays, misuses of abbreviations, 356
Home page, Web site, 182
Homonyms
  choosing the right word for your meaning, 215
  pronunciation and spelling and, 343–344
however
  correcting comma splices and fused sentences, 304–305
  subordination to distinguish main ideas of sentence, 198
  ways to coordinate information in sentences, 196

Humanities, styles for integrating source material into text, 150
Hyphens (-)
  hyphenated numbers considered a single word, 357
  uses of, 347–348
Hypothesis, formulating for use in survey, 76
Hypothetical conditions, 263

I

Ideas
  discovering and exploring, 18–19
  identifying connections in critical reading, 35
  organizing in planning and drafting phase, 107–109
  summarizing text, 37
Idioms, with prepositions, 216–217
ie vs. *ei*, spelling rules, 345
if
  conditional sentences, 261
  hypothetical conditions, 263
  subordination to distinguish main ideas of sentence, 198
Illustration or support, in paragraph development, 139
Illustrations. See also Graphics
  APA style, 443
  MLA style, 389
Images. See also Visuals and media
  databases and directories, 74–75
  selecting, 176
  using responsibly, 178
  visual aids in oral presentations, 188
Imperative mood, verbs, 263
Impromptu, presentation delivery methods, 187
in
  in expressions of time, 217
  preposition use in exact language, 217–218
in addition to, 268
in contrast, 136
Inc., uses of abbreviations, 356
including, 328
indeed
  adding interest by varying sentence beginnings, 204
  ways to coordinate information in sentences, 196

Indefinite pronouns
  antecedent agreement, 279–280
  identifying pronouns, 230
  subject-verb agreement, 269–270
  uses/misuses of apostrophe, 328–329
  verb endings and, 249
Indention
  APA style, 426, 441
  MLA style, 374, 405–406, 409
  writing format for academic audiences, 173
Independent clauses. See Main clauses
Indicative mood, verb mood, 263
Indirect objects, 239–240
Indirect questions, uses of periods in, 311
Indirect quotations
  deleting unnecessary commas, 323
  not using quotation marks with, 333
  tests for, 96
Indirect sources
  APA style, 425
  MLA style, 369–370
Induction (inductive reasoning), 118
Inference, rhetorical reading strategies, 8, 10
Infinitive phrases, 242
Infinitives
  capitalization conventions, 350
  pronoun case in, 276
  verbs with, 254–255
Information
  coordination of information in sentences, 196–198
  expected at beginning of sentences, 195
  gathering from sources, 91–92
  integrating background information into text, 149
  relating equal ideas using coordination, 196–198
  that does not need citation, 153–154
  that needs citation, 154–156
Informational sites, evaluating Web sites, 83–84
Informative essays, academic genres, 24–25

-ing
  case before gerund, 277
  gerunds, 254
  progressive tenses and, 258
  when helping verbs are required, 250
Insertion, dash marking, 336
Insights, responding to source material, 93
Instant messaging, 29
Instructors
  communicating with, 30–31
  roles as readers, 22–23
Insults, unfair uses in arguments, 119
Intellectual property, 151
Interjections
  comma use in, 319
  identifying, 235
  use of exclamation points, 312
Internet. See also Web sources, 153
Interpretation
  moving from description to analysis to interpretation, 19
  reading arguments, 39
  visuals, 44
Interrogative pronouns, 230
Interruption, dash marking, 336
Interviews
  APA style, 433–434, 439
  Chicago style, 465–466
  MLA style, 401–402, 404
  personal interviews as primary research, 76
Intransitive verb
  basic sentence patterns, 238–239
  easily confused verb forms, 248–249
Introductions
  analyzing a revised draft, 163
  colon use, 326–327
  dash uses with introductory series, 337
  effective openings, 143–144
  introduction-body-conclusion pattern, 108
  MLA paper format, 409
  MLA style, 392
  openings to avoid, 144
  organizing arguments, 122
  organizing presentation, 186–187
  paragraphs and, 142
  revision checklist, 160
  strategies for, 143

Introductory elements, uses of commas, 314–315
Irregular adjectives, 285–286
Irregular adverbs, 285–286
Irregular plurals, 267
Irregular verbs, 246–248
is because, 306
is when, 306
is where, 306
it
  conventions of academic language, 29
  indefinite antecedents and, 283
  pronoun use in paragraphs, 135–136
  vague reference to antecedent, 282
it is contractions
  punctuation errors, 166
  revising, 225
Italics
  overview of uses, 352–3534
  writing format for academic audiences, 174

J

Jargon
  rewriting for conciseness, 226
  standard English, 208–209
Journals
  APA style, 430–432, 434
  Chicago style, 459
  critical reading example, 36
  CSE style, 472, 473
  evaluating library sources, 79
  finding source material, 64–65
  keeping research journal, 52
  MLA paper format sample, 417–418
  MLA style, 363, 379–382
  reading to develop reading processes, 11
JSTOR, 66
Judgments, testing and making assertions, 40
just because, 307

K

Key terms, critical reading techniques, 35
Keywords
  developing search terms, 61–62

example search, 70–71
finding books and periodicals, 64–65
refining, 62–63
Koran, 353

L

Labels
  appropriate use of, 212–213
  parenthesis use, 337–338
Language
  academic. See Academic language
  culture and. See Culture and language issues
  exact. See Exact language
  standard American English. See English, standard American
  styles for integrating source material into text, 150
Latin
  abbreviations in citations, 356
  spelling rules for English words derived from, 346
lay, 248–249
Layout, writing format for academic audiences, 172
Lectures. See Addresses (lectures)
Legal documents, italicizing or underlining conventions, 353
Letters
  Chicago style, 465–466
  colon use in letter salutation, 327
  MLA style, 393, 404–405
Libraries
  evaluating library sources, 79–82
  finding books and periodicals, 64–65
  finding source material, 60–61
  sources for research project, 54–55
  visuals databases, 75
lie, 248–249
Limiting modifiers, 293
Line breaks, hyphenation use in dividing words at end of lines, 348
Line graphs, 177
Line spacing. See Spacing
Link, to video file, 175

Linking verbs
  adjectives and adverbs with, 285–286
  example of, 239
  subject-verb agreement and, 268–269
Lists
  CSE style for numbered lists, 470–471
  parallelism used with, 201
  parenthesis use, 337–338
  writing format for academic audiences, 174
Literacy narrative, 184
Literary works, MLA in-text citations, 370
Live performances, MLA style, 403–404
Locators (page numbers/reference numbers). See also Page numbers, 377
Logical thinking
  in arguments, 117
  combining rational appeals with emotional and ethical appeals, 119
  comparisons, 287–288
  correcting illogical equation using *be*, 306
  deduction (deductive reasoning), 118–119
  induction (inductive reasoning), 118
-ly
  uses of hyphenation with compound adjectives, 347
  word ending signifying adverb, 233

M

Magazines. See also Periodicals
  APA style, 433
  Chicago style, 461
  CSE style, 473, 474
  MLA style, 363, 384–385
Main clauses
  attaching sentence fragment to, 300
  commas in clauses linked by conjunctions, 313, 315
  in compound and complex sentences, 245
  in conditional sentences, 261

Main clauses (*continued*)
  for coordinating information in sentences, 196
  correcting comma splices and fused sentences, 301–302, 304–305
  deleting unnecessary colons, 328
  deleting unnecessary semicolons, 326
  overview of, 243
  pronoun case and, 274
  punctuation for two or more main clauses in a row, 301–302
  semicolons in, 324–325
  sentence types and, 244
  of sentences, 194, 245
  sequence of tenses between main clause and subordinate clause, 260–262
  subordination as means of adding variety, 203
  subordination to distinguish main ideas, 198–199
  when not to use commas in signal phrases, 321
Main verbs
  combining with helping verb, 251–252
  helping verbs and, 232, 250
  subject-verb agreement, 268
Maps. See also Charts; Diagrams; Graphics
  selecting visuals, 175–176
  using media responsibly, 178
Margins
  APA paper format, 441
  MLA paper format, 405
  writing format for academic audiences, 172, 174
may, 252–253
Meaning
  choosing the right word for, 215–216
  looking up, 35, 224
  revising sentences with mixed, 305–306
  word meaning and synonyms, 213
meanwhile, 136
Media/medium. See also Visuals and media
  analyzing the writing situation, 101
  finding source material, 73–75
  identifying in planning and drafting phase, 104
  multimodal use, 174
  in oral presentations, 188
  of portfolio, 185
  of text, 8
Memory, presentation delivery methods, 187
Men, avoiding sexist language, 210–212
Metacognition, 5
Metaphors, proper use of figurative language, 218
might, 262
Misplaced modifiers
  avoiding awkward placement of adverbs, 293–294
  clear placement of, 293
  limiting modifiers and, 293
  placing adverbs of frequency, degree, and manner, 294–295
Miss, forms of address and, 212
Mixed sentences
  overview of, 305
  revising sentences with mixed grammar, 306–307
  revising sentences with mixed meaning, 305–306
  revising sentences with repeated elements, 307–308
MLA Handbook, 365
MLA style
  analyzing revised drafts, 163, 165
  capitalization conventions, 350
  captions, 179
  documentation and format, 362
  documenting source material, 150, 157
  examining final draft, 169–170
  formatting final draft, 169
  italics or underlining conventions, 352
  writing format for academic audiences, 173
MLA style, in-text citations
  audio or video, 368
  authors, 366–368
  footnotes and endnotes, 373
  indirect sources, 369–370
  literary works, 370–371
  multivolume works, 369
  one page or entire work, 369

overview of, 365
placement of, 371–372
punctuation of, 372
two or more works in same citation, 371
MLA style, paper format
outline example, 408
overview of, 405–407
sample paper, 409–416
MLA style, works-cited
advertisements, 399
articles in magazines, 384–385
articles in newspapers, 382–384
articles in scholarly journals, 379–382
authors, 378–379
books, 385–393
comic strips/cartoons, 399
dissertations, 405
elements of works-cited entries, 374–378
film or video, 402
format of list of works cited, 374
government publications, 393–394
interviews, 401–402, 404
lectures, speeches, addresses, readings, 404
letters, 404–405
live performances, 403–404
maps, charts, diagrams, 400
overview of, 362–364
pamphlets or brochures, 405
in paper format sample, 417
podcasts, 403
radio programs, 401
social media, 397–398
sound recordings, 402–403
television episodes or series, 400–401
video games, computer software, and apps, 404
visual art, 398–399
Web sites, 394–397
writing list of works cited, 373–374
Modal helping verbs, 252–253, 268
Modern Language Association. See MLA style
Modifiers. See also by individual type
absolute modifiers, 287
absolute phrases, 243
adjective clauses, 243–244

adjective modifiers, 204, 284–285
adverb modifiers, 205, 284–285
appositive phrases, 243
choosing between *no* and *not*, 284–285
commas between adjectives modifying same word, 319–320
dangling, 296–297
dash uses, 336–337
irregular, 285–286
misplaced, 293–296
nonessential, 317
revising use of, 224–225
in sentence structure, 236
verb form functioning as, 250
verbal phrases (verbals) as, 241
Money, numeric conventions, 358
Months, misuses of abbreviations, 356
Mood. See Verb mood
Motion pictures, APA style. See also Films, 439
Mrs., forms of address, 212
Ms., forms of address, 212
Multimodal writing, 174
Multivolume works, MLA style, 369, 390
Music
APA style, 440
audio files, 75
conceiving Web composition, 180
database searches, 66
italics use for musical works, 353
MLA style, 402–404

N

Named words, italicizing or underlining for emphasis, 354
Names
commas in place names, 314, 320
communicating in the academic settings, 31
CSE documentation using name-year style, 470
misuses of abbreviations, 356
proper name abbreviations, 355
quotation marks used with words used in special sense, 334

Narration
  elements of visuals, 42
  literacy narrative, 184
  patterns for development of central idea in paragraphs, 138
Natural sciences, integrating source material into text, 150
Navigation, Web site, 183
Newsgroups, 73
Newspapers
  APA in-text style, 433–434
  Chicago style, 460
  CSE style, 473–474
  finding source material, 65
  MLA paper format sample, 417
  MLA works-cited style, 363, 382–384
Nicknames, 334
no, choosing between *no* and *not*, 285
Non sequitur, fallacies in arguments due to evasion, 120
Noncount nouns
  article use with, 290–291
  as collective noun, 271, 281
  determiner adjectives and, 289
  determiner use with, 291–292
  identifying, 230
  plural form and, 347
Nonessential elements
  dash uses, 336–337
  test for determing, 316–317
  uses of commas, 314–319
Nonprint sources, writing in-text citations, 367
nor
  coordinating information in sentences, 196–197
  plural/singular form agrees with near part of antecedent, 278–279
  semicolon use and, 325
  signaling need for parallelism, 200
  subject-verb agreement and, 268–269
not
  choosing between *no* and *not*, 285
  placement of adverbs, 295
NOT (-), boolean operators in refining keywords, 62–63
NOT, in custom searches, 70

not only.but also, 197
not.but, 201
Notes
  Chicago style, 456–458
  MLA style, 180
  primary research, 76
  writing captions and source notes, 179–180
Noun clauses, 244
Nouns
  absolute phrases, 243
  adjective clauses, 243–244
  adjectives modifying, 232, 284
  apostrophe uses/misuses, 329
  apostrophes to show possession, 328
  appositive phrases, 243
  arranging two or three adjectives before, 295–296
  article use, 290–291
  capitalization conventions, 350–352
  consistency of person, number, and tense, 136
  determiner adjectives, 289
  different forms of same word, 344–345
  generic, 279
  gerund phrases, 242
  gerunds, 254
  identifying, 230
  implied, 283
  infinitive phrases as, 242
  infinitives and, 255
  made from verbs, 193–194, 222–223
  prepositional phrases and, 233, 241
  pronoun antecedent and, 277
  replacing pronoun for clearer reference, 282
  revising sentences with mixed meaning, 306
  rewriting to avoid indefinite antecedents, 283
  in sentence patterns, 238–239
  as sentence subject, 236
  spelling rules for plural form, 346–347
  verb endings and, 249
  verbal phrases (verbals) as, 241
  words that can be noun or verb, 237
Novels, MLA in-text citations, 370

Number of noun, consistency in paragraphs, 136
Numbered sequences
  CSE style, 470–472
  MLA works-cited style, 376
Numbers
  abbreviations, 355
  commas in, 314, 320
  conventions for dates, addresses, and long numbers, 358
  expressing in written form (numerals), 357–358
  hyphenation for compound, 347
  overview of uses, 357
  pagination of publications. See Page numbers
  plural. See Plural form
  pronoun and antecedent agreement, 277
  singular. See Singular form
  subject-verb agreement, 266–267
Numerals
  conventions for dates and addresses, 358
  expressing numbers in written form, 357–358
Numeric arrangement, CSE reference list, 472

O

Object complement, basic sentence patterns, 240
Objective case
  defined, 272–273
  pronoun case in infinitives, 276
Objects
  active and passive voice, 264–265
  compound objects and pronoun case, 273–274
  deleting unnecessary commas, 322
  noun clauses as, 244
  of preposition, 241
  sentence patterns, 238–240
  in verbal phrases, 241
  who/whom, 275
Observations, primary research, 77
Occupational stereotypes, 211
Omissions, ellipsis indicating, 338–340

on
  in expressions of time, 217
  use in exact language, 217–218
Online audiences, 180
Online sources. See also Web sources
  citing, 156
  databases, 60–61
  evaluating source material, 88–90
  visuals, 175
On-screen, displaying presentations, 188
Opinions
  distinguishing facts from in critical reading, 35
  thesis statement as, 116
or
  coordinating information in sentences, 196–197
  plural/singular form agrees with near part of antecedent, 278–279
  preposition use in exact language, 217–218
  semicolon use and, 325
  signaling need for parallelism, 200
  subject-verb agreement and, 268–269
OR, boolean operator, 62–63
OR, in custom searches, 70
Oral presentations
  delivery methods, 187
  organizing, 186–187
  practice and stage fright, 190
  visual aids, 188–189
Organization
  of arguments, 122–123
  of essays, 108–109
  of ideas in planning and drafting phase, 107
  of oral presentations, 186–187
  outlines and tree diagrams for, 109–111
  of paragraphs, 134
  revision checklist, 160
  via general and specific ideas, 108
  of Web sites, 181–183
other, 287–288
Outlines
  formal, 110–111
  parallelism used with, 201

Outlines (*continued*)
  scratch or informal, 109
  tree diagrams, 109–110
Oversimplification, fallacies in arguments, 121–122

P

Page numbers
  APA paper format, 441
  APA reference lists, 427
  citing works lacking pagination or reference numbers, 369
  conventions, 358
  elements of MLA works-cited entries, 377
  MLA paper format, 405–406
  MLA works-cited style, 391
Painting, MLA style. See also Artwork, 398
Pamphlets, MLA style. See also Publications, 405
Papers. See also Publications
  APA format, 441–443
  MLA format. See MLA style, paper format
  research papers/reports, 25–26
Paragraphs
  analyzing revised drafts, 164
  checklist for revising, 131–132
  coherence of, 132–134
  conclusions, 144–146
  consistency, 136
  example of edited, 167
  introductions, 142–144
  in literacy narrative example, 184
  MLA paper format, 409–410
  organizing, 134
  parallelism for achieving coherence, 134–135
  patterns for development of central idea, 138–142
  pronouns in, 135–136
  relating to essay as whole, 131
  repetition and restatement, 135
  transitional expressions, 136–137
  unity of each, 132–133
  writing format for academic audiences, 172–173
Parallelism
  achieving coherence of paragraphs, 134–135
  in comparisons, 201

correlative conjunctions for, 201
defined, 200
for equal elements, 200–201
in lists, headings, and outlines, 201
Paraphrase
  avoiding plagiarism, 152
  borrowed material, 147
  information needs citation, 155
  managing sources, 28, 94–95
Parentheses (())
  abbreviations and, 356
  doubt indicated by question mark within, 312
  MLA style, 371–373
  uses of, 337–338
Parenthetical expressions
  comma use, 318
  dash use, 336–337
  parenthesis use, 337–338
Participial phrases, 241–242
Participles
  absolute phrases, 243
  as adjectives, 241–242, 288
  form of verbs, 231–232
  irregular verbs, 246–248
  passive verbs, 264
  perfect tenses with past participles, 259
  when helping verbs are required, 251
Particles, in two-word verbs, 255–256
Parts of speech
  adjectives and adverbs, 232–233
  conjunctions, 234–235
  interjections, 235
  nouns, 230
  overview of, 229
  prepositions, 233
  pronouns, 230–231
  verbs, 231–232
Passive voice. See also Verb voice
  changing to active, 222
  distinguishing from active, 194, 264
  overview of, 194
  using transitive verbs in, 239
  when to use, 265
Past participles. See also Participles
  as adjectives, 288–289
  easily confused verb forms, 248
  form of verbs, 231–232

irregular verbs, 246–248
participial phrases, 241–242
passive verbs and, 264
perfect tenses and, 259
when helping verbs are required, 250
Past perfect tense. See also Verb tenses
 of regular verb, 258
 sequence of tenses between main clause and subordinate clause, 261–262
Past tense
 easily confused verb forms. See also Verb tenses, 248
 form of verbs, 231–232
 irregular verbs, 246–248
 regular verbs, 257
 sequence of tenses between main clause and subordinate clause, 261–262
Patterns
 development of central idea in paragraphs, 138–142
 sentence, 237–240
 strategies for reading difficult text, 7
Peer review, 161–162
Percentages, numeric conventions, 358
Perfect tense. See also Verb tenses
 past perfect, 258
 present perfect, 257
 sequence of tenses between main clause and subordinate clause, 261–262
 uses of, 259
Period(.)
 combining main clauses, 303–304
 coordinating information in sentences, 196
 in signal phrases, 321
 use of decimal point in numbers, 358
Periodic sentences, 195–196
Periodicals
 databases, 65–66
 developing reading processes, 11
 finding source material, 64–65
 journals. See Journals
 locations of, 68–69
 magazines. See Magazines
 newspapers. See Newspapers

Permissions
 for using source materials, 74
 using visuals and media responsibly, 178
Person
 consistency in paragraphs, 136
 pronoun and antecedent agreement, 277
 pronoun errors, 166
 subject-verb agreement, 266–267
Personal essays. See also Essays, 25
Personal interviews. See also Interviews, 76
Personal names. See also Names, 356
Personal pronouns, 230
Personal Web sites. See also Web sites, 84
Photographs. See also Visuals and media
 conceiving Web composition, 180
 finding visuals, 74
 MLA style, 398–399
 in multimodal writing, 174
 reading visual arguments, 42
 selecting visuals, 175–176
 using media responsibly, 178
 visual aids in oral presentations, 188–189
Phrases
 absolute. See Absolute phrases
 appositive. See Appositive phrases
 of contrast, 318
 deleting unnecessary semicolons, 326
 nonessential, 317
 overview of, 240–241
 prepositional. See Prepositional phrases
 signal. See Signal phrases
 subject-verb agreement, 268
 subordination as means of adding variety, 203
 uses of commas, 314
 verbal. See Verbal phrases (verbals)
Physical delivery, oral presentations, 187
Pie charts. See also Graphics; Visuals and media
 selecting, 175–177
 using responsibly, 178

Place names, commas in, 314, 320
Plagiarism
  avoiding, 26, 96
  checklist, 152
  defined, 151
  deliberate and careless, 26–27, 151–153
  Internet and, 153
Plain form. See also Verb forms
  easily confused verb forms, 248
  irregular verbs, 246–248
  overview of, 231–232
  pronoun case in infinitives, 276
  subjunctive mood and, 263
Planning and drafting
  analyzing first draft, 112–114
  analyzing writing situation, 99–101
  choosing subject matter, 102–103
  creating first draft, 111–112
  defining purpose, 101–102
  developing thesis statement, 104–107
  identifying genre and medium, 103–104
  organizing ideas, 107–109
  outlines and tree diagrams, 109–111
Planning research project. See Research project, planning
Planning revisions, 158–159
Planning Web composition, 180–181
Plays
  MLA style, 370
  numeric conventions for scenes in, 358
Plural form
  antecedent agreement, 278–279
  antecedents joined by *and* they take plural pronouns, 278
  article use with plural count nouns, 290
  collective nouns and, 280–281
  conjunction *and* requires plural verb, 269
  determiner use with plural non-count nouns, 291–292
  indefinite pronouns and, 270, 279–280
  for nouns not adjectives, 285
  pronoun agreement, 277–278
  singular verbs with plural title, 272
  spelling rules, 346–347
  subject-verb agreement, 270–272
  subject-verb agreement and, 267
  uses/misuses of apostrophe, 329–330
Plural nouns
  article use with plural count nouns, 290
  collective nouns and, 280–281
  determiner use with plural non-count nouns, 291–292
  plural form for nouns not adjectives, 285
  subject-verb agreement, 270–271
Plural pronouns
  antecedents joined by *and* they take plural pronouns, 278
  indefinite pronouns and, 270, 279–280
  pronoun agreement, 277–278
  subject-verb agreement and, 270–272
Podcasts
  APA reference list, 440
  Chicago style, 465
  finding source material, 75
  MLA style, 403
Poetry
  MLA in-text style, 370
  MLA paper format for long quotations, 406–407
  omissions, 340
  slash use in, 340
Point by point, comparison and contrast, 141
Portfolio of writing, preparing, 185
Position arguments, 24
Positive form, adjective and adverbs, 233
Possession
  apostrophe showing, 328–331
  uses/misuses of apostrophe, 329
Possessive case
  defined, 272–273
  before gerund, 277
Possessive pronouns, 332
Post hoc fallacy, 122
Posts, social media
  CSE style, 475
  MLA style, 397–398

Practice and stage fright, oral presentations, 190
Predicates
  acceptable sentence fragments, 301
  in clauses, 243
  finding predicate verb when testing for sentence fragments, 298–299
  in phrases and in subordinate clauses, 241
  revising sentences with mixed meaning, 305–306
  sentence parts, 235–237
  sentence patterns, 238–240
  test for finding, 237
Predictions, conditional sentences, 261
Prefaces, MLA style, 392–393
Prefixes
  spelling rules, 346
  uses of hyphenation, 348
Preliminary response, to visuals, 41
Prepositional phrases
  commas in, 315
  in mixed grammar, 306–307
  as modifiers in sentence structure, 233
  overview of, 241
Prepositions
  appropriate use of case, 276
  capitalization conventions, 350
  in compound constructions, 201
  culture and language, 217–218
  deleting unnecessary colons, 328
  deleting unnecessary commas, 322
  gerund as object of, 242
  identifying, 233
  idioms with, 216–217
  list of common, 233
  objective case and, 272
  omitting in journal title citations, 472
  as particle, 255–256
  in prepositional phrases, 241
Present participle. See also Participles
  as adjective, 288–289
  form of verbs, 232
  participial phrases, 241–242
  when helping verbs are required, 251

Present perfect tense
  of regular verb, 257
  sequence of tenses between main clause and subordinate clause, 261–262
Present tense. See also Verb tenses
  of regular verb, 257
  sequence of tenses between main clause and subordinate clause, 261–262
  special uses of, 258–259
Presentation, evaluating Web sites, 85
Presentation, oral. See Oral presentations
Pretentious writing, avoiding, 209
Preview. See also Reviews
  text, 33–34
  visuals, 41
Prewriting, 13
Primary research
  conducting, 75–76
  observations, 77
  personal interviews, 76
  surveys, 76–77
Primary sources
  direct quotation, 95–96
  sources for research project, 55
Print publications (articles, journals, books. reports). See also Publications
  APA reference list for print books, 434
  APA reference list for print reports, 436
  Chicago style for articles in journal, 459
  Chicago style for print books, 461
  CSE reference list for print articles, 473
  CSE reference list for print books, 474
Prior knowledge, rhetorical reading strategies, 8–9
Privacy, communicating in the academic setting, 32
Process analysis, in paragraph development, 142
Progressive tenses, 259–260
Pronoun antecedents
  agreement in person, number, and gender, 277
  appropriate use of *you*, 283–284

Pronoun antecedents (*continued*)
  collective nouns and, 280–281
  indefinite pronouns and, 279–280
  making pronoun refer clearly to one antecedent, 281–282
  specific reference to antecedent, 282–283
  when joined by *and* they take plural pronouns, 278
  when joined by *or* and *nor* they agree with near part of antecedent, 278–279
Pronoun case
  common questions regarding, 275–277
  compound subjects and objects and, 273–274
  defining subjective, objective, and possessive cases, 272–273
  overview of, 272
  who vs. *whom*, 274–275
Pronouns
  absolute phrases, 243
  adjective clauses, 243–244
  adjectives modifying, 232, 284
  antecedents. See Pronoun antecedents
  apostrophe uses/misuses, 331
  appropriate use of, 283–284
  case. See Pronoun case
  checklist for editing, 166
  clear reference to one antecedent, 281–282
  identifying, 230–231
  implied nouns and, 283
  infinitives and, 255
  not confusing contractions with possessive pronouns, 332
  in paragraphs, 135–136
  in prepositional phrases, 233, 241
  in sentence pattern, 238–239
  as sentence subject, 236
  separable two-word verbs, 256
  singular pronoun to avoiding sexist language, 212
  specific reference to antecedent, 282–283
  subject-verb agreement, 269–270
  subject-verb agreement and, 270–272
  treatment of sentence subject in various languages, 299
  uses/misuses of apostrophe, 328–329
  verb endings and, 249
Pronunciation, 343–344
Proofreading
  to avoid omissions, 220
  final draft, 169
Proper adjectives, capitalization of, 350–352
Proper names, abbreviations, 355
Proper nouns. See also Nouns
  article use with, 291
  capitalization of, 350–352
  determiner adjectives and, 289
  identifying, 230
Proposal arguments, 24
ProQuest Research Library, 66
Prose
  conciseness of, 183
  final draft, 169
  first draft, 111
  introduction-body-conclusion pattern, 108
  MLA in-text style, 370
  MLA paper format, 405–407
  omissions, 340
  prose play as literary work, 370
Publication date
  APA reference lists, 427
  MLA works-cited, 377
Publications
  APA in-text reference lists, 436
  books. See Books
  CSE reference lists, 472
  fact check, 33
  government. See Government publications
  MLA works-cited guidelines, 393–394
  periodicals. See Periodicals
  previewing visuals, 41
  as source material, 73
  Web. See Web sources
Published letters, Chicago style. See also Letters, 465–466
Publisher (creator)
  APA reference lists, 427
  evaluating online sources, 88–89
  identifying Web site publisher, 84
  MLA works-cited, 377

Punctuation
  APA reference lists, 426
  apostrophe (in general), 328
  apostrophe for contractions and abbreviations, 331–332
  apostrophe for showing possession, 328–331
  brackets, 340
  colons, 326–327
  commas (in general), 313–314
  commas between adjectives modifying same word, 319–320
  commas between items in a series, 319
  commas in dates, addresses, place names, and long numbers, 320
  commas in main clauses linked by conjunctions, 313, 315
  commas in quotations, 321
  commas setting off introductory elements, 315
  commas setting off nonessential elements, 315–319
  dashes, 336–337
  deleting unnecessary colons, 328
  deleting unnecessary commas, 321–323
  deleting unnecessary semicolons, 326
  editing checklist, 166
  ellipsis mark, 338–340
  exclamation points, 312
  identifying and correcting errors, 207
  MLA style for parenthetical citations, 371–373
  parentheses, 337–338
  periods, 311–312
  quotation marks (in general), 332
  quotation marks enclosing words used in special sense, 334–335
  quotation marks indicating direct quotations, 332–333
  quotation marks indicating titles of works, 333–334
  quotation marks inside/outside other punctuation, 335–336
  semicolons, 324–325
  slashes, 340
  for two or more main clauses in a row, 301–302
Purpose
  analyzing the writing situation, 100
  conceiving Web composition, 180
  defining in planning and drafting phase, 101–102
  determing for academic participation, 22–23
  elements of rhetoric, 7
  evaluating online sources, 89
  identifying in Web sites, 84–85
  of portfolio, 185
  reading visuals, 41

Q

Question marks (?)
  doubt indicated by, 312
  ending direct questions, 312
  punctuation inside, 335–336
Questions
  comma use in tag questions, 318
  determining research questions, 53
  evaluating source material, 78–79, 88
  evaluating Web sites, 83
  generating about topics, 4
  periods in indirect questions, 311
  in primary research, 76–77
  rhetorical reading strategies, 8, 10
  visual analysis and, 43–44
  when to use *who* or *whom*, 274–275
Quotation marks (single and double)
  conventions for handling quotes, 96
  enclosing words used in special sense, 334–335
  indicating direct quotations, 332–333
  indicating titles of works, 333–334
  inside/outside other punctuation, 335–336
  MLA paper format for poetry or prose quotations, 406–407
  overview of uses, 332

Quotations
  analyzing a revised draft, 163
  APA paper format, 443
  bracket use, 340
  checklist for avoiding plagiarism, 152
  colon use, 327
  commas in, 314, 320–321
  conventions for handling, 96
  deleting unnecessary commas, 323
  direct quotation, 95–96
  ellipsis use, 338–340
  information needs citation, 155
  introducing borrowed material, 147
  in literacy narrative example, 185
  managing sources, 27
  MLA paper format, 406–407
  punctuation indicating direct quotations, 332–333
  summaries and, 94
  writing format for academic audiences, 173

R

Race, using appropriate labels, 212
Radio
  APA references, 420
  finding visuals and media, 73
  information that needs citation, 154
  MLA works-cited guidelines, 401–403
  primary research, 75
  punctuation of program title, 334, 353
raise, 248–249
Rational appeals. *See also* Logical thinking
  in arguments, 119
  strength of visual argument, 126
Readers
  conceiving Web composition, 180
  considering readers with vision loss, 173
  engaging, 117
Reading
  critical reading. *See* Critical reading
  critical response. *See* Critical response
  first read, 34
  processes, 5–7
  reading-writing connection, 3–4
  rereading, 34–35
  response assignment, 23–24
  summarizing, 16–17
  types of reading processes, 6
  visuals, 41–42
  into writing, 13–16
Reading arguments
  analyzing, 38–39
  critical analysis example, 48–50
  critical reading example, 35–36
  critical reading techniques, 32–33
  critical response, 38
  evaluating, 40
  evaluating visuals, 46
  first read, reread, annotate, 34–35
  interpreting, 39
  interpreting visuals, 44
  overview of, 32
  previewing material, 33–34
  previewing visuals, 41
  reading visuals, 41–42
  summarizing, 36–38
  synthesizing, 39–40
  synthesizing visuals, 44–45
  visual analysis, 40–44
  writing critical analysis, 46–48
Reading to learn
  discussions, 11–12
  elements of rhetoric, 7–8
  journals and reflections, 11
  processes for reading, 5–7
  reading-writing connection, 3–4
  rhetorical reading strategies, 8–10
  types of reading processes, 6
Readings, MLA style, 404
Reasoning (rationality). *See* Logical thinking
Record keeping, 91
Red herring fallacy, 120–121
Reductive fallacy, 121
Redundancy, 224
Reference librarians, 61
Reference lists
  APA. *See* APA style
  Chicago. *See* Chicago style
  CSE. *See* CSE style
  MLA. *See* MLA style
  preparing, 425–428

Reference numbers/pages. See Page numbers
Reference works
　APA style, 435
　Chicago style, 463
　finding source material, 63–64
　MLA style, 392
Reflections
　on reading processes, 11
　writing-to-learn strategies, 21
Reflexive pronouns, 231
Relationships (family), capitalization conventions, 351
Relative pronouns
　adjective clauses, 243–244
　identifying, 230
　subject-verb agreement, 269–270
　testing for sentence fragments, 299
Relevance, evaluating source material, 78–79
Reliability
　evaluating library sources, 80–81
　evaluating source material, 78–79
　of source material, 57
Repetition
　avoiding unnecessary, 224
　in paragraphs, 135
　revising sentences with repeated elements, 307–308
Reports
　APA in-text reference lists, 436–437
　APA style for research reports, 443–452
　CSE style, 475
　research papers/reports, 25–26
Reproductions (of art)
　Chicago style, 464
　MLA style, 398
Republished books, MLA style, 390
Reread, 34–35
Research
　arguments and, 24
　choosing subject matter, 52–53, 102
　conducting, 4
　determining research questions, 53
　papers/reports, 25–26
　primary. See Primary research

　for source material, 75–77
　strategies for writing academic genres, 26
　writing process, 51–52
Research guides, 61
Research journal, 52
Research project, planning
　determining research questions, 53
　developing working bibliography, 56–59
　finding researchable subject, 52–53
　overview of, 50
　process of research writing, 51–52
　search strategies, 53–56
Research reports, 25–26, 443–452
Response
　considering preliminary response in preview of text, 34
　critical. See Critical response
　deciding how to respond in critical analysis, 46
　previewing visuals, 41
　to reading, 4
　reading response assignment, 23–24
　sharing responses to what you read, 11–12
　to sources, 92
　writing, 16–17
　writing to learn and, 15–16
Restatement, in paragraphs, 135
Retrieval statement, in APA reference lists, 427–428
Reviews
　APA style, 433
　Chicago style, 461
　feedback, 161–162
Revisions. See also Editing
　analyzing a revised draft, 163–165
　checklist for, 159–160
　creating title during revision stage, 160–161
　peer review and, 161–162
　planning, 158–159
Rhetoric
　elements of, 7–8
　rhetorical analysis, 18
　rhetorical reading strategies, 8–10

Rhetorical situation. See Writing situation
rise, 248–249
Rogerian argument, 120, 122–123
Run-on (fused) sentences
 correcting, 303–305
 identifying, 301–303

S

-s ending. See also Plural form; Possession
 apostrophes for showing possession, 328–331
 singular nouns ending in -s, 271–272
 subject-verb agreement, 267
 verb endings, 231–232, 249
Sacred works, MLA style, 390
Salutations, in letter, 327
Sarcasm, in arguments, 119
Scenes (of a play), numeric conventions, 358
Scholarly sites, evaluating Web sites, 83
Scholarly sources, for research project, 55–56
Scores, numeric conventions, 358
Scratch outlines, 109
Search engines
 disadvantages of open-Web search, 69
 evaluating Web sites, 83
 finding images, 74
 public and custom searches, 70
Search strategies
 finding source material, 60
 library searches, 60–61
 search terms, 61–63
 setting goals for finding sources for research, 53
 types of sources, 54–56
 using own knowledge, 54
Search terms, 61–63
Searches
 database searches, 66–67
 Web searches, 69–72
Secondary sources
 direct quotation, 96
 for research project, 55
Self-reflection, 5
Semicolon (;)
 colon compared with, 325
 deleting unnecessary, 326

in main clauses, 324–325
outside quotation marks, 335
overview of uses, 324
Sentence fragments
 acceptable, 301
 correcting, 207, 300
 identifying, 207, 297–300
 overview of, 297
 when helping verbs are required, 251
Sentences
 adding needed words, 220
 analyzing revisions, 164
 beginnings and endings, 194
 capitalization of first word in, 349
 choppy, 197
 conciseness of, 225
 conditional, 261
 coordination of information in, 196–198
 correcting comma splices and fused sentences, 303–305
 creating Web sites, 182
 cumulative and periodic, 195–196
 editing checklist, 165–166
 fragments. See Sentence fragments
 identifying comma spices and fused sentences, 301–303
 in literacy narrative example, 184
 mixed. See Mixed sentences
 overview of, 235
 patterns, 237–240
 periods ending, 311
 punctuation. See Punctuation
 relating equal ideas using coordination, 196–198
 subjects and predicates, 235–237
 subordination to distinguish main ideas, 198–199
 types of, 244–245
 with unusual word order, 268
 using subjects and verbs effectively, 193–194
 varying beginning, 204
 varying length, 202–203
 varying structure, 203–204
 varying word order, 205
Sequence of tenses, between main clause and subordinate clause, 260–262

Series, of books or TV episodes
  APA reference list for TV series, 439
  Chicago style for works in, 463
  MLA works-cited style for books in a series, 390
  MLA works-cited style for TV series, 400–401
Series, of elements in sentences
  colon use, 327
  commas between items in, 319
  dash uses, 337
  deleting unnecessary commas, 323
  deleting unnecessary semicolons, 326
  uses of commas, 314
set, 248–249
Sexist language, eliminating, 210–212
she
  conventions of academic language, 29
  pronoun errors, 166
  pronoun use in paragraphs, 135–136
Shifts, dash marking, 336
Ships, italics or underlining with names of, 354
Shortcuts, texting and electronic communication, 207–208
Shortened notes, Chicago style, 466
should, 252–253
Signal phrases
  commas and other punctuation in, 321
  interpreting source material, 148–149
  tense use in, 150–151
Similes, proper use of figurative language, 218
since, 218
Single quotation mark (' '). See also Quotation marks (single and double), 333–334
Singular form
  article use with singular count nouns, 290
  collective nouns and, 280–281
  determiner use with singular noncount nouns, 291–292
  indefinite pronouns and, 279–280
  plural/singular form agrees with near part of antecedent, 278–279
  pronoun agreement, 277–278
  spelling rules, 346
  subject-verb agreement and, 267
  uses/misuses of apostrophe, 329–331
sit, 248–249
Situation. See Context
Skimming text. See also Preview, 33–34
Slang
  not used in academic language, 29
  quotation marks used with words used in special sense, 335
  when to use/when not to use, 208
Slashes (/), 340
Slides, visual aids in oral presentations, 188–189
so, 196
Social media
  APA in-text reference lists, 438
  Chicago style, 463–464
  CSE style, 474–475
  finding source material, 72–73
  MLA works-cited, 364, 397–398
Social networking sites
  finding source material, 72
  MLA works-cited, 397
Social sciences, integrating source material into text, 150
Social stereotypes, avoiding, 211
Software
  APA style, 440–441
  bibliography software, 158
  editions/versions, 376
  MLA style, 404
Songs, MLA style for sound recording, 402–403
Sound recordings. See also Audio; Visuals and media
  Chicago style, 465
  MLA style, 402–403
Sources
  abstracts, 67–68
  for bibliography, 57
  books and periodicals, 64–65, 68–69
  citing. See Citations

Sources (*continued*)
conceiving Web composition, 181
databases, 66–68
documenting, 156–158
government publications, 73
impartial and biased, 56
library or open Web, 54–55
managing, 27–28
MLA style, 180, 363–364
overview of, 59
primary, 55, 95–96
primary research, 75–77
reference works, 63–64
scholarly and popular, 55–56
search strategies, 60–63
secondary, 55
social media, 72–73
visuals and media, 73–75, 178
Web search strategies, 69–72
writing captions and source notes, 179–180

Sources, ethical use
academic participation and, 26–28
distinguishing between deliberate and careless plagiarism, 151–153
documenting sources, 156–158
information needs citation, 154–156
information that does not need citation, 153–154
visuals and media, 178

Sources, evaluating
developing perspective, 27
library sources, 79–82
online sources, 88–90
overview of, 78
reading to learn and, 4
relevance and reliability, 78–79
Web site evaluation, 82–87

Sources, integrating
interpreting borrowed material, 147–149
styles for, 149–151
into text, 146–147

Sources, synthesizing and summarizing
gathering information, 91–92
overview of, 90
paraphrasing, 94–95
quoting, 95–96
summarizing, 93–94
synthesizing, 92–93

Spacecraft, italics or underlining with names of, 354
Spacing
APA paper format, 441
APA reference lists, 426
CSE reference list, 471
MLA paper format, 405, 409
MLA works cited, 374
writing format for academic audiences, 172, 174
Spatial organization
of essays, 108
of paragraphs, 134
Specific words, 216
Specifics
organizing via general and specific ideas, 108–109
paragraph organization by general and specific, 134
Speculation, conditional sentences, 262
Speech, parts of. See Parts of speech
Speeches, MLA works-cited, 404
Spell checkers
for exact language, 215
using, 167–168
Spelling
British vs. American, 345
common problems, 343–344
editing checklist, 166
hyphenation and, 347–348
identifying and correcting errors, 207
overview of, 343
rules, 345–347
Split infinitives, 294
Spoken word, MLA works-cited, 403
Stage fright, 190
Standard American English. See English, standard American
Statements. See also Commands
drafting thesis statement, 105–106
example of thesis statement, 128
of fact and of belief, 116
functions of thesis statement, 104
outlines and thesis statement, 109–111
revising thesis statement, 107
thesis statement as opinion, 116

thesis statement in introduction, 143
use of exclamation points, 312
uses of periods, 311
Statistics
  numeric conventions, 358
  types of evidence, 116
Stereotypes
  avoiding, 210–211
  fallacies due to oversimplification, 121
Style checkers, 168
Styles
  APA. See APA style
  Chicago. See Chicago style
  CSE. See CSE style
  documenting sources, 157
  formatting final draft, 169
  for integrating source material into text, 149–151
  MLA. See MLA style
  writing format for academic audiences, 173
Subject by subject, compare and contrast, 141
Subject complement
  example of, 239
  pronoun case and, 273
  subject-verb agreement and, 268–269
Subject headings (subject terms)
  developing search terms, 62
  refining, 62–63
Subject matter
  analyzing the writing situation, 100–101
  choosing in planning and drafting phase, 102–103
  developing perspective on, 27
  elements of arguments, 115
  finding researchable subject, 52–53
Subjective case
  defined, 272–273
  pronoun case in comparisons, 276
Subjects
  absolute phrases, 231–232
  in acceptable sentence fragments, 301
  active and passive voice and, 264–265
  adding interest by varying sentence beginnings, 204
  agreement with verb. See Subject-verb agreement
  in clauses, 243
  compound subjects and pronoun case, 273–274
  conciseness of, 221–222
  correcting illogical equation using *be*, 306
  dangling modifiers, 296–297
  deleting unnecessary commas, 322
  effective emphasis, 193–194
  joined by conjunctions, 269
  noun clauses as, 244
  in phrases and in subordinate clauses, 241
  plural subject, 267
  revising sentences with mixed meaning, 305–306
  revising sentences with repeated elements, 307
  sentence parts, 235–237
  sentence patterns, 238
  test for finding, 237
  test for sentence fragments, 299
  verb endings and, 249
Subject-verb agreement
  collective and plural pronouns and, 270–272
  indefinite and relative pronouns and, 269–270
  in number and person, 266–267
  overview of, 266
  unusual word order and, 268–269
  when subjects are joined by conjunctions, 269
Subjunctive verb mood, 262–263
Subordinate clauses
  adjective clauses, 243–244
  adverb clauses, 244
  commas in, 315
  in compound and complex sentences, 245
  conditional sentences, 261
  correcting comma splices and fused sentences, 304–305
  correcting sentence fragments, 300
  deleting unnecessary semicolons, 326
  noun clauses, 244
  overview of, 243

Subordinate clauses (*continued*)
  sentence types and, 244
  sequence of tenses between main clause and subordinate clause, 260–262
  subject and predicate in, 241
  subjunctive mood and, 263
  subordination as means of adding variety to writing, 203
  testing for sentence fragments, 299–300
  who/whom in, 275
Subordinating conjunctions
  adverb clauses, 244
  list of, 234
Subordination
  adding variety to writing, 203
  correcting comma splices and fused sentences, 304–305
  to distinguish main ideas, 198–199
  effective use of, 199
Subtitles
  capitalization of, 350
  colon use in letter salutation, 327
such as, 328
Suffixes, 348
Suggestive titles, 161
Summary
  analyzing a revised draft, 163
  checklist for avoiding plagiarism, 152
  discovering and exploring ideas, 18–19
  examining final draft, 171
  information that needs citation, 155
  introducing borrowed material, 147
  in source management, 28
  of sources. See Sources, synthesizing and summarizing
  text, 36–38
  writing responses, 16–17
Superlative, adjective and adverb forms, 233, 286–288
Superscripts, 409
Supporting material, oral presentations, 186
Surveys, primary research, 76–77
Syllables, hyphenation and, 348
Syllogism, 118–119
Symbols, reading visuals, 41
Synonyms, 214
Synthesis
  in critical response, 39–40
  emphasizing in critical analysis, 47–48
  gathering information, 91–92
  overview of, 90
  of sources. See Sources, synthesizing and summarizing
  strategies for writing academic genres, 26
  visuals, 44–45

T

Tables. See also Graphics; Visuals and media
  MLA style, 180
  selecting visuals, 175–176
  using responsibly, 178
Tag questions, comma use in, 318
team, 270
Technical words, when to use/when not to use, 208–209
Television
  APA reference list for TV series, 439–440
  Chicago style, 463
  MLA style for TV episodes, 376, 400–401
Tense of verbs. See Verb tenses
Text
  annotating, 35
  creating Web sites, 183
  critical analysis, 24
  critical response, 47
  elements of rhetoric, 7–8
  integrating sources into, 146–147
  multimodal use of mediums, 174
  presentation delivery methods, 187
  preview, 33–34
  reading from different viewpoints, 4
  reading processes, 5
  strategies for reading difficult, 6–7
  in-text citations. See MLA style, in-text citations
  visual aids in oral presentations, 188

Text messages (texting)
  Chicago style, 464
  conventions of academic language, 29
  English shortcuts, 207–208
  MLA works-cited guidelines, 398
than
  parallelism in comparisons, 201
  pronoun case in comparisons, 276
that
  clear reference of pronoun to one antecedent, 282
  subject-verb agreement, 269–270
  subordination to distinguish main ideas of sentence, 198
  vague reference to antecedent, 282
the
  capitalization conventions, 350
  determiner adjectives, 289
  use with count nouns, 290
  use with noncount nouns, 290–291
  use with proper nouns, 291
  when to use, 221
them, 166
there, 268
there is contractions, 225
therefore
  subordination to distinguish main ideas of sentence, 198
  transitional expressions in paragraphs, 136–137
  ways to coordinate information in sentences, 196
Thesauruses, 214
Thesis
  acknowledging opposing views, 119–120
  analyzing a revised draft, 163–164
  drafting thesis statement, 105–106
  examining final draft, 169, 171
  example of thesis statement, 128
  formulating thesis question, 105
  functions of thesis statement, 104
  outlines and thesis statement, 109–111
  revising thesis statement, 107
  revision checklist, 160
  thesis statement as opinion, 116
  thesis statement in introduction, 143
they
  conventions of academic language, 29
  indefinite antecedents and, 283
  pronoun use in paragraphs, 135–136
  as singular pronoun to avoiding sexist language, 212
Third person subjects, 249
this, 282
thus, 196
Time
  colon use, 328
  numeric conventions, 358
Titles (personal)
  abbreviations, 355
  capitalization conventions, 352
  colon use in letter salutation, 327
  communicating in the academic settings, 31
Titles (of works)
  analyzing a revised draft, 163
  APA paper format, 441–442
  APA reference lists, 427
  building MLA citations, 375–376
  capitalization, 350
  Chicago style, 462
  citing sources by, 379
  comma use in, 321
  CSE reference list, 472
  descriptive and suggestive, 160–161, 183–184
  italicizing or underlining, 352–353
  MLA paper format, 406, 409
  MLA style for book titles, 390–391
  MLA style for government publications, 394
  MLA style for tables, 180
  MLA style for Web sites, 394–396
  quotation mark use, 332–334
  reflecting essay content, 160
  singular verbs with plural title, 272
  writing format for academic audiences, 172

to
  capitalization conventions, 350
  infinitives and, 254–255
to hide, 242
together with, 268
Topic sentence
  coherence of paragraph and, 134
  unifying feature in paragraphs, 132–133
Trains, italics or underlining with names of, 354
Transitional expressions
  adding interest by varying sentence beginnings, 204
  comma use in, 315, 318
  correcting comma splices and fused sentences, 304–305
  in MLA paper format sample, 413
  in paragraphs, 136–137
  semicolon use in, 324
  uses of, 137
Transitive verbs
  basic sentence patterns, 238–240
  easily confused verb forms, 248–249
  passive voice, 264–265
Translators
  APA reference list for books with, 435
  Chicago style for books with, 462
  MLA works-cited style for books with, 389
Tree diagrams, 109–111
Trite expressions, 219
TV. *See* Television
Tweets
  APA style, 438
  MLA style, 397–398
Two-word (or three-word) verbs
  inseparable and separable, 256
  particles and, 255
Type fonts
  considering readers with vision loss, 173
  writing format for academic audiences, 173

U

Underlining (underscore), 352–353
Units of measurement, 356

Unity
  qualities of paragraphs, 132–133
  revision checklist, 160
unless
  conditional sentences, 261
  hypothetical conditions, 263
  subordination to distinguish main ideas of sentence, 198
URLs
  hyphenation and, 348
  MLA style, 377
us, 276

V

Variety
  creating by adding details, 205
  sentence beginning, 204
  sentence length, 202–203
  sentence structure, 203–204
  word order, 205
Verb forms
  easily confused examples, 248–249
  endings, 249–250
  gerunds and infinitives, 254–255
  helping verbs, 250–253
  irregular, 246–248
  overview of, 246
  particles, 255–256
Verb mood
  consistency in use of, 263
  overview of, 262
  subjunctive, 262–263
Verb tenses
  consistency in use of, 136, 260
  editing checklist, 166
  overview of, 257
  perfect tense, 259
  progressive tense, 259–260
  for regular verbs, 257–258
  sequence of, 260–262
  signal phrases and, 148, 150–151
  special use of present tense, 258–259
Verb voice
  consistency in use of, 266
  overview of, 264–265
  passive, 194
  when to use active or passive voice, 265
Verbal phrases (verbals)
  commas in, 315
  helping verbs and, 232, 250

Index

overview of, 241–242
subject-verb agreement and, 267–268
Verbs
  adverb clauses, 244
  adverbs modifying, 232, 284
  agreement with subject. See Subject-verb agreement
  apostrophe uses/misuses, 331
  conciseness of, 221–222
  consistency of person, number, and tense, 136
  dangling modifiers, 296–297
  deleting unnecessary colons, 328
  deleting unnecessary commas, 322
  different forms of same word, 344–345
  editing checklist, 166
  forms. See Verb forms
  gerund phrases, 242
  gerunds, 254–255
  helping verbs, 250–253
  identifying, 231–232
  infinitive phrases, 242
  infinitives, 254–255
  mood. See Verb mood
  nouns made from, 193–194, 222–223
  particles, 255–256
  pronoun case in infinitives, 276
  in sentence patterns, 238–239
  in signal phrases, 148
  split infinitive, 294
  tense. See Verb tenses
  voice. See Verb voice
  weak, 194
  words that can be noun or verb, 237
Versions, MLA style, 376
Video. See also Visuals and media
  APA reference list, 439
  Chicago style, 465
  conceiving Web composition, 180–181
  designing for online audiences, 180
  finding source material, 73–75
  link to video file, 175
  MLA in-text citations, 368–369
  MLA works-cited, 364, 402
  multimodal use of mediums, 174
  selecting, 175
  visual aids in oral presentations, 188
Video games
  APA reference list, 440–441
  MLA works-cited, 404
Videocassette, MLA works-cited, 400–402
Vision loss, considering readers with, 173
Visual aids, oral presentations, 188–189
Visual analysis
  evaluation, 46
  interpretation, 44
  previews, 41
  reading visuals, 41–42
  synthesis, 44–45
  viewing critically, 40–41
Visual argument
  appeal and strength of, 126
  assumptions in, 125–126
  claims in, 123
  evidence in, 123–125
  fallacies in, 127
  overview of, 123
Visuals and media
  APA in-text reference lists, 439–441
  Chicago style, 464–465
  conceiving Web composition, 180–181
  critical analysis of, 24
  CSE reference list, 475
  elements of, 42–43
  finding source material, 73–75
  integrating, 178–179
  MLA works-cited, 364, 398–399
  selecting, 174–177
  supporting document, 178
  using in document design, 175–176
  visual aids in oral presentations, 188–189
Vocabulary, academic, 29
Vocal delivery, oral presentations, 187
Volumes (of a publication)
  Chicago style, 462
  MLA style, 376
  numeric conventions, 358

W

we, 276
Web composition, planning, 180–181
Web forums, 73
Web pages
  Chicago style, 463–464
  elements of, 45
  MLA style, 394
  visual analysis and, 44
  writing in-text citations, 367
Web reports, 436–437
Web searches
  disadvantages of open-Web search, 69–70
  example, 70–72
  finding sources, 69
  search engines and, 70
Web sites
  APA style, 437–438
  Chicago style, 463–464
  Chicago style for newspaper articles, 460
  considering and analyzing content, 85
  creating, 181–183
  CSE style, 474–475
  determining type of, 83–84
  evaluating source material, 82–83
  examples for evaluation, 86–87
  finding books and periodicals, 64–65
  finding source material, 60
  gauging purpose and biases, 84–85
  identifying author and publisher, 84
  MLA style, 364, 394–397
  organization of, 181
  posting to blogs or wikis, 183–185
  presentation of, 85
  public and custom searches, 70
  sources for research project, 54–55
  wikis, 64
Web sources. See also Online sources
  APA reference list, 425, 437–438
  APA reference list for TV programs, 440
  APA reference list for video on Web, 439
  APA reference list for Web books, 434
  APA reference list for Web publications, 436
  Chicago style, 463–464
  Chicago style for artwork, 464
  Chicago style for journal articles, 460
  Chicago style for reference works, 463
  Chicago style for Web books, 462
  Chicago style for Web recording, 465
  citing Web journal article, 430–431
  CSE reference list, 474–475
  CSE reference list for articles, 473
  CSE reference list for Web books, 474
  finding sources, 69
  MLA works-cited style, 394–397
  MLA works-cited style for video, 402
  MLA works-cited style for Web interview, 402
  MLA works-cited style for Web radio, 401
  MLA works-cited style for Web TV, 400
  sources for research project, 54–55
  using images responsibly, 178
Webcasts, 75
when, 261
whereas, 198
which
  clear reference of pronoun to one antecedent, 282
  subject-verb agreement, 269–270
  subordination to distinguish main ideas of sentence, 198
  vague reference to antecedent, 282
who
  clear reference of pronoun to one antecedent, 282
  pronoun case, 274
  pronoun use in paragraphs, 135–136
  in questions, 274–275
  subject-verb agreement, 269–270
  subordinate clauses and, 275
  subordination to distinguish main ideas of sentence, 198

whom
  pronoun case, 274
  pronoun errors, 166
  in questions, 274–275
  subordinate clauses and, 274–275
  subordination to distinguish main ideas of sentence, 198
Wikipedia, 64
Wikis
  APA reference list, 438
  MLA works-cited guidelines, 396
  posting to, 183–185
  Web sites, 64
Wildcards (*), 63
wish, 263
with, 350
Women, avoiding sexist language, 210–212
Words
  abstract, concrete, general, and specific, 216
  adding needed, 220
  capitalization. See Capitalization
  commas between adjectives modifying same word, 319–320
  compound words, 331
  dictionaries, 213–214
  different forms of same word, 344–345
  eliminating empty words to achieve conciseness, 223–224
  ending signifying adverb, 233
  expressing numbers as numerals, 357–358
  foreign. See Foreign words
  homonyms, 343–344
  hyphenation, 347–348
  indirect and pretentious writing and, 209
  italicizing or underlining for emphasis, 353–354
  looking up word meaning, 35
  meanings and synonyms, 213
  spell checkers, 215
  spelling. See Spelling
  technical words, 208–209
  that can be noun or verb, 237
  thesauruses, 214
  two-word (or three-word) verbs, 256
  unusual word order and subject-verb agreement, 268–269
  use in special sense, 332, 334–335
  varying order in sentences, 205
  wordiness and, 30, 221
Working bibliographies. See Bibliographies
Works cited. See MLA style, works-cited
would
  modal helping verbs, 252–253
  speculation, 262
Writing
  abbreviation use in nontechnical writing, 355–356
  academic. See Academic writing
  APA style, 422
  business. See Business writing
  convention for expressing numbers in written form (numerals), 357
  critical analysis. See Critical analysis
  genres, 23
  MLA style, 366–371, 373–374
  process of research writing, 51–52
  reading-writing connection, 3–4
Writing situation
  analyzing, 99
  audience, 99–100
  considering requirements and limits of, 178
  genre and medium, 101
  literacy narrative, 184
  purpose, 100
  subject matter, 100–101
Writing to learn
  discovering and exploring ideas, 18–19
  overview of, 12–13
  reading into writing, 13–16
  responses, 16–17
  sharing and collaborating, 19–21

Y

y, 346
Year, CSE style, 470
yet
  coordinating conjunctions signaling need for parallelism, 200
  using conjunctions to coordinate information in sentences, 196
you, 283–284

Culture and Language Guide

Throughout this handbook, *Culture and Language* boxes signal topics for students whose first language or dialect is not standard American English. These topics can be tricky because they arise from rules in standard English that are quite different in other languages and dialects. Many of the topics involve significant cultural assumptions as well.

Whatever your language background, as a college student you are learning the culture of US higher education and the language that is used and shaped by that culture. The process is challenging, even for native speakers of standard American English. It requires not just writing clearly and correctly but also mastering conventions of developing, presenting, and supporting ideas. The challenge is greater if, in addition, you are trying to learn standard American English and are accustomed to other conventions. Several habits can help you succeed:

- **Read.** Besides course assignments, read newspapers, magazines, and books in English. The more you read, the more fluently and accurately you'll write.
- **Write.** Keep a journal in which you practice writing in English every day.
- **Talk and listen.** Take advantage of opportunities to hear and use English.
- **Ask questions.** Your instructors, tutors in the writing lab, and fellow students can clarify assignments and help you identify and solve writing problems.
- **Don't try for perfection.** No one writes perfectly, and the effort to do so can prevent you from expressing yourself fluently. View mistakes not as failures but as opportunities to learn.
- **Revise first; then edit.** Focus on each essay's ideas, support, and organization before attending to grammar and vocabulary. See the revision checklist in 13.1 and the editing checklist in 13.4.1.
- **Set editing priorities.** Concentrate first on any errors that interfere with clarity, such as problems with word order or subject-verb agreement.

The following index leads you to text discussions of writing topics that you may need help with.

Academic writing, 3.4, 19.1
Adjective(s)
 clauses, repetition in, 38.3
 no, with a noun, 34.1
 no plurals for, 34.1
 order of, 35.1.3
Adverb(s)
 introductory, word order after, 18.1.2
 not, with a verb or adjective, 34.1, 35.1.3
 position of, 35.1.3

Argument, opinion and evidence in, 10.1
Articles (*a, an, the*), 20.2, 34.5
Audience, 9.5.2, 9.6, 13.2, 11.5, 4.1
Capital letters, 47.1
Collaboration, 13.2
Comma splices
 revision of, 37.1
 and sentence length, 37.1

Determiners (*a, an, the, few, a few, many, some,* etc.), 34.5
Dictionaries, ESL, 19.3.1
Forms of address (*Mrs., Miss, Ms.*), 19.2.2
Idioms, 19.3.4
Intellectual property, 12.2
Introductions, 11.5
Nonstandard dialect, 3.4, 19.1
Nouns
  collective: pronouns with, 32.4; verbs with, 32.4
  noncount: form of, 46.2.6
    list of, 34.5; verbs with, 30.5.1
  plural: forms of, 46.2.6; with *one of the,* 30.5.1
Numbers, punctuation of, 50.1
Omissions
  subject of sentence, 36.1
  there or *it* at sentence beginning, 21.4.2
Oral presentations, 15.2
Organization, 9.6
Paragraphs, 9.6, 11.1, 11.3, 11.5
Paraphrasing, 8.3.2
Plagiarism, avoiding, 12.2
Prepositions
  for vs. *since,* 19.3.4
  idioms with, 19.3.4
  in vs. *at* vs. *on,* 19.3.4
  to or *for* needed after some verbs, 23.2
Pronouns
  with collective nouns, 32.4
  matching antecedent in gender, 32.1
  needless repetition with, 23.1, 33.1, 38.3
  -self forms of, 31.1
Questions
  forming indirect, 39.1.1
  position of adverbs in, 35.1.3

Reading, critical, 4.1, 4.1.2, 8.1
Redundancy
  and implied meaning, 21.3
  in sentence parts, 38.3
Research writing, originality in, 8.1, 12.2
Spelling
  British vs. American, 46.1.3
  noncount nouns, no plurals of, 46.2.6
Standard American English, 3.4, 19.1
Subject of sentence
  agreement of verb with, 30.1
  needless repetition of, 23.1, 33.1, 38.3
  omission in sentence fragments, 36.1
Subordinating conjunctions, 22.3.2
Thesis statement, 9.5.2
Transitional expressions, 11.3
Verbs
  agreement with subjects, 30.1
  with collective nouns, 32.4
  gerund vs. infinitive with, 24.1.2
  with indirect objects, 23.2
  intransitive, 23.2
  irregular, 26.1
  with noncount nouns, 30.5.1
  participles of, 24.1.2
  passive voice of, 23.2, 29.1
  perfect tenses of, 27.1, 27.1.2
  progressive tenses of, 27.1
  tense formation of, 27.1
  transitive, 23.2, 29.1
  two-word, particles with, 26.6
Wordiness, vs. incorrect grammar, 21.1
Word order
  adjectives and adverbs, 18.1.2, 37.1
  questions, 35.1.3, 39.1.1
  subject-verb-object, 23.2

Contents

Preface v

1 Reading and Writing in College

1 Reading to Learn 3
- 1.1 Reading-writing connection
- 1.2 Process for reading
- 1.3 Rhetorical reading
- 1.4 Reading journals and reflections
- 1.5 Discussing readings

2 Writing to Learn 12
- 2.1 Reading into writing
- 2.2 Writing to respond
- 2.3 Discovering and exploring ideas
- 2.4 Writing to share and collaborate

3 Joining the Academic Conversation 21
- 3.1 Purpose and audience
- 3.2 Genre
- 3.3 Writing with sources
- 3.4 Academic language
- 3.5 Communication in academic settings

4 Reading Arguments 32
- 4.1 Techniques of critical reading
- 4.2 Summarizing
- 4.3 Critical response
- 4.4 Visual analysis
- 4.5 Writing a critical analysis
- 4.6 Sample critical analysis
  Sample critical analysis of a text 48

5 Planning a Research Project 50
- 5.1 Planning
- 5.2 Research questions
- 5.3 Search strategies
- 5.4 Working bibliographies
  Sample annotated bibliography entry 58

6 Finding Sources 59
- 6.1 Search strategies
- 6.2 Reference works
- 6.3 Books and periodicals
- 6.4 Web search strategies
- 6.5 Social media
- 6.6 Government publications
- 6.7 Visuals and media
- 6.8 Primary research

7 Evaluating Sources 78
- 7.1 Relevance and reliability
- 7.2 Library sources
- 7.3 Web sites
- 7.4 Other online sources

8 Synthesizing and Summarizing Sources 90
- 8.1 Interacting with sources
- 8.2 Synthesizing sources
- 8.3 Summary, paraphrase, and quotation

2 Writing with Sources

9 Planning and Drafting 99
- 9.1 Writing situation
- 9.2 Purpose
- 9.3 Subject
- 9.4 Genre and medium
- 9.5 Thesis
- 9.6 Organization
- 9.7 First draft
- 9.8 Sample draft

10 Organizing and Developing Arguments 114
- 10.1 Elements of argument
- 10.2 Engaging readers
- 10.3 Organization
- 10.4 Visual arguments
- 10.5 Sample argument
  Sample proposal argument 127

11 Paragraphs 131
- 11.1 Flow
- 11.2 Unity
- 11.3 Coherence
- 11.4 Development
- 11.5 Introductions and conclusions

12 Integrating and Using Sources Ethically 146
- 12.1 Integrating sources
- 12.2 Defining plagiarism
- 12.3 Information you do not need to cite
- 12.4 Information you must cite
- 12.5 Documenting sources

13 Revising and Editing 158
- 13.1 Revision plans
- 13.2 Peer review
- 13.3 Sample revision
  Sample revised draft 163
- 13.4 Editing
  Sample edited paragraph 1
- 13.5 Final draft
  Sample final draft 169

14 Designing Documents 171
- 14.1 Academic writing
  Sample paper in MLA format 172
- 14.2 Visuals and media
- 14.3 Writing online
  Sample literacy narrative blog post 184
- 14.4 Portfolios

15 Oral Presentations 186
- 15.1 Organization
- 15.2 Delivery
  Sample presentation slides 189

3 Clarity and Style

16 Emphasis 193
- 16.1 Subjects and verbs
- 16.2 Sentence beginnings and endings
- 16.3 Coordination
- 16.4 Subordination

17 Parallelism 200
- 17.1 Understanding parallelism
- 17.2 Equal elements

18 Variety and Details 202
- 18.1 Sentence length and structure
- 18.2 Details

19 Appropriate and Exact Language 206
- 19.1 Standard English
- 19.2 Sexist and biased language
- 19.3 Exact language

20 Completeness 220
- 20.1 Compounds
- 20.2 Adding needed words

21 Conciseness 221
- 21.1 Subjects and verbs
- 21.2 Empty words
- 21.3 Unnecessary repetition
- 21.4 Other strategies